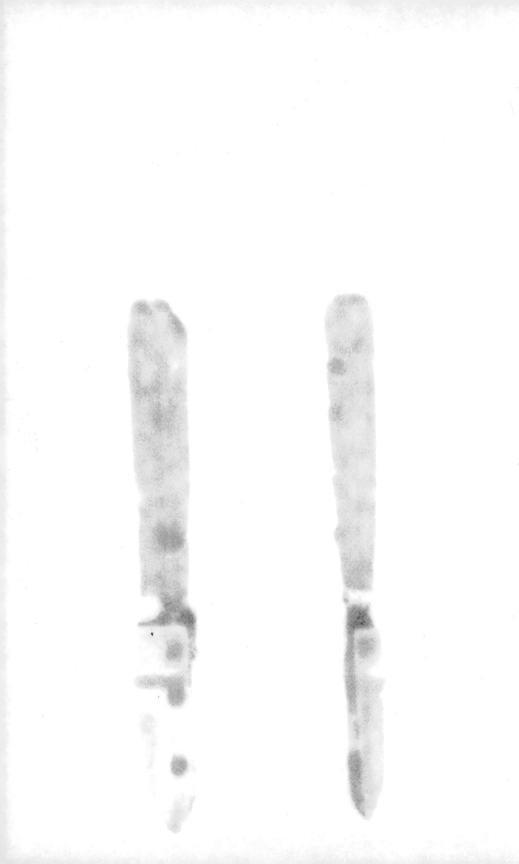

SHELLEY

MARY SHELLEY
MINIATURE BY REGINALD EASTMAN

By permission of the Bodleian Library

SHELLEY

BY

NEWMAN IVEY WHITE

VOLUME
II

OCTAGON BOOKS

A DIVISION OF FARRAR, STRAUS AND GIROUX

New York   1972

Reprinted 1972
by special arrangement with Alfred A. Knopf, Inc.

OCTAGON BOOKS
A Division of Farrar, Straus & Giroux, Inc.
19 Union Square West
New York, N. Y. 10003

Library of Congress Cataloging in Publication Data

White, Newman Ivey, 1892-1948.
   Shelley.
   Bibliography: p.
   1. Shelley, Percy Bysshe, 1792-1822.
PR5431.W5   1972   821'.7 [B]   72-7385
ISBN 0-374-98426-3

Manufactured by Braun-Brumfield, Inc.
Ann Arbor, Michigan

Printed in the United States of America

CONTENTS

VOLUME II

APPENDICES:

ILLUSTRATIONS

VOLUME II

SHELLEY

VOLUME II

Chapter XIX

SPRING AND SUMMER IN ITALY

JOURNEY ACROSS FRANCE; MILAN AND THE LAKE OF
COMO; TROUBLE OVER ALLEGRA; JOURNEY TO
LEGHORN; READING AND WRITING AT
THE BATHS OF LUCCA; NEWS FROM ENGLAND;
DEPARTURE FOR VENICE

THERE were eight in the little party of emigrants — Shelley and Mary and their two children, Claire and Allegra, the Swiss nurse Elise, and Amelia (" Milly ") Shields, who had been engaged as a second nurse some months earlier at Marlow. The passage was short, but rough. Allegra and William were seasick, and a Mrs. Hare, a fellow voyager, was both seasick and terrified. For the latter affliction she found comfort in repeating the Lord's Prayer, but growing too miserable to pray, she ordered prayers continued by her maidservant.

They landed at Calais on Thursday, March 12, 1818, and spent the night at the Grand Cerf hotel. The next day they bought a carriage, loaded their belongings, and set out in the afternoon for Saint-Omer. Here they found the city gates already closed for the night, but after an hour's delay they were admitted upon a promise of " remembering the guard." Thence to Lyon required seven days of rough, uncomfortable travel. On the 14th they slept at Douai, on the 15th at La Fère ("a miserable town," according to Claire), the 17th at Reims, the 18th at Saint-Dizier, the 19th at Langres, the 20th at Dijon (Le Chapeau Rouge), and on the 21st at Lyon. Between La Fère and Reims the road was so bad that the carriage was in constant danger of overturning. At Mâcon they were delayed

3

three hours by the breaking of a carriage-spring. Here, as previously, Shelley sought to beguile the tedium by reading Schlegel aloud.

Having arrived at Lyon, the party put up at the Hôtel de l'Europe and allowed themselves four days of rest and recreation. " Lyons," Claire wrote in her journal, " is a most Beautiful City, but its best parts are all the work of Napoleon." Mary wrote:

Sunday, Mar. 22. — A fine pleasant day. We agree with a voiturier to take us to Milan, and then walk out by the side of the river until its confluence with the Saone. We can see from here Jura and Mont Blanc, and the whole scene reminds us of Geneva. After dinner, our voiturier comes, and we have a long conversation with him about the state of Lyons, and passed events in it. He was here in the revolutionary times. After this, we ride out by the river-side, and see the moon rise, broad and red, and behind the Alps. Shelley writes to Lord Byron.

Monday, Mar. 23. — Walk out in the morning. After dinner, we ride to the Isle de Barbe, where there is a fête. In the evening we go to the Comédie, which is very amusing. [*L'homme Gris et le Physiognomisto,* according to Claire.]

After the weeks of strain and discomfort Shelley's spirits were again rising. From Lyon he wrote to Leigh Hunt:

We have journeyed towards the spring, that has been hastening to meet us from the south; and though our weather was at first abominable, we have now warm sunny days, and soft winds, and a sky of deep azure, the most serene I ever saw. The heat in this city to-day is like that of London in the midst of summer. My spirits and health sympathize in the change. Indeed, before I left London, my spirits were as feeble as my health, and I had demands upon them which I found difficult to supply.[1]

Shelley now took the first occasion to read *Foliage*, Hunt's recent volume of poems, and to record his pleasure. " The Nymphs," he thought was " truly *poetical*"; but he ventured gently to object to Hunt's use of the word " glib." He did not mention the sonnets to himself that he had undoubtedly seen

4

before leaving England, the re-reading of which must have helped raise his spirits.

A letter was dispatched to the indifferent Lord Byron informing him of Allegra's coming arrival at Milan, and the journey was resumed. They were now passing through wooded valleys dotted with white châteaux and scattered cottages. Everywhere they saw grapevines trellised upon huge stakes, and " lofty orchards of apple and pear trees, the twigs of which were just becoming purple with the bursting blossoms." [2] Early the first day (March 26) they reached the boundaries of Savoy at Pont Bonvoisin. Here, in the middle of a bridge guarded at one end by the soldiers of France and at the other by those of Savoy, they submitted with some misgivings to the customs examination. Shelley's luggage contained books by Rousseau and Voltaire, both proscribed authors in Savoyard territory. After some discussion the books were sent to Chambéry to be examined by the censor — a priest, as Shelley noted. Another priest, an English canon who had met Sir Timothy Shelley at the Duke of Norfolk's, came to Shelley's aid, and probably averted the usual fate of such books, destruction by fire. [3] The books were detained, but by the middle of July they were again in Shelley's possession. [4] While the party waited a day (March 27) at Chambéry, they were visited by the mother, father-in-law, and little daughter of Elise, their Swiss nurse.

They were now in the midst of such magnificent mountain scenery as had never failed to stimulate Shelley's imagination. They had crossed the Echelles to Chambéry over the high, winding road cut through the perpendicular rocks by Charles Emmanuel, Duke of Savoy, in 1582. " The rocks," as Shelley wrote of this passage,

which cannot be less than a thousand feet in perpendicular height, sometimes overhang the road on each side, and almost shut out the sky. The scene is like that described in the Prometheus of Aeschylus. Vast rifts and caverns in the granite precipices, wintry mountains with ice and snow above; the loud sounds of unseen waters within the caverns, and walls of toppling rocks, only to be scaled as he described, by the winged chariot of the ocean nymphs. [5]

In these words we have the definite starting-point of Shelley's greatest poem, which was to be begun five months later. Passing the same spot on her sad return to England in 1823, Mary Shelley wrote that " the dark high precipices towering above gave Shelley the idea of his Prometheus." [6]

Leaving Chambéry, they could see the sunlight flashing from the highest Alps. Soon they were enclosed by valleys as they followed the windings of a river higher and higher. At Saint-Jean-de-Maurienne, where they slept the first night, the town was deep in snow. As they ascended Mont Cenis next morning, the snow on the edges of the road was as high as their carriage. On March 30, two days after leaving Chambéry, they crossed Mont Cenis, blessing Napoleon for having improved the road, and stopped at Susa, the first town in cisalpine Italy.

To Mary, though she enjoyed the mountain scenery, there was " something dreadful " in travelling on the edge of an overhanging precipice that was " armoured from top to bottom with a cascade of ice." Shelley felt the cold of the higher altitudes as a discomfort, but he was elated. Marlow with its dampness and debts, Godwin with his incessant demands and ungracious lack of friendship, were far behind; over the Alps, as Napoleon had said, lay Italy. Like Cæsar's veterans singing their *Ecce Cæsar nunc triumphat* through the streets of Rome, Shelley sang all the way as they climbed the last heights of the pass over Mont Cenis:

> Now Heaven neglected is by Men
> And Gods are hung upon every tree
> But not the more for [loss] of them
> Shall this fair world unhappy be.[7]

The mountains, he asserted, were God's Corps de Ballet.[8]

The snow and ice of Mont Cenis were now behind them; ahead and below them were green, sunny slopes and wooded glades. Primroses were blooming everywhere. The air was full of the fragrance of fruit trees in full bloom — " A sky without one cloud — everything bright and serene — the cloudless sky of Italy — the bright and the beautiful." [9]

" No sooner had we arrived in Italy," Shelley wrote to Peacock, than the loveliness of the earth and the serenity of the sky made the greatest difference in my sensations — I depend on these things for life; for in the smoke of cities and the tumult of human kind and the chilling fogs and rain of our own country I can hardly be said to live. With what delight did I hear the woman who conducted us to see the triumphal arch of Augustus at Susa, speak the clear and complete language of Italy, tho half unintelligible to me, after that nasal and abbreviated cacophony of the French! A ruined arch of magnificent proportions in the Greek taste, standing in a kind of road of green lawn, overgrown with violets and primroses, and in the midst of stupendous mountains, and a *blonde* woman, of light and graceful manners, something in the style of Fuseli's Eve were the first things we met in Italy.[10]

Unsuspected as yet were the troubles into which Claire's relations with Byron were to plunge the whole party, or the deep mystery, perhaps never to be fully unravelled, which was to culminate nine months later in Naples.

A day's journey from Susa brought the party to Turin (March 31), where they attended a rather indifferent opera. Thence it was three days of leisurely travel to Milan, their first pause of more than one day since leaving Lyon on March 25. The countryside was now less picturesque, but they were still delighted with Italy. Mary wrote to the Hunts:

Italy appears a far more civilised place than France; you see more signs of cultivation and work and you meet multitudes of peasants on the road driving carts drawn by the most beautiful oxen I ever saw. They are of a delicate dove colour with eyes that remind you of, and justify the Homeric epithet, *ox-eyed Juno*. In France you might travel many miles and not meet a single creature. The inns are infinitely better and the bread, which is uneatable in France, is here the finest and whitest in the world. There is a disconsolate air of discomfort in France that is quite wretched. In Italy we breathe a different air and everything is pleasant around us.[11]

At Milan, which they reached on the evening of April 4, the party lodged at the Hôtel Reale. The next day they visited the cathedral. " The Cathedral here is something wonderful. I can conceive of no building that partakes more perfectly of the nature of air and heaven," Claire wrote in her journal. "The carved pinnacles whiter than snow rise into the clouds. The dazzling white of the marble and the immensity of the work impress one with the belief of the aid of some supernatural power." [12] Shelley's next letter to Peacock (April 20) described the cathedral even more enthusiastically. Mary's more laconic journal calls it simply " very fine."

The same evening (April 5) they were delighted with the ballet of the Milan opera. Even though they missed their favourite Mademoiselle Melanie of the London opera, Shelley thought the performance "'the most splendid spectacle I ever saw," and Mary called it " infinitely magnificent." [13] " I like this town," Mary added. " We think, however, of spending the summer on the banks of the lake of Como, which is only twenty miles from here. Shelley's health is infinitely improved and the rest of the chicks are quite well." Already Shelley's head was full of literary schemes to be put into practice as soon as they were settled. The first of these was a dramatic poem on the life of Tasso. On April 6 Shelley and Mary began reading Tasso's *Aminta* together, and Shelley began reading a life of Tasso.

After writing letters to the Hunts and Peacock, Shelley and Mary left Claire and the rest of the party at Milan and set out for the Lake of Como to find a house for the summer. " This lake," wrote Shelley after his return, " exceeds anything I ever beheld in beauty with the exception of the arbutus islands of Killarney." [14] Mary, who had never seen Killarney, wrote in her journal, " Nothing can be more divine than the shores of this lovely lake." They examined three houses, one of which was too small and one of which was out of repair, with a beautiful garden " full of serpents." The third, Villa Pliniana, they hoped to secure for the summer. Shelley sent Peacock an enthusiastic description of it in his next letter.[15]

While at Como it occurred to Shelley that his pistol had been loaded ever since the departure from England and that the charge might have become ineffective during the journey. Pistol in hand, he set out to find a solitary spot where he could

MILAN

Engraved by James Carter from a painting by C. Stanfield

discharge and reload it, not noticing at first that he was being followed by two men. The men came up, revealed themselves as police, and politely took him into custody for carrying fire-arms contrary to law. In spite of his expostulations they carried him before an equally polite local prefect, who released him from arrest but would not return the pistol until Madame Shel-ley came before him and certified that her husband had no intention of shooting himself with it.[16]

On the 12th of April Shelley and Mary were back in Milan, where Claire had beguiled their three days' absence in reading some nine plays of Molière and the life of Tasso, and in riding in the Corso in the evening and visiting the cathedral. The next two or three days passed uneventfully in reading, riding in the Corso, writing letters, and playing chess.

ALREADY there was trouble in the offing. Byron had not yet answered the letter written from Lyon asking his wishes with regard to Allegra. Shelley wrote him again on April 13:

Will you spend a few weeks with us this summer? Our mode of life is uniform, and such as you remember it at Geneva, and the sit-uation which I imagine we have chosen (the Villa Pliniana) is soli-tary, and surrounded by scenery of astonishing grandeur, with the lake at our feet. If you would visit us — and I don't know where you could find a heartier welcome — little Allegra might return with you.[17]

But Byron was resolved to have nothing more to do with Claire, and he was somewhat suspicious of Shelley's efforts. Writing to his friend Hobhouse shortly after the receipt of this letter, he remarked: " Shelley has got to Milan with the bastard, and its mother; but wont send the shild [*sic*] unless I will go and see the mother. I have sent a messenger for the shild, but I can't leave my quarters and have ' sworn an oath.' "[18] What Byron wrote to Shelley has been lost, but may be fairly well understood from Shelley's answer. Byron's letter arrived on April 21, on which day Claire wrote in her journal: " Letter from Albè. Nothing but Discomfort." Byron offered to take

Allegra and provide for her, but only on condition that Claire should resign her completely and absolutely to his care.

Shelley knew himself to be half-suspected by Byron; he regarded Allegra almost as one of his own children; and he was torn and agonized by Claire's distress. Under these circumstances the tact and humanity of his answering letter does him infinite credit:

Milan,
April 22, 1818.

My Dear Lord Byron,

Clare will write to you herself a detail of her motives and feelings relating to Allegra's being absent as you desire. Her interference as the mother of course supersedes *mine*, which was never undertaken but from the deep interest I have ever felt for all the parties concerned. Here my letter might well close, but that I would not the affair should finish so.

You write as if from the instant of its departure all future intercourse were to cease between Clare and her child. This I cannot think you ought to have expected, or even to have desired. Let us estimate our own sensations, and consider, if those of a father be acute, what must be those of a mother? What should we think of a woman who should resign her infant child with no prospect of ever seeing it again, even to a father in whose tenderness she entirely confided? If she forces herself to such a sacrifice for the sake of her child's welfare, there is something heroically great in thus trampling upon the strongest affections, and even the most unappeasable instincts of our nature. But the world will not judge so; she would be despised as an unnatural mother, even by those who might see little to condemn in her becoming a mother without the formalities of marriage. She would thus resign her only good, and take to herself, in its stead, contempt on every hand. Besides, she might say, " What assurance have I of the tenderness of the father for his child, if he treats the feelings of the mother with so little consideration? " Not to mention, that the child itself would, on this supposition, grow up either in ignorance, or in contempt of one of its parents; a state of things full of danger. I know the arguments present in your mind on this subject; but surely, rank and reputation, and prudence are as nothing in comparison to a mother's claims. If it should be recorded that you had sought to violate these, the opinion of the world might indeed be fixed on you, with such blame as your friends could not justify; and wholly unlike those ridiculous and unfounded tales which are told of every person of eminent powers, and which make your friends so many in England, at the expense of those who fabricated them. I assure you, my dear Lord Byron, I speak earnestly, and sincerely. It is not that I wish to make out a case for Clare; my *interest*, as you must be aware, is entirely on the opposite side. Nor have I in any manner influenced her. I have esteemed it a duty to leave her to the impulse of her own feelings in a case where, if she has no feeling, she has no claim. But in truth, if she is to be brought to part with her child, she requires reassurance and tenderness. A tie so near the heart should not be rudely snapt. It was in this persuasion that I hoped (I had a thousand other reasons for wishing to see you) that you would have accepted our invitation to the Pliniana. Clare's pain would then have been mitigated by the prospect of seeing her child with you, and she would have been reassured of the fears which your letter has just confirmed, by the idea of a repetition of the visit. Your conduct must at present wear the aspect of great cruelty, however you justify it to yourself. Surely, it is better if we err, to err on the side of kindness, than of rigour. You can stop when you please; and you are not so infirm of purpose that soothing words, and gentle conduct need betray you in essential matters further than you mean to go.

I am a third person in this painful controversy, who, in the invidious office of mediator, can have no interest, but in the interests of those concerned. I am now deprived of the power to act; but I would willingly persuade. . . .[19]

Even this letter did not entirely remove Byron's distrust and irritation. Perhaps it would have done so but for the wild letters that Claire was now writing him. Very likely these letters accused Byron of violating his promise at Diodati to leave the child in her possession until it was seven years old. Nevertheless Claire decided to accept Byron's terms. On April 30 Shelley wrote to Byron with a firmness that compelled respect:

Allow me also to *repeat* my assertion that Clare's late conduct with respect to the child was wholly unconnected with, and uninfluenced by me. The correspondence from which these misinterpretations have arisen was undertaken on my part solely because you refused to correspond with Clare. My conduct in the affair has been simple, and intelligible. I am sorry that I misunderstood your letter; and I

11

hope that on both sides there is here an end of misunderstandings.

You will find your little Allegra quite well. I think she is the most lovely and engaging child I ever beheld. Tell us what you think of her, and whether, or no, she equals your expectations. Her attendant is not the servant whom I alluded to in my last letter; but a Swiss, who has attended my own children, in whom Mrs. S[helley] entirely confides, and who even quits us somewhat unwillingly, and whom Mary parts with solely that Clare and yourself may be assured that Allegra will be attended almost with a mother's care.

Clare, as you may imagine, is dreadfully unhappy. As you have not written to her, it has been a kind of custom that she should see your letters; and I daresay you know that you have sometimes said things which I do not think you would have addressed to her. It could not in any way compromise you to be cautious in this respect, as, unless you write to her, I cannot well refuse to let her see your letters. I have not seen any of those which she has written to you; nor even have I often known when they were sent.[20]

In the same letter Shelley informed Byron that he had been unable to take the Villa Pliniana and that his party would leave next day for Pisa. Claire was wretchedly disconsolate, and the use of some letters of introduction at Pisa might serve to divert her melancholy. Her melancholy, and perhaps also something of the final outcome, had been foreseen by Shelley, who was further alarmed by an unfavourable account of Byron's life in Venice that he received from a Venetian with whom he fell into conversation at the Post Office. He had urged Claire not to part with Allegra on Byron's terms.[21] But Claire pinned her hopes on a future softening of Byron's attitude, and Allegra departed with Elise on April 28.

Shelley's state of health almost invariably reflected his emotional crises. He had arrived in Italy feeling unusually fit, but Mary now wrote in her journal for April 22: " Shelley unwell; he reads the ' Paradiso; ' writes to Albè." Other than this there is no indication in the reticent, impersonal journals of either Mary or Claire that the whole household was in a state of emotional strain. They rode in the Corso, walked in the public gardens with the children, visited the cathedral, enjoyed the opera, played chess, wrote and received letters, wrote Italian exercises, and read Dante and *Clarissa Harlowe* in Italian and Wieland's *Aristippus* in a French translation.

THE journey from Milan to Pisa occupied seven days, May 1–7. On the first night they slept at Piacenza, on May 2 at Parma ("a dear town," according to Mary), on the 3rd at Modena. Hitherto their road had been mostly through a fertile plain where the fields of grain were studded with trees up which grapevines were trained and then festooned from tree to tree. On May 4 they dined at Bologna and slept at a solitary inn high up in the Apennines.²² Very likely it was at this inn, while the keen winds whistled without, that Shelley wrote the fragmentary poem known as "Passage of the Apennines," his first poetic composition since leaving England:

> Listen, listen, Mary mine,
> To the whisper of the Apennine,
> It bursts on the roof like the thunder's roar,
> Or like the sea on a northern shore,
> Heard in its raging ebb and flow
> By the captives pent in the cave below.
> The Apennine in the light of day
> Is a mighty mountain dim and gray,
> Which between the earth and the sky doth lay [*sic*];
> But when night comes, a chaos dread
> On the dim starlight then is spread,
> And the Apennine walks abroad with the storm
> Shrouding . . .

Throughout the next day they travelled across chestnut-wooded ridges very different from the rugged Alps, and slept at the village of Barberino. On May 6 they began descending the valley of the Arno toward Pisa. That night they slept at La Scala, and next day they arrived at Pisa and put up at the Tre Donzelle. During their journey the sky had been regularly high and cloudless, in spite of constant winds. Claire, the most dejected member of the party, felt some hope that " the long strait road I see before me will take me to some place where I shall be happier." ²³

Pisa did not at first seem to be such a place. Wherever they went, Shelley, Mary, and Claire were always sensitive to any contrast between the beauty of nature and art and the degradation of man. It had been so in Switzerland and when they crossed Savoy. It could hardly be less so in Italy, a country, or rather ten countries, that had experienced the enlightened tyranny of Napoleon only to be returned by the Congress of Vienna to the reactionary domination of Austria, the Pope, and some five or six hereditary Habsburgs and Bourbons to whom the French Revolution was a nightmare they could neither forget nor successfully ignore.

In Milan Shelley had already begun to feel this contrast. "The people here," he had written to Peacock, "though inoffensive enough, seem both in body and soul a miserable race. The men are hardly men; they look like a tribe of stupid and shrivelled slaves, and I do not think that I have seen a gleam of intelligence in the countenance of man since I passed the Alps." [24] Though they admired the cathedral and the leaning tower of Pisa, they were far more impressed by a general air of poverty and wretchedness in the town. The streets were cleaned by a numerous gang of convicts, clad in red and chained together two-and-two. "All the day long one hears the slow clanking of their chains, and the rumbling of the cart they drag as if they were so many Beasts of Burden and if one goes to the window one is sure to see their yellow faces and emaciated forms." [25] The sight was to become a familiar one to Shelley during the rest of his life, but he never conquered the agitation which it caused him. [26]

THEY tarried at Pisa a few days, long enough to hear from Elise (May 8) of her safe arrival in Venice with Allegra. Proceeding next day to Leghorn (Livorno), they put up for a few days at the Acquila Nera and then took apartments. [27]

For nearly two months Shelley's party had been almost constantly on the move, meeting no one they knew, forming no new acquaintances except a very few which were immediately severed. Apparently they had received only one English letter, from Peacock. At Leghorn, though they did not originally intend it, they settled down for a month. Leghorn was a noisy trading city, a seaport containing a number of English business houses. The Shelleys were none too delighted with this "Wapping of Italy." Mary's journal on the day of their arrival labelled it "a stupid town," and Shelley described it to Peacock as "the most unattractive of cities." [28]

Here the Shelleys were to present a letter of introduction from Godwin to Mrs. John Gisborne, better known as Maria Gisborne. Long ago in London Mrs. Gisborne, then Mrs. Reveley, a beautiful young matron of unusual musical and artistic abilities, had been an admiring friend of both Godwin and Mary Wollstonecraft. When Mary Wollstonecraft died after childbirth and left a helpless, bookish widower in charge of the infant Fanny Imlay and the newly-born Mary Godwin, Mrs. Reveley had taken Mary into her own home. After her husband's death two years later she declined Godwin's almost immediate proposal of marriage. On the first evening that the Shelleys spent in Leghorn she called with her second husband on the young woman to whom she had been almost a foster-mother twenty years before. "She is reserved," Mary wrote in her journal that night (May 9), "yet with easy manners." The next day they had a long talk about Mary's parents, and thereafter the Shelleys and Gisbornes were constantly calling upon each other or taking long walks together. It was principally on her account that the Shelleys remained over a month in Leghorn.

Mary wrote to her father an account of her new friend that thrilled even his stoic mind with the memory of a time when he had been comparatively warm-hearted. "I was extremely gratified by your account of Mrs. Gisborne," he answered. "I have not seen her I believe these twenty years; I think not since she was Mrs. Gisborne; and yet by your description she is still a delightful woman. How inexpressibly pleasing it is to call back the recollections of years long past, and especially when the recollection belongs to a person in whom one has deeply interested oneself, as I did in Mrs. Reveley. I can hardly hope for so great a pleasure as it would be to see her again." [29] What

15

a pity, Mary must have thought on reading this, that he did not contrive to marry her instead of that odious Mrs. Clairmont.

Mrs. Gisborne, a woman of forty-eight, was not handsome, but her features were good; there was a pleasant expression about her mouth and eyes that marked her immediately as sensitive and intelligent. She had the calm, slightly reserved manner that can sympathize with enthusiasm without catching fire from it, and when she spoke, which was not too often, she dropped her words, as Leigh Hunt said, "deliciously."[30] She reminded Shelley of his early friend Mrs. Boinville, whose good sense and liberal principles he said she approached, but hardly equalled. After weeks of travel and mere day-to-day conversation with strangers the intelligent talk of such an understanding person was enough in itself to make Leghorn attractive to the Shelleys.

Mr. Gisborne was an unsuccessful merchant who had retired on the remainder of his property and had devoted himself for some years mainly to his books and the education of his stepson. He was a prosy, thin-lipped, placid man with a receding forehead and a nose, in Shelley's phrase, "quite Slawkenbergian" — a most prodigious nose, in fact, which Shelley could never forget. Nor could he completely forgive it, for it was "the sort of nose which transforms all the *g's* its wearer utters into *k's*."[31] Both the Shelleys thought him quite a bore; it amused Shelley to indulge in a classical pun for Hogg's benefit by describing him as "of the Erymanthian breed."[32] "Perhaps I do him an injustice," Shelley added after another such characterization, and Peacock commented: "I think he did. I found Mr. Gisborne an agreeable and well-informed man."[33]

Mrs. Gisborne's son by her first marriage, Henry Reveley, was a young man of about thirty, "an excellent fellow," as Shelley thought, "but not very communicative."[34] Henry was an engineer who had received the best training Italy could offer. In 1818 he was busily at work on the construction of a steamboat that he hoped would revolutionize maritime traffic in the Mediterranean. His room was a jumble of nautical instruments, books on mathematics, engine-models, "Great screws, and cones, and wheels, and groovèd blocks."[35] His talk, when he occasionally took part in the evening strolls, was doubtless of the project that filled his mind and time. On May 28 the Shelleys went with him and the Gisbornes to see his engine. Henry was full of high hopes, and Shelley, listening, lived again in his old dream of science regenerating the world. Within two years this engine was to damage his purse and all but wreck the longest and one of the most satisfying friendships that he formed in Italy.

There were a good many other English people in Leghorn, but Mary's journal mentions only two of them, a Mrs. Partridge, who accompanied them on their usual evening walk with the Gisbornes on June 5, and a Mr. Beilby, who called later in the same evening and who walked with them on May 17. By hearsay rather than by experience they made their first acquaintance with the Italian way of receiving callers. " They told us that whenever you call at an Italian house the servant always puts her head out of the window and demands, *chi è,* whatever time of day or night it may be. The proper answer to this question is *amici,* but those people [who] do not know the proper reply are terribly puzzled to know what to answer to this *chi è* which meets them at every corner." Assemblies, to the English, were not really assemblies. " There are no refreshments and the English complain that they do not know what to do when they come in, for there is no appearance of receiving visits; for the company instead of assembling together are dispersed in parties about the room." [36]

As usual, the Shelleys spent much of their time in reading. Shelley read the *Hippolytus* of Euripides, and the *Electra, Ajax,* and *Philoctetes* of Sophocles, Ariosto's sixth canto with Mary, and Manso's life of Tasso. " I have devoted this summer, and indeed the next year, to the composition of a tragedy on the subject of Tasso's madness, which I find upon inspection is, if properly treated, admirably dramatic and poetical," Shelley had written to Peacock.[37] Probably here or during the next two months at Bagni di Lucca he wrote the two short fragments which are all that he accomplished toward fulfilling one of his favourite projects. Mary, often the more extensive reader, read Lucian in translation and Terence's *Phormio* apparently in Latin, Gozzi's *Zobeide* and *Melarance,* the *Arabian Nights* in

17

French, Voltaire's *Zaïre, Alzire, Mahomet, Mérope,* and *Semiramis,* and several cantos of Ariosto. On May 25 she finished copying the manuscript history of Beatrice Cenci which was later to furnish the materials for Shelley's tragedy of *The Cenci.* Claire's journal in May and June trailed off into brief daily translations from her German reading and thereafter ceased (or at least is no longer extant) until August 1820.

Summer was now approaching, when all who could leave the hot lowland cities sought a retreat in the mountains. The Shelleys did not find Leghorn uncomfortably hot, but they did object to its noise and bustle. On May 26 Shelley departed with Mary or Claire for Bagni di Lucca, in the Apennines, about sixty miles north of Leghorn, to arrange for a summer home. He returned two days later and on June 11 the Shelleys travelled to Bagni di Lucca and settled in the house (Casa Bertini) that Shelley had engaged.

THE nine weeks during which they were settled at Bagni di Lucca were among the most comfortable weeks spent in Italy. They had a small house, but sufficiently commodious, clean, freshly painted and furnished, with a small garden at the end of which was a thick laurel grove.[38] After the grating noise of Leghorn it was soothing to hear only the sound of the river rushing through its valley below their little villa. The hills were picturesque and were covered with chestnut woods through which numerous paths offered opportunities for long quiet walks.

As yet the Baths were not crowded. The Casino, which usually offered every kind of amusement, particularly dancing, was still closed. Their only caller at first was a Signor Chiappa, probably their landlord. He was dull enough, but he was at least useful in providing them with servants — a cleaning-woman " to do the dirty work " at one paul a day, and a cook and general factotum named Paolo Foggi, at three pauls daily. Paolo was a great treasure. He cooked acceptably and managed all the little details of domestic economy so neatly and cleanly, without bothersome consultations, that he was able to cheat his employers from the first in comparative security. They knew his dishonesty, but ignored it, not realizing what a bitter price it was to cost them in the end.

All that was needed was the sympathetic company of the Gisbornes, whom they immediately tried to induce to join them. But the Gisbornes were now involved in exasperating complications of a legal or financial nature over Henry's steam engine and felt compelled to stay in Leghorn, where they amused themselves with a kaleidoscope built by Henry according to a description Shelley had received from Hogg.[39]

Throughout June, Shelley and Mary settled into their beloved quiet routine of reading and walking. Signor Chiappa appears to have troubled them only once or twice with his tiresome calls, and they saw no one else. Shelley continued to read mainly in the Greek classics, Xenophon's *Memorabilia,* and Aristophanes' *Clouds, Plutus,* and *Lysistrata,* and Barthélemy's *Anacharsis.*[40] He continued reading Ariosto with Mary. He also read aloud part of Spenser's *Shepherd's Calendar* and Hume's *History of England.* Mary read mainly Ariosto and the Latin classics — the *Æneid,* Horace, and Livy. But she also read in Gibbon, and Ben Jonson's *Every Man in His Humour* and *Volpone.*

Late June and early July brought to the Baths a considerable number of new people, particularly English people. " We see none but English," Mary complained to Mrs. Gisborne.

We hear nothing but English spoken. The walks are filled with English nursery-maids — a kind of animal I by no means like — and dashing, staring English-women, who surprise the Italians (who always are carried about in sedan chairs) by riding on horseback. For us, we generally walk, except last Tuesday [June 30], when Shelley and I took a long ride to *Il Prato Fiorito,* a flowery meadow on the top of one of the neighbouring Apennines. We rode among chestnut woods, hearing the noisy cicala, and there was nothing disagreeable in it except the steepness of the ascent. The woods about here are in every way delightful, especially when they are plain, with grassy walks through them. They are filled with sweet singing birds, and not long ago we heard a cuckoo. Mr. Shelley wishes to go with me to Monte Pellagrino, the highest of the Apennines, at the top of which there is a shrine; it is distant about twenty-two miles." [41]

Shelley's letter to the Gisbornes written a week or two later shows how little the increase of population and social activity at the Baths impinged upon their chosen manner of living:

We have spent a month here already in our accustomed solitude, (with the exception of one night at the Casino) and the choice society of all ages, which I took care to pack up in a large trunk before we left England, have revisited us here. I am employed just now, having little better to do, in translating into my fainting and inefficient periods the divine eloquence of Plato's Symposium; only as an exercise or perhaps to give Mary some idea of the manners and feelings of the Athenians — so different on many subjects from that of any other community that ever existed.

We have almost finished Ariosto — who is entertaining and graceful, and *sometimes* a Poet. Forgive me, worshippers of a more equal and tolerant divinity in poetry, if Ariosto pleases me less than you. Where is the gentle seriousness, the delicate sensibility, the calm and sustained energy without which true greatness cannot be? He is so cruel too, in his descriptions; his most prized virtues are vices almost without disguise. He constantly vindicates and embellishes revenge in its grossest form; the most deadly superstition that ever infested the world. How different from the tender and solemn enthusiasm of Petrarch — or even the delicate moral sensibility of Tasso, though somewhat obscured by an assumed and artificial style.

We read a good deal here and we read little in Livorno. We have ridden, Mary and I, once only, to a place called Prato Fiorito, on the top of the mountains: the road, winding through forests, and over torrents, and on the verge of green ravines, affords scenery magnificently fine. I cannot describe it to you, but bid you, though vainly, come and see. I take great delight in watching the changes of atmosphere here, and the growth of the thunder showers with which the moon is often over shadowed, and which break and fade away towards evening into flocks of delicate clouds. Our fire flies are fading away fast; but there is the planet Jupiter, who rises majestically over the rift in the forest-covered mountains to the south, and the pale summer lightning which is spread out every night, at intervals, over the sky. No doubt Providence has contrived these things, that, when the fire flies go out, the low-flying owl may see her way home.[42]

Through July and the middle of August the same calm, happy serenity continued. Mary read Vergil, *Anacharsis*, Livy, Horace, Ariosto, Tasso's *Aminta, Coriolanus*, Ben Jonson's *Tale of a Tub* and *The Case is Altered*, Montaigne, Wieland's *Peregrinus Proteus, The Revolt of Islam, Letters and Thoughts*, and Eustace's "*Travels in Italy*." [43] Shelley read *Anacharsis*, Aristophanes, Herodotus, *The Persians* of Æschylus, Theocritus, Vergil's *Georgics*, Hume, *The Maid's Tragedy, Philaster, Wife for a Month, Richard III, Henry VIII*, and Eustace's "*Travels*." In the evening he frequently read aloud from Hume or Shakespeare. The days succeeded each other with very few distinguishing incidents. Signor Chiappa called once (July 3), but they still knew practically none of the people who thronged the Baths. Three times (July 5, 12, and August 2) they visited the Casino, and once (July 27) they attended a *festa di ballo* in the evening. They took up horseback riding, a favourite amusement with the other summer residents, and Shelley rode over to see the adjacent city of Lucca. Claire fell off her horse twice, and injured her knee, but was able to ride with Shelley on one of his two visits to Lucca, July 17 and 18.

All this was in the mornings and evenings. As for midday, Shelley wrote:

In the middle of the day, I bathe in a pool or fountain, formed in the middle of the forests by a torrent. It is surrounded on all sides by precipitous rocks, and the waterfall of the stream which forms it falls into it on one side with perpetual dashing. Close to it, on the top of the rocks, are alders, and above the great chestnut trees, whose long and pointed leaves pierce the deep blue sky in strong relief. The water of this pool, which, to venture an unrythmical paraphrase, is "sixteen feet long and ten feet wide," is as transparent as the air, so that the stones and sand at the bottom seem, as it were, trembling in the light of noonday. It is exceedingly cold also. My custom [is] to undress, and sit on the rocks, reading Herodotus, until the perspiration has subsided, and then to leap from the edge of the rock

into this fountain — a practice in the hot weather excessively re-
freshing. This torrent is composed, as it were, of a succession of
pools and waterfalls, up which I sometimes amuse myself by climbing when I bathe, and receiving the spray over all my body, whilst
I clamber up the moist crags with difficulty.[44]

Shelley was full of ideas for writing. His plan of a drama on
Tasso's madness was still in mind. Very likely he was already
thinking of *Prometheus Unbound* and *The Cenci* and of a
tragedy based on the Book of Job.[45] As yet, however, he was
doing little writing. *Rosalind and Helen* was finished. Mary's
journal shows that she was copying it on August 14 and 16,
but she laid it aside until December 18. Shelley's only complete literary production at Bagni di Lucca was his translation
of Plato's *Symposium*.

From the very beginning of this dialogue Mary must have
wondered at the instinct that led Shelley to so sympathetic a
subject. The praise of the higher or Uranian love as the chief
inspirer to an excellent life, the analysis of love as a mystic,
universal force subsisting in all natures both animate and inanimate, were a prophecy of Shelley's own triumphant description of a similar " Light whose smile kindles the universe." [46] Aristophanes' fable of man's double, androgynous
nature, cleft asunder by the gods and seeking always to reunite
" in the pursuit of integrity and union . . . which we call love,"
might have reminded Mary of *Alastor*. She could easily recognize the Shelleyan quality of Agathon's tribute to love as the
power that " divests us of all alienation from each other and
fills our vacant hearts with overflowing sympathy." In the end,
when Diotima expounded to Socrates the highest state of Love,
the words might easily have been Shelley's own:

It is eternal, unproduced, indestructible; neither subject to increase nor decay: not, like other things, partly beautiful and partly
deformed; not at one time beautiful and at another time not; not
beautiful in relation to one thing and deformed in relation to another;
not here beautiful and there deformed; not beautiful in the estima-
tion of one person and deformed in that of another; nor can this
supreme beauty be figured to the imagination like a beautiful face,

or beautiful hands, or any portion of the body, nor like any discourse, nor any science. Nor does it subsist in any other that lives
or is, either in earth, or in heaven, or in any other place; but it is
eternally uniform and consistent, and monoeïdic with itself. All other
things are beautiful through a participation of it, with this condition,
that although they are subject to production and decay, it never
becomes more or less, or endures any change. When any one
ascending from a correct system of Love, begins to contemplate this
supreme beauty, he already touches the consummation of his labour.
For such as discipline themselves upon this system, or are conducted
by another beginning to ascend through these transitory objects
which are beautiful, towards that which is beauty itself, proceeding
as on steps from the love of one form to that of two, and from that
of two, to that of all forms which are beautiful; and from beautiful
forms to beautiful habits and institutions, and from institutions to
beautiful doctrines; until, from the meditation of many doctrines,
they arrive at that which is nothing else than the doctrine of the
supreme beauty itself, in the knowledge and contemplation of which
at length they repose.[47]

Shelley's own definition of love, evolved under the influence
of this reading, is stated in a fragment written almost immediately afterwards:

that profound and complicated sentiment, which we call love, which
is rather the universal thirst for a communion not merely of the
senses, but of our whole nature, intellectual, imaginative and sensitive; and which, when individualised, becomes an imperious necessity, only to be satisfied by the complete or partial, actual or supposed, fulfilment of its claims. This want grows more powerful in
proportion to the development which our nature receives from civi-
lisation; for man never ceases to be a social being. The sexual impulse, which is only one, and often a small part of those claims,
serves, from its obvious and external nature, as a kind of type of
expression of the rest, a common basis, an acknowledged and visible
link.[48]

Because the *Symposium* contains an episode in which Alci-
biades speaks of his homosexual love-making to Socrates, Shelley had no present intention of publishing his translation. It
was one of the most striking of several circumstances in which
the ancient and modern views of love differed, and it interested

Shelley in this respect very much as he had been (and was again to be) interested in the subject of incest. He immediately began his " Discourse on the Manners of the Ancients Relative to the Subject of Love," which Mr. Ingpen has privately printed, although only seven pages have been published. It deals in part with ancient homosexuality; Shelley called it " a subject to be handled with that delicate caution which either I cannot or I will not practice in other matters, but which I here acknowledge to be necessary." [49] In the introductory paragraphs Shelley gave full utterance to his great admiration for the ancient Greeks. " The period which intervened between the birth of Pericles and the death of Aristotle," he began, " is undoubtedly . . . the most memorable in the history of the world "; and after reviewing the contributions of that period toward human enlightenment, he concluded his tribute: " What the Greeks were, was a reality, not a promise. And what we are and hope to be, is derived, as it were, from the influence and inspiration of these glorious generations."

Nevertheless Shelley admitted that subsequent ages had improved upon Greek civilization in two important particulars, by a gradual abolition of human slavery and by a more elevated conception of love between the sexes. For these improvements, as in his later " Defence of Poetry," he gave the credit to Christianity and chivalry. Thus, while he was reading everything he could find that might conduce toward a fuller knowledge of Greek life, he was also making unexpected concessions to what he considered its destroyer. The explanation lies partly in the fact that the finest Greek ideals, as expressed by Plato, were occupying his mind at the same time that he was reading the best products of Christianity and chivalry in Italian literature — Dante, Petrarch, Tasso, and Ariosto. He could not escape their influence toward a greater sympathy and tolerance. Toward institutional Christianity his attitude continued unchanged, but he was now far better qualified to see the nobility of certain Christian ideals. This change had been gradually taking place since shortly after the publication of *Queen Mab*, and had perhaps already been expressed in the " Essay on Christianity," the date of which is uncertain; but it must have been greatly accelerated during his first months in Italy. Soon it was to find further expression in *Prometheus Unbound,* and a little later in *Hellas.*

HITHERTO the Shelleys had received only one or two letters from England. While they were at Bagni di Lucca letters reached them from Godwin, Peacock, the Hunts, and very probably others. Shelley had made an arrangement with his old friend Hookham whereby Peacock could send him a quarterly box of books and magazines from Hookham's shop and charge to Shelley's account. The first of these boxes probably arrived at Bagni di Lucca.⁵⁰ It contained Cobbett's *Register* and the *Examiner* to July, copies of the *Edinburgh* and *Quarterly* reviews, Constable's *Edinburgh Magazine,* and a few books, including Moore's *The Fudge Family In Paris.* Even if these were not yet at hand, both Peacock and Hogg wrote rather in detail about the political situation in England.

An election had just been called, and the government, out of ten members to be elected for London, Westminster, and Southwark, had failed to return a single supporter. This was cheering news for Shelley, convinced as he was that the policies of the Castlereagh administration were hurrying England toward a catastrophe. The *Quarterly,* he learned, was proclaiming that no country was ever in a more combustible state than England at that moment; the *Courier* was calling loudly for a censorship of the weekly press. Brougham had stood for Westmorland against the Tory candidate and had lost by a narrow margin, perhaps partly as a result of the activities of Wordsworth and Southey in support of the government candidate. Wordsworth had even published two addresses *To the Freeholders of Westmorland* arguing (in Peacock's interpretation) that Brougham's lack of wealth would make him an inferior representative and that the Commons should be chosen by the Peers — a pretty example, Peacock thought, of the moral degradation of which " self-sellers " were capable.⁵¹

All this provoked Shelley's deep interest and indignation. " I wish that I had health or spirits that would enable me to enter into public affairs," he wrote Godwin. "If the Ministers do not find some means, totally inconceivable to me, of plunging the nation in war, do you imagine that they can subsist?"[52] To Peacock, apropos of the Westmorland election, he burst out: "I wish you had sent me some of the overflowing villainy of those apostates. What a beastly and pitiful wretch that Wordsworth! That such a man should be such a poet! I can compare him with no one but Simonides, that flatterer of the Sicilian tyrants, and at the same time the most natural and tender of lyric poets."[53]

Peacock painted such a picture of a warm sunny summer in Buckinghamshire, cool, shady strolls through the woods near Marlow, solitary, moonlit evenings on the river, and excursions to the old haunts with Hogg, that Shelley was almost homesick. "What pleasure it would have given me," he answered, "if the wings of imagination could have divided the space which divides us, and I could have been of your party. I have seen nothing so beautiful as Virginia Water — in its kind. And my thoughts forever cling to Windsor Forest, and the copses of Marlow. . . ."[54] Godwin wrote in a mood that might well have made Shelley feel more warmly even toward such an iceberg as his father-in-law. Godwin was finishing his *Reply to Malthus*, which Shelley believed would restore to society some of the hopes Malthus had almost ruined. He was no longer nagging for money, though fully confident that "a tempest was brewing" for him "in the distance." He had thought of a book that he knew he could never write and that he urged Mary to undertake. This was to be a study of the lives of the Commonwealth men (Milton, Vane, Ireton, etc.) that would rescue their names from an inveterate and unjust prejudice. "Write to me as to your equal," he urged with a complacence not unnatural toward a young disciple, "and, if that word is not discordant to your feelings, your friend. It would be strange indeed if we could not find topics of communication that may be gratifying to both. Let each of us dwell on those qualities in the other which may contribute most to the increase of mutual kindness."[55] Shelley's reply ignored this rather gnarled olive-branch and maintained the same courteous, controlled, half-impersonal tone that he reserved for correspondents of antipathetic personality.

Both Godwin and Peacock sent the good news that Mary's *Frankenstein* was now receiving favourable notice. Even the most unfavourable review, the *Quarterly's*, granted the book considerable merit. This was much, considering that the reviewer believed Shelley to be the author, and took this occasion to condemn the way in which he usually employed his talents. A much clearer warning of what Shelley was to expect from the *Quarterly* appeared in its review of Leigh Hunt's *Foliage*, which appeared in the same number. A footnote referred to the production of one of Leigh Hunt's friends then before the reviewer, who doubted whether it " would be morally right " to " lend notoriety " to it by a review. He then gave an unfavourable picture of the author, still not mentioning Shelley's name, as the writer (John Taylor Coleridge) had known him at Eton. On the next page he referred to the author as one who wrote " *atheos* " after his name in an inn register.[56] Reviewing the same book, the *British Critic* for July also digressed briefly to characterize Mr. Percy Bysshe Shelley as a subject too vile, too dangerous to the public morals, to be discussed [57] — and carefully indexed the supposedly casual reference as " Mr. Shelley — an unmentionable subject." Shelley now knew what to expect when the conservative reviewers got to *The Revolt of Islam.* " Their notice of me," he said of the *Quarterly*, " and their exposure of the true motives for not noticing my book, shews how well understood an hostility must subsist between me and them." [58]

A note written to Charles Ollier on June 28 presents apparently an insoluble mystery which may be nothing more than Shelley's occasional love of mystery for its own sake, or a consequence of earlier furtive financial expedients.

> *Bagni di Lucca,*
> *June* 28, 1818

" In great haste "
Dear Sir,

I write simply to request you to pay ten pounds on my acount to a person who will call on you, and *on no account* to mention my name. If you have no money of mine still pay it at all events and cash the enclosed at the bank.

Ever most truly yours,

P. B. SHELLEY.

The person will bring a note without date signed A. B. It is of so great consequence that this note should be paid that I hope if there is any mistake with Brookes you will pay it for me, and if you have none of mine in your hands, that you will rely on my sending it you by return of Post.[59]

A similar note, undated, but postmarked " F. P. O., SE. 1 1818," directed Ollier to pay A. B. £20.[60] Whoever " this person " was, man or woman, he was not to know Shelley's name or, apparently, to divulge his own, yet he presumably received £30, not from Shelley's banker, but from his publisher, long after Shelley had left England. Unless the drafts were sent or carried from Italy he had probably received them some months before under an agreement not to present them for payment until notified. His being directed to Ollier instead of to Brookes and Co. suggests that he may have been known to Brookes and Co. but not to Ollier.[61]

SHELLEY still thought his health and spirits not quite equal to the task of original writing,[62] though it is a little difficult to see why. Both he and Mary had reported his health as wonderfully improved since entering Italy. He had been ill once at Milan under the strain of Claire's difficulties over Allegra, and again for one day, the day after arriving at Bagni di Lucca. Otherwise he seemed to be enjoying and profiting by the kind of life he loved best. Again it was Claire's troubles that set events in motion toward a disastrous sequel.

Claire was uneasy about Allegra. There seems to have been no special reason for this other than a mother's desire to see her child. Byron was already quite fond of the curly-haired, blue-eyed, high-spirited child of fifteen months, to whom he had referred so bluntly as " my bastard." He was proud of the way in which she accepted the admiration of Venetians, from the Governor's wife down, wherever she was shown. Obviously she was being spoiled by too much attention, and still more obviously Byron's disorderly household of caged wild animals and uncaged mistresses was hardly a fit place for her. Byron realized this himself and placed her in the home of his friends Mr. and Mrs. R. B. Hoppner.

Mr. Hoppner was the British consul at Naples, a son of the well-known portrait-painter, himself an amateur artist. Mrs. Hoppner, a Swiss, had a young child of her own and felt keenly the unfitness of Allegra's surroundings in Byron's household.

Claire received letters from Elise on August 14 and 16. Either Allegra had some soon-forgotten childish ailment, or else her situation outside of Byron's household overcame Claire with a desire to visit her. Whichever it was, Claire evidently made a scene. The same entry in Mary's journal that chronicles Elise's second letter records also the common result of unusual emotional strain: " Shelley is not well." Claire was determined to visit her child surreptitiously. Shelley was sure such a plan would fail and would irritate Byron into reprisals, but there was no arguing with Claire. Her determination may have found a secret ally in Shelley's own love of change.[63] On the next day, August 17, Shelley and Claire departed for Venice, accompanied as far as Florence by Paolo. En route Shelley seems to have persuaded her not to attempt a secret visit, but to wait in some neighbouring city while he entered Venice and tried to win Byron's permission for the meeting. Even this, he felt sure, would not succeed.[64]

Mary remained at Bagni di Lucca with the two children and the servants. She had probably opposed the wild journey and given signs of one of her occasional characteristic fits of despondency. En route Shelley seized the first opportunity to improve her spirits.

Well my dearest Mary, are you very lonely? Tell me truth, my sweetest, do you ever cry? I shall hear from you once at Venice and once on my return here [Florence]. If you love me you will keep up your spirits — and at all events tell me truth about it; for I assure you I am not of a disposition to be flattered by your sorrow, though I should be by your cheerfulness; and above all, by seeing [such] fruits of my absence as were produced when [we were] at Geneva.[65]

Before this letter reached Mary (August 23) she had already been disturbed by the illness of little Clara (August 21) and by her own illness the next two days. On the day of Shelley's departure she had written to urge the Gisbornes, once more, to visit the Baths. This time they accepted the invitation, arriving on August 25. They had been present only three days, however, when a letter was received from Shelley that completely altered all previous plans and required Mary's immediate departure with her household.

Chapter XX

MYSTERIES OF DEATH AND BIRTH

REUNION WITH BYRON; DEATH OF CLARA SHELLEY;
DEJECTION AT ESTE; "JULIAN AND MADDALO" AS
A RECORD OF DOMESTIC MISERY;
JOURNEY TO NAPLES; LIFE IN NAPLES;
SHELLEY'S NEAPOLITAN "DAUGHTER"

THE JOURNEY of about sixty miles from Bagni di Lucca to Florence seems to have occupied Shelley and Claire from August 17 until August 20. The last day's journey was accomplished in a "one-horse cabriolet almost without springs, over a rough road." [1] Claire was fatigued, but the effect on Shelley was the surprising one of making him forget the pain in his side that had afflicted him since the journey was decided on. The region over which they travelled consisted sometimes of farmland and vineyards with purpling grapes, at other times of high mountains crowned with impressive Gothic ruins. All this Shelley noted with an appreciative eye. At length they approached Florence, over a cultivated plain dotted with fine country-houses. "I have seldom seen a city so lovely at first sight," Shelley enthusiastically reported. "You see three or four bridges, one apparently supported by Corinthian pillars, and the white sails of the boats, relieved by the deep green of the forest which comes to the water's edge, and the sloping hills covered with bright villas on every side. Domes and steeples rise on all sides, and the cleanliness is remarkably great. On the other side there are the foldings of the Vale of Arno above, first the hills of olive and vine, then the chestnut woods, and then the

31

blue and misty pine forests which invest the aerial Apennines that fade in the distance." [2]

Venice, since the Congress of Vienna, was again Austrian territory; hence it was necessary to obtain a passport from the Austrian ambassador at Florence. This occasioned a delay of four hours or more, during which arrangements were made for continuing the journey to Padua. A more comfortable carriage was procured at a reasonable price, Paolo doing the bargaining. They expected to reach Padua, nearly two hundred miles distant, in three and a half days' travel. It is characteristic of Shelley that when he reported this first stage of the journey to Mary he had already found time to read *The Two Noble Kinsmen*, which he declined to believe was Shakespeare's.[3]

From Florence to Padua the journey provided no particular episodes. The inns were not always good; there were plenty of buzzing gnats to interfere with sleep where mosquito curtains had not been provided, and inside the curtains were sometimes other insects " inexpressible by Italian delicacy," which caused Shelley to pronounce an interdict against the Tre Mori at Bologna. Partly because the inns were bad, Claire again changed her plans and determined to accompany Shelley all the way into Venice.

From Padua to Venice the journey was completed by gondola, in nine hours of luxurious travel. " These gondolas," Shelley reported,

are the most beautiful and convenient boats in the world. They are finely carpeted and furnished with black and painted black. The couches on which you lean are extraordinarily soft, and are so disposed as to be the most comfortable to those who lean or sit. The windows have at will either Venetian plate-glass flowered, or Venetian blinds, or blinds of black cloth to shut out the light. . . . We past the laguna in the middle of the night in a most violent storm of wind, rain, and lightning. It was very curious to observe the elements above in a state of such tremendous convulsion, and the surface of the water almost calm; for these lagunas, though five miles broad, a space enough in a storm to sink a gondola — are so shallow that the boatmen drive the boat along with a pole. The seawater, furiously agitated by the wind, shone with sparkles like stars. Venice, now hidden and now disclosed by the driving rain shone dimly with its lights. We were all this while safe and comfortable, except that Clare was now and then a little frightened in our cabin.[4]

The gondolier, not knowing that they had any particular interest in Lord Byron, began talking of his own initiative about the wild young English milord whom he claimed to have carried in his gondola. Shelley and Claire learned that Byron had a *nome stravagante,* lived luxuriously, and had recently brought over from England two daughters, one of them almost as old as the gondolier himself. They had no sooner reached their inn in Venice than the waiter also began gossiping about Byron.[5]

Without waiting to see any of the sights of Venice, Shelley and Claire took a gondola immediately after breakfast and visited Mr. and Mrs. Hoppner, with whom Elise and Allegra were now domiciled. They were by no means sure of a cordial reception, for they came as unannounced strangers to friends of Byron who might be expected to be biased by his opinion of Claire. But they were received with a politeness that soon turned to active friendliness. Elise and Allegra were sent for immediately, and the Hoppners entered quite sympathetically into a discussion of the best way of approaching Byron. They were convinced that Claire's arrival, if known, would result in his immediate departure from Venice. It was therefore decided that Shelley should see Byron alone and that Claire's presence should be concealed.

Byron received Shelley with real cordiality on his own account and with unexpected good humour ·and reasonableness on Claire's. He objected mildly to Allegra's making a long visit to Claire at Florence, both because it would make the Venetians think he had grown tired of the child and because he thought it would entail fresh difficulties when Claire had to part with Allegra again. Supposing Claire and Mary to be then at Padua, he offered to allow Allegra to go there for a week. " In fact," he concluded, "after all, I have no right over the child. If Claire likes to take it, let her take it. I do not say what most people would in that situation, that I will refuse to provide for it, or abandon it, if she does this; but she must surely be aware herself how very imprudent such a measure would be! "[6] Byron

33

then proposed a horseback ride along the sands of the Lido. Shelley would have preferred returning to relieve Claire's impatience and anxiety, but Claire was supposed to be in Padua, and there was no excuse for not accepting Byron's suggestion.

Byron's gondola bore them through the canals and across the laguna to the long sandy island known as the Lido, where horses were waiting for them. It was a lonely spot, bare except for wrecks, a dwarfish tree or two, and the drying nets of a solitary fisherman. Here, over a thin strip of beach made firm and level by the tide, Byron and Shelley rode and talked until nearly sundown. It was their first meeting since the old familiar association at Geneva two years before, and there was much to tell. Byron was full of his wounded feelings and of the fourth canto of *Childe Harold's Pilgrimage,* which he was then writing. Shelley told the story of his wrongs at the hands of the Lord Chancellor. Byron exclaimed warmly that had he been in England at the time he would have moved heaven and earth to prevent such an unjust decision. There were lighter memories of the old days at Geneva to be renewed. Byron also had considerable fun, perhaps a little to Shelley's embarrassment, quizzing Leigh Hunt's *Foliage.*

All together it was a fine, genial reunion. As they recrossed the laguna to Venice in the sunset the Euganean hills in the distance were islands in a sea of fire, and the domes and towers of the city rose from the floor of the ocean as if by some enchantment. So powerfully was Shelley impressed by this view of Venice that he dwelt upon it not only in his next letter to Peacock but also in the poem which records this renewed association with Byron.[7]

The talk, which had turned to raillery, now grew serious. Old arguments that had beguiled long summer evenings at Villa Diodati came up again and found both disputants still standing on familiar ground.

> Concerning God, freewill, and destiny.
> Of all that Earth has been, or yet may be;
> All that vain men imagine or believe,

VENICE: GRAND CANAL, SHOWING BYRON'S PALAZZO MOCENIGO, LEFT

Lithographed by J. D. Harding

> Or hope can paint or suffering may achieve
> We descanted. . . .[8]

Shelley argued, as always, against despondency and pride, the
more earnestly because he thought they prevented Byron's great
genius from exercising its full power. No one really knew, he
maintained, the actual strength of the chains supposed to bind
the human spirit; there was a vast, unknown power in the human
will to suffer and to conquer.

> It is our will

he maintained,

> That thus enchains us to permitted ill.

But Byron still urged his belief in a dark destiny — "You talk
Utopia." He compared the human soul to the "black and dreary
bell" of a madhouse, that

> must toll
> Our thoughts and our desires to meet below
> Round the rent heart, and pray — as madmen do
> For what? they know not. . . .

How long Shelley stayed over such conversation at Byron's
palace after they returned is concealed by the fact that a part
of his account to Mary has been torn away. Byron, now
"changed into the livest and happiest looking man I ever met,"[9]
was so different from what everything had led Shelley to anticipate that he may have lingered longer than suited Claire, waiting impatiently since three o'clock in the afternoon. His letter
describing the meeting is dated "five o'clock in the morn" of
the next day, August 24.

At some time during the evening Byron had placed at Shelley's disposal "I Capuccini," his villa at Este, and Shelley had
accepted it. Since Byron supposed Claire and Mary to be near
by at Padua it was necessary to get them both to Este as soon
as possible. Not knowing that little Clara had been ill since his
departure, Shelley sent careful instructions to Mary for proceeding instantly to Este. "I have been obliged to decide on
all these things without you," he explained, " — I have done

for the best and, my own beloved Mary, you must soon come
and scold me if I have done wrong, and kiss me if I have done
right — for, I am sure, I do not know which — and it is only
the event that can show." Enclosing fifty pounds for the journey, he concluded: " Kiss the blue [eyed] darlings for me, and
dont let William forget me. Ca [Clara] cannot recollect me." [10]

This letter abolished their previous intention of proceeding
by boat or carriage to Naples soon after Shelley's return to the
Baths.[11] Its receipt by Mary on August 28 occasioned an immediate consultation with the Gisbornes. The next day Mary's
journal laconically records: " Bustle," and the next (August 30,
Mary's birthday): "Packing." Mrs. Gisborne accompanied
Mary and the children to Lucca, whence they proceeded under
Paolo's care to Este, arriving on Saturday, September 5.[12] The
weather had been hot, and there had been various delays, including one whole day at Florence waiting for passports.

Clara's illness, which was merely a teething ailment at Bagni
di Lucca, was converted by the heat and fatigue of the journey
into a serious attack of dysentery. Shortly after the arrival at
Este her condition was quite alarming. The local physician
seemed to Mary to be a stupid fellow, but after a more competent doctor was engaged to come from Padua, Clara's condition,
though still serious, seemed to be somewhat improved.[13] When
Mary arrived, Shelley was also quite unwell, " from taking poison in Italian cakes," [14] and Claire was finding it necessary to
visit a physician in Padua. Nevertheless, both Shelley and Mary
set immediately to work, the former on the first act of *Prometheus Unbound*, the latter on a translation of Monti's *A Cajo
Graccho*, which was apparently abandoned and is now lost.

The house in which they were living had formerly been the
home of the Hoppners, from whom Byron had taken it over without ever living in it. Twenty years later Mary Shelley described
it fully:

I Capuccini was a villa built on the site of a Capuchin convent, demolished when the French suppressed religious houses; it was situated on the very over-hanging brow of a low hill at the foot of a
range of higher ones. The house was cheerful and pleasant; a vine-
trellised walk, a *pergola*, as it is called in Italian, led from the hall-

door to a summer-house at the end of the garden, which Shelley made his study, and in which he began the *Prometheus;* and here also, as he mentions in a letter, he wrote *Julian and Maddalo.* A slight ravine, with a road in its depth, divided the garden from the hill, on which stood the ruins of the ancient castle of Este, whose dark massive wall gave forth an echo, and from whose ruined crevices owls and bats flitted forth at night, as the crescent moon sunk behind the black and heavy battlements. We looked from the garden over the wide plain of Lombardy, bounded to the west by the far Apennines, while to the east the horizon was lost in misty distance. After the picturesque but limited view of mountain, ravine, and chestnut wood, at the Baths of Lucca, there was something infinitely gratifying to the eye in the wide range of prospect commanded by our new abode.[15]

Mary Shelley's letter to Mrs. Gisborne dated " September, 1818 " shows that they found their environment agreeable and that Clara's health was somewhat better. Shelley wrote to Byron on September 13 to inform him that Clara's condition was improving, but would still delay his coming to Venice for four or five days more.[16] Meanwhile he had been writing steadily on the first act of *Prometheus Unbound* and possibly on " Julian and Maddalo." [17] The regular program of reading had been resumed on their arrival at Este, and no doubt continued. Mary had begun or planned to begin her projected drama on Charles I and a translation of Alfieri's *Myrrha.*[18]

During this period the Shelleys must have received the long, chatty double-letter of Leigh Hunt and Marianne Hunt written on Shelley's birthday (August 4) and characteristically delayed in sending; also Peacock's letters of July 19 and August 30.[19] Peacock reported that he was leading a quiet life: in the morning he wrote; in the afternoon he read classical poetry in the woods or on the river; at night he studied philosophy. He had finished *Nightmare Abbey* (in which he had not scrupled to turn some of Shelley's characteristics to amusing account) and was glad to make use of a motto from Ben Jonson that Shelley had sent him for the title page. Those disgraceful poets of the Lakes still roused his ire by their " dirty work " mending Lord Lonsdale's political fences.

Leigh Hunt sent as a birthday present a life-size portrait of his own head, done in chalk by young Thornton's drawing-master. In his old sympathetic, easy way he chatted with occasional touches of humour about personal matters — their friends in England, his literary plans and Shelley's, and the Italian literature that Shelley was reading or ought to read. Describing the veiled attack on Shelley that had appeared in the *Quarterly's* review of *Frankenstein,* he offered a more than sufficient antidote:

I can tell him that his name gets more known and respected every day, in *spite* of the *Quarterly Reviewers,* who have attacked him, and me, and Hazlitt (though not Shelley by name), in their old false, furious, and recoiling way. The candid part of their friends are, I believe, really ashamed of them, — one or two I know, are.

Somewhere, more probably from travellers' gossip than a letter, the Shelleys heard a false rumour that Sir Timothy Shelley was ill and was expected to die. This would have necessitated Shelley's immediate return to England. In his present poor health and spirits he dreaded the journey. "What will not be," he wrote Mary, " — if so it is destined — the lonely journey through that wide, cold France? But we shall see. As yet I do not direct to you *Lady* Shelley." [20]

By September 22 little Clara seemed well enough for Shelley to carry out his long-deferred return to Venice. On the way he wrote to Mary from Padua arranging for Claire to accompany Mary and the child to Padua, where he would meet them and accompany them to Venice. Claire was still attending a physician in Padua and was to return to Este. Shelley met Mary and Clara in Padua according to plan, but hardly had they set out again when the child grew rapidly worse. As her weakness increased and convulsive motions set in about the mouth and eyes, Shelley and Mary made all possible haste toward Venice in order to see a physician.

When they reached Fusina, where they were to take a gondola for Venice across the lagoon, the soldiers on duty demanded their passports. A desperate, frenzied search revealed that the passports had been forgotten. How Shelley, with his uncertain

Italian, overcame the objections of the soldiers and induced them to violate regulations probably neither he nor Mary ever clearly remembered. Mary simply recorded that " they could not resist Shelley's impetuosity at such a moment." [21]

As they crossed the lagoon Clara's condition became steadily worse. Mary hastened with the child to the inn where Shelley had reserved quarters, while Shelley rushed off from the dock to find Dr. Aglietti. When he returned, Mary was waiting for him in the inn hall in a state of dreadful distress. Another doctor was already with Clara, but the case was hopeless. In an hour the child was dead. The brief, restrained account of this tragedy which Shelley sent next day (September 25) to Claire concludes very characteristically: " All this is miserable enough — is it not? but must be borne [Here a line is erased in the original manuscript.] — And above all, my dear girl, take care of yourself." [22]

The Hoppners came instantly and took Shelley and Mary to their home. In Mary's state of complete despair Shelley was glad to accept so kindly an offer even from comparative strangers. [23]

For five days (September 24–9) the Hoppners, with some assistance from Byron, did what they could to keep their guests from dwelling on the recent tragedy. Visits to the Lido, to Byron's palace, the Bridge of Sighs, the Doge's Palace, the library, and the shops, and Shelley's reading aloud the fourth canto of *Childe Harold* are duly noted in Mary's journal as if nothing else had happened. For the day of Clara's death (September 24) she had written: " This is the Journal of misfortunes. . . . We go to Venice with my poor Clara, who dies the moment we get there. Mr. Hoppner comes, and takes us away from the inn to his house." No more than this at the time of her sorrow, and nothing afterwards.

Godwin wrote in due time (October 27) to condole somewhat aloofly on " the first severe trial of your constancy and the firmness of your temper," and to remind Mary that " we seldom indulge long in depression and mourning, except when we think secretly that there is something very refined in it." [24] The daughter of Godwin's stoicism hardly needed such advice, and the daughter of Mary Wollstonecraft's fatalistic depression could scarcely profit by it. On the surface both Shelley and Mary were stoically silent. But beneath the surface was a deep feeling of misery that was to have a far more important effect upon the events of the next few months than the trivial details that Mary so mechanically set down in her journal or the sightseeing that Shelley recorded so calmly in his letters to Peacock.

They returned to Este on September 29 and found that Claire had moved to Padua with the children during their absence. For twelve days they remained at Este, occupied as usual. Mary had brought from Venice the manuscripts of Byron's *Mazeppa* and " Ode to Venice," [25] which she copied for him. She read Livy and Vergil, Shakespeare, and the life and tragedies of Alfieri. Shelley read Shakespeare's *Cymbeline* and *The Winter's Tale* aloud. Reading by himself Malthus's *Essay on Population* he felt constrained, in spite of his abhorrence of the popular interpretation, to pronounced Malthus " a very clever man." [26]

The continued presence of Allegra may have offered some slight consolation for their recent sorrow. It was probably at this time that Shelley wrote his description of her as though he were playing and talking with her in Byron's Palazzo Mocenigo — where, apparently, they never saw each other:

> A lovelier toy sweet nature never made;
> A serious, subtle, wild, yet gentle being,
> Graceful without design, and unforeseeing;
> With eyes — Oh speak not of her eyes! — which seem
> Twin mirrors of Italian heaven, yet gleam
> With such deep meaning, as we never see
> But in the human countenance: with me
> She was a special favourite: I had nursed
> Her fine and feeble limbs when she came first
> To this bleak world. . . .[27]

Shelley was now writing again. " Lines Written among the Euganean Hills " and " Julian and Maddalo," as well as the first act of *Prometheus Unbound,* were all written at Este in 1818. The first of these was dated by Shelley " October, 1818," and hence follows Clara's death; the last was largely written before her death. There is no indication in Mary's journal or elsewhere that dates "Julian and Maddalo" definitely before or after September 24. Hitherto Shelley's letters had shown rare moments of deep despair, but his poetry had been strongly optimistic. Beginning with "Julian and Maddalo" and "Lines Written among the Euganean Hills," and for some months thereafter, his personal poems reached their greatest depths of despondency. If we include "Julian and Maddalo," Shelley completed seven poems in 1818 after Clara Shelley's death, and every single one of them is tinged with the same melancholy and despondence.

"Lines Written among the Euganean Hills" represents a partly successful struggle against utter despair. There must be green isles in the deep wide sea of Misery, he argues, or humanity would not continue to struggle. Shelley's own despair seems to proceed from the thought of a dead body by a "northern sea," which he speaks of as "unburied" and unlamented. This body might be Fanny Imlay's, on the Welsh coast, except that there was at this time no reason for reviving a grief long since healed. It must therefore be the body of Clara, which Mary Shelley's poem "The Choice" states was buried on the Lido, by the northern Adriatic. But the only death that Shelley commonly spoke of as unlamented was his own, hence the lines may suggest Shelley's feeling that he himself died at the same time with Clara. That might also explain the "unburied" — unless Shelley means (which was true) that Mary was in a state of mind which kept Clara's grave constantly open.

Turning in his poem from this despair, Shelley seeks his "flowering islands" in the beauties of sunrise over the plains of Lombardy, revealing a view of Venice, in a picture of Padua under the noontide sun, and of the gradually waning afternoon and evening as seen from his point of vantage among the hills. Both Venice and Padua are somewhat sombrely represented as trampled by tyranny, but Shelley thought that the tyranny would be eventually overthrown — and this, together with the beauty of the day, constituted "green isles" that enabled him to close with a faintly hopeful feeling that

> Other flowering isles must be
> In the sea of life and agony.[28]

41

I f " Julian and Maddalo " was written before the death of Clara, the extreme dejection expressed throughout most of its length by the Madman is either non-autobiographical or else must be referred to some other cause than the death of Clara. Mysterious and hitherto unexplained circumstances that occurred at Naples two or three months later make this poem, probably the first expression of the dejection that culminated at Naples, especially significant in any effort to understand the important hidden forces which both Shelley and Mary rigorously excluded from their letters and journal. Furthermore, it is a poem that is in itself mysterious and has never been fully explained.

" Julian and Maddalo " is usually regarded as a delightful account of the first two days of Shelley's renewed association with Byron, into which is soon introduced a deeply despondent Madman whose obscure conversation and history occupy the rest of the poem. There are strong indications, however, that the Madman is the real centre of the poem. Two-thirds of the six hundred and seventeen lines are devoted to him, and more than a third of the poem consists entirely of his broken monologue. The argument between Julian (Shelley) and Maddalo (Byron) is never concluded after the introduction of the Madman by Byron in support of his contention. Instead, Shelley seemed to consider that the conclusion of the Madman's history was the proper conclusion for the whole poem.

This desertion of the assumed initial purpose of the poem has been accepted as a more or less characteristic structural weakness.[29] But if Shelley had not considered the poem to be centred on the Madman he would never have prefixed to it the motto from Vergil's *Gallus* which asserts that Love is no more saturated with tears than meadows with streams, bees with thyme, or goats with the green leaves of spring. The Madman's story is a story of love and tears, a subject with which the conversation of Julian and Maddalo is totally unconnected. " The ' Julian and Maddalo ' and the accompanying poems are all my saddest verses raked up into one heap," Shelley informed his publishers.[30] Certainly this applies only to the so-called " episode " of the Madman and shows that Shelley considered it the real centre of the poem. It is quite possible (and, I suspect,

likely) that Shelley set out to write a poem about his conversations with Byron, that the first third of the poem was written
in this serene, unclouded spirit — and that something then occurred which completely changed the tone and made it in the
end a very different poem from the one originally intended. In
this case the first third of the poem must have been written before Clara's death, and the remainder, totally changed by that
event and its consequences, soon afterwards.

Such a supposition is supported by the practical certainty that
the Madman's story is autobiographical. The intense dejection
of the Madman, corresponding as it does with the professedly
personal passages of the same sort that dominated Shelley's poetry for the next few months, strongly suggests an autobiographical basis. In his letters Shelley once referred to the poem
as being based upon actual fact, and once to the Madman as a
real person, like Julian and Maddalo.[31] In the poem Maddalo
first speaks of the Madman as having been once very like Julian
(Shelley),[32] and the Madman himself refers to his youthful self-
dedication to love and justice,[33] as Shelley had twice before in
professedly autobiographical passages commemorated his own
youthful self-dedication. His general character is strikingly similar to the traits that Shelley later assigned himself in *Adonais*
and "Ode to the West Wind." The Madman's sensitiveness is
particularly like Shelley's, even to Shelley's occasional illusions
of seeing the absent as though present:

> But *me*, whose heart a stranger's tear might wear
> As water-drops the sandy fountain-stone,
> Who loved and pitied all things, and could moan
> For woes which others hear not, and could see
> The absent with a glance of phantasy . . .
> *Me* — who am as a nerve o'er which do creep
> The else unfelt oppressions of this earth.[34]

The centre of the poem, therefore, is an autobiographical portrait of Shelley in the grip of a "dreadful . . . reality."[35] What
this "reality" was for the Madman may not be literally the same
as what it was for his prototype, Shelley; but whatever it was, it
was the dominant fact in Shelley's life for several very impor-

tant months and lies at the root of his most despondent personal poetry.

Unless Shelley completely metamorphosed it in transferring it from himself to the Madman, it can hardly have been the death of Clara alone. The mental wreck of the Madman proceeded not from a dead child, but from a dead love. He had been accompanied from France to Venice by a lady whom he loved, and by whom he was spurned and deserted. It was her love that had first awakened his, and he had loved " even to mine overthrow "; but her love had turned to scorn and insult; she had rejected his embraces with physical loathing, and had left him. Under the lady's unwarranted scorn and insult he compares himself to a trodden worm which cannot die, but

> wears a living death of agonies!
> As the slow shadows of the pointed grass
> Mark the eternal periods, his pangs pass,
> Slow, ever-moving, making moments be
> As mine seem — each an immortality! [36]

Something very much like this morbid hypersensitiveness Shelley had already described as his own in a letter to Godwin (December 7, 1817): " My feelings at intervals are of a deadly and torpid kind, or awakened to a state of such unnatural and keen excitement that only to instance the organ of sight, I find the very blades of the grass and the boughs of the distant trees present themselves to me with a microscopical distinctness." But though the Madman writhes under pain and injustice with an intense sensitiveness, he protests like Shelley that he has no idea of revenge (he is in fact still in love) and that he will not allow his agony to silence his opposition to tyranny.[37]

Under these conditions the Madman thinks of suicide, as Shelley almost certainly did at the time, and as he later told Trelawny he did two months later at Naples. The Madman was restrained by the same responsibility that must have stayed Shelley's hand more than once:

> Do I not live
> That thou mayst have less bitter cause to grieve?
> I give thee tears for scorn and love for hate;

> And that thy lot may be less desolate
> Than his on whom thou tramplest, I refrain
> From that sweet sleep that medicines all pain.[38]

These lines completely abolish the old theory that the Madman's lady was Harriet Shelley. But they apply more particularly to Mary than even to the lady they purport to describe, for the Madman's lady was financially independent enough to leave him, whereas Mary was utterly dependent.

The cause of the lady's scorn and loathing is not stated. It could not have been infidelity.[39] Somehow, for her sake, he "had fixed a blot of falsehood" on a mind naturally devoted to truth. This blot was the cause of much of the Madman's agony, but not, apparently, of the lady's scorn, since there is no indication that she is aware of it. He asserts that the only road to peace is truth, and exclaims: "I must remove a veil from my pent mind."

Yet he dared not openly avow the falsehood, which not to avow was intolerable:

> O, not to dare
> To give a human voice to my despair
> But live and move, and wretched thing! smile on
> As if I never went aside to groan,
> And wear this mask of falsehood even to those
> Who are most dear — not for my own repose —
> Alas, no scorn or pain or hate could be
> So heavy as that falsehood is to me —
> But that I cannot bear more altered faces
> Than needs must be, more changed and cold embraces,
> More misery, disappointment and mistrust
> To own me for their father.[40]

From this passage it seems that the Madman's falsehood is not a particular lie, but a mask of falsehood under which he habitually lives.

There is another lady, however, "compassionate and wise" as the first is scornful and unrelenting:

> O Thou, my spirit's mate,
> Who, for thou art compassionate and wise,
> Wouldst pity me from thy most gentle eyes

45

> If this sad writing thou shouldst ever see —
> My secret groans must be unheard by thee,
> Thou wouldst weep tears bitter as blood to know
> Thy lost friend's incommunicable woe.[41]

Shelley concludes the poem by revealing that two years later the Madman's health began to fail, whereupon the scornful Lady who had left him returned, looking meek and remorseful — and departed again after his health had mended.

WE CAN hardly doubt that this Madman is Shelley and that his feelings are those of Shelley at Este. Lines 304–15, quoted above, show that Shelley has even forgotten his Madman in himself. In his physical isolation the Madman had no need to worry about "altered faces" and "changed and cold embraces" — the phrases apply only to Shelley, whose emotional loneliness he feared to increase. But how are we to relate the events that produced the Madman's condition to the events of Shelley's own life? The extreme importance of this hidden crisis, connecting (as we shall see later) with mysterious, hidden events at Naples two months afterwards, compels an excursion into subjective interpretations which the biographer fully realizes may be highly treacherous.

There is no word in Mary's journal or the letters of Shelley and Mary to help us; there is extant, in fact, only one letter written from Este after Clara's death. But twenty years later Mary commented briefly on the similarly despondent poems that Shelley resumed writing as soon as they were again settled:

Yet many hours were passed when his thoughts, shadowed by illness, became gloomy, and then he escaped to solitude, and in verses, which he hid for fear of wounding me, poured forth morbid but too natural bursts of discontent and sadness. One looks back with unspeakable regret and gnawing remorse to such periods; fancying that, had one been more alive to the nature of his feelings, and more attentive to soothe them, such would not have existed . . . and yet enjoying, as he appeared to do, every sight or influence of earth or sky, it was difficult to imagine that any melancholy he showed was aught but the effect of the constant pain to which he was a martyr.[42]

This comment must be as true of the poems and state of mind and health of Shelley at Este as to the plainly similar, continued conditions at Naples two months later. From Este in late September to Naples in late December the tone of Shelley's poems moderated somewhat, but remained otherwise completely uniform. In the last passage quoted above from " Julian and Maddalo " the Madman says that " this sad writing " may never be seen by his " spirit's mate " — and Mary's journal at Este shows no knowledge of either " Julian and Maddalo ". or " Lines Written among the Euganean Hills." [45] This suggests, as does the phraseology of the entire passage, that the second lady there appealed to is really Mary Shelley — the former Mary, to whom Shelley now regarded himself as a " lost friend," whose " gentle speech," expressive eyes, and " young wisdom " he had so eloquently praised in the dedicatory poem to *Laon and Cythna,* and whose full compassion (or, as he then called it, " all-powerful benevolence ") toward Claire he had recorded in their journal for December 19, 1814.

To identify the scornful Lady who deserted the Madman we must imagine Mary's thoughts at the time of Clara's death and the very probable effect of those thoughts on a brooding mind that was subject to attacks of deep despondency. Mary must have seen clearly and bitterly that Clara's death was directly traceable to Claire Clairmont's restless and reckless insistence upon visiting Allegra, to Shelley's yielding to Claire, and to his initial deception of Byron that had caused Shelley to insist upon the hot and hurried journey from Bagni di Lucca to Este, with its tragic results for their child. If she used bitter and scornful words toward Shelley, as the Madman's Lady did toward the Madman, and if she regarded Shelley for a while with a hysterical physical loathing, it would have been nothing so unnatural or unusual as the careless observer of life may suppose. Such bitternesses are usually repented later and are sealed up and as nearly as possible forgotten. Shelley's own condition at the time, however, would have prevented his viewing the situation normally.

If this all too probable sequence of thought and action really occurred, then the Madman's recalcitrant mate who deserted him at Venice was also Mary Shelley,[44] turned temporarily into a strange antagonistic personality by her grief. Shelley thought Mary had deserted him when Clara died at Venice, and Mary in the end professed remorse for something which even in her statement sounds like spiritual desertion. Such a desertion by Mary would have shattered Shelley at any time. Coming at a time of ill health and nervous hypersensitiveness it might well have been magnified by him into something far worse than it was.

But what of the Madman's "mask of falsehood," which looms so large in the poem? The only known falsehoods in Shelley's life in which one might be tempted to seek for an actual prototype are Shelley's falsehood against Harriet, when he overcame Mary's reluctance to elope by accusing Harriet of infidelity, and the more recent falsehood by which he had allowed Byron to suppose that his family had accompanied him to Padua. The first of these, if Shelley was ever conscious of it as a falsehood, was long past, and had been followed by several years of happy union with Mary. The second was no longer a falsehood, for Byron had been told of the arrival of Mary and the children at Este, after Shelley had summoned them. Neither fits the character of the falsehood described in the poem. That falsehood appears to be not a single falsehood, but a state of falsehood — a false appearance — of which the Lady is the cause, of which she is kept ignorant, and of which the Madman's friends must be kept ignorant lest they turn against him.

This precisely describes the false show which Shelley was at the moment keeping up with Mary and with all their friends about the situation between them. Such a state of mind was kept from Mary — she testified herself that he hid his dejected poems from her and that she had not realized his state of mind. No word of the situation was uttered to any outsider. If he had proclaimed that Mary no longer loved him, he knew he would encounter "altered faces" from the world and from their joint friends. The intensity of the poet's suffering from this lie could hardly apply to any experience except one actually existing as he wrote. No old affection for Harriet or old yet-to-be-demonstrated love for Claire will serve, for the cause of the Madman's

48

agony avowedly still existed.[45] It was so strong that the sufferer
was compelled to utter it, in spite of a determination to keep it
secret:

> I must remove
> A veil from my pent mind. 'Tis torn aside! [46]

And torn aside it was, for purposes of emotional relief, while
the fact that it had been so remained for a hundred years concealed. Later, in the most autobiographical part of *Epipsychidion,* he employed the same technique of proclaiming an autobiographical basis while concealing its real meaning.

The state of affairs between Shelley and Mary probably never
became as extreme as that described in the poem. In telling
Hunt that the third person in his story was from actual life Shelley added that he was, " with respect to time and place, ideal."
That is, his emotions at the time and place specified in the poem
were not literally and absolutely true. In some respects they
may have been heightened by the memory of former scenes with
Harriet, or even with Claire. They must have been heightened
by the intensity of Shelley's self-sympathy and by an abnormal
condition of both mind and body. Mary's statement that Shelley's mind was " shadowed " at Naples by illness must have been
starkly and almost frightfully true of the mind that uttered " Julian and Maddalo." The sudden violence and injustice to which
Shelley could give utterance under such conditions is well suggested by his conduct toward his mother in 1811, and by his
quick, bitter outbursts against the Gisbornes in 1820. Under
such conditions the extent of Mary's desertion is not to be measured by that of the Madman's Lady, but a desertion of some
extent is obvious. So deep was Shelley's dejection — so intensified, perhaps, by morbid self-pity — that he was not able to
make the Madman's later reconciliation with his Lady final or
complete.

Knowing that " Julian and Maddalo " contained some of his
best poetry up to this time, Shelley was probably loth to throw
it aside entirely. He felt safe enough in publishing it, so long as
it appeared without his name, for the story it concealed was one
that could be known to no one except possibly Claire Clairmont

and Mary.[47] If his judgment on this point seems rash, the repeated failure of critics to penetrate his meaning shows that it
was true for over a century. He could not anticipate the later
collection of hundreds of his letters which would finally furnish
the slight clues necessary for seeing this poem in its true light.

For four months after the death of Clara less than a dozen letters of Shelley's are extant, two of which are short business notes.
Beyond a record of movements and a few personal opinions
these letters give practically no hint of Shelley's misery while he
was writing, far less of its cause. They do, however, mention
a much worse state of health — and Shelley's health of body and
mind usually kept fairly parallel. Otherwise the letters are remarkably impersonal; one recalls the Madman's resolve [48] to
keep the life of the understanding free from that of the emotions and wonders at Shelley's success in doing so. His fine,
impersonal descriptions of Venice, Rome, and Naples are generally admitted to be among the best letters of the sort that English literature affords. Reading them before they were sent,
Mary added a postscript to Peacock: " Keep Shelley's letters, for
I have no copies of them and I want to copy them when I return
to England." [49] Like the Lady in the poem and like some of the
characters in *Prometheus Unbound,* Shelley had divided his personality. During these four months the intellectual, more impersonal side of his nature was producing an almost matchless
series of travel-letters, and at the same time the Madman was
giving more chastened utterance to his veiled sorrow in nearly
every poem Shelley wrote.

SHELLEY wrote to the Olliers that " The ' Julian and Maddalo '
and the accompanying poems are all my saddest poems raked
into one heap." [50] Thus we learn that when he sent the poem to
Hunt in August 1819, it was accompanied by poems which
Shelley not only associated with it, but desired to be printed
with it for that reason. The poem was never printed in this manner, but the significant accompanying poems may be easily identified as some or all of the poems known to have been written
between the death of Clara Shelley and the time Shelley sent

the manuscript to Hunt. One needs only to eliminate all poems
that are not sad and all poems already in print at the time of
Shelley's reference to " the accompanying poems." This leaves
only " The Past," " On a Faded Violet," " Invocation to Misery,"
" Stanzas Written in Dejection, near Naples," " Sonnet: Lift Not
the Painted Veil " — all written in 1818 — to which might possibly be added only " The Question," and " Death," both written
in 1820. All but the last two of these poems must also be the
same poems which (in her Note on the Poems of 1818) Mary
Shelley said Shelley hid from her for fear of wounding her feelings, for they are the only known poems of 1818 that could possibly have wounded her.

It is clear, therefore, that the poems which Shelley associated
with " Julian and Maddalo " were also poems which Mary associated with herself. In the light of this fact it is interesting to
see what Mary did with them when she afterwards published
most of them for the first time in *Posthumous Poems* (1824).
" Julian and Maddalo," the only long poem in the volume, naturally came first. Afterwards came sixty-six short poems, including four of the five " saddest poems " of 1818. One of the four,
" On a Faded Violet," had already been printed by Leigh Hunt;
the one omitted by Mary, perhaps the most revealing poem in
the group, was " Invocation to Misery," first published by Tom
Medwin in 1832. But did Mary print the related poems close to
" Julian and Maddalo," as Shelley had intended? Between " Julian and Maddalo " and the first one of this group she interposed
ten other poems. Ten poems intervene between the first and
second and also between the second and third. The fourth is the
last poem in the volume, separated from the third by sixteen intervening poems. It would have been impossible to dissociate
the poems more completely than Mary Shelley dissociated them,
nor have they ever yet been printed together as Shelley intended.

If we now consider these short poems as related to " Julian and
Maddalo " we see their real meaning for the first time, and confirm the meaning of the longer poem.

The first two of these poems speak plainly, like " Julian and
Maddalo," of a happy love that has turned to sorrow.

51

THE PAST

Wilt thou forget the happy hours
Which we have buried in Love's sweet bowers,
Heaping over their corpses cold
Blossoms and leaves instead of mould?
Blossoms which were the joys that fell,
And leaves, the hopes that yet remain.

Forget the dead, the past? O yet
There are ghosts that may take revenge for it;
Memories that make the heart a tomb,
Regrets which glide through the spirit's gloom,
And with ghastly whispers tell
That joy, once lost, is pain.

ON A FADED VIOLET

The colour from the flower is gone,
   Which like thy sweet eyes smiled on me;
The odour from the flower is flown,
   Which breathed of thee and only thee!

A withered, lifeless, vacant form,
   It lies on my abandoned breast,
And mocks the heart which yet is warm
   With cold and silent rest.

I weep — my tears revive it not.
   I sigh — it breathes no more on me;
Its mute and uncomplaining lot
   Is such as mine should be.

These two poems have hitherto been read without the slightest suspicion that the first is a direct remonstrance to the poet's wife for scorning the happy past which is dead, and the second an allegorizing of her apathy. When Shelley sent " On a Faded Violet " to Sophia Stacey in March 1820 in lieu of a promised poem on singing, he characterized the verses as " old stanzas . . . which, though simple and rude, look as if they were dictated by the heart. And so — if you will tell no one whose they

are, you are welcome to them." This is the same anonymity
Shelley wished for "Julian and Maddalo."

The third poem is a sonnet beginning,

> Lift not the painted veil which those who live
> Call Life . . .

and after describing life's deceptions and disappointments, continues:

> I knew one who had lifted it — he sought
> For his lost heart was tender, things to love,
> But found them not. . . .

In the fourth poem, "Invocation to Misery," Shelley may now
be seen again addressing Mary Shelley, whom the title so well
fitted. The first four stanzas are quite clear in their application:

> Come, be happy! sit near me,
> Shadow-vested misery!
> Coy, unwilling, silent bride,
> Mourning in thy robe of pride,
> Desolation deified! —
>
> Come, be happy! sit near me:
> Sad as I may seem to thee,
> I am happier far than thou,
> Lady, whose imperial brow
> Is endiademed with woe.
>
> Misery! we have known each other,
> Like a sister and a brother
> Living in the same lone home,
> Many years — we must live some
> Hours or ages yet to come.
>
> 'Tis an evil lot, and yet
> Let us make the best of it;
> If love can live when Pleasure dies,
> We two will love, till in our eyes
> This heart's Hell seem Paradise.

The next two stanzas summon Misery to be happy in the midst
of sights and sounds that were formerly sweet; then:

> Ha! thy frozen pulses flutter
> With a love thou darest not utter.
> Thou art murmuring — thou art weeping —
> Was thine icy bosom leaping
> While my burning heart was sleeping?

> Kiss me; oh! thy lips are cold:
> Round my neck thine arms enfold —
> They are soft, but chill and dead;
> And thy tears upon my head
> Burn like points of frozen lead.

The two following stanzas actually repeat the Madman's plea in
Julian and Maddalo, lines 384–390; and the two final stanzas present life as an illusion of puppets to be laughed at, concluding:

> What but mockery can they mean
> Where I am — where thou hast been?

" Stanzas Written in Dejection, near Naples," which will be considered later, shows that this strain in Shelley's poetry continued into December.

These poems, by the indirect testimony of both Shelley and
Mary, are autobiographical and are connected with " Julian and
Maddalo." When the attendant circumstances are considered
they could not possibly apply to anything except the relations
of Shelley and Mary in the autumn and winter of 1818. They
exclude, definitely and completely, both Claire Clairmont and
the absurd mysterious lady whom Medwin presented as the key
to the mystery of Shelley's dejection.[51] The poems show that
Mary probably abandoned the inimical attitude reflected in
" Julian and Maddalo " and sank into an apathy of grief, which
desolated Shelley, but which he soon came to regard with
mournful sympathy rather than with wild resentment, as at first.
It is this early antagonism on both sides that makes me suggest
that Mary at first held Shelley indirectly responsible for Clara's
death. The antagonism soon vanished, but the alienation, both

spiritual and physical, continued until the beginning of 1819. One sees at last why " Julian and Maddalo " and *Epipsychidion* were almost the only longer poems of Shelley about which Mary remained completely silent in her Notes. They were the poems which most needed elucidation, and which Mary alone could elucidate. But to do so would completely " remove a veil " which Mary was willing only to touch for one brief moment, as she had done in her poem " The Choice."

Though there is plenty of evidence of the mutual continued love and respect of Shelley and Mary thereafter, it was never the same as it had been before. There were later minor domestic crises. Neither Shelley nor Mary ever quite retraced all the steps by which they had withdrawn from their early rapturous union. At different times afterwards, in a number of poems that have commonly been supposed to have no particular personal significance, Shelley returned to the mood of mournful disappointment that followed upon the agonized resentment of his Madman.[52]

Mary, like Shelley, also felt the contradictory impulse both to conceal a private discord and to " remove a veil " from her " pent mind." Shortly after Shelley's death a possibly exaggerated remorse caused her to write her poem " The Choice," containing the following explanation and apology:

> — thou hast often sung,
> How fallen on evil days thy heart was wrung;
> Now fierce remorse and unreplying death
> Waken a chord within my heart, whose breath,
> Thrilling and keen, in accents audible
> A tale of unrequited love doth tell.
> It was not anger, — while thy earthly dress
> Encompassed still thy soul's rare loveliness,
> All anger was atoned by many a kind
> Caress or tear, that spoke the softened mind. . . .
> It speaks of cold neglect, averted eyes,
> That blindly crushed the soul's fond sacrifice: —
> My heart was all thine own, — but yet a shell
> Closed in its core, which seemed impenetrable. . . .[53]

Thus it is that for three vitally important months of Shelley's life the most significant circumstances have been concealed by

highly subjective confession-poems that were never intended
as full confessions, but were deliberately obscured by both Shelley and Mary. Neither Mary's journal nor Shelley's letters give
any hint of the abnormal emotional situation which both concealed from their friends, but which nevertheless dominated
most of Shelley's poetry at the time.

BEFORE the ill-fated journey from Bagni di Lucca to Venice it
had already been decided to go to Naples for the winter. This
plan was now resumed. On October 11 Shelley and Mary set
out for a last visit to Venice before their departure south, leaving William and Allegra en route at Padua, presumably with
Claire. For ten days they dined with the Hoppners almost every
day and spent most of the evenings with them, except for three
evenings (October 13, 21, 22) that Shelley spent with Byron.
It is of some possible significance in view of what happened
soon afterwards at Naples to know that the principal object of
his evenings with Byron was to secure Byron's consent to pro-
longing Allegra's visit. He argued and begged, but in vain. Byron, with whom he had at first been so delighted, was now a
great disappointment to him — a man dominated by obstinate,
self-willed folly, degrading himself with the lowest associations
and debaucheries, whose candour to his friends was not to be
fully trusted — and yet a great poet still.[54]
A frequent guest at the Hoppners was the Chevalier Men-
galdo, a veteran of Napoleon's campaigns, who talked of his experiences in Russia and related ghost-stories. While Shelley was
spending an evening with Byron (October 21), Mary was taken
by the Hoppners to see a comedy which she found " stupid beyond measure." On the 24th Shelley went to Este to fetch Allegra, who must now be returned to Byron, and on October 31,
the day after Shelley's return with Allegra, they took leave of the
Hoppners and set out for Este. November 5 saw them started
on the long overland trip to Rome and thence to Naples. They
travelled with less expense by having bought their own horses
and by using Paolo as coachman.[55]

Whoever wishes to see the effects of such a journey upon a lively and intelligent mind should read Shelley's detailed account in the letters, which even the usually unenthusiastic Peacock thought exceptionally fine.

At Ferrara on November 6–7 Shelley wrote Peacock a long and interesting account of the prosperous farms between Este and Ferrara and of the sights of Ferrara, rich in relics of Ariosto and Tasso. The fresh beauty of old illuminated manuscripts in the large public library, the armchair, the inkstand, and the handwriting of Ariosto are all thoughtfully described. Shelley even deduces the mental complexions of Ariosto and Tasso. " The handwriting of Ariosto is a small, firm and pointed character expressing, as I should say, a strong and keen, but circumscribed energy of mind; that of Tasso is large, free, and flowing except that there is a checked expression in the midst of its flow which brings the letters into a smaller compass than one expected at the beginning of the word. It is the symbol of an intense and earnest mind exceeding at times its own depths, and admonished to return by the chillness of the waters of oblivion striking upon its adventurous feet." The dungeon in which Tasso had been for so many years imprisoned seemed to him " a horrible abode for the coarsest and the meanest thing that ever wore the shape of man, much more for one of delicate sensibilities and elevated fancies." His pity was particularly aroused by a sight of some of the manuscripts in which Tasso flattered his persecutor: " There is something irresistibly pathetic to me in the sight of Tasso's own handwriting moulding expressions of adulation and entreaty to a deaf and stupid tyrant. . . ."[56]

From Ferrara to Bologna was a rainy day's travel (November 8) through a marshy, uninteresting country. At Bologna they spent the better part of two days in churches and palaces and in the Accademia delle Belle Arte looking at paintings. A long letter to Peacock is devoted almost entirely to an account of these paintings. Shelley was especially impressed with Guido's *Rape of Prosperine*.[57] A Guercino convinced him that the painter might surpass the writer in giving a true picture of religious austerity:

I never saw such a figure as this fellow [Saint Bruno, founder of the Carthusians]. His face was wrinkled like a dried snake's skin and drawn in long hard lines. His very hands were wrinkled. He looked like an animated mummy. He was clothed in a loose dress of death-coloured flannel such as you might fancy a shroud might be after it had wrapt a corpse a month or two. It had a yellow putrefied ghastly hue which it cast on all the objects around, so that the hands and face of the Carthusian and his companion were jaundiced in this sepulchral glimmer. Why write books against religion, when one may hang up such pictures. But the world either will not or cannot see.[58]

By November 14, after passing the night successively at Faenza, Cesena, and Catholica, they began the ascent of the Apennines. For six days (November 14–19) their road wound around and over mountains and ravines. Following the valley of the Metaurus through scenery that was "exceedingly beautiful," they passed along a road made by the Consul Æmilius, and through an ancient tunnel in which the Roman chisel-marks were still plainly discernible. They slept, generally without much comfort, at Fossombrone, Scheggia, Foligno, Spoleto, Terni, and Nepi.[59] Spoleto, with the large castle that had dominated it from Roman times and the high aqueduct connecting two mountain tops, seemed to Shelley "the most romantic city I ever saw."[60]

The falls of the Velino at Terni put Mary in mind of Sappho leaping from a rock and roused Shelley to one of his finest enthusiasms of description:

From Spoleto we went to Terni, and saw the cataract of the Velino. The glaciers of Montanvert and the source of the Arveiron is the grandest spectacle I ever saw. This is the second. Imagine a river sixty feet in breadth, with a vast volume of waters, the outlet of a great lake among the higher mountains, falling 300 feet into a sightless gulph of snow white vapour, which bursts up for ever and for ever, from a circle of black crags, and thence leaping downwards, made 5 or 6 other cataracts, each 50 or 100 feet high, which exhibit on a smaller scale and with beautiful and sublime variety the same appearances. But words, and far less could painting, will not express it. Stand upon the brink of the platform of cliff, which is directly opposite. You see the ever moving water stream down. It comes in thick and tawny folds, flaking off like solid snow gliding down a mountain. It does not seem hollow within, but without it is unequal, like the folding of linen thrown carelessly down; your eye follows it, and it is lost below; not in the black rocks which gird it around, but in its own foam and spray, in the cloud like vapours boiling up from below, which is not like rain, nor mist, nor spray, nor foam, but water, in a shape wholly unlike anything I ever saw before. It is as white as snow, but thick and impenetrable to the eye. The very imagination is bewildered in it. A thunder comes up from the abyss wonderful to hear; for, though it ever sounds, it is never the same, but, modulated by the changing motion, rises and falls intermittingly. We past half an hour in one spot looking at it, and thought but a few minutes had gone by.[61]

Two days after witnessing this sight Mary wrote in her journal:

Friday, Nov. 20. — We travel all day the Campagna di Roma — a perfect solitude, yet picturesque, and relieved by shady dells. We see an immense hawk sailing in the air for prey. Enter Rome. A rainy evening. Doganas and cheating innkeepers. We at length get settled in a comfortable hotel.

Since they intended to return to Rome for two or three months at the end of February,[62] the Shelleys remained there only a week (November 20–7) before resuming the journey to Naples. There were visits to St. Peter's, the Vatican, the Capitol, the Colosseum, the Forum, the Pantheon, and various other places of less note. The sight of galley slaves working among the ruins must have detracted somewhat from the pleasure of the scene.[63] On November 22 they attended the opera, which Mary condemned as " the worst I ever saw." Mary found time to continue her reading of Montaigne and to sketch some of the ancient Roman ruins. Shelley, who had been reading Plato's *Republic* on the journey, appears to have discontinued reading in favour of writing. Mary's journal for November 25 states: " Shelley begins the Tale of the Coliseum." [64]
Mary's almost bare record of places comes vividly to light in Shelley's later letter to Peacock. In this letter, after a detailed

picture of the Colosseum, Shelley proceeded to a more general picture:

Near it is the arch of Constantine, or rather of Trajan; for the servile and avaricious senate of degraded Rome ordered that the monument of his predecessor should be demolished in order to dedicate one to the Christian reptile, who had crept among the blood of his murdered family to the supreme power. It is exquisitely beautiful and perfect. The Forum is a plain in the middle of Rome, a kind of desert full of heaps of stones and pits; and though so near the habitations of men, is the most desolate place you can conceive. The ruins of temples stand in and around it, shattered columns and ranges of others complete, supporting cornices of exquisite workmanship, and vast vaults of shattered domes (laquearis) distinct with the regular compartments, once filled with sculptures of ivory or brass. The temples of Jupiter, and Concord, and Peace, and the Sun, and the Moon, and Vesta, are all within a short distance of this spot. Behold the wrecks of what a great nation once dedicated to the abstractions of the mind! Rome is a city, as it were, of the dead, or rather of those who cannot die, and who survive the puny generations which inhabit and pass over the spot which they have made sacred to eternity. In Rome, at least in the first enthusiasm of your recognitions of ancient time, you see nothing of the Italians. The nature of the city assists the delusion, for its vast and antique walls describe a circumference of sixteen miles, and thus the population is thinly scattered over this space, nearly as great as London. Wide wild fields are enclosed within it, and there are grassy lanes and copses winding among the ruins, and a great green hill, lonely and bare, which overhangs the Tiber. The gardens of the modern palaces are like wild woods of cedar, and cypress, and pine, and the neglected walks are overgrown with weeds. The English burying place is a green slope near the walls, under the pyramidal tomb of Cestius, and is, I think, the most beautiful and solemn cemetery I ever beheld. To see the sun shining on its bright grass, fresh, when we first visited it, with the autumnal dews, and hear the whispering of the wind among the leaves of the trees which have overgrown the tomb of Cestius, and the soil which is stirring in the sun warm earth, and to mark the tombs, mostly of women and young people who were buried there, one might, if one were to die, desire the sleep they seem to sleep. Such is the human mind, and so it peoples with its wishes vacancy and oblivion.[65]

SHELLEY left Rome for Naples on November 27, a day ahead of
the rest of the party, in order to secure lodgings into which they
could move directly upon their arrival. Travelling *vetturino*
with a Lombard merchant and a Neapolitan priest, he reached
Naples on November 29, three days ahead of his family.[66] If he
followed the route by which Mary arrived at Naples, he crossed
the Campagna to Velletri, traversed the Pontine Marshes, and
passed through Terracina and Gaeta, near which town Mary
was deeply impressed by the tomb and villa of Cicero. Part of
the journey lay through the most robber-infested district of Italy, and Shelley kept his pistol handy, but there were no incidents beyond the terror of the priest at sight of the pistol. All
that Shelley thought fit to record of his journey was an impression of the wild beauty of the country and the barbarous feroc-
ity of the inhabitants.

On entering Naples he was confirmed in his impression by
witnessing an assassination:

A youth ran out of a shop pursued by a woman with a bludgeon,
and a man armed with a knife. The man overtook him, and with
one blow in the neck laid him dead in the road. On my expressing
the emotions of horror and indignation which I felt, a Calabrian
priest who travelled with me laughed heartily and attempted to
quiz me as what the English call a flat. I never felt such an inclination to beat anyone. Heaven knows, I have little power, but he saw
that I looked extremely displeased, and was silent.[67]

The lodgings taken by Shelley were at No. 250 Riviera di
Chiaia,[68] in the better part of the city. Immediately in front of
them were the Royal Gardens, in whose shaded walks Mary
and Shelley often strolled, viewing Capri and Vesuvius across
the blue waters of the bay. The weather was mildly warm and
sunny and reminded Shelley of the best days of an English summer. Humanity in Naples might be base and degraded, but
external nature provided a fine compensation.[69] The scenery
seemed " more delightful than any within the immediate reach
of civilized man." [70] About three weeks after his arrival Shelley
concluded his first Neapolitan letter to Peacock by saying that
his spirits were depressed and his health not good, but that he
expected Naples to benefit him.

61

As for the people, Shelley thought less of the Neapolitans than of the other Italians, whom he rated low enough. Italian women, empty-headed and smelling of garlic, disgusted him particularly. For Leigh Hunt he summed up his impressions as follows:

There are *two* Italies — one composed of the green earth and transparent sea, and the mighty ruins of ancient time, and aërial mountains, and the warm and radiant atmosphere which is interfused through all things. The other consists of the Italians of the present day, their works and ways. The one is the most sublime and lovely contemplation that can be conceived by the imagination of man; the other is the most degraded, disgusting, and odious. What do you think? Young women of rank actually eat — you will never guess what — *garlick!* [71]

Though the climate and scenery of Naples continued to delight Shelley during January and February, his health did not improve. Standing or walking for hours in museums exhausted him. An English surgeon diagnosed his illness as a disease of the liver and gained some temporary success by a treatment based upon mercury and Cheltenham salts; and some improvement was also produced by painful applications of caustic to his side.[72] During a good part of the time he was confined to the house. Very likely it was on account of his health that Shelley bought carriage-horses about the middle of February, by which the sightseeing was made much easier.[73]

Externally, the life of Shelley's party in Naples consisted largely in sightseeing. Shelley's letters to Peacock constitute an almost matchless account of sightseeing excursions. The first of these was to Baiæ, on December 8. The party took boat early on a fine, cloudless morning when the sea was so calm that the seaweed upon the floor of the bay could be seen with a startling distinctness that came back to Shelley when he wrote his " Ode to the West Wind." Through the intense heat and light of the early afternoon they traversed a part of the Bay of Pozzuoli, past lofty, rocky islets and enormous sea-caverns to the promontory of Misenum, where they disembarked to view the Elysian Fields, already made memorable for Shelley and Mary by the sixth book of Vergil's *Æneid*. They entered the Bay of Baiæ and

THE BAY OF NAPLES AND MOUNT VESUVIUS

Engraved by E. Benjamin from a painting by G. Arnold

ROME FROM MONTE TESTACCIO, 1819

Showing Pyramid of Caius Cestius and Protestant Cemetery. Engraved by I. Byrns from a drawing by J. M. Williams

coasted down the left shore, landing occasionally to inspect
some of the picturesque ruins that line the bay. In the water
under their boat (as a result of ancient seismic disturbances
that had submerged a part of the shore) they could see "ruins
of its antique grandeur standing like rocks in the transparent
sea." Shelley saw this sight even more vividly in recollection
about a year later when he pictured the transparent "blue Mediterranean" in summer sleep, yet seeing

> — in sleep dim palaces and towers
> Quivering within the wave's intenser day,
>
> All overgrown with azure moss and flowers
> So sweet, the sense faints picturing them! [74]

On the same excursion they visited Lake Avernus, the cavern
of the sibyl, a ruined temple of Pluto, and various ruins at
Pozzuoli, the ancient Dicæarchia, where Shelley was reminded
of a description in Petronius. "After seeing these things," Shelley wrote, "we returned by moonlight to Naples in our boat.
What colours there were in the sky, what radiance in the evening star, and how the moon was encompassed by a light unknown to our regions!" [75]

On December 16 there was another long day's excursion to
Vesuvius. Shelley, Mary, and Claire took a carriage to Resina.
From this point Mary and Shelley rode mules, and Claire, who
had twice fallen from a horse at Bagni di Lucca, rode fearfully
in a chair carried by four fierce-looking men. Past the hermitage
of St. Salvador, where a rope-belted old hermit served them
lunch, they wound up the mountain, crossing a vast stream of
hardened lava, "an actual image of the waves of the sea,
changed into hard black stone by enchantment." Over rocks of
lava and declivities of ashes they reached the summit, "an ir-
regular plain, the most horrible chaos that can be imagined,"
of chasms, stones, cinders, and black, calcined boulders, with
smoke and "liquid fire" issuing steadily from a central cone.
They watched it in a sort of dreadful fascination until after
nightfall, noting that one of the slow lava streams was about
twenty feet broad and ten feet high. By daylight they could

scarcely see the fire for the volumes of white sulphurous smoke in which the lava streams were enveloped, but in the dark, as masses cracked off from the main stream, they could see the fiery glow extending from top to bottom.

The return journey, at ten o'clock by torchlight, was something of a Gothic nightmare. Against the lurid background of the volcano they picked their way among boulders and ashes. The savage guides shouted and yelled or sang wild songs and eventually threatened to deposit Claire by the roadside. They were prevented only by Paolo's liberal promises of a beating. Shelley was attacked by one of his sudden seizures and had to be taken to the hermitage until his intense suffering was relieved. The " worst effect " of this, he added characteristically, " was spoiling the pleasure of Mary and Clare." [76]

Shelley's memorable visit to the ruins of Pompeii occurred on December 22. His next letter to Peacock contains five printed pages of descriptive details of temples, streets, dwellings, the forum, and the amphitheatre. He did not limit himself, however, as in the two former excursions, to presenting a vivid and complete picture to the physical sense of a distant reader. Pompeii had been a Greek city, and Shelley was profoundly interested in the Greek manner of life. Viewing the modest but artistic dwellings, with their central open courts, the magnificent temples, "mostly upaithric," and the theatres open to the sun and the stars, Shelley stood amazed at what Athens must have been, if this was only a small Greek city of about twenty thousand people:

They lived in harmony with nature; and the interstices of their incomparable columns were portals, as it were, to admit the spirit of beauty which animates this glorious universe to visit those whom it inspired. . . . I now understand why the Greeks were such great poets; and, above all, I can account, it seems to me, for the harmony, the unity, the perfection, the uniform excellence, of all their works of art. They lived in a perpetual commerce with external nature and nourished themselves upon the spirit of its forms.[77]

Neither Mary's journal nor Shelley's letters mention a later visit to Pompeii in the company of Charles MacFarlane, a young

English traveller of nineteen then sojourning in Naples. Only a few days before Shelley left Naples he had formed a chance acquaintance with MacFarlane before a statue of a Roman matron in the Royal Bourbon Museum. They had been introduced to each other the next morning by Shelley's physician, Dr. Roskilly, and had spent the rest of the day in a visit together to Pompeii. The rapid journey from Naples, in a queer-looking *calesso* drawn by two black, spirited horses, brought the colour into Shelley's cheeks and exhilarated his spirits. Later, after several hours among the ruins, they seated themselves on a lava rock by the sea, and Shelley fell silent. A look of such intense, unconscious melancholy descended upon him that MacFarlane was ever afterwards convinced it was the mood that produced " Stanzas Written in Dejection." On the return journey Shelley recovered his high spirits, joked with the Italian driver, and displayed great interest in a macaroni-factory that they stopped to inspect. They were beset by beggars, for whom Shelley emptied his pockets of coins. " Poor creatures," MacFarlane commented; but Shelley responded: " Not a bit of it; they are happier than I — I dare say they are happier than you." [78]

The longest of the excursions from Naples was to the ruins of another Greek city, Posidonia (Pæstum), sixty miles to the south. The first day's journey (February 23) brought the party through the most romantic scenery, to Salerno. The weather, which had been bright and fair for two months, was now dark and stormy. A part of the journey during the night lay along the shore and was lighted only by the breaking of the waves. Fifteen miles beyond Salerno a swollen stream had carried away the bridge and rendered the ferry unsafe, so that the last seven miles (five in Mary's account) had to be traversed on foot over a rough, marshy road. This left only two hours for contemplating the ruins. Shelley came away with the impression of " some half-remembered dream " of columns and walls and dark purple Apennines in the background, but it was enough for a rather detailed description to Peacock.[79]

Between these longer excursions there were several visits to places of interest in Naples and near by. Herculaneum and the museum at Portici were visited on December 5, Vergil's Tomb and the Grotto of Pausilippo on December 15 and the former again on the 28th, the Lago d'Agnano, with its tame wildfowl, on February 11. On the same day (February 11) and again on February 14 they viewed the Caccia d'Ischieri, once (like the Lago d'Agnano) an active volcano, now a royal hunting preserve, in which they saw King Ferdinand in a shooting-box waiting for the wild boars to appear. At about the same date they saw the Grotto del Cane, where they refused to witness the usual exhibit of dogs being slowly and painfully asphyxiated by volcanic gas. On February 10 they went to Caserta. One visit to the opera (December 13) and two or three each to the Studii and the Royal Bourbon Museum apparently complete the record. The statues, particularly the ancient ones, Shelley admired greatly, but the Renaissance paintings he thought " sufficiently miserable," and overrated. It was on one of his later visits to the Museum that Shelley talked once, though without exchanging names, with Gabriele Rossetti, who was later to marry the sister of Dr. Polidori and become the father of one of Shelley's most distinguished expositors.[80]

BOTH Shelley in his letters and Mary in her journal furnish remarkably meagre information about their domestic life. They knew no one in Naples when they arrived, and they met almost no one there except one or two casual fellow sightseers. The only new acquaintances mentioned in Mary's journal or Shelley's letters for the entire period were a " M. Rosmilly," who dined with them on February 14, and " Madame Falconet," *passim*. Charles MacFarlane, who left a record of a casual acquaintance, is mentioned by neither Shelley nor Mary. Both Shelley and Mary read, of course, but hardly so much as usual. They read parts of Winkelmann's *History of Art* (in French) and two cantos of Dante's *Inferno* aloud to each other. Each read several books of Livy, and Madame de Staël's *Corinne*, and Shelley read a part and Mary all of Sismondi's *History of the Republics of the Middle Ages*. Shelley read separately in Euripides and in Plutarch's *Lives*, and Mary in Dante, Montaigne, Vergil's *Georgics*, " Adèle de Senanges " and " History of the two Viziera."

Claire Clairmont is mentioned only once or twice in Shelley's letters, and once in Mary's journal, as ill on December 27; neither William Shelley nor his dead sister Clara is mentioned. One domestic occurrence ignored by Mary in her journal, but destined to have important consequences, was the loss of two servants, Paolo and Elise, who were discharged because they were about to become the parents of an illegitimate child.[81]

The loneliness of their private lives was probably an unfortunate circumstance for the Shelleys, considering the state of mind in which they had left Este. It was somewhat mitigated, however, by letters. Mary maintained a rather reserved and contracted correspondence with Mrs. Gisborne; Madame Hoppner sent some details about Byron and Allegra. Byron, she informed Mary, continued to live " *dans une débauche affreuse* " which would sooner or later ruin him. He would certainly never consent to Allegra's return to Claire. Allegra suffered unnaturally from the cold; in spite of a warm room and flannel clothing her hands and feet were always " *comme des morceaux de glace* "; and she had become " *tranquille et sérieuse comme une petite vieille.* " [82]

Leigh Hunt wrote describing his new enterprise, *The Literary Pocketbook,* in which he had made bold to print Shelley's " Marianne's Dream," but without signature. With his usual tact, he must have guessed that Shelley felt the *Quarterly's* preliminary blasts more than he admitted. He warned Shelley that a more open assault was soon to be expected, and comforted him at the same time with the assurance that public disgust against the *Quarterly's* tactics was increasing every day. If Gifford and his allies continued their attacks, Hunt promised to " buckle on my old rusty armour, and give them such a carbonado as I know I am able to give, and they most capable of feeling." Shelley took note of this in his next letter by expressing the mistaken conviction that Southey was the anonymous *Quarterly* assailant and that he was animated by a deadly private hatred.[83]

Peacock wrote about his own literary plans, his methodical, simple manner of life at Marlow, and his expectations of a lucrative position with the East India Company which would probably make it impossible to accept Shelley's invitation to Italy.

More than any others, Peacock's letters kept Shelley informed of political conditions in England. Shelley was particularly pleased at Peacock's account of the Bank Note forgery trial:

There have been four capital trials for forgery of Bank Notes, and the Jury has found the prisoners " Not Guilty," expressly declaring that they could never believe the evidence of hired informers who betrayed men into crime; that they could not themselves distinguish the forged notes from the true; and that unless they were furnished with some certain criterion, they would not take the *ipse dixit* of the Bank Inspectors that the notes were forged. This is saying that they will hang no more men for the murderous paper-mill and that, if its wheel continues to turn, it shall be by other means than blood.[84]

To this Shelley's comment was: " Your news about the Bank-note trials is excellent good. Do I not recognize in it the influence of Cobbett? " Perhaps Shelley was reminded by such talk that his old sense of mission had reached a rather low ebb under his recent troubles. It was far from abandoned, however. He had cried out in his poetry and letters against the tyranny at Venice and Padua and in the very depths of his despair at Este he had proclaimed in " Julian and Maddalo " that he would never cease to cry out. To Peacock he exclaimed:

O, if I had health, and strength, and equal spirits, what boundless intellectual improvement might I not gather in this wonderful country! At present I write little but poetry, and little of that. . . . I consider Poetry very subordinate to moral and political science, and if I were well, certainly I should aspire to the latter; for I can conceive a great work, embodying the discoveries of all ages, and harmonising the contending creeds by which mankind have been ruled.[85]

Shelley was in fact writing little poetry, but the poems he did write are extremely important biographical documents. Of the few poems and fragments dated 1818 by Mrs. Shelley, only four or five may be referred more particularly to time and place. One of these is " Stanzas Written in Dejection, near Naples," dated by Mrs. Shelley " December, 1818." Shelley first describes the external beauty by which he is surrounded — warm sun, clear sky, snowy mountain-tops, blue isles, dancing waves, and the green and purple seaweed, clearly seen through the transparent water. So far he might have been — and to some extent was — translating into poetry the more enthusiastic passages of the letters by which the external world, including Mary, was supposed to judge the state of his mind. But the concluding line of these two opening stanzas comes directly to his inner dejection: " How sweet! did any heart now share in my emotion." Immediately following is one of Shelley's most mournful confessions:

> Alas! I have nor hope nor health,
>   Nor peace within, nor calm around,
> Nor that content surpassing wealth
>   The sage in meditation found
>   And walked with inward glory crowned —
> Nor fame, nor power, nor love, nor leisure.
>   Others I see whom these surround —
> Smiling they live and call life pleasure;
> To me that cup has been dealt in another measure.

Very probably some of the other poems that have previously been discussed in connection with " Julian and Maddalo " were written at this time. We have already seen that these poems are of a piece with the dejected poems written at Este and must have been among those that Mary afterwards said " he hid from fear of wounding me." [86]

These poems certainly show that the feeling of complete desolation and desertion that overpowered Shelley's inner consciousness at Este while he outwardly maintained an apparently unruffled front continued at Naples, under the same conditions. Yet it was at Naples, on December 18 and 19, that Mary finished making the fair copy of *Rosalind and Helen* and that Shelley wrote the Advertisement to that poem, dating it " Naples, Dec. 20, 1818." In that Advertisement he pays tribute to Mary as " a dear friend, with whom added years of intercourse only add to my apprehension of its value, and who would have had more right than anyone to complain, that she has not been able to extinguish in me the very power of delineating sadness." Unless the " Lines Written in Dejection " were written before December 20 and were followed almost immediately by a happier state of affairs between Shelley and Mary, this means that Shelley was not willing, in his public character, simply to maintain silence about the lack of sympathy that certainly existed, but that for the public he was even willing to suggest the contrary. After all, Shelley's public tribute was only suggestion — it merely states that Mary was unable to remove his melancholy, not that she tried. We have Mary's own confession that she did not try.

Shelley was indeed preserving the Madman's secret from both his Lady and the public, and still not violating the literal truth. "I never will be a party," he wrote Leigh Hunt in another connection, only two days after writing this Advertisement, "in making my private affairs or those of others to be topics of general discussion." [87] Perhaps he also thought that by suggesting a temporarily absent virtue he could expedite its presence. Mary herself has stated that this was often Shelley's principle of dealing with people.[88]

Biographers and critics have always half-suspected a particular reason for Shelley's dejection at Naples. But they have failed to consider its identity with the despair first expressed at Este and so have missed the true cause of both, while following a melodramatic false clue with which Shelley had supplied Tom Medwin. In 1821, long after the domestic crisis had been surmounted, Shelley showed his poems of dejection to Medwin, who very probably asked for an explanation of their background. At any rate Shelley told him a story which Medwin later advanced as the explanation and which has ever since been taken as a possible clue both to Shelley's despair and to another and more genuine mystery in Shelley's life at Naples.[89] A mysterious lady, Shelley said, had followed him first to Switzerland and had later met him at Naples only a few days before dying there. It was a story which Byron later scouted as pure imagination, and of which Shelley said Mary was still ignorant.

The poems that Medwin quoted as supporting his theory were the very ones that we have already seen prove that Mary Shelley, and no one else, was the source of Shelley's mysterious dejection. Shelley's own evidence abolishes the existence of the mysterious lady. Elsewhere I have shown its extreme improbability on other grounds.[90] It is exactly the kind of story Shelley would have told to mislead or forestall an embarrassing curiosity. Possibly he was also experimenting on Medwin with the plot of a poem he intended to write, but never wrote, about a " dreadful or beautiful " reality that occurred in Naples.[91] This " reality " may now be revealed. It was not told to Medwin, a fact which casts still further doubt upon the story that *was* told, since it is plainly the real centre of the so-called " Neapolitan mystery " in Shelley's life.

ACCORDING to Shelley's own statement before a Neapolitan magistrate, a daughter was born to Shelley and Mary at No. 250 Riviera di Chiaia, on December 27, 1818, at 7.00 p.m.[92] This child was given the name of Elena Adelaide Shelley, and was baptized in the parish of San Giuseppi, Chiaia, on February 27, 1819, exactly two months after its birth. The birth-record, bearing the same date, is signed by Shelley and by two witnesses from the neighbourhood — Francesco Florimonte, fifty-seven, a cheese-monger living at 128 Fondo Pennino, and Antonio di Lorenzo, twenty-three, a hairdresser living at 223 Riviera di Chiaia. The certificate of baptism states that the midwife was Gaetana Musto. Ordinarily at Naples when children were presented for registration both parents appeared, but Mary was not present upon this occasion. Except for the official account of the child's death and three puzzling references to his " poor Neapolitan " and his Neapolitan " ward," [93] in Shelley's later letters, this constitutes the sole documentary history of a hitherto unknown child officially declared by Shelley to be his daughter and Mary's.

Shelley's references to this child in 1820 in his letters to the Gisbornes show clearly enough — unless he deceived them — that the child was not his. Certainly the child was not Mary's. For two weeks before and after Elena's birth Mary's journal has its regular daily entries, which differ in no way from her usual entries except that they are perhaps briefer than usual. During the whole of her stay in Naples she never once recorded herself as ill. Nowhere in her journal or in any of her known letters did she ever refer to this child. Later events make it difficult to believe that she did not know of its existence, but if she did, she seems to have resolved never to mention it. Nevertheless, she herself furnished proof that Elena was not her child, for on June 29, 1819, when Elena was still alive, she wrote of Clara and William as her "two only and lovely children," and in November 1819 she wrote of herself as having been childless "for five hateful months."[94] It is also a fairly certain inference that Elena Shelley did not live at No. 250 Riviera di Chiaia for the two months that elapsed between her birth and its registration.[95]

Since both Shelley and Mary maintained a resolute reticence about Elena Adelaide Shelley, we are here forced to substitute hypothesis for authenticated biography. In the abstract, there are four hypotheses, one of which must be the solution of Elena Shelley's parentage. She must have been the daughter of Shelley and Claire, of Shelley and an unknown mother, of Claire and an unknown father, or of parents both of whom are unknown. Naturally only one of these possibilities can be the true solution, yet any one remains possible until the others are abolished. Further to complicate the difficulty created by the evident desire of both Shelley and Mary to conceal the whole episode, there is some dubious contemporary testimony which seems to support *both* the first and the second possibilities.

The second and third hypotheses may be dismissed rather briefly. The story of the mysterious lady who died at Naples while the Shelleys were there is obviously a false clue by which Shelley sought to distract Tom Medwin's curiosity. We have already seen that the poems Medwin associated with this lady are really to be associated with Mary Shelley. On other grounds it is practically impossible to credit the lady's existence.[96] The only lady in Shelley's life who could have died in Naples in December 1818 was the lady whom Shelley was at that time trying to resuscitate in his secret poems — the Mary Shelley he had known prior to the death of Clara. When this circumstance is properly understood, there remains not a single positive circumstance to support a belief that Elena was the daughter either of Shelley and an unknown mother or of Claire and an unknown father. If neither of these possibilities can be quite abolished, it would appear to be only because concrete documentary evidence of the true solution has very probably been destroyed.[97]

The possibility that Elena was the daughter of Shelley and Claire Clairmont gains powerful support from the so-called "Hoppner scandal," which is discussed in full in its proper chronological place in Chapter xxvii. Here it need only be summarized in its bare essentials. In the summer of 1820 the Shelleys' discharged servant Elise Foggi told Mrs. Hoppner in Venice that while the Shelleys were in Naples Claire Clairmont had borne Shelley a child, that the child had been born in Claire's room and had been immediately spirited into a foundling hospital, and that Mary Shelley had been kept in entire ignorance both at the time and later. She added also that while in Naples, Mary Shelley was treated by both Shelley and Claire with neglect and positive unkindness.[98] The official records of the existence of Elena Adelaide Shelley are sufficient proof that Elise's story can no longer be dismissed as an unfounded slander. There is the further fact, which is certainly startling enough, that on the very day of Elena's birth, according to the birth certificate, Mary Shelley's journal states that Claire was ill. In notes to Mrs. Hoppner and Mary Shelley, Elise afterwards denied having told any such story, but unfortunately it is her denial rather than her story which must be set aside as a total fabrication.

There are other more general circumstances that will immediately rise to mind to lend apparent verisimilitude to Elise Foggi's story. The situation between Shelley and Claire in 1815, Godwin's statement that all three of his daughters had been in love with Shelley, Claire's somewhat dubious statement in old age that she had been in love with Shelley,[99] Claire's probable identity with the Comet in *Epipsychidion*, and the well-known radical theories of both Shelley and Claire about marriage — all seem to support Elise Foggi's story. In March 1820, when he was corresponding with the Gisbornes apparently about Elena, Shelley asked to be addressed under a false name; and again in 1822, when Claire was in frequent conference with Elise and Elise was writing her repudiation of the story, Shelley made the same suggestion to Claire.[100]

Yet every single one of these considerations is dubious. The situation in 1815 is very far from a clear case of physical attraction, and even if it was, it must have been obliterated by Claire's affair with Byron immediately afterwards. The two statements that Claire loved Shelley are unconvincing and even if true carry no implication as to what Shelley felt. Shelley now smiled at the idea that he was willing to put his radical social and moral ideas into practice,[101] nor would he ever have been willing to practise them except openly. The position of Claire in *Epipsychidion* is not clearly anything more than adequate to the special circumstances. Emilia Viviani's letters show that she was devoted to Shelley, Mary, and Claire as a group, and to each one individually without much distinction between them, so that it was no more than natural that Shelley should assign all three women a place in the regulation of his life — and a definitely subordinate one to Claire. As to the false addresses, Shelley may have used them either because the subject was one of which Mary must be kept ignorant (which presumes the truth of Elise's story) or because it was a subject known to Mary and known to exasperate her (which is capable of a different interpretation, as will be seen later). The latter seems more probable, since Mrs. Gisborne, Mary's foster-mother and best friend, would have been an unnatural confidante for a really guilty secret, and also because it was Shelley's habit, when Mary's nerves were likely to be upset, to keep disturbing communications away from her.[102]

The journals of Mary and Claire would not of course be expected to offer direct support of Elise's story, if it were true, but they should afford unconscious evidence which could be adduced in its support — some indication of Claire's unusual feeling for Shelley, of Mary's suspicion of Claire (rather than mere occasional irritation), of Claire's special interest in Naples as long as Elena was alive there, or of Claire's disturbed state of mind when Elena died. Nothing of the sort occurs. From a close study of all the journals and letters of Shelley, Claire, and Mary the only justifiable conclusion seems to be that Shelley regarded Claire both as a sister and as a ward; that he sometimes drew sympathetic comprehension from her when Mary was apathetic, but probably never felt physically attracted to her; that Claire felt similarly toward Shelley with the possible exception of a dawning physical attraction in 1815 which was consumed (if it existed) by her affair with Byron; and that the attitude of Mary and Claire toward each other, which continued many years after Shelley's death, was one of general sisterly affection and duty interrupted by sharp spells of antagonism due principally to Claire's propensity sooner or later to quarrel with nearly everyone with whom she associated.

Neither does the previous conduct of Shelley and Claire accord satisfactorily with the theory of their guilt. Knowing that a child was to be born, it is incredible that they would risk everything by not arranging for Claire's absence during the period of danger — if they really hoped to conceal the matter from Mary. As a matter of common sense they could not have anticipated anything except discovery, sooner or later. Their only hope would have lain in winning Mary's co-operation after having convinced her in advance that the child was not Shelley's. Mary had co-operated similarly at the birth of Allegra and would have done so again. If she did so again in Naples she might have pretended ignorance as a part of a general effort to deceive the servants — foolhardy as such an attempt seems. Only by supposing that Elise was deceived can one accept the good faith of her allegation that Mary never knew of a birth under the circumstances described. Doctors agree that it is not impossible for such births to happen undetected, but it is wildly improbable; and it is even more difficult afterwards to conceal from a daily associate that a birth has occurred. If Elena Shelley was really the daughter of Shelley and Claire, it may be taken for granted that Mary knew of her birth (if not her identity) in advance. Her co-operation, however, was a strange one if her journal for the day in question is to be trusted. It reads: " Finish 2nd book of the ' Georgics.' Clare is not well. Shelley reads Winklemann. Walk in the Gardens."

When Elise's charges were repeated to Mary Shelley she denied them with a passionate vigour that has hitherto been considered a complete refutation. She stated frankly that Claire had been ill for two days at the time in question, but asserted that she had attended her, that the illness was a familiar one for which she had administered familiar medicines, and that no such birth as Elise described could have occurred. This completely demolishes Elise's story — unless Mary was deliberately lying. But if Mary believed that Elena was indeed Claire's child either by Shelley or by an unknown father, it is not improbable that she would have lied rather than ruin either Claire or Shelley, and in the latter case herself, by telling the truth. For suspicious minds the "Hoppner scandal" will not be abolished as possible truth unless the truth of Mary's denial can somehow be demonstrated. In Chapter xxvii I have quoted and analysed the correspondence between Shelley and Mary and have concluded that their letters are genuinely sincere. My main reason for this conviction is their tone of passionate trust and confidence in each other. For if Elise's story is substantially true, then Shelley and Mary both knew it was true, and each knew that the other knew. They might agree in denying its truth to the world. But they were both persons of unusual sincerity and integrity; there was no reason to lie passionately to each other when each would have known the other to be lying. It is doubtful if either could have made to the other such a barefaced exposure of moral bankruptcy even if it had seemed needful, but to have done so for no reason at all is incredible.

This conclusion seems to be supported by a significant piece of negative evidence. Shelley wrote a number of poems in Naples reflecting an unusual state of his domestic emotions. If Claire had recently borne him a child one would expect the poems in some manner to point to Claire as a centre of emotional disturbance, but instead they point clearly to Mary and continue a state of mind begun at Este three months earlier.

The breakdown of Elise's story in spite of its apparent support by several circumstances and the obvious truth of several of its details can only be due to one of two facts. Either Elise believed her story and misreported certain facts because she misunderstood them, or else she was wilfully perverting facts in a skilful effort to damage the Shelleys. Both Shelley and Mary asserted the latter. When Elise's husband tried with the same story to blackmail Shelley in 1820, Shelley wrote to the Gis-

bornes that Paolo was "taking advantage of my situation at
Naples in December 1818 to attempt to extort money by threatening to charge me with the most horrible of crimes." And
Mary Shelley, writing to Shelley about the Hoppner scandal,
said: "They are as cunning as wicked." [103]

The incontestable facts supporting Elise's story are (1) the
existence of a child, (2) the state of strain within the household,
(3) the illness of Claire at the time, and (4) the fact that the
child did not live within the house. Either an honest effort to
account to herself for these facts or a dishonest effort to use them
against the Shelleys led most reasonably to her other assertions.
Evidently Elise did not herself see a baby or attend Claire in
her illness, or she would have said so. Either honestly, to satisfy
herself, or dishonestly, to impress others, she pieced together
these facts with a logical chain of incidents necessary to complete her story. Assuming or pretending that the child was
Claire's followed naturally enough from Claire's illness at the
time. This involved assuming that the child was born in the
house, and this involved assuming Mary's ignorance. The fact
that Elise had never seen the child in the house involved supposing it to have been immediately spirited away. The foundling hospital was the natural place to take it, and so Elise may
have believed it was taken there.

Indeed, the child may actually have been in the foundling hospital before its baptism and official registration two months
later. It was certainly not with the Shelleys, and Shelley was
very probably visiting it somewhere else. If Shelley visited
Elena at the foundling hospital, the clever, unscrupulous Paolo,
Elise's husband, probably knew of the visits. He may also have
known (what I suspect to be the truth) that the child was obtained from the hospital in the first place. Shelley's three known
references to the child were as "my poor Neapolitan," "my
Neapolitan," and "my Neapolitan charge," [104] which suggests
that Elena was a Neapolitan, not merely that she came under his
care at Naples. Also he named her Elena, the Italian form of
an English name under which he had recently written of Mary
in *Rosalind and Helen*.[105] If circumstances had not furnished
Elise with a ready basis for concluding that the child was born

to Claire in Shelley's lodgings she might have concluded that it came from the foundling hospital, but to Elise (or to those she may have hoped to deceive) such a hospital was primarily a place for depositing children; there was no problem about obtaining them.

It has seemed necessary to linger so long over the " Hoppner scandal " because of the extraordinary combination of factors that give it such superficial credibility. It was a practically perfect basis for blackmail and will perhaps still attract honest believers. For a time I believed it myself, before I perceived that its basis, upon closer analysis, grew weaker rather than stronger, as any true basis should have grown. Even so it cannot be absolutely discredited on the evidence I have given unless another hypothesis of Elena's parentage can be made to appear more probable, by evidence more substantial than the comparative weakness of competing possibilities.

The fourth hypothesis, that Elena was the child of parents unknown to us and probably unknown to Shelley, seems to me to fulfil the conditions of acceptance. These conditions are: (1) that it must be in character, (2) that it must fit the peculiar circumstances in which the Shelleys found themselves in Naples, (3) that it must provide a reasonable explanation for all the peculiar circumstances that made the " Hoppner scandal " credible, and (4) that it must introduce no fresh improbabilities for which acceptable explanations are not forthcoming.

The conclusion that Elena was an adopted child fits the known characteristics and behaviour of the principal parties so much better than other explanations that it must be the true one, even though it is supported by no evidence other than inference. Shelley was intensely lonely as the result of a peculiar estrangement from Mary that was never openly admitted and was probably partly pathological on both sides. Elise noticed this without understanding it. Very likely Claire noticed also and remonstrated with Mary, being naturally Shelley's partisan, or perhaps Elise saw one of Claire's tantrums. Shelley was so despondent at Naples that he is said to have attempted suicide.[106] In his loneliness he must have thought of

78

a desire that had formerly been almost an obsession with him. This long-standing desire was to adopt a little girl. As a small boy he had scoured the neighbourhood for a gypsy girl to adopt; as a youth he had with difficulty been dissuaded by Gibbons Merle from adopting and educating *two* little girls. At Marlow he had adopted Polly Rose, so far as circumstances permitted. Now that his daughter was dead, the idea recurred. He had already tried, and failed, to persuade Byron to allow Allegra to remain with him. Perhaps an adopted daughter might win Mary back to her usual self. He would name her Elena, after his portrait of Mary in *Rosalind and Helen.*

Normally Mary would have been consulted at this point. But Shelley in one of his tense emotional strains would have been quite capable of adopting a child without informing Mary at the time. If Mary was consulted, she evidently refused to accept an obscure little Italian infant as a substitute for the lost Clara. In any event Shelley probably decided to adopt a little girl without Mary's immediate consent — for Mary's consent at the time would have resulted in the child's living with its foster-parents, which was not the case.

Shelley must have known already the impossibility of legal adoption in England. Not until the next year, 1819, did England possess a statute legalizing adoption. Previous to this the relationship was without legal status.[107] Fearing, as he did, that the Court of Chancery might deprive him of his own children by Mary, and expecting to return to England with a child not his own, Shelley had every reason to make the child's position secure. This could only be done by disguising a *de facto* adoption as a legal birth and preserving the utmost secrecy about what had been done. Even to-day, with legal adoption secure and easy, and without Shelley's special reasons, adoptive parents have been known to employ the same method.[108] In Naples, where life was cheap, the scheme should have been easy enough for a native, but whether or not it was easy for a foreigner and a non-Catholic is uncertain. Elise Foggi would appear to have known something definite about a foundling hospital, which suggests that Shelley had no difficulty in securing his little girl directly. If difficulties arose, a child could easily enough have been secured from some willing family through the bribery of a midwife.

Such a child could not have been brought into the home until Mary's consent and co-operation were obtained. In two other details also Mary's co-operation would be needed. In case of any perfunctory official questions she would have to pretend that Claire's illness on the day of the child's alleged birth was her own, in which she would have been supported by the midwife, Gaetana Musto, whose name appears on the birth-registration. Also, before it was too late their English friends should be informed that Mary had given birth to a child or expected soon to do so. There was plenty of time for this, however, since it would probably be a year or two before the child would appear in England, and they were safe enough with the Gisbornes, the only people in Italy to whom Mary might have been expected to send such a letter. One might assume that Mary's formal consent, however grudging, was won by February 27, the day on which the child was baptized and registered, without the supposed mother's attendance. These two acts involved Mary irretrievably. If she did not know about Elena before, she was now bound to know sooner or later — and not only to know, but to act her part as mother. Few people except a Shelley would have dared go so far without a previous understanding, and it seems doubtful that even a Shelley would do so.

In all Mary's voluminous journals or letters there remains no shred of direct evidence to show that she even knew of Elena Adelaide's existence. Yet, just as her letters to Marianne Hunt demonstrate by inference that she was not Elena's natural mother, so her letter to Shelley on the "Hoppner scandal" proves clearly that she understood all about Elena. She could never have described the Foggis' machinations as dangerously cunning without understanding the factors that made them so — otherwise, like all the subsequent commentators, she would have regarded them as mere stupid malignity.[109]

At the time of registering the child Shelley would have to be prepared with the precise time and date of Elena's "birth"; and since he was claiming that she was born in his lodgings he must have thought it a clever idea (in case of any perfunctory question) to give the only date on which any possible mother for the child had been ill. If Claire had been the actual mother, it would have been far better to falsify the date.

Paolo either helped with the arrangements or was alert and ingenious enough to discover them. In no other way could he have acquired a basis for his later attempts at blackmail. Had Paolo known of the secret birth of a child of Shelley and Claire, Shelley would never have discharged him under antagonizing circumstances. But Paolo did know of Claire's illness and of an adopted child and he knew that a combination of these two facts would receive the worst interpretation from people who knew Shelley's reputation. Later he might even persuade Elise of the truth of these charges. Elise was at the time an expectant illegitimate mother herself and might naturally find a secret liaison the best explanation for a puzzling domestic strain which we know to have been due to other causes. Hence the story told later by Elise, but told much earlier by Paolo, without Elise's participation. Probably neither Paolo nor Elise knew of the registration or christening of Elena, which took place after their discharge. Before these events Paolo was a known rascal and Elise a reliable and respected servant, but their stories seemed to the Shelleys to tar them both with the same brush.

Before coming to Naples the Shelleys had intended to return to Rome in the early spring. Their recent bitter experience with Clara had given them a dread of travelling in Italy with very young children. It was better to leave Elena in good hands at Naples and return in a few months for a longer sojourn.[110] By February 19 the Shelleys had already seen most of what was to be seen at Naples[111] and were ready to carry out their original intention of returning to Rome. On February 27 Mary entered in her journal the one word: " Pack." While she was packing, Shelley was attending to the registering and christening of Elena Adelaide. Possibly she was already domiciled with a family living at Vico Canale, No. 45, where she was living at the time of her death. But tragic events were to prevent their return, and Shelley was never to see Elena Adelaide again. On an occasion totally unconnected with Medwin's interest in the

Naples mystery, Shelley once remarked to him that when he left Naples he was in fear of arrest.[112] This, at least, must have been true, on account of the false birth certificate.

Meanwhile it was time for Mary Shelley to write to her English friends that she had become a mother, if she ever intended doing so. Only the Godwins and Hunts, with Hogg and Peacock, would have expected any such announcement, and it is possible that Mary never intended deceiving them. Such false news would have been hard to write, since Mary was obviously opposed to the scheme. She would have been safe enough in deferring her letters a few weeks until she felt more equal to it. Yet within a month after leaving Naples Mary must have learned that she was to become an actual mother in November. It was still possible to pretend that she had become a mother in December of 1818, but it was probably even more distasteful. At any rate, Mary never wrote. When Shelley wrote to the Gisbornes on April 6 it was evident that they had decided not to deceive the Gisbornes about Elena's parentage, and Shelley's later references to Elena in letters to the Gisbornes indicate that they had been told the truth. Thereafter any idea of persuading their friends in England that Elena was their own daughter must have been abandoned. Nevertheless documents were still available at Naples to defeat any attempt in England to deprive Shelley of Elena on the grounds that she was not legally his child.

NOTE

IN THIS solution of the mystery of Elena Adelaide Shelley I have frankly stated the last hypothesis as if it were a proved fact, and I shall hereafter refer to it as such. In the present and possibly final state of the evidence the conclusion I have reached seems practically inevitable, but it still remains hypothetical because of the paucity of documentary and testimentary evidence. This fact should not be overemphasized, however. Any reader called upon to reach conclusions in a similar matter involving a neighbour or kinsman would probably be forced to do so upon less " evidence " than the present case affords. In considering every possible hypothesis I have been forced into an unbiographical style and a prolixity of detail for which the importance of striving for the exact truth must be sufficient ex-

cuse. No fact or possible fact in my possession tending to support
any one of the four possible conclusions has been ignored or consciously slighted except a few comparatively insignificant matters
which have been treated in later chapters and to which due reference has been made.

Chapter XXI

ROME AND VILLA VALSOVANO

THE SIGHTS OF ROME; DEATH OF WILLIAM SHELLEY;

GRIEF AND DESPAIR AT VILLA VALSOVANO;

GODWIN AND CHARLES CLAIRMONT; PUBLISHING

ARRANGEMENTS; THOUGHTS OF ENGLAND

ON February 27, 1819 Mary packed clothes and other belongings while Shelley attended to the baptism and birth-registration of Elena Adelaide. The next day, at two o'clock in the afternoon, the party set off for Rome, driving behind their own horses, as formerly. A new driver, named Vincenzo, supplied the place of the accomplished but unscrupulous Paolo. They slept the first night at Capua and the second at Gaeta, where they tarried all the next day, playing chess, strolling about the woods and seashore, and thinking thoughts of Cicero, who had once owned a villa on the very spot occupied by their inn. On March 3 they slept at Terracina, and on the next night, after an arduous day's travel, at Velletri. Thence it was only a day's journey, over the hills of Albano and across the Campagna, to Rome. Here they stayed for two days at the Villa di Parigi, removing on March 7 to the Palazzo Verospi, on the Corso. From this central position they immediately set about sightseeing. "'All that Athens ever brought forth wise,'" Mary quoted in her journal,

> All that Afric ever brought forth strange
> All that which Asia ever had of prize
> Was here to see.[1]

Throughout the remainder of March not a day passed without its record of sightseeing in the journals of Mary and Claire.

84

Again and again, in sunlight, moonlight, or rain, they visited the Colosseum, with its weed-grown arena and broken arches overgrown with wild olive, myrtle, and fig. Next to the Colosseum Shelley was most impressed by the Baths of Caracalla. "Never was any desolation more sublime and lovely," he thought, than the high, straight walls of its six enormous chambers, their fissures sending forth vegetation, their floor now a level green in which elm trees had grown up. Through a crumbling stairway in one of the buttresses he ascended to the top, and from this viewpoint later described the scene to Peacock:

There grow on every side thick entangled wildernesses of myrtle, and the myrletus, and bay, and the flowering laurustinus, whose white blossoms are just developed, the wild fig, and a thousand nameless plants sown by the wandering winds. These woods are intersected on every side by paths, like sheep tracks through the copse wood of steep mountains, which wind to every part of the immense labryinth. From the midst rise those pinnacles and masses, themselves like Mountains, which have been seen from below. In one place you wind along a narrow strip of weed-grown ruin; on one side is the immensity of earth and sky, on the other a narrow chasm, which is bounded by an arch of enormous size, fringed by the many coloured foliage and blossoms, and supporting a lofty and ir-regular pyramid, overgrown like itself by the all-prevailing vegeta-tion. Around rise other crags and other peaks, all arrayed, and the deformity of their vast desolation softened down, by the undecaying investiture of nature. Come to Rome. It is a scene by which expres-sion is overpowered; which words cannot convey.[2]

Often, in all lights and weathers, Shelley walked among the ruins of the Capitol and the Forum, which then stood in an open plain, with the modern city on one side. The Temple of Con-cord, with its eight granite columns, and the Arches of Septimius Severus and of Constantine were the objects of his almost daily admiration.

I walk forth in the purple and golden light of an Italian evening, and return by star or moonlight, through this scene. The elms are just budding, and the warm spring winds bring unknown odours, all sweet from the country. I see the radiant Orion through the mighty columns of the temple of Concord, and the mellow fading light softens down the modern buildings of the Capitol, the only ones that interfere with the sublime desolation of the scene. . . . This walk is close to our lodging, and this is my evening walk.[3]

By moonlight on March 9, " a beautiful and mild spring Evening," [4] they entered the Pantheon, admired its perfect proportions and its sixteen fluted columns of polished yellow marble, gazed through its roofless dome at the open sky, and felt mildly critical that its perfect unity should have been flawed by providing twelve niches for such trivial creatures as the gods. Temples, baths, tombs, and arches were all visited, sometimes with guide-book in hand.[5]

But there was a modern city also, which had its attractions. Merely the fountains of Rome seemed to Shelley worth a long journey. He sent Peacock detailed descriptions of several of them — one a tall obelisk supported by boulders between which the water gushed forth, another the Fontana di Trevi, surmounted by a great statue of Neptune, and particularly the Quirinal fountain, with its obelisk of red granite and its " vast basin of porphyry in the midst of which rises a column of the purest water." [6] The palaces and temples of modern Rome, though inferior to its ruins, yet seemed superior to those of any other city. But Saint Peter's, its greatest glory, proved disappointing. There were fine details, such as the colonnade, but even its loftiness failed somehow to seem emphatic. " Externally, it is inferior in architectural beauty to St. Paul's, though not wholly devoid of it; internally it exhibits littleness on a large scale, and is in every respect opposed to antique taste." [7]

At the Palazzo Doria, the Palazzo Raspigliosi, the Palazzo di Spada, the Palazzo Borghese, St. Peter's, the museum of the Capitol, and various other public and private buildings they saw a wealth of painting and statuary. Shelley's favourite statue, in the museum of the Capitol, was an Apollo leaning backward with feet crossed and head thrown up in the very act of being inspired to fresh music.[8] Among the paintings of Guido Reni, Domenichino, Raphael, and Michelangelo, Shelley thought those of Raphael probably the finest in the world. Michelangelo he disliked sharply because he seemed to lack "moral dignity and loveliness." "His famous painting in the Sixtine Chapel seems to me deficient in beauty and majesty, both in the conception and the execution. It might have contained all the forms of terror and delight — and it is a dull and wicked emblem of a dull and wicked thing. Jesus Christ is like an angry pot-boy, and God like an old ale-house keeper looking out of window." [9]

Best of all the pleasures of modern Rome, however, were the Gardens of the Villa Borghese, with their ilex and laurel shades, their fountains and statues. Here, beside a quiet pool, stood the ancient temple of Esculapius the Saviour. Claire's comment repeated Shelley's sensations at Pompeii: "Here then I caught a glimpse of the ancients."

On March 12 the party heard Mass and a sermon at Saint Peter's. "The Music of the Mass," Claire wrote, "is divine, and the voices of the Singing Boys sounded in this vast edifice like flutes. We saw the Pope Pius VII a poor old man upon the brink of the Grave, and many Cardinals almost as old and trembling." The next day, as they were returning from a visit to the Baths of Caracalla, they again saw the Holy Father, who had descended from his carriage to walk. And about two weeks later (March 25) Claire wrote in her journal: "Fiesta of the Annunziata, Lady-day — Go to the church Maria Sopra Minerva. See the Pope and the Cardinals." The Emperor of Austria was expected to arrive in Rome on the afternoon of April 3. They went to the Ponte Molle to see the pavilion that was being prepared for his reception, and hoped to get tickets for some of the accompanying fiestas, but none was to be had. Perhaps tickets were unnecessary or were actually secured later, for Mary furnished Mrs. Gisborne with a rather lively description of the fireworks, the silk hangings, and the abundant feasting.[10]

Shelley's health had materially improved; life in Rome was less solitary and in all respects more pleasing than in Naples. "The Romans please me much," Shelley informed Peacock, "especially the women: who though totally devoid of every kind of information or culture of the imagination or affections or understanding, and, in this respect a kind of gentle savages — yet contrive to be interesting. Their extreme innocence and naïveté, the freedom and gentleness of their manners; the total absence of affectation makes an intercourse with them very like an intercourse with uncorrupted children, whom they resemble in loveliness as well as simplicity." [11] This was perhaps faint praise, but it gains considerable strength by comparison with his previous utterances on the Italians.

The centre of such social life as Shelley's party enjoyed in Rome was the salon of the Signora Marianna Candida Dionigi, an elderly Roman bluestocking who was rather uncharitably described by Mary to Mrs. Gisborne as " a painter and authoress, very old, very miserly, and very mean." [12] Her *conversazioni* were attended by both Italians and foreigners and were visited by members of Shelley's party as often as two or three times a week. " In the Evening go to the Conversazione of the Signora Marianna Dionigi," Claire wrote in her journal on March 28, " where there is a Cardinal, and many proportionate Englishmen, who after having crossed their legs and said nothing the whole Evening, rose all up at once, made their bows and filed off." Possibly it was through Signora Dionigi that the Shelleys became acquainted with Signor Amarone, who called on March 18, and the painter Milani, on whom they called on March 22. Lord Guildford called on the Shelleys on March 10. A more fruitful acquaintance was begun on March 22 with Dr. J. Bell, a well-known Scotch physician, with whom the Shelleys thereafter had considerable contact, both professional and social.

ALL this amounted to less for Shelley than for Mary, who always depended more upon social life than Shelley did. Her journal entries still carried some slight suggestion of the stoical, clipped repression that had characterized them for three months after Clara's death, but her letters were now showing a more lively interest in the life about her. The change seems to have begun shortly before the departure from Naples, for Godwin, who had been alarmed at the state of mind shown in her earlier letters, was greatly pleased at a " vivifying principle " in her letter to him dated January 31.[13] But Mary still suffered from

PENCIL SKETCH IN *PROMETHEUS UNBOUND* MS.

By permission of the Bodleian Library

low spirits. "God knows why," she wrote, "but I have suffered more from them, ten times over, than I ever did before I came to Italy. Evil thoughts will hang about me — but this is only now and then." [14] In general, Mary was finding Rome a place of "perpetual enchantment," whose delights made her whole previous life seem almost blank by contrast. [15] Under such influences, with both Shelley and Mary in improved health and spirits, the former morbid, unacknowledged strangeness that had followed Clara's death was apparently put aside.

Shelley, Mary, and Claire all continued to read, but not very extensively. Since March 19 Claire was again taking singing-lessons, and Mary (March 24) had taken up drawing and painting. Though neither of the two journals mentions the fact, Shelley was spending a large part of his time writing the second and third acts of *Prometheus Unbound,* which were finished by April 6. [16] This poem, with the other important poems written in 1819 and published the following year, represents the summit of Shelley's poetic power and calls for special consideration in a separate chapter.

The month of April glided by much as March had done. After finishing the third act of *Prometheus Unbound* Shelley was probably taking a short rest from composition before beginning *The Cenci.* Visits to the *conversazioni* of Signora Dionigi continued, a few new acquaintances were formed (for example, with Signor Delicati, an artist, and two musicians from Arpino named Fanelli), visits were received and repaid from time to time. A Mr. and Mrs. Davies called occasionally, and the acquaintance with Dr. and Mrs. Bell became more intimate. Godwin's friend, Sir William Drummond, whom Shelley already admired as the author of *Academical Questions,* called on April 22. An extract from Mary's journal for the week following Easter will give a fair picture of the whole month. For the sake of added detail I have bracketed with it the corresponding entries in Claire's journal:

Monday, April 12 — Drawing lesson. Draw in the Borghese Gardens. Visit the Signora Dionigi. [No lesson in music. Letter from Mrs. Hoppner concerning Mrs. Vavasour. Drive in the Borghese Gardens.

In the Evening go to the conversazione of the Signora Dionigi. Music by two from Arpino. Mr. Davies and the Principessa Belvidera.]

Tuesday, April 13 — Draw in the Borghese Gardens. Signor Chiappa calls. Read Livy. In the evening Mr. Davies calls. [Arrange some little matters — Signor Chiappa call [*sic*]. Drive in the Borghese. Walk to the Campi D'oglio. In the evening Mr. Davies calls.]

Wednesday, April 14 — Drawing lesson. Visit Monte Cavallo. Finish the 23rd book of Livy. Visit the Signora Dionigi. [A lesson in Music. Read S —'s translation of Plato's Symposium. Go to Monte Cavallo — Drive in the Borghese Gardens. In the Evening go to the Signora Marianna Dionigi.]

Thursday, April 15 — Draw all the morning in the Gardens Borghese. Walk to the Coliseum. Read " Huon de Bordeaux " and " Roman de la Chevalerie." [Practise. Read Plato's Symposium. Drive in the Borghese Gardens. In the Evening visit the Signora — Dionigi. Music by two from Arpino.]

Friday, April 16 — Paint; read Livy. Draw in the Borghese Gardens. The Neapolitan and his Sister walk about with us. After dinner, Shelley reads the first book of " Paradise Lost " to me. Visit the Signora Dionigi. [Finish the Symposium of Plato — Two Fanelli of Arpino call. In the Evening Practise.]

Saturday, April 17 — Drawing lesson. Read Metastasio. Shelley reads " Paradise Lost " aloud. Visit the Signora Dionigi in the evening. [A lesson in Music. Read La Fleur des Batailles a history of Chivalry — Drive in the Borghese Gardens.]

Sunday, April 18 — Draw. Signor Delicati comes. Afterwards ride to the Vatican, and walk through it. In the evening, visit the Signora Dionigi. [Read Regnes Lodbrog [? — indecipherable] a history of Chivalry. Go to the Vatican Meet there the two from Arpino. Drive in the Borghese. In the Evening at the Conversazione of the Signora Marianna. The two from Arpino called Fanelli two Irish Ladies and Mr. Davies.]

On April 23, as Claire and Mary were driving in the Borghese Gardens, they thought they recognized Miss Amelia Curran, the

daughter of Godwin's old friend and Shelley's Irish acquaintance, John Philpot Curran. Shelley had met her once on one of
his earlier visits to Godwin's with Harriet, and Claire and Mary
knew her somewhat better. The next day they found that it was
indeed Miss Curran and left cards at her lodgings. This was
the beginning of an association that quickly ripened into friendship. The ladies exchanged calls frequently and visited various
places together. Miss Curran, an amateur painter, began portraits of Shelley, Mary, William, and Claire. Her portraits of
Claire Clairmont and William were finished; Claire's still survives as her only extant portrait.[17] The portrait of Shelley was
thrown aside unfinished, but after the poet's death it was resur-
rected and completed, and now hangs in the National Portrait
Gallery in London. It is the principal basis for nearly all of the
engraved portraits of Shelley that later became current.[18]

Shelley was again busy writing. Just when he began is uncertain, but on May 14 Claire's journal mentions her reading
of the manuscript history of the Cenci family that Mary had
copied for Shelley at Leghorn almost a year before, and on
the same day Mary wrote: "Shelley writes his tragedy." On
April 22 the party had visited the Colonna Palace and had seen
there the supposed portrait of Beatrice Cenci by Guido. Later,
on May 11, they had visited the old Casa Cenci, in which the
early action of Shelley's drama was to be laid. Conversations
at the Signora Dionigi's salon convinced him that Italians, at
least, were still deeply interested in the story, and Guido's portrait greatly stimulated his interest. He went briskly to work.[19]

PROBABLY on Elena's account the Shelleys had planned to return to Naples late in May and remain there until winter.[20] On
April 20, however, Shelley was again " very unwell," and, though
there are no further reports of his illness, it seemed wise to
advance the date of their departure from Rome. Mary believed
that the Roman air produced " cold, depression and even fever "
in Shelley, and the doctors recommended Naples.[21] Mary wrote
to Mrs. Gisborne to urge her to accept the invitation to visit

them in Naples. They now expected to leave Rome on May 7. Meanwhile Shelley's health again improved and the pleasant intimacy with Miss Curran developed, so that the last week of May found the family still in Rome. The Roman climate was well known to be dangerous in warm weather, and Clara's death was still a very recent memory, but it seems never to have occurred to either Shelley or Mary that there was any risk in the delay except for Shelley.

On May 25 William Shelley fell ill. At first his parents were not particularly alarmed: hitherto William had always enjoyed excellent health and spirits.[22] The next day he was better, but it was two or three days more before he could be pronounced convalescent from an attack of worms. As the doctors were of the opinion that he suffered from the heat of the southern climate, his parents thought it unwise to take him still farther south, to Naples. Moreover, Mary Shelley was expecting another baby in November and was already under the care of a surgeon who intended to be in Pisa or Florence at that time. Thus a new plan was formed, to leave Rome early in June for Lucca, spend the summer at the Baths of Lucca or the Baths of Pisa, and settle down for the winter in Pisa, which was especially recommended for Shelley's health.[23] A letter was dispatched to Mrs. Gisborne explaining the new plan and commissioning her to engage a servant.

It was too late, however, to save William. His convalescence was only temporary. Two days after Mary wrote to Mrs. Gisborne she wrote in her journal (June 2): "William becomes very ill in the evening," and Claire's journal adds: "Mr. Bell calls three times. — I sit up with Willy." The next day William was still very ill. Thereafter for some days there was no thought of keeping a journal. "(The journal ends here. P. B. S.)" stands in place of the regular entry for June 4, and Claire's journal is interrupted from June 2 to June 10.

The occurrences of the intervening days are best told in two hurried letters that are tragically brief. The first of these, hitherto printed as by Amelia Curran, was really written by Claire Clairmont:[24]

Rome, Thursday, June 3, 1819

Dear Mrs. Gisborne,

Mary tells me to write for her for she is very unwell and also afflicted. Our poor little William is at present very ill and it will be impossible to quit Rome so soon as we intended. She begs you therefore to forward the letters here and still to look for a servant for her as she certainly intends coming to Pisa. She will write to you a day or two before we set out. William has a complaint of the Stomach but fortunately he is attended by Mr. Bell who is reckoned even in London one of the first English Surgeons. I know you will be glad to hear that both Mary and Mr. Shelley would be well in health were it not for the dreadful anxiety they now suffer.

[No signature]

[On the same sheet two days later Mary added the following note:]

June 5.

William is in the greatest danger — We do not quite despair yet we have the least possible reason to hope — Yesterday he was in the convulsions of death and he was saved from them — Yet we dare not must not hope —

I will write as soon as any change takes place — The misery of these hours is beyond calculation — The hopes of my life are bound up in him —

Ever your affectionately
M. W. S.

I am well and so is S. although he is more exhausted by watching than I am — William is in a high fever.

On June 8, 1819 Shelley wrote to Peacock as follows:

Rome,
June 8, 1819.

My dear Friend,

Yesterday, after an illness of only a few days, my little William died. There was no hope from the moment of the attack. You will be kind enough to tell all my friends, so that I need not write to them. It is a great exertion to me to write this, and it seems to me as if, hunted by calamity as I have been, that I should never recover any cheerfulness again.

If the things Mary desired to be sent to Naples have not been shipped, send them to Livorno.

We leave this city for Livorno to-morrow morning, where we have written to take lodgings for a month. I will then write again.

Yours ever affectionately,

P. B. SHELLEY.

The gap in Claire's journal from June 2 to 10 is broken by one notation: "Monday, June 7, at noonday," which probably indicates the hour of William's death. For "sixty miserable, death-like hours" without once closing his eyes, Shelley watched William's hopeless struggle for life, and emerged almost a wreck, all the great improvement that had taken place in his own health in the last month quite demolished.[25] On June 10, according to Claire's journal, the Shelleys and Claire left Rome for Leghorn. Several weeks later Shelley wrote Hogg: "I had been slowly recovering a certain degree of health until this event, which has left me in a very weak state, — and Mary bears it, as you may naturally imagine, worse than I do."[26]

This was in answer to a prompt, slightly formal, but evidently sincere letter of condolence from his old friend.[27] Leigh Hunt was equally prompt and considerably more perceptive. He tried gently to reason with Mary's extreme depression. "Not that I wonder at it under such sufferings; but I know, at least I have often suspected, that you have a tendency, partly constitutional perhaps, and partly owing to the turn of your philosophy, to look over-intensely at the dark side of human things; and they must present double dreariness through such tears as you are now shedding. Pray consent to take care of your health, as the ground of comfort; and cultivate your laurels on the strength of it."[28]

All this did little or no good. For months after William's death Mary's letters show her mood to have been predominantly hopeless and dead. She abandoned her journal and very likely much of her reading. Claire's journal, except for three days in June and two in July, also falls silent until the beginning of 1820. Mary's letters tried to keep her desolation in the background, but to no avail. "I no sooner take up my pen," she wrote to Miss Curran on June 27, "than my thoughts run away with me, and I cannot guide it except about *one* subject, and that I must

avoid. . . . Let us hear also, if you please, anything you may
have done about the tomb, near which I shall lie one day, and
care not, for my own sake, how soon. I shall never recover that
blow; I feel it more than at Rome, the thought never leaves me
for a single moment; everything on earth has lost its interest
to me. You see I told you that I could only write to you on one
subject; how can I, since, do all I can (and I endeavour very sincerely) I can think of no other, so I will leave off." [29]

To Marianne Hunt, two days later, it was the same: "We
went from England comparatively prosperous and happy; I
shall return broken hearted and miserable. I never know one
moment's ease from the wretchedness and despair that possesses me. May you, my dear Marianne, never know what it is to
lose two only and lovely children in one year — to watch their
dying moments, and then at last to be left childless and for ever
miserable. It is useless complaining and I shall therefore only
write a short letter, for as all my thoughts are nothing but
misery it is not kind to transmit them to you." But before the
letter was ended she had returned to her grief: " I feel that I
am not fit for anything and therefore not fit to live." [30]

By August 4, Shelley's birthday, Mary had overcome her
apathy sufficiently to resume her journal, but with one of the
bitterest entries it ever received:

Wednesday, August 4 — Leghorn (Mary) I begin my Journal on
Shelley's birthday. We have now lived five years together; and if
all the events of the five years were blotted out, I might be happy;
but to have won, and then cruelly to have lost, the association of
four years is not an accident to which the human mind can bend
without much suffering.

Toward the end of the month she wrote to Marianne Hunt: " I
never am in good spirits — often in very bad; and Hunt's portrait has already seen me shed so many tears that if he had his
heart as well as his eyes, he would weep too in pity." [31]

Finally William Godwin, whose opinions had great weight
with Mary except on the one subject of Shelley, claimed the
privilege of " a father and a philosopher" in speaking out
plainly. He was bitterly disappointed, he wrote, to see one who

was so far above the majority of her sex subject herself to " so inglorious a change," by joining a class of people who " sit with their arms crossed, a prey to apathy and languor, of no use to any earthly creature." "Remember, too," he concluded, "though at first your nearest connections may pity you in this state, yet that when they see you fixed in selfishness and ill humour and regardless of the happiness of every one else, they will finally cease to love you, and scarcely learn to endure you." [32] This true but rather heavy-handed admonition might have done more good had it not been accompanied by a reminder that he and some others did not think any too highly of her husband's character. Also throughout the whole period of Mary's deepest depression Godwin did not scruple to add to it by laying his own renewed financial troubles at her feet.

THE SHELLEYS and Claire had left Rome for Leghorn (Livorno) on June 10 and had remained there a week, seeing the Gisbornes frequently and making arrangements for a house. Since June 17 they had been living in a house called Villa Valsovano, about half-way between Leghorn and Monte Nero. The house stood at the end of a green lane in the middle of a cultivated field, where sun-browned, bare-legged peasants worked alternately with their cabbages and grapes and sang Rossini's music in competition with the more ancient and insistent noise of the cicalas and the creaking of a water-wheel supplying the irrigation ditches. At the top of the house was a small terrace, roofed and glazed, which Shelley took as his study. Here on the hottest days of a hot Italian summer Shelley wrote steadily on *The Cenci* or desisted for a while to watch some sudden summer squall sweep over the waters of the Mediterranean.[33] It amused him to refer to this study as Scythrop's tower, in good-natured reference to Peacock's caricature of Shelley as Scythrop in *Nightmare Abbey.*

Life in Villa Valsovano was quite simple. The Gisbornes, whom the Shelleys saw frequently, were almost the only callers. Twice only does Mary's journal mention any others — a " Madame du Plantis and Zoide " who took tea with them on Septem-

ber 15 and 16. Claire Clairmont was still with them, but she
is mentioned only once (in one of Mary's letters), as continuing
her music-lessons. Toward the end of August, Shelley gave Peacock the following description of a daily routine, which differed
very little from the one practised at Marlow two years earlier:
" I awaken usually at 7. read half an hour then get up, breakfast, after breakfast *ascend my tower* and read or write until
two. Then we dine — after dinner I read Dante with Mary,
gossip a little, eat grapes and figs, sometimes walk, though seldom, and at one half past five pay a visit to Mrs. Gisborne who
reads Spanish with me until near seven. We then come for
Mary, and stroll about till supper time." [34] While Shelley was
at work in his tower Mary spent the morning in writing and in
reading Latin. The reading of Dante with Shelley usually consisted of two cantos. Generally Mr. and Mrs. Gisborne called
in the evening.[35]

The death of William had been a heavy blow to Shelley. " O
that I could return to England! " he exclaimed. " How heavy
a weight when misfortune is added to exile, and solitude, as
if the measure were not full, heaped high on both." [36] In England, at least there were a few friends whose letters always assured him of a welcome back. But his health still demanded a
warmer climate than England's, and there were also prudential
reasons against his return. He had supposed all but one of his
debts in Marlow settled by Longdill, his solicitor, but he now
learned that there were several debts still unpaid, and he was
not secure against an arrest for debt if he returned.[37]

Not until July did Shelley feel equal, either in health or in
spirits, to his usual program of reading and writing.[38] Amelia
Curran had been instructed to see that a small pyramid of stone
should be set up over William's grave in the English burying-
ground at Rome,[39] but before the instructions could be carried
out Shelley had written two stanzas of his unfinished poem
" To William Shelley," possibly also the six undated lines of
his second poem of that title.

Mary Shelley once expressed a guarded belief that Shelley
did not entirely disbelieve in a future existence.[40] This opinion
was shared by Byron and is supported by certain passages in

Shelley's later works. One would expect to find some support for it in his fragmentary verses on the death of his son, but the strongest faith in survival that he could muster was an essentially pagan faith in a reunion with nature:

> Where art thou, my gentle child?
>   Let me think thy spirit feeds,
> With its life intense and mild,
>   The love of living leaves and weeds.
> Among these tombs and ruins wild
>   Let me think that through low seeds
> Of sweet flowers and sunny grass,
> Into their hues and scents may pass,
> A portion —

About the streets of Rome he had heard workmen chanting a sad *ritornello*, importing that Rome could never be the same again. Byron had been moved by the same chant. It kept recurring to Shelley in his grief. At the top of his unfinished manuscript poem he wrote: " With what truth may I say —

> Roma! Roma! Roma!
> Non è piu come era prima! "

At times it must have seemed that Mary also would never be the same again — that she had withdrawn into a world of blank listlessness from which she was almost unwilling to emerge. In July he wrote the two unfinished poems entitled " To Mary Shelley " seeking to recall her to his need of her companionship:

> My dearest Mary, wherefore hast thou gone,
> And left me in this dreary world alone?
> Thy form is here indeed — a lovely one —
> But thou art fled, gone down the dreary road,
> That leads to Sorrow's most obscure abode;
> Thou sittest on the hearth of pale despair, where
> For thine own sake I cannot follow thee.

And again:

> The world is dreary,
> And I am weary

> Of wandering on without thee, Mary;
>   A joy was erewhile
>   In thy voice and thy smile,
> And 'tis gone, when I should be gone too, Mary.
>   O why do we rest on the world's cold breast
>   Thy name is like the   sweet heart . . .

By midsummer, however, Mary was forced to begin taking thought about the child whose birth was expected in October or November. Certain clothes and other necessaries had to be purchased for her by friends in England and plans had to be made for removing to Florence in time to have the attendance of Dr. Bell, almost the only available doctor whom she or Shelley trusted. Shelley pinned his hope of restoring Mary's normal spirits upon the birth of her child.

Matters might have been a bit more cheerful in Shelley's household if Godwin, after a quiescence of a year and a half, had not resumed his old nagging on financial affairs. There had been for some time a misunderstanding over Godwin's lease of his house in Skinner Street, which was not ended until 1822, but which in July 1819 had already brought Godwin into court as an anxious defendant. Shelley felt that he had discharged all his financial obligations to Godwin at the time he left England, but Godwin claimed otherwise. At about this time Shelley wrote to Godwin, after a year's silence, asking him to do what he could to alleviate Mary's terrible depression. The sequel is best stated in Shelley's indignant relation to Leigh Hunt:

The *very* next letter, received yesterday, and addressed to her, called her husband (me) "a disgraceful and flagrant person," tried to persuade her that I was under great engagements to give him *more* money (after having given him £4700), and urged her if she ever wished a connection to continue between him and her to force me to get money for him. — He cannot persuade her that I am what I am not, nor place a shade of enmity between her and me — but he heaps on her misery, still misery. — I have not yet shown her the letter — but I must. I doubt whether I ought not to expose this solemn lie; for such, and not a man, is Godwin. But I shall, as is our custom, (I mean yours and mine), err on the side of patience and endurance. I suspect my character, if measured with his, would sustain no diminution among those who know us both. — I have bought bitter knowledge with £4700. I wish it were all yours now.[41]

THOUGH the death of William was to both Shelley and Mary a heavier blow than the death of Clara, it did not, as Clara's death had done, produce a feeling of estrangement and injustice between them. They were confident of their mutual love and esteem, even though they may also have suspected that it might never again be quite what it had been before Clara's death. Shelley, moreover, had his work, in which he tried to obtain Mary's interest.[42] *The Cenci,* which was completed in August, was the only one of his poems about which he consulted Mary constantly while it was in progress. There were also the daily conversations and readings with Mrs. Gisborne, whom both the Shelleys liked and praised more and more. Mrs. Gisborne taught Shelley enough Spanish to read the plays of Calderón, which he did with great enthusiasm, for a time almost forgetting his Greek.

The arrival of Charles Clairmont on September 4, consistent sponge as he was, added a new interest to the rather forlorn household. In his frugal, cheerful way Charles had probably been living partly on Shelley's bounty ever since Shelley in 1817 had declined to finance his marriage with the daughter of his French landlady. He was now on his way to Vienna, where he expected to earn a living by his linguistic ability. He lingered with the Shelleys until about November 10 — long enough to fall in love, again unsuccessfully, with another landlady's daughter.[43] Since early August, Mary had returned to her reading and writing, to which Charles's optimistic and really interesting conversation was doubtless a welcome addition. Shelley for once found Charles's arrival particularly opportune. He had spent fifteen months in Spain and of course knew Spanish. Together, and sometimes with the addition of Mrs. Gisborne, they spent many evenings over Calderón. Shelley became quite proficient, and by the end of September had read twelve plays, some of which he was inclined to rank "among the grandest and most perfect productions of the human mind." [44]

Shelley's correspondence during the summer and autumn was concerned rather largely with the poems he had recently completed. "Julian and Maddalo" was sent to Leigh Hunt "for publication, but *without my name.*"[45] Charles and James Ollier had been rather listless in their relations with Shelley during his first year in Italy, and it was necessary to find out if they really wished to continue as his publishers. They still did, in spite of the poor report on previous sales they had to make; but apparently they were more anxious to become Mary's publishers, since her *Frankenstein* had outsold all of Shelley's books. Shelley, however, was now able to offer them a book of his own which he thoroughly believed would become popular. He was having two hundred and fifty copies of *The Cenci* printed at Leghorn, where the work could be done more cheaply than in England and where he could correct the proofs himself. These were to be sent to England as a kind of advance edition, to be kept a strict secret even from the Olliers until the fate of Shelley's more ambitious design of a stage production was determined.

In July Peacock was given the task of procuring a stage production. Only Covent Garden was to be considered, since Shelley could think of no one except his favourite Miss O'Neill in the rôle of Beatrice. If accepted — and Shelley was inclined to think that the story was too compelling and too clearly and delicately handled to be rejected — it was on no account to be known as Shelley's. Eliza Westbrook alone, as Mary wrote to Miss Curran, would hire enough people to damn any play known to be Shelley's. Peacock had some acquaintance at Covent Garden and procured a reading of the play by Harris, the manager. Harris's judgment was a bitter disappointment, though the reviews that appeared later showed that he was right. He thought the subject much too horrible for contemporary audiences; too objectionable, in fact, even for Miss O'Neill to read — but he would like to consider and would "gladly accept" a play by Shelley on a more acceptable subject.[46] Not until after it had been rejected by the theatre did Shelley mention the play to Ollier except in one vague reference.

The first three acts of *Prometheus Unbound* were also ready for publication. "My 'Prometheus,' which has been long finished," he wrote to Ollier on September 6, "is now being transcribed, and will soon be forwarded to you for publication. It is, in my judgment, of a higher character than anything I have yet attempted, and is perhaps less an imitation than anything that has gone before it." Two weeks later he sent the manuscript to Peacock, with instructions to withhold it from Ollier until he received further notice. Late in December Ollier received his instructions to publish *The Cenci* if it had been rejected by the theatre and to begin printing *Prometheus Unbound* at once, with the additional fourth act that he would soon receive. "My 'Prometheus,'" he concluded, "is the best thing I ever wrote." Both volumes appeared in the following year, *The Cenci* toward the end of March and the *Prometheus* in September. Ollier already had his instructions to send copies (and also copies of anything else Shelley published) to Hunt, Godwin, Hogg, Peacock, Keats, Thomas Moore, Horace Smith, and Byron.[47]

THE LETTERS which the Shelleys received from England during the summer and autumn of 1819 were principally from Leigh Hunt. Probably because he realized the distress of his friends Hunt formed a resolution of writing to them every Monday. Almost every letter contained some tactful indirect argument against indulging sorrow, and all were filled with amiable efforts to amuse and divert. "I wish in truth I knew how to amuse you just now, and that I were in Italy to try," he confessed to Mary. "I would walk about with Shelley wherever he pleased . . . I should be merry or quiet, chat, read, or impudently play and sing you Italian airs all the evening."[48] As far as these things could be done in letters Hunt endeavoured to do them. He discussed points of literature and art, quoted, gossiped about the opera and about common friends, and made a special point of saying encouraging things to Shelley about the rise of his reputation. Young Henry Hunt (Leigh Hunt's nephew) had astonished his father's dinner guests by a passionate defence of Shelley against the aspersions of one of them; Leigh Hunt himself had indignantly declined to meet a friend of Peacock's who had declined to meet Shelley. Lamb's friend Charles Lloyd spoke highly of Shelley's poetry and defended it against criticism; Lamb himself, who had formerly declined to meet Shelley, greatly admired *Rosalind and Helen*. "Your reputation is certainly rising greatly in your native country," wrote Hunt, "in spite of its honest Promethean chains." [49] Despite Hunt's encouragement, there was little in the public prints about Shelley, either for or against. Hunt himself had published in the *Examiner* of May 9 a glowing tribute to *Rosalind and Helen*.

The London *Chronicle*, the *Commercial Chronicle*, the *New Times*, and the *Gentleman's Magazine* had published practically identical reviews of *Rosalind and Helen* in June, bitterly condemning it as an effort "to bring a poetic sanction to the basest passions of the human heart." *Blackwood's Edinburgh Magazine* for June condemned its "strange perversion of moral principle," but expressed confidence that a "highly gifted man" who could write such undeniably beautiful poetry would soon outgrow his faults of opinion and take his proper place among the greatest living poets. None of these reviews, except his own, did Hunt call to Shelley's attention, nor is there any proof that Shelley ever saw them.

To each of Hunt's little encouragements Shelley paid some particular notice in his letters. He expressed the highest opinion of Lamb's *Rosamund Gray*, which he had just read, and lamented that "the malice of an enemy" (Godwin?) had prevented his knowing Lamb in England. He recollected with pleasure an acute comment in one of Charles Lloyd's books that Southey had lent him years earlier, and he deeply appreciated Hunt's favourable review of *Rosalind and Helen*. "Your kind expressions about my Eclogue gave me great pleasure, indeed my great stimulus in writing is to have the approbation of those that feel kindly towards me." [50]

All of Hunt's little reminders of how the Shelleys were missed — at the opera, or during a discussion when someone would be sure to say: "What would Shelley say?" or "If Mary were only here now" — all of Hogg's accounts of his pleasure in reading Greek and his long Sunday rambles with Peacock, Coulson, or

Hunt, when someone would deplore Shelley's absence, occasionally came together in Shelley's mind to form a brief, intense nostalgia. "Social enjoyment," he assured Peacock, "in some form or other, is the alpha and omega of existence. All that I see in Italy — and from my tower window I now see the magnificent peaks of the Apennine half enclosing the plain — is nothing — it dwindles to smoke in the mind, when I think of some familiar forms of scenery little perhaps in themselves over which old remembrances have thrown a delightful colour. How we prize what we despised when present! So the ghosts of our dead associations rise and haunt us, in revenge for our having let them starve, and abandoned them to perish." [51] Such feelings were probably intensified by the fact that both Byron and the Hoppners were now acting as if they had never known the Shelleys. In spite of pressing entreaties from Claire and Mary, not a line had reached them from Venice since March. As late as October 18 the Shelleys did not know the residence of either Byron or Allegra.[52]

HUNT said nothing about the political situation in England, and Peacock was for a while too busy with his new duties at the East India Company to write; but Hogg gave Shelley a brief account of the trial of Richard Carlile for publishing Paine's *Age of Reason.* Hunt's *Examiner,* which now arrived regularly (though two months late), and Cobbett's *Political Register* gave much fuller information. Shelley also read *Galignani's Messenger,* a Paris newspaper in English.

From all these sources it appeared that England had gradually reached a serious crisis that might easily produce a revolution. As early as 1816 the Lord Mayor of London had presided over a public meeting in which it was declared that England stood face to face with "either bloody revolution . . . or a military despotism." Since then the situation had steadily grown worse, and Shelley had been moved to comment upon it in two published pamphlets in 1817 and 1818. By the autumn of 1819 it seemed to many that the inevitable explosion was fully prepared and needed only a match to set it off.

On August 16, 1819 a large reform meeting outside the city of Manchester was scheduled to be addressed by Mr. " Orator " Hunt, a former manufacturer turned agitator. A considerable body of local militia was assembled by the authorities and an attempt was made to arrest Mr. Hunt in the midst of his crowded audience. A panic ensued during which the militia lost their heads and charged the crowd of workingmen. At least nine people were killed and four hundred and eighteen injured. The country rang with alarm as an official inquiry whitewashed the conduct of the local officials. Radicals like Hunt and Cobbett voiced the popular indignation, while Tories like Lord Grenville warned the House of Lords that England was " inundated with inflammatory and poisonous publications " and " deluged with sedition and blasphemy." It was moved in Parliament to appoint a commission to inquire into the state of the country. Public journals did not disguise their apprehension that the country was on the verge of revolution.[53]

Shelley heard of the Manchester Massacre, as it was called, early in September, and boiled with indignation.[54] " The tyrants here, as in the French Revolution, have first shed blood," he exclaimed to Peacock. " May their execrable lessons not be learnt with equal docility." But though such disturbances seemed clearly enough to be " the distant thunder of a terrible storm," Shelley did not expect the storm to break until the financial situation grew worse.[55] By the last week in September he had completed a poem on the crisis, The Masque of Anarchy, which he sent to Hunt to be inserted in the Examiner.

Like the triumphs or masques of Petrarch, which he had recently been reading,[56] the poem is in the nature of a vision into which both real persons and abstractions are introduced. Its language and imagery are studiously plain, almost stark, as became direct appeal to the common people rather than to the " esoteric few " for whom Epipsychidion was written, or " the more select class of poetical readers " to whose " highly refined imagination " he addressed Prometheus Unbound. These stanzas, as he informed Hunt, were " exoteric "; [57] but they are none the less typically Shelleyan.

In the poem Murder, Fraud, and Hypocrisy, in the guise of

Lords Castlereagh, Eldon, and Sidmouth, pass slowly by in a
ghastly masquerade, followed by a deathly-pale personification
of Anarchy, riding a white horse splashed with blood. As the
pageant passes over England, it is attended and cheered by an
array of applauding bishops, lawyers, peers, spies, and hired
murderers. They waste the country in the name of Anarchy,
whom they proclaim to be both God and Law. Ahead of the
procession flees a maniac maid whose name is Hope, proclaiming:

> " My father Time is weak and grey
> With waiting for a better day;
> See how idiot-like he stands,
> Fumbling with his palsied hands! "

She throws herself before the horses' feet, expecting to be trampled. Then, as in *Prometheus Unbound*, an apparent miracle
takes place. Between her and the oncoming hoofs rises a misty
form, small and weak at first, but soon growing into a bright,
mailed Shape before whom the forces of Anarchy are suddenly
annihilated. It was that same Spirit of Liberty which Shelley
could never think of as quite extinguished, which, nearly two
years before, he had imagined as possibly arising from the tomb
of Princess Charlotte to become the true Queen of England.

As if from the long-suffering and indignant Earth itself a
voice arises. Having already shown by his pageant that in the
mysterious nature of things annihilation inevitably waits upon
Anarchy and Tyranny, Shelley employs this voice of Nature for
the remaining two-thirds of his poem to administer a practical
stimulation and guidance that should hasten the victory. Thus
the voice summons the men of England to arise:

> " Rise like Lions after slumber
> In unvanquishable number,
> Shake your chains to earth like dew,
> Which in sleep had fallen on you —
> Ye are many — they are few."

It paints a picture of their present slavery in plain terms that
no labourer could misunderstand — undernourishment, exploi-

tation, and a fraudulent currency — evils to which even savages
and wild beasts are superior. It then pictures the freedom to
which they are entitled — clothes, fire, food, and decent living,
Wisdom, Justice, Peace, and Love, in which the virtues flourish
and Science and Poetry lead mankind forward. Finally it proposes the means for achieving freedom — a great assembly
at which Englishmen would simply and solemnly announce
their intention to be free. Such an assembly would be beset
by artillery, scimitars, and fixed bayonets, but it should rely
upon the old laws of England that guarantee a certain amount
of freedom and upon its own unalterable will to freedom. Let
the tyrants slash and stab and maim till they were glutted; if
the people only abjured retaliatory bloodshed, the hired soldiers,
being human after all, would eventually become worn out and
ashamed. Firm resolution would achieve freedom, as Shelley's
heroes always achieve it, by superior moral strength.

Shelley's remedy is both simple and desperate, but it is one
at which the Christian, at least, should forbear to sneer, since
Christ Himself was profoundly convinced of the power of non-
resistance. It is a power whose practical effectiveness for purposes not unlike Shelley's has been demonstrated by millions
of Indians. Yet it is doubtful if the English workingman would
have understood Shelley's remedy half so well as his description
of the disease. " Rise like Lions after slumber " — the ringing
lines which Shelley repeated as his conclusion — is a rather confusing battle-cry in such a cause. So it must have seemed to
Leigh Hunt, who quietly neglected to publish the poem in his
Examiner. In view of the fact that he had printed strong statements of his own on the same subject his decision can hardly
be charged to cowardice. When he later published the poem
in a separate volume in 1832, he explained that he had formerly
suppressed it because the public of 1819 would have misunderstood it, distorting its indignation while minimizing its counsel of restraint, to the further prejudice of Shelley's reputation.

During the autumn Shelley wrote six other poems equally
vigorous and simple.[58] His desire was to publish them for the
direct inspiration of the common people in the revolution that
he thought was approaching. None of them was published until

after his death. "In those days of prosecution for libel," Mrs. Shelley wrote later, "they could not be printed." [59] The *Prometheus* volume, however, contained his "Ode, before the Spaniards had Recovered Their Liberty," and his "Ode to Liberty," both of which reflect Shelley's strong political excitement in terms sufficiently general to escape prosecution.

QUIETLY, and somewhat painfully for Shelley, dully and miserably for Mary, June wore into July, and the months of August and September passed by. By August, Mary's dejection had given way to the resumption of her regular reading and writing, but she expected never to be happy again, and she looked forward to her approaching confinement with apprehension, because one child only was "a fearful risk on whom all one's hope and joy is placed." [60] Shelley, depressed and ailing, was almost helpless in the face of Mary's melancholy. He knew now that there was a wall between himself and Mary that not even their mutual love and confidence could surmount. He had his work, however, and before the end of the autumn he had been considerably restored in health and spirits.[61] Probably because of the danger to Mary of a journey to Naples and the danger to Elena of a journey from Naples, nothing appears to have been done about Elena Adelaide Shelley.

Dr. Bell was now in Florence. He had attended Mary in Rome and it was much desired that her child should be born under his care. On September 23 Shelley and Charles Clairmont went to Florence to engage apartments there for six months. A note to Claire en route shows that Shelley was still suffering from the pain in his side and required opium in order to sleep. On the 25th they were back at Livorno, and on the 30th the party set out for Florence, which they reached after two days' slow and easy travel.

The journey to Florence was broken by a one-day stop at Pisa, where the Shelleys made an acquaintance destined to be of great value to them and to Claire as long as they remained in Italy. In Ireland many years earlier Mary's mother, Mary

Wollstonecraft, had been the much-loved teacher of a young girl who later became Lady Mountcashell. Afterwards Lady Mountcashell had entertained Godwin in Ireland and had ever since been in sporadic correspondence with him and the second Mrs. Godwin. She was a woman of extraordinary mind and appearance. In the early days Godwin had described her as a stern democrat, a republican of unusual understanding and good nature, but rather liable to caricature on account of the combination of these qualities with a handsome countenance and a tall, brawny figure most oddly and carelessly clothed.[62] She had separated from her husband, and when the Shelleys met her had been living for many years in a free-love union with Mr. George William Tighe, the son of an Irish M.P. and a cousin of Mary Tighe, the author of *Psyche*. For eight years "Mr. and Mrs. Mason," as they called themselves, had been living a life of quiet, decent retirement in Italy, devoted to each other and to their two daughters, Laura and Nerina. They were both held in general respect by all who knew them.

Mr. Mason was now something of an invalid, but time had dealt more kindly by Mrs. Mason. Claire Clairmont described her as "very tall, of a lofty and calm presence. Her features were regular and delicate; her large blue eyes singularly well-set; her complexion of a clear pale, but yet full of life, and giving an idea of health. Her countenance beamed mildly, with the expression of a refined, cultivated, and highly cheerful mind. In all my intercourse with her I never saw the smallest symptom of the melancholy and discontent which was so striking both in Byron and Shelley." [63]

Mrs. Mason already knew all about the Shelleys from her correspondence with the Godwins. She welcomed them — and particularly Mary — with a warmth that must have been very heartening to people who had already spent a year and a half in Italy without forming more than one friendship that had any roots in the country itself. Thereafter she was in constant correspondence with them when not in their company, and from the first her advice and opinions were always sound and sensible. Almost immediately she helped guide Shelley toward far better medical treatment than he had previously received. She dropped a wise, matter-of-fact observation to Mary that nursing mothers could not indulge melancholy without risking their children's health; she wrote letters to smooth Charles Clairmont's way in Vienna,[64] and she·became the best friend, except Shelley himself, that Claire Clairmont ever had.

Chapter XXII

ANNUS MIRABILIS

PROMETHEUS UNBOUND; COMPARISON WITH

QUEEN MAB; THE CENCI;

A PHILOSOPHICAL VIEW OF REFORM

THE POEMS written by Shelley mostly in 1819 and published in two volumes in 1820 are so important in themselves and are such an impressive exhibit of his powers that any biography of the poet would be out of focus without giving them separate and detailed consideration. Of few writers more than Shelley can it be said that his works are the man himself. At this point, therefore, midway between the composition and publication of two of his greatest volumes, it is necessary to pause somewhat at length to consider these works as examples of his artistic and intellectual maturity and as expressions of that inner life that Shelley was coming to regard as the more important side of reality. This chapter may be safely ignored by those who seek in biography only "material" facts; it is written primarily for those who agree with Diogenes Teufelsdröckh. For "what," exclaimed that emphatic sage, "are your historical Facts; still more your biographical? Wilt thou know a Man, above all a Mankind, by stringing together beadrolls of what thou namest facts? The Man is the spirit he worked in; not what he did, but what he became."

EVER since his arrival in Italy Shelley had been meditating a long dramatic poem in which he hoped to do justice to the old myth of Prometheus. Unlike Satan, who was also an indomi-

111

table rebel, Prometheus was untainted by ambition, envy, revenge, or selfishness. Yet Æschylus, one of Shelley's favourite dramatists, was known to have ended the story with the partial surrender of Prometheus, for in his lost *Prometheus Unbound* Æschylus makes Prometheus purchase freedom by revealing a secret that enabled Jupiter to perpetuate his power. Shelley was far too well acquainted with classical literature not to realize that to the Greek mind Prometheus, though a great champion, had nevertheless been guilty of the sin of presumption and was only recognizing the hard realities of existence by his compromise. But this seemed to him actually to destroy the moral value of the fable. " I was averse from a catastrophe so feeble as that of reconciling the Champion with the Oppressor of Mankind," he wrote in his Preface. By this he meant only that he could tolerate no surrender of the *principle* of resistance to injustice; his letters of the time and his *Philosophical View of Reform* show that he was willing to tolerate individual abuses indefinitely, as a matter of practical necessity, provided only the principle of reform were kept alive and advanced.

At Este Shelley had completed the first act, over eight hundred lines of the best poetry he had ever written. He had shown Prometheus tortured for his benevolence and resistance to tyranny, but he had moved a step beyond Æschylus in the nature of Prometheus's sufferings. The really exquisite, subtle pain, as Shelley had learned, takes place in the mind. Shelley's Prometheus was compelled to witness a banding together of nations in the name of truth, liberty, and love that was turned to bitterness by the intrusion of deceit and fear — the very sight which Shelley had already pictured and tried to correct in *Laon and Cythna*. Worse still, Prometheus beholds Christ on the cross, no longer an impostor, as Shelley had once considered Him, but a would-be benefactor like Prometheus — and His suffering is made to appear absolutely futile. He is pointed to by one of the Furies as an emblem that those who endure most for the sake of humanity merely heap greater torment upon themselves and others. The sight is almost unendurable to Prometheus as he exclaims that the very name of Christ has been turned into a curse by the persecutions practised in His name

112

against those who are most like Him. Yet though Prometheus sees clearly how " All best things are thus confused to ill," his deepest pity is not for those who are tortured by the sight, but for those who are unaffected by it.

According to Shelley's creed, true freedom can never coexist with hatred and revenge. These were the passions that had ruined the fair prospects of the French Revolution. Prometheus therefore wished to recall a deep curse he had formerly pronounced on Jupiter. He now pitied Jupiter for his blindness and deliberately renounced the curse he had formerly pronounced upon him — an act of generosity and strength which his mother, the Earth, mistakenly interpreted as a surrender. But he still refused to yield up the secret that would make Jupiter more secure on his throne. He knew that he himself had conferred upon Jupiter the power that was being abused, and he knew that power to be limited:

> O'er all things but thyself I gave thee power
> And my own will.

There was an internal weakness in such a power that guaranteed its eventual overthrow, even though Shelley was unwilling to go as far as the Psalmist in proclaiming that " the ungodly are not so." To this purely negative basis of faith Shelley added a positive one, certain

> subtle and fair spirits,
> Whose homes are the dim caves of human thought.

These instinctive hopes were the spirits that comforted Prometheus, as they have comforted oppressed humanity for ages. One spirit brought hope from a battlefield on which the banner of tyranny was torn, another from a shipwreck that had furnished an instance of unselfish heroism, another from the bedside of wisdom, and a fourth from a poet who, out of strange wildernesses of thought, was able to create " Forms more real than living man." Like Prometheus in his agony, these spirits had also seen ruin follow upon the footsteps of love. The hopeful signs they saw, though unmistakable, were so slight, encompassed as they were by evil and ruin, that Shelley seems to be using the episode to emphasize the difficulty of hope almost as much as its ineradicable vitality. Nevertheless, the spirits were confident that Prometheus would restore the reign of Love and Justice. "How know ye this will be?" Prometheus asked them. They answered that Wisdom, Justice, Love, and Peace, once they give even faint signs of growing, foretell a better day to the human spirit as naturally and infallibly as the first mild winds of spring foretell the blossoming of the whitethorn.

At the same time that Shelley was writing this first act he was also arguing with Byron against cynicism and despair, and the argument, as we have seen, was the same:

> It is our will
> That thus enchains us to permitted ill.[1]

Then came the death of Clara Shelley and the strange domestic situation which made Shelley write of himself under the guise of an almost hopeless madman and even think of suicide. Not until he had returned to Rome from Naples was he able to resume *Prometheus Unbound*.

Now, however, the situation was again favourable. With improving health and a calm mind, while spring marched slowly and irresistibly across a warming countryside, Shelley could have imagined no better place than Rome to fill his mind with the grandeur that his subject demanded. Here good and bad were timeless. On the same day he might pass the Arch of Constantine "loaded with reliefs of captives in every attitude of humiliation and slavery" and the Square of St. Peter's with its three hundred fettered criminals at work under guard, hoeing out weeds against the coming visit of the Austrian Emperor.[2] Everywhere were the ruins of a magnificence "by which expression is overpowered, which words cannot convey." And all this destruction, Shelley thought, was due to Christianity, that pernicious and rapid perversion of perhaps the greatest human hope. In the midst of the ruins of Græco-Roman civilization sat the Pope, a living symbol to Shelley, "a poor old man," in Claire's phrase, "upon the brink of the Grave, and many Cardinals almost as old and trembling."[3] Jupiter, a foul, false deity substituted for a fair one by man's own mind, seemed almost palpable in his viceroy; his blighting power and his inherent weakness were visible to the physical eye.

In this general environment Shelley could not have chosen a better spot in which to do his writing than the deserted ruins of the Baths of Caracalla. Here, as we learn from the Preface, the second and third acts were written, among flowery glades and blossoming thickets. He must have worked rapidly and enthusiastically, for March 13 is mentioned in both journals as apparently the first visit to the Baths of Caracalla, and on April 6 he informed Peacock that the two acts were " just finished."

" The bright blue sky of Rome," Shelley said in his Preface, " and the effect of the vigorous awakening spring in that divinest climate, and the new life with which it drenches the spirits even to intoxication were the inspiration of this drama." Almost inevitably he resumed writing with Asia's address to spring:

> From all the blasts of heaven thou hast descended:
> Yes, like a spirit, like a thought, which makes
> Unwonted tears throng to the horny eyes,
> And beatings haunt the desolated heart,
> Which should have learnt repose: thou hast descended
> Cradled in tempests; thou dost wake, O Spring!
> O child of many winds! As suddenly
> Thou comest as the memory of a dream,
> Which now is sad because it hath been sweet;
> Like genius, or like joy which riseth up
> As from the earth, clothing with golden clouds
> The desert of our life.[4]

It is in fact spring that dominates these two acts, furnishing not only much of the physical imagery and the enthusiasm, but also something of the motivation. For, as Shelley had already made clear in the first act, there were deep human impulses, inscrutable and undying, which when once awakened could overcome the world of evil as victoriously as spring swept over the ruins of winter. The same imagery underlies Shelley's " Ode to the West Wind," published in the same volume, only there the seasons are reversed and the west wind of autumn is the symbolic destroyer of the old order, at the same time sowing seeds of the new which spring will quicken into a new birth.

Asia, who had been separated from Prometheus since Jupiter's triumph, was joined by her sister nymph Panthea, who had been by the side of Prometheus during the first act and had therefore seen the beginning of his triumph without realizing it. But a vision that Panthea reported to her, in which Prometheus appeared transfigured by love, was instantly understood by Asia as foreshowing her reunion with Prometheus. Panthea had seen another vision: a figure had appeared and summoned her to follow, and the buds of spring had suddenly overcome the frost and burst into blossom, every petal stamped: " Follow, follow." This recalled to Asia similar voices with which nature had seemed to call to her.

As the two sisters talked, the refrain of " Follow, follow " was taken up by a chorus of Echoes, in probably the most beautiful lyric that Shelley had written up to this time. The Echoes foretold Asia's reunion with Prometheus and summoned the sisters to follow far and deep, into a strange world, where Asia's step alone could awaken an unknown voice. Presumably this unknown voice was that of Demogorgon, by whose " mighty law " (as a semichorus explains in the next scene) certain destined spirits are awakened and irresistibly impelled to follow to his throne while they imagine themselves drawn only by their own desires. Since Shelley nowhere else suggests the nature of Demogorgon's " mighty law," we must conclude from these scenes that it is Spring itself — not the literal, physical spring, but the mysterious, invincible power of which spring was the only adequate symbol. Only thus, by symbol instead of direct exposition, could Shelley have thought it possible to impress upon even " the highly refined imagination " of his " select classes of poetical readers " the inevitability of a resurgence of the human spirit — a rebirth as mysteriously powerful and beautiful as the spring and as much a " mighty law " of destiny.

Having followed the Echoes to a mountainous crag, Asia and Panthea were further directed by spirits who sang:

> To the deep, to the deep,
> Down, down!
> Through the shade of sleep,

> Through the cloudy strife
> Of Death and Life;
> Through the veil and the bar
> Of things which seem and are
> Even to the steps of the remotest throne,
>   Down, down! [5]

At length they appeared before Demogorgon, a formless darkness in the innermost recesses of thought and space, beyond the " veil " of things which merely " seem " and the " bar " of things which actually exist. Here Asia demanded of Demogorgon an answer to two questions that Shelley well knew were incapable of adequate explanation in human language. What was the ultimate source of evil, beyond its existence in the mind of man? When would good, in the person of Prometheus, be released and enthroned?

Up to this point the meaning of the poem is quite clear. Jupiter, the active agent of evil, owes his power to Prometheus; and an inherent, ineradicable impulse in man's nature and in the whole universe stands always ready to free humanity from its sufferings (really self-imposed) when the human spirit, like Prometheus, demonstrates its worthiness by steadfastness and generosity. In answer to her questions Asia is now informed that " God " made the living world and all that it contains, including the sense of love and sympathy which alone renders life tolerable. But when she demands to know the author of all the evil under which humanity labours, Demogorgon becomes unfortunately cryptic and answers simply: " He reigns." He seems to agree, however, with her conclusion that Jupiter does not really reign, since he is a slave to evil and has not established his supremacy over the will of Prometheus. Pressed to state who then is really responsible, he replies that " the deep truth is imageless " — the answer cannot be stated in human language — but there are impersonal forces, " Fate, Time, Occasion, Chance, and Change," to which all things but Love are subject.

Thus Shelley fails, necessarily, to give a definite answer to a question by which most other inquiries have been thrown back upon a conclusion that the deep truth is imageless. The philo-

sophic basis of his poem remains what it had been from the first
— absolute faith in a tide of change that sets in as inevitably as
the spring when conditions are made ripe for it. It is very clear
(in the last lines of the poem) what these conditions were to
Shelley so far as human behaviour is concerned; and it is also
quite clear that Shelley recognized their severity and difficulty.
But Eternity alone (which Demogorgon later avowed himself
to be) could know the answer to Asia's two questions. And
Eternity could be comprehensible to mortals only in mortal
language and images, which were inadequate for a clear statement of "the deep truth." Truths could exist, and even be partially apprehended, Shelley clearly implies, without passing
through the limited medium of human language.

To Asia's eagerness to know the hour of Prometheus' restoration Demogorgon responds by indicating the Spirit of the Hour,
then standing ready to convey Asia and Panthea to Prometheus.
They enter his chariot, and as they sweep toward their destination Panthea notices that Asia has become as insupportably
bright and beautiful as she was reported to have been during
her first happy union with Prometheus, before evil fell upon
the world with Jupiter's domination. Voices in the air sing a
song addressing Asia in terms that establish her identity with
Shelley's earlier conception of Intellectual Beauty, or, as he now
called it, slightly modified, Love. She is the Life of Life, so
intolerably beautiful that she is never seen except partially
veiled:

> Fair are others; none beholds thee,
>   But thy voice sounds low and tender
> Like the fairest, for it folds thee
>   From the sight, that liquid splendour,
> And all feel, yet see thee never,
> As I feel now, lost for ever!
>
> Lamp of Earth! where'er thou movest
>   Its dim shapes are clad with brightness,
> And the souls of whom thou lovest
>   Walk upon the winds with lightness,
> Till they fail, as I am failing,
> Dizzy, lost, yet unbewailing! [6]

118

The second act closes with Love on its way to a triumphant
union with wisdom, courage, and endurance, as typified by
Prometheus.

Meanwhile Jupiter on his throne, knowing that his despotism
is incomplete because he has never subdued the human will,
rejoices in the conviction that his expected offspring by Thetis
will mark his complete triumph over humanity. It is at this
point that Shelley departs most strikingly from the myth used
by Æschylus, in which Prometheus purchases freedom by revealing to Jupiter the danger of his union with Thetis. When
Demogorgon arrives in the Car of the Hour, Jupiter hails him
gladly as his expected offspring. But Demogorgon gives his
name as Eternity, and informs Jupiter that his reign is for ever
ended. There is a struggle, and Jupiter is overcome, for the
issue has been predetermined from the moment when Prometheus recalled his curse. In the hour of defeat Jupiter realizes
that Prometheus, " Gentle and just and dreadless," is indeed the
monarch of the world. His disappearance is marked by a repetition of Shelley's earlier symbol, in *Laon and Cythna,* of the
eternal struggle between good and evil:

> We two will sink on the wide waves of ruin,
> Even as a vulture and a snake outspent
> Drop, twisted in inextricable fight,
> Into a shoreless sea.[7]

Hercules, announcing that strength is subservient to wisdom,
courage, and love, frees Prometheus from his chains. Prometheus turns to the waiting Asia and hails her as

> . . . thou light of life,
> Shadow of beauty unbeheld [8]

— thus again identifying her as the approximate impersonation
of that Intellectual Beauty, or Love, which Shelley had long
since thought of as too bright a vision ever to be completely
realized. Prometheus then paints a glowing picture of the
peaceful, retired life that he and Asia will lead henceforth, hearing echoes of the human world as " veil by veil, evil and error fall " before the mind's gradually widening perception of
Beauty, through

> . . . Painting, Sculpture, and rapt Poesy,
> And arts, tho' unimagined, yet to be.[9]

The rejoicing Earth summons the Spirit of the Earth (an innocent child beloved of Asia before the reign of evil), who guides Prometheus, with Asia and her two sister nymphs, to the retired cavern that is to be their home — the very cave in which Earth had formerly mourned the triumph of Jupiter. This Spirit has noticed already the great change that has taken place everywhere. Men and women have dropped their evil masks, and what once seemed ugly or poisonous throughout the whole of nature now seems harmless and beautiful.[10]

The same story is brought back by the Spirit of the Hour, who had been sent by Prometheus to sound a magic shell over the earth as a sign of humanity's new freedom. His report concludes the poem as Shelley first planned it and gives Shelley's picture of human freedom as he expected it ultimately to be accomplished:

> I wandering went
> Among the haunts and dwellings of mankind,
> And first was disappointed not to see
> Such mighty change as I had felt within
> Expressed in outward things; but soon I looked,
> And behold, thrones were kingless, and men walked
> One with the other even as spirits do.
> None fawned, none trampled; hate, disdain, or fear,
> Self-love or self-contempt, on human brows
> No more inscribed, as o'er the gate of hell,
> " All hope abandon ye who enter here; "
> None frowned, none trembled, none with eager fear
> Gazed on another's eye of cold command,
> Until the subject of a tyrant's will
> Became, worse fate, the abject of his own,
> Which spurred him, like an outspent horse, to death.
> None wrought his lips in truth-entangling lines
> Which smiled the lie his tongue disdained to speak;
> None, with firm sneer, trod out in his own heart
> The sparks of love and hope till there remained
> Those bitter ashes, a soul self-consumed,
> And the wretch crept a vampire among men,

Infecting all with his own hideous ill;
None talked that common, false, cold, hollow talk
Which makes the heart deny the *yes* it breathes,
Yet question that unmeant hyprocrisy
With such a self-mistrust as has no name.
And women, too, frank, beautiful, and kind
As the free heaven, which rains fresh light and dew
On the wide earth, past; gentle radiant forms,
From custom's evil taint exempt and pure;
Speaking the wisdom once they could not think,
Looking emotions once they feared to feel,
And changed to all which once they dared not be,
Yet being now, made earth like heaven; nor pride,
Nor jealousy, nor envy, nor ill shame,
The bitterest of those drops of treasured gall,
Spoilt the sweet taste of the nepenthe, love.

Thrones, altars, judgment-seats, and prisons; wherein,
And beside which, by wretched men were borne
Sceptres, tiaras, swords, and chains, and tomes
Of reasoned wrong, glozed on by ignorance,
Were like those monstrous and barbaric shapes,
The ghosts of a no-more-remembered fame,
Which, from their unworn obelisks, look forth
In triumph o'er the palaces and tombs
Of those who were their conquerors: mouldering round,
These imaged to the pride of kings and priests,
A dark yet mighty faith, a power as wide
As is the world it wasted, and are now
But an astonishment; even so the tools
And emblems of its last captivity,
Amid the dwellings of the peopled earth,
Stand, not o'erthrown, but unregarded now.
And those foul shapes, abhorred by god and man, —
Which, under many a name and many a form
Strange, savage, ghastly, dark and execrable,
Were Jupiter, the tyrant of the world;
And which the nations, panic-stricken, served
With blood, and hearts broken by long hope, and love
Dragged to his altars soiled and garlandless,
And slain amid men's unreclaiming tears,

Flattering the thing they feared, which fear was hate, —
Frown, mouldering fast, o'er their abandoned shrines:
The painted veil, by those who were, called life,
Which mimicked, as with colours idly spread,
All men believed or hoped, is torn aside;
The loathsome mask has fallen, the Man remains, —
Sceptreless, free, uncircumscribed, — but man:
Equal, unclassed, tribeless, and nationless,
Exempt from awe, worship, degree, the King
Over himself; just, gentle, wise: but man:
Passionless? no: yet free from guilt or pain,
Which were, for his will made, or suffered them,
Nor yet exempt, tho' ruling them like slaves,
From chance, and death, and mutability,
The clogs of that which else might oversoar
The loftiest star of unascended heaven,
Pinnacled dim in the intense inane.[11]

His great poem had been brought to a natural and inspiring conclusion. But Shelley had thought too long and too intently upon it to leave it so. His mind was still stored with materials he had not fully used. He had imagined many subtle ways of suggesting the unity of all animate and inanimate existence in the spirit of Love and Freedom. The inexpressible beauty and happiness of life when so united seemed to demand a fuller expression than it had received. Enthusiasm for perfection needed to be given a more profound stimulus; the reign of evil in Act I needed a more impressive counterbalance than it had received.

Several months later, in the autumn and early winter, he added a fourth act, in which he repeated his conception of the liberated human spirit and the means by which the liberation had been achieved and could be preserved. Man, " one harmonious soul of many a soul," subjects his own evil passions; " All things confess his strength," and Nature's last secrets vanish before his intelligence and will. Then Demogorgon reappears and summons in succession the Earth, the Moon, even all creatures beyond the solar system, the dead, the elemental genii of the mind, and the spirits of all living creatures. They gather as a vast, all-inclusive audience to hear his last word on how human freedom is won and kept:

> Gentleness, Virtue, Wisdom, and Endurance,
> These are the seals of that most firm assurance
>   Which bars the pit over Destruction's strength;
> And if, with infirm hand, Eternity,
> Mother of many acts and hours, should free
>   The serpent that would clasp her with his length;
> These are the spells by which to re-assume
> An empire o'er the disentangled doom.
>
> To suffer woes which Hope thinks infinite;
> To forgive wrongs darker than death or night;
>   To defy Power, which seems omnipotent;
> To love, and bear; to hope till Hope creates
> From its own wreck the thing it contemplates:
>   Neither to change, nor falter, nor repent;
> This, like thy glory, Titan! is to be
> Good, great and joyous, beautiful and free;
> This is alone Life, Joy, Empire and Victory! [12]

This poem has far greater intellectual integrity than most critics have granted it. Mrs. Shelley led the way to underestimation when she stated in her note to the poem that " The prominent feature of Shelley's theory of the destiny of the human species was, that evil is not inherent in the system of the creation, but an accident that might be expelled." This may have been true of Shelley's conversation with Mary, though it seems more likely that she unconsciously warped his opinions in restating them twenty years afterwards. Nowhere in his published works or in his letters do we find any similar statement, and it is certainly not true of *Prometheus Unbound.* In the first act (lines 293–4) Prometheus is quoted as pronouncing evil and good " Both infinite as is the universe." When in the third act Jupiter describes himself as sinking to ruin " twisted in inextricable fight " Shelley is repeating an image far more elaborately developed in *Laon and Cythna,* which he definitely explained was to typify the constantly repeated, never ceasing struggle of the two opposing principles. And Demogorgon's last words, in the conclusion of the drama, clearly envisage the possibility of Jupiter's return to power. Nor does Shelley minimize the power of evil. Nowhere is this power more truly seen, especially in its deadly effect upon the mind, than in *Prometheus Unbound.* Shelley's letters also show the same consciousness.

If in *Prometheus Unbound* the victory seems too easily achieved, or achieved more as a sudden *coup* than as the result of long, toilsome, positive effort, it is largely the fault of Shelley's original fable and the timelessness and spacelessness of its setting. As far as words may serve, the duration and intensity of Prometheus' sufferings are emphasized. It makes little difference if Jupiter's final struggle seems brief — though it need not seem so, when we recall that his antagonist called himself Eternity — for the issue was already clearly settled earlier, by Prometheus' renunciation of his curse.

The Prometheus fable gave Shelley little opportunity to show the liberation of humanity as the result of such toilsome gradual building-up as history shows to have been responsible for partial and transient victories in the past. If he quite definitely follows Christ and anticipates Gandhi in stressing the passive virtues, it is not to be assumed in his case any more than theirs that he placed no proper value on the positive ones. In his own life he realized the value of positive action. Few poets have ever laboured so long and earnestly as Shelley to fit themselves for a mission. No movement for human betterment, however unpromising, ever came to his attention without receiving either his encouragement or his active assistance. Here we must also recall the purpose that Shelley professed in the Preface to *Prometheus Unbound.* Admitting a " passion for reforming the world," he denied that his poems were dedicated to the direct enforcement of reform or were intended to convey a reasoned philosophy of life. " My purpose has hitherto been simply to familiarize the highly refined imagination of the more select classes of poetical readers with beautiful idealisms of moral excellence."

Shelley did not view the liberation of humanity from its age-old oppressions as something to be lightly or quickly won. It was to be a " slow, gradual, silent change," as he had earlier made clear in the Preface to *Laon and Cythna*. In his opinion excessive expectations were sure to create dangerous reactions by minimizing the real power of evil. Still earlier he had realized that a great change must first be produced in men's habits of thought. Under the conditions prevailing in 1819, and with his closely limited object in view, Shelley may well have considered that the virtues of endurance and patience were those most in need of emphasis.

This would be especially true if one believed, as Shelley did, that Eternity held in store some Hour whose ultimate causes were beyond human reason, which would liberate the human spirit as inevitably as the arrival of spring. In the vast reaches of time and in the almost limitless capacities of the human spirit that he envisaged, Shelley confidently and joyously foretold a rendezvous between a destined Hour and a human spirit made ready for it by a courageous resistance of evil. The readiness of the human spirit might possibly hasten the readiness of the Hour; but the Hour would certainly never arrive until the spirit had been made ready for it. This is optimism, certainly — and when we consider the terribly depressing events taking place in Shelley's life as he wrote, it is evidence of a far greater optimistic bias in the writer. It is not unphilosophic or unrealistic optimism, however; on the contrary, it is the optimism of an invincibly hopeful nature restrained by a powerful and very subtly comprehensive intellect.[15]

The poem, therefore, is not only consistent in its philosophy; it is even moderate. Surely the faith that there is an inextinguishable spark within the human spirit is intellectually as respectable as the contrary belief, when neither is capable of absolute proof by the ordinary laws of reason.

A comparison between *Prometheus Unbound* and *Queen Mab* shows how greatly many of Shelley's ideas had changed in the seven years' interval, while others remained essentially the same. Vegetarianism, once an important gospel, was now no longer worth a word. On the evils of marriage Shelley was also silent in *Prometheus Unbound,* though he showed later in *Epipsychidion* some residue from his earlier ideas. Christ, who had been sneered at as an impostor in *Queen Mab,* is treated sympathetically in *Prometheus Unbound*. In both poems hatred and revenge, hypocrisy, fear, custom, and faith (meaning theological faith) are compound causes and results of evil; and in both poems these forces are closely linked with kingcraft, priestcraft, and warcraft. The significant difference is that in *Prometheus Unbound* evil is far more powerfully realized as a subtle perversion of thought than in *Queen Mab*. A note to *Queen Mab* practically denies the freedom of the will, which is asserted in the text, whereas *Prometheus Unbound* makes freedom of the will the one quality that bulwarks humanity against an eternity of oppression. Here, perhaps, lies the clue to one of the greatest differences between the two poems, the substitution of Love for Necessity. Necessity left no place for freedom of the will and was an impersonal force without sympathy or variation. Since 1816 Shelley had been steadily working toward a more sympathetic, less mechanistic belief, which he had first expressed in his " Hymn to Intellectual Beauty." In *Prometheus Unbound* the phrase " intellectual beauty " does not occur, but the word " love," meaning universal sympathy, is endowed with all its functions, to which has been added a nearer sense of sympathy not perceptible in Shelley's idea of intellectual beauty. Thereafter Shelley's god is Love.

IT is quite possible to reject or misunderstand the meaning of *Prometheus Unbound* and consider it a great poem on account of the lyrical or descriptive beauty of many of its passages. To do so has become almost a critical commonplace, endorsed by the poet's only authorized biographer,[14] who misunderstands the poem by assuming that Shelley considered evil purely an external matter. Such a view does not underestimate the powerful stimulus that the poem offers to some of the finest human virtues. And undoubtedly, as even hostile contemporary critics admitted, the poem abounds in passages of the greatest poetic beauty. These passages, considered merely as separate poems, would alone mark Shelley as one of the great English poets. No other single volume of English poetry contains a finer range of effective rhythms. Shelley was a great poet before he wrote *Prome-*

theus Unbound, but in this volume he suddenly far surpassed himself, especially as a lyric poet.

But to judge the poem on this basis alone is to mistake the clothes for the man. There is no lack of unity between the thought and its vesture. Mrs. Shelley remarked that Shelley's views were more particularly developed in the lyrics, and Shelley complained of typographical errors in the lyrics not because they marred the lyrical effect but presumably because they assisted " the obscurity " of the poem as a whole.[15] Considering them as something apart merely falsifies Shelley's intention. If the poem lacked philosophic integrity or reasonableness we might indeed rescue from it enough splendid bits of wreckage to justify calling it a great poem, but unnecessarily to do so is to mutilate one of the most highly integrated unions of noble thought and subtle expression by which English literature has ever been enlarged.

The reason why *Prometheus Unbound* has from the first been so commonly misunderstood lies in the boldness and originality of the imagery. Had the contemporary critics been entirely without other prejudices they would still have misunderstood and underestimated the poem on this ground. Except for William Blake, who was disregarded, no English poet since Milton had ventured far beyond the narrow bounds of subject-matter and expression that were perhaps best stated by Dr. Johnson in his *Rasselas.* The efforts of Wordsworth and Coleridge to expand these limits had been comparatively modest and had dealt with material rather than expression, except for Wordsworth's theory of poetic diction, with which even Coleridge disagreed. Even so, they had aroused misunderstanding and resentment.

Shelley was fully aware of his imaginative daring and did not expect *Prometheus Unbound* to sell more than twenty copies. When his own friends considered it too wild and perplexed with imagery he clung to his opinion that it was his best and most original poem.[16] He was quite aware also that the originality was largely a matter of the imagery. He explained in the Preface that many of his images were " drawn from the operations of the human mind, or those external actions by which they are expressed." Such imagery, he added, was un-usual in modern poetry except in Dante and Shakespeare, but abounded in Greek poetry, from which he professed to have borrowed it.

Mary Shelley also noted the peculiar nature of Shelley's imagery, and sought to throw some light upon it in her note on the poem. She insisted that the poem was not vague, but subtle; it required a mind " as subtle and penetrating " as Shelley's own to understand all its finer shades of meaning. It was obviously as a partial clue to this subtlety that she commented upon his unusual imagery, the source of which she attributed to Sophocles. To her its essence seemed to be an effort " to gift the mechanism of the material universe with a soul and a voice, and to bestow such also on the most delicate and abstract emotions and thoughts of the mind." Instead of illustrating this very general statement with images drawn from the poem (and thereby forestalling a good bit of mistaken criticism) Mrs. Shelley quoted from one of Shelley's notebooks an image from Sophocles with Shelley's comment. The image, as translated by Shelley, reads: " Coming to many ways in the wanderings of careful thought." " What a picture does this line suggest," Shelley had written in his notebook, " of the mind as a wilderness of intricate paths, wide as the universe, which is here made its symbol, a world within a world. . . ."

Here, then, apparently, is the severe and difficult model for much of the imagery of *Prometheus Unbound*. We have already seen [17] that Shelley had for some years been convinced of the inadequacy of ordinary language to convey the fullness and the finer shadings of thought, and had developed a supplementary use of symbols. From the publication of *Alastor* his succession of caves, streams, boats, veils, etc., were plainly intended to carry a meaning beyond the purely literal ones. These symbols, which should have been nothing new to any habitual reader of Shelley, are also present in *Prometheus Unbound*.

But Shelley was no more content than the ancient Greeks whom he praised in his Preface to neglect any resource for " awakening the sympathies " of his readers. He wished his imagery to reflect " the operations of the human mind, or those external actions by which they are expressed." His extensive, continuous reading made him far more familiar than most scholars with the rich results of all that the human mind had achieved. Prominent among these achievements were those scientific investigations which, as a youth, Shelley had thought of as the future liberators of the human spirit. Though he now read far less science than literature, philosophy, and even history, and though he now realized that freedom was not so easy of attainment (for could not science, like Christianity, be another of those blessings easily convertible into a curse?), he had not totally abandoned his early interest nor had his tenacious memory relaxed its hold on his earlier scientific reading. Was he not at the moment promoting steam navigation? Only recently has it been perceived that *Prometheus Unbound* echoes again and again with the best scientific knowledge of Shelley's generation.[18] One illustration may here be given for several possible ones.

Perhaps the most complicated and puzzling passages in the poem are the descriptions of the moon and the earth, in the fourth act (lines 206–318), which sound like apocalyptic visions but are in reality only visualized, condensed images of these bodies as they would appear to the physical senses if scientific knowledge and speculation about them were combined into physical, visible entities. Thus the earth is first described as a sphere consisting of numerous orbs, expanding, contracting, revolving, in a manner that clearly illustrates Davy's theory of the " dance of matter." [19] Shelley then proceeds to describe a spirit asleep within the sphere in terms which correspond closely with various current scientific facts and speculations about electricity.[20] He concludes the composite picture by showing within the sphere relics of the forgotten civilizations and extinct forms of life that have marked the earth's history. Thus in one daring picture, not at all necessary to the main thought of the poem, Shelley sought to objectify the salient facts of the earth's nature and history. The original suggestion for this complicated image may well have been from Canto xxviii of Dante's *Paradiso* or from Ezekiel's well-known vision of the wheel.[21]

129

Similarly Shelley makes use of metaphysical speculation. In the first act (lines 190–210) he postulates a world of shades in which all living beings have coexistent "phantasms," or shadows, with which they are united at death. Thus Prometheus is enabled to hear his curse repeated by the Phantasm of Jupiter while Jupiter himself still reigns.[22]

It should now be clear that Shelley gave his imagery a far greater range than his contemporaries perceived or might reasonably have been expected to perceive. To him anything that was intellectually or transcendentally comprehensible was possible; in fact, it was desirable as a means of expanding the imagination; but to his reviewers imagery had to be physically possible. Again and again in his poetry, but more often in *Prometheus Unbound* and afterwards, Shelley's imagery presents mental phenomena in terms of the physical, physical phenomena in terms of the mental, and even fuses matter and spirit in the same image.[23] The first of these types is not so unusual, though there have been few if any English poets who employed it so consistently as Shelley. Thus in *Prometheus Unbound* the soul is a judgment-throne, the heart a vine, the mind a sun or an ocean, thought a cavern, and all manner of thoughts and emotions are endowed with objective existence. It is the second category that Shelley considered unusual enough to mention in his Preface as "imagery . . . drawn from the operations of the human mind." He likens the descent of spring to the advent of thought or the "memory of a dream"; feet are "sandalled with calm"; and the physical avalanche, accumulated flake by flake, is likened to an accumulation in "heaven-defying minds,"

> As thought by thought is piled, till some great truth
> Is loosened, and the nations echo round.

When in such imagery Shelley sometimes fuses the physical and spiritual or mental in the same image it is as if he thought the distinctions either unreal in fact or at least not worth preserving in imagery. In his downfall Jupiter exclaims:

> And like a cloud, mine enemy above
> Darkens my fall with victory!

Here, as Professor Firkins has pointed out, it is not a physical cause (the bodily presence of Prometheus, casting a shadow) but an immaterial one (victory) that produces a physical effect of darkening the fall of Jupiter.[24]

There is no evidence that Mary Shelley or any of the poet's friends fully understood his symbolism or imagery, though it seems probable that Mary understood more of it than one or two recent writers have been willing to concede. That contemporary reviewers, even those without a hostile bias, could understand it was not to be expected. *Blackwood's Edinburgh Magazine* passed the point without comment, but the *London Magazine and Monthly Critical and Dramatic Review* was obliged to qualify an extraordinarily enthusiastic admiration of the poem by calling it " a vast wilderness of beauty " and admitting that the dialogue between Asia and Demogorgon was obscure and metaphysical. The *Literary Gazette*, the *Monthly Review*, and the *Quarterly Review*, however, concentrated a fierce attack upon the poem's alleged obscurity. Their protestations in turn that it was " inflexibly unintelligible," " only *nonsense*, pure, unmixed *nonsense*," and "*drivelling prose run mad*" must be discounted by their own uncanny ability to understand its danger to conservative theories of church and state. Nevertheless they devoted columns to demonstrating the intellectual anarchy of Shelley's style. Among the numerous passages analysed as absurd occur most of those instanced earlier in this chapter as illustrations of Shelley's attempts to refine and extend the meaning of poetic expression. The *Literary Gazette* thus concludes a series of such illustrations:

An' these extracts do not entitle the author to a cell, clean straw, bread and water, a strait waistcoat, and phlebotomy, there is no madness in scribbling. It is hardly requisite to adduce a sample of the adjectives in this poem to prove the writer's condign abhorrence of any relation between that part of speech and substantives: sleep-unsheltered hours; gentle darkness; horny eyes; keen faint eyes; faint wings; fading waves; crawling glaciers, toads, agony, time, &c.; belated and noontide plumes; milky arms; many-folded mountains; a lake-surrounding flute; veiled lightning asleep (as well as hovering); unbewailing flowers; odour-faded blooms; semi-vital worms; wind-

less pools, windless abodes, and windless air; unerasing waves; un-
pavilioned skies; rivetted wounds; and void abysms, are parcel of the
Babylonish jargon which is found in every wearisome page of this
tissue of insufferable buffoonery.

The *Quarterly*, after a similar display, concludes:

We have neither leisure nor room to develop all the absurdities
here accumulated, in defiance of common sense, and even of gram-
mar; whirlwind harmony, a solid sphere which is as many thousand
spheres, and contains ten thousand orbs or spheres, with intertran-
spicuous spaces between them, whirling over each other on a thousand sightless (alias invisible) axles; self-destroying swiftness; intelligible words and wild music, kindled by the said sphere, which also
grinds a bright brook into an azure mist of elemental subtlety;
odour, music, and light, kneaded into one aerial mass, and the sense
drowned by it!

Oh quanta species! et cerebrum non habet.

But this is only a partial conclusion; other demonstrations follow, summarized by a statement which in itself is quite an
accomplishment of critical absurdity, yet must have seemed a
logical consequence to most readers:

In short, it is not too much to affirm, that in the whole volume there
is not one original image of nature, one simple expression of human
feeling, or one new association of appearances of the moral with
those of the material world.[25]

Mary Shelley and Leigh Hunt had foreseen something like
this. More than once they had advised Shelley to write more
concretely. Very likely their concern was to prevent his giving
his opponents another stick with which to belabour him. They
also desired to see Shelley's beliefs becoming immediately influential. Shelley realized the force of such opinions and admitted that the poem would probably find not more than twenty
qualified readers.[26] Thus he deliberately pleased himself and
jeopardized the effectiveness of a poem through which he
was carrying on a lifelong sense of mission. Perhaps he knew
and defiantly subscribed to Burke's dictum that "a clear idea

WILLIAM GIFFORD

Engraved by S. Freeman from the painting by J. Hoppner

JOHN MURRAY

Artist unknown

is therefore another name for a little idea." His self-justification appears only incidentally a year later, in his "Defence of Poetry": "The jury which sits in judgment upon a poet . . . must be composed of his peers; it must be impanelled by time from the selectest of the wise of many generations." Leigh Hunt made a partial reply to the *Quarterly,* but neither Shelley's friends, nor his authorized biographer, nor his later Victorian admirers ever demonstrated the real integrity of his imagery and symbolism. Only after a century was Shelley's jury (who were critics rather than poetic peers) ready to bring in a just verdict. An understanding that Shelley's imagery is not vague, but intelligible and profound, is necessary if we are to see him in his true proportions.

Queen Mab had been written in hard, clear, comparatively inflexible blank verse and free verse. Soon thereafter Shelley had acquired the ability to write really distinguished blank verse and stanzaic verse. His stanzaic verse, however, had shown no extraordinary variety or harmony before the *Prometheus Unbound* volume appeared — no poems that sang themselves so instantly and compellingly that their lyric qualities alone seemed to ensure them immediate and lasting preeminence. That the blank verse of *Prometheus Unbound* should surpass in majesty and strength even the extraordinary blank verse of *Alastor* is in itself a great accomplishment, though hardly surprising. But the sudden burst of lyrical genius in *Prometheus Unbound* is genuinely astonishing. The poem contains thirty-six different verse forms, all handled perfectly. Most of them Shelley had apparently never employed before. Several of them are either unique or extremely rare in English poetry before Shelley. Any reader would probably make additions to the following passages, but hardly anyone would deny that each of them is entitled to a high position among the best English lyric poems: "On a poet's lips I slept" (I, 737); "Hast thou beheld the form of Love" (I, 763); "O follow, follow" (II, i, 173); "To the deep, to the deep" (II, iii, 54); "Life of Life" (II, v, 48); "My soul is an enchanted boat" (II, v, 72); "Weave the dance" (IV, 69); and "Thou art speeding round the sun" (IV, 457). In the same volume also appeared " To a Skylark," " The Sensitive Plant," " Ode to the West Wind," and " The Cloud." How many other single volumes in the whole range of English literature have provided as much sheer lyric beauty or such an astonishing range of effective rhythms?

The intellectual depth, subtlety, and unity of the poem may be accounted for by the steady growth of an extraordinarily fine mind, but the sudden lyrical splendour is practically unexplainable. Very likely Shelley learned something from the choral passages in the many Greek dramas that he studied in 1818 and 1819. Greek lyrics, however, differ so radically from English lyrics in metrical basis that any suggestions Shelley may have received from them involved total reconstruction in English. There had been Greek dramas in English before, but practically none of them was of the type Shelley was attempting. Byron's recently published *Manfred* (1817), though not in the Greek dramatic form, was probably nearest to *Prometheus Unbound*, and from this drama, indeed, we find slight traces of metrical influences. The seven spirits in the first act of *Manfred* serve a function vaguely similar to the four voices in the first act of *Prometheus Unbound*. Byron's first and seventh spirits speak in a tetrameter stanza similar to one of those used by Shelley's four voices and re-employed later by the furies and by the four spirits in Act II. The basic form is a fairly common one, and the parallelism would mean nothing except that the uncommon verse-forms employed by Byron's second, fourth, and fifth spirits are evidently the basis for the verse-form employed by Shelley in " The Cloud." Shelley may also have adapted other stanzas found in his wide reading in English poetry and even in Gothic novels, but if so, they have never yet been discovered. It is quite possible that some of his verse-forms were suggested directly by music rather than by poetry. He was a fairly constant patron of the opera, and *Prometheus Unbound* at times suggests the opera rather than the drama. The poem contains cumulative effects of changing rhythms far commoner to music than to poetry. Such a source of inspiration, like the Greek choruses, would be transposed almost beyond recognition when turned into English poetry. But these are all vague guesses. There seems to be no adequate explanation of the lyrical richness of *Prometheus Unbound* other than a sudden flowering of pure lyric genius.

In one other particular *Prometheus Unbound* is an important landmark in Shelley's development. It is the first public expression of a decided change in his philosophy. Shelley had never in his life fully accepted reality for what it seemed to be. As a boy he had sought in various ways to escape its dullness and oppression. As a youth he had vowed war against some of its aspects, and as a young man he had vigorously prosecuted his warfare. His rationalistic reading at that time never suggested to him to doubt the nature of reality, nor did he feel any psychological need for such doubt, while there was a hope of victory. When he first came into contact with Berkeley's doctrine of immateriality he rejected it. But the disastrous consequences of his first marriage must have convinced him that he could not conquer on the battlefield he had originally chosen. A revolution must first be accomplished in men's minds. At about the same time he became a convert to Berkeley and projected his idea of an Intellectual Beauty whose real essence was never perceived, whose mere shadow was only inconstantly apprehended. Why might not life itself and all the phenomena commonly assumed to be real be after all only distorted shadows of reality? Plato, now his favourite philosopher, so argued in *The Republic*, in his wonderful image of the cave. In Plato and the Neo-Platonists, for whom he had now largely abandoned the rationalist mentors of his youth, he found abundant encouragement for the new tack which the circumstances of life forced upon his invincible optimism and sense of rectitude. Perhaps the forces that had checked him were really, like the ungodly, "not so." Perhaps life itself was merely a shadow of the mind, and the mind only a shadow of the Eternal Mind. "You know," he wrote to Peacock, shortly after finishing the first act of *Prometheus Unbound*, "I always seek in what I see the manifestation of something beyond the present and tangible object." [27]

Prometheus Unbound is full of this feeling. It is the *mind* of man that is invincible. A revolution in the mind of Prometheus, by which he abjures hatred and revenge, calls into action inscrutable and invincible forces that act automatically once they are released. Evil is a "loathsome mask" upon reality and falls "veil by veil" — veils being almost always with Shelley a symbol of the concealment of truth. Asia's beauty is "unveiled" to Panthea after they leave the cave of Demogorgon; life itself is a veil upon reality, or rather

> Death is the veil which those who live call life:
> They sleep, and it is lifted.[28]

A sonnet published by Mrs. Shelley as written in 1818 begins:

> Lift not the painted veil which those who live
> Call Life; though unreal shapes be pictured there.

In this poem, probably a result of the same mood that produced "Stanzas Written in Dejection, near Naples," Shelley expressed his own disillusion and disappointment in life. Acts II and III of *Prometheus Unbound* were written shortly after Clara's death and its disastrous consequences, and Act IV followed an even greater personal calamity. Yet in these acts Shelley reasserted more strongly than ever an optimism based upon a new philosophy of reality that could recognize fully the strength of evil while perceiving that it was not for ever invincible, because it rested upon a distortion of truth.

A few months later, in time to include it in the *Prometheus* volume, Shelley wrote "The Sensitive Plant" with a wistfully beautiful conclusion in which he plainly stated his new philosophy:

>   . . . but in this life
> Of error, ignorance, and strife,
> Where nothing is, and all things seem,
> And we the shadows of the dream,
>
> It is a modest creed, and yet
> Pleasant if one considers it,
> To own that death itself must be
> Like all the rest, a mockery.

That garden sweet, that lady fair,
And all sweet shapes and odours there,
In truth have never pass'd away:
'Tis we, 'tis ours, are changed! not they.

For love, and beauty, and delight,
There is no death nor change; their might
Exceeds our organs, which endure
No light, being themselves obscure.

Having long been unable to follow his earlier belief and
tactics and being equally unable to change his own fundamental
faith and nature, Shelley was gradually and unconsciously compelled to this new philosophy. To a certain extent it may have
been an escape from an untenable position. But it was a reforming of the lines rather than a retreat. To view freedom
only *sub specie æternitatis* and omit to promote it in the here
and now was to impoverish the will by which alone freedom
could be called into being. The same volume in which he declared his new position also showed that he would not utterly
abandon the old. It contained his " Ode, Written October 1819,
Before the Spaniards had Recovered Their Liberty " and his
" Ode to Liberty," both of which show that Shelley's warfare
against oppression had not entirely abandoned the old *Queen
Mab* spirit.

While *Prometheus Unbound* was yet unfinished, Shelley was
already writing his *Philosophical View of Reform*, designed as
a practical contribution to the reform movement. One of the
ideas urged earnestly in that work was that every true patriot
should feel the necessity of doing everything in his power to
keep alive the love of freedom and justice in the common people.
At the same time he was urging this course on others he was
himself writing a letter intended as a public protest against the
conviction of Richard Carlile, and also six poems in a radically
different, popular style, describing the state of England in 1819
and appealing to the English to resist their oppressors (like
Prometheus) with an invincible and hateless passive resistance.
None of these was printed in his lifetime, but the longest and

most fervent, *The Masque of Anarchy,* was sent to Leigh Hunt
to be printed in the *Examiner.*

THE BURST of energy that produced the second and third acts
of *Prometheus Unbound* was not exhausted with their completion. Shelley turned immediately to another project. Before
he resumed *Prometheus* to add the fourth act he had produced
The Cenci, written rapidly between May 14 and August 8, 1819.
Both volumes were published in 1820, *The Cenci* in March or
April and *Prometheus Unbound* probably in August.

For some time Shelley had been interested in the horrible
Renaissance story of Count Francesco Cenci and his heroic
daughter. No criminal or degenerate of Shelley's extensive
youthful reading in the school of horror could have equalled
the historical truth of the Cenci story, the full enormity of which
is abated in Shelley's manuscript source and was further abated
in his drama. Moreover, it was a story well suited to the thought
that inspired *Prometheus Unbound.* Here was an indubitable
historic example of wickedness in alliance with the church
against virtue — for in Shelley's manuscript source the historical
facts unfavourable to the character of Beatrice Cenci are
omitted. He was from the first enthusiastic about its dramatic
possibilities, but he considered that he was " too metaphysical
and abstract — too fond of the theoretical and the ideal, to
succeed as a tragedian." [29] Mary, he thought, could do it better.
It was only in Mary's default that he undertook the task himself.

How Count Cenci, old in years and in wickedness, rejoiced
publicly at the death of his sons and sought to crown his villainy
with the debauchery of his daughter; how Beatrice, surrounded
by wickedness and cowardice, is raped by her father and
sets about planning and executing his destruction, how in-
exorably she is forced to the scaffold by the guardians of right-
eousness, and how bravely she resists, is a story too well
known to need detailed summary. Deeply moved himself, and
noting that after two hundred years the Romans were still stirred
by the story, Shelley concluded that it was a tragic theme suited
to the English stage.

The essentially tragic nature of the story as Shelley retold it may well be doubted. If we waive the fact that the character of Count Cenci is too monstrous to be credible to many readers after they have removed themselves awhile from the hypnotic persuasion of Shelley's lines, there still remains the matter of motivation. Tragedy cannot exist without adequate, acceptable motive. Count Cenci committed violent incest upon his daughter not from lust, a dramatic motive comprehensible enough, but from a deep, unexplained hatred and a love of evil for its own sake. Beatrice is motivated by revenge, the tragic flaw in her character. "Revenge, retaliation, atonement," Shelley asserted in his Preface, "are pernicious mistakes. If Beatrice had thought in this manner she would have been wiser and better; but she would never have been a tragic character." Revenge was indeed to Shelley the great tragic flaw in human society, but it was not necessarily so in the conventions of drama. Very likely it was to emphasize the fallacy of revenge that Shelley departed from his manuscript source by having Cenci's murder followed immediately by the arrival of envoys to arrest him. Yet in writing the drama Shelley is so sympathetic with his heroine that he can scarcely tolerate his own notion of revenge as a part of her character. Her real motive for the murder is self-protection and an almost religious mission to rid her family and the world of a dangerous monster. It is only by a narrow margin that she escapes the dramatic fault of being a flawless character.

To several contemporary reviewers and also to some of the newspaper critics who witnessed the performance of *The Cenci* in 1886 Beatrice's determined denial of her guilt proved a serious flaw in characterization.[30] Why should she not have avowed and defended her action, thus making the tragic issue a clear-cut one between environment and personality? The difficulty seems not to have occurred to Shelley, possibly because the situation is similarly handled in Webster's trial scenes, which he appears to have been using as models. Leigh Hunt, answering contemporary criticisms, maintained that Beatrice's lie was evidence of extreme subtlety of characterization. The sort of guilt that her inquisitors had in mind was naturally so abhorrent to her that it actually had no reality in her mind — hence confession might be an even greater falsehood than denial. This explanation accords so ingeniously with Shelley's own psychology that it is virtually convincing to a Shelleyan, but an audience of theatre-goers is quite another matter.

Structurally the play is far less suitable to the theatre than Shelley supposed. It lacks consistent progression, and in one important detail it lacks unity. All three scenes of Act I barely fall short of being pure character scenes. They do little more than set the stage for action that is to follow. In the second act the first scene brings us no closer to the accomplishment of Cenci's design, while the second scene, in which Giacomo and Orsino are both shown to be thinking of Cenci's murder, has only the slightest bearing on the murder as later executed under the direction of Beatrice. Thus Shelley consumes two whole acts with interesting characterization and background, but with practically no progress in the action. In the third act Count Cenci has accomplished his crime and Beatrice reaches her resolution to kill him. The first plan for Count Cenci's murder miscarries and new murderers are engaged. The fourth act opens with Cenci's wife, Lucretia, vainly trying to change his course of persecutions, and succeeding only in eliciting an intense prayer to God for the utter destruction of his daughter. This scene, evidently intended to create suspense by offering Cenci a chance of life, shows clearly enough that self-preservation, rather than revenge, is the principal motive for Count Cenci's murder. Thereafter the act moves swiftly through three scenes in which the murderers approach Cenci's couch, recoil, and are induced by Beatrice's reproaches and determination to complete the deed. One of the murderers is soon arrested with an incriminating note, and the arrest of Beatrice and Lucretia follows. These three scenes, so like *Macbeth* in structure and even occasionally in diction, have nevertheless a vitality of their own which places them high in the ranks of English tragic scenes. The fifth act, after wasting the first scene, proceeds rapidly and impressively through three scenes describing the trial, the conviction, and the preparations for the execution. Very probably influenced by a similar situation in Webster's

The White Devil,[31] these scenes are hardly less powerful than the three scenes in which the murder is executed and detected.

Most of the theatrical and dramatic effectiveness of the whole play is concentrated in these two groups of three scenes each. In actual presentation, however, it was found that the play seemed to fall apart with the death of Count Cenci. His character had so dominated the first part of the play that the substitution of judges and Pope as Beatrice's antagonists seemed almost to begin a new play. His inexperience probably prevented Shelley's realizing this, but had he done so he could hardly have overcome the difficulty for a modern audience as Shakespeare managed to do in *Julius Cæsar.* This theatrical flaw is far more perceptible to the spectator than to the reader, but it had been perceived from the first by managers who considered staging the play.[32]

So much has been loosely written about *The Cenci* as one of the great English tragedies and about Shelley as potentially a great writer of stage plays [33] that it has seemed well to set the matter straight. *The Cenci* can hardly be called a tragedy at all, in anything like the traditional meaning of the word. In spite of an intelligent and clever use of the materials, it is obviously defective in structure, when considered as a play for the stage. Shelley had read extensively in English and Greek drama, and also a little in Spanish, French, and German; he wrote dramatic speeches and even a few scenes comparable to those of any English dramatist except the two or three greatest; but he was totally devoid of experience behind the footlights and was a rare and uncomfortable spectator of plays. To such a writer the drama must be primarily literature, not theatre. Probably no such person has ever written or could write great drama that was at the same time " good theatre."

It matters little, however, that *The Cenci* is not a good acting play and according to formal criteria is essentially melodrama rather than tragedy. It is still great literature. The speeches and the pivotal scenes are on a par with those of all but the very greatest English tragedies. The emotional tone and the poetry are such as are never associated with melodrama, but always with great tragedies. The feeling of several contemporary reviewers that it should arouse only righteous horror because it involved incest was due partly to special conditions and was scarcely justified even from the viewpoint of those conditions. Any unprejudiced reviewer even then should have seen that the incest was handled tactfully and without morbid exploitation. In Count Cenci and Beatrice the play contains two really great character creations. Count Cenci, almost impossibly monstrous according to traditional criticism, was made so compelling by good acting and by the power of Shelley's verse that none of the critics who witnessed the 1886 performance thought to question its credibility. Beatrice fired more than one English actress to attempt to organize a production of the play in order to act the part.[34]

Though Shelley did not agree with his wife's opinion that *The Cenci* was " the finest thing he ever wrote " [35] he felt some justifiable pride in having written it without " diffuseness, a profusion of inapplicable imagery, vagueness, generality and as Hamlet says, *Words — words*." [36] It is indeed remarkable that a poem practically every line of which is immediately clear to the average reader should have been written between the acts of *Prometheus Unbound*. Such a fact speaks volumes for the command of expression that Shelley had acquired at the age of twenty-seven.

Nevertheless, except in style, Shelley was not nearly so far from his characteristic bent in *The Cenci* as even Mary seems to have supposed. *Prometheus Unbound* embodied a conception of evil as a human perversion of ideas that were originally good, such as Christ's doctrines perverted and the ideals of the French Revolution betrayed. *The Cenci* sets forth an historical example of similar perversions. Beatrice was for Shelley the victim of an evil society and an evil religion. It was not even necessary to go the full length of his historical source to emphasize sufficiently the evil of Count Cenci and the Pope. Thus Shelley omitted Count Cenci's three convictions for sodomy and some of the Pope's cruelty and vindictiveness. Had he not decided to end the drama on the eve of the execution he could have rendered the Pope's cruelty almost insupportably shocking by incorporating from his source the effects upon Bernardo of being compelled to witness the execution of his mother, sister, and brother.

Shelley's few additions to his source-material, however, indicate quite clearly the significance he wished to give the story. Orsino, who helps plan the murder, is in the original narrative a priest who appears to be motivated by sympathy and friendship. Shelley, whose numerous references to priests throughout his works never once contain a favourable adjective, converts him into a sly false friend actuated by avarice and lust. He is made a part of the net of evil by which Beatrice is surrounded. Count Cenci, described in the manuscript source as an atheist, is endowed by Shelley with a peculiarly horrible piety. Living in virtual alliance with the Pope, who profits by occasionally fining him for his crimes, he also feels an alliance between his own interests and those of his God. Were they not both fathers? As one father to another he prays earnestly to his God to heap curses upon a rebellious daughter. Nothing could be stronger evidence than this curse of Shelley's idea of the extent to which an evil nature perverts ideas of good. Significantly, it was one of Shelley's favourite passages.[37] In this one respect *The Cenci* story offered Shelley greater scope for his ideas of evil than *Prometheus Unbound.* The latter provided no place for parental tyranny, a *bête noire* at least of Shelley's youthful reading and experience. But the Pope, even in Shelley's source, is motivated partly by a desire to uphold the principle of parental authority. Shelley expands this motive to the extent of making Count Cenci suppose it a valid bond of sympathy between his own wickedness and God. This is possible because Cenci's God is the wicked God of perverted human ideas, like Jupiter.

In *Prometheus Unbound* Shelley had emphasized his belief that the evil in men's minds corrupts the institutions by which men are governed. In *The Cenci* he gave objective, dramatic representation to what he was otherwise presenting as an abstract theory, and extended the area of corruption to include parental authority in the evil alliance of secular and religious oppressions. It would be hard to name two other poems in English in which the power and the subtlety of evil are more poignantly realized.

It has been commonly said that Shelley's experience of life was too limited to allow him to understand the real nature of evil. Very possibly this is true to the extent that in practical affairs he may have been less cautious and suspicious than if he had possessed a more abundant association with highwaymen, swindlers, and defaulters. A character like Count Cenci's, motivated by love of evil for its own sake, lends some support to such a view. But in fact what young man ever reached the age of twenty-seven without enough personal experience of evil to justify reflections upon its nature — provided only that he was capable of analysis and reflection? The absence of a more extensive experience was in Shelley's case more than balanced by extraordinary perceptive and analytical powers and a voluminous and penetrating knowledge of literature, history, and philosophy.

The final proof that Shelley was not ignorant of the real nature of evil, however, is the view of evil which he expressed. He was now quite clear that the seat of evil was in the mind of man itself, and not primarily in the evil institutions that were merely a result of that fact. He was so far from regarding evil as a flimsy antagonist that he has been recently regarded almost as a pessimist.[38] Had he really been one, however, he must have ended *The Cenci* with the moral and spiritual destruction of Beatrice instead of a moral triumph. He had become in fact that rare type of optimist who realizes and overcomes the tremendous difficulties of optimism.

AT THE very time when Shelley was writing *Prometheus Unbound* and *The Cenci* he also wrote a part or all of his *Philosophical View of Reform.*[39] This unfinished prose work remained unpublished, though not quite unknown, for a hundred years, and was not included in any " complete " edition of Shelley's works until the appearance of the Julian edition in 1926–7.[40] Had it appeared earlier it might well have modified a distorted impression of Shelley's views and mental powers that has been all but established by mistaken Victorian critics. A brief examination of its contents lends support to my previous remarks on Shelley's other writings in 1819 and emphasizes both Shelley's optimism and its firm, practical, and temperate basis.

The introductory chapter of fifteen pages traces the degeneration of governments and institutions in Europe and Asia since the overthrow of the ancient Greek city-democracies. The Roman Empire, "that vast and successful scheme for the enslaving [of] the most civilized portion of mankind," laid the foundation for subverting the genuine liberty and equality of Christ's doctrines, and its evil influence was perfected and handed down to the nineteenth century by an alliance of the church with various dynasties. For a while the Italian republics and city governments offered successful opposition to this combination of selfish interests, but they were inevitably overpowered. An equally inevitable resistance to oppression began elsewhere with "that imperfect emancipation of mankind from the yoke of priests and kings called the Reformation." The republics of Holland and Switzerland sprang up as glorious examples; the growth of a spirit of liberty in England was accompanied as always and everywhere by a flowering of intellectual and artistic energy.

The fluctuations of the cause of freedom in England represented by the Restoration and the Revolution of 1688 contributed probably little more than was lost by confirming some of the usurped privileges of the oppressors; but they at least clearly established the legal right of the people to change their government. During the seventeenth and eighteenth centuries philosophy established the principles of utility, liberty, and equality, even though society failed to live by these principles. An astonishing development in commerce and science, instead of adding to human happiness, actually increased misery. On account of a vicious social and economic system modern society became an engine "which, instead of grinding corn or raising water acts against itself and is perpetually wearing away' or breaking to pieces the wheels of which it is composed."

As he looks over the world in his own generation, Shelley finds in the United States of America a bright flower of the new philosophy — a country without king, hereditary oligarchy, or established church, where the assemblies represent the will of the people and where the Constitution provides for its own amendment without the necessity of revolution. Much of South America was also free, or soon would be. In France, though the Revolution had been reversed, Freedom had lost only a part of what it had gained. Its partial failure was due to the fact that in completely overthrowing oppressive institutions it had failed to extinguish the passions on which they were founded and had even encouraged the spirit of revenge. Germany, caught in the reaction after the French Revolution, possessed such a power and depth of knowledge and literature that the ultimate triumph of Freedom was certain in the revolution that must inevitably come to such a nation. Spain was suffering under the most oppressive tyranny in Europe, " the rapidly passing shadows, which forerun successful insurrection." The Turkish Empire was in its death-throes already, and even India and China, far more deeply mired in hopelessness than Europe, showed some signs of the intellectual awakening that always precedes or accompanies Freedom.

Against this optimistic view of the vitality of Freedom throughout history and its hopeful prospects in the face of present discouragements Shelley proceeded to examine the present state of England. Practically everyone in England, he truthfully asserted, realized the inevitability of a fundamental change in government, and most people except those with a vested interest in existing institutions hoped for it.

Clearly and soberly Shelley explained how in his opinion England had arrived at this state of affairs. A much larger proportion of the people than ever before were now unrepresented in the government. A proportion of one voter to eight potential voters in 1641 had become one to twenty by 1688 and one to " many hundreds " by 1819. The House of Lords, which represented the privileged classes, also possessed great influence, as landed proprietors, over the election of the Commons.

Since 1688 the relative power and influence of the wealthy had enormously increased. The principal cause of this increase was the device of public credit first systematically applied by William III. The paper money issued by the government had so far exceeded its physical basis, with a resulting increase in prices, that an English workman must now work twenty hours to earn the same bare physical necessities he had formerly earned in eight. One result of this — since a twenty-hour workday could not be endured — was the hideous spectacle of child-labour, which was ruining the future manhood of the nation. Another was the creation of a new aristocracy of speculators, government pensioners, bankers, and brokers, in addition to the old one based upon the land. Their wealth arose from no useful occupation, but from manipulations in the funds. The English labourer, who produced the country's real wealth, was now saddled with a new class of drones. Overworked, ill-clothed, and undernourished, steadily degenerating in physical, mental, and moral stamina, the British workman was now advised by a leading economist (Malthus) to improve his condition by refraining from almost the only pleasures and comforts left him — those of sexual gratification and parenthood. It was even suggested that the poor-laws might be invoked to enforce such a program.

This intolerable state of affairs could result only in violent revolution, if the privileged classes would not yield to reform, or a more gradual, peaceful improvement, if they showed reason. The reforms that must be achieved were, in Shelley's opinion:

1. The restoration to the people of their former liberties.
2. Improvements in government that would preserve these rights.

Specific approaches to these ends were the abolition of the national debt, and of sinecures, tithes, and religious inequalities, the disbanding of the standing army, the extension of the jury system, and the speeding-up of legal processes. So far was Shelley from being a radical revolutionist that he proposed practically nothing that could not be regarded as a restoration rather than an innovation.

In the incomplete nature of Shelley's essay it is impossible to state the steps by which these changes were to be realized. Concerning only one of them, the abolition of the national debt, does he present anything like detailed suggestions. The large bulk of this debt, he pointed out, was the result of the wars against America and France that had been waged without the real approval of the people, and contrary to their interests. The principal was now owed to the privileged classes of England and was secured by the physical property of England, also largely owned by the same classes. The interest was paid in taxes mainly by the working classes, who owned little physical property. Thus it was to the advantage of the real workers of England to abolish the principal and of the privileged classes to retain their stranglehold on the economic life of the country by retaining the principal. Let the mortgagee foreclose, Shelley urged. It would not be such an economic wrench as was pretended, because he would be largely foreclosing on himself, and such physical goods as would be confiscated were goods to which no title had been earned by honest labour. Half the earnings of British labour would then no longer be diverted to the maintenance in vicious luxury of two idle aristocracies.

Naturally payment of the principal would involve confiscation of property. If this occurred, all property in England would have to be listed. The actual present value of the debt would have to be adjusted on some such basis as the price of corn at the times of contracting and of settling the debt. Local tribunals would fix the proportions to be paid by individuals, presumably taking into account Shelley's principle that property earned by physical or mental labour had a more valid title than property acquired through inheritance or financial manipulation. The result would be that "such a gentleman must lose a third of his estate, such a citizen a fourth of his money in the funds; the persons who borrowed would have paid, and the juggling and complicated system of paper finance would be suddenly at an end." Knowing that governments faced by dire necessity will confiscate what is necessary, and knowing also that they were themselves both the mortgagers and the mortgagees, the privileged classes might even arrange their debts among themselves. In fact, " One of the first acts of a reformed government would undoubtedly be an effectual scheme for compelling these to compromise their debt between themselves."

This, and the abolition of tithes, are the only specific reforms recommended in the document that have not since been put

into effect by " conservative " governments in England and elsewhere, and the abolition of tithes is even now being sought
in England by farmers who are otherwise conservative. If the
only program of immediate and practical reform that Shelley
ever drew up for public consideration is to be called radical,
it must be because he proposed paying a public debt — which,
it must be admitted, most nations still consider heinous. On the
other hand, since Shelley wrote, various governments by no
means radical have sought to solve the same difficulty by means
more indirect but no less radical than Shelley's. Practically con-
fiscatory taxes on large inheritances and incomes, and deliberate
manipulation of financial systems for the purpose of " liquidat-
ing " certain economic classes, would probably have seemed to
Shelley too radical, and in the latter case dishonest.

In instituting these reforms Shelley was willing to proceed
with a caution that many of his critics will find surprising. The
important point was to reverse the trend of events without violence. To achieve this Shelley was willing to postpone or even
forgo a great deal. He believed both in universal manhood
suffrage and in suffrage for women, but he thought England so
far from ready for either that he wished to relegate them to
an indefinite future. Universal suffrage would almost certainly
stimulate an attempt to set up a republic, with resultant violence and bloodshed. Extreme caution was necessary:

> If reform shall be begun by the existing government, let us be con-
> tented with a limited *beginning*, with any whatsoever opening . . .
> it is no matter how slow, gradual and cautious be the change; we
> shall demand more and more with firmness and moderation, never
> anticipating but never deferring the moment of successful opposition,
> so that the people may become habituated [to] exercising the func-
> tions of sovereignty in proportion as they acquire the possession of it.

If Parliament would not itself initiate the reforms — and Shelley greatly feared that it would not — he was for universal
suffrage with all its consequences, even if it involved abolition
of the existing government. An intelligent privileged minority,
he observed, will not stand out against a determined majority
possessed of overwhelming force. For this reason every means

of encouraging, unifying, and informing the people should be
sedulously cultivated by all true patriots. But the privileged
minority might be so ignorant and the people already so bru-
talized and misled by demagogues that the desired result might
not be practically attainable. In that case every means of petition and passive resistance should be cultivated, even to the
extent of passively defying armed force. Soldiers faced by
either force or flight are likely to be mere instinctive tools of
oppression, but soldiers faced firmly by non-resistant fellow
countrymen will eventually make common cause with them.
If such preliminary skirmishes should incline the oppressor to
make concessions,

the people ought to be exhorted by everything ultimately dear to
them to pause until by the exercise of those rights which they have
regained they become fitted to demand more. It is better that we
gain what we demand by a process of negotiation which would
occupy twenty years, than that by communicating a sudden shock
to the interests of those who are the depositaries and dependents of
power we should incur . . . civil war.

Only as the last possible resort could Shelley tolerate the
idea of armed insurrection. " If there had never been war, there
could never have been tyranny in the world." Armies, as in the
case of the French Revolution, were tools ready to hand for
would-be tyrants; any war, from whatever motive, extinguished
reason and justice and might soon lose its sense of direction.
But the English people, without Reform, were tending surely
toward an Asiatic condition of moral and political degradation.
To avoid such a destiny, and in default of all other remedies,
Shelley says firmly and reluctantly that the last recourse is
armed insurrection. Not even at this point should the idea of
revenge be tolerated. . . . Here Shelley left his manuscript
unfinished, just as he was launching himself upon his favourite
doctrine that revenge is under all circumstances a suicidal
policy.

A *Philosophical View of Reform* expressed an idea of modern
government, particularly in England, which Shelley intended

as a public utterance. His utterances in private correspondence at the same time leave no doubt as to the strength and consistency of his opinions. In November 1819 he wrote to Leigh Hunt:

> The great thing to do is to hold the balance between popular impatience and tyrannical obstinacy; to inculcate with fervour both the right of resistance and the duty of forbearance. You know my principles incite me to take all the good I can get in politics, for ever aspiring to something more. I am one of those whom nothing will fully satisfy, but who [are] ready to be partially satisfied [by] all that is practicable.

HAVING now seen " the Man " in some detail both in " what he did " and " what he worked in," we may return in other chapters to the beadroll of " facts." First, however, we should consider certain possible conclusions. Knowing how often the hypnotism of Shelley's verse has betrayed his admirers into wild generalizations, are we not nevertheless compelled to wonder if any poet except Shakespeare in any one year has ever contributed more great poetry to the wealth of English literature than Shelley did in the year 1819? No poet since Shakespeare has followed his own desire for perfection so far beyond the immediate comprehension of the ordinary reader while still leaving him so fully certain that he has been in the presence of great poetry. This Shelley did at a time when he was also writing another great poem in a totally different style, and when he was often in great physical and mental distress. Obviously such an accomplishment proves a will-power and understanding, an instant command of wide resources of thought and expression, that far exceed the power of biography to explain or even to state clearly. Such a climax is inadequately prepared for by even the most careful and detailed study of all the preceding " facts " available. It is the dominant, too easily forgotten factor which gives significance to the usual details of daily life that compose the bulk of biography. The remaining three years of Shelley's life produced no such concentrated exhibit of these powers, but they produced clear evidence that the powers at least of thought and expression were not diminished and were even in some respects still developing.

Nor is it without significance to any true or unified view of Shelley's life that an examination of " the real Shelley " in 1819 confirms an impression made quite clear by the "facts" of his earlier life, though temporarily somewhat obscured in the years following his second elopement — namely, that his life was extraordinarily dominated by the purpose he had first formulated for himself as a schoolboy at Syon House Academy or Eton. It goes farther and adds a harmony and thoughtful wisdom to that purpose which the earlier Shelley lacked and which the world has not yet sufficiently conceded to the mature Shelley. *Prometheus Unbound,* so significantly different in several ways, flows from the same clear source as *Queen Mab; The Cenci,* so brilliantly different in style and probably even in intention, is still closely linked to the *Prometheus Unbound. A Philosophical View of Reform* is a thoroughly harmonious practical counterpart to the highly idealistic *Prometheus Unbound* and is at the same time a quite logical culmination of Shelley's earlier addresses to the Irish and of the Marlow pamphlets. In fact, as I have shown in Chapter vii, *Prometheus Unbound, A Philosophical View of Reform,* and various other works of Shelley's maturity are clearly forecast by his letters of 1811 and 1812. The three superficially different works we have considered all converge with perfect harmony, from widely different angles, upon a few simple propositions that, taken together, constitute the essential Shelley.

These are that the present state of man and society is predominantly evil, that this condition can and must be improved, that the fault lies primarily in the distortions of truth in the human mind and only secondarily in the institutions produced by the distortion, that the complete remedy lies far in the future and in an emancipation of the mind, and that it is the practical duty of all right-thinking people never to concede the principle that existing evils are permanent, while at the same time they must proceed toward reforming practical abuses with a full sense of the present power of evil. Over and above all these was a growing conviction that the so-called " realities " of life were mere illusions from the point of view of truth and Intellectual Beauty, even though they must still be dealt with on a practical plane of living as if they were genuine realities.

At the same time that Shelley was preaching these doctrines he was doing what he could to bring them into effect by addressing the " highly refined imaginations " of a " select class," the considerably less refined imaginations of the practical reformers, and even the English working classes, each within its own vocabulary and intellectual range.

Chapter XXIII

LIFE IN FLORENCE

GETTING SETTLED; THE REVIEWERS;

BIRTH OF PERCY FLORENCE SHELLEY; FAMILY AND

FINANCIAL DIFFICULTIES; INTEREST IN

ENGLISH POLITICS; SOPHIA STACEY

ON October 2, 1819 the Shelleys and Claire took possession of their apartment in Florence, in the Palazzo Marini, at 4395 Via Valfonda, a narrow, picturesque street near Santa Maria Novella.[1] The Palazzo Marini was a lodging-house kept by the Madame Merveilleux du Plantis who with her daughter, Zoide, had taken tea with the Shelleys at Villa Valsovana on September 15 and 16.[2] On further acquaintance Mary formed an unflattering opinion of her as a brainless goose: "Her head is a sieve, and her temper worse than wildfire — it is gunpowder and blows up everything."[3] The Shelleys saw less of her, however, than of her daughter Louise, whom Mary considered sensible and attractive, but lazy. Charles Clairmont, who had accompanied the party to Florence, succumbed to the charms of another landlady's daughter and was soon in love with Louise. But, in Shelley's phrase, Louise, "Not so fair but I fear as cold as the snowy Florimel in Spenser," was "in and out of love with Charles as the winds happen to blow."[4]

Charles was on the point of leaving for Vienna. Claire settled down at once to her singing-lessons. The Shelleys knew no one in Florence, and the Masons and Gisbornes, who had been somewhat acquainted there in earlier years, were now able to produce only one letter of introduction between them. This

154

was to Signor and Madame Tonelli, friends of Mrs. Gisborne's whom Shelley was at first unable to see. Mary's condition also confined the party somewhat closely to home. Accordingly the first weeks at Florence were rather lonely ones.

Shelley went several times to the art galleries. One of the chief advantages he hoped from Italy was to achieve a better notion of ideal beauty as suggested by ancient and modern sculpture.[5] He evidently intended a systematic detailed study. Mary recorded later that Shelley spent several hours daily in the Florentine galleries,[6] but her contemporary journal mentions only three or four such visits, and Shelley's uneven notes on his observations hardly suggest a much greater number.[7] Occasionally he dropped into Delesert's reading-rooms, to read the English papers.

LONG ago, in the *Examiner*, Shelley had seen Leigh Hunt's favourable criticism of *The Revolt of Islam*, and Horace Smith's warm sonnet to the author. Very probably he had not seen a friendly review that had appeared in a Canterbury weekly, the *Man of Kent*, in November 1818.[8] What the *Quarterly Review* was likely to say about the volume he knew already from his correspondence with Hunt. But the book had been in print almost a year and a half before Shelley saw any of the hostile criticism. One day in early October Lord Dillon, an English visitor in Florence, observed a rather delicate-looking young man in Delesert's reading-rooms poring intently over the *Quarterly*. Suddenly the reader burst into hysterical, uncontrollable laughter and hastily left the room.[9] The reader was Shelley, and the *Quarterly* was the number for April 1819, containing the review of *Laon and Cythna* under both its titles now known to have been written by John Taylor Coleridge.[10] Shelley concealed his hurt as best he could by comparing the conclusion to the bombastic first act of an opera: " It describes the result of my battle with their Omnipotent God; his pulling me under the sea by the hair of my head, like Pharaoh; my calling out like the devil who was *game* to the last; swearing and cursing in all comic and horrid oaths, like a French postillion on Mont

Cenis; entreating everybody to drown themselves; pretending not to be drowned myself when I *am* drowned and, lastly, *being* drowned." It seemed to amuse Shelley particularly that the *Quarterly* proclaimed that his " chariot-wheels " were broken. He suggested that Ollier publish a solemn denial, as coming from Mr. Charters, of Bond Street, the injured chariot-maker.[11]

All this was merely pretending that he was not hurt; he had been expecting this blow for some time, and preparing himself for it. In the same letters in which he made light of it to Ollier he made it the principal subject of remark. He began a letter of remonstrance to the editor of the *Quarterly*,[12] and he deeply appreciated the *Examiner's* reply to the *Quarterly*. No periodical in Great Britain, except the *Edinburgh Review,* spoke with anything like the authority of the *Quarterly*. Its lead was sure to be followed by almost all the conservative or timid-minded reviewers. To be damned by the *Quarterly* just as he was publishing two volumes that far surpassed his previous work was a heavy misfortune for a poet with a strong sense of mission.

The *Quarterly's* excommunication was indeed only a little less thorough than the famous one read aloud by Mr. Shandy. Eleven pages were devoted to demonstrating the dullness, obscurity, and moral delinquency of the poem. The reviewer claimed to know that Shelley's private history and character afforded a disgusting and convincing corroboration of the strictures he had just passed on the poem. With an appearance of sincerity he admitted the occasional presence of real beauty in the poem and quoted five stanzas in proof of it, but " As a whole, it is insupportably dull, and laboriously obscure; its absurdities are not of the kind which provoke laughter, the story is almost wholly devoid of interest, and very meagre; nor can we admire Mr. Shelley's mode of making up for this defect — as he has but one incident where we should have ten, he tells the one so intricately that it takes the time of ten to comprehend it." Having thus repudiated its own admission of beauty, the *Quarterly* examines the poem in detail, and thus states its indictment of the poet:

FLORENCE

Engraved by Redaway from a drawing by Harding

He has indeed, to the best of his ability, wounded us in the tenderest part. — As far as in him lay, he has loosened the hold of our
protecting laws, and sapped the principles of our venerable polity;
he has invaded the purity and chilled the unsuspecting ardour of
our fireside intimacies; he has slandered, ridiculed and blasphemed
our holy religion; yet these are all too sacred objects to be defended
bitterly or unfairly.[13]

The *Monthly Review* had also condemned the poem on the
same general grounds:

It is lamentable, indeed to see the waste of so much capability of
better things. . . . The author has many poetical talents, but he
does not seem to have rendered a just account of a single one. His
command of the language is so thoroughly abused as to become a
mere snare for loose and unmeaning expression; and his facility of
writing, even in Spenser's stanza, leads him into a licentiousness of
rhythm and of rhyme that is truly contemptible.[14]

There is no evidence that Shelley ever knew of the attack in
the *Monthly Review*. Fortunately when he received the *Quarterly* article it was accompanied by Leigh Hunt's reply to it.
Hunt had indeed kept his promise to buckle on his "rusty old
armour" in Shelley's defence. He exposed the hypocrisy of the
Quarterly in dragging forth the suppressed *Laon and Cythna*
in order to condemn alleged immorality which according to
its own theories should have been left to oblivion; he analysed
several passages in the *Quarterly* to demonstrate the weakness
or unfairness of its conclusions; and he entered upon a bold
and spirited defence of Shelley's principles and personal character as compared with those of his reviewers. Against the reviewer's assertion that Shelley was "shamefully dissolute in his
conduct" Hunt opposed a detailed account of Shelley's daily
life at Marlow, as he himself had seen it while Shelley was
writing *The Revolt of Islam*.[15] While Hunt's method in the
main was calmly expository, he made no attempt to conceal his
feelings, and such expressions as "half-sighted and whole-
clawed meanness" and "Heavy and swelling, and soft with
venom, it creeps . . . like a skulking toad" show a hearty willingness to meet the enemy on his own ground.

Consoling as this defence was to Shelley, he valued it most as an act of personal friendship. No such consideration tempered the encouragement he received at about the same time from the review that appeared in *Blackwood's Edinburgh Magazine* for January 1819. *Blackwood's* was indeed a Tory magazine, in some ways as conservative or reactionary as the *Quarterly* itself and far more reckless. Its treatment of Keats was a shade more brutal even than the *Quarterly's*. It was already involved in a fierce crusade against the "Cockney School of Poetry," with which Shelley was known to be closely affiliated by personal ties. But John Wilson ("Christopher North"), John Gibson Lockhart, and William Maginn, who wrote most of its reviews of poetry, were all poets of sorts. The two latter were merely clever verse-writers, but Wilson enjoyed a fairly high contemporary reputation as a poet. Moreover, they were also literary snobs, and as there was a social as well as an artistic distinction between Shelley and the "Cockneys," they were not disinclined to exploit the difference. Being as reckless as they were clever, they cared little about following the lead of the *Quarterly*, which in fact had not then fully declared its position.

It was a particularly fortunate accident for Shelley that *Blackwood's* sent the book to Thomas De Quincey for review. De Quincey had not met Shelley at Keswick in 1812, but he almost certainly knew of him from common friends there. He was by temperament and experience far better equipped than most of his contemporaries to review Shelley intelligently. Though he declined writing the review, he read and admired the book and furnished Wilson with some of his opinions.[16] Wilson, ever an adept at using other men's ideas, wrote a review that was probably based on De Quincey's suggestions.

In this review *Blackwood's* yielded nothing to the *Quarterly* in condemning Shelley's theories. "A pernicious system of opinion," it began, "concerning man and his moral government, a superficial audacity of unbelief, an overflowing abundance of uncharitableness toward almost the whole of his race, and a disagreeable measure of assurance and self-conceit . . . in the character of any one person might, at first sight, be considered as more than sufficient to render that one person utterly and entirely contemptible." Mr. Shelley, it admitted, was such a person. But Mr. Shelley, though "weak and worthless" as a philosopher, was "strong, nervous, and original" as a poet; he was far superior to the other Cockneys; he had a strong genius that placed him already "near to the great creative masters" of the age. In this spirit the reviewer proceeded to describe the poem at length, dealing out equally generous praise of the poetry and condemnation of the principles.

Blackwood's deeply admired Shelley's power as a poet of love:

It is in the portraying of that passionate love, which had been woven from infancy in the hearts of Laon and Cythna, and which, binding together all their impulses in one hope and one struggle, had rendered them through life no more than two different tenements for the inhabitation of the same enthusiastic spirit; — it is in the portraying of this intense, overmastering, unfearing, unfading love, that Mr. Shelley had proved himself to be a great poet. Around his lovers, moreover, in the midst of all their fervours, he has shed an air of calm gracefulness, a certain majestic monumental stillness, which blends them harmoniously with the scene of their earthly existence, and realizes in them our ideas of Greeks struggling for freedom in the best spirit of their fathers.

The concluding sentences of the review not only reaffirm *Blackwood's* belief in Shelley's genius as a poet, but give a clear hint of the policy of temptation that the magazine maintained toward Shelley as long as there seemed any possibility of "converting" him:

Mr. Shelly [*sic*] has displayed his possession of a mind intensely poetical, and of an exuberance of poetic language, perpetually strong and perpetually varied. In spite, moreover, of a certain perversion in all his modes of thinking, which, unless he gets rid of it, will ever prevent him from being acceptable to any considerable or respectable body of readers, he has displayed many glimpses of right understanding and generous feeling, which must save him from the unmingled condemnation even of the most rigorous judges. His destiny is entirely in his own hands; if he acts wisely, it cannot fail to be a glorious one; if he continues to pervert his talents, by making them the instruments of a base sophistry, their splendour will only contribute to render his disgrace the more conspicuous. Mr. Shelley, whatever his errors may have been, is a scholar, a gentleman, and a poet; and he must therefore despise from his soul the only eulogies to which he has hitherto been accustomed — paragraphs from the Examiner, and sonnets from Johnny Keats. He has it in his power to select better companions; and if he does so, he may very securely promise himself abundance of better praise.[17]

It is not unlikely that Shelley read both this review and the equally favourable review of *Rosalind and Helen* that followed it in *Blackwood's* for June, though there is no mention of them in his letters. In its second review *Blackwood's* praised *Rosalind and Helen* highly, with frequent excerpts of beauties, but expressed deep concern over the " monstrous perversity " of the author. It reiterated its faith in his ultimate triumph — only to be achieved, however, by abandoning his vices. " His fame will yet be a glorious plant if he do not blast its expanding leaves by the suicidal chillings of immorality." [18]

In September, however, *Blackwood's* reached the crest of its really well-meant effort to save wayward genius from its own perversity. It ferreted out for review a copy of *Alastor,* published the year before *Blackwood's* was established, and announced that it did so in order to give its readers an idea of the progress already achieved by " a mind destined, in our opinion, under due discipline and self-management, to achieve great things in poetry." The detailed description of the poem that followed deplored a general obscurity of meaning but found passage after passage to be praised for its intrinsic beauty. In conclusion, *Blackwood's* turned upon the *Quarterly* a long and spirited rebuke for its review of *The Revolt of Islam.* Such reviewing, it roundly asserted, was both infamous and stupid; a mere comparison of the reviewer's prose with Shelley's poetry made one think of " a dunce rating a man of genius." The *Quarterly's* praise of one passage in Shelley's poem was denounced as a mere hypocritical dodge which should expose the reviewer to the scorn and contempt of all true lovers of genius. " He *exults,*" *Blackwood's* charges, " to calumniate Mr. Shelley's moral character, but he *fears* to acknowledge his genius," and so shows himself " as far inferior to Mr. Shelley as a man of

JOHN WILSON ("CHRISTOPHER NORTH"), *c.* 1820

Unsigned contemporary sketch

worth, as the language in which he utters his falsehood and
uncharitableness shows him to be inferior as a man of intellect."
Both Shelley and the *Quarterly* reviewer are assured that England will pardon much to genius, but will not pardon a dishonest attempt to obscure genius. And " It is not in the power
of all the critics alive to blind one true lover of poetry to the
splendour of Mr. Shelley's genius." To understand the greatness
of the poet and the littleness of his traducer it was only necessary
to read " six successive stanzas " of *The Revolt of Islam,* " so
full of music, imagination, intellect, and passion." [19]

This persistent and extraordinary wooing of Shelley by the
most powerful monthly of the day was a more significant thing
than either Shelley or his biographers have realized. It was
clear evidence that a genius like Shelley's could not be wasted,
no matter how dull or biased the majority of the reviewers
might be. It showed also that in 1819, before his best works
were published, it was possible for Shelley to achieve a fairly
general recognition as a great poet. Shelley was really yielding
to a persecution complex in the letters in which he spoke of his
case as if it were hopeless. Had the two volumes then in press
been as free from his political, religious, and moral theories as
the *Alastor* volume the story might have been different. Even
so, it was not until 1821 that the opportunity vanished. But
Shelley was incapable of accepting *Blackwood's* already implied invitation to win recognition by modifying his opinions.
Prometheus Unbound reiterated most of the doctrines that en-
sured attack from the conservatives; and *The Cenci,* rigidly
objective and " popular " as Shelley supposed it to be, nevertheless repeated the theme of incest against which the reviewers
had already rebelled.

Shelley was acquainted at least with *Blackwood's* review of
Alastor and was considerably puzzled and encouraged by it.
" I am glad however, to see the *Quarterly* cut up, and that by
one of their own people," he wrote to Ollier. ". . . Do you
know, I think the article in *Blackwood* could not have been
written by a favourer of Government and a religionist. I don't
believe any such one could sincerely like my writings. After
all, is it not some friend in disguise, and don't you know who

wrote it?" [20] At about the same time Mary sent Maria Gisborne copies of the *Quarterly* and *Blackwood's* reviews, which she called "the bane and [the] antidote." It seemed singular, she remarked, that a journal fully as furious as the *Quarterly* should take up Shelley's defence. "We half think that . . . it must be Walter Scott, the only liberal man of that faction." [21]

MARY'S fourth and last child was born on the morning of November 12, 1819. The next day Shelley wrote to Leigh Hunt: "Yesterday morning Mary brought me a little boy. She suffered only about two hours' pain, and is now so well that it seems a wonder that she stays in bed. The babe is also quite well, and has begun to suck. You may imagine that this is a great relief and a great comfort to me amongst all my misfortunes past present and to come. . . . Poor Mary begins (for the first time) to look a little consoled. For we have spent as you may imagine a miserable five months." A few days later, in announcing the event to Miss Curran, Shelley reported that Mary was "exceedingly well." [22]

Young Percy Florence, as he was christened, grew rapidly, indeed quite prodigiously, by Mary's account. He resembled his mother and was such a fine, healthy child that it seemed absurd to worry about him, yet Mary had been through too much not to worry. She shuddered with horror to think of the five bleak, childless months that had preceded Percy's birth, and it was a bitter thought that only one frail life stood between her and a repetition of that misery. Though her spirits and energy were now much improved, some of this morbid dread still lingered in her letters. At length Mrs. Mason interjected a plain, sensible warning: "I am very sorry to find that you still suffer from low spirits. I was in hopes the little boy would have been the best remedy for that. Words of consolation are but empty sounds, for to time alone it belongs to wear out the tears of affliction. However, a woman who gives milk should make every exertion to be cheerful, on account of the child she nourishes." [23]

There were other more substantial worries for the Shelleys in Florence. Godwin was writing disturbing letters about his lawsuit. On October 19 the case was decided against him, and he was called upon to pay several years' back rent for a property he had supposed himself holding rent-free. The judgment, Godwin informed Shelley, would involve the payment sooner or later of between £600 and £2,000.[24] Mary's journal for November 9 reads: "Bad news from London. Shelley reads Clarendon aloud, and Plato. He writes to Papa." "Papa" naturally expected Shelley to rescue him again, and Shelley, whose affairs were too much involved to assume the burden without borrowing, thought he might have to return to England to settle the matter.[25] A notion of Shelley's or Mary's that Godwin might do well to give up his Skinner Street business entirely and live abroad was fortunately referred to Mrs. Mason for her judgment. Mrs. Mason agreed that Godwin would do well to retire from business, but on the basis of her own experience and observation as an exile she advised strongly that the Godwins remain in England.[26]

At no time since Shelley had come to Italy could Godwin's troubles have been revived so inconveniently. For the rest of Shelley's life they interfered with Mary's recovery of cheerful spirits and but for Mary's faith in him might have produced the open breach between them which Godwin did not hesitate to risk. Moreover, Shelley had just rendered himself doubly unable to come to Godwin's rescue, by involving himself in the straitened finances of the Gisbornes.

THE GISBORNES had been living on a small income a part or all of which was invested in the funds of the English government. Somewhat alarmed at the possible insecurity or future inadequacy of his investments, Mr. Gisborne had recently taken a journey to England to look into the situation and had returned after the Shelleys left Leghorn for Florence. Shelley was tireless in urging him to withdraw his money from the public funds as quickly as possible. The taxes, he argued, were failing and in any case could no longer meet the expenses of the government. The standing army was being increased; a bloody struggle seemed imminent. If the government won, it would be compelled to reduce the interest on the national debt, and if the people won, they would abolish most of the government's present financial obligations. Even if there were some sort of last-minute compromise between the government and the people the interest on government bonds would certainly be reduced.[27] Mr. Gisborne was not fully convinced, and was in any case powerless to do anything without the consent of Henry Reveley's uncle, who apparently did not share Shelley's alarm.

But there was another way in which the Gisbornes might be aided. Why not make Henry Reveley's steam-engine a source of income? Already in England, in New York, and even in Italy the first steamboats were beginning a revolution of water-transport. The Shelley who as a freshman had dreamed of balloons over Africa and who a few years later had lent his enthusiasm to the Tremadoc Embankment dreamed another dream of progress. There seemed no reason why Henry Reveley should not build a steamboat to ply between Leghorn, Genoa, and Marseilles. There was no reason, in fact, except the lack of funds. A few days before the Shelleys left Leghorn Mary's journal states (September 22): "Shelley reads Calderon and talks about the steam engine." One day after the Shelleys left, a contract was signed for the fitting and launching of the boat. Henry and his assistant were going ahead with the engine, but were handicapped by lack of cash. Mrs. Gisborne had already advanced all she could — a hundred and forty crowns.[28]

Shelley's financial assistance must have been arranged shortly before he left Leghorn. Its total extent is uncertain, but he actually furnished a hundred pounds on December 7 and another hundred on December 23.[29] These sums had been promised much earlier, but were delayed by a temporary snarl in Shelley's banking accounts.[30] Eventually, after some letters to England, the matter was corrected without actual loss of money, but not without some inconvenience. Henry Reveley found himself unable to buy certain materials when needed, and lost some excellent workmen because they could not remain idle until funds arrived.

Shelley's letters to the Gisbornes were full of eager inquiries about the steamboat; Mrs. Gisborne's answering letters communicated Henry's eagerness, energy, and resourcefulness. After examining the new steamboat from Genoa and talking with its engineer about the practical difficulties of operation Henry still felt confident. He also obtained a detailed account of the Trieste boat.

Henry himself was now a correspondent of Shelley's. Recognizing his deficiencies in written English, he had accepted Shelley's offer to criticize a series of letters. But when Henry described his boat or gave a vivid account of casting the cylinders for his engine Shelley was roused to a very uncritical enthusiasm: "Your volcanic description of the birth of the cylinder is very characteristic both of you and of it. One might imagine God, when he made the earth, and saw the granite mountains and flinty promontories flow into their craggy forms, and the splendour of their fusion filling millions of miles of the void space, like the tail of a comet, so looking, so delighting in his work." [31]

THE STATE of mind that had caused Shelley to write *The Masque of Anarchy* continued during the autumn and early winter of 1819. His sonnet " England in 1819 " pictures a country with a mad and dying King, disgraceful princes, and heartless ministers, its people starved and assassinated, its religion meaningless, and its standing army dangerous to oppressor and oppressed alike. From all this might soon arise the " glorious Phantom," freedom. In the Preface to *Prometheus Unbound* Shelley had half-promised to undertake a systematic statement in prose of his ideas of society. He now made considerable progress on his *Philosophical View of Reform* (discussed in the preceding chapter), which amply shows the moderation with which he thought reform should be accomplished. Shelley wanted reform without revolution, but he was very much afraid that the rulers would induce revolution. " I fear that in England things will be carried violently by the rulers, and [that] they will not have learned to yield in time to the spirit of the age. The great thing to do is to hold the balance between popular impatience and tyrannical obstinacy; to inculcate with fervour both the right of resistance and the duty of forbearance." If it came to an open struggle, he wrote to Hunt, "*We* cannot hesitate which party to embrace; and whatever revolutions are to occur . . . our party will be that of liberty and of the oppressed." [32]

As he wrote these words Shelley was already coming to the defence of the oppressed. Hogg had recently sent him a brief account of the trial of Richard Carlile for blasphemy in publishing Palmer's *Principles of Nature* and Paine's *Age of Reason*. This was the second of Carlile's several martyrdoms at the hands of the law, and he received a very severe sentence. [33]

Carlile had conducted his own defence and had insisted upon reading to the jury the whole of Paine's *Age of Reason*. His wife had then published an account of his trial in which Carlile's " defence " was repeated — a technically legal method of publishing Paine which resulted in her prompt trial and conviction. Many of the details were probably unknown to Shelley, who only needed to know that Carlile was unjustly imprisoned. It was the Peter Finnerty case over again. Immediately he dashed off a long letter to Leigh Hunt to be inserted in the *Examiner*. Why Hunt failed to print so moderate and able a paper has not been explained.

" In the name of all we hope for in human nature what are the people of England about? " Shelley demanded. Briefly summarizing the disastrous news of post after post, he introduced Carlile's case as the most recent outrage: " And thus at the same time we see on one hand men professing to act by the public authority who put in practice the trampling down and murdering an unarmed multitude without distinction of sex or age, and on the other a tribunal which punishes men for asserting that deeds of the same character, transacted in a distant age and country were not done by the command of God."

Shelley held no brief for Carlile individually. He admitted that the defence might have been deficient in dignity and that the books for whose publication Carlile was sentenced might well contain offensive matter. The real points were that Carlile had been denied his constitutional right to a trial by a jury of his *peers,* that the terms of the indictment (" wicked, malicious," and blasphemous libel) had been practically ignored and were certainly unproved, and that Carlile's conviction was really a case of class oppression which violated the principle of equal justice for all. On all these points Shelley argued more like a temperate and skilful lawyer than an enthusiastic reformer. How could a jury of orthodox churchmen be called peers of a man whose case their very orthodoxy forced them to prejudge? If it were contended that a jury of deists might be his peers but would be equally predetermined for acquittal, what could be said against a jury half orthodox and half deist, on the model of the half-foreign juries which were regularly impanelled to try criminal cases involving foreigners? The argument that a deist could not take the oath to be impanelled was absurd — deists and unitarians regularly did so, regarding it as a matter of form. Why had the government not prosecuted the writings of Hume and Gibbon? Why had it not haled into court Sir William Drummond, William Godwin, and Jeremy Bentham, all of whom treated Christianity as " an exploded superstition "? Among the very men who prosecuted booksellers like Carlile were persons who Shelley said he could testify of his own knowledge were themselves deists.

Shelley contended further that Carlile not only had failed to receive a trial by his peers, but had also been denied *equal* justice. The reason was that by attacking more powerful deists the government risked defeat. By making sure of Carlile's conviction they bolstered the power of an Established Church, which was a principal prop of their various political oppressions. They cared little for religion except as a mask of worldly power. " In prosecuting Carlile they have used the superstition of the jury as their instrument for crushing a political enemy." Twenty years later, when the government was employing a similar partiality in prosecuting radicals for publishing *Queen Mab*, such radical admirers of Shelley as Henry Hetherington actually forced the trial of Edward Moxon on the same charges, and by the threat of compelling equal justice helped abolish the discrimination against which Shelley protested in Carlile's case.[34]

Under such conditions, with England trembling in the balance between despotism and free government, it seemed to

Shelley that the case of Carlile forced every lover of freedom to speak out. But meanwhile Carlile was in prison, financially ruined. Let a good subscription be raised, not only to relieve Carlile, but to defeat the government's purpose of ruining him and thus damaging the cause of freedom in which he suffered. Shelley offered to deny himself some intended lessons in German and devote the money to Carlile's relief.[35]

IT IS very probable that Shelley's "Peter Bell the Third," which was written within the same fortnight as the letter on Carlile,[36] was not so completely a mere play of fanciful humour as it appears, though its origin was not very serious. Wordsworth's *Peter Bell: A Tale in Verse,* after lying nineteen years in manuscript, was published in 1819; but its publication was actually preceded by John Hamilton Reynolds's burlesque *Peter Bell: A Lyrical Ballad.* The review of both poems in the *Examiner* for April 26 and May 3 furnished Shelley with the idea of creating a third Peter Bell. Mary finished copying it on November 2, and it was immediately sent off to Hunt. Ollier was to publish it, but as it was a "party squib" written carelessly in a few days' time, Shelley's name must not be mentioned. As a matter of fact, the poem was not published until 1839.

Mrs. Shelley's note on the poem states Shelley's great admiration for Wordsworth as a poet and seems anxious to show that the poem is not a personal attack on Wordsworth. The very words in which she states Shelley's purpose serve also partly to veil it:

> He conceived the idealism of a poet — a man of lofty and creative genius — quitting the glorious calling of discovering and announcing the beautiful and the good, to support and propagate ignorant prejudices and pernicious errors; imparting to the enlightened, not that ardour for truth and spirit of toleration which Shelley looked on as the sources of the moral improvement and happiness of mankind; but false and injurious opinions, that evil was good, and that ignorance and force were the best allies of purity and virtue. His idea was that a man gifted even as transcendently as the Author of Peter Bell, with the highest qualities of genius, must, if he fostered such errors, be

WILLIAM WORDSWORTH

Engraved by Henry Meyer from a painting by R. Carrothers

infected with dulness. The poem was written as a warning, not as
a narration of the reality.

This states Shelley's opinions only half-way. The truly humorous description of the poet's dullness undoubtedly bears
little relation to Shelley's opinion of Wordsworth's earlier poems.
But Shelley and everybody else knew that since about 1814
Wordsworth was becoming duller. Shelley certainly thought
Peter Bell a ridiculous product of nineteen years' incubation.
He used to quote the poem, beginning with chuckles of amusement and reaching a point of almost uncontrollable laughter
with the stanza beginning " It is a party in a parlour " and ending " All silent and all damned," which he used as a motto for
"Peter Bell the Third." [37] But Shelley also thought Wordsworth was becoming more dangerous. He had already characterized him to Peacock as an odious flatterer of tyranny. Under the surface, as he remarked in his introductory poem to
" The Witch of Atlas," Peter was

> a fellow
> Scorched by Hell's hyperequatorial climate
> Into a kind of sulphureous yellow.

In " Peter Bell the Third," beneath the odd Shelleyan horse-
play and occasional cutting parody, is plainly to be seen not
only Shelley's warning that a poet who deserts the cause of
freedom must necessarily grow dull, having committed a sort
of spiritual suicide, but his very plain conviction that Wordsworth was already growing dull for this reason.

It is a curious fact that *The Masque of Anarchy,* the letter on
Carlile, and " Peter Bell the Third " were all sent to Leigh Hunt
for publication, within a few months of each other, and yet
none was published until many years later. As late as April 5,
1820 Shelley complained to Hunt that he had not even acknowledged receipt of " Peter Bell the Third " and the letter on Richard Carlile. Hunt probably acted within the vague discretion-
ary powers assigned him by Shelley in suppressing these
writings, but why did he do so? He had fearlessly published
similar opinions of his own on all three subjects. Hardly any
answer is possible except that Hunt believed that Shelley at

this time had a real opportunity to win public recognition as a great poet, and that this opportunity should not be lost through relatively minor publications that were not sufficiently valuable to justify such a risk.

" I HAVE deserted the odorous gardens of literature to journey across the great sandy desert of Politics," Shelley lightly informed the Gisbornes on November 6. He was, in fact, more excited over political matters than at any time since his first expedition to Ireland. Mrs. Mason, with a better notion than anyone else of the close connection between Shelley's health and his state of mind, wrote: " I am very sorry to hear such a bad account of Mr. Shelley, and fear that the interest he takes in the political state of England is very injurious to his health. I speak feelingly on this subject, as my nerves have never recovered the shake they got about twenty years ago on a similar occasion." [38] Mrs. Gisborne was also concerned about Shelley's health: " Messere! I am not quite satisfied with the account of your health. What occasions the fixed pain in your side? You must move heaven and earth to get rid of it." [39] Mary's letters had evidently been disquieting, as they generally were on the subject of Shelley's health. The physicians in Florence thought his condition delicate enough to require forbidding his return to England during the winter.[40]

The weather, too, was unfavourable; Florence was having one of its coldest and most disagreeable winters for many years. " Nothing," Shelley wrote to Tom Medwin,[41] " reconciles me to the slightest indication of winter: much less such infernal cold as my nerves have been racked upon for the last ten days." At the same time Mary Shelley was writing to Mrs. Gisborne that Shelley's health, although better, still showed the effects of the cold in an " extreme nervous irritability." [42] In a less exasperated mood Shelley described the winter as " an epic of rain, with an episode of frost, and a few similes concerning fine weather." [43]

Yet Shelley's health was not bad enough to prevent considerable activity. Besides the writing already discussed he wrote the **fourth act of *Prometheus Unbound*,** the " Ode to the West

Wind," [44] and several exquisite short lyrics. For a day or two he returned to his old unfinished task of translating Spinoza with Mary. Nor had he deserted his reading so much as he gave Mrs. Gisborne to understand. He kept up his new-found interest in Calderon and had read some half-dozen new plays by November 16.[45] He read Massinger, Beaumont and Fletcher, Shakespeare, and Sophocles, but his more constant reading was in the Earl of Clarendon, Plato's *Republic,* and the New Testament, all of which (and sometimes Shakespeare and Sophocles) he sometimes read aloud to Mary.

As Mary recovered strength she occasionally accompanied Shelley on his frequent strolls in the Cascine Forest. Most of her time, however, was consumed by the needs of her rapidly growing baby. Claire was busy with her singing-lessons and with reading Spanish, though she seems to have found more time for social life than either Shelley or Mary. Except for the lodgers in the house, the life of the Shelleys was almost as solitary as it had been at Villa Valsovano. Milly Shields, the only remaining servant who had accompanied the Shelleys from England, left them shortly before the middle of December and was replaced by a much better nurse, a German-Swiss, who spoke excellent Italian. The Shelleys had made no Italian acquaintances. Madame du Plantis, their landlady, they saw occasionally, and her rather attractive daughter, Louise, more often. They had a calling acquaintance with several English people — a Mr. and Mrs. Meadows, a Mr. and Mrs. Harding, and a Mr. Tomkins. Mr. Harding, a clergyman, christened young Percy Florence on January 25. Mr. Tomkins, an amateur portrait-painter, sketched a portrait of Shelley on January 7 and 9.[46] Claire Clairmont's journal mentions other English people with whom she associated and who were probably known to the Shelleys — Mr. Dalton, Mr. Baxter, Mr. Pidwell, and a Mrs. Pollok. A more familiar caller, on January 23, was Elise Foggi, who had come to Florence to live some time after leaving the Shelleys in Naples. As yet it was five or six months before she was to tell her damaging story to the Hoppners. The Shelleys received her and even recommended Paolo's employment by Henry Reveley.

Early in November, shortly before the birth of Percy Florence, a visitor came to Florence in whom the poet took an immediate interest. She was Miss Sophia Stacey, the ward of one of Shelley's favourite uncles, Mr. Robert Parker. Miss Stacey was accompanied by an older friend, Miss Corbet Parry-Jones. Having spent three years with her guardian at Bath and Brighton, Miss Stacey was rather fond of social life and enjoyed the gaiety to be found among English circles at Florence. She had an excellent, well-trained voice, and some superficial interest in ideas and events; but if one may judge from such extracts from her journal as have been preserved [47] she was fundamentally a simple, ingenuous English girl, with the touch of sentimentalism that was rather fashionable for young ladies at the time. Mr. Parker had told her enough about Shelley to stimulate her curiosity. Two days after her arrival in Florence she called at the Palazzo Marini and received the impression that the Shelleys often communicated, that " They see no company and live quite to themselves.'" On the next day (the day before Percy Florence was born) she and Miss Jones removed to the same house, after which a considerable intimacy arose.

This intimacy was at first more with Shelley than with Mary. Shelley talked often on politics and religion, and " Love, Liberty, Death." Sophia found him deliciously " mysterious " and " interesting " — his room was cluttered with Greek books; he always had a book under his arm or in his hand; and a little table with pen and ink stood always by his bed.

The somewhat sentimentally romantic charm that Shelley had scarcely had opportunity to exercise since Hogg had observed its effect upon the young ladies of the Boinville-Newton circles claimed another delighted victim. Two days after she had moved to the same pension (November 13), Sophia wrote in her journal: " Saw Mr. Shelley: ' Louisa can you give me some paper? ' — He walked on the terrace before the house with Mlle. du Plantis and Mlle. Clermont: after dinner (ho veduto il signa: lumiere del lampo — ho parlato dei sue sorrelle — Devo ritornare i suoi ricordanze al Signor Parker, Di suoi avventure [?] nella sua gioventù — Gli scrittori — Inchiostro. Si parlò della musica. Ha ascoltata le canzonette [?]. Uomo molto interessante). . . ." [48]

Once (November 22) Shelley visited the Uffizi Gallery with Sophia Stacey and Mr. Tomkins and walked with them afterwards in the Cascine groves. He helped her with her Italian. Mary Shelley, who at the time of Sophia's arrival seemed only "very delicate and interesting," soon grew strong enough to accompany Shelley to one of her tea parties and to walk with Shelley and Sophia in the Cascine (December 11). They were Sophia's guests for Christmas dinner. Mary's opinion of Sophia and her friend was expressed in a letter of December 1 to Maria Gisborne: " There are some ladies come to this house who knew Shelley's family, the younger one was *enthousiasmée* to see him; the elder said that he was a very shocking man, but, finding that we became the mode, she melted, and paid us a visit. She is a little old Welshwoman, without the slightest education. . . . The younger lady . . . is lively and unaffected. She sings well for an English *débutante,* and, if she would learn the scales, would sing exceedingly well, for she has a sweet voice." [49]

Shelley took great delight in Sophia Stacey's singing. He particularly enjoyed hearing her sing "*Non temer, o madre amata* " and de Thierry's ballad "Why declare how much I love thee," often to her own accompaniment on the harp. His lyric " Thou art fair and few are fairer," which he entitled " To Sophia," was written for her to sing. Sometimes she asked him for a song or a poem. Two months after her departure from Florence Shelley complied with one such request by sending her, in a postscript to one of Mary's letters, his lyric " On a Faded Violet ": " I promised you what I cannot perform; a song on singing: — there are only two subjects remaining. I have a few stanzas on one which though simple and rude, look as if they were dictated by the heart." [50] Already (on December 28) he had presented her with a copy of Leigh Hunt's *Literary Pocketbook* for 1819, in which he had written out three poems: " Good-Night," " Love's Philosophy," and " Time Long Past," all of which have somewhat the air of having been written for music. [51]

These poems may or may not have been written originally for Sophia Stacey; there is a stanza evidently intended as part of " Love's Philosophy " which Shelley did *not* present to Miss Stacey and which would indicate that the poem given her may have been adapted from one already written.[52] But there can be no question about his first and most famous poetic gift to her, the passionate lyric " I arise from dreams of thee," whose title, " Indian Serenade," suggests that it, too, was written to be sung. Miss Stacey's journal states that on November 16 Shelley promised to write her some poetry, and that on the next evening after hearing her sing, he handed her the famous lyric. A more personal meaning belongs to the little poem entitled " To ——," which obviously related fragments in Shelley's notebooks show to have been intended for Sophia Stacey:

> I fear thy kisses, gentle maiden,
>   Thou needest not fear mine;
> My spirit is too deeply laden
>   Ever to burden thine.
>
> I fear thy mien, thy tones, thy motion,
>   Thou needest not fear mine;
> Innocent is the heart's devotion
>   With which I worship thine.

Whether or not the declaration in the last two lines was made to Sophia Stacey personally or only to himself, it shows Shelley stating the same attitude he had formerly stated to Elizabeth Hitchener and was soon to state again to both Emilia Viviani and Jane Williams. Shelley's striking consistence in endeavouring to prevent the misunderstanding of such poems has not been sufficiently noted by his more suspicious critics.

It is to be regretted that we know so little of the songs that Shelley enjoyed hearing Sophia Stacey and Claire Clairmont sing; they might furnish some useful clues to the feeling, imagery, and particularly the rhythms of many of Shelley's finest short lyrics. The stanzas " To Sophia," for example, might possibly have been intended to be sung to the same tune as de Thierry's " Why declare how much I love thee? " since the first lines — all that can be checked — are metrically equivalent. Certainly Shelley was charmed with the company of Sophia Stacey, but the beautiful lyrics that she inspired, and even, for the most part, the poem directly addressed to her, were not personal tributes, but tributes to the power of music. Some other lovely voice singing impassioned or sentimental lyrics would have done as well, as Claire Clairmont's had done before, at Marlow. The most impassioned of them all, "The Indian Serenade," was written within a week of the time he first saw Sophia Stacey.

Shelley continued to squire his attractive quasi-kinswoman about Florence until her departure for Rome. "Mr. Shelley walked with me to see our carriage for Rome," Sophia wrote in her journal for December 23, "and the step being high he lifted me out of the carriage." This apparently was only a visit of inspection. On the 29th Sophia and Miss Parry-Jones departed, bearing with them a letter in which Shelley recommended them to the good graces of the Signora Dionigi.

Not long afterwards the Shelleys themselves began to talk seriously of departing for Pisa, though they had come to Florence to remain six months. Florence in January was so cold and rainy, and so socially cheerless, that there seemed no virtue in remaining. Had it not been for a reluctance to interrupt Claire's satisfactory progress in music they would have left earlier. When in the middle of January the frost was broken by a sudden and rapid thaw they decided to depart for Pisa at once. At eight o'clock on the morning of January 26 they set out, descending the Arno by boat to Empoli, thirty miles in five hours. Four hours more by carriage brought them to Pisa,[53] in or near which city Shelley was to pass the rest of his life.

Chapter XXIV

PISA AND LEGHORN:

OLD TROUBLES REVIVE

QUIET IN PISA; REVOLUTIONARY HOPES;

THE CENCI REVIEWS; ATTEMPTED BLACKMAIL;

DEATH OF ELENA; WORRY OVER GODWIN

PISA in 1820 was a sleepy, shrunken old city, much less noisy and bustling than Leghorn. Mary Shelley spoke of it as half-unpopulated.[1] Following the French Revolution and the Napoleonic Wars its population had decreased from 120,000 to 18,000. The Shelleys' first view of Pisa in 1818 had left a rather unfavourable impression. There were no great museums or art galleries and its best architecture was mainly Gothic, which Shelley rather despised in comparison with Græco-Roman remains. Only in his " Tower of Famine," describing the prison of Ugolino, and in " Evening: Ponte al Mare, Pisa," does the city of Pisa make any impression on Shelley's poetry. Nevertheless, he was attracted to its quiet peacefulness and expected to be greatly benefited by its mild climate and good water. The surrounding hills and neighbouring forest, and the yellow Arno, flecked with foam from mountain freshets in spring or flashing like fire beneath a summer sunset, offered occasional thrills of natural beauty that compensated for the absence of the ruins of Rome or Naples and the art galleries of Florence.

On January 29 the party left their temporary quarters at the Tre Donzelle and moved into lodgings at Casa Frasi, Lung' Arno. But Shelley was " irritated to death for the want of a study,"[2] and in little more than a month (March 4) they moved to more commodious quarters on the top floor of the same building, where they remained till the middle of June.

Pisa was the home of one of the most distinguished physicians in Italy, Dr. Vaccà Berlinghieri, a man with a really international reputation who had the added merit, in Shelley's eyes, of being a political and philosophic radical. Here, too, lived the Masons, already good friends of the Shelleys. At Leghorn, distant only three and a half hours' travel, lived the Gisbornes. There were other English at Pisa, but to the Shelleys and Masons they seemed rather a dull lot. Only one of them, Walter Savage Landor, seemed likely to prove interesting, but he, unfortunately, was even more averse to English society than the Shelleys, who were merely indifferent. He declined to meet them. In Claire's journal (May 5) he is represented as saying he would not see a single English person. He had in fact only recently contracted a strong prejudice against Shelley, based upon an account of Shelley's treatment of Harriet probably furnished him by Southey.[3] Of the other "odd English" in Pisa, not omitting Shelley, Claire's journal furnishes an amusing glimpse:

Shelley, who walks about reading a great quarto Encyclopedia with another volume under his arm, Mr. Tatty [Mr. Tighe, known as Mason] who sets potatoes in Pots, and a Mr. Dolby who is rejoicing that he is escaped from Suflano [?] at last although he is 70 some say 80 yrs. of age — he is short and thick and goes about with his pockets stuffed out with books, singing, and a pair of spectacles hung by a gold chain round his neck. He is learned and tells everyone that he would put on a better coat to visit them in if he had another in the world besides the one he wears.

To this account may be added Mrs. Mason's "very amusing stories of English Prudery. Of a Lady who 'mounts her Chastity and rides over us all.' "[4] Claire might have added the name of "the Reverend Colonel [Calicot] Finch," who had been for some time a flitting resident of several Italian cities and was occasionally in Pisa in 1820. The Shelleys had met him before, on April 25, 1819, at Signora Dionigi's, and considered him a ridiculous bore. They bestowed the name of Calicot upon him from the character of that name in Moore's *The Fudge Family In Paris*. One day as Claire and Shelley were taking a walk they became aware of a grand commotion. A tall gentleman with an umbrella was chasing a blacksmith's boy, crying: "Seize him! Seize him!" The boy was cornered and his pursuer began calling loudly for the Governor. Shelley intervened to see that justice was done, but when Claire recognized the Reverend Colonel he allowed her to drag him away, preferring even the jeopardy of justice to the risk of being recognized by such a bore.[5]

A much more violent encounter with a fellow Englishman that has been reported of Shelley in Pisa probably never happened at all. Medwin was told by Shelley of an assault by an English officer of the Portuguese army, supposedly as a result of the *Quarterly's* review of *Laon and Cythna*.[6] Overhearing Shelley call for his mail at the post office, this man, a tall, powerful fellow, exclaimed: "What! Are you that d—d atheist, Shelley?"—and straightway knocked him down. While Shelley lay stunned the man vanished. Mr. Tighe, or Mason, as he preferred to be called, traced him to his inn, whence he had also vanished, and Shelley and Mr. Mason followed him at once to Genoa, whence he had again vanished, this time without trace. It would appear that the story of this fleeing assailant (the third in Shelley's life) should vanish also when we consider its utter absence from the journals and letters of the Shelleys and Claire. In fact, such a journey as one to Genoa and back would have consumed the better part of a week and is totally disproved by the almost daily mention in the journals of Shelley's presence in Pisa.

In such society as Pisa afforded, the Shelleys went about very little. "I ought to tell you," Shelley warned Tom Medwin in inviting him to Pisa, "that we do not enter society. The few people we see are those who suit us, — and I believe nobody but us. I find saloons and compliments too great bores; though I am of an extremely social disposition."[7] Even from their correspondents the Shelleys were somewhat more isolated than usual. Sophia Stacey wrote several letters for a few months

SHELLEY'S HOUSE IN LUNG' ARNO, PISA (first, left), AUTUMN 1820

As photographed in 1905 by Professor W. Hall Griffin

PISA

Engraved by J. T. Wellmore, from a drawing by C. Stanfield

after the separation at Florence, but the correspondence with Amelia Curran had lapsed. Leigh Hunt, oppressed with his own worries, wrote only infrequently, and Hogg, too lazy for much letter-writing, wrote only once to decline Shelley's warm invitation to visit him. One or two letters arrived from Horace Smith and Elizabeth Kent, but Peacock, full of India House business and immersed in matrimony, was more than usually lax in his correspondence.

A great part of the Shelleys' time was spent with the Masons. Mrs. Mason in particular they found delightful company. "We see no one but an Irish lady and her husband, who are settled here," Shelley wrote to Leigh Hunt on April 5. "She is everything that is amiable and wise, and he is very agreeable. You will think it my fate either to find or to imagine some lady of 45, very unprejudiced and philosophical, who has entered deeply into the best and selectest spirit of the age, with enchanting manners, and a disposition rather to like me, in every town that I inhabit. But certainly such this lady is."

Mrs. Mason not only possessed sound common sense, learning, and a humorously tolerant view of life; she was also a calm friend of freedom, though her greatest enthusiasm had died with Robert Emmet. With her reminiscences of the Irish revolt of '93 she set Mary and Claire reading the Irish pamphlets with which her library was still stocked. Looking into the past she could recall an amusing story of how Thomas Holcroft's daughter, employed by her family as a governess, wrote ridiculous poetry and eloped with a nameless man about whom she knew only that he wore a green coat. She remembered how, when Hardy had been acquitted of treason in 1794, she called at his shop to buy shoes of him that proved uncomfortable, and how she accused his lasts of being too aristocratic for her democratic feet. She could also touch lightly on the mildly scandalous details of Lady Oxford's Continental travels. Turning to the more immediate present she could tell of calling upon an old priest whose mistress had just died, and how sympathy gave way to laughter as they listened to his praise of her virtues — "una fresca donna di sessant' anni." Mrs. Mason possessed a good library, and was quite at home reading the _Agamemnon_ of Æschylus with Shelley. The Masons lived at Casa Silva, Via Mala Gonella. Almost every day for six months the Shelleys and Claire went there for tea, dinner, or an afternoon or morning call. Mrs. Mason's personality, and her garden, very probably contributed something to Shelley's " The Sensitive Plant." [8] Claire was especially attracted. She occasionally took it upon herself to straighten out the library and frequently went walking or driving with Laurette and Nerina, the Masons' attractive young daughters.

Except for the Masons, Mary's journal mentions practically no other acquaintance in Pisa from February to June 1820, and Claire's journal mentions only three or four. A Signor Tantini called once and a Signor Gianitti once. Dr. Vaccà, in addition to professional calls, appears to have called several times socially. One of these times was on April 21 during a two days' visit of the Gisbornes, whom Vaccà had known ten years earlier. On this occasion, according to Claire, Shelley and Vaccà engaged in " a very profound and atheistical conversation." At some other time Shelley and Vaccà must have talked about agriculture, one of Vaccà's hobbies, for on April 23 Shelley wrote to the Gisbornes: " I have been thinking, and talking, and reading Agriculture this last week." [9]

The Gisbornes' visit of April 20 was their second, the first having been a visit of one day, on February 28. Shelley made several short visits to Leghorn, January 31–February 2, March 3–6, and April 21. Correspondence between the two families was frequent. Mrs. Gisborne acted as a kind of shopping agent for the Shelleys in attending to many small purchases more easily made in Leghorn, and even in the securing of a new maidservant. But the Gisbornes were about to make a journey to England. As the time for their departure approached, Mary conceived the idea that it would be far better for all concerned if Mrs. Gisborne were to remain behind with the Shelleys. Several urgent letters argued the hardships and expenses of the journey and the uselessness of Mrs. Gisborne's presence in England on a financial mission that could be perfectly well handled by Mr. Gisborne and Henry Reveley. As far as self-respect would allow she urged that her own low spirits would be greatly improved by Mrs. Gisborne's remaining in Pisa. Shelley seconded Mary's arguments, but Mrs. Gisborne remained firm in her decision.[10] On April 28 the Shelleys went to Leghorn to say good-bye, and on May 2 the Gisbornes departed for England, having promised to keep a journal partly for the Shelleys' benefit.

In one matter in which the Gisbornes served Shelley's interests, letters have been either lost or destroyed. One or both of Shelley's visits to Leghorn in February and March seem to have been concerned with Elena Adelaide Shelley, still in Naples. The Shelleys had been prevented from returning to Naples first by the death of William Shelley and then by the birth of Percy Florence. Since they feared to submit Percy Florence to the dangers of travel that had proved so fatal to Clara, some more permanent arrangement must be made for Elena than the one made in anticipation of an early return to Naples. In such a matter, since Shelley had violated Neapolitan law in making a false birth-registration, it might be as well to have the counsel of a lawyer. On March 8, two days after returning from Leghorn, Shelley wrote to the Gisbornes:

> I inclose an outside calculation of the expenses at Naples calculated in ducats. I think it is as well to put into the hands of Del Rosso, or whoever engages to do the business 150 ducats — or more, as you see occasion — but on this you will favour me so far [as to] allow your judgment to regulate mine.

Whatever the " expenses at Naples " were, they had evidently been discussed with the Gisbornes before, and Federico del Rosso, a distinguished attorney at Leghorn,[11] had been either discussed or consulted in connection with it. It is difficult to suppose that the expenses at Naples could refer to anyone except Elena. Shelley's evident desire not to handle the matter from his own home at Pisa becomes clearer in a postscript to his next extant letter to the Gisbornes, eleven days later:

> If it [is] necessary to write again on [letter torn] Del Rosso, ad-dress not *Medwin,* nor Shelley, but simply " Mr. Jones."

This shows the Gisbornes, good friends of Mary as they were, frankly collaborating with Shelley in concealing from Mary something connected with del Rosso which could hardly be anything except the affairs concerning Elena. In a correspondence otherwise well preserved, the previous letter addressed to "Medwin" and Shelley's assumed answer to it are both missing. Neither Mary's journal nor Claire's, at this or any other time, breathes a word of Elena. Either Mary still did not know of Elena or she did know and the subject was so painful that it had to be kept from her attention. That she did know, at least by July, seems certain from Shelley's postscript of July 2 to the Gisbornes, in which he stated that Elena was to join him on her recovery. It is just possible that Mary's antagonistic attitude, either expressed or unexpressed, is criticized in a cryptic line of Claire's journal for February 9, at a time when Mary's journal contains no entries from February 3 to 10: "A Greek author says 'A bad wife is like Winter in a house.'"

WHEN the Shelleys moved to Pisa, Shelley was still suffering from the effects of the severe winter in Florence.[12] This physical and mental depression, in a diminishing degree, continued in Pisa until the return of spring. From January 27 until June Claire's journal mentions no illness of Shelley's, and Mary's journal mentions Shelley only as "unwell" on February 25, "not very well" on March 26, "ill" on April 4, and "not Well" on May 27. Her letters to Mrs. Gisborne show that he was also "ill" on April 8 with "a very bad nervous attack." These expressions seem hardly in tone with those of Shelley. To Medwin Shelley wrote on April 16: "You will find me a wretched invalid unless a great change should take place"; and on May 1: "I have been seriously ill since I last wrote you, but I am now recovering." But even in his own more serious view of his illness, the return of warm weather made Shelley describe his health as "materially better." He added: "I am on the whole greatly benefited by my residence in Italy, and but for certain moral causes, should probably have been able to reinstate my system completely."[13]

The wise and competent Vaccà evidently thought that Shelley's illness was at least partly nervous, and to some extent de-

pendent on his state of mind. He "could only guess" at the
cause, but he enjoined Shelley to abstain from all physicians
and medicine, and trust to Nature. Warm baths and a still
warmer climate than Pisa's seemed highly desirable.[14] In the
spring Shelley began taking the baths at the Baths of Pisa, with
some slight benefit, and in June the family planned to go to the
Baths of Lucca for the summer months. The hotter climate of
southern Italy, however, was for the present out of the question,
on account of the risk to young Percy Florence.

The "moral causes" that Shelley himself recognized as having injured his health previously must have been the distresses
following the deaths of Clara and William, and the situation
created by Godwin's financial crisis. The first of these had
somewhat abated, but it had not vanished, nor was its first shock
of disillusion and disappointment a thing that could ever be
completely obliterated. The problem of Elena must have served
occasionally to reopen the wound.

Godwin's situation was dragging on hopelessly. His letters
were to be dreaded. It is not without significance that when
Mary wrote in her journal for April 4: "Shelley ill," it was immediately preceded by "Letter from Papa." Letters from Elizabeth Kent and Leigh Hunt showed that Hunt's finances were
again desperate, and Shelley was now too straitened himself to
help. He did what he could by writing to Ollier about the debt
of Hunt's that he had guaranteed shortly before leaving England.[15]

Old debts of his own were cropping up in embarrassing profusion. Payment was due on the piano he had bought at Marlow on a deferred-payment plan negotiated through Vincent
Novello. Two money-lenders of Bath, from whom Shelley had
borrowed over five hundred pounds in 1817 demanded a large
payment, reproached him for selling his furniture at Marlow and
departing without leaving an address, and threatened legal
action. Money was still owing to Madocks at Marlow, a debt
which Shelley thought Longdill should pay but which that
"insolent rascal" referred to Shelley through Peacock. Rey-
nell, the printer of A Six Weeks' Tour, pressed for payment,
and when Shelley sought to pay him out of a supposed bal-

ance in Ollier's hands he found that his balance was too trifling to apply. Before July Samuel Hamilton of Weybridge was clamouring for his money for printing *Alastor* in 1816. Sir Timothy heard of these debts and informed Whitton with a certain grim satisfaction: " It is not likely he will soon visit England with so many unwelcome guests to ask how he does by a gentle tap."

Though Shelley was now living economically and well within his income, it was impossible to meet any of these debts at the moment. He sent the Bath money-lenders a plain statement of the case that evidently pacified them, asked Leigh Hunt to arrange another postponement of payment for the piano, directed the publishers of *Alastor* to pay Samuel Hamilton out of a balance probably more trifling than Ollier's, and promised Maddocks full payment in the future, with interest, offering " any security." [16] The creditors, either generous or hopeless, seem to have stayed their hands for a while on these slender reassurances.

To financial worries were added increasing domestic discord between Mary and Claire. Mary's frequent low spirits sorted ill with Claire's vivacity and her critical attitude toward Mary's treatment of Shelley. Quite likely there were frequent little domestic clashes that both ladies were careful to omit from their journals. But, with all their reticence, two or three brief lapses tell a clear story. One recalls Claire's remark of February 9: " A bad wife is like Winter in a house." On June 8 Mary wrote: " A better day than most days, and good reason for it, though Shelley is not well. Clare away at Pugnano." On July 4 Claire's journal began:

> Heigho the Clare and the Ma
> Find something to fight about every day.

At one time, only a few days after the removal to Leghorn, it would appear that Claire was on the verge of leaving, but whether as a result of domestic friction or in fulfilment of her wish to visit Allegra at Ravenna is uncertain. Her journal for June 17 states: " All this Week employed in packing and arranging," and Mary's journal for the same date, showing no signs of packing on her part, remarks only: " We are unhappy and discontented."

Both Mary and Claire were in somewhat worse health than usual, and Claire's nerves were not improved by the fact that there were fresh difficulties with Byron over Allegra. Between January and June some ten letters were exchanged between Claire and Madame Hoppner, who was Claire's none too adequate agent in matters concerning Allegra. Claire also wrote five or six letters to Byron. Since Allegra had visited her mother in 1818 Byron had given up miscellaneous profligacy and had settled down to his comparatively respectable liaison with the Countess Guiccioli. He had grown fonder and prouder of Allegra and had rejected the offer of an English lady to adopt her. Claire was uneasy and wished for another visit from Allegra. Byron's refusal, delivered through the Hoppners, was most decisive. He totally disapproved of the treatment of children in Shelley's family. " Have they *reared* one? " he harshly demanded. Certainly he would not allow Allegra to join them and " perish of Starvation, and green fruit, or be taught to believe that there is no Deity." He conceded only that Claire might see Allegra when there was " convenience of vicinity and access," and said that he was thinking of placing the child in a convent to be educated.[17]

Upon receipt of this " strange jumble " from Mrs. Hoppner Claire spent a day in cogitation and then sent Byron a most emphatic protest against his plan. Sick and miserable as she was, she would forgo seeing Allegra, was " willing to undergo any affliction rather than her whole life should be spoilt by a convent education." What she felt about Byron as she wrote may be judged from her journal entry (May 1): " Write to my damned Brute," which she scratched through with belated prudence that might not have been exercised had she known that Byron was soon to characterize her to Hoppner as " a damned Bitch." Byron's answer to this letter is unknown, except inasmuch as it can be inferred from Claire's journal for May 19 — " Brutal letter from Albè " — and from Shelley's reply to it. Drawn again into his trying rôle of mediator, Shelley wrote Byron the following letter:

Pisa,
May 26th, 1820

My Dear Lord Byron, — On a return from an excursion among the mountains, I find your letter. Clare tells me that she has already answered what relates to the differences of opinion between you and her about Allegra; so I am spared the pain of being an interlocutor in a matter over which, I believe, I have no influence either as it regards her, or you. I wish you had not expressed yourself so harshly in your letter about Clare — because of necessity she was obliged to read it; and I am persuaded that you are mistaken in thinking she has any desire of thwarting your plans about Allegra — even the requests that annoy you spring from an amiable and affectionate disposition. She has consented to give up this journey to Ravenna — which would indeed have been a material inconvenience, and annoyance to me, as well as you — but which, for such a purpose, I hardly felt that I could refuse. When we meet, I can explain to you some circumstances of misrepresentation respecting Allegra which, I think, will lead you to find an excuse for Clare's anxiety. What letters she writes to you I know not; perhaps they are very provoking; but at all events it is better to forgive the weak. I do not say — I do not think — that your resolutions are unwise; only express them mildly — and pray don't *quote me*.

I have read your "Don Juan" in print, and I observe that the *murrain* has killed some of the flock, *i.e.*, that your bookseller has omitted certain passages. The personal ones, however, though I thought them wonderfully strong, I do not regret. What a strange and terrible storm is that at sea, and the two fathers, how true, yet how strong a contrast! Dante hardly exceeds it. With what flashes of divine beauty have you not illuminated the familiarity of your subject towards the end! The love letter, and the account of its being written, is altogether a masterpiece of portraiture; of human nature laid with the eternal colours of the feelings of humanity. Where did you learn all these secrets? I should like to go to school there. I cannot say I equally approve of the service to which this letter was appropriated; or that I altogether think the bitter mockery of our common nature, of which this is one of the expressions, quite worthy of your genius. The power and the beauty and the wit, indeed, redeem all this — chiefly because they belie and refute it. Perhaps it is foolish to wish that there had been nothing to redeem. My tragedy you will find less horrible than you had reason to expect. At all events it is matter-of-fact. If I had known you would have liked to have seen it, I could have sent you a copy, for I printed it in Italy, and sent it to England for publication. Did you see a little poem called "Rosalind and Helen" of mine? It was a mere extempore thing, and worth little, I believe. If you wish to see it, I can send it you.

I hope you know what my feelings, and those of Mary have ever been, about Allegra. Indeed, we are not yet cured of our affection for her; and whatever plans you and Clare agree upon, about her future life, remember that *we*, as friends to all parties, would be most happy to be instrumental to her welfare. I smiled at your protest about what you consider my creed. On the contrary, I think a regard to chastity is quite necessary, as things are, to a young female — that is, to her happiness — and at any time a good habit. As to Christianity — there I am vulnerable; though I should be as little inclined to teach a child disbelief, as belief, as a formal creed. You are misinformed, too, as to our system of physical education; but I can guess the source of this mistake. I say all this, not to induce you to depart from your plan (nor would Clare consent to Allegra's residing with us for any length of time), but only to acquaint you with our feelings on the subject — which are, and must ever be, friendly to you, and yours.

It would give me the greatest pleasure to come into your part of the world and see you in any other character than as the mediator, or rather the interpreter, of a dispute. At all events we shall meet some day in London, I hope *auspicio meliore*. Mary desires not to be forgotten, and I remain,

Dear Lord Byron,
Yours very sincerely,
P. B. SHELLEY

It is no wonder that on the same day on which this letter was written Shelley saw more clearly than before the connection between his health and his state of mind. Mentioning to the Gisbornes his course of baths at the Baths of Pisa as somewhat soothing, he added: "I ought to have peace of mind, leisure, tranquillity; this I expect soon." [18]

DAILY life during the first six months at Pisa was regular and uneventful. Mary's time was divided between her baby (who had a light attack of measles in March), her reading, and her friends the Masons. Her journal records reading about thirty books — novels, memoirs, politics, and Latin. One suspects that the reading may have been partly mechanical. On one day, April 23, she wrote: " Read — I am sure I forget what." On April 1 she finished reading Machiavelli's *Life of Castruccio,* on which her own novel of *Valperga* is based, and in the latter part of the month she began writing her novel and wrote almost daily throughout May. At various times from March to June she also helped Shelley in his translation of Spinoza. The idea that Mary and Shelley had in February of studying mathematics together was apparently abandoned.

Claire had her music, and after March 16, dancing-lessons also. She went about more than Mary, particularly with the Mason children, Laurette and Nerina, and kept up a correspondence with friends in Florence. She, too, was engaged in literary work, translating a French book and composing a work now lost, which she called " Letters from Italy." Her reading was if anything more extensive than Mary's, running to drama, dramatic history, and politics.

Shelley read (but apparently not so much as either Claire or Mary), wrote about half a dozen short poems and a number of letters, spent a good deal of time with the Masons, and from March 17 to April 8 devoted a part of most of his days to translating Spinoza with Mary. Almost half the books that Mary mentions as read by Shelley during the first six months at Pisa were read aloud to Mary in the evening, probably after Claire had retired to her own room. Those read aloud were Isaiah, Jeremiah, *Henry IV,* " Catiline's Plot," Ezekiel, one and a half books of Vergil, Wisdom of Solomon, Beaumont and Fletcher's *Bonduca* and *Thierry and Theodoret,* and *Paradise Regained.* To himself he read " Las Casas on the Indies," " Æschylus," " Athenaeus," " Plato," Soli's *History of Mexico,* " Hobbes," *Political Justice,* Voltaire's *Memoirs* and Condorcet's *Life of Voltaire,* the *Phædrus* and *Phædo* of Plato, and Theocritus — several of which were also read by Mary and Claire.

This is for Shelley a slight record of reading, or of all activities combined, for six months. A part of his comparative inaction Shelley explained to Hunt [19] as due to the lack of a

study previous to changing lodgings on March 14. The ill effect
of the winter upon Shelley's vitality lasted longer and probably
accounts for more. Possibly a still greater reason, on which both
Mary and Claire were silent and on which Shelley affords a
clue only in his letters to the Gisbornes, was the lack of " peace
of mind " and " tranquillity."

Among the four poems known to have been written by Shelley in the first half of 1820 all but the " Ode to Liberty " are
identical with or similar to the poems discussed in Chapter xx,
some or all of which Shelley at one time intended publishing
together with " Julian and Maddalo " as " all my saddest poems
raked up into one heap." " The Sensitive Plant," written in
March, has already been mentioned in this connection. " A
Vision of the Sea," written in April, is a strange, detailed picture
of a shipwreck in which a mother and her child are finally left
alone on a sinking ship whose cargo of tigers has been loosed
by the storm. This may or may not reflect Shelley's view of
Mary's withdrawal into herself. The 124-line fragment " Orpheus " presents the search for a lost Eurydice with almost
autobiographical poignance:

> . . . so Orpheus, seized and torn
> By the sharp fangs of an insatiate grief,
> Mænad-like waved his lyre in the bright air,
> And wildly shrieked " Where she is, it is dark! " [20]

Even the beautiful, apparently playful little poem called " An
Exhortation," dated 1819 when published by Mrs. Shelley, but
" Pisa, April 1820 " in Shelley's hand in the Harvard manu-
script, contains the significant lines,

> Where light is, camelions change!
> Where love is not, poets do:
> Fame is love disguised: if few
> Find either, never think it strange
> That poets range.

Mary Shelley printed three other poems as written in 1820, all
of which touch upon the same theme — " The Question," " The

189

Two Spirits — An Allegory," and " Time Long Past." She dated
none of these three poems more specifically than 1820. We
have seen in Chapter xxiii that " Time Long Past " was written
at least as early as December 1819. Since Mary Shelley also
post-dated two other poems presented to Sophia Stacey in December 1819 (" Love's Philosophy " and Good-Night ") one is
justified in not accepting her dates too confidently.

In the absence of more objective data these poems, hitherto
ignored as having a bearing upon Shelley's domestic life, may
easily be overemphasized. The surrounding circumstances indicate that they do reflect moments of dejection and unhappiness connected with the earlier crisis. But they do not indicate
a fresh crisis so much as a considerably milder aftermath of the
first one. More of them than we know may actually have been
written earlier and misdated by Mary when later published.

THOUGH Mary was not what she had been before Clara's death,
she was still more than anyone else; and though Shelley had
his moments of bitter disillusion, he also had hopes. He wore
a ring with the motto " *Il buon tempo verrà* " (The good time
will come) as a kind of symbol of his belief that " There is a
tide both in public and private affairs, which awaits both men
and nations." [21]

In one brief comment to Hunt at this time Shelley condensed
much of the disillusion and continued faith that had gone into
his poetry of the preceding year:

> The system of society as it exists at present must be overthrown
> from the foundations with all its superstructure of maxims and of
> forms before we shall find anything but disappointment in our inter-
> course with any but a few select spirits. This remedy does not seem
> to be one of the easiest. But the generous few are not the less held
> to tend with all their efforts towards it. If faith is a virtue in any case
> it is so in politics rather than religion; as having a power of producing
> a belief in that which is at once a prophecy and a cause.[22]

A strong inspiration to Shelley at this time, and also to Mary
and Claire, was the growth of the spirit of freedom in Spain.

190

They received Galignani's Paris weekly *Messenger* and scanned it eagerly for news of revolutionary progress. On March 16 Claire's journal recorded two insurgent victories, and on March 26 Mary wrote to inform Mrs. Gisborne of the triumph of freedom in Spain: " The beloved Ferdinand has proclaimed the Constitution of 1812, and called the Cortes. The Inquisition is abolished, the dungeons opened and the patriots pouring out. This is good. I should like to be in Madrid now." [23] Shelley even thought of a voyage to Spain on account of his health and also " on account of the glorious events of which it is at this moment the theatre." [24]

These " glorious events " stirred Shelley to produce his lofty " Ode to Liberty."

> A glorious people vibrated again
> The lightning of the Nations —

bringing to the poet a vision. He saw all the rude, blind savagery of the world before the spirit of freedom was born, the splendid birth of Liberty in Greece and its rebirth later in Rome, the thousand years of darkness during which it seemed dead, and its mysterious resurrection in Saxon England and mediæval Italy, to shine with greater glory in such later spirits as Luther and Milton. Then he saw another reign of oppression; it was confusedly broken by the French Revolution, which in turn came to be dominated by Napoleon, a mightier tyrant still, the " Anarch " of Freedom's " own bewildered powers.'" At nearly the same time Shelley was making a similar survey of the progress of freedom in his *Philosophical View of Reform,* and he was to do it later in his " Defence of Poetry," this time emphasizing more fully the relationship between Art and Freedom implicit in the fourth and fifth stanzas of the " Ode to Liberty." From the history of freedom Shelley turns in his ode to its present prospects, as he was also doing at greater length in his *Philosophical View of Reform.* He seeks to awake the spirit of Liberty which he says yet lives in " king-deluded " Germany; and in words that must sound strangely modern to critics of a more recent English government he calls upon England to take inspiration from Spain:

England yet sleeps: was she not called of old?
Spain calls her now. . . .

In this poem we have yet another evidence of the intense
unity of Shelley's artistic purpose in 1819 and 1820. In spite
of personal distractions that in 1818 had caused him to consider
suicide and to write of himself as a madman, he held with utter
concentration to his purpose announced in "Julian and Maddalo" of continuing his fight against Tyranny. The "Ode to
Liberty" overleaps Shelley's philosophic and æsthetic growth
of eight years and shows that in his war against oppression Shelley was very little changed from the inexperienced youth who
had written *Queen Mab* and the letters to Elizabeth Hitchener.
The fifteenth and sixteenth stanzas, but for their greater perfection, might easily be mistaken for passages from *Queen Mab*.
The fifteenth stanza begins:

Oh, that the free would stamp the impious name
Of *King* [25] into the dust! or write it there,
So that this blot upon the page of fame
Were as a serpent's path, which the light air
Erases, and the flat sands close behind! . . .

and the sixteenth:

O, that the wise from their bright minds would kindle
Such lamps within the dome of this dim world,
That the pale name of *Priest* might shrink and dwindle
Into the hell from which it first was hurled. . . .

But Shelley's old disharmony between free will and Necessity
had vanished when Intellectual Beauty supplanted Necessity in
his mind, and now (stanza xvii), as in *Prometheus Unbound* and
earlier in "Julian and Maddalo," Shelley insisted that oppressions were founded upon the consent of man's "own high will."
To do his own share toward awakening the England that yet
slept, Shelley asked Hunt if he could suggest any bookseller
who would publish his *Philosophical View of Reform* — "boldly
but temperately written — and I think readable" — and also
"a little volume of *popular songs* wholly political, and destined

to awaken and direct the imagination of reformers." [26] It is
only in connection with the intense strength and unity of Shelley's poetry and prose of 1819 and 1820 that his nearest perfect
poem, "Ode to the West Wind," can be fully appreciated.
Written in the autumn of 1819 and published with *Prometheus
Unbound*, its description of himself as a frail form scarcely able
to sustain the weight of the " superincumbent hour " loses much
of its appearance of sentimental self-pity when seen as a deep
realization of the disparity between the tremendous things that
must somehow be done and the inadequacy of one mind and
body to such a task. The poem is in fact a reaffirmation of faith
in spite of discouragement, and a sustained prayer for power
and opportunity to carry out the purposes that he had resolved
upon in childhood:

> Drive my dead thoughts over the universe
> Like withered leaves to quicken a new birth!
> And, by the incantation of this verse,
>
> Scatter, as from an unextinguished hearth
> Ashes and sparks, my words among mankind!
> Be through my lips to unawakened earth
>
> The trumpet of a prophecy! O, Wind,
> If Winter comes, can Spring be far behind?

Like *Prometheus Unbound*, this poem finds in the revolution
of the seasons a semi-mystical assurance of social regeneration.
Like *Prometheus Unbound* again, it was no sudden outburst,
but a thoroughly natural and logical culmination of thoughts
that had long been germinating. In March 1812 (as I have
previously quoted him in Chapter viii) he had rebuked the
pessimism of the Malthusians with the same argument. And
in 1817, in two consecutive stanzas in *The Revolt of Islam*
(IX, 21, 22), he had fully anticipated both the regenerative
significance of autumn and spring in the " Ode to the West
Wind " and the apostrophe to Spring which begins Act II of
Prometheus Unbound.

During the first six months of 1820 Shelley devoted a little
attention to the practical aspects of scattering his words among

mankind. Besides seeking information about a publisher for his *Philosophical View of Reform* and his " popular songs," he gently chided Hunt for having completely ignored receipt of " Peter Bell the Third " and the letter on Carlile.[27] He sent new poems to be published with *Prometheus Unbound* and arranged for Mr. Gisborne, who had heard it read, to read the proof after his arrival in London.[28] It was his favourite poem, he said, and required fine ink, good paper, and especial care in printing, even though he realized it would not sell. He was indifferent about the publication of " Peter Bell " and " Julian and Maddalo," provided they were not published over his name. In a comparative sense Shelley was also indifferent to *The Cenci*, as not close enough to his most vital interests in writing, but he was pleased with its sales and even with a false report that a pirated edition had appeared in Paris. He urged a new edition at once. When adverse criticisms of the play reached him he protested, in spite of his indifference. To Ollier he asserted that it was *not* unfitted for the stage, and to Leigh Hunt that its scenes were as delicate and free from offence as those of Sophocles, Massinger, Voltaire, and Alfieri.

Shelley was still somewhat dissatisfied with Ollier as a publisher. Though Ollier was generous as to royalties, allowing twenty per cent when Shelley would have accepted ten, he was dilatory and unenterprising. " I am afraid his demerits are very heavy," Shelley told Hunt, but at the same time he realized that he was practically in Ollier's power, since probably no other publisher would take over his books. There was really nothing to do, he concluded, except to " make the best of a bad business." [29]

Prometheus Unbound was still in the press, but *The Cenci* appeared about the middle of March and received immediately far more critical attention than any previous work of Shelley's. Ten reviews appeared between March 19 and July 26, 1820.[30] It did Shelley no good with the conservatives that the play was dedicated to Leigh Hunt and that the first notice it received was a brief note in the *Examiner* calling it " undoubtedly the greatest dramatic production of the day" and promising a fuller review later. The promised review appeared in the *Indicator*, July 19 and 26. It was a full and sympathetic tribute. The *Theatrical Inquisitor* for April also admired the play greatly, without reservation. "If purity of praise," it concluded,

> can atone to Mr. Shelley for the rough terms in which it is delivered, we beg him to believe us sincere, though unpolished, in its application. As a first dramatic effort "The Cenci" is unparalleled for the beauty of every attribute with which drama can be endowed . . .

At the other extreme stood the *Literary Gazette*, a powerful weekly with a keen eye for impiety and immorality, both of which it professed to find in *The Cenci*. It began: "Of all the abominations which intellectual perversion, and poetical atheism, have produced in our times, this tragedy appears to us to be the most abominable." And without having once wandered from this theme it reached its conclusion: "We now most gladly take leave of this work; and sincerely hope, that should we continue our literary pursuits for fifty years, we shall never need again to look into one so stamped with pollution, impiousness, and infamy." Thus the *Literary Gazette* embarked upon an unintermittent, single-minded, pious, and unscrupulous effort to exterminate the Amalekite that lasted until after Shelley's death. The *Monthly Magazine* granted Shelley's "original and extensive genius" but felt mainly "sentiments of horror and disgust" for the play on account of its subject. The *London Magazine and Monthly Critical and Dramatic Review*, the *New Monthly Magazine*, the *Edinburgh Monthly Review*, and the *London Magazine* were all horrified by the shocking story and by Shelley's "moral perversity." Yet all of them acknowledged the very great genius of the author. "The doctrines they inculcate," said the *London Magazine and Monthly Critical and Dramatic Review*, referring to Shelley's previous poems, "are of the most evil tendency, the characters they depict are of the most horrible description; but in the midst of these disgraceful passages, there are beauties of such exquisite, such redeeming qualities, that we adore while we pity — we admire while we execrate. . . ." The *New Monthly* felt that "every honest

heart " must feel wonder and disgust at the strange perversity
of Shelley's theme, yet it freely admitted that there was " great
power in many parts of this shocking tragedy " and singled out
Shelley's own favourite passage, Cenci's curse, as a touch of
" singularly profound and sublime " insight. The *London Magazine,* while fully castigating the play's "radical foulness of
moral composition," treated it as the "production of a man of
great genius, and of a most unhappy moral constitution." At
some length it anticipated Hazlitt's later suggestion that personal vanity, aggravated perhaps by a tinge of disease, formed
the basis of the author's faults.

The *Edinburgh Monthly Review,* also mixing moral abhorrence with æsthetic appreciation, concluded by letting an important cat out of the bag: "Not a few of our contemporaries
. . . seem to us to labour under a foolish timidity, which prevents them doing justice to the genius, at the same time that they
inflict due chastisement on the errors of this remarkable young
man. . . . His genius is rich to overflowing in all the nobler
requisites for tragic excellence, and were he to choose and
manage his themes with some decent measure of regard for the
just opinions of the world, we have no doubt he might easily
and triumphantly overtop all that has been written during the
last century for the English stage." This exposure of an element
of hypocrisy in the criticism of Shelley, and even the implied
bribe, is suggestively similar to the attitude already taken by
Blackwood's Edinburgh Magazine.

An author less predisposed to consider himself the prey of
hostile reviewers might have found more encouragement in the
criticism of *The Cenci* than Shelley perceived. But Shelley was
far more concerned with propagating the ideas which the reviewers generally assailed than in securing recognition of the
" genius " which they generally admitted and praised. Yet when
Ollier sent him some or all of these reviews a few months later,
his comment did not entirely ignore their more favourable elements:

The reviews of my " Cenci " (though some of them, and especially
that marked " John Scott," are written with great malignity) on the

JOHN SCOTT, EDITOR OF THE *LONDON MAGAZINE*

Lithograph by Edward Morton from an original drawing

whole give me as much encouragement as a person of my habits of thinking is capable of receiving from such a source, which is, inasmuch as they coincide with, and confirm, my own decisions. My next attempt (if I should write more) will be a drama, in the composition of which I shall attend to the advice of my critics, to a certain degree, but I doubt whether I *shall* write more. I could be content either with the Hell or the Paradise of poetry; but the torments of its purgatory vex me, without exciting my power sufficiently to put an end to the vexation.[31]

It may have some bearing upon the real impression made upon Shelley by the reviews of *The Cenci* that he chose the time of their appearance to write a letter to Robert Southey that should ordinarily have been written much earlier:

> *Pisa,*
> *June 26, 1820*
>
> Dear Sir,
> Some friends of mine persist in affirming that you are the author of a criticism which appeared some time since in the *Quarterly Review* on the " Revolt of Islam."
> I know nothing that would give me more sincere pleasure than to be able to affirm from your own assurance that you were not guilty of that writing. I confess I see such strong internal evidence against the charge, without reference to what I think I know of the generous sensibility of your character, that had my own conviction only been concerned, I should never have troubled you to deny what I firmly believe you would have spurned to do.
> Our short personal intercourse has always been remembered by me with pleasure, and (when I recalled the enthusiasm with which I then considered your writings,) with gratitude for your notice. We parted, I think, with feelings of mutual kindness. The article in question, except in reference to the possibility of its having been written by you, is not worth a moment's attention.
> That an unprincipled hireling, in default of what to answer in a published composition, should, without provocation, insult the domestic calamities of a writer of the adverse party — to which perhaps their victim dares scarcely advert in thought — that he should make those calamities the theme of the foulest and the falsest slander — that all this should be done by a calumniator without a name — with the cowardice, no less than the malignity, of an assassin — is too

common a piece of charity among Christians (Christ would have taught them better), too common a violation of what is due from man to man among the pretended friends of social order, to have drawn one remark from me, but that I would have you observe the arts practised by that party for which you have abandoned the cause to which your early writings were devoted. I had intended to have called on you, for the purpose of saying what I now write, on my return to England; but the wretched state of my health detains me here, and I fear leaves my enemy, were he such as I could deign to contend with, an easy, but a base victory, for I do not profess paper warfare. But there is a time for all things.

I regret to say that I shall consider your neglecting to answer this letter a substantiation of the fact which it is intended to settle — and *therefore* I shall assuredly hear from you.

> Dear Sir, accept the best wishes of
> Yours truly,
> P. B. SHELLEY

Thus began an interchange of criticisms and reproofs between two former friends that lasted until September and altered the opinions of neither. Southey denied authorship of the *Quarterly Review* article, but seized upon the occasion to make a vigorous and apparently well-meant criticism of Shelley's opinions and conduct. Like the reviewers, he accused Shelley of debasing real genius by devoting it to monstrous and pernicious ends, and he pointed to Shelley's own experience as proof that such doctrines and conduct lead to unhappiness — Christian principles might have saved him and might still save him. These admonitions, he warmly protested, were dictated neither by personal animosity nor by party spirit, but by a genuine, sympathetic interest surviving from the old friendship at Keswick.

Shelley replied that he could never think well of Christianity as long as its effects seemed to be to transform men of amiable manners and high accomplishments into men of the most unChristlike violence and harshness. Southey himself had been so betrayed into a presumptuously cruel condemnation of his private life. " You select a single passage out of a life otherwise not only spotless, but spent in an impassioned pursuit of virtue, which looks like a blot, merely because I regulated my domestic arrangements without deferring to the notions of the vulgar, although I might have done so quite as conveniently had I descended to their base thoughts — this you call *guilt*." Most solemnly Shelley protested that this accusation was false, that he had been in no way responsible for Harriet's ruin, and that he could, if he wished, tell a tale that would open Southey's eyes. As for the calamities that Southey believed to be the fruit of his opinions, " The immediate fruits of all new opinions are indeed calamity to the promulgators and professors; but we are the end of nothing, and it is in acting well, in contempt of present advantage, that virtue consists." Some day, he concluded, he hoped for a conversation with Southey in London, but meanwhile their differences were too great to make further correspondence useful.

Nevertheless Southey returned stoutly to the attack, insisting that Shelley was morally responsible for Harriet's ruin, and pointing to orthodox Christianity as the only proper guide.[32] To this Shelley did not reply. Two letters of Southey's written much later show that his view of Shelley's character hardened with the years. " With all his genius (and I think *most* highly of it)," he wrote to Sir Henry Taylor on February 28, 1830, " he was a base, bad man." The next day he amplified his phrase thus: " I meant that he was a liar and a cheat: that he was a coward was less [word illegible] unfortunate [word illegible] not his fault — but he paid no regard to truth nor to any kind of moral obligation. It was mortifying to discover this, for I never saw a youth of whom I could have hoped better things." [33]

THE GISBORNES were now in London, where they had arrived on June 4. On their overland journey they had met a Swiss banker named Heinsh who claimed to have been Shelley's banker in Geneva and who informed them that Shelley was both an evil and an ignorant man. In London they soon gathered other personal impressions. At first Godwin was comparatively reticent about Shelley. He conceded that Shelley had genius and some benevolence, but accused him of immorality, instability, and irresponsible enthusiasm, failure to fulfil a solemn promise on which Godwin had depended, and of "a particular enmity against truth, so that he utters falsehoods and makes exaggerations even when no end is to be answered by them." As he saw more of Mrs. Gisborne he seldom missed an opportunity of showing his dislike for Shelley. Finally, just before the departure of the Gisbornes in early September, Godwin called and gave them a detailed history, which he had also written out for their benefit, of his financial dealings with Shelley from the beginning. He maintained that Shelley had constantly misled him with false hopes and "would certainly be the death of him."

Coleridge, Mrs. Gisborne found, knew Shelley only from Southey's accounts and admired his genius while condemning his conduct and principles. Mr. Fenwick had formed a similar opinion at second hand (Mrs. Gisborne thought from Lamb), but was "staggered in his opinion when we told him how much we admired S . . . and that there was not a person in the world that we preferred to him." [34]

The Gisbornes found Mrs. Godwin far more bitter toward Mary than Godwin was toward Shelley. She considered Mary her greatest enemy in the world and held Mary responsible for the defection of Claire, on whom she had built high hopes for the future. Though she had no personal feelings against Mrs. Gisborne, she explained through Godwin and Mr. Fenwick that she found it impossible ever to talk with one who was so much a friend to Mary.

With the Hunts, however, the Gisbornes found Shelleyan conversation most congenial. "We talked much in praise of the S—s . . . we laughed at S's little occasional aristocratical sallies, but we agreed that in general it is the aristocracy of superior with regard to inferior intellect." Hunt told them that he had ready for delivery a blast against Gifford (his *Ultra-Crepidarius*?) that would silence the *Quarterly's* attacks upon Shelley, and that he had only withheld it so far on account of Gifford's serious illness. Hunt's opinion of Shelley expressed at this time is startlingly in advance of the criticism of his day. It suggests some understanding of Shelley's effort to expand the means of appealing to the imagination (as in *Prometheus Unbound*, then

just published). Mrs. Gisborne reported that he considered
Shelley

> as the discoverer of a pure original exposing of human knowledge,
> from whence other men, having perceived its existence, will dig
> channels in which rivers of knowledge will flow, in all directions, less
> pure than at their source, but more adapted to the gross senses and
> comprehension of the multitude.[35]

IN ITALY, meanwhile, fresh troubles were accumulating for the
Shelleys. On June 12 Mary wrote in her journal: " Paolo. Dine
and spend the evening at Casa Silva; sleep there "; and on the
next day: " Read ' Fleetwood.' Shelley goes to Leghorn, and
returns." Claire's journal notes Shelley's visit to Leghorn, but
does not mention Paolo. Shelley had just returned from Ca-
sciano on June 11, where presumably he was making final arrangements for a house there during the summer months. The
one word " Paolo " in Mary's journal, however, is the key to a
complete revision of the Shelleys' plans for the next few months.
On June 14 Mary wrote in her journal: " Read ' Fleetwood.'
Pack. Read ' Vicar of Wakefield.' " And on June 15: " Pack.
Go to Leghorn."

These bare details are made fairly intelligible by turning to
passages in two letters written by the Shelleys to the Gisbornes,
who already knew about Paolo and the earlier events in Naples
of which he was now taking advantage. On June 18 Mary wrote
to Mrs. Gisborne from Casa Ricci, the Gisbornes' home on the
outskirts of Leghorn:

> Where am I? Guess. In a little room, before a deal table, looking
> out on a podere. . . . Nay, here we are; we have taken possession.
> What do you say? The truth is, my dear Friend, a variety of cir-
> cumstances have occurred, not of the most pleasant nature, since you
> left us, and we have been obliged to reform our plans. We could
> not go to the Baths of Lucca, and finding it necessary to consult an
> attorney, we thought of Del Rosso, and came here. Are you pleased
> or vexed? Our old friend Paolo was partly the cause of this, by en-
> tering into an infamous conspiracy against us. There were other cir-
> cumstances that I shall not explain till we meet. That same Paolo is

a most superlative rascal. I hope we have done with him, but I know not, since as yet we are obliged to guess as to his accomplices.[36]

Except for a distressed passage about Godwin's financial difficulties and the remark that Shelley's recent troubles had " of course " induced a bilious attack, the rest of Mary's long letter consists of humorous chatter about the Gisbornes and their Livornese neighbours and servants. In later letters to the Gisbornes that are extant Mary made no further references to Paolo, nor did she ever refer to the illness of Elena Shelley in Naples, which was an additional distress to Shelley at the time.

Shelley's comment on Paolo's attempted blackmail adds little to Mary's account and is mentioned almost as a footnote to more distressing news from Naples. On June 30 he wrote to the Gisbornes:

My poor Neapolitan, I hear has a fever of dentition. I suppose she will die and leave another memory to these which already torture me. I am waiting the next post with anxiety but without much hope. What remains to me? Domestic peace and fame? You will laugh when you hear me talk of the latter; indeed it is only a shadow. The seeking of a sympathy with the unborn and the unknown is a feeble mood of allaying the love within us; and even that is beyond the grasp of so weak an aspirant as I. Domestic peace I might have — I may have — if I see you I shall have — but have not, for Mary suffers dreadfully about the state of Godwin's circumstances. I am very nervous, but better in general health. We have had a most infernal business with Paolo whom, however, we have succeeded in crushing. I write from Henry's study, and I send you some verses I wrote the first day I came, which will show you that I struggle with despondency.[37]

A postscript to this letter, dated July 2, 1820, adds: " I have later news of my Neapolitan. I have taken every possible precaution for her, and hope that they will succeed. She is to come to us as soon as she recovers." But Elena did not recover. She had died, according to the official records of Naples, on June 9, at three o'clock in the morning.[38] Her death, like her life, is entirely ignored in the journals of Mary and Claire. From Shelley it drew a bitter comment in an undated letter written early in

July: " My Neapolitan charge is dead. It seems as if the destruction that is consuming me were an atmosphere which wrapt
and *infected* everything connected with me." [39] After these
words no member of the Shelley or Gisborne families ever
wrote or spoke a single word about Elena Adelaide Shelley
that has survived. When Mary Shelley passionately denied
Elise Foggi's story of Elena's birth she confined her denial to
Elise's version of the story and continued to ignore Elena
Adelaide.

Shelley's last words about his " Neapolitan " are immediately
followed by his conclusion of the episode with Paolo:

The rascal Paolo has been taking advantage of my situation at
Naples in December 1818 to attempt to extort money by threatening
to charge me with the most horrible crimes. He is connected with
some English here who hate me with a fervor that almost does credit
to their phlegmatic brains, and listen and vent the most prodigious
falsehoods. An ounce of civet good apothecary to sweeten this dunghill of a world.

Neither Mary nor Shelley mentioned the precise nature of
Paolo's " prodigious falsehoods " about " horrible crimes." Anyone who already knew about Elena could hardly fail to understand what they were, and any other reader of the letters would
hardly see the connection between Paolo and Elena. Mrs. Gisborne's journal for August 28, 1820 seems to show that she knew
the true story, for she inferred from what the Shelleys had
written that if Paolo made his charges public, Claire's reputation would be damaged as well as Shelley's. This supports the
inference from Shelley's letters that the Gisbornes knew the
story of Elena substantially as it has been reconstructed in
Chapter xx, and it shows that Paolo's activities failed to shake
their confidence in it.[40]

THE SAME letters that record the death of Elena and the villainy
of Paolo show that the Shelleys were in perhaps even greater
distress over Godwin's catastrophic finances. Godwin was begging with a kind of tragic dignity to be relieved at once, or

else allowed to face his catastrophe without false hopes. " Do not let me be led into a fool's paradise. It is better to look my ruin full in the face at once than to be amused for ever with promises, at the same time that nothing is done." [41] The Gisbornes had been anxiously charged to make a full and prompt report of Godwin's real situation. Shelley now regarded Godwin as "the only sincere enemy" he had in the world and yet felt more than ever compelled to admiration of his intellectual powers and even the moral resources of his character.[42] His old dream of being the means of preserving the world's greatest living apostle of truth had turned bitter when the means of preservation were no longer at hand and when the apostle himself was a domestic enemy and a financial vulture whose implacable demands even if granted seemed unlikely to promise a rescue. Yet Shelley, probably more on Mary's account now than on Godwin's, wished to do all he could. Mary's· state of mind was almost frantic. Immediately following her account of Paolo (June 18) she complained of Mrs. Gisborne's failure to send her journal as· promised, and added:

Tell my Father I have not heard from him a long long time, and am dreadfully anxious. The path of our life is a very thorny one, as you well know, nor is my anxiety concerning him the least of my troubles. You will imagine how teazed we were when I tell you that the fright I had gave our poor Percy a violent diarrhœa; he is now well; but we were much alarmed, as the poor little thing suffered, but he had no fever, so he has lost none of his strength, and is now blither than ever — he is the merriest babe in the world.[43]

It was on June 30 that Mary's journal recorded receipt of a "letter from Papa" that calamitously made up for his former epistolary lapses. Unless Godwin could raise £500 at once to effect a compromise with his creditors, he would be ruined. On June 30 also Mary wrote an agonized letter to the Gisbornes, beseeching them to advance £400 against Shelley's· enclosed note, which, with a hundred pounds already paid by Horace Smith on Shelley's account, might be Godwin's salvation. Very likely without Mary's knowledge Shelley also wrote to the Gisbornes on the same day:

It is needless that I should explain to you the kind of letter which a real embarrassment makes Godwin write to Mary, or the degree in which this cause combines with a thousand greater and lesser accessories to disquiet me. With respect to the [Mary's] proposal itself, I can only say that by accepting it you will confer on me an equal good, and impress me with no less of your kindness, than if the money were destined to the relief of some beloved friend, as it will now be applied to the need of my bitterest enemy.[44]

Shelley felt bitterly humiliated to be compelled to ask help from the Gisbornes under such circumstances. He knew that their own finances were not flourishing; he even doubted that the money, if obtained, would confer any real benefit on Godwin. His principal reason in writing separately from Mary, he explained, was to insist that no money should actually be paid over to Godwin until the papers of release were drawn up and signed. All he could do himself was to endeavour to keep his written engagement to pay Godwin fifty pounds a quarter. He suggested that the Gisbornes write to him under cover to Mrs. Mason, "if you have any communications unfit for Mary's agitated mind." [45]

The Gisbornes were either unable or unwilling to come to the rescue, and Godwin's miserable situation remained unchanged. Whatever frantic or stoical letters he wrote to the Shelleys during the next two months have been lost, but they resulted on August 7 in a long letter from Shelley in which he gave full reasons for the very firm stand he was resolved thenceforth to maintain.

In this letter Shelley reviewed his whole financial relationship with Godwin and stated at length why he both could not and should not yield to continued demands. His own finances, he asserted, had become more involved than even Mary knew. Any fresh drain upon his resources would involve him in personal peril. He owed nearly £2,000 to creditors, most of whom were importunate and some of whom were now threatening suit. Within a few years he had given Godwin between £4,000 and £5,000 procured largely from money-lenders at an actual cost of nearly four times the amount realized. His credit with money-lenders was practically gone and his fortune almost wrecked. Godwin had been benefited by the sacrifice no more than if the money had been thrown into the sea. The only result, Shelley bitterly remarked, was the *good will* created by the sacrifice. He denied Godwin's assertion that he had promised £500 out of his present year's income; he denied, with one exception, ever promising Godwin anything, save on condition of ability to pay.[46] He promised still to do what he could, but he could not produce the £400 that Godwin demanded.

Finally, Shelley insisted firmly that he would not allow Mary to be further tormented by letters that almost seemed to be written with that purpose:

Mary is now giving suck to her infant, in whose life, after the frightful events of the last two years, her own seems wholly to be bound up. Your letters from their style and spirit (such is your erroneous notion of taste) never fail to produce an appalling effect on her frame. On one occasion agitation of mind produced through her a disorder in the child, similar to that which destroyed our little girl two years ago. . . . On that occasion Mary at my request authorised me to intercept such letters or information as I might judge likely to disturb her mind. That discretion I have exercised with the letter to which this is a reply. The correspondence, therefore, rests between you and me, if you should consider any discussion of a similar nature with that in which you have lately been engaged with Mary necessary after the full explanation which I have given of my views, and the unalterable decision which I have pronounced. Nor must the correspondence with your daughter on a similar subject be renewed. . . . She has not, nor ought she to have, the disposal of money; if she had, poor thing, she would give it all to you.[47]

Shelley's firmness with Godwin, and the almost desperate state of his finances, lend lustre to his generous behaviour toward the Gisbornes at the same time. Throughout the year Shelley had urged Henry Reveley forward in the construction of his steamboat. But if it should be to Henry's advantage to remain in England, Shelley was quite willing to sacrifice the boat and the considerable sums he had invested in it. It was for Henry's good, he said, that he had encouraged the project and he wanted no attention to a " mere form " (that is, a debt

of several hundred pounds) to influence the decision as between Italy and England.[48]

THE SHELLEYS and Claire remained in the Gisbornes' home from
June 15 to August 5. Daily life there was even more uneventful
than at Pisa, for they knew few people at Leghorn, and Claire
and Mary were both in worse health than usual. For ten days
after their arrival Mary was " too much oppressed and too lan-
guid to do anything." [49] Soon afterwards, however, she was
studying Greek with Shelley.[50] As for Shelley, he wrote Godwin
on August 7: " I am tormented beyond all expression by nephritic pains. . . . The surgeon here assured me that my disease
is nephritic, and adds, as my consolation, that it has no tendency
to shorten life." [51] Occasionally they took walks in the surrounding country or to the seaside, sometimes with one another, sometimes with members of the Ricci family, the Gisbornes' neighbours and landlords. Shelley and Claire each made two or
three short trips to Pisa, and on July 20 Mr. Mason, his eleven-
year-old daughter Laurette, and Miss Field visited them for the
day. As usual, all three read every day. Shelley read Euripides,
the Greek romances, Lucretius (with Mary), and Forteguerri's
Ricciardetto aloud. On July 14 he finished his translation of
the Homeric " Hymn to Mercury." Claire was still writing her
" Letters from Italy " and was still endeavouring vainly to secure
some satisfaction about Allegra.

A touch of humour was occasionally added to the predominantly dreary tone of existence by the presence of the Gisbornes'
neighbours and servants. Mary pretended in her letters that
the Signorina Appolonia Ricci was pining dreadfully for the
absent Henry Reveley. The servants Giuseppe and Annunziata
had just become the parents of a son for whom a lively christening party was given; Giuseppe insisted with ridiculous earnestness that he looked the very image of Mr. Gisborne. If the
Shelleys found private amusement in this circumstance, Giuseppe's turn came later. A sudden violent dispute having broken
out between Giuseppe and Annunziata, Shelley endeavoured
in vain to compose the matter and in a pretended rage chased

Giuseppe from the house with a pistol. With Shelley in close pursuit, threatening murder, Giuseppe darted round a corner and hid in the shrubbery while Shelley raced ahead. Shelley returned to the house to find the couple in the most amicable conversation, using many " *caro's* " and " *carissima's,*" as if nothing had occurred. They denied, in fact, that anything had occurred, and with Mary's help half persuaded him that the whole episode must have been an illusion.[52]

Shelley had immediately taken over Henry Reveley's study. Thence, surrounded by mysterious pieces of machinery — " Great screws, and cones, and wheels, and groovèd blocks " — he wrote his rhymed " Letter to Maria Gisborne " that touches so lightly upon the troubles by which he was surrounded and so gracefully upon his life with the Gisbornes and his absent friends in England. He pictured himself humorously as " plotting dark spells and devilish enginery " such as would " pump up oaths from clergymen " and grind " the gentle spirit of our meek reviews " into violent outbreaks — a " war of worms " of which he could remain heedless. Old pleasures with his friends crowded into his mind to produce a delightful picture of former days with the Gisbornes:

> — how on the sea-shore
> We watched the ocean and the sky together,
> Under the roof of blue Italian weather;
> How I ran home through last year's thunder-storm,
> And felt the transverse lightning linger warm
> Upon my cheek — and how we often made
> Feasts for each other, where good will outweighed
> The frugal luxury of our country cheer,
> As well it might, were it less firm and clear
> Than ours must ever be; — and how we spun
> A shroud of talk to hide us from the sun
> Of this familiar life, which seems to be
> But is not, — or is but quaint mockery
> Of all we would believe, and sadly blame
> The jarring and inexplicable frame
> Of this wrong world: — and then anatomize
> The purposes and thoughts of men whose eyes
> Were closed in distant years; — or widely guess

The issue of the earth's great business,
When we shall be as we no longer are —
Like babbling gossips safe, who hear the war
Of winds, and sigh, but tremble not; or how
You listened to some interrupted flow
Of visionary rhyme, — in joy and pain
Struck from the inmost fountains of my brain,
With little skill perhaps; — or how we sought
Those deepest wells of passion or of thought
Wrought by wise poets in the waste of years,
Staining their sacred waters with our tears;
Quenching a thirst ever to be renewed!
Or how I, wisest lady! then indued
The language of a land which now is free,
And winged with thoughts of truth and majesty,
Flits round the tyrant's sceptre like a cloud,
And bursts the peopled prisons, and cries aloud,
" My name is Legion! " — that majestic tongue
Which Calderon over the desert flung
Of ages and of nations; and which found
An echo in our hearts, and with the sound
Startled oblivion; — thou wert then to me
As is a nurse — when inarticulately
A child would talk as its grown parents do.
If living winds the rapid clouds pursue,
If hawks chase doves through the æthereal way,
Huntsmen the innocent deer, and beasts their prey,
Why should not we rouse with the spirit's blast
Out of the forest of the pathless past
These recollected pleasures? . . .

But the Gisbornes were now in London, where they were
meeting some of their old friends and several of Shelley's
friends, to all of whom Shelley had already written to recommend them. Each of these receives in turn a brief appreciative
sketch in the poem. Even Godwin is here pictured, " though
fallen," as inferior to none in his ability to face " the dread tribunal " of fame. Coleridge, a former friend of the Gisbornes', is " a
hooded eagle among blinking owls "; Hunt " the salt of the
earth." Hogg, " a pearl within an oyster shell," is " one of the
richest of the deep "; Peacock's " fine wit " is " too wise for selfish

bigots "; and Horace Smith has a combination of virtues that might " make this dull world a business of delight." [55]

Shelley ends his poem with a very optimistic forecast of the next winter:

> Next winter you must pass with me; I'll have
> My house by that time turned into a grave
> Of dead despondence and low-thoughted care,
> And all the dreams which our tormentors are.
> Oh! that Hunt, Hogg, Peacock, and Smith were there,
> With everything belonging to them fair! —
> We will have books, Spanish, Italian, Greek,
> And ask one week to make another week
> As like his father, as I'm unlike mine,
> Which is not his fault, as you may divine.
> Though we eat little flesh and drink no wine,
> Yet let's be merry: we'll have tea and toast;
> Custards for supper, and an endless host
> Of syllabubs and jellies and mince-pies,
> And other such lady-like luxuries, —
> Feasting on which we will philosophize!
> And we'll have fires out of the Grand Duke's wood,
> To thaw the six weeks' winter in our blood.
> And then we'll talk; — what shall we talk about?
> Oh! there are themes enough for many a bout
> Of thought-entangled descant; — as to nerves —
> With cones and parallelograms and curves
> I've sworn to strangle them if once they dare
> To bother me — when you are with me there.
> And they shall never more sip laudanum
> From Helicon or Himeros; — well, come,
> And in despite of God and of the devil,
> We'll make our friendly philosophic revel
> Outlast the leafless time; — till buds and flowers
> Warn the obscure inevitable hours
> Sweet meeting by sad parting to renew; —
> " To-morrow to fresh woods and pastures new."

It was probably on the evening of June 22, just a week after this poem was written, that Mary and Shelley walked among the myrtle hedges near Casa Ricci and took a momentary joy in

the flashing of the fireflies in the hedges and the singing of the
skylarks overhead.[54] Though Mary's journal for the day mentions only "Walk to the sea," such a walk toward the sea seven
years later led the Gisbornes through a meadow they had formerly visited with Shelley where the sky was alive with skylarks. Very probably Shelley and Mary were revisiting the same
spot when Shelley was inspired to write his famous lyric, "To
a Skylark."

There had been few times in Shelley's life when a symbol
of joy could have been more welcome to him. From the first
line of his poem the skylark is such a symbol — "Bird thou
never wert." He is in fact a poet, and a poet to whom the world
will listen. Languor, which particularly oppressed both Shelley
and Mary at the time, had no existence for this skylark-poet.
Annoyance — a mild name for Shelley's importunate creditors
— never came near him; he could love without feeling the sadness of too much love. More than Shelley and Mary he was a
stranger to tears and a scorner of hate and fear — the hate of
the reviewers and the fear of Paolo's slanders and of Godwin's
impending ruin. In the end he is an example to his panegyrist:

> Teach me half the gladness
>   That thy brain must know,
> Such harmonious madness
>   From my lips would flow
> The world should listen then, as I am listening now.

All the shadows and miseries which surrounded Shelley as he
wrote have their echoes in the poem. Far more clearly than
is apparent from the poem alone it is an instinctive reaction
from an immediate, definite environment.

THE PLAN to spend the summer months at the Baths of Lucca
had been abandoned when it was found necessary to go to
Leghorn. But as the weather grew hotter at Leghorn it was
decided to go for at least three months to the Baths of San
Giuliano di Pisa, four miles above the city of Pisa. On July 30
Shelley took an apartment there which he described as "very

pleasant and spacious," for a period of three months at a rental of forty sequins quarterly. And on August 5 the Shelleys and Claire left Leghorn and entered their new quarters,[55] known as Casa Prinni. Two of Shelley's last actions before the removal were to write to Tom Medwin (July 20) insisting upon his promised visit, and to write to John Keats (July 30) offering sympathy and encouragement. Having just heard from Mr. Gisborne [56] of Keats's pulmonary attack, he urged him warmly to conserve his health by spending the winter in Italy as the guest of the Shelleys. He added a word of encouragement and advice about poetry which Keats, in his illness and sensitiveness, may not have taken exactly as meant:

I have lately read your "Endymion" again and ever with a new sense of the treasures of poetry it contains, though treasures poured forth with indistinct profusion. This, people in general will not endure, and that is the cause of the comparatively few copies which have been sold. I feel persuaded that you are capable of the greatest things, so you but will.

I always tell Ollier to send you copies of my books. . . . In poetry I have sought to avoid system and mannerism; I wish those who excel me in genius would pursue the same plan.[57]

Keats replied appreciatively on August 10, without definitely accepting the invitation. After some brief account of his health and his attitude toward his own poetry, he reminded Shelley of the latter's earlier advice to him to restrain his desire to publish and ventured to return the same advice, after reading *The Cenci.* He wished that Shelley would curb his impetuosity and "load every rift of your subject with ore." Without having yet seen *Prometheus Unbound* he admitted he would be happier if he could think of Shelley as not yet half-way through writing it. At the same time he confided to Charles Cowden Clarke that his sole motive in not accepting Shelley's invitation was a fear that in his company he could not remain a free agent.[58]

Chapter XXV

AUTUMN AND WINTER OF 1820

THE BATHS OF PISA; "THE WITCH OF ATLAS,"

"ODE TO NAPLES," AND *ŒDIPUS TYRANNUS;*

RENEWED ASSOCIATION WITH MEDWIN; OPINIONS,

HABITS, AND TRAITS; NEW FRIENDS

THE BATHS OF PISA, or the Baths of San Giuliano (for they went under either name), were warm natural springs at the foot of the mountain of San Giuliano, four miles from Pisa. They were supposed to be particularly soothing for nervous ailments. Though the Baths of Lucca, only about ten miles distant, were more fashionable, the Baths of Pisa were still in Shelley's day in considerable esteem with the surrounding gentry. Their hot summer climate suited Shelley exactly.

Casa Prinni, the commodious house which Shelley had secured, was conveniently situated at the lower side of the square containing the little casino in which the life of the resort was centred. To the rear of the house, a garden extended to a canal connecting the river Serchio with the Arno. Across the canal the low, flat fields, under frequent threat of inundation, were not a particularly inspiring view, but there were mountains close by, and in summer the neighbouring slopes of Monte San Giuliano were covered with the bloom of myrtle.

On the evening of August 5 [1] the Shelleys and Claire moved into their new quarters, where they were to remain until October 29. They were near enough to Pisa, Lucca, and even Leghorn for occasional callers, especially from Pisa, and to visit those places practically as often as they desired. Few days passed without some such visit, sometimes on pleasure, sometimes, in Shelley's case, on business. There were still some matters in Leghorn that necessitated dealings with Federigo del Rosso, and also a Mr. Jackson who is several times mentioned in the journals and letters as if he were both a social and a business acquaintance. Possibly he was Shelley's banker. Mr. and Mrs. Mason came several times to visit them at the Baths, sometimes alone, once or twice with the children, and once with Miss Field. Madame Tantini, whom they had known in Pisa, was in residence at the Baths, and exchanged occasional calls with the Shelleys. Once Madame Tantini brought with her the English nun Betsy, on whom Claire had called in Pisa; once Claire's dancing-teacher, Lanetti, called with his wife.

About the only entertainment furnished by the resort was a St. Bartholomew's celebration on August 24, with horse races in the evening. Otherwise there.was little to do except walk, bathe, read, and write. The Shelleys and Claire enjoyed walking before breakfast or· in the evening on the mountainside or along one of the several roads leading from the Baths. Occasionally they rode. Their one excursion to Lucca occupied two days (August 11 and 12) and was devoted by Mary and Claire to sightseeing, with some special attention to relics of Castruccio, on account of Mary's novel about him. Shelley left the others at Lucca and went on to climb Monte San Pellegrino alone, returning to the Baths on August 13 considerably fatigued, but inspired with the idea for his "Witch of Atlas," which he wrote during the three days following his return.

Claire remained at the Baths only until August 31, when she removed to Leghorn for her health,[2] apparently because she thought sea-bathing might be more beneficial to her. Shelley accompanied her to install her in Casa Ricci and apparently to attend to matters of business with del Rosso and Jackson. Thereafter Claire remained at Casa Ricci, exchanging letters and visits with the Shelleys and going occasionally to Pisa to visit the Masons.

Shelley's health improved with the summer temperature, warm baths, and a life more in the open air. Only once while at the Baths (September 17) does Mary record: "Shelley is not well." The recent death of Elena Adelaide, sad as it was for

Shelley, may have terminated a strain in his life with Mary. Claire's absence removed an occasional domestic irritation, and Paolo Foggi seemed definitely silenced. Writing to Amelia Curran, Mary mentioned Paolo's recent threat in a tone almost of self-confidence:

> Do you know, we lose many letters? — having spies (not the Government ones) about us in plenty. They made a desperate push to do us a desperate mischief lately, but succeeded no further than to blacken us amongst the English; so, if you receive a fresh batch (or green bag) of scandal against us, I assure you it will be a lie. Poor souls! we live innocently, as you well know; if we did not, ten to one we should not be so unfortunate.[3]

In the same letter Mary described their situation at the Baths as quite pleasant, with delightful scenery near by, and reported Percy Florence as thriving and Shelley as in improving health. "We go on in our old manner," she adds, "with no change. I have had many changes for the worse — one might be for the better — but that is nearly impossible." What the one change possibly for the better might be, since Claire was then still with them, is hard to imagine, unless Mary was thinking of the removal of Elena Adelaide as a source of domestic difference. Going on "in the old manner," of course, meant regular reading and study and occasional writing. Mary was reading Greek, Lucretius, Vergil's *Georgics*, Boccaccio, a few books of travel and history, *Don Juan*, Keats's poems, and *Prometheus Unbound*. Shelley was reading alone Apollonius Rhodius, Plato's *Republic*, Herodotus, "Robertson's America," "Gillie's Greece," and "Ancient Metaphysics"; aloud he was reading *The Double Marriage*, *Love's Progress*, Boccaccio, and Keats's *Hyperion*. Claire's reading was somewhat similar to Mary's. In addition she was writing a "Don Juan" of her own, all record of which she later sought to obliterate, even in her journal. During September and October Mary wrote occasionally, presumably on *Valperga*.

UPON his return from Monte San Pellegrino Shelley immediately set about writing down the delightful poem "The Witch of

Atlas," which he had imagined during his solitary expedition. Three days (August 14, 15, 16),[4] as he playfully boasted to Mary in his introductory poem, were sufficient, though Wordsworth took nineteen years in "dressing" Peter Bell. Of late Mary had reasoned earnestly with Shelley that he should address his poems more to the average intelligence and so convince the world he was not the idle, even reckless dreamer that he was supposed to be. She did not wish him to compromise with his principles, but merely to lay a broader foundation in the popular mind for their just reception. She also felt that Shelley's own mind and health might be greatly benefited if he could be convinced that his writings were not so totally scorned as he supposed.[5] The reception of *The Cenci,* violent as it was in some respects, offered solid basis for her opinion, in the clear recognition of Shelley's genius by some of the reviewers. Better than most others Mary was in a position to understand that Shelley's protestations of indifference to the reviewers were too constant to mean anything except a despairing desire to be indifferent. Twenty years later she still thought she was right, and it is fairly plain from their letters that Hunt, Horace Smith, Byron, and Peacock would have agreed with her.

But Shelley, while reasonable and practical enough to begin planning " Charles I " [6] — exactly the sort of thing Mary wished him to do — was never the person to be diverted from his bent. Laughingly he began his introductory poem, " To Mary ":

> How, my dear Mary, — are you critic-bitten
>   (For vipers kill, though dead,) by some review,
> That you condemn these verses I have written,
>   Because they tell no story, false or true!
> What, though no mice are caught by a young kitten,
>   May it not leap and play as grown cats do,
> Till its claws come? Prithee, for this one time,
> Content thee with a visionary rhyme.

In the " visionary rhyme " that follows, Shelley developed a delicately beautiful little semi-myth that seems almost Puckishly to desert the world of flesh and blood that Mary wished him to cultivate. In a cavern of the Atlas Mountains, beside a secret fountain, dwelt a " lady-witch " whom Shelley does not trouble to name, other than to identify her as the daughter of one of the Atlantides. To this "lady-witch" and Apollo is born a daughter,

> A lovely lady, garmented in light
> From her own beauty.

All creatures — cameleopards, serpents, elephants, lionesses, Silenus, Dryope, Faunus, Pan, Priapus, pygmies, polyphemes, centaurs, satyrs, kings, herdsmen, and mountain maidens — came in succession to witness and be chastened by her beauty, which was of the same insupportable quality as Asia's in *Prometheus Unbound:*

> For she was beautiful: her beauty made
>   The bright world dim, and everything beside
> Seemed like the fleeting image of a shade:
>   No thought of living spirit could abide,
> Which to her looks had ever been betrayed,
>   On any object in the world so wide,
> On any hope within the circling skies,
> But on her form, and in her inmost eyes.

Perceiving this, the Witch wove a subtle magic veil as "a shadow for the splendour of her love." She was the mistress of many charms and spells, which Shelley described with a careful elaboration suggestive (like a number of specific details) of both Edmund Spenser and John Keats. At first she lived alone; later she created for herself a winged, sexless creature called Hermaphroditus, who propelled with its wings the magic boat in which she journeyed through mountain streams and austral oceans. Millions of her ministering spirits in the clouds built for her an imperial magic tent of vapour, light, and fire, whence she observed with pleasure or delight all that happened between the earth and the moon. But her chief delight was to visit in sleep the spirits of human beings. To the most beautiful she offered a crystal bowl whose contents made them live thereafter under the control of some mighty power beyond them, and live on even after death. The less beautiful she would visit with strange dreams, wherein priests, kings, and soldiers would see them-

selves for the cheats they were, and timid lovers would overcome their timidity and yet take no harm from doing so. She
was herself as ignorant of the love of the sexes as if she were a
sexless bee, but later, Shelley says, she knew what love was.
Thus ends one of Shelley's lightest, airiest, most graceful im-
aginings. It is a description rather than a story, and can hardly
be called the creation of a new myth so much as the creation of
a lovely goddess, with the myth still to come.

Who is this Witch then, and what is her significance? How
can she be any other than the only goddess in Shelley's pantheon, Intellectual Beauty, or Love? She is far more playful and
youthful than in his other accounts of her, but otherwise her
attributes are exactly the same. Like Asia and the Intellectual
Beauty of his early "Hymn to Intellectual Beauty," her beauty
is veiled because otherwise it would be insupportable. Like the
Intellectual Beauty or Love of *Adonais,* she wields the world to
her purposes, but only to the extent to which the reluctant mass
is capable of being so moulded.

In concluding his introductory stanzas to the poem Shelley
remarks that "If you strip Peter" [Wordsworth's *Peter Bell*]

> you will see a fellow,
> Scorched by Hell's hyperequatorial climate . . .

but

> If you unveil my Witch, no priest nor primate
> Can shrive you of that sin, — if sin there be
> In love, when it becomes idolatry.

This stanza is not, as the most recent critic of the poem has supposed,[7] a statement that "The Witch of Atlas" is a deliberate
mystery, to be unveiled at the reader's peril. It is merely two
assertions that Shelley had often made before, in prose and
poetry; namely, that Wordsworth's *Peter Bell* only partly conceals the poet's spiritual degeneration, and that to unveil Love or
Intellectual Beauty is the sin of Actæon — perhaps not really a
sin when due to the idolatry of love, but nevertheless certain to
be punished within the year. Shelley was soon to describe himself as so punished, in *Adonais:*

218

. . . he, as I guess,
Had gazed on Nature's naked loveliness,
Actæon-like, and now he fled astray
With feeble steps o'er the world's wilderness,
And his own thoughts, along that rugged way,
Pursued, like raging hounds, their father and their prey.

In "Peter Bell the Third," written less than a year before
"The Witch of Atlas," and in *Swellfoot the Tyrant,* written only
a few days after "The Witch of Atlas," Shelley was unable, in
spite of comparatively frivolous intentions, to avoid a serious
undernote where his own theories of society were involved. No
more was he able to do so in "The Witch of Atlas," the lightest
and most elfish of all his poems. In the end he dwells lightly,
but with unmistakable meaning, upon the old evils of human
society that he could never put completely out of his mind.
Beyond this there are suggestions of the unreality, or dream
quality, of physical phenomena, that had become quite usual in
Shelley's poetry since 1818.

Thomas Medwin noticed that the poem was touched with
Shelley's usual philosophy. Mary Shelley could not have missed
noticing the same fact, but evidently considered it too obvious
or too light to mention in her note on the poem. This is a trivial
fault indeed, but it is a greater pity that she failed to mention
a circumstance that would have made the graceful lightness of
the poem more intelligible and would have gone far toward explaining a tone that Shelley had never applied and would never
afterwards apply to Intellectual Beauty.

Throughout July and August, up to within about three weeks
of the time "The Witch of Atlas" was written, Shelley and
Mary were reading aloud the *Ricciardetto* of Niccolò Forteguerri, a three-volume, half-serious epic-romance, professedly
an imitation of Pulci. On June 30 Shelley expressed his admiration for the book in a letter to the Gisbornes. While reading
Ricciardetto Shelley was translating the Homeric "Hymn to
Mercury," with a playful turn of language somewhat less like
the original than like the tone of "The Witch of Atlas" and
Ricciardetto. Both the translation of the "Hymn" and "The
Witch of Atlas" employed the same stanza as *Ricciardetto,*

ottava rima, which Shelley had never used in a long poem before.[8] The single large fact to be explained about the poem is the Witch herself, and the Witch is clearly Shelley's one and only goddess, Intellectual Beauty, transparently veiled in the cloudy, semi-mischievous magic of *Ricciardetto*. There are details that are not so explained. In fact, almost every detail of the poem has been given a profound Shelleyan significance inconsistent with a connection with *Ricciardetto*. Some of these connections may still be possible, but *Ricciardetto* and Shelley's own introductory poem establish the tone of the poem, and the tone, as Mary Shelley perceived, requires the poem to be viewed more as fancy than as philosophy.[9]

A further examination of *Ricciardetto* shows various other possible " influences " upon " The Witch of Atlas." There is no one of them which Shelley did not fully assimilate and transmute in the "borrowing," if indeed the borrowing could be clearly established for the individual details, some of which are probably complicated by Miltonic and Spenserian reminiscences. But the sum of the details is undoubtedly of significance in Shelley's poem. Why, for instance, should Shelley call his beautiful creature a witch? Nothing is more· evident than the fact that she is not a witch in the usual unpleasant English meaning of the word. But the Italian *maga*, translated as sorcerer, witch, or hag, is employed in *Ricciardetto* in both a good and a bad sense. The suspicion that Shelley's " Witch " is the Italian *maga* in its good sense is borne out by the fact that two of the good witches in *Ricciardetto* have·some points of resemblance to Shelley's Witch. One of them, the *maga* Stella, like Shelley's Witch, is the most beautiful lady alive, and " knows not love." She comes forth to greet the paladins singing the praises of freedom from love, and later gives one of them a charm against its power. Another, the *maga* Lirina, after showing some initial desire to frustrate Ricciardetto and Despina, becomes their principal guardian and rescues them by her magic from numerous evils. Like Shelley's Witch, she journeys to Egypt and exercises her magic there — hence it is not necessary to assume with Professor Grabo that the Egyptian scenes in Shelley's poem are due to an interest in Egyptian mythology and its moon-goddess, Isis,[10] which Shelley nowhere else exhibits.

Ricciardetto abounds in witches and sorcerers both good and bad, incantations, lakes, fountains, caves, and grottoes. There is a Grotto of Sleep, a Perfect Island, an Island of Necromancers, an Island of Portents, and a Palace of Fortune. If it seems strange that Shelley should combine this background with a touch of classical mythology, there is a trace of the same combination in *Ricciardetto*. Where else should Shelley, who had never before dealt in magic (unless *Queen Mab* is an exception), have drawn the impulse at this particular time except from *Ricciardetto* and possibly from Spenser?

ALMOST immediately Shelley turned from his Witch to a more familiar type of poetry. During the summer the cause of Freedom in Italy, never quite extinguished by the partial failure of the French Revolution, flared forth in a brilliant *ignis fatuus* that seemed at the time to be a true illumination. The success of the Spanish insurgents stimulated the Neapolitans. In July an incipient revolt broke out, which the soldiers of King Ferdinand refused to suppress. Most of the army went over to the revolution, and King Ferdinand was compelled to grant a constitution to Naples. On July 16, before the removal from Leghorn, Claire's journal received the following enthusiastic entry:

> Report of the Revolution at Naples; the people assembled round the palace demanding a Constitution; the King ordered his troops to fire and disperse the crowd; they refused, and he has now promised a Constitution. . . . This is glorious, and is produced by the Revolution in Spain.

In the sister Kingdom of Sicily (Naples and Sicily were then known as the Kingdom of the Two Sicilies) there was more violence, but the result was the same. Shelley wrote to Mary on July 30: " The soldiers resisted the people, and a terrible slaughter amounting, it is said, to four thousand men, ensued. The event however was as it should be — Sicily like Naples is free."

It was a false dawn. The attitude of Austria, backed by Russia, became definitely threatening within two months, and though the Congress of Leybach withheld violence for a while, Neapolitan freedom was bloodily stamped out by the Austrians early in 1821. But while Freedom still shone bright Shelley wrote his " Ode to Naples." According to Mary's journal it was finished on August 24.[11] His earlier " Ode to Liberty " had been mainly an invocation; the " Ode to Naples " is an impassioned greeting:

> Naples! thou Heart of men, which ever pantest
> Naked, beneath the lidless eye of Heaven!
> Elysian City, which to calm enchantest
> The mutinous air and sea! . . .
>
> .   .   .   .
>
> Thou which wert once, and then didst cease to be,
> Now art, and henceforth ever shall be, free,
> If Hope, and Truth, and Justice can avail, —
> Hail, hail, all hail! [12]

But in this ode, as elsewhere, Shelley realized that liberty, like the Mohammedan's paradise, lay under the shadow of a sword. Already he saw a vision of the Austrian armies on the march:

> The Anarchs of the North lead forth their legions
> Like Chaos o'er creation, uncreating.

They desolate the Alps, trample beautiful cities into dust, and leave only the fire-blackened fields behind them. The poem concludes with a moving invocation to Love to protect the spirit of freedom against brutish oppression:

> Great Spirit, deepest Love!
> Which rulest and dost move
> All things which live and are, within the Italian shore;
> Who spreadest Heaven around it,
> Whose woods, rocks, waves, surround it;
> Who sittest in thy star, o'er Ocean's western floor;

> Spirit of beauty! at whose soft command
> 　The sunbeams and the showers distil its foison
> 　　From the Earth's bosom chill;
> Oh, bid those beams be each a blinding brand
> 　Of lightning! bid those showers be dews of poison!
> 　　Bid the Earth's plenty kill!
> 　　Bid thy bright Heaven above
> 　　Whilst light and darkness bound it,
> 　　Be their tomb who planned
> 　　To make it ours and thine!
> Or, with thine harmonizing ardours fill
> And raise thy sons, as o'er the prone horizon
> Thy lamp feeds every twilight wave with fire —
> Be man's high hope and unextinct desire
> The instrument to work thy will divine!
> 　　Then clouds from sunbeams, antelopes from leopards,
> 　　　And frowns and fears from thee,
> 　　　Would not more swiftly flee,
> 　　Than Celtic wolves from the Ausonian shepherds. —
> Whatever, Spirit, from thy starry shrine
> 　　Thou yieldest or withholdest, oh let be
> 　　This City of thy worship ever free!

The " Ode to Naples " did not, as Shelley's editors have supposed, remain unpublished until the appearance of *Posthumous Poems* in 1824. It was immediately sent to England and appeared on October 1 and 8, signed P. B. S., in a weekly journal where certainly no one would look for the first edition of one of Shelley's poems — *The Military Register and Weekly Gazette, Historical, Literary*, etc. *for the Army, Navy, Colonies, and Fashionable World*, edited and published by R. Scott, 3 Pall Mall Court. There is no evidence that Shelley was acquainted with Mr. R. Scott. Hunt had already disappointed Shelley by failing to print *The Masque of Anarchy* and the letter on Carlile. Possibly Shelley sent the poem to Horace Smith at the same time that he sent *Swellfoot the Tyrant* and it was published with or without Smith's knowledge. The publication could hardly have been authorized by Shelley or his publisher, because four months later (February 22, 1822) Shelley offered it to Ollier for publication in his *Literary Miscellany*.

On August 24, while Shelley was writing the "Ode to Naples," Mrs. Mason happened to be visiting the Shelleys. On that day also the local farmers brought their pigs to a small fair, held in the square of the village just beneath the Shelleys' windows. Undertaking to read his recent "Ode to Liberty" to Mrs. Mason, Shelley found himself riotously accompanied by the grunting of the pigs. Laughingly he compared them to the chorus of frogs in Aristophanes, and then in a spirit of burlesque he imagined a drama on the sordid trial of Queen Caroline in which the pigs should serve as chorus. So began, on October 24, his *Œdipus Tyrannus, or Swellfoot the Tyrant.*[13]

For some time Shelley's letters had been showing a considerable interest in the trial of Queen Caroline for infidelity. His interest in political events at home had always been lively, and the coming trial was not only a political event, with the Whigs violently championing the Queen; it was also probably the most complete public display of dirty royal linen that England ever witnessed.

The Princess Caroline, separated from her royal husband, the Prince Regent, had long been travelling in Mediterranean countries with a fairly complete disregard of decorum. Not much attention was paid to her; in fact, English ambassadors were instructed to ignore her so far as possible. When the coronation of George IV was being planned, it was decided by the King and his Tory ministers to provide no place for her in the ceremonies. Caroline, who was no coward, returned to England to insist upon her royal position, and the ministers thereupon brought her to trial for infidelity. The Whigs, who hated her husband, took up her cause with alacrity. The country teemed with coarse cartoons and anonymous satires in verse and prose, some of which went beyond fifty editions. George IV was riotously lampooned as Nero, Glorious Georgie, and Gorgeous Whelp. Ministers were mobbed, processions were formed, houses were stoned, and the notorious Italian witnesses that the ministers introduced were assaulted on landing. Henry Brougham, one of the Queen's defenders, sardonically suggested that certain days should be set apart for the transaction of business. Wherever English newspapers and travellers went,

it was incumbent on all good Englishmen to pronounce upon
the question of the Queen's virtue. Byron scouted the charges;
Scott, a Tory, believed them true. Mary Shelley was a strong
partisan of Caroline. Shelley, this time not so warm as Mary,
thought the charges probably exaggerated. His principal feeling, however, was one of disgust that "a vulgar cook-maid"
should somehow become a symbol in the fight against oppression. Nevertheless, her enemies were worse than she, and were
also the enemies of Freedom. Though he scorned her, he was
technically on her side.

Mary mentions the beginning of *Swellfoot* in her journal for
August 24 and records reading it on August 30. It was sent at
once to Horace Smith in London, who had it printed as a pamphlet and published by J. Johnson, 98 Cheapside, probably in
December 1820. After only seven copies had been sold, the
Society for the Prevention of Vice threatened a prosecution,
which the publisher averted by surrendering all remaining
copies.[14]

Against a background of the privation and oppression of the
masses, represented as a chorus of swine, Shelley presented the
King's ministers seeking to ruin the Queen by pouring over her
head the poisonous contents of a green bag full of perjured testimony. The Queen, however, turned the tables by pouring
the bag's contents over their heads and riding forth in triumph
on the Ionian Minotaur (John Bull). Written as a mere *jeu
d'esprit,* it is in a sense the least Shelleyan of all Shelley's mature
poems. There is hardly an original device in it. Even as Shelley was writing, his apparently impromptu chorus of pigs was
being used as an instrument of satire against George IV by
Professor Porson, in an article in the *Examiner* for June 30. The
green bag, the Rat, the Leech — in fact practically all of Shelley's characters — appear again and again in similar rôles in
the numerous cartoons and other satires with which England
was being flooded. Somewhere, probably among the English
at Leghorn, Shelley must have seen a number of them. Even
Shelley's old enemy Lord Eldon, satirized as Dakry ("Tear"),
is treated impersonally as the same sentimental wheedler and
weeper who appears in the contemporary satires. The similari-

ties are so general and so close that some of Shelley's characters may be confidently identified from their parallel treatment in cartoons and other anonymous satires.[15]

But in another sense the poem is so peculiarly Shelleyan that no one could possibly mistake it for one of the anonymous school to which it otherwise belongs. Shelley could not debase his verse to march *pari passu* with his subject, nor could he be boisterously, coarsely humorous in the way that was natural to most of the pamphleteers. No one but Shelley would have been capable of writing contemporary political satire in the grotesquely Gothic stage-setting that he employed. No more than in "Peter Bell" could he really abandon himself to trifling upon a subject that was fundamentally so serious for him. His attacks upon government spies, paper money, corrupt courts, and the repression of the masses have an undernote of suppressed earnestness that the mere partisans lacked. A serious sense of impending revolution underlies the entire action and hints that the author's jesting is almost consciously against the grain.

"The Witch of Atlas," *Swellfoot,* and the "Ode to Naples" were all written between August 14 and August 30. During September and October Shelley wrote little if any poetry, though the beautiful lyric "Autumn — A Dirge," would seem to have been written in either late October or early November.

CLAIRE Clairmont's unequal contest with Byron over the education of Allegra still dragged on. Her journal shows that she wrote to Byron on August 16 and received letters from him on August 30 and October 14. On August 25 Byron wrote to Shelley a short note declining further correspondence with Claire, "who merely tries to be as irrational as she can be," and saying he preferred hearing from Shelley.[16] Shelley agreed that Claire's letters were probably childish and absurd. But after all, he reminded Byron, Claire's wish to see her child was natural, and she should be treated as indulgently as possible on account of her unhappiness and bad health. He politely declined to become Claire's means of communicating her sentiments to Byron, but suggested that for the present there was no need of Byron's doing more than sending news of Allegra at fairly regular intervals.[17]

In the latter part of October Claire secured a situation in the home of Dr. Bojti, who lived in Florence, opposite the Pitti Palace, and was one of the court physicians to the Grand Duke. Her position was apparently not that of a paid governess, for her journal records payments to the Bojtis, nor was it one of complete independence, to judge from Shelley's references to it in letters to Claire. Very likely she was a " paying guest " with light duties which somewhat reduced the pay. Probably Claire owed her new situation to the good offices of Mrs. Mason, who must have been aware of her occasional unhappiness in the same home with Mary. On October 20 Claire set out for Florence with Shelley, and on the next day, having seen her installed at Casa Bojti, Shelley returned. He arrived at the Baths on October 22 with Tom Medwin, whom he had picked up at Pisa on his return journey.

Medwin had been resident with the Shelleys less than a week when they were all compelled to leave the Baths and return to Pisa. Since the middle of October there had been constant rains. The Serchio rose steadily. On October 25 Mary wrote in her journal: " Rain all night. The banks of the Serchio break, and by dark all the baths are overflowed. Water four feet deep in our house." From the rear of the house came another flood caused by the overflow of the canal connecting the Arno and the Serchio. The water in the house rose to six feet. From an upper window the inmates seemed more impressed by the sight than the danger. " It was a picturesque sight," Mary wrote later, " at night to see the peasants driving the cattle from the plains below to the heights above the baths. A fire was kept up to guide them across the ford; and the forms of the men and the animals showed in dark relief against the red glare of the flame, which was reflected again in the waters that filled the Square." [18] Shelley urged Medwin to do a sketch of it. Next morning they stepped from an upstairs window into a boat and after landing proceeded by carriage to Pisa.[19]

Here, on October 29, the Shelleys and Medwin entered new lodgings, Palazzo Galetti, which Shelley described to Claire with some optimism:

We are now removed to a lodging on the Lung Arno, which is sufficiently commodious, and for which we pay thirteen sequins a month. It is next door to that marble palace, and is called Palazzo Galetti, consisting of an excellent mezzanino, and of two rooms on the fourth story, all to the south, and with two fireplaces. The rooms above, one of which is Medwin's room and the other my study (congratulate me on my seclusion) are delightfully pleasant, and to-day I shall be employed in arranging my books and gathering my papers about me. Mary has a very good room below, and there is plenty of space for the babe. I expect the water of Pisa to relieve me, if indeed the disease be what is conjectured.[20]

IN THE same letter Shelley stated that much of his time lately had been occupied by Medwin, "who relates wonderful and interesting things of the interior of India." It had been nearly seven years since Medwin and Shelley had seen each other. Once, in India, Medwin had found in a Parsee bookstall a copy of *The Revolt of Islam*, shipped out of England with other unsalable books. This had stirred his enthusiasm for his old friend, to whom he wrote from Geneva shortly after learning his address. His friends at Geneva, Edward John Trelawny and Lieutenant Edward Williams, heard so much of his enthusiasm that they too desired Shelley's acquaintance.[21]

Medwin did not find in his friend the hopeless invalid that Shelley had told him to expect. " His figure was emaciated, and somewhat bent, owing to near-sightedness and his being forced to lean over his books with his eyes almost touching them; his hair, still profuse, and curling naturally, was partially interspersed with grey; . . . but his appearance was youthful, and his countenance, whether grave or animated, strikingly intellectual. There was also a freshness and purity in his complexion that he never lost." [22] Shelley had probably forgotten that he had outgrown Medwin intellectually even while still at Eton, and it was too soon for him to reach his later conclusion that

THE BATHS OF PISA: HOUSE SUPPOSEDLY OCCUPIED BY THE SHELLEYS
As photographed in 1905 by Professor W. Hall Griffin

THE BATHS OF PISA: CANAL BETWEEN SERCHIO AND ARNO RIVERS
As photographed in 1905 by Professor W. Hall Griffin

Medwin was, after all, a bore. He had recently criticized Medwin's mediocre poems with delicate tact and excessive respect;
he was soon (November 10) to recommend one of them to
Ollier as "a very elegant and classical composition." He and
Medwin planned to begin at once the study of Arabic together,
and Shelley wrote to both Claire in Florence and John Gisborne
in Leghorn seeking Arabic grammars, dictionaries, manuscripts,
and from Leghorn "any native Arabs capable of teaching
the language."²³ By the middle of November the studies had
begun.²⁴

Suddenly now the Shelleys were no longer the close friends
with the Gisbornes that they had been. On their return to Leghorn the Gisbornes had reached Genoa by October 3, where
they probably received Mary's letter inviting them to come immediately to the Baths to recuperate from the fatigues of the
journey. They returned straight to Leghorn, however, arriving
there about October 6, but without notifying the Shelleys,
though Mr. Gisborne had written Mary a note from Genoa concluding: "We are very anxious to see you." When Shelley heard
from Claire that they were in Leghorn he wrote to renew Mary's
invitation. But he was puzzled and a little hurt: "We do not
quite understand your silence; if you are less desirous to see
us than we are to see you, you can send whatever letters and
papers you have brought us to Claire at Mrs. Masons. . . ."²⁵

Still a strange silence from the Gisbornes. They were always
negligent letter-writers, and it may be that their silence meant
nothing. It may be, however, that they were somewhat offended
by supposing that Shelley had mentioned their indebtedness to
him as one of the reasons why he could not succour Godwin,
and it seems certain that in London John Gisborne had been at
least partly converted to Godwin's point of view on Shelley's
financial obligations to Godwin.²⁶ Finally, just before the Shelleys left the Baths, they received a call from Henry Reveley that
threw Shelley into a real passion. Henry came with a proposal
of Mr. Gisborne's that the steamboat be abandoned and the
engine used in an iron foundry. Otherwise four hundred crowns
more would be needed to complete the boat. Shelley refused to
invest any more money and declined to have anything more to

do with the project if it was to be carried on through Mr. Gisborne. He obtained Henry's agreement that the needed funds be raised " upon the materials of the engine," whether a mortgage or the sale of excess materials is not clear. On the same day on which Shelley informed Claire of Henry's visit he also wrote a brief, impersonal business note to Mr. Gisborne in which he ignored the steamboat. But to Claire his indignation was so excessive that it indicates either additional unknown causes or else one of the sudden, irrational outbursts of which his earlier friends had sometimes been obliged to take note: " The Gisbornes are people totally without faith. — I think they are altogether the most filthy and odious animals with which I ever came in contact. — They do not visit Mary as they promised, and indeed if they did, I certainly should not stay in the house to receive them." [27]

Mary's journal shows nothing of this except the remark on November 4: " Inexplicable conduct of the Gisbornes " and the mention of visits by Henry Reveley on November 5 and 6. Later in the month Shelley's ire was still very much alive. " Henry Reveley," he informed Claire, " has been frequently at Pisa, and always dines with us, in spite of a conversation which I had with him, and which was intended to put an end to all intercourse between me and that base family. — I have not the heart to put my interdict in effect upon Henry, he is so very miserable, and such a whipped and trembling dog." [28] By the beginning of December all intercourse with the Gisbornes had been broken off. Mary so informed Marianne Hunt, adding that it was not entirely " an affair of pelf," but that the Gisbornes had behaved with a folly and baseness that was extremely painful and disappointing.[29] In a few months, however, the two families were again on friendly terms.

The Shelleys had heard seldom from their English friends during the autumn at the Baths, and continued to hear but seldom in the following winter at Pisa. Medwin said later that he never knew of an author who had less correspondence.[30] The Hunts once or twice wrote letters that distressed Shelley by his inability to relieve Hunt in his deepening financial troubles. Horace Smith wrote that he intended to emigrate and was con-

sidering coming to Italy to be Shelley's neighbour.[31] Shelley still
expected to be Keats's host and mentor in Italy, in spite of Keats's
failure to accept his invitation and in spite of the fact, unknown
to him, that Keats rather feared his influence.[32] Keats's early
poetry was in Shelley's opinion deeply flawed by Cockneyisms,
which he detested even in the poetry of Hunt,[33] but he thought
Hyperion really magnificent.[34] "If the *Hyperion* be not grand
poetry," he assured Peacock, "none has been produced by our
contemporaries." He also deeply sympathized with Keats as a
victim of unjust criticism and wrote (but seems not to have
sent) a letter to William Gifford in which he sought to persuade
the *Quarterly Review* to deal more justly with him. Nothing
could be more generous and benevolent than the eagerness with
which he looked forward to aiding a brother poet.

"Where is Keats now?" Shelley asked the Hunts at the time
he was moving back to Pisa. "I am anxiously expecting him
in Italy when I shall take care to bestow every possible attention
on him. I consider his a most valuable life, and I am deeply
interested in his safety. I intend to be the physician both of
his body and his soul, to keep the one warm and to teach [the]
other Greek and Spanish. I am aware indeed in part, that I am
nourishing a rival who will far surpass [me;] and this is an
additional motive and will be an added pleasure." [35]

Soon, however, Shelley had another patient to tend. Medwin's health, weakened by his long stay in the East, broke down
as a result of the hardships of his journey to Pisa. On November 5 he suffered a severe attack of illness and was thereafter
confined to his room for six weeks. During this time Shelley
nursed him as if he were a brother. "He applied my leeches,
administered my medicines, and . . . was assiduous and unin-
termitting in his affectionate care of me," Medwin testified
later.[36]

During his illness Medwin read all of Shelley's poetry and
became an enthusiastic admirer of it. Shelley was surprised
that anyone could admire his poems after what the reviews had
said. He was, he said, "disgusted with writing, and were it not
for an irresistible impulse, that predominates my better reason,
should discontinue so doing." [37] Medwin had previously awak-

231

ened an admiration for Shelley in an unnamed wealthy friend who wished the Shelleys to join him on a cruise he proposed taking in his own ship among the Greek islands. The idea of such a trip had presented itself to Shelley even before Medwin's arrival and he had asked Byron for letters, in case he went.[38] The cruise never developed, but Shelley was sufficiently attracted by the idea to explain it to Claire Clairmont.[39]

THE SHELLEYS had chosen Pisa for their winter residence not only on account of its good water, but also because of its excellent repute for winter climate. Lying in a depression, it was sheltered from the cold " tramontanes " that had made Shelley miserable in Florence. "Pisa is a pretty town," Mary had informed Marianne Hunt during the previous spring,

but its inhabitants would exercise all Hogg's vocabulary of scamps, rafts, etc. etc. to fully describe their ragged-haired, shirtless condition. Many of them are students of the university and they are none of the genteelest of the crew. Then there are *Bargees*, beggars without number; galley slaves in their yellow and red dress with chains, the women in dirty cotton gowns trailing in the dirt . . . and fellows with bushy hair, large whiskers, canes in their hands, and a bit of dirty party-coloured ribband (symbol of nobility) sticking in their buttonholes. . . . The Pisans I dislike more than any of the Italians, and none of them are as yet favourites with me.[40]

In November her opinion was much the same:

Sunday, Nov. 12. Percy's birthday. A divine day; sunny and cloudless; somewhat cold in the evening. It would be pleasant enough living in Pisa if one had a carriage, and could escape from one's house to the country without mingling with the inhabitants; but the Pisans and the Scolari, in short, the whole population, are such, that it would sound strange to an English person if I attempted to express what I feel concerning them — crawling and crab-like through their sapping streets.[41]

Shelley, with his extreme sensitiveness, was at times acutely aware of the squalor and degeneracy that could be met on the streets. He was very much affected by the sight of fettered con-

victs clanking their chains as they cleaned the streets under the
eyes of armed guards. " So sensitive was he of external impressions," wrote Medwin, " so magnetic, that I have seen him, after
threading the carnival crowd in the Lung' Arno Corsos, throw
himself half-fainting into a chair, overpowered by the atmosphere of evil passions, as he used to say, in that sensual and
unintellectual crowd." [42] He was equally intense in his reaction
to physical beauty. Many times he and Medwin watched a
gorgeous Pisan sunset from their upper windows and saw the
grim prison of the Torre del Fame turn to a bright gold. At
such times Shelley seemed completely dead to his immediate
surroundings in merging himself with the beauty of the scene.
Returning to himself he would exclaim: " What a glorious world!
There is, after all, something worth living for. This makes me
retract the wish that I had never been born." [43]

Medwin fell easily into the reading habits of Shelley and
Mary. While he was still ill he was soothed and delighted by
Shelley's habit of reading aloud to him. " No one ever gave
such emphasis to poetry. His voice, it is true, was a cracked
soprano, but the variety of its tones, and the intensity of feeling
which he displayed in the finest passages, produced an effect
almost electric." [44] Later Shelley translated aloud for him the
Prometheus of Æschylus, " reading it as fluently as if it were
written in French or Italian," often in extemporized blank
verse.[45] Medwin had learned a little Spanish in India, and he
and Shelley revelled in the " starry autos " of Calderon and also
in his tragedy of *Cisma d'Inghilterra*.[46] From Calderon they
turned to Dante, and Shelley read the *Divine Comedy* aloud,
lamenting at the time the inadequacy of English translations
and showing Medwin a copy of his own exquisite translation
from the 28th canto of the *Purgatorio*.[47] He also read with Medwin Cervantes's Little Novels, which he deemed inferior, and
Schiller's *Maid of Orleans,* which he admired for its bold treatment of Christianity as a mythology.[48]

Naturally there was much talk of literature. Shelley expressed
a great respect for Scott's novels and was an enthusiastic admirer of Manzoni's *I Promessi Sposi*. He also praised Thomas
Hope's *Anastasius,* a picaresque novel of modern Greece, but

he was no longer the indiscriminate reader of novels that he had been in his youth. Bad novels and bad verse, he now believed, should be avoided by a writer who desired purity in his own style. He was a constant reader of the older English dramatists, and particularly admired Webster's *The Duchess of Malfi.* The Latin poets he rather slighted, except Lucretius and Vergil, considering them poor copyists of the Greeks, and even Vergil's *Eclogues* inferior to the *Pastorals* of Theocritus. Among Italian poets other than Dante he had lost much of his earlier interest in Tasso and Ariosto, but admired Petrarch intensely and frequently quoted his " Ode to Italy." Milton was his idol among English poets. " So far, far above all other Poems indeed did he class the *Paradise Lost,* that he even thinks it a sacrilege to name it in speaking of any other Poem, and in his admiration of *Cain* said we had nothing like it since the *Paradise Regained* — a work which he frequently read and compared to the calm and tranquil beauty of an autumnal sunset, after the meridian glory and splendour of a summer's day." [49]

He regarded contemporary English poetry with mixed feelings. Wordsworth was still a great poet to him, though a bad man; Byron had written some supremely great poetry and some that was bad; and " Moore's *Irish Melodies* were great favourites with him." But Campbell and Rogers were simply spoiled favourites of public taste; and the attempts of the Cockneys to write in a new poetic jargon falsely imitated from the Lakists was disgusting madness. From this criticism he did not exempt Leigh Hunt and the early poems of Keats, though he sang the praises of Keats's last volume and thought Hunt, in his *Indicator,* an excellent prose essayist. Barry Cornwall's style (though Medwin does not mention him) Shelley thought particularly execrable.[50]

It was Shelley's idea that a good library should consist of only a few well-chosen titles. " I'll give you my list," he told Medwin — " catalogue it can't be called: — The Greek Plays, Plato, Lord Bacon's Works, Shakespeare, The Old Dramatists, Milton, Göthe and Schiller, Dante, Petrarch and Boccaccio, and Machiavelli and Guicciardini, — not forgetting Calderon; and last, yet first, the Bible." [51]

LIKE Hogg, Hunt, and Sophia Stacey before him, Medwin was deeply impressed with Shelley's studious habits. Never since leaving Oxford had Shelley ceased to be a more ardent student, perhaps, than he would have been had he remained:

> He was indeed ever engaged in composition or reading, scarcely allowing himself time for exercise or air; a book was his companion the first thing in the morning, the last thing at night. He told me he always read himself to sleep. Even when he walked on the *Argine,* his favourite winter walk, he read — sometimes through the streets, and generally had a book on the table by his side at dinner, if his temperate meal could be called one. . . . He arose fresh in the morning to his task; the silence of the night invited him to pursue it, and he could truly say that food and rest were not preferred to it. No part gave him uneasiness but the last, for then he grieved that the work was done. — He was indeed an indefatigable Student. So little impression did that which contributes one of the main delights of ordinary mortals, make on him, that he sometimes asked, " Mary, have I dined? " [52]

Shelley's studiousness was scarcely less impressive than his occasional melancholy and despondency. It was perhaps natural for Tom Medwin, years later, to look upon Shelley through the medium of the pathetic tradition that had grown up around him. Medwin remarked himself that it might be easy to mistake for melancholy the moods of deep reflection or reverie in which Shelley sometimes sank himself.[53] But the tradition, though possibly exaggerated in retrospect, is substantiated by Shelley's own poems, letters, and conversations. In the " Stanzas Written in Dejection, near Naples," Shelley had described himself as one " whom men love not," lacking hope, health, and even inward peace; in *Adonais* he was to call himself a " herd-abandoned deer, struck by the hunter's dart." To Peacock he had written: " I am regarded by all who know or hear of me, except, I think, on the whole, five individuals, as a rare prodigy of crime and pollution, whose look even might infect. This [is] a large computation, and I don't think I could mention more than you, Hogg, and Hunt." [54]

These words were written at a time when Shelley would certainly have included Byron, Mr. and Mrs. Hoppner, Elizabeth Kent, Horace Smith, Keats, John Williams, and the Gisbornes in any thoughtful list of those who liked and admired him — not to mention, of course, Mary and Claire. Yet they reflect a mood in which Medwin must have seen him more than once. Few people, he told Medwin, had not been tempted at one time or another to commit suicide, adding that four of his friends had done so. Medwin thought, quite truly, that Shelley himself sometimes dwelt on the idea. Such moods, he added, were " most distressing to witness," they could not be dissipated, and they bowed Shelley to the earth in an utter " prostration of spirits." [55] It was partly to help combat these moods with cheerful society that Medwin urged his friends Captain Edward Ellerker Williams and his common-law wife to come to Pisa.[56]

Like all of Shelley's other friends who noticed these melancholy fits, Medwin was also conscious of Shelley's liveliness and playfulness at other times. " At times he was as sportive as his child, (with whom he would play by the hour upon the floor,) and his wit flowed in a continuous stream, — not that broad humour which is so much in vogue at the present day, but a genuine wit, classical I might say, and refined, that caused a smile rather than a laugh." [57] He could be almost boisterously mirthful in deriding Wordsworth's *Peter Bell*, Elizabeth Hitchener's poetic enthusiasm for woman's rights, or Count Taafe's heavy-footed translation of Dante.

Perhaps reversing or over-simplifying the relations of cause and effect, Medwin suggested that Shelley's physical sufferings induced or aggravated his mental ones.[58] Be that as it may, Shelley's physical condition, as usual with him in cold weather, grew steadily worse with the approach of winter. About the middle of November he " suffered horribly " from the pain in his side (now diagnosed by Dr. Vaccà as due to a kidney ailment), but felt that his general health was improving. A month later Mary Shelley wrote Mrs. Gisborne that he was " by no means well," and Mary's journal for December 22, 24, and January 10 mentions him as ill on those days. During the latter part of December and most of January his letters show him suffering from a severe ophthalmia not mentioned in Mary's journal. The spasms in his side were so intense that while they lasted Shelley rolled on the floor in agony,[59] yet they seem to have been of short duration, for Mary's journal seldom mentions Shelley's illness without speaking of other activities, inconsistent with disability, on the same or the following day. " Scott's vitriolic acid baths," a popular remedy at that time, were tried without success.

About this time Tom Medwin came unexpectedly to the rescue. In the East he had seen hypnotism (or " animal magnetism ") practised with some success. More recently he had dabbled in the writings of Friedrich Mesmer, who was then regarded by his own profession as an impostor. Having picked up some of the rudiments of hypnotism, Medwin consented to try its effects upon Shelley. The next attack occurred when Mary Shelley and another lady (Claire or Mrs. Mason) were present. No sooner had Medwin placed his hand on Shelley's forehead than the spasms ceased. Shelley fell into a deep state of somnambulism, with his eyes open. He followed Medwin to a couch at the other end of the room, answered questions in the same pitch and tone in which they were asked, and (during a second experiment) even improvised verses in Italian — all of which, after he was awakened, he denied having done.[60] On December 15 Claire Clairmont saw one of these hypnotic experiments and heard Shelley beg not to be asked more questions, lest he should say what he ought not.[61] Shelley became philosophically interested in the phenomenon and thought it a proof of the power of the mind under certain conditions to separate itself from the body. Medwin asserted, perhaps too broadly, that Shelley considered it a further argument in favour of immortality, of the truth of which "no man was more fully persuaded." [62]

MEANWHILE Claire Clairmont had from the first been bored and discontented with her position in Florence. Within a fortnight Mary Shelley was writing in her journal (November 4): " Letters from —— complaining of dullness." On one evening (November 8) Claire tried to amuse herself with hints for a series of cartoons on Byron, and one on Shelley; [63] and for five days beginning November 16 she wrote all her journal entries in what seems at first glance a strange new language, but is in reality only English spelled backwards. She complained to Shelley about her health, about being neglected, and about the prospects of a cold winter in Florence. Friends returning to Pisa from Florence reported that Claire felt and looked wretched.

As Claire's self-appointed and only protector Shelley took up his everlasting duty of consolation and advice. Claire was hoping, through a letter to be furnished by Mrs. Mason, to obtain a position in the household of the Princess Montemelitto. But Mrs. Mason, when sounded out by Shelley, was inclined to think that Claire should remain at Florence for the present. Any abrupt departure might offend Mrs. Mason, as well as the Bojtis. Claire's present engagement was on a trial basis for one month; her decision would have to be made before being re-engaged for three months. On all these difficulties Shelley gave her full and sound advice. The Bojtis were coming to Pisa after Claire's first month would have elapsed, so Shelley urged Claire to find some excuse to precede them, in order to settle a policy within the month.

The sympathy and consolation he offered were hardly so wise as his advice. He assured Claire that her presence in Pisa and on the projected excursion to Greece with Medwin's friend would make him much happier. This was in itself a harmless way of refuting Claire's sense of neglect, and was probably quite true, but it was coupled with a caution not to mention the Greek trip to Mary and with a statement that had Mary not " taxed " his letter with a postscript he could have said many things that were perforce left unsaid. It seemed to be a matter of tacit agreement, born of previous experience, that Mary was excluded from some of their mutual sympathies.

No one can say whether this was a cause or a result of Mary's attitude toward Claire. If Shelley's language to Claire at this time is typical of the relations between the two from the first, it is at least easy to understand Mary's dislike of Claire's continual presence in her home. And when we consider that in 1814 Shelley had deliberately supplanted Mrs. Godwin with

Claire and that he showed in his will of 1816 how seriously he took his responsibilities, we must conclude that these letters to Claire represent his habitual language to her. It were as well that Mary did not see such expressions as " my best girl," " my poor girl," " your kind love," " how I long to see you again, and take what care I can of you," " request you to love me better than you do," " only to thank you, and if you will, kiss you for your kind attention to me." [64] One passage, possibly more ardent, was deleted by Claire. Yet Shelley referred to himself only as Claire's " one ever affectionate friend." He was in fact expressing himself to a petulant and spoiled child, in an oddly combined rôle of mother and elder brother, with a characteristic warmth of language that Mary would have found displeasing rather than alarming. So far as any epistolary record remains, this was consistently Shelley's tone to Claire from first to last, and it was also the tone of his references to Claire in his letters to Byron.

CLAIRE returned to Pisa on November 21 and remained until December 23, when she returned to her old position in Florence. Her arrival in Pisa coincided almost exactly with a sudden enlargement of the Shelleys' circle of acquaintances. Here we may well follow a section of Mary's journal, with supplementary details in brackets condensed from Claire's contemporary account:

Thursday, Nov. 23. — (Mary) — Write. Read Greek and Spanish. M— ill. On Monday walk. Play at chess. [Claire and Mary call upon Mrs. Mason.]

Friday, Nov. 24. — Read Greek, Villani, and Spanish with M. — Bill against the Queen Thrown out in the Lords. Pacchiani in the evening. A rainy and cloudy day.

At this point Mary's journal shows a hiatus of six days. Claire's journal for the missing days records a trip to Leghorn with Shelley on the 25th, calls by Pacchiani on the 26th and 28th, and walks with Mary on the 22nd and 28th. For the next two days Claire wrote:

Wednesday, Nov. 29th. Go with M. — funzioni in the church of San Nicolo. Pacchiani Fudge and Campbells [word crossed out].

Then with Pacchiani to the Convent of St. Anna. The beautiful Teresa [Emilia] Viviani, Madame Aust and Bapanti. Call upon Madame Mason see Madame Vacca, then with Miss F[ield] upon Madame Tantini. In the evening go upstairs. Esopo calls.

Thursday, Nov. 30th. Call upon Madame M[ason]. Walk with Titta fuori Porta Mare to Porta Firenze. Call in Convent St. Anna upon Teresa Emilia Viviani. A letter from the same. Esopo and Pacchiani sup. Read the [two words crossed out] Novella of Belfegor da Macchiavelli.

Here Mary's journal resumes:

Friday, Dec. 1. — Read Greek, "Don Quixote," Calderon and Villani. Pacchiani comes in the evening [to supper, with Esopo and Sgricci]. Visit La Viviani. Walk [with Claire]. Sgricci is introduced. Go to a funzione on the death of a student. [Claire calls with Pacchiani upon the Greek Archbishop and the Princess Argiropoli. She also calls on Mrs. Mason and her companion, or guest, Miss Field, and meets a Signor Foggi. Sgricci improvises after supper upon the future independence of Italy.]

Saturday, Dec. 2. — Write an Italian letter to Hunt. Read "Oedipus," "Don Quixote," and Calderon. Pacchiani and a Greek Prince call — Prince Mavrocordato. Delightful weather. [Claire calls with Pacchiani upon the Countess Pecori and upon the Signora Tadioli. She also calls on Mrs. Mason, where she meets the Tantinis. Writes to the Viviani and receives an answer, and reads English with Esopo.]

Sunday, Dec. 3. — Read Greek, Calderon, and "Don Quixote." Visit Emilia [with Shelley and Claire]. Mr. Taafe in the evening. A cloudy day.

Monday, Dec. 4. — Read "Don Quixote" and Greek. Walk out. A delightful day. [Claire calls upon Emilia and on the Masons.]

Tuesday, Dec. 5. — Ride to Ponte Serchio [with Shelley and Claire]. Read Greek. Sgricci in the evening. Cloudy, but mild. [Claire calls upon Emilia and records that Mary, Shelley, and Medwin did also. Esopo calls in the evening, and Claire writes to Madame Bojti.]

Wednesday, Dec. 6. — Read Greek and "Don Quixote." Ride out. A warm, cloudy day. Shelley reads. [Claire calls upon Emilia and upon Mrs. Mason.]

Thursday, Dec. 7. — Read Greek. Call upon the Princess Argiropoli [with Claire]. Sgricci dines with us. Fazzi [Foggi?] calls in the evening. [Claire calls upon Emilia, and records calls by Signor Tantini and by Foggi, who spent the evening.]

Friday, Dec. 8. — Read Greek. Walk. [Claire calls upon the Viviani and upon Mrs. Mason. She receives a letter and flowers from Emilia in the evening, and goes to the theatre with Mary and Titta. Receives a letter from Ravenna (probably Byron's secretary's report on Allegra).]

Saturday, Dec. 9. — Read Greek and Spanish with Emilia Viviani in the evening. [Claire calls upon Mrs. Mason, plays chess. Esopo and Madame Tantini both call.]

Sunday, Dec. 10. — Read Greek. The Greeks [Prince Mavrocordato, Princess Argiropoli, and her brother] call. Call on Mrs. Mason [with Claire]. Read "Don Quixote." ["Mr. Taafe in the Evening."]

Monday, Dec. 11. — Read Greek, Spanish, and Calderon. Pacchiani in the evening. [Claire calls on Emilia. "Pacchiani sups and shows us the reverse of the medal that is to say an inquisitive and indelicate character. Write to Albè and Madame Bojti. Also a letter from her."]

Tuesday, Dec. 12. — Read Greek. Copy the "Witch of Atlas." Sgricci in the evening. [Claire writes to Emilia and receives a drawing from her as a present. She reads Hunt's *Indicator* and writes down some bitter "Hints for Don Juan." Mentions call by Vaccà.]

Wednesday, Dec. 13. — Read Greek. Not well. Read "Indicators." Pacchiani in the evening. [Claire calls upon Emilia.]

FOR the first time since leaving England the Shelleys were now members of a little circle of friends and acquaintances. Four of them were distinctly remarkable characters. Professor Francesco Pacchiani, known as "Il Diavolo Pacchiani," was a somewhat disreputable wreck of once brilliant prospects whom the Shelleys did not immediately recognize for quite what he was. He was a tall, thin man of fifty-one, dark almost as a Moor, with regular, strongly marked features, black eyes, and a recklessly witty tongue of which both his friends and his enemies stood in awe. His stories, like his conduct, were occasionally dissolute. Some time previous to his acquaintance with the Shelleys he had been questioned in the streets as he was returning home with some gay companions and had given the watch an answer that passed into local tradition: " I am a public man, in a public street, with a public woman."

In his youth Pacchiani had become a canon at Prato. He still remained in orders and was confessor to the household of the Governor of Pisa, but he thought so meanly of the priesthood that he scoffingly called his beret his " Tartuffemestro," or " measure of hypocrisy." As a young man he had invented a new method of producing muriatic acid. His early experiments in chemistry and galvanism had attracted the attention of Volta, Cuvier, and Humboldt. He had undertaken in 1818 to found a grandiose Società Letteraria in Florence, and when the idea was discouraged by the authorities he had the audacity in a public address to quote them in its support. He was a poet, also, and made frequent reference to a tragedy he had written the existence of which seemed to be confirmed only by his own quotations from it. Having been appointed Professor of Logic and Metaphysics at the University of Pisa in 1801, he was transferred in the following year to the chair of physical chemistry. Brilliant and lazy, he neglected his duties and antagonized his colleagues. Within a year after the Shelleys met him he was retired on a pension, with the poisonous stipulation that he was to return to Prato and remain there " under the surveillance of his own bishop." [65]

Thomas Medwin viewed him, at least afterwards, with a disapproving eye, as a person inquisitive about everyone's business, hopelessly in debt, recommending hotels, shops, and lodgings to travellers and collecting later from the tradesmen — perhaps even a government spy. Yet he was undoubtedly a man of extensive knowledge and great conversational powers. Shelley, who had never heard Coleridge talk, thought that Pacchiani might be his equal. On December 3, about ten days after meeting Pacchiani, Mary Shelley gave an enthusiastic account of him to Marianne Hunt:

I must tell you, dear friend, of a professor with whom we have become acquainted at Pisa. He is really the only Italian who has a heart and soul. He is very high spirited, has a profound mind and an eloquence which enraptures. The poor people of Pisa think him mad and they tell many little stories about him, which make us

FRANCESCO PACCHIANI

Reprinted by permission from Enrica Viviani Della Robbia:

Vita di una Donna

THOMAS MEDWIN

Reprinted by permission of Mr. M. B. Forman from H. B.

Forman: Medwin's Revised Life of Shelley

believe that he is really somewhat extravagant or, as the English say, "eccentric." . . . Every evening he comes to our house and always delights us with his original ideas.[66]

Pacchiani made himself very useful in taking the party to places of interest and introducing them to other people. Soon they became acquainted with "the other side of the medal," as Claire said, and experienced his occasional indelicacy and curiosity.[67]

Some of his recklessness they had learned first-hand from Madame Tantini. She told how he had once begged a bed at her house and had disappeared while it was being prepared, not to return for four years; also how he had once sent Signor Tantini an urgent summons to his bedside in the middle of a cold winter night, only to inform him on his arrival that he could not sleep and desired "a little pleasant conversation." [68] Before the middle of December, Pacchiani had already revealed the "inquisitive and indelicate" side of his character; on December 14 Claire remarked in her journal that his conduct during an evening call was indecent. "Pacchiani is no great favourite of ours," Mary informed Mrs. Gisborne in January. "He disgusted Shelley by telling a dirty story." [69] On December 23 he accompanied Claire on her return to Florence, and remained absent from Pisa until the latter part of February,[70] after which his calls upon the Shelleys practically ceased.

It was with Pacchiani that the improviser Tommaso Sgricci first visited the Shelleys, on December 1, 1820. Sgricci was at that time a young man of thirty-one who for seven years had been reciting his improvised poems in many of the principal cities of Italy. His vogue had continued after the attack upon the *improvvisatori* made by Giordani in 1816. He was especially able in improvising tragic scenes and even whole tragedies, reaching his greatest heights in passages of invective.[71]

Mary Shelley mentioned with enthusiasm his advent into their circle: "We have further made the acquaintance of an Improvisor, a man of great talent, very well up in Greek and of an incomparable poetic mind. He improvises with admirable fervour and justice. His subject was the future destiny of

Italy. . . ." [72] On December 20 Sgricci gave a public performance in the theatre at Pisa. The pit was only half-filled, mostly
with students, and the boxes were almost entirely empty, except
for a few foreigners. Pisa was indifferent, partly because of
ignorance, partly because Professor Rossini, Pacchiani's greatest
enemy, industriously decried the improviser. The Shelleys,
however, were enthusiastic. "A most wonderful and delightful
exhibition," Mary wrote in her journal. "He poured forth a
torrent of poetry clothed in the most beautiful language."
Claire's journal for the next day described it as "wonderfully
fine . . . it seemed not the work of a human mind, but as if
he were the instrument [words crossed out] played upon by
[and] interpreting the superhuman inspiration of a God." Quite
likely it was to hear Sgricci at the Accademia at Lucca that Mary
Shelley visited that city on January 5.

From December 1 till his departure from Pisa on January 24
or 25 Sgricci was a frequent caller in Shelley's lodgings. In her
next letter after Sgricci's performance of December 20 Mary
Shelley gave Marianne Hunt the following glowing account
of him:

Conceive of a poem as long as a Greek Tragedy, interspersed with
choruses, the whole plan conceived in an instant. The ideas and
verses and scenes flowing in rich succession like the perpetual gush
of a fast falling cataract. The ideas poetic and just; the words the
most beautiful, *scelte* and grand that his exquisite Italian afforded.
He is handsome; his person small but elegant, and his motions graceful beyond description; his action was perfect; and the freedom of
his motions outdo the constraint which is ever visible in an English
actor. The changes of countenance were of course not so fine as
those I have witnessed on the English stage, for he had not conned
his part and set his features, but it was one impulse that filled him;
an unchanged deity who spoke within him, and his voice surpassed
in its modulations the melody of music. The subject was Iphigenia
in Tauris. It was composed on the Greek plan (indeed he followed
Euripides in his arrangement and in many of his ideas) without the
division of acts, and with choruses. Of course if we saw it written
there would have been many slight defects of management — defects
amended when seen, but many of the scenes were perfect; and the
recognition of Orestes and Iphigenia was worked up beautifully. . . .

God knows what this man would be if he labored and became a poet for posterity instead of an Improvvisatore for the present.[73]

For Mary, the most delightful of their new acquaintances was Prince Mavrocordato, who had also been introduced by Pacchiani. Having been compelled by the Turks to flee from Greece, Prince Mavrocordato was compiling a lexicon at Pisa while waiting for a better turn of events at home. His very appearance was romantic. His somewhat small size was balanced by huge mustachios and whiskers. His hair, over which he wore a turban, was bushy and jet black, his eyebrows thick and heavy. His head, large for his size, was finely modelled, and his large eyes, sparkling with intelligence and wit, carried also an impression of benevolence.[74] He continued to see the Shelleys often from his first advent on December 2 till his departure for Greece early in June. "Do you not envy my luck," Mary exulted to Mrs. Gisborne, "that, having begun Greek, an amiable, young, agreeable, and learned Greek Prince comes every morning to give me a lesson of an hour and a half?"[75] Mary taught him English in return.[76] Shelley played chess with him occasionally, and read *Paradise Lost* and the *Agamemnon* with him, but had little liking for his modern Greek accent or for his emendations and comments on the *Agamemnon*. He gave him credit for the highest qualities of courage and conduct,[77] and in 1822 dedicated his *Hellas* to him; but he could never fully like "our turbaned friend," as he called him.[78] "I reproach my own savage disposition," he confessed to Claire, "that so agreeable, accomplished, and amiable a person is not more agreeable to me"; and when Mavrocordato departed for Greece: "He is a great loss to Mary, and *therefore* to me . . . but not otherwise."[79]

Except Emilia Viviani, who will be discussed later, little is known of the other persons mentioned frequently at this time in the journals of Mary and Claire. Esopo was a language-teacher, a young man who seemed to depend upon Pacchiani for his engagements and who was supposed to be kept in a kind of personal and financial subjection to him. The Princess Argiropoli was Mavrocordato's cousin, who with her husband was also an exile. Miss Field, an English schoolteacher, was a protégée of Mrs. Mason. Foggi (certainly not Paolo) was an Italian gentleman, possibly the same as the Foggi praised seven years later in Mr. Gisborne's journal for the generosity of his friendship.[80] The Tantinis, occasional callers, had been known to the Shelleys since their earlier residence in Pisa, as had also Count Taafe.

From the autumn of 1820 Count Taafe was frequently in the Shelleys' company whenever they were in Pisa. The Shelleys, and a little later Byron, considered him a bore, but a good fellow. He fancied himself as a poet and was the author of several ridiculously banal occasional poems, besides a translation of Dante equipped with a two-volume Commentary. Shelley and his friends used to laugh secretly at the translation,[81] but they regarded his Commentary with more respect. Both translation and Commentary were recommended to Ollier by Shelley, but Ollier seems not to have been tempted. Byron's recommendation of the Commentary to Murray resulted in the publication of the first volume.[82]

In this new circle of acquaintances, in which the friendship with the Masons continued and that with the Gisbornes somewhat revived, life went on rather pleasantly through November, December, January, and into the next spring. A severe attack of ophthalmia, lasting from some time in December until about January 20,[83] kept Shelley from all but the most necessary writing and reduced the time usually given to reading. There was much talk about literature, the trial of Queen Caroline, and the precarious future of the new Neapolitan revolution. When the King of Naples went to the conference at Troppau, Shelley mistakenly regarded it as a prelude to peace. Shelley sought to convince the doubtful Mavrocordato that a successful revolution was also near at hand in Greece. The greatest interest of Shelley's household, however, was in a suppression of liberty much nearer home. In Pisa, in the convent school of St. Anna, languished the beautiful and accomplished Teresa Emilia Viviani, to be kept there by a tyrannical father until released by an unwanted marriage.

PRINCE ALEXANDER MAVROCORDATO

Artist unknown

Chapter XXVI

SPRING IN PISA, 1821

EMILIA VIVIANI AND *EPIPSYCHIDION;* "DEFENCE OF

POETRY"; NEAPOLITAN AND GREEK REVOLUTIONS;

SHELLEY'S INCOME THREATENED;

EDWARD AND JANE WILLIAMS

It was on the evening of November 29, 1820 that Claire Clairmont and Mary Shelley were taken by Professor Pacchiani to the Convent of St. Anna and there introduced to the beautiful Teresa Viviani.[1] Pacchiani had been her tutor and confessor when she was still living at home in the Governor's mansion, and he had formerly been one of the faculty of the convent school. Her elderly father, Niccolò Viviani, was not only the Governor of Pisa, but also head of one of the four civil and military districts under which the Grand Duchy of Tuscany was administered. Dignified and proud, with a quick temper, he carried an external air of hardness that was by no means proof against the domination of a wife thirty years his junior. When Teresa was sixteen years old, a bright and beautiful girl with a sensitive mind unusually eager for affection, her mother had easily prevailed upon Niccolò Viviani to place her and her sister in separate convent schools.

At the time Pacchiani told her story to the Shelleys, Teresa, or Emilia as they came to call her, was between nineteen and twenty years of age and had been a " prisoner " for nearly three years. That is, like most Italian girls who were educated, she had been in a convent school. To Shelley it seemed more a prison than the one from which he had formerly rescued Harriet Westbrook and afterwards schemed to rescue his " two heiresses." That she was there awaiting, like most Italian girls of the time, the conclusion of marriage arrangements in which she had no voice seemed peculiarly horrible to people whose views on marriage were those of Shelley, Mary, and Claire. Mary took the trouble, in her next letter to Marianne Hunt, to copy an Italian marriage contract, in all its insensitiveness to the doctrines of Mary Wollstonecraft.[2]

The heavily barred, curtainless windows of the Conservatory, the high wall surrounding the garden, the large, echoing entrance hall, the cloisters, and the narrow, meagre cells of the students [3] did nothing to dispel the Shelleys' impression. Emilia herself did less, because she shared it. She was, in fact, much more a victim than the other students. She had become a " *convittrice* " at nearly four years under the regular age at which inmates of her class were permitted to enter. She was of a higher social station than her companions, and far above them in intellect and sensibility. In 1820 she had already written several poems, and a short prose rhapsody on Love [4] that is quite in the same vein as the famous poem, *Epipsychidion,* that Shelley was soon to address to her. This hypersensitive young girl was under the special tutelage of two instructors, one of whom was extraordinarily naïve and indulgent and the other hard and austere, in a school that had recently been shaken by internal disorders, where it was easier and cheaper to leave girls indefinitely rather than provide a dowry. Her father, Professor Pacchiani told the Shelleys, was an avaricious man, somewhat depleted in fortune by the extravagance of a young wife, and intended leaving her there till a suitor was found who would take her without a *dot.*[5] Add that Emilia was beautiful, with faultlessly regular Greek features, high forehead, profuse black hair, and a clear white complexion that was almost pallid [6] — and it is evident that at no time in his life except when he met the daughter of Godwin and Mary Wollstonecraft had Shelley met anyone who upon early acquaintance seemed half so likely to send him into one of his intense idealizing enthusiasms.

For the next ten months, until Emilia's marriage, frequent letters passed between Emilia and Shelley, Mary, and Claire. During December, January, February, and March, Mary called upon Emilia twice or even more often in nearly every week. Once (December 9) she read Greek and Spanish with Emilia; at other times she brought or sent her books and other gifts. Claire, equally interested, undertook to teach Emilia English and corresponded regularly with her after returning to Florence. Shelley probably accompanied Mary on many of her visits, but there is slight record of his seeing her without Mary until after the Shelleys returned to the Baths of Pisa in May. In *Lodore,* however, where Mary Shelley later represented the friendship of Shelley and Emilia, the two are described as meeting daily, in the presence of a chaperon. Once (February 2) Mary's journal records: "Emilia Viviani walks out with Shelley in the evening."

By a natural affinity of temperaments Emilia immediately struck the right chord for intensifying the new friendship. Medwin, accompanying Shelley and possibly Mary and Claire in an early visit to the convent, tells how she compared her own captive lot to that of a caged bird whose cage attracted her attention at the moment.[7] Shelley remembered and echoed the sentiment in his *Epipsychidion* when he addressed her as "poor captive bird." In many of her letters thereafter the note of unhappy captivity was almost unintermittent. "Unhappy Corinne," she commented, in returning to Mary the novel of that name, . . . "but how many unhappy ones whose lot is the same as thine? . . . How profoundly I feel my sorrows! And those of my Friends! The prospect which Destiny holds before my eyes is indeed terrible." At another time she wrote: "Oh! how many things make me anxious! I am unhappy and shall always be so; I see that it is inevitable."[8] These and other similar expressions occur more in letters to Mary than to Shelley, but one whole letter to Shelley (or all that is left of it, for it lacks a regular conclusion) is an agony of sensitiveness only to be matched by Shelley's characterization of himself in "Julian and Maddalo" as a single nerve for feeling "the else-unfelt oppressions of this earth":

My dear Friend,

I am indeed unhappy! What a fate! I suffer heavily, and am the cause of a thousand griefs to others. O God! Were it not better that I should die? Then I should cease to suffer, or at least to make others suffer. Now I am the object of hatred to others and to myself. I afflict the most courteous and beloved persons. O my incomparable Friend, "*Angelica Creatura*," did you ever suppose that I should be the cause of so much anguish to you? You see what a person you have come to know. Pardon me, my friend, pardon me! You are obliged to bear so many pains and anxieties on my account that your health even suffers through them. How remorse is torturing me! How many misfortunes have I caused! It would be better if you had never known me!

Thus Emilia was as sensitive to the misfortunes of others as to her own, and particularly to the agony which Shelley allowed her to perceive he felt over her sufferings. More than once she besought him to take care of his health. When she knew him to be suffering with ophthalmia she begged him to "rest from this long reading!" One of her letters to Shelley begins: "How are you? You must have suffered horribly from those spasms. May Heaven grant that they have now ceased!"

Claire was to Emilia "mia Chiara"; Mary was "Carissima Sorella Mia," "Mia Mary adorata," "mia cara Sorella ed Amica," and "Mia adorata Amica." Shelley was "mio caro fratello," "Caro Amico e Fratello mio," or "Caro Amico mio." To Shelley and Mary alike she generally signed herself "la tua Sorella ed Amica," sometimes with the adjectives "constante" or "aff.-ma." This was all in accord with one of her first letters to Shelley (December 10) in which she said: "Call me always, if you like, your Sister . . . and I too will always call you my dear brother."

In these early letters, which constitute all but three or four of those extant, Emilia showed a deep sense of gratitude for the friendship of the Shelleys — for "tua famiglia," however, rather than for Shelley or Mary exclusively. Her warmest expressions of devotion were for Mary rather than Shelley. Shelley apparently realized that her affection for him was genuinely that of a sister. Once, after he had evidently expressed a feeling that his language might seem too ardent or familiar, she reassured him: "To show you that your familiarity does not displease me, but on the contrary, gratifies me, and in order that you should not take as a rebuke my treating you in any other way, I write to you in your own tone of confidence and sweet friendship."

With Latin intensity Emilia thought her new friends practically perfect, and frankly said so. "You have much talent, my Mary, which, together with your virtue and your excellent heart, makes you one of the loveliest of God's or Nature's creatures." Shelley, as Emilia informed Mary (anticipating certain similar expressions of Mary and the Hunts several years later), was really more than human. "His many misfortunes, his unjust persecutions, and his firm and innate virtue in the midst of these terrible and unmerited sorrows filled my heart with admiration and affection and made me think, and perhaps not untruly, that he is not a human creature; he has only a human exterior, but the interior is all divine." These words were written on the 14th of December, about a fortnight after her first meeting with Shelley.

Deeply stirred by Emilia's situation and rendered really ill at times by his sense of helplessness, Shelley sought unsuccessfully to effect her liberation. What chance had a foreigner, petitioning the Grand Duke, to frustrate the will of one of the four district governors of Tuscany? Nevertheless, Shelley drew up a petition, and sought Claire's aid in presenting it to the Grand Duchess. Since Dr. Bojti, at whose home Claire was living in Florence, was court physician, Claire came into occasional contact with ladies of the court. "My dearest girl," Shelley urged Claire on February 18, "I wish you would contrive some means of causing the Petition of Emilia to be presented to the Grand-Duchess. I have engaged that I will procure its presentation, and although perhaps we may conceive little hope from the application, there is yet the possibility of success. — She made *me* write the Petition for her, though she could have done it a thousand times better herself; for she has written to the Princess Rospigliosi to entreat her to second the prayer of the petition in a manner that I am persuaded must produce some effect — it is so impressive and pathetic. — Pray do something for me about this, otherwise I must come to Florence, which does not suit me in any manner." [9]

The petition, if ever presented, came to nothing, as Emilia

had predicted of a similar project that had been discussed more than two months earlier. At that time (December 12) Emilia had frankly stated that liberation, if it meant separation from the Shelleys, would be no blessing: " You say that my liberation will perhaps *divide* us. Oh, my Friend! My soul, my heart, can never be parted from my brother, from my dear sister. . . . I do not love, nor shall I ever be able to love anything or person so much as your family; for it I would abandon everything and should lose nothing. . . . I pray always to God to grant that I may live with you always. . . . Yes, my soul is simple and sincere like the blue of the sky on a fine day of Spring. I am happy that you know it, and I know that, since you do, you will do me justice."

No letters from the Shelleys or Claire to Emilia have been preserved. Shelley's letters to Claire after her return to Florence show the strength of his interest in Emilia without at all matching the ardour of Emilia's expressions, or of his own in his poems. " She continues to enchant me infinitely," he informed Claire on January 2. Two weeks later: " I am deeply interested in her destiny, and that interest can in no manner influence it." Remembering what she had seen, however, and knowing Shelley, Claire seems to have expressed some warning against the danger of falling in love with Emilia, for Shelley added: " There is no reason that you should fear any mixture of that which you call *love*. My conception of Emilia's talents augments every day. Her moral nature is fine — but not above circumstances — yet I think her tender and true — which is always something. How many are only one of these things at a time! " [10]

Among Shelley, Mary, and Emilia it seems to have been well understood that the affection was a Platonic one. But even so the situation cannot have been always entirely comfortable for Mary. She thought at first that Emilia had talent, if not genius,[11] and she deeply sympathized with her in her troubles. She had some of her mother's strong emotional nature, but she had also her father's strong stoical inclination to repress emotional display. Quite likely she was somewhat disgusted by Emilia's demonstrative affection for her; probably no wife, however confident of her husband's fidelity, could have fully sympathized with Emilia's unrestrained adoration of Shelley. Otherwise Mary found much that was admirable in Emilia, and a strong sense of justice kept her assiduous in her efforts to render Emilia's position less miserable. This would hardly have been possible had she doubted the honesty of either Emilia or Shelley. Throughout December and January until past the middle of February, when the mutual admiration of Shelley and Emilia was most fervent, Mary continued to refer to Emilia in her journal as Emilia; but thereafter, though visiting Emilia almost as often as ever as long as she remained in Pisa, she regularly referred to her as Emilia Viviani.

Emilia soon noticed a reserve in Mary's manner, and frankly and gently remonstrated. Naïvely she discussed it with both Shelley and Mary as "freddezza," a milder word than the English word "jealousy" that Shelley and Claire had used under similar conditions in 1815 and that Shelley had frankly written into their journal for Mary to see. Shelley assured Emilia that Mary's apparent coldness of manner was "only the ashes that cover an affectionate heart," and Emilia was naïve enough to quote this to Mary. She seems never to have suspected that such a feeling might be founded on jealousy, but considered it a defect of temperament ("the only trait lacking in your perfections"), a matter for friendly raillery only. "Accept my most tender kisses, which, being distant, will not be too *warm* for you, and will not have the effect of the *Sun* upon your *ice,* or limpid *drop from a frozen fountain.*" [12] If so sensitive a person as Emilia failed to recognize jealousy it may have been because she was unusually naïve, or because there was none to recognize until *Epipsychidion* was written.

FAR otherwise was the effect of Emilia's emotional intensity upon Shelley. When Emilia, seeking to return some of the kindnesses she had received, sent a present of flowers, he began a poem, "To Emilia Viviani," in a vein of intense sentimental sympathy matching her letters.[13] A far more passionate stanza, but of more uncertain date, occurs in the *Verse and Prose* recently (1934) rescued from Shelley's notebooks by Roger Ingpen and Sir John C. E. Shelley-Rolls:

> Thy gentle voice, Emilia dear,
>   At night seems hovering o'er mine.
> I feel thy trembling lips — I hear
>   The murmurs of thy voice divine.
> O God, why comes the morning blank
>   To quench in day this dream of peace
> From which the joys my being drank
>   Yet quiver thro' my burning face?

Not yet was Shelley's judgment sufficiently detached to suggest to him that Emilia was no better than a "slave" in her religious feelings, that (as Mary observed at the outset) she had studied little, that her reactions might be poetic but were always intuitive rather than philosophic, and particularly that she seemed totally uninterested in the great cause of freedom except her own. Except for a strong natural championship of the oppressed, one fact, and one fact only, now governed Shelley's feelings toward Emilia. Whoever reads such poems as *Alastor,* the "Hymn to Intellectual Beauty," and "Julian and Maddalo" (not to mention certain passages in Shelley's letters) will realize that Intellectual Beauty, or universal sympathy, was closely related with Shelley to an intense desire for personal sympathy. It is quite possible that Shelley's almost preternatural sensitiveness and desire for sympathy are the original basis not only for his occasional self-pity, but also for his devotion to Freedom and to Intellectual Beauty. In his essay "On Love" Shelley had written: "There is something within us which, from the instant that we live, more and more thirsts after its likeness," and he added his personal testimony: "With a spirit ill-fitted to sustain such proof, trembling and feeble through its tenderness, I have everywhere sought sympathy, and have found only repulse and disappointment." [14] The title *Epipsychidion* ("soul of my soul") merely translates into Greek a phrase Shelley had used in the same essay — "a soul within our own soul." Practically the same phrase occurs earlier, in Shelley's letter of January 10,

1812 to Godwin: " the sublime interest of poetry . . . the prose-
lytism of the world . . . were to me soul of my soul." And at
the time of using this phrase, Shelley was evincing in his letters
to Elizabeth Hitchener the same fervent sympathy and craving
for sympathy that he later exhibited toward Emilia Viviani in
Epipsychidion. Shelley's disillusion in Elizabeth Hitchener
came gradually, without sudden shock. " Julian and Maddalo "
is the intense testimony of the shock Shelley could experience
from such a disappointment. Far more than anyone else had
been, Emilia Viviani was the natural and almost perfect answer
to Shelley's desire for complete, unreserved personal sympathy.
The close spiritual kinship of Shelley and Emilia in this one particular is the personal foundation of Shelley's *Epipsychidion,* as
the Dantean, Petrarchan, and Platonic conceptions of love are
its intellectual basis.

SHELLEY's *Epipsychidion* was written very probably during the
first two weeks of February 1821,[15] and was sent to Ollier for
limited publication on February 16. The fair copy, apparently,
was in Shelley's hand rather than that of Mary, his usual copyist.
Only a hundred copies were to be printed, a large estimate, Shelley felt, for the number of people, " the esoteric few," capable
of judging rightly a poem " of so abstruse a nature." Its author's
name was to be kept secret, " to avoid the malignity of those who
turn sweet food into poison, transforming all they touch into the
corruption of their own natures." In a sense, Shelley added, it
really was, as the introduction pretended, the work of an author
already dead.[16] This means, if anything, that immediately after
writing the poem Shelley felt that he had exalted himself and
Emilia far above actual conditions. During the same spring
Shelley characterized his spirits as being alternately depressed
and seized by " almost supernatural elevation " — " I live, however, for certain intoxicating moments." [17] In such a moment
he must have written *Epipsychidion,* just as " Julian and Maddalo " is the product of the opposite extreme. In the one case
he recognized a perfect sympathy he had given up hopes of
finding, and in the other he recognized the loss of the most

perfect sympathy he had then found. In both cases he exceeded himself, and very probably the facts, in his expression. Many lines written for *Epipsychidion* and later rejected show that it began in a conversational, almost matter-of-fact mood very different from that of the completed poem.

For the intoxicating moment, however, the poem was in its main aspect literally and intensely true. Shelley's youthful vision of a complete sympathy seemed possible; after experience had almost demonstrated its impossibility it seemed actually present. The main purpose of *Epipsychidion* was to express this magnificent truth and to share it with the one person fully capable of sympathizing. Far wiser now than when he had eloped with Mary under a similar domination, Shelley proposed an elopement with Emilia only in spirit, but he dwelt lovingly and at length upon their spiritual union on the Ionian island to which he wished to escape, as he said, from " the world," or reality. Even so, Shelley probably intended Mary, and possibly even Claire, to accompany them. There is no mention of either in the actual vision of such a life, but the vision is preceded in the poem by an invocation to Mary to share equally with Emilia the control of his life. Claire, as the Comet, was to have some influence also, along with Emilia and Mary, the Sun and the Moon respectively. A cancelled advertisement speaks of the drowned author as having been accompanied to the island by his wife. As the enthusiasm of the poem overmastered Shelley's original mood he must have forgotten the inconsistency of its attitude toward Mary.

Had Shelley intended it, Emilia would not have eloped with him as Mary had done.[18] She had made it as plain as possible in her letters that her affections were only sisterly and spiritual. On that point she and Shelley agreed, and understood each other perfectly. Each believed (whether mistakenly or not the psychiatrists may argue if they like) that there was nothing fleshly in their mutual attraction. Not for Emilia, probably, but for others, Shelley stated his denial of any such feeling:

> To whatsoe'er of dull mortality
> Is mine, remain a vestal sister still. (389–90)

256

Had not Emilia described Love as " an essence eternal, spiritual, pure, celestial," with no wish but for virtue, and averse to illicit affections? The words, from her little essay " True Love," must have been before Shelley as he wrote, for he quoted a passage from the essay as a motto for his poem.

It would instruct any reader of Shelley's poem to read all of Emilia's essay. Here, in its immediate context (about a third of the essay) is Shelley's motto:

He [the lover] becomes a supereminent being, and as such altogether incomprehensible. The universe — the vast universe, no longer capable of bounding his ideas, his affections, vanishes from before his sight. The soul of him who loves disdains restraint — nothing can restrain it. *It* [the soul in love] *lances itself out of the created, and creates in the infinite a world for itself, and for itself alone, how different from this obscure and fearful den!* — is in the continued enjoyment of the sweetest extasy, is truly happy. All that has no relation to the object of its tenderness — all that is not that adored object, appears an insignificant point to his eyes. But where is he, susceptible of such love? Where? Who is capable of inspiring it? Oh love! I am all love. I cannot exist without love! My soul — my mortal frame — all my thoughts and affections, all that which I am, transfigures itself into one sole sentiment of love, and that sentiment will last eternally." [19]

Some readers of Emilia's letters may feel, as Mary Shelley did, that they are excessive and emotionally unbalanced. Nevertheless, they are remarkably like many passages in Shelley's letters and poems. Mary's deficiency of sympathy with this side of Emilia was also a lack of sympathy for one of the most powerful springs in her husband's character. She recognized the phenomenon for what it was, or she would never have continued her friendship for Emilia for months after the writing of *Epipsychidion,* but she was innately incapable of the same feeling, and thought it slightly ridiculous. " Shelley's Italian Platonics " was her phrase for it shortly afterwards [20] — an admirable critical phrase, but definitely superior and patronizing. Had *Epipsychidion* been written before the death of Clara Shelley, it might have been addressed to Mary, for even in the extreme enthusiasm of the poem Shelley paid tribute to her for qualities he knew Emilia lacked. But the quality that Mary lacked and Emilia possessed was paramount at the moment and actually did produce more spiritual kinship while it reigned than Shelley ever felt for Mary or anyone else. No one can read Emilia's letters, and particularly her essay, taking them at face value, as Shelley did, and deny their utter kinship, almost identity, with a vital part of Shelley. Shelley's poem is the expression of the frustrated, impossible longing of a whole life, miraculously come true:

> I never thought before my death to see
> Youth's vision thus made perfect, Emily. (41–2)
>
> .   .   .   .
>
> Spouse! Sister! Angel! Pilot of the Fate
> Whose course has been so starless! Oh too late
> Beloved! O too soon adored, by me!
> For in the fields of immortality
> My spirit should at first have worshipped thine,
> A divine presence in a place divine. (130–5)
>
> .   .   .   .
>
> We – are we not formed, as notes of music are
> For one another, though dissimilar? (142–3)

We need not pause over the initial somewhat sentimentalized sympathy with Emilia merely as beauty and innocence oppressed. Shelley would have done as much for anyone; his last essay of the sort had been to defend a blacksmith's apprentice from a gentleman with an umbrella, the irate Colonel Finch. The central point is spiritual affinity. From this everything else in the poem proceeds — the rehearsal of Shelley's spiritual history leading up to this overwhelming discovery, the outbursts of adoration, the attempted reconciliation of the discovery with the positions of Mary and Claire in Shelley's actual life, the escape from actual life in a purely ideal elopement, and the epilogue, again suggesting the non-physical quality of "true" Love and gently urging Mary and his other intimates to abandon erroneous opinions and join the poet as true guests of Love.

For one brief, intense moment, Shelley had seen Intellectual Beauty in the flesh:

> Seraph of Heaven! too gentle to be human,
> Veiling beneath that radiant form of Woman
> All that is insupportable in thee
> Of light, and love, and immortality!
> Sweet Benediction in the eternal Curse!
> Veiled Glory of this lampless Universe!
> Thou Moon beyond the clouds! Thou living Form
> Among the Dead! Thou Star above the Storm!
> Thou Wonder, and thou Beauty, and thou Terror! (21–9)

This was far more intense adoration than anyone had stirred in Shelley before, but he could not be content without returning to the theme:

> In her mild lights the starry spirits dance,
> The sun-beams of those wells which ever leap
> Under the lightnings of the soul — too deep
> For the brief fathom-line of thought or sense.
> The glory of her being, issuing thence,
> Stains the dead, blank, cold air with a warm shade
> Of unentangled intermixture, made
> By Love, of light and motion; one intense
> Diffusion, one serene Omnipresence,
> Whose flowing outlines mingle in their flowing
> Around her cheeks and utmost fingers glowing
> With the unintermitted blood, which there
> Quivers, (as in a fleece of snow-like air
> The crimson pulse of living morning quiver,)
> Continuously prolonged, and ending never,
> Till they are lost, and in that Beauty furled
> Which penetrates and clasps and fills the world;
> Scarce visible from extreme loveliness. (87–104)

THE DIFFICULTIES which make *Epipsychidion* such a nightmare to the literalist all lie outside its relatively clear main significance. Shelley declared boldly (148–59) his repudiation of the modern view that love should be limited strictly to one person,

consigning all others, "though fair and wise," to "cold oblivion."
This statement is followed by the famous passage beginning:

> True love in this differs from gold and clay,
> That to divide is not to take away.
> Love is like understanding, that grows bright,
> Gazing on many truths. (160–3)

To take these declarations as a repetition of the anti-matrimonial
thesis of *Queen Mab* is easy, but fallacious, even though an
earlier draft for this passage reads "free love" for "true love."
It is the old position applied to ideal instead of physical love,
and describes no more than the situation in which Shelley was
living as he wrote. He was simply asserting a belief that to love
Mary for her qualities and to love Emilia with a different kind
of love for totally different qualities did not detract from either
love. It could be nothing else without violating the clear logic
of the poem's general meaning. Coming as it does immediately
after the "Spouse! Sister! Angel!" passage, it may be something of a justification of that passage to Mary.

This interpretation is further borne out by an examination of
Shelley's phrase "true love." The phrase, like the word "witch"
in "The Witch of Atlas," runs counter to conventional English
usage. The poem itself is the clearest possible demonstration
that by "true love" Shelley meant ideal love. In his mind as
he wrote, if not actually before his eyes, was Emilia's little essay
describing ideal love and calling it true love (*Il vera Amo*).
Possibly Shelley was unconsciously translating, as in the case
of his "witch." But he had implied the distinction between love
and true love before and was to do so later. To Claire he had
written that he did not love Emilia "as you use the word love,"
and to another he was to write soon,

> I can give not what men call love,
> But wilt thou accept not
> The worship . . .

proceeding thence to a fine expression of ideal love as described
in *Epipsychidion*.[21] One of Shelley's letters shows that he expected many readers to pervert the poem's meaning by turning

" sweet food into poison." [22] Unconsciously he aided many of them in doing so by using in a new and peculiar sense the phrase " true love," which since ballad times has been a conventional phrase for faithful love of the usual kind.

In one of the rejected passages of the poem Shelley expressed some glee at the baffling quality of the poem for " dull pedants." For this different type of misinterpreter he may have had specially in mind the autobiographic part of the poem, which furnishes much of the poem's obscurity. That the poem is an idealized history of what Shelley was and had been we have Shelley's own word to John Gisborne.[23] And in lines 319–20 of the poem we have his declared intention of being obscure in tracing his own spiritual history. Because this section of the poem is professedly both autobiographical and obscure it must be explored by the biographer with particular care, despite Shelley's gibe at " dull pedants."

The supernatural Being to whom Shelley dedicated his youthful search need puzzle no one. The passage (lines 190–255) is far too suggestive of *Alastor* and the " Hymn to Intellectual Beauty " to indicate any other divinity than Intellectual Beauty. There are similarities also to the poem to Mary used as the introduction to *The Revolt of Islam*. Shelley's awakening to his mission to fight tyranny and his recognition of Intellectual Beauty were really only two aspects of the same experience, both growing out of his childhood's intense capacity for sympathy and longing for sympathy. The attempt to realize this vision in human form is also similar to *Alastor*, where the woman of his vision is followed as if she were human.

Before he mentions his experience with the " many mortal forms " in which he had sought to realize Intellectual Beauty, or Love, Shelley speaks first of " One whose voice was venomed melody" and whose "touch was as electric poison " (lines 256 ff.). It is difficult to apply this phrase to either Elizabeth Hitchener or Harriet Westbrook, apparently the only parallel possibilities in Shelley's life. Nor is it necessary to do so, for the natural presumption should be that Shelley is not here referring to any person in his own life. It is not until several lines later that he begins seeking his ideal " in many mortal forms."

This earlier form, like his ideal, must be an immortal form, a false ideal, which for a time he followed in his youth and whose "electric poison" was spiritual poison only.[24] It could have been a reference to his early subjection to rationalistic philosophy, except that there is elsewhere no sign that he regarded his earlier beliefs with revulsion. It could have been an early worship of Life instead of Perfection, or it could have been Venus Pandemos (Earthly Love) as opposed to Venus Urania (Spiritual Love). Shelley had first intended to call his autobiographical "Prince Athanase" "Pandemos and Urania"; and in "Una Favola" (1820) he had written a little prose allegory — also partly autobiographical — turning upon a similar contrast between Life (or imperfection) and Death (or perfection) as false and true loves. It is of course possible that Shelley associated Harriet Westbrook with the love of Venus Pandemos.

Next come the "many mortal forms" in which the poet sought his ideal and found only disillusion:

> And some were fair — but beauty dies away:
> Others were wise — but honeyed words betray:
> And One was true — oh! why not true to me?

There is not enough definite detail in the first two lines for anything like positive identification. In the first category one thinks of Harriet Westbrook and possibly of Cornelia Turner; in the second, of Elizabeth Hitchener and Mrs. Boinville, though Shelley seems never to have expressed any disappointment in the latter. The third person, however, can hardly be any but Harriet Grove. In an earlier autobiographical fragment [25] Shelley refers to her in almost the same language as "dear, but false to me." This was his attitude in life toward Harriet Grove and to no other person whom he idealized.

The next person introduced is treated at length (lines 277–320) in comparison with the Moon, her influence over the poet's spirit being likened throughout to the various natural influences of the moon. Here the obscurity is not with the identification, but with the treatment. After Shelley's death, in her journal for October 5, 1822, Mary Shelley accepted the identification: " — and then, maybe, I may join him. Moonshine may be united

to her planet and wander no more, a sad reflection of all she
loved on earth." This character, unlike the others, is not again
dismissed. After Emilia is recognized as the impersonation of
his vision Shelley invites her as the Sun and Mary as the Moon
to share the control of his destiny. Without question, then, the
Moon is Mary, and she is not a discarded influence, even in the
ecstasy of idealizing Emilia. But Shelley's account of Mary's
influence is so puzzling that it demands careful analysis. Professedly (line 319) it concerns a buried chapter of Shelley's life.

In the beginning of this autobiographical passage Mary's
advent into Shelley's life is hailed as enthusiastically as it was
in the tribute to her used as the introductory poem to *Laon and
Cythna*. She resembled his Vision as the Moon resembled the
Sun — that is, she was the reflection of his Vision, but without
its warmth. A few lines describe the Moon as " the cold chaste
Moon," whose " soft, yet icy flame " " warms not but illumines."
As the Moon hid the night from its own darkness, Mary is described as having hidden Shelley until all was bright. Like
Endymion in his subjection to the Moon, Shelley was laid asleep,
" spirit and limb," " within a chaste, cold bed." This time there
can be no doubt — Mary's influence is described as chaste and
cold. He was neither alive nor dead; that is, he was experiencing
neither the fullness of complete love nor its absence, but was
living in a trance-like illusion.

Whatever the meaning of this passage in terms of Shelley's
life with Mary, it is of all things least likely to be physical, both
because it was not true physically and because Shelley has given
evidence again and again, both in the poem and out of it, that
Epipsychidion is the history of spiritual, not physical love. This
being true, what else can Shelley mean but that his life with
Mary was at first happy, a genuine " deliverance " from his sorrows, and that he was " asleep " to the fact that complete sympathy was lacking? The chasteness and coldness was spiritual
and was not at first perceived because of the intense brightness
of the intellectual light which Mary shed upon him. How intense Shelley felt this light to be is clear from letters to Hogg and
Mary shortly after his elopement, acknowledging himself Mary's
intellectual inferior. In actual life, before meeting apparently

complete sympathy in Emilia, Shelley came to a poignant realization of Mary's defective sympathies, and made bitter record
of it in " Julian and Maddalo." [26]

An even more obscure passage follows Shelley's discovery
that with Mary he has not fully experienced either Death or
Life:

> What storms then shook the ocean of my sleep,
> Blotting that Moon, whose pale and waning lips
> Then shrank as in the sickness of eclipse;
> And how my soul was as a lampless sea,
> And who was then its Tempest; and when She,
> The Planet of that hour, was quenched, what frost
> Crept o'er those waters, till from coast to coast
> The moving billows of my being fell
> Into a death of ice, immovable; —
> And then — what earthquakes made it gape and split,
> The white Moon smiling all the while on it,
> These words conceal: — If not, each word would be
> The key of staunchless tears. Weep not for me! (307–20)

This is professedly autobiography, and professedly cryptic.
The period it describes must be subsequent to the summer of
1817, when Shelley wrote his introductory poem to *Laon and
Cythna*, his earlier spiritual autobiography. In that poem Mary
was still his perfect " deliverance " and he was still " asleep,"
without then knowing it, to her inability to furnish the complete
sympathy he sought. When Shelley awoke to this deficiency we
have already seen in our discussion of " Julian and Maddalo." [27]
That poem, if any poem ever did, records a spiritual storm, and
a storm in which Mary was " blotted." Also, like the present
passage, it is autobiography that Shelley thought concealed.
Shelley's life between 1817 and 1821 is too well known for the
storms he described to have been anything except those following Clara Shelley's death and repeated possibly after the
death of William Shelley. Under these blows, it is a known fact
that Mary's spirits " shrank as in the sickness of eclipse," and
Shelley's soul was often " as a lampless sea."

The identity of the Tempest and the Planet is not so certain,

because the lines in which they are mentioned do not absolutely
exclude any one of three possible meanings. The sentence is
phrased so vaguely that the Tempest and the Planet might be
the same, or the Planet might be Mary (for in Shelley's astronomy the moon was a planet) or a person otherwise unknown.
If we try to resolve this difficulty from the known facts of Shelley's life in 1819 and 1820, Sophia Stacey must be considered
a possibility, though there is no indication that she was ever
" quenched " or in fact that Shelley ever idealized her to anything like the extent implied in the passage. In an earlier chapter we have seen that not even all of the few poems with which
her name is associated were inspired by her. Mary was never
" quenched," for Shelley says the "white Moon " continued
smiling. Nor could Mary, for the same reason, be a planet only
" of that hour."

But Elena Adelaide Shelley, whose life was concealed just as
Shelley says the truth behind these allusions is concealed, might
well have been a Tempest in the life of Shelley and Mary. She
alone was definitely " quenched," and her influence could most
properly be limited to " that hour." The " frost " which at her
death afflicted Shelley's spirits may be inferred from Shelley's
words at the time: " It seems as if the destruction that is consuming me were as an atmosphere which wrapt and *infected*
everything connected with me — An ounce of civet good apothecary to sweeten this dunghill of a world." [28] Elena Adelaide
fits into the pattern of the passage and of Shelley's life far better
than any other known person, but she conforms rather badly to
the pattern set by Shelley's other Incarnate Sympathies. Against
this may be set the known fact that she entered his life at the
precise moment when the need of sympathy was most des-
perately felt.

The earthquakes that split the ice-pack of the poet's frozen
spirit are hard to explain because it is not clear whether they
are to be regarded as further catastrophes or a deliverance. If
the former, one thinks of the troubles in 1820 over Godwin and
Paolo Foggi; if the latter, one thinks of the appearance of Emilia.
On the whole it would seem that the earthquakes were internal

265

rather than external forces and were an agency of deliverance. At any rate Emilia immediately appears, " Soft as an Incarnation of the Sun," and Shelley hails her by name as

> . . . the Vision veiled from me
> So many years.

Emilia and Mary are then given complete dominion of the poet's spirit as " twin Spheres of light." They are to rule with " alternate sway " his day and night, and their influence is to be " equal, yet unlike." If Mary Shelley, an exclusive and possessive wife by nature, resented Shelley's burning tributes to Emilia and their terribly frank implications, here was a tribute which she could value more justly than many subsequent critics have done, and her actions indicate that she did. In the very ecstasy of recognizing his most perfect Incarnate Sympathy Shelley, for the first time in his life, admitted the equal sway of his former ideal. Under similar circumstances seven years earlier he had eloped with Mary, offering Harriet only a friendly sympathy similar to that offered Claire in *Epipsychidion*. The proposed partnership of Mary and Emilia in his life was little more than an intensification of Emilia's own attitude. It was not Shelley alone, but " tua famiglia," that she had protested her desire to follow to the ends of the earth.

Quite in line with Emilia's words, Shelley invited Claire, Emilia's " mia bella Chiara," to " float into our azure heaven again." For Emilia, as for Shelley, Claire was a part of the circle, and Claire was the only person once a part of an " azure heaven " including Emilia who could have been invited back " again." Claire and Emilia had been in correspondence ever since Claire's return to Florence. Shelley's letters to Claire show that Emilia was contantly asking about her, and they also repeat Shelley's own desire for her presence. Claire had not been alluded to in the preceding spiritual autobiography,[29] nor was she given equal dominion with Emilia and Mary, but she was offered the loving sympathy of the three others. The Comet of the following lines must without a doubt indicate Claire Clairmont:

> Thou too, O Comet beautiful and fierce
> Who drew the heart of this frail Universe

> Toward thine own; till, wreckt in that convulsion,
> Alternating attraction and repulsion,
> Thine went astray and that was rent in twain;
> Oh, float into our azure heaven again! (368–73)

Here is the same terrible frankness with which Mary had been treated. In the autumn of 1814 and the spring and summer of 1815 the journals of Claire and Mary, as we have seen earlier, indicate pretty clearly a state of " alternating attraction and repulsion " between Shelley and Claire. Whether on Shelley's part this was more than his regular half-motherly, half-brotherly affection seems doubtful, but on Claire's part it was attended by distinct emotional disturbance. Shelley complained of her perverse " incapacity for the slightest degree of friendship " and added some moralizing on " the danger of giving way to trivial sympathies," which may have been intended as a warning to himself. That it was not entirely unneeded is indicated by his ability in 1817, in such poems as " To Constantia Singing," partly to idealize Claire as she sang. The attractive and repulsive sides of Claire had been gently stated to her by Shelley himself in the spring of 1816, in words that Claire repeated to Byron.

Against this background it must be evident that the lines just quoted constitute a surprising autobiographical revelation. They seem to state Shelley's opinion that Claire's liaison with Byron was a reaction from a frustrated love for himself. All trace of the liaison with Byron, including naturally its effects on the emotions of Shelley and Mary, was excluded from their journals, but Shelley could not have avoided a deep sense of grief at the spiritual infidelity of one of his disciples. He can be speaking of nothing else when he speaks of Claire's heart as going " astray " and his own as being " rent in twain " by that fact. It was at this moment that, according to Medwin, a new feminine disciple enlisted under his banner and followed him to Switzerland. This mythical person, stepping promptly into Claire's place, has been discussed in earlier chapters. In her second appearance, at Naples, she would seem to be a deliberate revival for the purpose of diverting Medwin's curiosity, but in her first appearance she may have been genuine in Shelley's mind, a wish-fulfilment like the elopement in *Epipsychidion.*

The imaginary elopement of Shelley and Emilia provides none of the veiled autobiography which has detained us so long with the poem. Beautiful as it is, it throws the poem out of proportion, occupying more than two hundred of its six hundred and four lines. Its inconsistency with the rest of the poem in its ignoring of Mary has already been observed. This fact suggests that it was added, like the fourth act of *Prometheus Unbound,* because Shelley was too much absorbed in his poem to quit it.

Still another circumstance turns this possibility into a probability. As we have seen, Shelley regarded the poem as a spiritual autobiography. The autobiography ends naturally with the recognition of Emilia as the realization of Shelley's ideal, and the establishment of an " azure heaven " with Emilia, Mary, and Claire. Immediately following this we encounter the following lines:

> Lady mine,
> Scorn not these flowers of thought, the fading birth
> Which from its heart of hearts that plant puts forth
> Whose fruit, made perfect by thy sunny eyes,
> Will be as of the trees of Paradise. (383–7)

Here the poem should end if it is a spiritual autobiography, as Shelley asserted. On the contrary, however, this passage is followed by more than two hundred lines describing the imaginary elopement with Emilia — lines in which Mary, an integral part of the poem hitherto, is ignored in a manner contradictory to the sentiments expressed earlier in the poem. Let us now compare the lines just quoted with the beginning of the poem. The poem begins:

> Sweet Spirit! Sister of that orphan one,
> Whose empire is the name thou weepest on,
> In my heart's temple I suspend to thee
> These votive wreaths of withered memory.

No more exact return to this opening passage could have been written than the lines already quoted as the natural conclusion to the poem. Artistically, as well as logically, these lines form such a perfect conclusion that it is very difficult to suppose they were not at one stage so intended. The long imaginary elopement was an addition imperfectly welded to a poem already artistically and logically complete.

Emilia, when she wrote her essay on Love, had never read Plato's *Symposium* [30] and perhaps not Dante's *Vita Nuova* and *Divine Comedy.* Shelley was an adept in all three and had already developed his idea of Love, largely on these bases, before he saw Emilia's essay. *Epipsychidion* and its Advertisement contain a number of echoes from Dante, and Shelley's own translation of Plato's *Symposium* furnishes one of the best commentaries on his poem — though Plato might have been a little surprised at the intense passion blazing forth from his calm and beautiful philosophy.

EMILIA VIVIANI had only begun to learn English and hence could not read the poem she had inspired. There is no evidence that she ever saw it, but it is to be presumed that Shelley read it to her, translating as he read. Although Trelawny's belief that the poem was first written in Italian is fantastic, there is evidence that Shelley set about making an Italian translation of the poem, presumably for Emilia. [31]

By early May, Ollier had published a small edition of *Epipsychidion,* adding a hundred or more to Shelley's suggested one hundred copies. It did not pass quite unnoticed, as most of Shelley's editors and biographers have stated, but received three reviews. [32] The Brighton *Gossip* on June 23 expressed high admiration for the poet's talents and closed the poem " with a pang of regret that his mind should be harassed and wasted " by such impracticable and unsocial ideas. Shortly afterwards (July 14) it published a longer article in which a gentleman of conventional taste dissected the poem for a sentimental girl who admired it, demonstrating with easy good humour that its imagery was perfectly anarchic. There is no evidence that Shelley was aware of either of these notices or the one in *Blackwood's Magazine* the following February. The latter would undoubtedly have amused him, for in one of the rejected passages of the poem he enjoyed the prospect of seeing its reviewers perplexed by " all sorts of scandals." The writer of this review was generously appreciative of the poem's " delicious beauty " in the parts not obscured by " impenetrable mysticism," but he took its object to be a defence of marrying one's sister, and evidently attributed it to Byron. The latter error was corrected in a footnote signed by Christopher North, who said that none but " the unfortunate Mr. Shelley " was capable of " wasting such poetry on such a theme."

Even as *Epipsychidion* was being written Shelley was conscious of gossip about his relations with Emilia. In a town of eighteen thousand people an eccentric foreigner, a married man, too, does not without notice pay such particular attention to the beautiful young daughter of the Governor of the entire district. One of the passages rejected from the completed poem refers to this local interest, saying that some believe Emilia a " familiar spirit " and others " Hint that, though not my wife, you are a woman." In another such passage he refers to those, evidently among his circle, " who taunt me with your love." Whatever rumours existed continued throughout the spring and summer and until Emilia's marriage on September 8. Shortly before that date, as will appear later, Emilia's family required her to terminate her intimacy with Shelley and his family. If Mary Shelley knew of the rumours, which is probable, the knowledge made no difference in her consistently friendly treatment of Emilia. As early as May, however, even while continuing their friendship with Emilia, both Mary and Claire clearly regarded it as a misfortune. Early in that month, while trying to dissuade Claire from a wild attempt to rescue Allegra from Byron, Mary argued that spring had always been an unlucky season, and instanced Emilia as an unlucky element in the present spring.[33]

ON THE day before sending *Epipsychidion* to his publisher Shelley wrote a letter to Peacock which showed that he had another literary enterprise also in mind. He had just received Peacock's letter of December 4 stating his view that poetry had become so debased that it should no longer be written or read by anyone

270

with intellectual qualifications. Some time earlier Shelley had received Peacock's essay: "The Four Ages of Poetry," which appeared in 1820 in Ollier's promising shortlived new journal, the *Literary Miscellany*. Here he found the same views expressed. With Peacock's views of particular poets, especially Barry Cornwall, Shelley cordially agreed, but the attack upon poetry itself excited him to " a sacred rage," as he now informed Peacock. " I had the greatest possible desire to break a lance with you, within the lists of a magazine, in honour of my mistress Urania; but God willed that I should be too lazy." This, he added with good-humoured irony, deprived Peacock of a ready victory, " since first having unhorsed poetry, and the universal sense of the wisest in all ages, an easy conquest would have remained to you in me, the knight of the shield of shadow and the lance of gossamere." [34] In fact, Shelley had already promised Ollier to write such a paper, and on February 22 he again promised to deliver the essay, " within a week." [35] After another postponement, caused by the essay's growth beyond its original conception, he sent the manuscript to Ollier on March 20. Mary's journal shows that she was copying it for Shelley on March 12, and from March 14 to 20 inclusive.

Mary made an extra copy for Peacock, which was sent to him on March 21, with the hope that Peacock would not find its views in utter disagreement with his own: " But read and judge; and do not let us imitate the great founders of the picturesque, Price and Payne Knight, who, like two ill-trained beagles, began snarling at each other when they could not catch the hare." [36]

The manuscript sent to Ollier was complete in itself, but was intended only as the first part of an essay in three instalments. Before it could be published, however, the *Literary Miscellany* was discontinued, hence the other parts were never written.[37]

There had been other famous essays on poetry in English before Shelley's, notably Sir Philip Sidney's *Apologie for Poetrie* (*c*. 1581) and Wordsworth's Preface to *Lyrical Ballads* (1800). To both of these Shelley's essay shows some relationship, as it does also to Plato's *Ion*. These similarities, however, are only incidental to Shelley's reading habits; he was familiar with all three and he had only recently been reading the *Ion* and the

Apologie for Poetrie.[38] A poet, as he once said to the Gisbornes, unconsciously takes some of his tone from the books he feeds on.[39] But far more important than any such incidental colouring is the fact that the " Defence of Poetry," like *Prometheus Unbound* and *Epipsychidion*, is a homogeneous and intensely unified expression of Shelley's own character and views. For this reason, as well as for its high literary value, it requires somewhat detailed consideration in any estimate of the man and his works.

Shelley's first concern in the essay is to inquire into the foundation and nature of poetry. Imagination, as distinguished from reason, he defines as mental action which synthesizes rather than analyses; it is an active, creative agent, as compared with reason, which is the mere instrument employed by the agent. Poetry is the " expression of the imagination." Thus Shelley laid a definite psychological foundation that is only implied in the other two essays. Like Sidney, Shelley then proceeds to show the antiquity and universality of poetry, but where Sidney is most concerned to show by this means the power of poetry, Shelley's object is to suggest the nature and basis of that power.

Children and savages, Shelley continues, seek by voice and motion to imitate and prolong pleasurable impressions; their actions in so doing fall into natural rhythms; and their very language, until it is dulled by later mechanical repetition, is " vitally metaphorical " and is in itself poetry. The poet is merely he who possesses this re-creative faculty most fully. " To be a poet is to apprehend the true and the beautiful, the good which exists in the relation . . . between existence and perception and . . . between perception and expression." Thus in the most elemental sense all artists are poets to the extent that they " imagine and express this indestructible order." So also were the early lawmakers, inventors, and religious teachers, for the same reason. Like Sidney, Shelley comments on the ancient identity of prophet and poet, and even carries the point further:

For he [the poet] not only beholds intensely the present as it is, and discovers those laws according to which present things ought to be ordered, but he beholds the future in the present, and his thoughts are the germs of the flower and the fruit of latest time. . . . A poet participates in the eternal, the infinite, and the one. . . .

Turning to poetry in its narrower and more modern sense, Shelley defines it as imagination expressed in language usually metrical. Like Sidney he holds that metre is not an absolute essential and that such men as Plato and Herodotus are poets in many passages of so-called prose. Because language is a more flexible and durable medium than stone, paint, motion, or sound, Shelley regards poetry in this restricted sense as superior to the other arts whose expression is also poetry in the broader, more elemental meaning of the word.

Having defined poetry in a more social sense and far more basically than either Sidney or Wordsworth, Shelley proceeds to examine its effects upon society. This is the main purpose of his essay; it occupies two-thirds of its bulk, comprises Shelley's defence against the only two attacks that he notices (as against four considered by Sidney), and involves a disproportionately long historical view of poetry as an enlightening agent.

Sir Philip Sidney had argued against the moral objection to poetry expressed in Plato's *Republic,* asserting that though individual poets might be open to this criticism, poetry itself was not; that the good in poetry far outweighed the evil; and that Plato's praise of poetry in the *Ion* as something divine proved that the passage in his *Republic* was not aimed at poetry, but at bad poets. Shelley meets the same argument on other and unique grounds. The criticism is based, he says, on a misunderstanding of the way in which poetry produces the moral improvement of humanity. Unlike ethical science, which acts didactically, poetry " acts in another and diviner manner " by awakening and enlarging the mind itself; it " lifts the veil from the hidden beauty of the world, and makes familiar objects be as if they were not familiar." In the following passage, explaining clearly *how* poetry " lifts the veil," Shelley reveals not only the heart of his " defence," but also the guiding principle of his own conduct as a poet:

The great secret of morals is love; or a going out of our own nature, and an identification of ourselves with the beautiful which exists in thought, action, or person, not our own. A man, to be greatly good, must imagine intensely and comprehensively; he must put himself in the place of another and of many others; the pains and pleasures of his species must become his own. The great instrument of moral good is the imagination; and poetry administers to the effect by acting upon the cause. Poetry enlarges the circumference of the imagination by replenishing it with thoughts of ever new delight, which have the power of attracting and assimilating to their own nature all other thoughts, and which form new intervals and interstices whose void for ever craves fresh food. Poetry strengthens that faculty which is the organ of the moral nature of man, in the same manner as exercise strengthens a limb. A poet therefore would do ill to embody his own conceptions of right and wrong, which are usually those of his place and time, in his poetical creations, which participate in neither. By this assumption of the inferior office of interpreting the effect, in which perhaps after all he might acquit himself but imperfectly, he would resign the glory in a participation in the cause.

This argument returns logically to Shelley's initial demonstration that poetry in its broad elemental sense is the language of the imagination and that poetry in its more restricted sense is the most powerful form of imaginative expression. If these positions are true, the argument would seem to be closed. One understands at least why Shelley wrote in the Preface to *Prometheus Unbound:* " didactic poetry is my abhorrence," and why Claire Clairmont listed didactic poetry as one of the three things he hated most — the others being institutional Christianity and Lord Eldon.[40]

But Shelley was far from closing the argument with this demonstration. He believed that history supported the position he had just stated. Almost a third of his essay is devoted to a rapid survey of history from Greek times to his own, showing that poetry, at least in its broader sense, has always attended every great awakening of the human spirit. His greatest enthusiasm, naturally, was lavished upon the Greeks; his least upon the Romans, where his position was most difficult to maintain. The poetry of the Romans, however, was to be found in their laws and institutions. Even Christianity, in its original purity, was to Shelley a great imaginative, or poetic, movement, and deserved credit for eliminating the one great blot of Greek civilization — the servile state of women. His own age seemed

also an age of great poetry, and it must therefore be the beginning of another great awakening of the human spirit. It
mattered little that particular poets at particular times might
seem in some of their works to be bad men or bad influences.
The poet, as he was to maintain later in the essay, was not always quite conscious of what he was doing; he was not, in fact,
quite identical with his poetry. Moreover, he was a creature of
his own time and partook of its limitations. If he could really
deliver his poem in the original purity in which he saw it himself, the truth [like Intellectual Beauty] would be too powerful
for his contemporaries to perceive or accept.

To some readers of the essay this historical argument may
seem too long and too elastic, but certainly not so to Shelley.
To him it was a philosophy of history, the reason why, in spite
of his great sensitiveness to the amount of evil in the world, he
wore his ring with the motto " *Il buon tempo verrà.*" Poetry, in
the larger meaning Shelley gave it, would surely bring an awakening, it mattered little whether sooner or later, since it was
certain. Thus Shelley could wait for the world to understand
Prometheus Unbound; it was in the nature of things that the
" jury of his peers impanelled from the selectest spirits of all
time " would eventually recognize merit. In his *Philosophical
View of Reform,* a professedly practical treatise in which mere
æsthetics had no place, Shelley developed precisely the same
panoramic view of history as in the " Defence of Poetry," and
lingered on the subject just as disproportionately. The two
passages are quite similar. In the former he argued that great
political and social awakenings were periodically inevitable
and were always attended by a new life in the imaginative
arts; he even felt confident that Germany was on the eve of
such an awakening because her arts were already awake. His
view of history was, in fact, dictated by a semi-mystical faith
which linked it to his theory of poetry.

Proceeding to the second alleged fault of poetry, Peacock's
argument that in the modern world it lacked utility, Shelley
analysed the real meaning of utility with a wisdom that is still
insufficiently regarded. His doctrine had been foreshadowed,
rather than anticipated, by Sir Philip Sidney's shrewd, incidental

blow against the usurpation of the " serving sciences." " Whatever strengthens and purifies the affections, enlarges the imagination, and adds spirit to sense," Shelley earnestly contended,
is more useful than whatever ministers merely to creature comforts, valuable as he conceded this lower form of utility to be.
This hardly goes beyond Sir Philip Sidney, and had Shelley been
writing in the sixteenth century it is possibly as far as he would
have gone. But since Sir Philip's day, as Shelley had already
pointed out in detail in his *Philosophical View of Reform,* a
narrowing view of utility had brought England to the verge of
spiritual and even physical bankruptcy. " While the mechanist
abridges and the political economist combines, labour," Shelley
now warned again, " let them beware that their speculations, for
want of correspondence with those first principles which belong
to the imagination, do not tend, as they have in modern England, to exasperate at once the extremes of luxury and want."

Even more significant today than in 1821 is Shelley's final
pronouncement on the subject of " utility ":

We have more moral, political, and historical wisdom than we
know how to reduce into practice; we have more scientific and eco-
nomical knowledge than can be accommodated to the just distribu-
tion of the produce which it multiplies. The poetry in these systems
of thought, is concealed by the accumulation of facts and calculating
processes. There is no want of knowledge respecting what is wisest
and best in morals, government, and political economy, or at least,
what is wiser and better than what men now practise and endure.
But we let " *I dare not* wait upon *I would,* like the poor cat in the
adage." We want the creative faculty to imagine that which we
know; we want the generous impulse to act that which we imagine;
we want the poetry of life: our calculations have outrun conception;
we have eaten more than we can digest. The cultivation of those
sciences which have enlarged the limits of the empire of man over
the external world, has, for want of the poetical faculty, propor-
tionally circumscribed those of the internal world; and man, having
enslaved the elements, remains himself a slave. To what but a cultivation of the mechanical arts in a degree disproportioned to the
presence of the creative faculty, which is the basis of all knowledge,
is to be attributed the abuse of all invention for abridging and combining labour, to the exasperation of the inequality of mankind?

From what other cause has it arisen that these inventions which
should have lightened, have added a weight to the curse imposed
on Adam? Thus Poetry, and the principle of Self, of which Money
is the visible incarnation, are the God and Mammon of the world.
. . . The cultivation of poetry is never more to be desired than at
periods when, from an excess of the selfish and calculating principle,
the accumulation of the materials of external life exceed the quantity of the power of assimilating them to the internal laws of human
nature. The body has then become too unwieldy for that which
animates it.

Up to this point Shelley's argument is finely idealistic, but
also finely rational. His contention for the paramount utility
and the vital necessity of poetry in society is skilfully and reasonably deduced from his distinction between imagination and
reason. Sir Philip Sidney had reached similar conclusions by
a fuller appeal to experience, examining the effects of poetry
rather than the reason for the effects. So practical was Sidney's
point of view that he expressly declined to follow Plato's declaration in the *Ion* that poetry was divine in its origin and operation. But Shelley's argument even when most rational carried
also an overtone of mystical faith. Moreover, in many of its
passages it conformed to his own definition of poetry in the
broader sense by the nobility and imagination of its "vitally
metaphorical" language, appealing beyond reason to a transcendental, imaginative realization of the profound importance
of poetry. "A poet participates in the eternal, the infinite, and
the one"; poetry "acts in another and diviner manner"; poetry
"acts in a divine and unapprehended manner." These phrases
show clearly Shelley's sympathy with Plato's point of view in
the *Ion*. It is significant that in acknowledging the receipt of
Peacock's essay Shelley remarked that he had not felt greatly
dejected by its materialistic view of poetry, because he was
reading *Ion* at the time. He somewhat dryly suggested that
Peacock re-read it himself, as the refutation of his own arguments.

In the end Shelley absorbs Plato's view and makes it his own.
"Poetry is indeed something divine. It is at once the centre and
circumference of knowledge; it is that which comprehends all

science, and that to which all science must be referred." Continuing this tribute Shelley launches into a series of comparisons quite suggestive of one he was to make soon afterwards of Liberty, which I quote from *Hellas* as another example of the unity of Shelley's æsthetic and political philosophy:

> Yet were life a charnel where
> Hope lay coffined with Despair;
> Yet were truth a sacred lie,
> Love were lust —
>   If Liberty
> Lent not life its soul of light,
> Hope its iris of delight,
> Truth its prophet's robe to wear,
> Love its power to give and bear.[41]

Stripped of its rhyme and metre, with " Poetry " substituted for " Liberty," this passage could replace undetected the passage in the " Defence of Poetry " that it resembles. Nor would such a substitution in any degree violate the integrity of Shelley's thought, for to him Liberty was the child, and Poetry the voice, of the imagination.

Being " something divine," poetry " comprehends all science " and " is at the same time the root and blossom of all other systems of thought." From this position Shelley arrives logically enough at a prose counterpart of the verses I have just quoted: " What were Virtue, Love, Patriotism, Friendship — what were the scenery of this beautiful Universe which we inhabit; what were our consolations on this side of the grave, and what were our aspirations beyond it, if Poetry did not ascend to bring light and fire from those eternal regions where the owl-winged faculty of calculation dare not ever soar? " [42] At this point it is clearly to be seen that poetry is to Shelley simply the voice of Intellectual Beauty, that Intellectual Beauty is itself the sum of all true Imagination conceivable and inconceivable, that the individual human imagination flows from this fountain and back into it and is the nearest human contact with the Divine. It is this contact, in Shelley's view, that both stimulates Freedom and is stimulated by it.

Thenceforward, in a dozen repeated assertions whose appeal is more transcendental than rational, Shelley continually suggests the presence of divinity in poetry. It is "the interpenetration of a diviner nature through our own"; it "makes immortal all that is best and most beautiful in the world"; it "redeems from decay the visitations of the divinity in Man"; "it strips the veil of familiarity from the world, and lays bare the naked and sleeping beauty which is the spirit of its forms"; it "defeats the curse which binds us to be subjected to the accident of surrounding impressions"; it "creates for us a being within our being" and "purges from our inward sight the film of familiarity which obscures from us the wonder of our being."

It is a consequence of the immortal element in poetry that even the greatest poet cannot compose poetry to his own order. He is an instrument through which poetry is produced, and an imperfect instrument at that. "The most glorious poetry that has ever been communicated to the world is probably a feeble shadow of the original conception of the Poet." It is true of poetry in the narrower sense, and even truer of the plastic and pictorial arts, that the mind is "incapable of accounting to itself for the origin, the gradations, or the media of the process." The frequent recurrence of poetical power makes of the poet a superior man, and it is "incontrovertible" that, inasmuch as he is a poet, he is "the wisest, the happiest, and the best" of mankind. In the intervals of inspiration the poet becomes a man rather than a poet and may even be guilty of some of the sins that have been charged against individual poets. But even so, he is by nature "more delicately organized than other men," and hence the cruder vices, such as "cruelty, envy, revenge, and avarice," have seldom been charged against the conduct of poets.

At this point, after summarizing his essay, Shelley concludes with the statement: "Poets are the unacknowledged legislators of the world." So fully had he stressed the super-rational element in poetry that he completely ignored a point made by Wordsworth with which he would certainly have agreed: namely, that a poet "must have thought long and deeply." Such long, deep thought was for Shelley a prerequisite to true inspiration, but by no means a substitute. In another respect also Shelley was closer to Wordsworth than he realized. The older poet had written, but not published, his definition of the Imagination as:

> But another name for absolute power,
> And clearest insight, amplitude of mind,
> And Reason in her most exalted mood.[43]

PERHAPS enough has already been said in the course of this analysis to show how thoroughly this essay is a part of Shelley's life and thought. He had decided early in life that he had a paramount mission and somewhat later that it could best be accomplished through poetry. For years his reading and study had been constantly directed to this end. The nature of this preparation shows clearly that from the first he conceived of the poet as the "unacknowledged legislator of mankind" through his ability to "lift the veil from the hidden beauty of the world." As early as June 5, 1811 he had read, and recommended to Elizabeth Hitchener, George Ensor's discussion of poetry in his *National Education* (1811), which also regards poetry as the unacknowledged legislator of mankind. Politics and poetry had been allied in his practice long before he so regarded them in his "Defence of Poetry." He had stated the connection in his *Philosophical View of Reform* and clearly implied it in *Prometheus Unbound* and the "Ode to Liberty." More and more, poetry had become for Shelley a matter of the inspiring imagination rather than of didactic reason, until didactic poetry became one of his greatest abhorrences. The distinction between the poet as a man and as the sometimes divinely inspired mouthpiece of Intellectual Beauty appeared in his letters as well as in this essay.[44] His skylark, soaring into regions of light and fire, foreshadowed not only the idea but even to a slight degree the language of one of the passages quoted above in which Shelley emphasized the divine, super-rational quality of poetry. The greatest of all Shelley's shorter poems, the "Ode to the West Wind," was his personal prayer that as a poet he might have his share in producing one of the

280

great human revolutions it was the function of poetry to produce. The intensity of this desire (which is also suggested by
the conclusion of " The Skylark ") is the measure of his deep dejection as he became convinced that his voice was failing to
find an audience. It is psychologically connected with his despondent self-portrait in *Adonais,* where he identifies his own
fate with that of Keats, and it is a possible reason why in such
poems as *Prometheus Unbound* he turned deliberately to a
more distant audience of the " highly refined imaginations " of
the " more select " readers.

EXCEPT for the exciting episode of Emilia Viviani the spring
of 1821 passed quietly enough for the Shelleys. On March 5
they moved to new lodgings, Casa Aulla. Mary was still studying Greek and writing *Valperga;* and Shelley and Mary both
were reading, though somewhat less than formerly.[45] After the
departure of Medwin, Sgricci, and Pacchiani they still passed
many more evenings with others than formerly. They were at
home, as before, with the Masons. Henry Reveley called or
dined occasionally, oblivious of the fact that Shelley no longer
felt very cordial toward him. Count Taafe called frequently.
So did Prince Mavrocordato, often with news of affairs in
Greece.

Austrian proclamations and marching armies now clearly
foretold the doom of Neapolitan liberty. Shelley viewed the
gathering storm with a clear vision, but would not abate his faith
in freedom. " I need not tell you," he informed Peacock, " how
little chance there is that the new and undisciplined levies of
Naples should stand against a superior force of veteran troops.
But the birth of liberty in nations abounds in examples of a re-
versal of the ordinary laws of calculation." It angered him that
Sgricci and other Tuscans sneered at the Neapolitans as brutal
and savage. So some of them were, he admitted, but they had
been made so by the oppression they were now abolishing.
What if the Austrians were well disciplined and strong? Such
considerations, " if the Spirit of Regeneration is abroad, are
chaff before the storm, the very elements and events will fight

against them, indignation and shameful repulse will burn after
them to the valleys of the Alps." The Austrians could and would
win if they marched straight to Naples without serious check,
but one real defeat would ruin them, " for the good spirit of the
World is out against them." [46]

In Greece, however, freedom seemed prospering, as news
arrived of local insurgent successes. On April 1 Mavrocordato
called with news that made him " as gay as a caged eagle just
free." [47] Mary lost no time communicating it to Claire:

> Greece has declared its freedom! Prince Mavrocordato has made
> us expect this event for some weeks past. Yesterday he came *rayon-
> nant de joie* — he had been ill for some days, but he forgot all his
> pains. Ipselanti, a Greek general in the service of Russia, has col-
> lected together 10,000 Greeks and entered Wallachia, declaring the
> liberty of his country. The Morea — Epirus — Servia are in revolt.
> Greece will certainly be free. The worst part of this news to us is that
> our amiable prince will leave us — he will of course join his country-
> men as soon as possible — never did man appear so happy — yet he
> sacrifices his family — fortune — everything to the hope of freeing his
> country.[48]

The same ardour overflowed into a note which she immediately dispatched to Mavrocordato's lodgings, offering to surrender the remaining Greek lessons due her to the great cause of
Greek freedom. Mavrocordato accepted, with strong gratitude
for her generous sentiments and for his happy association with
her and her husband.[49]

On January 16 Medwin's friends the Williamses had arrived at
Pisa, and they immediately became a part of the Shelleys' circle.
Very soon they were dining together, walking together, and
visiting each other several times a week. Like Medwin, the
Williamses accompanied the Shelleys at least once to call on
Emilia Viviani. Lieutenant Edward Ellerker Williams was a
half-pay lieutenant in the Eighth Dragoons, in the army of the
East India Company. A year Shelley's junior, he had been
briefly at Eton in 1805, where Shelley may have seen him with-
out recognizing one of the most congenial of his future friends.

EDWARD ELLERKER WILLIAMS

Sketched by himself in 1820 or 1821.   By permission of the British Museum

His frank, lively countenance and manly good sense and good taste appealed to Shelley from the start. He was himself a writer and a fairly clever painter in water-colours. His common-law wife, Jane, was sister of General John Wheeler Cleveland, of the Madras Army. She had been deserted by a husband with whom she was unhappy, and had subsequently become the "wife" of Lieutenant Williams. When they reached Pisa the Williamses had one child, Edward Medwin, almost a year old. A second child, Rosalind, was born in Pisa on the 16th of March 1821.

Jane Williams was beautiful, sympathetic, and possessed of a pleasant singing voice. Her interests were quite domestic, and at first Shelley seems only to have tolerated her. "W[illiams] I like," Shelley informed Claire in May, "and I have got reconciled to Jane." [50]

Edward Williams had been acquainted with Shelley only about two months when he sent his friend Edward Trelawny the following impression:

Shelley is certainly a man of most astonishing genius, in appearance extraordinarily young, of manners mild and amiable, but withal full of life and fun. His wonderful command of language, and the ease with which he speaks on what are generally considered abstruse subjects, are striking; in short, his ordinary conversation is akin to poetry, for he sees things in the most singular and pleasing lights: if he wrote as he talks, he would be popular enough. Lord Byron and others think him by far the most imaginative poet of the day. The style of his lordship's letters to him is quite that of a pupil. . . .

Some months later Williams entered in his journal the opinion that Shelley was one of the greatest living English poets, and would be the greatest "if he applied himself to human affections." [51]

THERE were few letters from England that spring. Peacock wrote once or twice rather briefly and generally. Godwin (January 30) wrote Mary a long, tranquil letter in which, obedient to Shelley's stern warning, he omitted to attack Shelley and

283

to complain about his financial situation, which was still *in statu quo.*

Depressing news arrived from the Hunts. Leigh Hunt was in financial difficulties and had been ill for months. One of his children was seriously ill, and his brother John had just been imprisoned for a year for attacking the House of Commons in the *Examiner,* of which he was now, fortunately for Leigh, technically sole owner as well as printer. Overwork had driven Leigh Hunt into a nervous fever that compelled him to give up the *Indicator* and drop most of his writing for the *Examiner.*[52] His wife wrote to the Shelleys in a tone of almost frantic desperation: "He is irritable beyond anything you ever saw in him, and nervous to a fearful extent. Oh! how much I wish we could come over to you! I think of such a thing in a sunshiny moment, but the clouds soon gather, and the thoughts soon vanish. Ask Mr. Shelley, my dear Mr. Shelley, to *urge it to him.*" [53] In spite of his consistent prudence in money matters since the previous summer, Shelley sent the Hunts money that he could hardly spare.[54]

Horace Smith wrote to Shelley on April 3 primarily to announce that his proposed emigration to Italy would have to be deferred a few months. Almost incidentally he explained his failure to enclose Shelley's quarterly allowance:

I called to-day at Brooks and Co. for your money, as usual and was not a little surprised to be told that they had received notice *not to advance anything more on your account, as the payments to them would in future be discontinued,* but they could give me no information why this alteration had occurred or whether you were apprised of it. Perhaps you have been, though you could hardly fail to have mentioned it to me, but I will call again and endeavour to get some solution of the apparent mystery. Meantime, if you are in any straits, you had better draw on me at the Stock Exchange for what you want. I would remit you, but that knowing you are not over regular in matters of business, you may, perhaps, have made new arrangements for your money, and by some inadvertency omitted to apprise me.[55]

Receipt of this letter is marked by Mary's journal entry for April 11: "A letter that overturns us." On the next day Claire, in Florence, wrote in her journal: "News of the stopping of Shelley's income. Very unhappy all day." Fortunately Horace Smith's vigorous investigation cleared up the difficulty within about a fortnight, and his letter of explanation reached the Shelleys only two days after their original alarm. The trouble had arisen through the failure of Dr. Hume, the guardian appointed by Lord Eldon for Ianthe and Charles Shelley, to receive their regular quarterly allowance of thirty pounds. The money had been available all the while, but had not been paid because some slight unauthorized incidental charges, perhaps for postage, had diminished it a trifle below the exact thirty pounds. Shelley had been briefly in arrears once before.[56] Dr. Hume, apparently without investigating, had applied to Longdill, Shelley's solicitor. That gentleman, also without investigating and without communicating with Shelley, had agreed with Whitton, the Shelley family lawyer, to start Chancery proceedings, meanwhile stopping Shelley's whole income. Mr. Westbrook and Sir Timothy Shelley had been made parties to the suit, the latter without his knowledge. The bankers informed Horace Smith that legal charges had already been incurred and that the suit could not be stopped. In Horace Smith's opinion it was all a cooked-up affair between fee-hungry lawyers, one of them Shelley's own. His indignation knew no bounds, and it was entirely due to his prompt and vigorous action that the truth was brought to light and Shelley's income continued.[57]

Shelley wrote at once to reassure Claire and to promise her next monthly allowance immediately. During the first part of the spring Claire seemed much more contented than formerly with her position in Florence. Her duties were light, and she circulated almost gaily in Florentine society, either by herself or with Dr. and Madame Bojti. Occasionally she saw Pacchiani, Sgricci, and Captain Thomas Medwin. She kept up a frequent correspondence all spring with Mary Shelley and Emilia Viviani and one only a little less frequent with Mrs. Mason and Shelley.

Much of Claire's time was given to the study of German, in which she made good progress and for which she sacrificed some of her usual reading. She had formed a plan, which Shelley took pains to encourage, of preparing herself to go to Germany as a ladies' companion. Twice she received "ridiculous" anonymous love letters from Pisa. The fact that they bore rude sketches of trees in the border made her suspect a practical joke by Shelley and she sent them to Mary to inquire. But Shelley remarked aloofly that the letters seemed meant for someone else and indignantly repudiated the trees as beneath his style of ornamentation.[58]

As summer approached, Claire began to think more and more of Allegra. To recover Allegra, she wrote in her journal on April 12, would be to "come back to the warmth of life after the stiffness of the grave." A week later (April 21) she dreamed that Allegra actually had been brought back to her by Mr. Mason. At the same time she permitted herself some destructive remarks in her journal on Byron's character both as a man and as a poet. Throughout most of May she was constantly dejected. She wished the Shelleys to come to Florence to aid her in some wild scheme, evidently quite hazy in her own mind, of stealing Allegra and hiding her from Byron. Mary answered with sensible sympathy, agreeing with her strictures on Byron, but arguing that her fears for Allegra's health were without basis. She pointed out that Claire's scheme was utterly hopeless and, even if it could succeed, would very likely involve Byron and Shelley in a duel.[59]

As USUAL, Shelley's health improved with the appearance of warmer weather. Dr. Vaccà recommended buying a saddlehorse, but Shelley much preferred a boat, as less expensive of both care and money. Early in April he called on Henry Reveley in considerable excitement and said that he was tired of walking fourteen miles backwards and forwards [60] and must have a small, inexpensive boat. Henry secured for a few pauls a small, flat-bottomed boat about ten feet long, a frail structure of lath and pitched canvas, of the type commonly used by hunters in the marshes, but regarded as quite unsafe among waves or rapid currents. He fitted it with a rudder, mast, and sails.

On April 16, when the boat was ready, nothing would do but

Shelley and Williams must sail it from Leghorn to Pisa through the canal by moonlight. Mrs. Gisborne flatly forbade any such undertaking unless Henry, an unusually good swimmer, accompanied them. It was well he did, for about half-way to Pisa Williams, reflecting small credit on his youthful years in the navy, stood up, lost his balance, and overturned the boat by seizing the mast to steady himself. Williams could swim well enough to make shore; Henry, a much better swimmer, undertook the rescue of Shelley. As in the storm on Lake Leman in 1816, Shelley was quite calm and unafraid. " Never more comfortable in my life," he assured Henry; " do what you will with me." Once ashore Shelley fainted, but recovered while Henry was regaining and securing the boat. At a house near by they were hospitably received, fires were blown up, dry clothes provided, and a good breakfast was cooked while their own clothes were drying. Before they set off on foot for Pisa, Shelley was quite merry over the adventure.

Henry Reveley took the boat back to Leghorn, where he soon received two letters from Shelley, the first reporting that he had suffered no ill effects and was still enthusiastic, the second giving intelligent and fairly precise directions for making the boat safer.[61] Williams was probably the consulting marine architect. The location of the rowlocks was changed, a false keel was added, and within a fortnight the boat had been made safe enough for Henry and Shelley to sail her down the Arno from Pisa and by sea to Leghorn. On another trip Mary accompanied Shelley down the river to the sea.

The Shelleys' curious estrangement from the Gisbornes had lost some of its sharpness during the winter. It had never interfered with the free use of the Gisbornes as purchasing and paying agents in Leghorn nor with Henry Reveley's frequent calls on the Shelleys. Though both Mary and Shelley no longer communicated personal information with the former fullness and affection, Mary did not cease to invite the Gisbornes to visit them. A new trip to England was now necessary for the Gisbornes. In late April (April 26–30) they visited the Shelleys almost for the last time.

Ten days before their arrival Shelley had written Henry

Reveley with seeming cordiality: "We expect with impatience the arrival of our false friends who have so long cheated us with delay; and Mary unites with me in desiring that, as *you* participated equally in the crime, you should not be omitted in the expiation." [62] Yet with the Gisbornes in the house Shelley could write to Claire: "The Gisbornes are going to England. They have been here for two days on a visit proposed by themselves, and return tomorrow. My manners to them have been gentle, but cold. Not a word of the Steam Boat, in fact my money seems to be as irretrievable as Henry's character, and it is fortunate that I value it as little." [63] If Mary shared Shelley's smouldering resentment she had so far forgotten it by 1839 as to say: "Leghorn had lost its only attraction, since our friends who had resided there were returned to England." [64]

Chapter XXVII

SUMMER AND AUTUMN, 1821

ADONAIS; THE *QUEEN MAB* PIRACY;
SHELLEY AND THE REVIEWERS; VISIT TO BYRON;
THE "HOPPNER SCANDAL"; MARRIAGE
OF EMILIA VIVIANI

No DOUBT remembering the happy boating days on Lake Geneva, Shelley had written on May 4 to urge Byron to join him for the summer, taking care to mention that Claire was absent. But Byron, who seems to have suggested first that Shelley visit him, was not yet quite ready to leave Ravenna. Shelley wrote again on July 16 to suggest that he might visit Byron at Ravenna. In both letters Shelley commented rather dejectedly on his own poems and their lack of success. Despite his altered opinion of Byron's character since the visit to Venice in 1818, Shelley's opinion of Byron as a poet was unchanged. With undiminished earnestness he repeated his old exhortations of 1816:

I still feel impressed with the persuasion that you *ought* — and if there is prophecy in hope, that you *will* write a great and connected poem, which shall bear the same relation to this age as the " Iliad," the " Divina Commedia," and "Paradise Lost " did to theirs. . . . You know the enthusiasm of my admiration for what you have already done; but these are " disjecti membra poetae " to what you may do, and will never, like that, place your memory on a level with those great poets. Such is an ambition (excuse the baseness of the word) alone worthy of you.[1]

On May 8, 1821 the Shelleys returned to the Baths of Pisa for the summer months, and remained there until about the first of

November.[2] The summer and autumn passed quietly, in much the same calm, uneventful manner as the previous summer and autumn at the Baths. Shelley's spirits were more often depressed than in the previous summer, and there is somewhat more mention in the letters and Mary's journal of his poor health. As Mary Shelley looked back upon this period she remembered it as "a pleasant summer, bright in all but Shelley's health and inconstant spirits; yet he enjoyed himself greatly, and became more and more attached to the part of the country where chance appeared to cast us. Sometimes he projected taking a farm, situated on the height of one of the near hills, surrounded by chestnut and pine woods and overlooking a wide expanse of country: or settling still further in the maritime Apennines, at Massa." [3]

Even Pisa seemed much more pleasing to Shelley than in the previous year. In an unfinished, undated poem of 1821 he noted with almost caressing detail the calm beauty of a summer or autumn evening as observed from the Ponte al Mare:

> The sun is set; the swallows are asleep;
>   The bats are flitting fast in the grey air;
> The slow soft toads out of damp corners creep;
>   And evening's breath, wandering here and there
> Over the quivering surface of the stream,
> Wakes not one ripple from its summer dream.
>
> There are no dews on the dry grass to-night,
>   Nor damp within the shadow of the trees;
> The wind is intermitting, dry, and light;
>   And in the inconstant motion of the breeze
> The dust and straws are driven up and down,
> And whirled about the pavement of the town.
>
> Within the surface of the fleeting river
>   The wrinkled image of the city lay,
> Immovably unquiet, and for ever
>   It trembles, but it never fades away. . . .[4]

Four miles away, at Pugnano, Edward Williams was writing his play, "The Promise; or A Year, A Month and A Day,[5] and

Jane Williams was bustling about among her pots and pans
and cheerfully tending her two children. Almost every day
the Shelleys and Williamses were in each other's company.
The intervening distance was only a pleasant summer walk, or
a still more delightful journey in Shelley's boat, by way of the
canal joining the Serchio and the Arno. The canal was full and
deep, shaded by overhanging boughs and played upon by multitudes of ephemera. During the heat of day its quiet was emphasized by the almost unnoted hum of cicalas; in the evening
fireflies gleamed fitfully in the bordering shrubbery and the silence was occasionally broken by the cooing call of aziolas.[6]
When Mary first called Shelley's attention to the cry of the
aziola Shelley thought the name referred to "some tedious
woman," but

> . . . Mary saw my soul,
> And laugh'd and said, " Disquiet yourself not,
> 'Tis nothing but a little downy owl."

> Sad Aziola! many an eventide
>   Thy music I had heard
> By wood and stream, meadow and mountain-side,
>   And fields and marshes wide, —
> Such as nor voice, nor lute, nor wind, nor bird,
>   The soul ever stirr'd;
> Unlike, and far sweeter than them all —
> Sad Aziola! from that moment, I
>   Loved thee, and thy sad cry.[7]

Jane Williams was as yet a person whom Shelley tolerated
rather than liked.[8] Edward Williams, with his high spirits and
high principles and his love of outdoor life, particularly boating, was far more to Shelley's taste. Together they embarked
on many a brief excursion in the little canvas-covered sailboat.
The flavour of one of these excursions survives in one of Shelley's
most cheerful unfinished poems of 1821, " The Boat on the
Serchio." The poem begins with a fine description of early
morning, when Shelley and Williams (Lionel and Melchior)
had intended to start on a trip to the sea. They arrive late; the
boat is " asleep on Serchio's stream "; and as they throw the bal-

last overboard and stow their food and other luggage they speculate light-heartedly on what the boat is dreaming. Then:

> The chain is loosed, the sails are spread,
>   The living breath is fresh behind,
> As, with dews and sunrise fed,
>   Comes the laughing morning wind; —
> The sails are full, the boat makes head
> Against the Serchio's torrent fierce,
> Then flags with intermitting course,
>   And hangs upon the wave, and stems
>   The tempest of the —
> Which fervid from its mountain source
> Shallow, smooth, and strong doth come. —
> Swift as fire, tempestuously
> It sweeps into the affrighted sea;
> In morning's smile its eddies coil,
> Its billows sparkle, toss and boil,
> Torturing all its quiet light
> Into columns fierce and bright.[9]

These verses and those previously quoted suggest that Shelley's occasional fits of illness and depression were only brief interruptions of a season predominantly happy. Never before had Shelley's verse dwelt quite so steadily upon the substantial comfortable details and even the light-heartedness of life. Possibly his recent admiration of Keats's poems had increased in his eyes the poetic value of earthy materials.

IN HIS earlier letter of May 4 to Byron Shelley confirmed the rumour of Keats's death in Rome.[10] While freely admitting that Keats had written "bad verses," Shelley had defended him against an unfavourable opinion which he knew Byron shared;[11] but he had not mentioned the poem he was then cogitating in Keats's defence. With the letter of July 16 he sent Byron a copy of *Adonais*, admitting at the same time that his praise of Keats as a poet, though genuine, might be excessive:

. . . Yet I need not be told that I have been carried too far by the enthusiasm of the moment; by my piety, and my indignation, in

JOHN KEATS

Miniature by Joseph Severn. By permission of the National Portrait Gallery

panegyric. But if I have erred, I console myself with reflecting that it is in defence of the weak — not in conjunction with the powerful. And perhaps I have erred from the narrow view of considering Keats rather as he surpassed *me* in particular, than as he was inferior to others: so subtle is the principle of self! [12]

Shelley informed Byron in the letter just quoted that *Adonais* was "written, indeed, immediately after the arrival of the news " — that is, about April 19. He must have meant that some parts of it were then written in rough draft, for on June 5 he told the Gisbornes: " I have been engaged these last days in composing a poem on the death of Keats which will shortly be finished. . . . It is a highly wrought *piece of art,* perhaps better in point of composition than anything I have written." [13] On June 8 Shelley informed Ollier that it was finished,[14] and it was soon afterwards sent to London in a printed copy, in order to obviate the proof-reading errors that " *assist* the obscurity of the ' Prometheus.' "

Shelley's later opinion that *Adonais* was the " least imperfect " of his poems must raise a question in some minds as to the possibly greater perfection of both *Prometheus Unbound* and " Ode to the West Wind," but the argument would be a fruitless one. Certainly it is by common consent one of Shelley's two or three greatest poems and one of the greatest elegies in English.

In general structure the poem is quite simple. Twenty-two Spenserian stanzas express not only the poet's desolation at the death of Adonais, but the desolation of all the natural and imaginative forces that he had made beautiful in his poetry. The next fifteen stanzas emphasize the same pity and sorrow, as expressed by the Muse Urania and by brother poets, ending with a peculiarly Shelleyan curse upon the assassin — a curse that renounces vengeance in the confidence that self-knowledge is the worst possible punishment for such a " noteless blot on a remembered name."

At this point (stanza xxxviii) the discovery is made that physical death is not really the extinction of life for such as Adonais. From the viewpoint of Eternity, physical life is itself a living death, and actual life lies beyond. Adonais still lives as a part of the Nature which he helped to make more lovely and as a part of that great Spirit, Intellectual Beauty, or Love, which eternally shapes all forms of life to its purposes, as far as they are capable of feeling its influence. The supposedly alive are seen to be really less alive than Adonais. Rome, the sepulchre not only of Keats, but of empires and religions, is a visible proof that the only part of the past which can never die is those spirits, like Adonais, "Who waged contention with their time's decay." The only ultimate reality to Shelley was Intellectual Beauty; human life was real and lasting only inasmuch as it was identified with her. Thus he reached one of his highest points of expression in the climax of *Adonais:*

> The One remains, the many change and pass;
> Heaven's light for ever shines, Earth's shadows fly;
> Life, like a dome of many-coloured glass,
> Stains the white radiance of Eternity.

It has not been previously remarked that in this brilliant image Shelley condensed almost the whole spirit of Petrarch's *Triumphs.* In five separate masques, all leading toward one conclusion, Petrarch had described the triumphal processions of Love, Chastity, Death, Fame, and Eternity, and had emphasized the vanity and emptiness of earthly aspirations *sub specie æternitatis.* Eternity in these *Triumphs* was the one lasting perfection; earthly life, in the light of Eternity, was a procession of shadows. Shelley had since 1818 steadily expressed his high admiration for Petrarch as one of the greatest of poets; [15] it is more than possible that *The Masque of Anarchy* owes its structure to the Petrarchan triumphal procession. Petrarch's works are not mentioned in Mary Shelley's annual lists of Shelley's reading, but her journal for September 7, 1819 states that Shelley read the triumph of Death aloud to her. Throughout the poem Shelley's notion of Life and Death is impressively similar to that found in Petrarch's *Triumphs.* In the concluding lines of the triumph of Death, Part II, Petrarch states that Death is called so only by the unwise, and that Laura, dead, is really alive, whereas her living lover is in truth dead. So thoroughly had Shelley made this idea his own that he expressed it in an image suggested by Shakespeare's *Macbeth* which at

the same time conveys the significance of Petrarch's poem and
of Shelley's own creed:

> Peace, peace! he is not dead, he doth not sleep —
> He hath awakened from the dream of life —
> 'Tis we, who, lost in stormy visions, keep
> With phantoms an unprofitable strife
> And in mad trance strike with our spirit's knife
> Invulnerable nothings. . . .

The three stanzas that conclude the poem transmute the author's personal despondency into something like ecstasy. Since
his own earthly hopes were dead, why hesitate to join Adonais
in an eternal Life?

> The massy earth and sphered skies are riven!
> I am borne darkly, fearfully, afar;
> Whilst burning through the inmost veil of Heaven,
> The soul of Adonais, like a star,
> Beacons from the abode where the Eternal are.

The very essence of this Eternity is Intellectual Beauty, the
One which remains steadfast in a universe of change and decay.
In the fifty-fourth stanza, immediately preceding the concluding lines quoted above, Shelley gave impassioned utterance
both of the power of Intellectual Beauty and of the manner in
which it operates:

> That Light whose smile kindles the Universe,
> That Beauty in which all things work and move,
> That Benediction which the eclipsing Curse
> Of birth can quench not, that sustaining Love
> Which through the web of being blindly wove
> By man and beast and earth and air and sea,
> Burns bright or dim, as each are mirrors of
> The fire for which all thirst; now beams on me,
> Consuming the last clouds of cold mortality.

Adonais, like *Epipsychidion*, bears evidence of having gen-
erated some of its own fire. Shelley began, and continued
half-way through the poem, under the influence of Bion and
Moschus. Among Shelley's fragments occur two undated translations, one of a part of Bion's *Lament for Adonis* and one of

295

a part of Moschus' *Elegy on the Death of Bion*. From the former of these poems comes not only Shelley's title (a Doric form of Adonis) but the machinery of loves, echoes, etc., the sympathetic grief of inanimate nature, the picture of the corruption of physical death, the reabsorption of the victim into the cycle of natural change, Cythera's grief (changed by Shelley to Urania's), and the horror at the brutal slaughter. Moschus furnished in addition mainly the grief of brother poets. There are a few verbal echoes from the Greek elegies, mingled with several from Keats, Milton, and Spenser. Though Shelley changed and elaborated with the freedom of a truly great poet and produced some beautiful stanzas based partly upon borrowed materials, the poem does not attain its full power until it becomes more fully Shelleyan.

Shelley's personal relations with Keats had been friendly, but quite limited until shortly before Keats's death. They had then been somewhat intensified on Shelley's part by sympathy and by a more appreciative re-reading of Keats's poems. Shelley's praise of Keats to Byron and in the Preface to *Adonais* is based rather more on Keats's promise than on his achievement. Even in the poem Urania gently echoes Shelley's earlier advice to Keats against too precipitate publication.[16] Making full allowance for Shelley's recently increased critical esteem, it is still difficult to think that he would have written *Adonais* had he not thought of Keats as assassinated by the reviewers.

Possibly all of Shelley's championing of oppressed individuals was strengthened by his constant view of himself as a victim of persecution. In the case of Keats there is hardly room for doubt that this was particularly so. Clear evidence outside the poems shows that Shelley regarded himself as having been completely ruined by the reviewers. If he felt any natural impulse to fight back in his own behalf it must have been inhibited by his principle that revenge was one of the greatest of all human errors. In his own behalf he was limited to forgiveness and indifference, both of which he protested a shade too much to conceal the hurt. In defending Keats, however, he was at the same time defending himself. Very probably this was a subconscious, rather than a deliberate impulse. In the first draft of his Preface

he linked his own wrongs from the reviewers with those of
Keats and omitted his personal grievances only on the advice
of Count Taafe. Among the brother poets who come to weep
for Adonais Shelley disposes of Byron, Moore, and Hunt in not
more than four lines each, but requires four stanzas to present
the "pardlike Spirit," or "Love in desolation masked," that is
his own impassioned self-portrait. Considerably more than
these four stanzas of self-portraiture were written but were
omitted in the final draft.[17] Shelley presents himself, like Keats,
as a "herd-abandoned deer, struck by the hunter's dart," and
he realizes that he is one "who in another's fate now wept his
own." Under such circumstances it was impossible to elegize
Keats without elegizing himself. Once the amalgamation of
Keats and Shelley is fairly complete, the classical "influences"
are dropped almost entirely. The poem gathers intensity and
sweeps forward to its perfect conclusion in a manner characteristically Shelleyan.

SHELLEY frequently left the Baths to spend part of the day or
evening in Pisa. He was often with the Masons at Casa Silva,
and occasionally in Leghorn. Twice a week he called on Emilia
Viviani. In the delays attending negotiations for her marriage,
Danielli, the less fortunate of Emilia's two suitors, became almost frantic, and Shelley found himself cast in the odd rôle of
pacifier. "Danielli almost frightens her to death," he wrote
Claire, shortly after removing to the Baths, "and she handed
him over to me to quiet and console. — It seems that I am
worthy to take my degree of M.A. in the art of Love, for I have
contrived to calm the despairing swain, much to the satisfaction
of poor Emilia, who in that convent of hers sees everything as
through a mist, ten times its natural size."[18] Her marriage,
Shelley informed Claire, would remove "a great and painful
weight" from his mind,[19] and yet Italian marriages were in his
opinion so tyrannous that he "trembled" at her approaching
fate.[20] Mary, as well as Shelley, continued to visit Emilia in her
convent, and Claire's correspondence with her continued.

On June 19 Claire Clairmont arrived in Pisa on a vacation

that was to last until November 1. Most of this time she spent in Leghorn, taking the sea-baths, learning to swim, and exchanging calls with a number of Italian and Russian acquaintances. She seems to have seen nothing of the Gisbornes, who were in Leghorn until the last week of July. Shelley and Mary each visited her a number of times. Several times she visited for a week or more with her friends in Pisa, staying generally with the Masons, twice with the Shelleys at the Baths, and once with the Williamses at Pugnano. During her earlier visits she made several calls upon Emilia Viviani.[21]

Claire's first visit to the Baths was signalized by a quarrel with Mary, insignificant in itself and soon mended, but interesting in the glimpse it affords of Shelley as a peacemaker: " I hear from you but seldom now you cease to correspond with Mary," Shelley wrote to Claire on June 22. ". . . I am trying to persuade Mary to ask your pardon. . . . In the meantime, as you were in the wrong you had better not ask hers, for that is unnecessary, but write to her — if you had been in the right you would have done so." [22]

In Pisa and at the Baths the Shelleys continued most of their former associations. Count Taafe was a fairly frequent caller whose visits both amused and bored the Shelleys. Sending Mary a present of two guinea-pigs, he accompanied them with a gallant note in which he wished to be a guinea-pig himself in order to enjoy her company. " Mr. Taafe rides, writes, invites, complains, bows and apologizes," Shelley reported to Claire. "He would be a mortal bore if he came often." [23] This was shortly after the removal to the Baths; Count Taafe did come fairly often thereafter, and Shelley thought enough of his literary judgment to request his criticism of *Adonais*. It was on his advice that Shelley sensibly suppressed a passage in the original Preface in which he attacked the reviewers for their treatment of him.[24] There was some vague talk of the Shelleys' accompanying him on a visit to Lake Como. Amelia Curran wrote from Rome proposing a visit to the Baths, but the Shelleys found it inconvenient to receive her at the time.[25]

Both Prince Mavrocordato and the Gisbornes were leaving Italy. The Prince was head over heels in his preparations and in revolutionary correspondence. He was unable to see the Shelleys as often as formerly, but he wrote Mary frequent letters in French, full of war news and respectful friendship. He sailed for Greece on June 26 after promising Mary to write whenever he could.

The Gisbornes, with some assistance from Mary and Shelley, had sold off most of their household goods by the end of July and were now ready to depart. Under the surface of his politeness, however, Shelley was still resentful. He reported to Claire that the Gisbornes were selling all their goods, " and mine too. I wonder how much they will have the face to offer me as the produce of the wreck of the steamboat." [26] Yielding to repeated and seemingly cordial invitations from both Mary and Shelley, the Gisbornes came to the Baths on July 26 for a final visit of three days, after which Shelley accompanied them to Florence.

Both Shelley and Mary were reading rather lightly, for them. Shelley complained that reading no longer held his attention, which could only be absorbed in writing poetry.[27] Mary was busy trying vainly to finish writing *Valperga* (her novel on Castruccio) so that the Gisbornes could take the manuscript to England. Letters from England were few, and not encouraging. Godwin had been silent for months, but from Horace Smith the Shelleys at least knew that he had encountered no fresh disasters. He had sent them his long-awaited *Reply to Malthus,* which Shelley considered "victorious and decisive," " a dry but clever book, with decent interspersions of cant and sophistry." [28] Hogg wrote once about his Greek studies and pedestrian excursions, and two letters arrived from Leigh Hunt with further details of the misfortunes of his family and the *Examiner.* Both family and fortunes were now on the mend, however, and if the *Examiner* continued to recover its lost circulation Hunt had some hopes of joining the Shelleys in Italy. Peacock wrote that Shelley's old debts were still troublesome. Beck and English, he believed, could be satisfied with a simple post-obit. Madocks at Great Marlow was on the verge of financial ruin and was pressing hard for payment. Hookham had submitted a bill of £ 67 6s. 6d. for books, periodicals, and opera tickets, with a refusal to continue his services till paid. Peacock had settled a bill of £45 for silver plate bought for Harriet in 1813 and had given Shelley's address to a Mrs. Lyon, probably another creditor on Harriet's account.[29] The Shelleys wished to settle these accounts. Since the spring of 1820 they had been economizing consistently in order to meet their financial obligations, which could only be reduced gradually. Shelley promised to refund Peacock's disbursements within the month.[30] Hookham's account was still unpaid at Shelley's death.[31]

THERE is no indication in Shelley's letters that he read any of the reviews of *The Cenci* that continued throughout 1821, or any of the seven reviews which *Prometheus Unbound* received in 1820 and 1821. In her journal for May 6 and also for May 7 Mary Shelley wrote the bare word " Reviews," without further detail. Shelley knew from Hunt[32] that Hazlitt had attacked him in his essay on " Paradox and Commonplace "[33] and that Hunt had remonstrated and threatened to attack Hazlitt if he continued. Shelley's letters consistently professed the indifference of a man who felt himself already sentenced to nothing but neglect or abuse.[34] If he heard the current quip that *Prometheus Unbound* was well named because none would take the trouble to bind it, he probably accepted it as a true index of public opinion.

The three later reviews of *The Cenci*, which had gone into a second edition in 1821, continued the same tone of mixed praise and censure that marked the 1820 reviews.[35] *Prometheus Unbound* was reviewed in 1820 by the *London Magazine* (June), the *London Magazine and Monthly Critical and Dramatic Review* (September and October), the *Literary Gazette* (September 9), *Blackwood's Edinburgh Magazine* (September), and the *Lonsdale Magazine* (November). In 1821 the reviews continued, with articles in the *Monthly Review* (February) and the *Quarterly Review* (October).[36]

The inability of these reviews to understand Shelley's style has already been discussed in Chapter xxii, so that it only remains to summarize their general attitude toward the poem. Of the seven magazines, three (the *Literary Gazette, Monthly Review,* and *Quarterly*) were almost entirely denunciatory. The *Literary Gazette* bitterly attacked the poem for its obscurity, pronouncing Shelley little better than a lunatic and the poem " a mélange of nonsense, cockneyism, poverty, and pedantry." The *Monthly Review* denounced the title poem as " *nonsense, pure, unmixed nonsense.*" It also pronounced the poem impious, but nevertheless admitted Shelley's genius and " benevolent feeling, beautiful language, and powerful versification." The *Quarterly* found it quite dull and unoriginal — " drivelling prose run mad." Its " total lack of meaning," however, did not prevent the reviewer (W. S. Walker) from asserting that the meaning was thoroughly impious and immoral. Somewhat more colourlessly and impartially the *Lonsdale Magazine and Provincial Repository* acknowledged Shelley's genius while condemning his principles. *Blackwood's Edinburgh Magazine* continued its policy of mixing stern criticism of Shelley's ideas with enthusiastic praise of his genius, and sought once more to win from his errors a poet " destined to leave a great name behind him."

Two of the reviews were enthusiastic almost without qualification. The *London Magazine,* somewhat briefly, praised *Prometheus Unbound* as " unsettled, irregular, magnificent," and the *London Magazine and Monthly Critical and Dramatic Review* gave it two full-sized reviews, the first praising " the extreme force and freshness " of the shorter poems and the second summarizing and copiously quoting from the title poem as " one of the most stupendous . . . works of modern poetry," " a vast wilderness of beauty." Few poems have received more extreme praise than Shelley's in this review, which apparently neither Shelley nor any of his biographers ever read. Another eulogistic review was written, but not published. Henry Colburn, owner of the *New Monthly Magazine* and part-owner of the *Literary Gazette,* turned it back upon the hands of the reviewer, Thomas Noon Talfourd, because he considered the book " full of Jacobinism and blasphemy." [37]

In addition to these reviews and those of *Queen Mab, Epipsychidion,* and *Adonais,* Shelley received in 1820 and 1821 a considerable amount of general and incidental notice.[38] The *Dublin Magazine* (November 1820) printed some general, predominantly unfavourable " Critical Remarks on Shelley's Poetry." In the same year the *Retrospective Review*, taking an enthusiastic view of the poetry of the present age, praised Shelley's poetry. It is pleasing to know that Shelley probably read this brief comment,[39] which was copied by one of the provincial journals and by the *New York Literary and Scientific Repository*. Other American journals began to take notice of Shelley by printing extracts from reviews or poems. The *Honeycomb*, in a series entitled " Portraits of the Metropolitan Poets," treated Shelley not unfavourably in the third essay. An appreciative general article " On the Philosophy and Poetry of Shelley " appeared in the *London Magazine and Theatrical Inquisitor* for February 1821. The pious Quaker poet Bernard Barton published in 1820 his " Stanzas Addressed to Percy Bysshe Shelley," a dull, well-meant attempt to convert erring genius. Horace Smith's sonnet " To the Author of The Revolt of Islam," published first in the *Examiner* in 1818, was republished under another title in 1820 in his volume *Amarynthus the Nympholept* and was quoted with approval by the *London Magazine and Theatrical Inquisitor*. Arthur Brooke (John Chalk Claris) printed an enthusiastic sonnet to Shelley in the *Examiner* for November 5, 1820, which was reprinted in the *Tickler* for April 1, 1821.

In the two years 1820 and 1821 Shelley received in all about thirty reviews and about forty brief incidental notices. Several journals quoted his poems independently of reviews, others published poems which were addressed to him, and one book was published about him. Granted that the *Quarterly* and possibly the *Literary Gazette* exerted more influence in condemning Shelley than any two friendly journals in his defence, the amount of favourable criticism and the recognition of Shelley's power and genius even by unfriendly critics offer a convincing demonstration that Shelley greatly underrated the impression he was beginning to make upon the British public. He prejudged the case against himself, and his judgment has been uncritically accepted as true by all subsequent critics and biographers. At this point, had he finished and published "Charles the First" instead of "The Witch of Atlas" it would have been possible for Shelley to have received far more general recognition.

THE PUBLICATION of *Adonais* late in 1821 undoubtedly helped swing the tide more strongly against Shelley. Instead of giving any wavering reviewer an opportunity for praise by presenting a non-controversial poem, Shelley threw down the gage of battle by assailing reviewers as the assassins of Keats. Rather significantly, only three journals reviewed *Adonais* in 1821.[40] The liberal *Literary Chronicle and Weekly Review* reviewed it before it had been published, quoted almost all of it, and praised it as a poem of "transcendent merits" by a poet of "no ordinary genius." The *Literary Gazette* (December 8) scorned it as an unrelieved farrago of nonsense and impiety, quoting excerpts illustrating six different types of nonsense. This was to be expected, since the *Literary Gazette* had consistently assailed Shelley from the first. But *Blackwood's Magazine*, which had been even more savage with Keats than the *Quarterly*, now abandoned its efforts to "save" Shelley and joined his most furious enemies. In the December issue it rained contempt and sarcasm upon him, quoted a whole column of his "absurdities," and offered two brutal parodies of *Adonais*. Having previously omitted to review *The Cenci*, it included in the same article a furious brief review of that poem as well.

Very probably the reviewers felt that *Adonais* should be treated as a declaration of war; Shelley, on the other hand, felt that his "least imperfect poem" was the final test of his ability to win public acceptance. "I am especially curious to hear the fate of 'Adonais,'" he wrote to Ollier on November 11. "I confess I should be surprised if *that* poem were born to an immortality of oblivion." Before he knew how the poem had been reviewed he wrote to Hunt (January 25, 1822): "My faculties are shaken to atoms, and torpid. I can write nothing; and if *Adonais* had no success, and excited no interest what incentive can I have to write?"[41]

In the spring of 1821 another circumstance occurred to make it still more difficult for Shelley to receive fair treatment from the reviewers. In 1819 the radical printer Richard Carlile had discovered Shelley's *Queen Mab* and had asked and been refused permission to reprint it. He had respected Shelley's wishes, but his former employee William Clark was less scrupulous. He brought out and advertised two slightly variant editions,[42] and the notorious radical piratical publisher William Benbow anonymously brought out still another edition under a false New York imprint.[43]

Shelley learned that *Queen Mab* was selling "by the thousands," and considered it rather a droll circumstance.[44] He was nevertheless somewhat annoyed to be judged in 1821 by his comparatively crude artistic standards of 1813 and by beliefs which did not adequately represent him in 1821. It had been ruled in the case of Southey versus the piratical publishers of his *Wat Tyler* that books liable to conviction for blasphemy or sedition were not entitled to legal protection; hence it was impossible to suppress the piracy, though Horace Smith seems to have made some tentative efforts. Shelley contented himself with a letter in the *Examiner* disavowing and disapproving the publication, condemning the book as immature both artistically and philosophically, but reaffirming in general terms his opposition to social, political, and religious oppressions.[45]

From this moment Shelley's *Queen Mab* became an important weapon in the arsenal of British working-class radicalism. *John Bull's British Journal,* a radical weekly published by William Benbow, gave it a sympathetic review on March 11. The *London Magazine and Theatrical Inquisitor,* though only mildly radical, and not a workingman's magazine, reviewed it favourably in the March issue and prophesied that the author was meant to fulfil a high destiny.[46] Within twenty years fourteen or more separate editions were issued by piratical radical publishers. The book took an honoured place with Volney's *Ruins of Empire,* Palmer's *Principles of Nature,* Byron's *Cain,* and the works of Tom Paine in the little radical "libraries" constantly offered for sale.

In 1821 responsible authorities in England were far too nervous over the condition of the country to ignore such a publication. William Clark was immediately indicted by the Society for the Prevention of Vice, that active and virtuously named association which genuine liberals like Sydney Smith regarded rather as a society for preserving aristocratic vices. Instead of awaiting his trial, selling the books meanwhile, the unheroic William Clark disgusted his fellow radicals by binding himself to good behaviour in the interim,[47] and publishing the anonymous *Reply to the Antimatrimonial Hypothesis and Supposed Atheism of Percy Bysshe Shelley, as Laid Down in Queen Mab* (1821), as a demonstration that his interest in *Queen Mab* was financial rather than propagandistic. At his trial on November 19, 1822 Clark made the most of this publication and of his willingness to surrender all copies of the offending book, but was nevertheless sentenced to four months' imprisonment.[48]

Two conservative journals, the *Literary Gazette* for May 19 and the *Monthly Magazine* for June, vigorously denounced the poem; and the rather liberal *Literary Chronicle and Weekly Review* for June 2 reviewed the author, rather than the poem, as a striking example of perverted genius, powerful, but wicked. Two published poems were elicited by the *Queen Mab* piracy. A reader of the review in the *Literary Gazette* sent in a short poem entitled " The Atheist," wondering why the author of such a line as " There is no God " should not immediately have been blasted by Heaven's lightnings " to his native hell." On the other side John Watson Dalby, in the *Literary Chronicle* for June 9, 1821, published two eight-line stanzas commenting sarcastically on the " clearest proofs " being offered that Shelley was either the devil or his equal.[49] All this happened in the very year, 1821, when Southey, in the Preface to his *Vision of Judgment,* was urging public opinion to emphasize decency and order by suppressing the " Satanic School " for just such utterances as *Queen Mab.* Thus the effect of the piracy of *Queen Mab* was less " droll " than Shelley supposed.

WHEN the Gisbornes set out on July 29 on their journey to England, Shelley accompanied them as far as Florence, where he remained for several days investigating the possibilities of securing a suitable house there for the winter.⁵⁰ During his absence Mary spent most of her time with the Williamses, partly at the Baths and partly at Pugnano, while Edward Williams was painting a water-colour portrait of her that was to be her birthday present to Shelley on August 4.

Shelley returned on August 2, but he was off again before his birthday. On the day of his return a letter arrived from Byron, informing him that the Countess Guiccioli's father and brother had been expelled from Ravenna for Carbonarist sympathies and that she herself had fled to Florence. Byron requested Shelley to visit him, and as Shelley knew Byron himself would soon be leaving Ravenna, he must have thought at once of what would become of Allegra in her convent at Bagnacavallo. On the next day he set out to visit Byron. He arrived that night at Leghorn and spent the next morning with Claire Clairmont, celebrating his birthday by rowing in the bay.⁵¹

During the tiresome night journey in an open carriage from Leghorn to Bologna, the carriage overturned. " The old horse stumbled and threw me and the fat vetturino into a slope of meadow over the hedge. My angular figure stuck where it was pitched but my vetturino's spherical form rolled fairly to the bottom of the hill, and that with so few symptoms of reluctance in the life that animated it, that my ridicule (for it was the drollest sight in the world) was suppressed by my fear that the poor devil had been hurt. But he was very well, and we continued our journey with great success." ⁵² Shelley offered Mary the suggestion, which was accepted, that Claire be invited to stay with her during his absence.

Shelley reached Ravenna on August 6. On the very first evening Byron imparted some profoundly disturbing information. He showed Shelley a letter he had received from Mr. R. B. Hoppner eleven months before. In all that pertains to Shelley the letter was as follows:

. . . You are surprised, and with reason, at the change of my opinion respecting Shiloe: it certainly is not that which I once entertained of him: but if I disclose to you my fearful secret, I trust, for his unfortunate wife's sake, if not out of regard to Mrs. Hoppner and me,

that you will not let the Shelleys know that we are acquainted with
it. This request you will find so reasonable that I am sure you will
comply with it, and I therefore proceed to divulge to you, what
indeed on Allegra's account it is necessary that you should know, as
it will fortify you in the good resolution you have already taken
never to trust her again to her mother's care.

You must know then that at the time the Shelleys were here Clara
was with child by Shelley: you may remember to have heard that
she was constantly unwell, and under the care of a Physician, and I
am uncharitable enough to believe that the quantity of medicine
she then took was not for the mere purpose of restoring her health.
I perceive too why she preferred remaining alone at Este, notwithstanding her fear of ghosts and robbers, to being here with the
Shelleys. Be this as it may, they proceeded from here to Naples,
where one night Shelley was called up to see Clara who was very
ill. His wife, naturally, thought it very strange that he should be
sent for; but although she was not aware of the nature of the connexion between them, she had had sufficient proof of Shelley's indifference, and of Clara's hatred for her: besides as Shelley desired
her to remain quiet she did not dare to interfere. A Mid-wife was
sent for, and the worthy pair, who had made no preparation for the
reception of the unfortunate being she was bringing into the world,
bribed the woman to carry it to the Pietà, where the child was taken
half an hour after its birth, being obliged likewise to purchase the
physician's silence with a considerable sum. During all the time of
her confinement Mrs. Shelley, who expressed great anxiety on her
account, was not allowed to approach her, and these beasts, instead
of requiting her uneasiness on Clara's account by at least a few expressions of kindness, have since increased in their hatred of her,
behaving to her in the most brutal manner, and Clara doing everything she can to engage her husband to abandon her. Poor Mrs.
Shelley, whatever suspicions she may entertain of the nature of their
connexion, knows nothing of their adventure at Naples, and as the
knowledge of it could only add to her misery, 'tis as well that she
should not. This account we had from Elise, who passed here this
summer with an English lady who spoke very highly of her. She
likewise told us that Clara does not scruple to tell Mrs. Shelley she
wishes her dead, and to say to Shelley in her presence that she wonders how he can live with such a creature. Thus you see that your
expression with regard to her is *even too delicate;* and I think with
you, not only that she is a —— ——, but any thing worse even

that you can say of her. I hope this account will encourage you to persevere in your kind attentions to poor little Allegra, who has no-one else to look up to. I cannot conceive what Clara can mean by her impertinence to you. She ought to be too happy to reflect that the child is so well taken care of. Mrs. Hoppner was so angry when she heard the above account that it was with difficulty she was prevailed upon not to write to the Shelleys and upbraid them with their infamous conduct. However, as this could have been productive of no good, it was better to leave them to themselves, the more particularly as she had already written to decline interfering in the affair of her child, and there was every probability of our not being troubled any more with them. Besides that, in pity for the unfortunate Mrs. Shelley, whose situation would only have been rendered worse by the exposure, silence on these matters was still more incumbent on her. I think after this account you will no longer wonder that I have a bad opinion of Shelley. His talents I acknowledge: but I cannot concur that a man can be, as you say, " crazy against morality," and have honour. I have heard of honour among thieves, but there it means only interest, and though it may be to Shelley's interest to cut as respectable a figure as he can with the opinions he publickly professes, it is clear to me that honour does not direct any one of his actions. I fear my letter is written in a very incoherent style, but as I really cannot bring myself to go over this disgusting subject a second time; I hope you will endeavour to comprehend it, as it stands.[53]

At the time Byron had expressed an opinion that the story was no doubt true, because " just like them," even though Elise seemed to him a very shaky witness.[54] But contact with Shelley evidently made him ashamed of this judgment; he broke his promise to keep Hoppner's counsel, and laid the letter before Shelley. " Lord Byron," Shelley immediately informed Mary, " has also told me of a circumstance that shocks me exceedingly; because it exhibits a degree of desperate and wicked malice for which I am at a loss to account. When I hear such things my patience and my philosophy are put to a severe proof, whilst I refrain from seeking out some obscure hiding place where the countenance of man may never meet me more." After summarizing Hoppner's story as given above, he concluded:

As to what Reviews and the world says, I do not care a jot, but when persons who have known me are capable of conceiving of me — not that I have fallen into a great error and impudence, as would have been the living with Clare as my mistress — but that I have committed such unutterable crimes as destroying or abandoning a child, and that my own — imagine my despair of good, imagine how it is possible that one of so weak and sensitive a nature as mine can run further the gauntlet through this hellish society of men. *You* should write to the Hoppners a letter refuting the charge, in case you believe, and know, and can prove that it is false; stating the grounds and proofs of your belief. I need not dictate what you should say; nor, I hope, inspire you with warmth to rebut a charge, which you only can effectually rebut. If you will send the letter to me here, I will forward it to the Hoppners. Lord Byron is not up, I do not know the Hoppners' address, and I am anxious not to lose a post.[55]

Two days later, before receiving Mary's reply to his former letter, Shelley commented further:

I dare say the subject of the latter half of my letter gave you pain: but it was necessary to look the affair in the face, and the only satis-factory answer to the calumny must be given by you, and could be given by you, alone. This is evidently the source of the violent de-nunciations of the Literary Gazette — in themselves contemptible enough, and only to be regarded as effects which show us their cause, which until we put off our mortal nature we never can de-spise — that is, the belief of persons who have known and seen you, that you are guilty of the most enormous crimes.

A certain degree and a certain kind of infamy is to be borne, and, in fact, is the best compliment which an exalted nature can receive from the filthy world of which it is its hell to be a part — but this sort of thing exceeds the measure, and even if it were only for the sake of our dear Percy I would take some pains to suppress it. In fact, it shall be suppressed, even if I am reduced to the disagreeable necessity of prosecuting Elise before the Tuscan tribunals.[56]

Mary Shelley's reply to the first of these letters was prompt and passionate:

My dear Shelley,

Shocked beyond all measure as I was, I instantly wrote the enclosed. If the task be not too dreadful, pray copy it for me. I cannot.

Read that part of your letter which contains the accusation. I tried, but I could not write it. I think I could as soon have died. I send also Elise's last letter: enclose it or not as you think best.

I wrote to you with far different feelings last night, beloved friend. Our barque is indeed " tempest-tost "; but love me, as you have ever done, and God preserve my child to me, and our enemies shall not be too much for us. Consider well if Florence be a fit residence for us. I love, I own, to face danger; but I would not be imprudent.

Pray get my letter to Mrs. Hoppner copied for a thousand reasons. Adieu, dearest! Take care of yourself — all yet is well. The shock for me is over, and I now despise the slander; but it must not pass uncontradicted. I sincerely thank Lord Byron for his kind unbelief.

Affectionately yours,

M. W. S.

Friday.

Do not think me imprudent in mentioning Clare's illness at Naples. It is well to meet facts. They are as cunning as wicked. I have read over my letter; it is written in haste; but it were as well that the first burst of feeling should be expressed. No letters.[57]

With this letter was enclosed the following:

Pisa, August 10, 1821.

My Dear Mrs. Hoppner, — After a silence of nearly two years I address you again, and most bitterly do I regret the occasion on which I now write. Pardon me that I do not write in French; you understand English well, and I am too much impressed to shackle myself in a foreign language; even in my own my thoughts far outrun my pen, so that I can hardly form the letters. I write to defend him to whom I have the happiness to be united, whom I love and esteem beyond all creatures, from the foulest calumnies; and to you I write this, who were so kind [and] to Mr. Hoppner; to both of whom I indulged the pleasing idea that I have every reason to feel gratitude. This is indeed a painful task.

Shelley is at present on a visit to Lord Byron at Ravenna, and I received a letter from him to-day containing accounts that make

my hand tremble so much that I can hardly hold the pen. It tells
me that Elise wrote to you relating the most hideous stories against
him, and that you have believed them. Before I speak of these falsehoods permit [me] to say a few words concerning this miserable
girl. You well know that she formed an attachment with Paolo when
we proceeded to Rome, and at Naples their marriage was talked
of. We all tried to dissuade her; we knew Paolo to be a rascal, and
we thought so well of her that we believed him to be unworthy of
her. An accident led me to the knowledge that without marrying
they had formed a connexion; she was ill, we sent for a doctor who
said there was danger of a miscarriage. I would not turn the girl
on the world without in some degree binding her to this man. We
had them married at Sir W. A'Court's — she left us; turned Catholic
at Rome, married him, and then went to Florence. After the disastrous death of my child we came to Tuscany. We have seen little
of them; but we have had knowledge that Paolo has formed a scheme
of extorting money from Shelley by false accusations — he has
written him threatening letters, saying that he w^d be the ruin of
him, etc. We placed these in the hands of a celebrated lawyer
here who has done what he can to silence him. Elise has never interfered in this, and indeed the other day I received a letter from
her, entreating with great professions of love that I would send her
money. I took no notice of this; but although I knew her to be in
evil hands, I would not believe that she was wicked enough to join
in his plans without proof.

And now I come to her accusations — and I must indeed summon
all my courage while I transcribe them; for tears will force their way,
and how can it be otherwise? You knew Shelley, you saw his face,
and could you believe them? Believe them only on the testimony
of a girl whom you despised? I had hopes that such a thing was
impossible, and that although strangers might believe the calumnies
that this man propagated, none who had ever seen my husband
could for a moment credit them.

She says Clare was Shelley's mistress, that — upon my word, I
solemnly assure you that I cannot write the words, I send you a part
of Shelley's letter that you may see what I am now about to refute —
but I had rather die that [sic] copy anything so vilely, so wickedly
false, so beyond all imagination fiendish.

I am perfectly convinced in my own mind that Shelley never had
an improper connexion with Clare — at the time specified in Elise's

letter, the winter after we quitted Este, I suppose while she was with us, and that was at Naples, we lived in lodgings where I had momentary entrance into every room, and such a thing could not have passed unknown to me. The malice of the girl is beyond all thought — I now remember that Clare did keep her bed there for two days — but I attended on her — I saw the physician — her illness was one that she had been accustomed to for years — and the same remedies were employed as I had before ministered to her in England.

Clare had no child — the rest must be false — but that you should believe it — that my beloved Shelley should stand thus slandered in your minds — he the gentlest and most humane of creatures, is more painful to me, oh far more painful than any words can express.

It is all a lie — Clare is timid; she always showed respect even for me — poor dear girl! She has some faults — you know them as well as I — but her heart is good, and if ever we quarrelled, which was seldom, it was I, and not she, that was harsh, and our instantaneous reconciliations were sincere and affectionate.

Need I say that the union between my husband and myself has ever been undisturbed. Love caused our first imprudence, love which improved by esteem, a perfect trust one in the other, a confidence and affection which, visited as we have been by severe calamities (have we not lost two children?) has encreased daily, and knows no bounds.

I will add that Clare has been separated from us for about a year. She lives with a respectable German family at Florence. The reasons of this were obvious — her connexion with us made her manifest as the Miss Clairmont, the mother of Allegra — besides we live much alone — she enters much into society there — and solely occupied with the idea of the welfare of her child, she wished to appear such that she may not be thought in aftertimes to be unworthy of fulfilling the maternal duties. You ought to have paused before you tried to convince the father of her child of such unheard-of atrocities on her part. If his generosity and knowledge of the world had not made him reject the slander with the ridicule it deserved what irretrievable mischief you would have occasioned her!

Those who know me will believe my simple word — it is not long ago that my father said in a letter to me, that he had never known me to utter a falsehood — but you, easy as you have been to credit evil, who may be more deaf to truth — to you I swear — by all that I hold sacred upon heaven and earth by a vow which I should die to write if I affirmed a falsehood — I swear by the life of my child, by my blessed and beloved child, that I know these accusations to be false.

Shelley is as incapable of cruelty as the softest woman. To those who know him his humanity is almost as a proverb. He has been unfortunate as a father, the laws of his country and death has [*sic*] cut him off from his dearest hopes. But his enemies have done him incredible mischief — but that you should believe such a tale coming from such a hand, is beyond all belief, a blow quite unexpected, and the very idea of it beyond words shocking.

But I have said enough to convince you, and are you not convinced? are not my words the words of truth? Repair, I conjure you, the evil you have done by retracting your confidence in one so vile as Elise, and by writing to me that you now reject as false every circumstance of her infamous tale.

You were kind to us, and I shall never forget it; now I require justice; you must believe me, I solemnly entreat you, the justice to confess that you do so.

MARY W. SHELLEY [58]

When Mary's letter reached him, Shelley added the following to a letter that was waiting for the post:

I have received your letter with that of Mrs. Hoppner. I do not wonder my dearest friend that you should have been moved with the infernal accusation of Elise. I was at first but speedily regained the indifference which the opinion of anything, or any body, except our own consciousness amply merits and day by day shall more receive from me. I have not recopied your letter; such a measure would necessarily destroy its authenticity; but have given it to Lord Byron, who has engaged to send it with his own comments to the Hoppners. People do not hesitate it seems to make themselves panderers and accomplices to slander, for the Hoppners had exacted from Lord Byron that these accusations should be concealed from *me*. Lord Byron is not a man to keep a secret good or bad — but in openly confessing that he has not done so he must observe a certain delicacy, and therefore he wishes to send the letter himself, and indeed this adds weight to your representations. Have you seen the article of the Literary Gazette on me? They evidently allude to some story of this kind — however cautious the Hoppners have been in preventing the calumniated person from asserting his justification, you know too much of the world not to be certain that this was the utmost limit of their caution. So much for nothing.[59]

The letters here quoted, if their statements and omissions can be correctly interpreted, should throw additional light upon the mystery of Elena Adelaide Shelley, as treated in Chapter xx. By their intensity of emotion they have convinced all previous biographers that Elise Foggi's story was a complete fabrication. We now know that such was not the case; Elise's story concerned a child whose reality is incontestable. The letters must be re-examined in the light of this fact. How do they accord with each of the four possible explanations of Elena Adelaide Shelley?

If Elena was the child of Shelley and Claire, or of either and an unknown mother or father, Mary Shelley would most likely have known it at the time, as has been pointed out earlier. But if she did not know it then, she would certainly have been pretty sure of it after Paolo's attempted blackmail in 1820. If she knew or believed in either of these three possibilities she might have felt it necessary to lie passionately to Mrs. Hoppner, in order to protect her whole family. If, as is most probable, Mary knew the truth in Naples, or if she only learned it after the Paolo episode, Shelley must have known that she knew, and she must have been aware of Shelley's knowledge. In fact, if Elise's story is compared with Mary's — and probably even if Mary's story were entirely disregarded — the child could hardly have been born in the house without Mary's knowledge and connivance. Such being the case, though Mary and Shelley might lie to Mrs. Hoppner, they could hardly have enacted such fervent lies to each other as these letters would, in that case, exhibit, because each would have known that the other despised his hypocrisy. For this reason it seems very unlikely that this correspondence concerns an illegitimate child of either Shelley or Claire.

But if Elena was an adopted child of other parentage the letters contain no such difficulty. Mary could assert truly: " Claire had no child." She did not say: " There was no child," because she knew that there had been a child and that Elise and Paolo also knew. Thus she could very properly call Elise and Paolo " as cunning as wicked," for their story would have been rather preposterous than cunning except for the actual existence of a

child. It has in fact been so considered by everyone unfamiliar
with Elena's existence, even by Byron, after reflection, with all
his distrust of Claire.

Why, then, did not Mary tell Mrs. Hoppner the true story as
an antidote for the false? There were several excellent reasons.
It would have confessed to breaking the laws of Naples. To
have done so while the child was still alive would have been
to sacrifice all the considerations for which the law had been
broken; and now that Elena was dead, the truth would violate
a habit of secrecy that had obtained for two years. To minds
suspicious enough to believe Elise's story the truth would seem
odd enough to provide an additional doubt rather than an antidote. It would require full explanation, and this would involve
a confession of all the strange private miseries that had followed
the death of Clara Shelley. Mary could never have brought
herself to this point, and it would have been unwise to do so even
if she could.

SHELLEY's visit to Byron continued from August 6 to about
August 22.[60] Something, but not quite all, of the old friendship
immediately revived. Every day Shelley arose at twelve, and
Byron at two in the afternoon. After breakfast they talked until
six, and then rode for two hours in the pine forest between
Ravenna and the sea. After dinner they sat up and talked until
six in the morning.[61] The strain of such a life was probably not
minimized for Shelley by the fact that Byron's household was
practically a menagerie — "ten horses, eight enormous dogs,
three monkeys, five cats, an eagle, a crow, and a falcon; and all
these, except the horses, walk about the house, which every
now and then resounds with their unarbitrated quarrels, as if
they were the masters of it. . . . I find that my enumeration
of the animals in this Circean Palace was defective, and that
in a material point. I have just met on the grand staircase five
peacocks, two guinea hens, and an Egyptian crane." [62]

In every way Byron was much improved over the man Shelley
had observed at Venice in 1818. He had given up reckless dis-
sipation and was no longer subject to the indigestions, fevers,

315

and debilities of the earlier period. His secret activities in behalf of Italian freedom commanded Shelley's unstinted admiration. In their views of poetry, however, Shelley and Byron differed perhaps more than before — Shelley felt that Byron's best poetry was written in defiance of his own principles. *Marino Faliero*, a part of which Byron read to him on the first night, seemed to Shelley to suffer from false critical views, nor did he care greatly for Byron's prose letter to Murray on Pope and Bowles; but he was extremely enthusiastic over the fifth canto of *Don Juan*. Here was the very poem, he assured Mary, that he had long urged Byron to write — something on the scale of Milton or Dante that should be completely original and thoroughly express its own age. As in the old days at Geneva, Byron's excellence added to Shelley's dejection over his own fancied inferiority. " I write nothing," he told Peacock in the letter quoted above, " and probably shall write no more. It offends me to see my name classed among those who have no name. . . . My motive was never the infirm desire of fame; and if I should continue an author, I feel that I should desire it. This cup is justly given to one only of an age; indeed, participation would make it worthless: and unfortunate they who seek it and find it not."

Byron told Shelley all about La Guiccioli and showed him some of her letters. He even engaged Shelley to write to her and try to dissuade her and her brother, Count Pietro Gamba, from their desire to settle in Switzerland. "An odd thing enough," Shelley commented dryly, " for an utter stranger to write on subjects of the utmost delicacy to his friend's mistress." [63] Shelley in turn told Byron some details about Emilia Viviani that he later cautioned him not to repeat to Mary for fear they would annoy her. [64] He also used Emilia's experience and her unfavourable stories of convents for whatever effect they might have on Byron's disposal of Allegra. On this point Byron's response was comforting. The Countess Guiccioli, he assured Shelley, was very fond of Allegra, nor was he himself willing to depart for Switzerland and leave the child in an Italian convent. At first Byron was undecided where he should go; he would have preferred Pisa, but Shelley was stopped from urging Pisa upon him by Claire's proximity. Within a week, however, he had decided on Pisa and commissioned the Shelleys to secure him a " large and magnificent house " there.

Byron's decision raised the question of whether or not the Shelleys should abandon their plan for passing the winter in Florence. It had been decided to stay in Florence partly because Horace Smith was to live there. A house had already been all but engaged. Arguments of health favoured Pisa, and they had friends there. " Our roots never struck so deeply as at Pisa, and the transplanted tree flourishes not," Shelley observed, as he weighed the question in one of his letters to Mary. His greatest content, which he somewhat bitterly admitted was impracticable, would have been utterly to desert all human society. " I would retire with you and our child to a solitary island in the sea, would build a boat, and shut upon my retreat the floodgates of the world. I would read no reviews, and talk with no authors. If I dared trust my imagination it would tell me that there were two or three chosen companions besides yourself whom I should desire. But to this I would not listen — where two or three are gathered together the devil is among them. And good far more than evil impulses — love far more than hatred, has been to me, except as you have been its object, the source of all sort [sic] of mischief." [65]

A more pressing question raised by Byron's decision was what to do about Allegra. Wishing to hold Byron to his earlier promise not to leave her at Bagnacavallo when he left the country, Shelley felt it necessary to be able to suggest some practicable place for her in Pisa. " Is there any family," he inquired of Mary, " any English or Swiss establishment, any refuge in short, except the convent of St. Anna where Allegra might be placed? Do you think Mrs. Mason could be prevailed on to *propose* to take charge of her? I fear not. Think of this against I come. If you can now see or write to Emilia ask her if she knows anyone who would be fit for this purpose." [66] All this anxiety came to nothing, however, for when Byron came he left Allegra at Bagnacavallo.

Before leaving Ravenna Shelley made a visit to Allegra. In the three years since he had seen her Allegra had grown taller and slighter and had developed a curious manner of mingled pensiveness and wild vivacity. With her light, airy figure, graceful motions, and pale beauty she seemed to belong to a different order of humanity from the children with whom she was associated. She was at first diffident; then, won over by the gold chain and basket of sweetmeats that Shelley brought, she raced wildly about the place with him until he was exhausted, and concluded the romp by ringing the tocsin that usually summoned all the nuns from their beds. Shelley had known her as self-willed, and Byron had complained of the same trait only a few days before, but the nuns had brought about a considerable improvement in discipline. This, and the kindness with which she seemed to be treated, must have been a welcome surprise for Shelley. On the other hand, " Her intellect is not much cultivated here — she knows certain orazioni by heart, and talks and *dreams* of Paradise and angels and all sorts of things and has a prodigious list of saints, and is always talking of the Bambino. This [——] will do her no harm, but the idea of bringing up so sweet a creature in the midst of such trash until sixteen! " Shelley asked her what he should say to her mother. " That I want a kiss and a beautiful dress," was the prompt answer. " And what kind of dress? " " All of silk and gold," was the reply. These messages were doubtless delivered, but not the message to Papa — " To make me a visit and bring *mammina* with him." [67]

WHEN Shelley wrote to Medwin immediately after his return to Pisa: " Whilst you were with me, that is during the latter period, and after you went away, I was harassed by some severe disquietudes, the causes of which are now I hope almost at an end," [68] he must have been referring to his distresses over Emilia Viviani, and her approaching wedding. One wonders what hysterical words may have been said in some of the unrecorded scenes in which Shelley sought to reconcile Emilia to a marriage that she did not desire and that he desired only as the lesser of two evils. Possibly it was Shelley's relation of some such scene to Byron, in the confidence of their post-midnight conversations, that he warned Byron not to repeat to Mary, because the full truth might annoy her. Emilia, if one is to trust Mary Shelley's fictional portrait of her in *Lodore*, was impetuous. Perhaps some such scene was overheard, or perhaps general rumour only was responsible for a temporary interdict on further visits from the Shelleys. Emilia's letter is undated, but it must have been written shortly before Shelley's departure for Ravenna, probably in July.[69] " I beg you," Emilia wrote, " to come no more to St. Anna, neither you, nor any of your family. My parents desire that I should henceforth see no one. Every attempt would be in vain; we should be humiliated without obtaining anything. Signora Eusta agrees with them; she treated me yesterday in a most insolent manner and uttered an impertinence to me which not even a servant-maid would have endured. . . ."[70]

Emilia was married on September 8 to Luigi Biondi,[71] rather than to the other suitor, Danielli, whose despair in May Emilia had asked Shelley to assist in calming. After her marriage she left Pisa to live with her husband's family at Pomerance, about sixty miles southeast of Pisa. The Shelleys seem not to have been invited to any of the wedding festivities, and the marriage is ignored by both Mary and Claire in their journals. A week later Shelley informed Byron of the marriage " after a great deal of tumult, etc.," and added that Emilia's brother-in-law watched her·with great assiduity.[72] " My convent friend . . ." he informed John Gisborne four months later, " is married, and I [am] in a sort of morbid quietness." [73]

Some of the " tumult " took place in Shelley's own mind. Some five or six of his shorter poems written in 1821 are either certainly or possibly to be connected with Emilia's wedding. An unfinished epithalamium of about thirty lines exists in three different versions, as if Shelley had tried to write a conventional, impersonal marriage ode and had given it up as a failure. A longer poem of 219 lines, " Ginevra," is the tragic story of a bride who stole forth from the marriage festivities to listen to the reproaches of her former lover and returned to her chamber to die quietly on her bed before the guests had left the house. The story is not of Shelley's invention; it had appeared in 1821 in *L'Osservatore Fiorentino;* but Shelley's poem about it could not have been written near the time of Emilia's wedding without being psychologically connected with that event. Ginevra answers her disappointed lover's reproaches thus:

> . . . Friend, if earthly violence or ill,
> Suspicion, doubt, or the tyrannic will
> Of parents, chance, or custom, time, or change,
> Or circumstance, or terror, or revenge,
> Or wildered looks, or words, or evil speech,
> With all their stings and venom, can impeach
> Our love, — we love not: — if the grave, which hides
> The victim from the tyrant, and divides
> The cheek that whitens from the eyes that dart
> Imperious inquisition to the heart
> That is another's, could dissever ours,
> We love not. . . .[74]

In " The Fugitives " Shelley attempted once more to realize the elopement he had proposed in *Epipsychidion.* It is a poem of rather spirited action, but falls far below the emotional intensity of *Epipsychidion.*

It was Shelley's belief that a poet was really two people, the poet and the man. The man could and did see that a union with Emilia was impossible and probably not even to be desired, that it was better for Emilia to marry Biondi. He had written Claire (April 29) that Emilia's marriage would remove " a great and painful weight " from his mind, and he had expressed to Mary (August 16) his desire to retire utterly from the world with Mary and their child. This was the man; the poet had proposed a purely imaginary elopement to Emilia. To the poet Emilia's marriage was another beautiful idealism shattered upon the rocks of reality. The intense idealizing fire of *Epipsychidion* still smouldered, even though much of its original heat had vanished, as it had risen, in the act of writing. To the poet Emilia's marriage could only have seemed, like the defection of Elizabeth Shelley nine years earlier, another addition to his poignant disillusions with life, a kind of death.

Here one may well pause for a thoughtful reading of several of Shelley's finest brief lyrics, all written in 1821.

A LAMENT

O World! O life! O time!
On whose last steps I climb,
    Trembling at that where I had stood before;
When will return the glory of your prime?
        No more — Oh, never more!

Out of the day and night
A joy has taken flight:
    Fresh spring, and summer, and winter hoar,
Move my faint heart with grief, but with delight
        No more — Oh, never more!

REMEMBRANCE [75]

Swifter far than summer's flight,
Swifter far than youth's delight,
Swifter far than happy night,
    Art thou come and gone;
As the wood when leaves are shed,
As the night when sleep is fled,
As the heart when joy is dead,
    I am left lone, alone.

The swallow Summer comes again,
The owlet Night resumes her reign —
But the wild-swan Youth is fain
    To fly with thee, false as thou.
My heart each day desires the morrow,
Sleep itself is turned to sorrow,
Vainly would my Winter borrow
    Sunny leaves from any bough.

Lilies for a bridal bed,
Roses for a matron's head,
Violets for a maiden dead,
    Pansies let *my* flowers be:
On the living grave I bear,
Scatter them without a tear,
Let no friend, however dear,
    Waste one hope, one fear for me.

TO ——

When passion's trance is overpast,
If tenderness and truth could last
Or live, whilst all wild feelings keep
Some mortal slumber, dark and deep,
I should not weep, I should not weep!

It were enough to feel, to see
Thy soft eyes gazing tenderly,
And dream the rest — and burn and be
The secret food of fires unseen,
Couldst thou but be as thou hast been.

After the slumber of the year
The woodland violets reappear;
All things revive in field or grove,
And sky and sea; but two, which move,
And form all others, life and love.

TO ——

Music, when soft voices die
Vibrates in the memory;
Odours, when sweet violets sicken,
Live within the sense they quicken.

Rose leaves, when the rose is dead,
Are heaped for the belovèd's bed;
And so thy thoughts, when thou art gone,
Love itself will slumber on.

A biographer may in any case quote these poems as examples of Shelley's finest personal lyrics, admitting that their connection with Emilia is a matter more of belief than of proof. If the connection exists, however, it would seem to indicate that all of the poems except " A Lament " were written shortly before the marriage.

Without his experience with Emilia, Shelley's sense of the tragic difference between the ideal and the real could have given rise to such well-known lyrics of melancholy as " To —— Music when soft voices die," " Mutability," " A Lament," " Re- membrance," and " To —— When passion's trance is over- past." [76] But there was no actual death or known melancholy event in 1821 which could have given definite occasion for these lyrics at that time — nothing except the marriage of Emilia. With this marriage a " soft voice " would die, to vibrate only in memory, and Emilia would be " gone " both physically and spiritually, leaving only the " thought " of her as food for Love's slumbers. Its near approach *did* set, for the poet, a terminus to certain dreams, from which the awakening would be sad; a " maiden " *would* have died into a " matron," terminating a swift, beautiful interlude for the poet; a particular " joy " *had* " taken flight "; and for him, when the " passion's trance " of this marriage had " overpast," there *would* be an end of the " tenderness and truth " he had known in Emilia. " I knew a very interesting Italian lady last winter," Shelley wrote to Hogg on October 22, 1821, " but she is now married; which, to quote our friend Peacock, is you know, the same as being dead." [77] Except for Emilia's marriage, what would be the point of the association of death and bridal-beds in these poems? Two of these poems are actually entitled " To —— " with the name left blank. Emilia's name fits the blank perfectly, and no other name does.

IT SEEMS a pity that the story of Shelley and Emilia does not end with these poems. Five days before her marriage Emilia had written to Shelley: " I have received your very dear letter. I am most disappointed that you are not in good health. Oh God! we are indeed unfortunate in this world." After her mar- riage, she concluded, she would be pleased to receive his letters if he wished to write — " but please be very prudent in all your expressions." This was quite consistent with their previ- ous correspondence. The bulk of her letter, however, concerned a very unusual request that had been advanced in a preceding letter now lost. A friend of hers, a lady, needed a sum of money which Emilia had undertaken to secure for her. The whole sum was evidently considerable, since Emilia thought Shelley might require Byron's assistance in providing it, but a part would be better than none, and the sum could be handled by a third party in order not to compromise Emilia. Failure to provide the money would greatly disappoint her and compel her to witness the suffering and destruction of a virtuous, sensitive friend to whom she had promised aid.

It is improbable that Shelley granted Emilia's request, for the simple reason that no considerable sum was at his disposal. What this unusual request really meant will perhaps always remain doubtful. Emilia was impulsive and naïve enough to have written it to rescue a friend from distress and to expect her friends to receive it in the same spirit. Had not Shelley assured her long before, in words which she had approved and quoted back to him, that " in *friendship* everything must be in common "? Her biographer considers Emilia's letter a proof of her unselfish, impulsive generosity. Prior to its writing, however, there is no evidence of anything but friendship toward Emilia on the part of Mary Shelley, whereas afterwards Mary Shelley's few recorded expressions about Emilia are unfriendly and injurious. Six months after the wedding she wrote to Mrs. Gisborne:

" Emilia married Biondi; we hear that she leads him and his mother (to use a vulgarism) a devil of a life. The conclusion of our friendship (*a la Italiana*) puts me in mind of a nursery rhyme, which runs thus —

> As I was going down Cranbourne lane,
> Cranbourne lane was dirty,
> And there I met a pretty maid,
> Who dropt to me a curtsey;
>
> I gave her cakes, I gave her wine,
> I gave her sugar-candy,
> But oh! the little naughty girl,
> She asked me for some brandy.

Now turn ' Cranbourne Lane ' into Pisan acquaintances, which I am sure are dirty enough, and ' brandy ' into that where-

324

withal to buy brandy (and that no small sum, *però*), and you have the whole story of Shelley's Italian Platonics." [78]

From this letter it seems clear that Mary's revulsion of feeling toward Emilia was connected with Emilia's request for money. It is not clear that the revulsion followed immediately upon receipt of Emilia's request five days before her marriage. Four months later, as we have seen, Shelley's letter to John Gisborne mentions no disillusion. But within three months after Mary's letter Shelley expressed a similar revulsion, his last reference to Emilia: "The *Epipsychidion* I cannot look at; the person whom it celebrates was a cloud instead of a Juno; and poor Ixion starts from the centaur that was the offspring of his own embrace." [79]

One can only say that Mary and possibly Shelley thought that Emilia tried to obtain money from them for false or unworthy purposes, but whether or not such suspicions were just is another matter. It is possible that Mary was misled by a latent jealousy and that Shelley's revulsion was only a psychological phenomenon, similar to several other sudden revulsions in his affections. To turn the beautiful Emilia into a centaur was not very different from turning Elizabeth Hitchener into a brown demon or "an artful, superficial, ugly, hermaphroditical beast of a woman." Shelley's idealization of Emilia may have crashed to earth simply as a result of its hyperintensity. "I think one is always in love with something or other," Shelley concluded, in the same letter quoted above. "The error . . . consists in seeking in a mortal image the likeness of what is perhaps eternal."

Whatever the cause of Shelley's revulsion against Emilia and the *Epipsychidion*, its genuineness is attested by the previously uncertain fact that he actually withdrew the poem from publication after only a few copies had been sold. In February of 1822, about a month before Mary Shelley wrote the letter quoted above, *Blackwood's Edinburgh Magazine* spoke of the poem as having been "suddenly withdrawn" from circulation. By itself this might be regarded as irresponsible literary gossip, but it is rendered conclusive by a letter from Charles Ollier to Mary Shelley after Shelley's death: "As it was the wish of Mr.

Shelley that the whole of the *Epipsychidion* should be suppressed, I would not, though it was printed at our expense, suffer the remainder to be disposed of." [80]

Evidently it was no exaggeration when Shelley assured John Gisborne a few months later that he could not look at the *Epipsychidion.*[81]

Chapter XXVIII

WINTER AND SPRING IN PISA, 1821–2

HELLAS; THE SHELLEY–BYRON CIRCLE; TRELAWNY;

SHELLEY AND JANE WILLIAMS;

EPISODES WITH THE CHURCH AND THE MILITARY;

DIFFICULTIES WITH BYRON;

DEATH OF ALLEGRA

THE SHELLEYS remained quietly at the Baths of Pisa until October 25, when they moved back into the city. Claire had arrived from Leghorn on October 9, and from October 11 to 30 was the guest of the Williamses at Pugnano. Almost every day the two families were together for at least a part of the time, either at the Baths or at Pugnano, at breakfast, at dinner, or in the evening. The days passed smoothly in walking, boating, or discussing. Mary was busy copying her novel, which had already been offered to the Olliers, and acquiring furniture for their house, for they were now fully decided to settle in Pisa and its neighbourhood indefinitely. Though this decision was reached shortly after Shelley's return from Ravenna in August, he nevertheless wrote to Peacock inquiring about the possibilities of going to India in the employ of the East India Company. Peacock replied congratulating Shelley on his " recent fixedness to one spot " and pointing out the practical impossibility of the Indian project.[1] Within a week of settling down in Pisa they were also thinking of taking up their abode in Greece if the Greeks won their independence.[2]

Godwin's financial troubles once more reached the edge of disaster, but he was granted a temporary reprieve before he had time to unload them upon Shelley and Mary. On the score of Mary's novel, however, he was able to cause them some justifiable uneasiness. "Respecting Ollier," he wrote on October 10, "it is perhaps right I should say that I do not think him a very safe man, and I doubt whether you will ever get any money he promises you."[3] After long and irritating delays Ollier offered three hundred pounds for Mary's novel, but on such vague conditions of deferred payment that Mary was obliged to decline.[4] The book was eventually published in 1823 by G. and W. B. Whittaker.

THE KNOWLEDGE that Prince Mavrocordato was now fighting for Greek independence gave an additional fillip to Shelley's interest in that cause. Late in October a number of Greek revolutionaries, escaped from a recent defeat in Wallachia, passed through Pisa and were honourably treated by the government. Shelley was at that moment just finishing his *Hellas,* which he described as "a sort of imitation of the *Persæ* of Aeschylus, full of lyrical poetry," "a mere improvise," "a sort of lyrical, dramatic, nondescript piece of business," "written without much care, in one of those few moments of enthusiasm which now seldom visit me."[5] Edward Williams made the fair copy between November 6 and 10 and suggested the title, *Hellas,* on October 25.[6]

In his Preface Shelley apologized for the thin and inaccurate "newspaper erudition" on which he was forced to rely for the factual basis of the poem. In truth, the obscure battles Shelley describes resemble those in the *Persæ* of Æschylus far more than they resemble any conflicts described by the historians of the modern Greek war of independence. Similarly Shelley's Greeks really belong to the world of Plato and the Greek historians and dramatists. To Shelley this period was "the most memorable in the history of the world."[7] "We are all Greeks," he asserted in his Preface. "Our laws, our literature, our religion, our arts, have their root in Greece. . . . The human form and the human mind attained to a perfection in Greece which has impressed its image on those faultless productions whose very fragments are the despair of modern art, and has propagated impulses which cannot cease, through a thousand channels of manifest or imperceptible operation, to ennoble and delight mankind until the extinction of the race."

Probably the only modern Greeks whom Shelley knew were Prince Mavrocordato, to whom *Hellas* was dedicated, and several of his relatives. To him the modern Greek (as he said in his Preface) was "the descendant of those glorious beings whom the imagination almost refuses to figure to itself as belonging to our kind." He had seen more ignoble Greeks, no doubt, in the busy markets of Leghorn. Soon Edward Trelawny was to give him a view of the squalor and dirt of a Greek trading vessel which he acknowledged reminded him more of Hell than of Hellas.[8] Such revelations could never discourage a Shelley, for to him the Idea was more true than any factual representation of it limited to a particular time and place. The real Greece, as his chorus sang, was

> Based on the crystalline sea
> Of thought, and its eternity.

He had read Thomas Hope's *Anastasius* (1819), with its unflattering picture of the modern Greeks, as well as Byron's realistic comments on Greece in the notes to the second canto of *Childe Harold*. He probably knew, in one corner of his mind, more of the "facts" than Trelawny supposed, but regarded them as relatively insignificant. In his Preface he even admitted the inferiority of the modern Greeks. But what of that? As he had previously asserted of the French and Neapolitan revolutionists, their present lack of grandeur was only a temporary condition, a natural result of the very tyranny they were striving to overthrow.

Hence the outcome of this particular revolution seemed to Shelley not half so important as the fact of revolution itself. He could not foresee the intervention of the Khedive of Egypt on the Turkish side and the counter-intervention of England, France, and Russia which was to establish Greek independence seven years later at the battle of Navarino. He evidently thought that the Greeks stood a fair chance of losing. Yet they had revived the spirit of freedom, whose losses were only temporary losses as long as the spirit itself survived. This was the doctrine of revolution as expounded in the parable of the Serpent and the Eagle in the first canto of *Laon and Cythna*, the same doctrine that is implicit in Demogorgon's concluding speech in *Prometheus Unbound*, in *A Philosophical View of Reform*, in the "Defence of Poetry," and in Shelley's view of the contemporary Italian and Spanish revolutions.

Though he had written rapidly, in the midst of arranging for Byron's residence in Pisa and while still trying to keep warm the dying embers of "Charles the First," Shelley had a fondness for *Hellas* out of proportion to the care he had bestowed upon it. It represented the union of two of his greatest passions, liberty and Greece. He hoped that it would be published promptly, but Ollier was most irritatingly and uncommunicatively dilatory. It was published in the spring (probably March) of 1822, and by April 10 Shelley had received a copy, which he pronounced the most accurately printed of any of his works.[9] *Hellas* received only one review, a very stupid and hostile one on June 30 in a shortlived London weekly entitled the *General Weekly Register of News, Literature, Law, Politics, and Commerce*.[10]

The plot of *Hellas* is too slight to require more than passing notice. The Turkish Sultan, Mahmud, is oppressed with vague fears for the future of his rule; these are increased by the reports of land and sea battles brought to him by four successive messengers. He talks with an old and learned Jew named Ahasuerus, who is no other than the Wandering Jew of Shelley's youthful enthusiasm dignified and ennobled by all that Shelley had learned between 1811 and 1822. Through him Mahmud talks with the founder of his line and learns that its end is near. Interspersing the thin action, a chorus of Christian slaves comments upon the struggle, not in its present aspects so much as *sub specie æternitatis*. Though the drama contains some fine passages of blank verse, it is in these choruses that it reaches a height showing that Shelley's poetic powers were not declining. The first full chorus, " In the great morning of the world," relates one of Shelley's favourite stories, the progress of Freedom, from its dawn in ancient Greece. The next, "Worlds on worlds are rolling ever," presents both the evanescence and the distortions of human creeds and asserts that the star of Mahomet "arose and it shall set." The concluding chorus, "The world's great age begins anew," forecasts a new golden age and a revitalized Greece, but concludes significantly that possibly hate and death may still return. Such a conclusion is not merely a reflection of Shelley's uncertainty about the outcome of the present struggle. Like Demogorgon's last speech in *Prometheus Unbound*, it suggests that in Shelley's view no golden age was ever perfectly secure against relapse.

These choruses are more objective than most of Shelley's great lyrics and suggest Byron at his lyrical best almost as much as they do Shelley. It may not be without significance that when he was writing them he was reading with extreme enthusiasm the third canto of Byron's *Don Juan,* containing "The Isles of Greece." [11] Nothing could be more genuinely Shelleyan, however, than the underlying ideas of the drama or some of the shorter choral passages. The semichorus in the first scene is an almost perfect summary of Shelley's philosophy of living. Though Hope, Truth, and Love may be obscured, it sings, they are never finally defeated or abolished — Liberty is the spark that preserves their life and beauty. But Shelley had long since reached the conclusion that living, or rather the time, space, and physical entities that environ living, are really only functions of thought. In *Hellas* he gave his final and most beautiful expression to this idea:

> . . . This Whole
> Of suns, and worlds, and men, and beasts, and flowers,
> With all the silent or tempestuous workings
> By which they have been, are, or cease to be,
> Is but a vision; all that it inherits
> Are motes of a sick eye, bubbles, and dreams;
> Thought is its cradle and its grave, nor less
> The future and the past are idle shadows
> Of thought's eternal flight — they have no being;
> Nought is but that which feels itself to be.

.   .   .   .

Mistake me not! All is contained in each.
Dodona's forest to an acorn's cup
Is that which has been or will be, to that
Which is — the absent to the present. Thought
Alone, and its quick elements, Will, Passion,
Reason, Imagination, cannot die;
They are what that which they regard appears,
The stuff whence mutability can weave
All that it hath dominion o'er — worlds, worms,
Empires, and superstitions. What has thought
To do with time, or place, or circumstance? [12]

Hellas is also Shelley's last utterance on another subject of lifelong interest — Christianity. The unfinished Prologue, the choruses, and the prose notes present a sympathetic view of Christ. In relation to Mohammedanism and the ancient pagan creed Shelley is even tolerant of Christianity; but in a universal aspect he still regards it as a monstrous perversion of Christ. "The sublime human character of Jesus Christ," he asserts in one of his notes on the poem, "was deformed by an imputed identification with a Power who tempted, betrayed, and punished the innocent beings who were called into existence by His sole will; and for the period of a thousand years the spirit of this most just, wise, and benevolent of men has been propitiated with myriads of hecatombs of those who approached the nearest to His innocence and wisdom, sacrificed under every aggravation of atrocity and variety of torture." This view is quite consistent with the view of Christ in *Prometheus Unbound* and in the "Essay on Christianity," a prose fragment of some length whose date of composition is extremely uncertain, but which may have been written as early as 1815.[13]

By THE end of October the Shelleys were comfortably settled in Pisa on the north side of the Lung' Arno, in the top floor of a house known as the Tre Palazzi di Chiesa. Their outlook was south, over open country toward the sea, rather than over the jumbled city streets that both Mary and Shelley found at times unpleasant. They had installed their own furniture, bought

with the savings of two years' economy, but they were still trying vainly to get possession of books and two desks that had
been left behind in England. The Williamses had also furnished their own lodgings, in the same building, on the floor
beneath the Shelleys. Immediately opposite the Shelleys stood
the Palazzo Lanfranchi, which had been taken for Byron.[14]
The Countess Guiccioli and Count Gamba, her brother, had
already settled in Pisa. On November 1 Byron had arrived,
bringing at least part of his household furnishings and menagerie in a train of eight wagons that Shelley had sent to him
from Pisa.[15] Claire had simultaneously departed for Florence,
and had seen Byron probably for the last time as her carriage
drew to the side of the road near Empoli to watch Byron's
cortège pass toward Pisa.[16] Byron brought with him his *Cain,*
which seemed to both Shelley and Mary to be a poem of the
very highest order. It was probably after reading *Cain,* with
the third canto of *Don Juan* also freshly in mind, that Shelley
wrote his fulsome and self-abasing " Sonnet to Byron."

The following letter from Shelley to Peacock, undated, but
written probably on January 11, 1822, leaves little to be added
to the picture of the life led by the Shelleys in the autumn and
early winter of 1821–2:

My dear Peacock,

Circumstances have prevented my procuring the certificate and
signature which I inclose, so soon as I expected, and other circumstances made me even then delay. I inclose them, and should be
much obliged by your sending them to their destination.

I am still at Pisa, where I have at length fitted up some rooms at
the top of a lofty palace that overlooks the city and the surrounding
region; and have collected books and plants about me, and established myself for some indefinite time, which, if I read the future
will not be short. I wish you to send my books by the very first opportunity, and I expect in them a great augmentation of comfort.
Lord Byron is established now, and we are constant companions;
no small relief this after the dreary solitude of the understanding
and the imagination in which we past [*sic*] the first years of our
expatriation, yoked to all sorts of miseries and discomforts.

Of course you have seen his last volume, and if you before thought
him a great Poet, what is your opinion now that you have read *Cain?*

The Foscari and Sardanapalus I have not seen, but as they are in the style of his later writings, I doubt not they are very fine. We expect Hunt here every day, and remain in great anxiety on account of the heavy gales which he must have encountered at Christmas. Lord Byron has fitted up the lower apartments of his palace for him, and Hunt will be agreeably surprised to find a commodious lodging prepared for him after the fatigues and dangers of his passage. I have been long idle, and, as far as writing goes, despondent, but I am now engaged in " Charles the First," and a devil of a nut it is to crack.

Mary and Clara, (who is not with us just at present,) are well, and so is our little boy, the image of poor William. We live, as usual, tranquilly. I get up, or at least wake, early; read and write till two; dine; go to Lord B.'s, and ride, or play at Billiards, as the weather permits; and sacrifice the evening either to light books or whoever happens to drop in. Our furniture, which is very neat cost fewer shillings than that at Marlow did pounds sterling; and our windows are full of plants, which turn the sunny winter into spring. My health is better — my cares are lighter; and although nothing will cure the consumption of my purse, yet it drags on a sort of life in death, very like its master, and seems, like Fortunatus's, always empty yet never quite exhausted. You will have seen my Adonais, and perhaps my Hellas, and I think, whatever you may judge of the subject, the composition of the first poem will not wholly displease you. I wish I had something better to do than furnish this jingling food for the hunger of oblivion, called verse, but I have not; and since you give me no encouragement about India, I cannot hope to have.

How is your little star, and the heaven which contains the milky way in which it glimmers?

Adieu — Yours ever, most truly,
S.[17]

Mary saw Byron but seldom, as Byron's dinners were usually for men only. She saw the Countess Guiccioli rather frequently, however, and described her to Mrs. Gisborne as " a nice pretty girl without pretensions, good-hearted and amiable." To Shelley she was " a very pretty, sentimental, innocent, superficial Italian, who has sacrificed an immense fortune to live for Lord Byron; and who, if I know anything of my friend, of her, and of human nature will hereafter have plenty of leisure and opportunity to repent her rashness." [18] The Williamses and Shelleys continued seeing each other as frequently as at the Baths. Shelley now thought Jane Williams " more amiable and beautiful than ever, and a sort of spirit of embodied peace in our circle of tempests." [19] Occasionally one or both of the Shelleys called on the Masons at Casa Silva.

A Mrs. Beauclerc, a daughter of the Duchess of Leinster, who had been a neighbour of the Shelley family in Sussex, was spending the winter in Pisa with her daughter. Shelley called on her somewhat unwillingly in late December, " after much solicitation," and was disgusted at her effusive reception of him.[20] By spring, however, Mary's journal shows that Mrs. Beauclerc was a fairly regular member of the Shelley-Byron circle. Medwin had returned to Pisa on November 15 to something like his former intimacy with the Shelleys. With Count Gamba, Count Taafe, Shelley, and Williams he was a regular member of Byron's riding party and was already taking the occasionally inaccurate and gullible notes of Byron's conversation that were later to bring down upon his head the wrath of Byron's friends.

The Hunts, delayed in England by bad weather and Mrs. Hunt's ill health, were expected daily. With Mary's help the lower floor of Byron's palace had already been made ready for their reception. From various places between September and March Hunt wrote to Shelley explaining each new delay, but always enthusiastic about the project of establishing a new liberal review in Italy with Byron's and Shelley's co-operation: " What? Are there not three of us? And ought we not to have as much strength and variety as possible? We will divide the world between us, like the Triumvirate, and you shall be the sleeping partner, if you will; only it shall be with a Cleopatra, and your dreams shall be worth the giving of kingdoms." [21]

November passed pleasantly in a succession of mild autumn days. Fires were unlighted and windows were kept open to the breeze as late as December 20; not until the middle of December were there any very authentic signs of winter. Mary had resumed her Greek studies late in November and often read Herodotus with Shelley in the evening. By day she enjoyed the conveniences of the city and " all the delights of friendly and social intercourse "; [22] and by night she enjoyed the quiet and solitude to be obtained by sitting up late. Shelley wrote none too brightly to Claire of his health and spirits, but that was possibly because he craved more sympathy than he received. On December 21 Mary reported to Mrs. Gisborne: " You will be glad to hear that Shelley's health is much improved this winter; he is not quite well, but he is much better. The air of Pisa is so mild and delightful, and the exercise on horseback agrees with him particularly." Tom Medwin, on his return to Pisa, " found him an altered man. His health had sensibly improved, and he had shaken off much of that melancholy and depression to which he had been subject during the last year." [23] In November Shelley was translating Spinoza again, this time with Williams.

Constantly the Shelley-Byron party of men dined together, rode together, talked, and indulged in pistol practice. Shelley was an awkward horseman, but he was better with a pistol, having a quicker and firmer aim than Lord Byron. He delighted both in the shooting and in preparing the targets. Conversation at the Palazzo Lanfranchi was lively and interesting. Occasionally the party was augmented by some travelling friend of Byron's, as it was by Samuel Rogers toward the end of April.[24] Byron's talk, like his letters and his *Don Juan,* was full of gay sharp flippancies and rapid changes from grave to gay, and from the comic to the almost sublime. He scoffed at nearly everything except freedom and religion.

Medwin, like Claire Clairmont, noted in Byron a basically superstitious attitude toward religion, and for that reason could not quite agree with Shelley's opinion that Byron was to be compared with Voltaire. Whenever Byron's talk turned upon subjects that to Shelley's finer sensibilities seemed gross and indelicate, he would depart with scarcely concealed disgust. He was also baffled and somewhat annoyed by Byron's constant flitting from subject to subject, his unwillingness to stick to the point and argue. Medwin, taking his unequal part in the conversation, was, like Taafe, occasionally the victim of a little mystification and leg-pulling; yet his comparison of Shelley and Byron shows that he was something more than the mere *sec-*

catura that Mary Shelley thought him: " There was something enchanting in his [Byron's] manner, his voice, his smile — a fascination in them; but on leaving him, I have often marvelled that I gained so little from him worth carrying away; whilst every word of Shelley's was almost oracular; his reasoning subtle and profound; his opinions, whatever they were, sincere and undisguised; whilst with Byron, such was his love of mystification, it was impossible to know when he was in earnest." [25]

Despite his opinion that *Don Juan* and *Cain* were almost supernatural achievements, and despite the charm of Byron's personal presence, Shelley had no illusions about the fundamental fickleness and instability of Byron's character. Nor did he hesitate to disagree with Byron on questions of literary opinion. When Byron showed him *The Deformed Transformed* Shelley stated frankly " that he liked it the least of all his works; that it smelt too strongly of *Faust;* and besides that there were two lines in it, word for word from Southey." Perhaps it was the last statement, rather than Shelley's lack of enthusiasm, that caused Byron to turn deathly pale and immediately throw the manuscript into the fire — only to reproduce it later. Shelley disagreed completely with the high rank assigned by Byron to Campbell and Rogers as poets, and with the low opinion Byron sometimes expressed of both Dante and Shakespeare.[26]

Byron, on his part, had a high respect for Shelley's character and judgment. According to Medwin, he consulted Shelley on most of his personal and private affairs.[27] He could be capricious, annoying, and rude with Shelley as with anyone; but despite his disagreement with most of Shelley's ideas of religion and society, he was compelled to respect and admire him. In answering occasional criticisms from his English correspondents Byron consistently defended Shelley against the current misunderstanding of his character.

As WINTER storms descended upon Pisa toward the end of December, Mary was seized with a " rheumatism of the head " from which she suffered severely. For several nights she was entirely deprived of sleep. Shelley also reported himself to Claire

Clairmont as having "suffered considerably from pain and depression of spirits." [28] But within less than a fortnight he was writing to Peacock: "My health is better — my cares are lighter," [29] so that the letter to Claire may be regarded as in part the expression of the for ever dissatisfied craving for sympathy which is to be found more in his letters to Claire than anywhere else except in his poetry.

Something of the same feeling crops out in an earlier letter to John Gisborne, in which Shelley expressed his extreme admiration for Antigone. "Some of us," he concluded, "have in a prior existence been in love with an Antigone, and that makes us find no full content in any mortal tie." [30] In a fragmentary poem called "The Zucca" written in January 1822, this sentiment is more clearly expressed in the third stanza:

> I loved — oh no, I mean not one of ye,
> Or any earthly one, though ye are dear
> As human heart to human heart may be: —
> I loved I know not what — but this low sphere,
> And all that it contains, contains not thee,
> Thou whom, seen nowhere, I feel everywhere,
> From Heaven and Earth, and all that in them are
> Veiled art thou, like a   star. . . .

By 1822 Mary's journal had gradually drifted into more and more desultory mention of Shelley's reading and writing. Perhaps this tendency, which first becomes noticeable immediately after Clara Shelley's death in the autumn of 1818, is a sign on Mary's part (as his poems are on Shelley's) that the union of Shelley and Mary had lost some of its original sympathy. If so, it was only normal and seems to have been generally so considered by Shelley; he knew well enough that his ideal was not to be found in flesh and blood. But the unsatisfied craving still persisted, and he was even now beginning to see in Jane Williams at least a symbol of its possible fulfilment. Having already informed John Gisborne that Jane Williams was "a sort of spirit of embodied peace in our circle of tempests," he wrote to Horace Smith two weeks later to commission him to buy in Paris a harp of seventy or eighty guineas' value, with some sheets of harp music,[31] which he intended as a present for Jane. Poems somewhat like those to Emilia Viviani were soon to follow.

EARLY in December two episodes occurred which brought passing excitement to the Shelley-Byron circle. On December 12 Medwin heard at a bookseller's a rumour that in Lucca a man was to be burned alive for stealing consecrated wafers from an altar. Shelley, out walking with the Williamses, heard the same rumour at the same time. Both went immediately to Byron. Byron suggested that Lord Guildford, then at Leghorn, be asked to appeal to the Grand Duke, whose liberal and humanitarian feelings would certainly cause him to stop the execution. Believing that the culprit was to be burned next day, Shelley was all for organizing a band to ride to Lucca and effect a rescue by force, to which Byron agreed, if it should be necessary. Meanwhile Taafe undertook to ride to Lucca to ascertain the truth of the rumour, and the others agreed to submit a written appeal to the Grand Duke, who was in Pisa at the time. The next day, probably from Taafe, news arrived which made violent action unnecessary. The thief had escaped from Lucca into the Tuscan dominions, where he had been arrested at Florence. The Grand Duke's officers, true to his reputation for humanity, had consented to surrender him only on condition of his being tried according to Tuscan laws. He was eventually sent to the galleys.[32]

On a lower floor of the same house with the Shelleys lived the Reverend Dr. Nott, a prebend of Winchester Cathedral and author of a life of Surrey. He had once been subpreceptor to the Princess Charlotte and, according to a story believed by Medwin and Byron, had lost his position through abusing it for ambitious ends. Earlier, according to Medwin, he had earned the name of " Slip-knot " for his dexterity in evading matrimonial engagements. Every Sunday Dr. Nott held religious services for the benefit of the fourteen or fifteen English people who wished to attend. He gave Mary Shelley a personal and particular invitation, which she accepted, for three ser-

mons.³³ These sermons, according to Medwin, constituted a
trilogy against atheism. They were directed so pointedly at
Mary Shelley that everyone felt that Shelley was being assailed
through his wife. She wrote him a note and obtained his denial
of any such purpose, but apparently she never returned to his
services. Shelley only laughed, even when Dr. Nott later referred to him at Mrs. Beauclerc's as a " *scelerato.*" Not so Byron,
who regarded the sermon as a shabby example of priestly malice. Dr. Nott, he said, had revised one of the Ten Command-
ments to read: " Thou shalt, Nott, bear false witness against
thy neighbour." He wrote a nine-stanza satire, beginning: " Do
you know Doctor Nott," which rehearsed various gossip at his
expense and concluded:

> You may still preach and pray
> And from bishop sink into backbiter.³⁴

SHORTLY after this episode, a young Cornishman named Edward
John Trelawny arrived in Pisa. He was already acquainted with
the Williamses and Medwin, having met them in Geneva in
1820. He had read and admired Shelley's *Queen Mab* and *The
Cenci* and had been further interested in Shelley by Medwin's
constant enthusiastic talk and by similar reports from Williams
after the latter had settled in Pisa.

Trelawny had intended to hunt in the Maremma marshes
during the winter with Williams and another friend, Captain
Daniel Roberts, of the Royal Navy; but correspondence with
Williams stimulated his desire to know both Shelley and Byron,
so he set out early, planning to spend some time in the intellectual society of Pisa and to hunt later. On January 14, 1822
he turned up at the Williamses' apartment in the Tre Palazzi.

Within a few minutes thereafter he became conscious that
a young man in the darkened hallway beyond the open door
was gazing upon him with a peculiar steadiness. It was Shelley; Mrs. Williams called him in and furnished the necessary
introductions. Trelawny was astonished. He could hardly believe that this tall, thin, boyish-looking person could be the
deadly enemy of church and state that reviews had pictured.

EDWARD J. TRELAWNY IN 1838

Pen sketch by Joseph Severn. By permission of the National Portrait Gallery

Jane Williams asked Shelley to read a little from the book he
held in his hand, Calderon's *El Mágico Prodigioso*, and Shelley
complied in a manner that immediately told Trelawny that
he was in the presence of genius: "The masterly manner in
which he analyzed the genius of the author, his lucid interpretation of the story, and the ease with which he translated into
our language the most subtle and imaginative passages of the
Spanish poet, were marvellous. . . ." [35] After the reading Shelley vanished as silently as he had appeared, but reappeared
almost immediately with Mary.

In the following days Trelawny soon became well acquainted
with the Shelleys and Byron. From the first he was in their company practically every day, though he seems not to have dined
with them before January 23. He was pleased with Mary's intellectual quality, and her engaging, alert, and witty conversation
among her friends, even though he soon learned that she was
often melancholy when alone. He greatly admired Shelley
for his sincerity, his deep sympathies, and subtle intellectual
penetration. He even admired Shelley's idealizing tendencies,
though he often tried rather ineffectually to bring the poet into
closer touch with his own notion of the realities of life.

The Shelleys were perhaps a little longer making up their
minds about Trelawny. Five days after the first meeting Mary
set down in her journal an unusually long sketch showing how
much already he had stimulated her imagination. A little later,
February 9, she elaborated the same account in a letter to Mrs.
Gisborne:

. . . Trelawny, a kind of half-Arab Englishman, whose life has been
as changeful as that of Anastasius, and who recounts the adventures
as eloquently and as well as the imagined Greek. He is clever; for
his moral qualities I am yet in the dark; he is a strange web which
I am endeavouring to unravel. I would fain learn if generosity is
united to impetuousness, probity of spirit to his assumption of
singularity and independence. He is 6 feet high, raven black hair
which curls thickly and shortly, like a Moor's, dark grey expressive
eyes, overhanging brows, upturned lips, and a smile which expresses
good nature and kind heartedness. His shoulders are high, like an
Oriental's, his voice is monotonous, yet emphatic, and his language,

as he relates the events of his life, energetic and simple, whether the tale be one of blood and horror, or of irresistible comedy. His company is delightful, for he excites me to think. . . .[36]

Some of the tales of violence that Trelawny told were doubtless those later recorded in his *Adventures of a Younger Son,* which Mary Shelley helped Trelawny to publish years later. There, and in his subsequent career, one may see that he had in his nature a recognizable strain of ruffianism. Yet both Mary Shelley and Claire Clairmont were soon to learn that he did indeed possess " generosity . . . united to impetuousness." By the second week in April the Shelleys and Williamses talked of a romantic drama to be founded upon his singular adventures,[37] as those of " a Pirate, a man of savage but noble nature." Some 250 lines of it were written by Shelley before it was abandoned for more serious affairs.

Even before Trelawny's arrival the Shelleys, Williamses, and Byron had resolved to spend the summer on the Bay of Lerici, and Shelley and Williams were counting upon the help of Trelawny in building the boat which they were planning. The next day after his arrival Trelawny produced a model of an American schooner and was authorized to write at once to his friend Captain Roberts in Genoa, directing him to build a thirty-foot undecked boat on the same model. Mary and Jane listened to this fateful decision without enthusiasm. Somewhat laughingly Mary said to Jane: " Our husbands decide without asking our consent, or having our concurrence; for, to tell you the truth, I hate this boat, though I say nothing." Jane replied: " So do I, but speaking would be useless, and only spoil their pleasure."

Byron at once decided to build a similar boat, but larger, and decked. Williams, however, was so much in love with a boat design he had brought with him from England that he ultimately prevailed against the judgment of both Trelawny and Roberts. At this stage, Shelley, Williams, and Trelawny were to be joint owners. During the months when the two boats were building Shelley and Williams continued their naval exploits in the small boat that had already given them so much pleasure. But they were boyishly eager and impatient for larger sea-room and a larger boat. Time and again they repaired with Trelawny to the banks of the Arno to sketch in the sand her lines and compartments; then with a chart of the Mediterranean spread before them they planned extended cruises. They talked of the exploits of Diaz, Drake, and Commodore Bligh, all accomplished in small boats. Byron stood by with a wicked smile and speculated on the amount of salvage Shelley's boat would fetch after *his* boat had rescued and towed it into port.[38]

At this time Shelley also expressed a desire to learn to swim. After watching Trelawny perform a series of difficult aquatic feats he remarked wistfully: "Why can't I swim . . . ?" — upon which Trelawny proposed to give him a first lesson. Shelley shed his clothes briskly and plunged in, but made no effort to rise from the bottom of the pool. Upon rescuing him Trelawny found that he had regarded the prospect of death rather comfortably. "I always find the bottom of the well," he remarked, "and they say Truth lies there. In another minute I should have found it, and you would have found an empty shell. It is an easy way to get rid of the body."[39]

IN HIS almost daily walks, rides, and meals with the Shelleys and Williamses Trelawny would not necessarily have perceived a somewhat unusual emotional situation between Shelley, Mary, and Jane Williams — at least he wrote nothing to show that he did. Yet by early January Shelley's admiration for Jane Williams had produced two poems, "To Jane: The Invitation," and "To Jane: The Recollection," which show that it was to Jane, rather than Mary, that he now looked for his bright moments of spiritual sunshine. The two poems reflect Shelley's pleasure in a walk through the neighbouring woods with Jane and Mary, apparently on February 2. Mary's participation in the walk, however, is virtually ignored in Shelley's two poems. It is Jane who is hailed as "best and brightest" and who is "ever fair and kind"; if Mary's presence is indicated at all it is only as the "envious wind" which "Blots one dear image out" and causes the poet to lament his lack of spiritual calm.

Possibly it was during the stroll so commemorated that Shel-

ley came across the secluded spot to which he loved to repair
later in order to compose in entire solitude. One fine spring
morning when Shelley had vanished in this direction Mary engaged Trelawny's assistance in finding him. After some fruitless searching Trelawny found an old man who had seen "*l'inglese malincolico*" and undertook to guide the searcher. While
Mary waited near the edge of the wood Trelawny and his guide
plunged on until they reached a deep dark pool surrounded by
stunted and twisted trees. Near by lay Shelley's hat, books, and
papers. A few paces beyond, in the lee of a pine that had toppled
over into the pool, sat the poet, gazing into the water in a mood
of such abstraction or concentration that he had not noticed Trelawny's approach. "Is this your study?" Trelawny demanded.
Shelley launched forth into fanciful praises of the spot. Trelawny reminded him that a "forsaken lady," his wife, was waiting at the entrance to the grove. Shelley jumped up and stuffed
his books and papers into his jacket pockets. "Poor Mary!" he
exclaimed in rueful contrition, "hers is a sad fate. Come along;
she can't bear solitude, nor I society — the quick coupled with
the dead." When they rejoined Mary she scolded Shelley affectionately as "a wild goose" with no sense of social obligations; then the party started back for Pisa in spirits as wild and
high as Shelley's had been previously silent and abstracted.

Shelley had been working on a poem beside his fallen pine
tree, and Trelawny had picked up the manuscript. But it was
such a frightful scrawl that he could read only two lines. With
its smears, deletions, additions, and so forth, it reminded him
of a marsh overgrown with bulrushes in which the blots appeared as wild ducks. Shelley explained:

"When my brain gets heated with thought, it soon boils, and
throws off images and words faster than I can skim them off.
In the morning, when cooled down, out of the rude sketch, as
you justly call it, I shall attempt a drawing. If you ask me why
I publish what few or none will care to read, it is that the spirits
I have raised haunt me until they are sent to the devil of a
printer. All authors are anxious to breech their bantlings." [40]

When more fully drawn, the "rude sketch" later emerged as
one of Shelley's most delicately beautiful fancies, the poem now

known as " With a Guitar: to Jane." The guitar itself had been
purchased and presented when Horace Smith, about the end of
January, had declined Shelley's request to buy for him in Paris
a pedal harp to be presented to Jane.⁴¹ The following poem
shows that the poetic inspiration of Jane's guitar was not limited
to its presentation:

TO JANE

The keen stars were twinkling,
And the fair moon was rising among them,
Dear Jane!
The guitar was tinkling,
But the notes were not sweet till you sung them
Again.

As the moon's soft splendour
O'er the faint cold starlight of heaven
Is thrown,
So your voice most tender
To the strings without soul had then given
Its own.

The stars will awaken,
Though the moon sleep a full hour later,
To-night;
No leaf will be shaken
Whilst the dews of your melody scatter
Delight.

Though the sound overpowers,
Sing again, with your dear voice revealing
A tone
Of some world far from ours,
Where music and moonlight and feeling
Are one.

The beneficial effects of Jane Williams upon Shelley were not
confined to her music and her cheerful, happy disposition. She
had learned from Medwin something of the art of hypnotizing

("magnetism") and was able to use it in combating Shelley's occasional attacks of pain from his side. In a poem entitled "The Magnetic Lady to her Patient" Shelley gives a specimen of the soothing, sympathetic talk with which her "magnetic" ministrations were accompanied. In the second stanza Jane is made to say plainly: "I love thee not." At the same time she expresses deep pity that his case is so different from hers and Williams's in that Shelley's consolation in distress must come from a hand not his wife's. One cannot be certain that any such conversation actually happened except in Shelley's mind, but a later letter of Jane's shows that it could have happened. "You, I imagined," she wrote to Leigh Hunt, "as well as myself, had seen that the intercourse between Shelley and Mary was not as happy as it should have been." [42]

Another poem, which Shelley sent to Edward Williams on January 26, shows that he was equally frank with both the Williamses, as he was a few months later with John Gisborne. Here Shelley seems clearly to be speaking of Mary's objection to his intimacy with the Williamses. "The serpent is shut out from Paradise," he begins the first stanza, and concludes it:

> I, too, must seldom seek again
> Near happy friends a mitigated pain.

He expresses the despondency of spirits he felt in his "cold home" (the same phrase he had previously applied to his home with Harriet) and apologizes for the necessity of seeing his friends less often. The poem was sent to Edward Williams with a note requesting that it be shown to no one except Jane — and, on second thought, not even to her. [43] The Williamses, seeing Mary's deficient sympathy and Shelley's excessive reaction to it, sympathized with both parties while condemning neither.

Shelley paid another strong tribute to Jane in the tenth stanza of "The Zucca," yet in the third stanza he quite clearly disposed of the question of love. This poem, which was written in January, is a fairly clear statement both of Shelley's sense of obligation to Jane and also of the fact that he was not in love with her:

JANE WILLIAMS

Painting by George Clint. By permission of the Bodleian Library

> I loved — oh no, I mean not one of ye,
> Or any earthly one . . .

— which is but a slight variation from the passage from St. Augustine that had been prefixed to *Alastor* six years before: "*Nondum amabam, et amare amabam, quærebam quid amarem, amans amare.*"

The clue to Shelley's state of mind as expressed in his poems of this spring was his own intense idealizing nature, which magnified both sympathetic and non-sympathetic moods far beyond any reality except the intensified transient reality of the moment in which he wrote. It is unlikely that the Williamses, Gisbornes, and Mary Shelley misunderstood, even though Mary may well have thought the situation dangerous in its future possibilities.

AT THE same time there were anxieties and irritations that were more tangible and were not at all exaggerated by a hopeless craving for perfect sympathy. The Olliers had completely exhausted Shelley's patience by their delays and indifference. On January 26 Shelley gave John Gisborne instructions to terminate the connection — "extract me from his clutches." But both Hogg and Mrs. Gisborne were of the opinion that Mary should allow Ollier to publish her novel.[44] Mr. Gisborne found himself obliged to temporize with Shelley's instructions as Ollier, wishing to retain the business, made fair promises and delayed submitting an account. Shelley again insisted upon receiving his account from "this infinite thief," but Ollier again delayed. The change to a new publisher was still unaccomplished at the time of Shelley's death.[45]

Now that Horace Smith had left London and Peacock was becoming more and more absorbed in East India Company affairs, it was to John and Maria Gisborne that the Shelleys turned to get their various London commissions executed. Eventually they were even able to prod Ollier into sending Shelley's books and Mary's desk, about which delays had been most irritating. Mr. Gisborne was a business man in whose judgment Shelley now seemed to have considerable confidence; the old miserable affair of Henry Reveley's steamboat was evidently forgiven. He consulted Mr. Gisborne's opinion about employing a legal business agent to try to bring more order into his financial affairs and expectations than the unsatisfactory and exorbitant Mr. P. W. Longdill had accomplished. At this time Shelley expected to inherit an estate worth from £5,000 to £7,000 a year which was burdened with about £22,500 in debts (mostly Shelley's post-obits) and £10,000 devised to his sisters, besides an annual charge of "some hundreds a year" on his mother's jointure. The debts, Shelley thought, might by negotiation be reduced to £14,000 or £15,000.[46]

Since early in 1820 the Shelleys had been living within their income, but with little to spare. Leigh Hunt's expenses in coming to Italy raised financial demands which Shelley could not meet alone. With considerable difficulty he got together £150 to send to Hunt on January 25. Byron had already paid the expenses of furnishing rooms to be assigned the Hunts, and it was for several reasons infinitely galling for Shelley to have to call upon him for more. Nevertheless, it was necessary, and Byron made no objection to advancing £250 on Shelley's security. Shelley promised £50 more of his own in the future.[47] On May 13 Hunt finally set sail from Plymouth. Long before this his various delays had assumed Odyssean proportions in Hogg's humorous point of view. "I would have written by Hunt," Hogg wrote to Shelley on January 28, "but I was unable to muster up sufficient gravity to address a grey-headed, deaf, double, tottering, spectacled old man, for such I was persuaded you would be before he reached Pisa . . . and I was unwilling to interrupt, by any recollections of 'poor Hogg, who has been dead these fifty years,' the meeting of Shelley and Old Hunt, which might possibly take place about the close of the nineteenth century."[48]

SHELLEY's anxieties over Hunt's affairs and his irritation with the Olliers was coincidental with a considerably deeper worry. Claire Clairmont had returned to Florence upon Byron's first arrival at Pisa. But from the moment Byron left Ravenna her fears about Allegra had redoubled. Early in February she was pressing Shelley and Mary to help her do something about Allegra. Mr. Mason had made a secret trip to Bagnacavallo on her behalf and had returned with disquieting impressions. Both he and Mrs. Mason urged vigorous steps to recover Allegra, but Shelley, although extremely angry with Byron, clung to a policy of watchful waiting.[49] Shelley urged her to keep as tranquil as possible and to come and spend the summer with him and Mary. He could offer little hope for improving Allegra's situation:

> Mary tells you that Lord Byron is obstinate and *awake* about Allegra. My great object has been to lull him into security until circumstances might call him to England. But the idea of contending with him in Italy, and defended by his enormous fortune, is vain. I was endeavouring to induce him to place Allegra in the institute at Lucca, but his jealousy of my regard for *your* interests will, since a conversation I had with him the other day, render him inaccessible to my suggestions. It seems to me that you have no other resource but time and chance and change.[50]

Meanwhile Claire was forming wild schemes, apparently with the help of Elise Foggi, Allegra's former nurse, who was living in Florence and whom Claire had first met on February 7. When taxed by Claire with having told scandalous stories to Mrs. Hoppner in the summer of 1820, Elise probably lied, since she eventually wrote notes to both Mrs. Shelley and Mrs. Hoppner denying ever having told such stories.[51] For two months Claire was in constant contact with Elise. Nowhere in her journal is there any mention of Allegra, but many entries briefly record her low spirits. On February 18 she wrote to Byron, who disregarded her letter.[52] She then made a four days' visit to Pisa (February 21–5), but it is unknown what schemes, if any, she proposed at this time.

After her return to Florence and renewed conferences with Elise, Claire proposed a mad new plan which evidently required kidnapping and a forged letter. It evoked one of Shelley's sternest admonitions. "I know not what to think of the state of your mind," Shelley wrote, "or what to fear for you. Your plan about

Allegra seems to me in its present form, pregnant with irremedi-
able infamy to all actors in it except yourself; — in any form
wherein *I* must actively co-operate, with inevitable destruction.
I *would not* in any case make myself the party to a forged letter.
I *could not* refuse Lord Byron's challenge; though that, however to be deprecated, would be the least in the series of mis-
chiefs consequent upon my pestilent intervention in such a plan.
I say this because I am shocked at the thoughtless violence of
your designs, and I wish to put my sense of this madness in
the strongest light." There was now no way of securing Allegra from Byron, he assured her, and he urged her to see the
situation as it was and accommodate herself to it, at least for
the present. " If you would take my advice, you would give up
this idle pursuit after shadows, and temper yourself to the
season, seek in the daily and affectionate intercourse of friends
a respite from these perpetual and irritating projects. Live from
day to day, attend to your health, cultivate literature and liberal ideas to a certain extent, and expect that from time and
change which no exertion of your own can give you." [53]

This was good advice, and surprisingly Horatian from a Shelley, but the distracted Claire could not calm herself so easily.
She did circulate briskly among her Florentine friends, and she
continued in a desultory way a translation from Goethe for
which Byron was to pay (not knowing her hand in it) and for
which he was to furnish a sketch of Goethe by way of introduction. But she continued seeing Elise, and she dropped for the
present a design she had formed of joining her brother Charles
in Vienna. In April she was still unsettled, and Shelley wrote to
repeat his former advice and to urge her to join the Shelleys and
Williamses at Lerici for the summer.[54]

In the case of both Claire and Leigh Hunt, Shelley stood in
an awkward relationship to Byron. He had been the cause of
Hunt's emigration, and even before Hunt arrived he had seen
Byron vacillate again and again in his desire to set up a liberal
journal of opinion. The Tory journals in England were de-
nouncing the *Liberal* in anticipation; strong pressure both direct and indirect had been put upon Byron. His friends had
warned him not to cheapen himself by a public association with

Leigh Hunt and Shelley. One or two such letters he had shown to Shelley. Knowing Byron's inconstant nature, Shelley was very much afraid that he might withdraw from the enterprise. Knowing also Byron's mixture of penuriousness and generosity, he was also embarrassed about making financial arrangements with him, and yet it was he on whom Hunt relied for the arrangements. It was an even greater strain to preserve friendly relations with Byron when he felt so keenly the harshness of Byron's treatment of Claire Clairmont and knew that he was suspicious of any suggestion about Allegra.

Matters reached the point where Shelley's dearest wish was to be able to separate himself from Byron without an open break — and yet Leigh Hunt's dependence rendered even this impossible. " It is of vital importance," Shelley wrote to Claire, " both to me and to yourself, to Allegra even, that I should put a period to my intimacy with L[ord] B[yron], and that without *eclat*. No sentiments of honour or justice restrain him (as I strongly suspect) from the basest insinuations, and the only mode in which I could effectually silence him I am reluctant (even if I had proof) to employ during my father's life." Some two months later he informed Claire that in his opinion " a great gulph " existed between him and Byron and that it must daily grow wider.[55]

From the second week in February, however, it was fairly clear that Byron could hardly be a member of the Shelley-Williams summer colony. Shelley and Williams left Pisa on February 7 to investigate housing possibilities at Spezia. After three days' inquiring and inspecting in Spezia and neighbouring towns, they could find only two houses that were at all possible, and only one of these was for rent. Toward the end of April, when the Williamses and Shelleys were actually departing for Spezia, they were still uncertain of a house.[56] Meanwhile an occurrence had taken place at Pisa which looked for a while as if it might terminate all such plans.

ON SUNDAY afternoon, March 24, Byron's usual riding party, consisting of Lord Byron, Shelley, Trelawny, Captain Hay,

Count Gamba, and Mr. Taafe, were returning toward Pisa, followed at a short distance by Mary Shelley and the Countess Guiccioli in a carriage. As they neared one of the city gates a mounted dragoon (afterwards identified as Serjeant-Major Masi) dashed through the riders and seemed to brush insolently and defiantly against Taafe. That gentleman, always pompous and slightly ridiculous, could brook no derogation from his dignity; he called to Byron: " Shall we endure this man's insolence? " and Byron answered: " No, we will bring him to an account." The dragoon continued toward the city gate. Byron's party (except Taafe, who remained prudently behind) put spurs to their horses, stopped the man, and demanded an explanation. He was half-drunk, however, and cursed them for " *maladetti Inglesi*." He announced that he could cut them all to pieces, but would merely arrest them. Whereupon Byron laughed: " Arrest, indeed! " and with Count Gamba rode on toward the gate. Before the others could pass, the dragoon placed himself in the gateway and called on the guard to stop them. Byron and Count Gamba rode on, intending to arm themselves and return for the expected scuffle. Behind them the dragoon again grew violent. He made a vicious sabre-cut at Shelley, who warded or dodged the blade but took a blow on the head from the hilt and was knocked off his horse. The man cut at him again, but Captain Hay warded the blow with his stick, only to receive a cut across the nose when the sabre cut through the stick.

After a few cuts and slashes at the empty air the man rode on into Pisa. Here he met Byron returning to the scene with his sword-stick. The dragoon put up his sword and begged Byron to do the same, which Byron did only on being given his name, that he might require satisfaction later. One of Byron's servants had caught Masi's bridle. Byron ordered him to let go, and the dragoon immediately put his horse to the gallop. By now, however, it was dusk, and Byron's servants, watching from his house, thought that another affray had taken place and that Byron had been killed. As Masi passed, one of them dashed out with a pitchfork and wounded him in the abdomen. He fell

LORD BYRON AFTER HIS DAILY RIDE AT PISA AND GENOA
Cut-paper silhouette by Marianne Hunt

from his horse and was carried to the hospital, where for several days his recovery seemed doubtful.

In such a small, quiet city as Pisa rumours immediately began to circulate. Some Englishmen had placed themselves at the head of a peasant insurrection and had made a fruitless assault upon the guard; Trelawny had been killed and Byron mortally wounded. Taafe had assassinated a dragoon and was being guarded against arrest by Byron's bulldogs. When word arrived on Tuesday that Serjeant-Major Masi was dying, the English all armed themselves against a possible attack from the mob. This soon gave rise to another story. Lord Byron and all his servants, with four English gentlemen, armed with stilettos and forty brace of pistols, had all been captured after a desperate resistance. Shelley received a message from a nervous lady, probably Mrs. Beauclerc or Mrs. Mason, warning him that friends of the wounded man might assassinate him if he visited her home after nightfall. From Rome the affray was reflected back to Pisa as an assassination executed by Byron upon a Tuscan colonel who had challenged him.

Meanwhile all was not well among the English. Shelley's wound was of no consequence, but Captain Hay and the Countess Guiccioli required physicians, the one for a face badly bruised and cut, the other for nerves. Taafe, having caused the fray and then carefully withdrawn from it, was first to exculpate himself by a statement to the police. But among the English he also boasted so constantly of his valour that Jane Williams took to referring to him as False-Taafe. To Byron he even said: "My Lord, if you do not dare ride out today, I will alone." Needless to say, Byron regarded him with a bilious eye for some days thereafter; not until April 3 was he willing to shake hands with him. Vaccà, who attended the wounded man, believed and quoted his story that he would not have drawn his weapon if one of the party had not struck him with a riding-whip, and Captain Hay privately admitted that Count Gamba had struck the man with his whip. Vaccà was willing to testify in court that Masi's wound was given with a stiletto rather than a pitchfork.

Soon Justice began to move with rather more than customary blindness. Depositions were taken on all sides, from fifteen participants and witnesses. A commissioner arrived from Florence who interviewed Mary Shelley for six hours, the length of the interview, however, being due less to rigour than to politeness. English officials in Florence, called into the case by Byron, rather pooh-poohed the danger. No one of the witnesses could or would name Masi's assailant. The Pisan authorities arrested one of Byron's servants and one of Countess Guiccioli's. Both were perfectly innocent, but one of them unfortunately possessed a rather villainous look — "*aveva lo sguardo fiero, quanto un assassino.*" This man was soon ordered released by the commissioner from Florence, but the relatively meek-visaged servant of the Countess Guiccioli was kept in solitary confinement for some time afterwards. The Tuscan government, though liberally administered, had never regarded with enthusiasm the presence of such known Carbonari as the Gambas. It hinted that in view of the threats of vengeance Byron's party would be safer in another city. Since Lerici had already proved impossible, Byron decided to do his summer boating from Leghorn. On April 9 he rented for himself and the Gambas a house in Montenero, about four miles from Leghorn, but did not himself take up residence there until about the end of May.[57]

As Serjeant-Major Masi began to recover and the excitement died down, the Shelleys and Williamses turned again to their plans for a summer on the coast. But news arrived on April 15 that the two houses Shelley and Williams had considered renting were abruptly withdrawn — in Byron's opinion, because the Piedmont government objected to Shelley as a radical. The same day Claire Clairmont arrived on a visit from Florence, probably with the intention of accompanying the Shelleys to Spezia. In the uncertainty of their situation it was decided that the Williamses and Claire should make another trip to Spezia to attempt to find suitable quarters there. They returned on April 25, having achieved nothing. During their absence, as Williams guessed from Shelley's face, disastrous news had reached the Shelleys.

CLAIRE'S worst fears had been realized. Allegra had been stricken with typhus fever in her convent school at Bagnacavallo and had died on April 19, at the age of five years and three months. The Shelleys and Claire had not even known of her illness, though she had been ill for weeks. Byron had known, but thought the danger past. Under no circumstances, Shelley felt, could the news be broken to Claire when she was in the same neighbourhood with Byron. Though there was only one house, unfurnished, to be rented near Spezia, it was better to go there in all haste and then break the news. This was Shelley's opinion; the others were doubtful. But Shelley was not to be denied; he was " like a torrent hurrying everything in its course." [58] Mary, Claire, and Trelawny went ahead on April 26. Shelley and Williams remained a day longer in Pisa to superintend the loading of the two boats that had been engaged to carry their furniture. Next day Shelley and Williams were at Lerici, straightening out customs difficulties about their furniture and seeking vainly for another house. Shelley wrote thence to Mary urging that she lose not a minute in securing Casa Magni, the one available house in San Terenzo. It was none too large for the Shelleys alone, but they contrived to allow the Williamses one of the three bedrooms, and the party settled down in one house as best they could.

It was now Shelley's task to break to Claire the news that had been for days such an oppressive secret among her friends. On May 2, a day after the Williamses were installed with the Shelleys, the two families were in a back room, planning how best to perform this sad duty. The door opened and Claire walked in. One look at their faces was enough to make her guess the truth.

In the first moments of bitterness and desolation she must have said to Shelley and Mary some of the things that are adumbrated in her journals and letters many years afterwards. She always regarded Byron as the murderer of her child. Mary and Shelley, by not falling in with her wild schemes of rescue, had been to some extent Byron's accomplices. Many years later, in a cryptic, bitter passage in one of her journals, Claire condemned Mary for calmly witnessing the execution of a child at Pisa, and afterwards shaking hands with the executioner.[59] Without consulting the others she wrote Byron a letter of searing denunciation. Byron sent it on to Shelley — this time, it is to be hoped, without his usual comments on Claire. The shock of his own grief softened Byron into an attitude temporarily more generous. He granted at once all of Claire's last requests — for a miniature of Allegra, a lock of her hair, and the right to see the body before it was shipped to England. He even agreed that she might dictate the funeral arrangements. But Claire was willing to leave this to Byron, and Shelley was even able to persuade her not to go to Leghorn to see Allegra's body.

After the first wild outbursts, during which Shelley feared she might lose her reason, Claire settled at first into a state of apparent bewilderment; then she called to her support a fortitude which was quite surprising. Within a week or two she had become far more tranquil and had returned to Florence, though she expected to come back to San Terenzo for the summer.

THE INCREASED interest in Shelley shown by the English reading public in 1820 and 1821 which has been discussed in a previous chapter continued with some slight abatement in 1822. The four current editions of *Queen Mab* then available, and the anticipation of the *Liberal*, lent a somewhat more furious tone to the Tory journalists. Leigh Hunt came vigorously to the defence in four letters in the *Examiner* and in a favourable review of *Adonais*.[60] Exclusive of five poems inspired by his death, Shelley was in 1822 the subject of an unfavourable epigram and a neutral parody stanza; also of two poetic eulogies, by Arthur Brooke [John Chalk Claris] and J. W. Dalby respectively.[61] But Shelley had been comparatively isolated from English opinion in Pisa and was almost completely so at San Terenzo. His publishers neglected to keep him informed. By this time it hardly mattered, for his mind was made up that the public and the reviewers would have none of him. The failure of *Adonais* to receive adequate recognition had extinguished his last hope.

Chapter XXIX

LAST DAYS

SHELLEY IN 1822; THE NEW ENVIRONMENT;
TROUBLES AND PLEASURES; "THE TRIUMPH
OF LIFE"; ARRIVAL OF HUNT; SHELLEY'S DEATH;
DISPERSAL OF THE SURVIVORS

WHEN the Shelleys left Pisa on May 1, 1822, they had already been in almost daily association with Edward Trelawny for four months. For two months more they were to be in correspondence and occasional personal contact with him. From the first, Trelawny had been a sharp, almost fascinated observer, recording in his retentive memory details and anecdotes without which the story of Shelley's later life would be seriously incomplete. At this point, therefore, it is well to pause for a moment for a general picture of Shelley as Trelawny saw him.[1]

There was nothing particularly arresting about Shelley's appearance until he spoke. His first sentence, however, was apt to rivet one's attention, because the deep earnestness and clarity of his utterance were perfectly mirrored by the ever changing aspect of his mobile features.[2] This, however, was only when Shelley was interested. Though his manner was uniformly courteous, he dreaded bores almost as much as in the old days. He consistently avoided miscellaneous society, and when Mary "threatened" him with a party he was woebegone. His oversensitiveness led him to an exaggerated impression that people shunned his society, but to those who sought it in spite of his own aloofness he was frank, cordial, and, in all worthy cases, almost excessively friendly. He would make extreme sacrifices to serve a friend, and in congenial company was generally social and cheerful. Towns and crowds generally distracted him or threw him into dejection. To the rough and ready Trelawny he seemed as ignorant of the "working-day world" as a schoolgirl — so much so that Trelawny undertook more than once to enlighten him. Such "distractions," as Shelley called them, usually resulted in a state of mirth and high spirits.

From the city Shelley generally sought to escape during the day-time to the solitude or semi-solitude of the woods or his boat.[3] His daily routine was simple. He was "up at six or seven, reading Plato, Sophocles or Spinoza, with the accompaniment of a hunch of dry bread; then he joined Williams in a sail on the Arno, in a flat-bottomed skiff, book in hand, and from thence he went to the pine forests, or some out-of-the-way place. When the birds went to roost he returned home, and talked or read until midnight." This monotonous routine was somewhat alleviated by social contacts with Byron and his companions and visitors.

Like Medwin, Trelawny was immensely impressed by Shelley's thirst for knowledge. "He set to work on a book, or a pyramid of books, his eyes glistening with an energy as fierce as that of the most sordid gold-digger. . . ." At ten o'clock one morning Trelawny left Shelley standing in front of a mantelpiece, with a dictionary in hand, studying a German folio resting on the mantelpiece; returning at six in the evening he found Shelley in exactly the same position, fully believing that he had eaten the food that stood untouched on a tray near by. He paid little attention to meal-times, and only ate — rather absent-mindedly — when hungry. "If not writing or sleeping, he was reading; he read whilst eating, walking, or travelling — the last thing at night, the first thing in the morning. . . ."

Nothing impressed Trelawny more deeply than Shelley's mental powers. "Sometimes he would run through a great work on science, condense the author's laboured exposition, and by substituting simple words for the jargon of the schools, make the most abstruse work transparent."[4] "He kept your brain in constant action." His mental activity was infectious; it converted Williams from a sportsman to a scholar and writer; it elevated the tone of Byron's conversation whenever Shelley was present; it imposed upon Byron an unwonted docility toward Shelley's critical judgment. His excessive mental labour, in Trelawny's opinion, "impeded, if it did not paralyze, his bodily functions. When his mind was fixed on a subject his mental powers were strained to the utmost." The occasional spasms which Trelawny thought were Shelley's only physical complaint were in his opinion caused by "the excessive and almost unremitting strain on his mental powers, the solitude of his life, and his long fasts, which were not intentional, but proceeded from the abstraction and forgetfulness of himself and his wife." Trelawny believed that his intense brooding damaged both his bodily and his mental health.

Like Medwin again, Trelawny was constantly drawing a comparison between Shelley and Byron, always to Shelley's advantage. In the rare social gatherings Shelley attended he was easier and less self-conscious than Byron.[5] Unlike Byron, he was completely unselfish. Where Byron, with large means, was petty in money matters, Shelley, with a limited income, was generous to a fault. In argument Byron was quick and shifty, Shelley acute and steady; where Byron was superficial, Shelley was bold and profound. "Shelley had a far loftier spirit. His pride was spiritual. When attacked he neither fled nor stood at bay, nor altered his course, but calmly went on with heart and mind intent on elevating his species. . . . His words were, 'I always go on until I am stopped, and I never am stopped.'"

Shelley was no atheist to Trelawny. "If his glorious conception of gods and men constituted an atheist I am afraid all that listened to him were little better." Trelawny remonstrated with Shelley for accepting the title and received the answer: "It is a word of abuse to stop discussion, a painted devil to frighten the foolish, a threat to intimidate the wise and good. I used it to express my abhorrence of superstition; I took up the word, as a knight took up a gauntlet, in defiance of injustice."

THE GULF OF SPEZIA, which Shelley and Williams had selected for their summer sailing, was at that time completely neglected by tourists. This considerable bay is divided by wooded rocky promontories into numerous smaller ones, the most beautiful of which was the little bay of San Terenzo, which was almost completely landlocked. Here was the primitive hamlet of San Terenzo, not more than two hundred yards distant from the house Shelley had rented, called Casa Magni. The surrounding scenery was lonely and romantic. Behind rose rocky foothills, extending down to the beach; in front lay the blue, tideless Mediterranean. Immediately behind Casa Magni rose a hill on which the owner had planted a young forest of chestnut and ilex trees.

Casa Magni was a two-storey structure about twice as long as it was deep, with the lower storey projecting in front several feet beyond the upper one, forming an open porch across the entire front of the house. It looked almost as much like a large boat-house as like a residence. The ground floor was unpaved and fit only for storage purposes. The upper floor was reached by two stairways, one leading to a large dining-room which occupied the entire centre of the floor, and another, in the right rear corner, leading to Mary's bedroom. There were three bedrooms, each occupying a corner of the upper floor. Shelley's room occupied the left front corner, separated by the dining-room from the right front room occupied by Mary and Percy Florence. The Williamses, with two children, had the rear room. This whole storey had once been whitewashed, but the walls were now splotchy, the ceiling cracked, and the floor broken. There were an outbuilding for cooking, and separate quarters for the servants. This house now had to accommodate not only the three Shelleys and Claire, but the four Williamses as well. Mary and Jane groaned and complained when they first entered it and with difficulty were induced to stay. But there was nowhere else to go, and they knew that Shelley and Williams had set their hearts on a summer's boating in the bay.[6]

The neighbouring hamlet of San Terenzo was too small and poor to be of any advantage as a source of supplies. Nearly four miles away, on the other side of a little river, a limited amount of provisions could be bought at Sarzana; Lerici, a mile away, could be reached by following a rocky, winding footpath near

VILLA MAGNI, SHELLEY'S LAST RESIDENCE

Reprinted by permission from the Illustrated London News, *August 6, 1892*

the shore. The natives of San Terenzo were so crude of speech
and manners that Mary thought them the most savage people
she had seen in Italy. At night they gathered on the beach and
the women danced among the waves while the men leaned
against the rocks and joined them in a wild chorus. Once or
twice Shelley and Trelawny joined them, much to Mary's disgust. " Had we been wrecked on an island of the South Seas,"
wrote Mary Shelley almost twenty years later, "we could
scarcely have felt ourselves further from civilization and comfort; but where the sun shines the latter becomes an unnecessary
luxury, and we had enough society among ourselves. Yet I confess housekeeping became rather a toilsome task, especially as I
was suffering in my health and could not exert myself actively." [7]

This was putting it mildly. From the first, Mary hated the
place with an intense, almost morbid loathing. She complained that the natives were wild and hateful, that the living-
arrangements were extremely inconvenient, and that the Tuscan
servants would soon leave — which some of them did. The
Shelley and Williams servants quarrelled among themselves
" like cats and dogs." Jane Williams was dissatisfied also; she
longed for her own pots and pans, which could not be unpacked,
now that the Williamses had been compelled to accept a room
instead of a house of their own. Shelley, in turn, reproached
Mary for her antagonism to a situation in which he felt his health
and spirits better than ever before. The wise Mrs. Mason
showed a true estimate of this situation when she wrote Shelley
that she dreaded Claire's return to Casa Magni and wished the
Williamses at least half a mile away. Mary precipitated several painful domestic scenes that were witnessed by the Williamses and were later reported to Leigh Hunt by both Shelley
and Jane Williams. Hunt considered them serious enough to
produce a temporary coldness in his attitude toward Mary, yet
nothing which a few words from an old friend might not easily
smooth over. The Williamses, though unaware of Mary's subsequent private apologies to Shelley, seem not to have taken the
situation very seriously. [8]

Mary was really in a state of nervous and physical ill health
for which the others possibly made insufficient allowance. She

was expecting another baby in December, and her pregnancy was proceeding very unsatisfactorily. Her languor and irritability were disturbing; she sometimes had alarming hysterical affections.[9] After May 4 she wrote nothing in her journal until June 1.

Shelley confided to John Gisborne that the only flaw in his present happiness was " the want of those who can feel, and understand me. Whether from proximity and the continuity of domestic intercourse, Mary does not." [10] As people who were friends of both Mary and himself, who understood their recent domestic life probably better than anyone else, the Gisbornes could be trusted not to misunderstand the situation, whatever they may have thought of Shelley's wisdom in mentioning it to others. Not to blame Mary unduly, Shelley continued: " The necessity of concealing from her thoughts that would pain her, necessitates this, perhaps. It is the curse of Tantalus that a person possessing such excellent powers and so pure a mind as hers, should not excite the sympathy indispensable to their application to domestic life."

The oldest of Mary's imperfect sympathies with Shelley — Godwin's affairs — now raised its head for the last time. Godwin's lawsuit had finally reached its miserable conclusion, though the Shelleys as yet did not know the result. Mary was disturbed and anxious. Shelley felt obliged to protect her nerves from Godwin's importunities, as he had done in 1820 with Mary's consent. In this both Mrs. Mason and the Gisbornes concurred, though it is not certain that Mary did. At any rate she wrote to William Godwin, Jr., for a complete statement of the situation.

Mrs. Godwin had sent an alarming account to Mrs. Mason, requesting that she transmit it to Mary. Instead, Mrs. Mason thought it best to send it to Shelley, and Shelley wrote Mrs. Godwin a courteous letter explaining why her news must for the present be withheld from Mary, and promising such assistance to Godwin as seemed possible in his own circumstances.[11] He wrote to Horace Smith, asking if the loan of £400 which he had formerly offered Shelley for Godwin's benefit was still available. This sum, added to Mary's expectations from her recent novel, would just about make up the £900 Godwin was adjudged to pay. But Horace Smith had already loaned this sum elsewhere and was unable to provide another similar sum. Moreover, he was strongly of the opinion that Godwin should take advantage of the Insolvency Act.[12]

The situation was finally cleared by the arrival of young William Godwin's answer to Mary's letter. In the long-drawn-out suit of Godwin's landlord for disputed arrears of house-rent, judgment had been given against Godwin early in April. His motion for a new trial had been denied on May 1. On the same day Godwin had been served with two writs, one for the costs of the trial and one for repossession of the house. A few days later, just as the Godwins were being put out of the house, a third writ was served for the arrears of rent. They had moved to 195 Strand, and with generous assistance from their printers and stationers were able to continue in business, with nothing to threaten them except the payment of rent in arrears, which was not compulsory before October.[13]

DESPITE worries and occasional fits of depression and pain, the winter and spring of 1821–2 were the happiest time of Shelley's life in Italy. Certainly his health was better than ever before.[14] For this his outdoor life and his congenial association with the Williamses was mainly responsible. Williams was a frank, manly, healthy-spirited young man who far surpassed the rest of the Pisan circle in understanding Shelley and sympathizing with him. Jane, though intellectually somewhat shallow,[15] possessed a sunshiny, affectionate disposition unfortunately in contrast with Mary's occasional moodiness and self-absorption, pardonable as the latter was after the removal to San Terenzo. Though Jane was also petulant on occasion, when her domestic instincts were offended by the makeshifts of semi-communal housekeeping, she was more often bright and cheerful. In the still, warm evenings, either on the water or along the rocky shores, her guitar and her singing could create for the moment a brighter world of thought and feeling than that with which they were otherwise surrounded.

There was a moment, probably in May, when Shelley and Jane seem at least slightly to have overstepped the bounds of conventional propriety. What this moment was is obscurely hinted at in two of Shelley's last poems, " Lines Written in the Bay of Lerici," and " Lines: We Meet Not as We Parted." The first records a parting in the purple night from a " guardian angel " whose presence "made weak and tame All passions " and inspired thoughts the poet dared not speak. Whether the " guardian angel " was Jane Williams or Intellectual Beauty, or a combination of the two, is not clear. It does seem clear, however, that the poet dared not speak his thoughts to her. But the other poem, " We Meet Not as We Parted," appears to be a sequel, and clearly indicates that either by word or by action the poet did declare a feeling which he was forbidden to cherish.[16]

If this was to Jane, as seems probable, it was the Jane of " The Keen Stars Were Twinkling," who lived in

> . . . some world far from ours
> Where music and moonlight and feeling
> Are one.

In the actual world Shelley lived too close to Jane to idealize her completely or to fall completely in love with her in any other sense. He realized that she was intellectually somewhat commonplace, and he was occasionally uncomfortably aware of her domestic discontents. Writing of these to Claire on May 29, he commented: " It is a pity that anyone so pretty and amicable could be so selfish — [But] don't tell her this. . . ."[17] It seems to have been well understood by all the others that Shelley's devotion to Jane, even at its height, was limited. Her own exclusive love for Edward Williams was unquestioned even by Mary and was explicitly granted by Shelley in most of his poems to her.

With her combination of music, sympathy, and beauty Jane could create moments of divine forgetfulness for Shelley; but if he had been compelled to choose between her and Edward he would probably have chosen the latter. Together Shelley

GUITAR GIVEN BY SHELLEY TO JANE WILLIAMS

By permission of the Bodleian Library

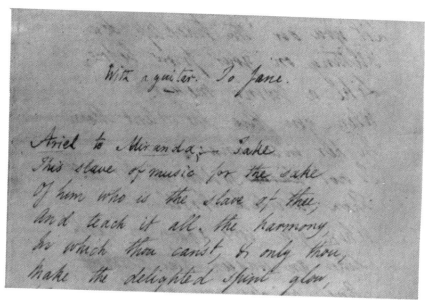

FROM SHELLEY'S MS. OF "WITH A GUITAR TO JANE"

By permission of the Bodleian Library

and Williams were having a glorious time, almost every day. At first Shelley's boat was not yet finished, and her delivery at San Terenzo was further delayed by heavy weather, so that for the first fortnight they were obliged to depend upon the little flat-bottomed skiff that had given them so much pleasure on the Arno and the Serchio. When the sea was relatively calm the small boat was adequate for inshore sailing or rowing, but more than once, when the waves were high, the sailors were drenched in launching or landing their craft. Williams did a little ineffective shooting and fishing. The matter of provisions was occasion for frequent walks along the shore to Sarzana or Lerici. All the surroundings were magnificently grand and lonely. In heavy weather the seas boomed upon the beach like heavy artillery.

On May 12, as Williams and Shelley were walking upon the terrace after dinner, they noted a strange boat entering the bay. As she came closer they identified her as the long-expected *Don Juan*. At once they set off to Lerici to take possession and make a trial sail, which had to be deferred one day because of rough weather. Of the three men who were in charge of her they retained only one, a young English sailor named Charles Vivian. The boat was a strongly built, trim-looking, undecked craft, Torbay-rigged, twenty-four feet by eight, with a four-foot draught. To overcome her tendency to ride too high in the water two tons of iron ballast had been fixed in her keel. Though somewhat cranky in a breeze, she was fast for her size, and handled well.[18]

Both Shelley and Williams were delighted with her. " The Don Juan is arrived," Shelley hastened to write to Trelawny, " and nothing can exceed the admiration she has excited. . . . Williams declares her to be perfect, and I participate in his enthusiasm, in as much as would be decent in a landsman. We have been out now several days, although we have sought in vain for an opportunity of trying her against the feluccas or other large craft in the bay; she passes the small ones as a comet might pass the dullest planet in the heavens." He begged Trelawny to express his warmest gratitude to Captain Roberts,

received very cheerfully the information that the cost had probably exceeded the original estimate of fifty pounds, and promised a prompt remittance.[19]

There was one small fly in the ointment. In the original plan
Trelawny and Williams were to have been part owners of the
boat, but Byron had then engaged Trelawny to sail the *Bolivar*
for him, and Shelley had taken over sole ownership. At Trelawny's suggestion the boat was to have been named the *Don
Juan*. When Trelawny retired, Shelley decided to call it the
Ariel from his favourite play, *The Tempest*. Whether or not
Byron knew of this contemplated change, he persuaded Captain
Roberts, who was superintending the construction, to print the
name *Don Juan* on the mainsail. As a point of fact, the name of
the boat was never changed; it was consistently referred to by
the Shelley circle as the *Don Juan*. But Byron's " contemptible vanity," as Williams called it, had defaced a beautiful white
mainsail. The blot must be removed, no matter what Byron
thought. With help and advice from Signor Maglian, the
friendly harbour-master at Lerici, Williams sought vainly to
erase the letters. A sailmaker was then found and consulted,
with similar results. In the end they were forced to remove a
section of the sail itself.[20]

After the arrival of the *Don Juan* both friends were constantly
on the water. Scarcely an entry in Williams's journal of these
days failed to record some sailing expedition within the confines
of the bay. Shelley kept books and papers on board and did
most of his writing there. Mary, who hated almost everything
else about the neighbourhood, felt more at ease in the boat than
elsewhere. At times when they could not sail, Williams was
busy making a small, light boat of reeds, to be carried on the
Don Juan and used as a tender. Finally (June 12) he completed a boat that answered all requirements and weighed only
eighty-six pounds. Next day, between the straits of Porto Ve-
nere, they encountered the *Bolivar* as Trelawny and his crew
were taking her from Genoa to Leghorn. Proudly they received
her salute of six guns and raced alongside for a while, only to
find that the larger vessel was also the speedier. " But I think
we keep as good a wind," Williams boasted.[21]

TRELAWNY and Roberts appear to have utilized this meeting for a visit to Casa Magni. Trelawny made a short visit and then sailed the *Bolivar* back to Leghorn, but Roberts remained to help Williams change the *Don Juan's* rigging.[22] On a second visit about a week later Trelawny had a good opportunity to judge the *Don Juan* and the seamanship with which she was handled. Already her navigators were considering the Mediterranean too small a sphere of operations; they talked of the broad sea-room of the Atlantic. Shelley was still a most indifferent steersman. He had a book in his hand, as usual, and when Williams yelled: "Luff," he brought her into the wind's eye. He was promptly demoted by the skipper and told to attend the mainsheet. On the next order: "Let go the mainsheet," the sheet was jammed and Shelley was almost swept overboard. This did not affect Shelley's high spirits, nor were they depressed by Williams's disgust at his seamanship. "You will do nothing with Shelley," Trelawny warned Williams, "until you heave his books and papers overboard, sheer the wisps of hair that hang over his eyes; and plunge his arms up to the elbows in a tar-bucket." Williams was actually a somewhat better sailor than Trelawny had expected to find, but was out of practice. The boy, Charles Vivian, was quick and handy. Nevertheless, Trelawny suggested that the boat needed also a Genoese sailor to help handle her in heavy weather. But Williams was as touchy about the boat's character as if she had been his wife — "as if we three seasoned salts were not enough to manage an open boat!"[23]

About a fortnight before Trelawny's arrival Shelley had written to Claire, who was feeling ill and depressed, urging her to make a visit to Casa Magni. Claire had arrived about June 6[24] — a new Claire, no longer petulant and oppressed with forebodings, but vivacious and talkative.[25]

Two or three days after Claire's arrival, during a spell of hot, sultry weather, Mary was threatened with a miscarriage. After a week of wretched health the miscarriage occurred on June 16. For seven hours she lay almost lifeless. Claire and Jane applied restoratives and stimulants while others sought frantically for ice and a doctor. The ice arrived first, but Claire and Jane were

afraid to make use of it without a doctor's directions. For a
short while it looked as if nothing could save Mary's life. Shelley, who had read medical books and who had only recently
acted as doctor in some minor emergency of Jane's, took the
responsibility of making Mary sit in ice. The doctor arrived
only in time to commend Shelley's decision and to prescribe
for Mary after the emergency was over. Thereafter her convalescence was slow, and her state of mind even more depressed
and apprehensive than before.[26]

In spite of his surface pleasure and his very obvious physical
improvement Shelley had himself felt far more disturbed than
he probably realized. A month before Mary's miscarriage,
when he was compelled to repress his feelings in dealing with
Byron about the death of Allegra, they had asserted themselves
in a waking vision. As he was walking with Williams on the
terrace in front of the house he had seen a naked child, like
Allegra, rise up from the sea and clap its hands at him as if in
joy. " There it is again — There! " he cried to Williams. He was
so shaken that for some time he could not tell what he had
seen, and it was with some difficulty that Williams persuaded
him that it was a trance and not reality.[27]

Following the emergency of Mary's miscarriage Shelley saw
several visions. He met his own figure walking on the terrace,
and the phantasm demanded of him: " How long do you mean
to be content? " Another time, in the middle of the night, he
screamed loudly and rushed into Mary's room. He continued
to scream in spite of Mary's efforts to waken him, until Mary,
still almost too ill to walk, fled to the Williamses in a panic and
collapsed at their door. Shelley was now awake and explained
that he had had two visions. In the first the Williamses had
appeared to him, mangled and battered, and had warned him
that the sea was flooding the house and pounding it to pieces.
Then he saw a vision of himself strangling Mary, and he had
rushed into her room and had been awakened by her flight.
Mary thought them dreams, but Shelley could not be persuaded
that they were not waking visions. A strong subconscious tension seemed to be gripping almost everyone except Ned Williams. Even the unimaginative Jane was not exempt; she was

THE *DON JUAN* (above) AND THE *BOLIVAR* (below)

Sketch by Edward Ellerker Williams. By permission of the British Museum

sure she had seen Shelley walk across the terrace, followed a few minutes later by his phantasm.[28]

This tension was certainly not seriously recognized, except by Mary. To the end Shelley considered the life at Casa Magni extraordinarily happy. ". . . We drive along this delightful bay in the evening wind, under the summer moon, until earth appears another world. Jane brings her guitar, and if the past and the future could be obliterated, the present would content me so well that I could say with Faust to the passing moment, 'Remain, thou, thou art so beautiful.'" Shelley's last extant letter from Casa Magni concluded: ". . . My only regret is that the summer must ever pass, or that Mary has not the same predilection for this place that I have, which would induce me never to shift my quarters." [29]

THE SUBCONSCIOUS apprehension which still dogged them was perhaps partly propitiated, for Shelley, by his unfinished " Triumph of Life." In the midst of his pleasure Shelley was writing his last long poem, a fragment which contains a powerful picture of human unhappiness and delusion. Some six months earlier he had been thinking of a tragedy founded on the story of Timon of Athens, which would have given him an equal opportunity to depict human meanness and depravity.[30] " My firm persuasion," he had written about a month later, " is that the mass of mankind, as things are arranged at present, are cruel, deceitful, and selfish, and always on the watch to surprise those few who are not. . . ." [31] It is such a humanity that Shelley describes in the 547 lines of " The Triumph of Life " that he was able to write before he laid the poem aside for a temporary interruption that was to be perpetual.

Approximately the first half of the fragment is devoted to the description of a weird and saddening triumphal procession, that of Life. Her chariot is driven madly by a Janus-faced charioteer whose eyes are bandaged. Millions of figures, young and old, dance madly and disgracefully before and after her chariot. Eventually they sink into the dust and the chariot passes over them. Along with the meaner captives of life move great emperors, philosophers, and religious leaders — even Plato is there, and several of the fathers of the Christian church "who rose like shadows between man and God" until the eclipse they created was taken for the religion which it obscured. Only a few, like Christ and Socrates, were totally exempt from the vile bondage which Life imposed.

"Struck to the heart by this sad pageantry," the poet is addressed by one of the captives who identifies himself as Rousseau. The remaining half of the fragment is devoted to Rousseau's symbolic story of how he became enslaved to Life after having once seen a brighter vision which is surely the Intellectual Beauty that Shelley had recently given a more definite form as the Witch of Atlas:

> A Shape all light, which with one hand did fling
> Dew on the earth, as if she were the dawn,
> And the invisible rain did ever sing
>
> A silver music on the mossy lawn;
> And still before me, on the dusky grass,
> Iris her many-coloured scarf had drawn:
>
> In her right hand she bore a crystal glass,
> Mantling with bright Nepenthe; the fierce splendour
> Fell from her as she moved under the mass
>
> Out of the deep cavern. . . .

The cave, the fountain (the "burning Fountain" of *Adonais,* whence all beauty arises and to which it returns), the crystal glass which she offers to a few chosen spirits, the effects of its contents and of her presence, are all clearly recognizable properties of Shelley's beautiful Witch. Rousseau drank from her crystal glass; but soon a new vision came over him as the beautiful shape grew dim before his eyes. Still as he moved along through the wilderness he was conscious that the Shape kept its "obscure tenor" beside his path. After a while the new vision supplanted the former one; the triumphal car of Life swept across his way and he was caught up in her wild mob of singing, dancing sycophants. The grove grew dense with shadows, the earth grey with phantoms; soon from every form in the procession the beauty began slowly to wane. Weary of the madness, he dropped by the wayside where the poet later discovered him. Almost his last words before the fragment ends were: "'Then what is life?' I cried. . . ."

Whether the answer, if any, was to be in Rousseau's words or Shelley's is uncertain. If Shelley's, one may suppose that the answer would conform to his previous answers that life was a dream, a shadow, a stain upon the "white radiance of Eternity," a "painted veil" mistakenly called life by those who think they live, a "loathsome mask" as long as the world is dominated by ignorance and error, a fair garden which at least to earthly eyes seemed abandoned by a celestial mistress until rank weeds flourished and the sensitive plants drooped. Entering it he called "the eclipsing Curse of birth"; leaving it he called lifting a veil from reality. He had stated his conviction in his essay "On the Devil and Devils" that "the most admirable tendencies to happiness and preservation are forever baffled by misery and decay," and in his "Essay on Christianity" that it was indisputably true that "some evil spirit has dominion in this imperfect world." To Trelawny he had characterized human life as "a perpetual torment to ourselves and to every living thing."[32] Even as he was writing "The Triumph of Life" Shelley asked Trelawny to secure for him some prussic acid, stating that he had no present intention of suicide, but that a time might come when he would find life insupportable.[33]

Certainly it is an unavoidable conclusion that when Shelley wrote "The Triumph of Life" he had a profound and almost morbid conviction of the pains and penalties of living. But it is a misconception of Shelley's character and writings to assume either that this was something new or that it negates his fundamental optimism. He held these same beliefs, and expressed them with equal poignance, in *Prometheus Unbound,* which asserts the perfectibility of the human spirit. Only a few months before "The Triumph of Life" he had written *Hellas,* which is anything but despondent. All of his associates regarded him as one whose view of human life was fundamentally optimistic.

The two extremes have their parallels in Shelley's expression at different times about, or to, his associates. His father, his mother, Elizabeth Hitchener, Hogg, Harriet, the Gisbornes, Godwin, Mrs. Mason, Byron, Emilia Viviani, even Mary, if I have correctly interpreted " Julian and Maddalo," were all subjects at various times of attraction and revulsion that were in most cases extreme. It is very probable that both phenomena owe a great deal to Shelley's conviction of persecution and to what modern psychologists would undoubtedly call a manic-depressive psychology — the violent fluctuations between depression and " almost supernatural elevation " which Shelley himself seemed to regard as characteristic.[34] One would be ill-advised to take either extreme for the whole outlook. According to his own testimony and that of most other witnesses, when Shelley wrote " The Triumph of Life " and desired to procure prussic acid he was in the best health he had felt for years and was finding his happiest enjoyment of life.

After all, " The Triumph of Life " is a fragment. Its conclusion is not to be assumed, but may only be guessed at in the light of Shelley's known character and beliefs, and in relation to its model, the *Triumphs* of Petrarch.[35] The first test does not indicate that the poem, if it was to be of similar length to *Prometheus Unbound,* would have been any less optimistic in conclusion. *Prometheus Unbound* shows a realization of human evil fully as profound as that in " The Triumph of Life." If only the first 547 lines had survived, there would be scarcely a hint of its triumphal conclusion — only the picture of Prometheus, after three thousand years of agony, recalling his curse and being subjected thereafter to worse tortures. The fragment would end with the statement that the words of the greatest benefactor in history had been converted into deadly spiritual poison. Similarly, if all but the first 547 lines of Petrarch's *Triumphs* had been lost, there would have been no hint of the triumph of true spiritual grandeur to which the poems as a whole conduce. Thus, if Shelley had followed his model to the end, or if he had followed his own previous, fundamentally consistent bent, he would have reached a conclusion anything but pessimistic, though perhaps, like Petrarch's, " pinnacled dim in the intense inane " of an Eternity rather far removed from man's earthly hopes and fears. Once before, in *Adonais*, he had expressed a Petrarchan idea of eternity and immortality, substituting only his own Intellectual Beauty for Petrarch's God. And, as we have seen, Intellectual Beauty had been early introduced into "The Triumph of Life," ready to perform her customary ministry.

But fortunately one does not have to put one's own interpretation on an unfinished, highly subjective poem to obtain Shelley's final opinion of the world and the possibility of its improvement. Only a few days before his death, while he was still composing "The Triumph of Life," he wrote in his last letter to Horace Smith:

It seems to me that things have now arrived at such a crisis as requires every man plainly to utter his sentiments on the inefficacy of the existing religions, no less than the political systems, for restraining and guiding mankind. Let us see the truth, whatever that may be. The destiny of man can scarcely be so degraded that he was born only to die — and if such should be the case, delusions, especially the gross and preposterous one of the existing religion, can scarcely be supposed to exalt it. If every man said what he thought, it could not subsist a day. But all, more or less, subdue themselves to the element that surrounds them, and contribute to the evils they lament by the hypocrisy that springs from them. . . .

England appears to be in a desperate condition, Ireland still worse; and no class of those who subsist on the public labour will be persuaded that *their* claims on it must be diminished. But the government must content itself with less in taxes, the landholder must submit to receive less rent, and the fundholder a diminished interest, or they will all get nothing. I once thought to study these affairs and write or act in them — I am glad that my good genius said *refrain* — I see little public virtue, and I foresee that the contest will be one of blood and gold, two elements which however much to my taste in my pocket and my veins, I have an objection to out of them. . . .[36]

This is far from the rosy optimism with which Shelley had invaded Ireland ten years before. His sense of mission had suffered serious setbacks. He had found by experience that life cannot be lived in entire immunity from cross-currents that thwart or divert even the most determined will. He no longer felt obliged to take an immediate hand in events. But the liberation of the human mind, through which alone true freedom could be attained, was an object still to be pursued. He held it his duty and every man's duty to speak his mind against error. Whether or not he still wore the ring he had described to Peacock two years before, he had not renounced its motto: " *Il buon tempo verrà.*"

ON JUNE 20 Shelley heard that the Hunts had arrived at Genoa. On the 24th Shelley and Williams were on the point of setting sail for Genoa when Mary suffered a relapse caused largely by Shelley's sleep-walking experience of the night before, which has been previously described. About the end of the month the Hunts sailed from Genoa to Leghorn, and as soon as the news reached Lerici Shelley and Williams prepared to join them. Shelley had grave doubts about Byron's constancy in the project for the *Liberal* and wished to be on hand promptly to see that everything was as propitious as possible at the start. In the spring he had done some translations from Goethe, Homer, and Calderon for the *Liberal,* but he was resolved to write little or nothing more for it, lest his unpopularity have a bad effect on the journal's circulation.

Mary had wished to accompany Shelley to greet the Hunts, but she was still far too weak to do so. Depressed and apprehensive as she was, she could hardly bear the thought of Shelley's departure. She gave Shelley or Williams a note to Leigh Hunt, begging him in hysterical terms not to accept Shelley's all too probable invitation to visit " this dungeon " where she thought of herself as chained.[37] She called Shelley back several times, and wept bitterly when he finally stepped on board.[38]

No such forebodings oppressed Shelley as he and Williams weighed anchor at two o'clock on July 1, made a short run over to Lerici to pick up Captain Roberts, and then laid their course for Leghorn. In seven and a half hours they had completed the run of forty-five or fifty miles. But the health office was closed when they reached Leghorn at nine o'clock and the Italian

quarantine laws were far too strict to permit landing without
an inspection. So they anchored astern of the *Bolivar* and made
shift to sleep on board.

Next morning they heard (probably from the health officers)
that Count Gamba's family was being exiled from Tuscany. As
they landed they encountered Count Gamba's group leaving
the police office, having just been given short notice to quit
Tuscany. This was bad news for Shelley and the *Liberal,* for it
meant that Byron's present household at Monte Nero was dis-
agreeably upset and that Byron might accompany the Gambas
into exile.

They met the Hunts, who welcomed them gladly. Marianne
Hunt was seriously ill and was soon to be pronounced dying by
the celebrated Vaccà, whom she outlived by many years. It did
not help her state of mind or her husband's that Byron had
welcomed her with almost insulting coldness and hauteur.[39]
Young Thornton Hunt, now a keen, quick lad of twelve, noticed
that Shelley had changed greatly since the old days at Marlow;
he was far stronger and healthier-looking; he had added some
three or four inches to his chest measure; his voice was stronger;
and his manner much more confident and downright.[40]

On the morning of July 3 Shelley accompanied the Hunts to
Pisa, and Byron returned to his Pisan residence. Getting the
Hunts settled in their new quarters was less difficult than tying
Byron down to a definite mode of operation for the *Liberal.*
At first Byron said he did not wish to publish anything in it
over his own name. He considered that the expulsion of the
Gambas was also an attack upon himself, and talked of moving
to America, to Genoa, Geneva, and finally Lucca. With Byron
everything was confusion; with the Hunts everything was despair. Shelley's own state of mind was depressed by at least one
semi-hysterical letter from Mary, urging his early return and
saying that she was haunted by a feeling of impending disaster.[41] Gradually, under Shelley's tactful persistence, Byron
came round to a definite agreement which was satisfactory.
He offered for the first number the copyright of his *Vision of
Judgment.* This was more than enough to start the journal, and

when Shelley called on Mrs. Mason on July 7 before returning
to Leghorn, he was in the best spirits she had ever seen him
exhibit.[42]

WILLIAMS had been waiting at Leghorn, impatient to return
home, but unwilling to accept Shelley's permission to return
ahead of him. Mary had begged Shelley to see if he could not
rent another house near Pugnano, but Shelley had no time to
make inquiries, and he hoped Mary would consent to remain
at San Terenzo at least through the summer. On the morning
of July 8 Shelley and Williams were busy buying supplies for
the little colony at San Terenzo — food, milk for the children,
and a hamper of wine to be presented to Signor Maglian, the
friendly harbour-master at Lerici. Trelawny accompanied Shelley first to a bank [43] and then to a store, and at about one
o'clock [44] they boarded their respective boats, Trelawny with
the intention of accompanying the *Don Juan* into the offing
with the *Bolivar*.

The weather had been hot and unsettled. Captain Roberts,
who did not quite like the look of it, suggested that they wait
till next day. But Williams was impatient to be off, the wind was
fair for Lerici, and Shelley was in high spirits to meet Williams's
desire for a quick run before the wind. At the last minute Trelawny was prevented by the authorities from taking out the
Bolivar, because he had not yet got his port clearance papers.
Two Livornese feluccas left port at about the same time and in
about the same direction. Roberts walked out to the end of the
mole, to watch the *Don Juan* out of sight; the *Bolivar* furled
her sails as Trelawny watched the *Don Juan* through his glass.
His Genoese mate remarked that a squall was coming up and
that the *Don Juan* was too close inshore and carried too much
sail. About three o'clock Roberts saw the squall entering the
bay and obtained permission to go up in the watch-tower and
follow his friends with the glass. The *Don Juan* was then about
ten miles out at sea, off Viareggio, and the crew were taking
in sail. Then he lost sight of her in a swirl of fog and cloud
and was unable to pick her up again. Trelawny, in the *Bolivar*,

THE PORT OF LEGHORN

Engraved by J. C. Bentley from a painting by Sir A. W. Callcott

had lost sight of her a little earlier and had retired to his cabin and gone to sleep.

When Trelawny awoke at about half past six the sky had darkened, the sea was smooth and lead-coloured, flat and quiet under the fitful gusts and raindrops that preceded a heavy squall. With a crash the storm broke, and for about twenty minutes the thunder roared and rain fell in sheets. Looking out to sea it was impossible to see any vessel through the smother. When the skies cleared there were still no ships to be seen in the offing. All the other boats that had put out ahead of the squall had returned to port in time; only the *Don Juan* was missing. No one of the feluccas that had returned to port would admit having seen the *Don Juan,* though Trelawny's mate saw on one of them an English-made oar which he thought might have belonged to the *Don Juan.*

The *Don Juan* was never seen again from shore after Captain Roberts lost sight of her in the fog and smother at about three o'clock. If Trelawny is correct in stating that all the Livornese boats were safely in harbour when the main storm broke out about half past six, the wreck of the *Don Juan* must have occurred shortly after Roberts lost sight of her, before the storm had really broken. Two Livornese boats, however, appear to have seen Shelley's craft shortly after Captain Roberts retired from his watch-tower. The captain of the first of these, doubting the ability of the *Don Juan* to weather the squall, offered to take the crew aboard, but was refused. Then, as a large wave broke over the little boat, he shouted: ". . . For God's sake reef your sails or you are lost." One of the gentlemen (supposed to be Williams) started to lower the sails, but the other (supposedly Shelley) seized his arm and restrained him.[45] The crew of the second vessel to see the *Don Juan* kept their own counsel, but when the boat was finally salvaged it was only too clear that she had sunk as the result of a collision. Her starboard timbers were broken, her gunwale was stove in, and both masts and bowsprit had broken off at the base.[46] One large wave the next moment would have been sufficient to fill and sink her instantly.

It would appear, therefore, that Shelley's end came very quickly. He would not have had time, as when he faced drowning in the Channel in 1816, " to reflect and even to reason upon death," or to reach the conclusion then reached that " it was rather a thing of discomfort than horror to me." Byron had seen him resolve to drown rather than risk another's life on Lake Geneva. Trelawny, within the last few months, had been deeply impressed with his indifference to both the idea and the physical discomfort of dying and had heard him speak of going down with the *Don Juan* like a piece of ballast in case she were wrecked.[47] In poems, letters, and conversation he had shown for several years that he regarded death primarily as a release and an opportunity and that his desire to live was based mainly upon his personal obligations. " If I die tomorrow," he had remarked to Marianne Hunt on the previous day, " I have lived to be older than my father; I am ninety years of age." [48] It seems certain that he died calmly, probably with little or no effort to save himself.

That night in Pisa Mrs. Mason dreamed that Shelley, whom she had seen looking so cheerful the day before, appeared before her, wearing a look of utter melancholy and speaking vague words of disaster. This dream soon merged into another, in which she thought that Percy Florence was dead. She awoke crying so bitterly that she wondered if the actual death of the child would have affected her so deeply.[49]

Trelawny was now definitely alarmed. Another day of waiting produced no news. Thinking that Byron might have received some message from Shelley, Trelawny mounted his horse and rode to Pisa. Byron had heard nothing; he was visibly shaken by Trelawny's report. Trelawny then sent word to the *Bolivar* to cruise along the coast toward Viareggio and set out in the same direction himself, after dispatching a courier along the coast toward Nice. At Viareggio a punt, a water-keg, and some bottles had been washed up on the beach. With a sinking heart Trelawny recognized them as belonging to the *Don Juan*. Yet there was still some room for hope. These articles might have been washed overboard or thrown out to lighten the boat, and the boat might have been driven across to Corsica. Or the boat's crew might have been rescued by some vessel outward bound.[50] The search of the coastline was intensified; rewards were offered. Trelawny was indefatigable. But though the *Don Juan* had left Leghorn on July 8, it was July 18 before any further news was obtained.

MEANWHILE Trelawny had been doing all he could to keep up the spirits of Mary, Jane, and Claire. On Monday, the 8th, they had received Ned Williams's letter written the preceding Saturday, saying that he at least would be back in San Terenzo by Tuesday at the latest, and probably Shelley with him. When no one appeared on Monday or Tuesday they supposed the *Don Juan* storm-bound in Leghorn. But Wednesday and Thursday provided fine sailing weather, and the waiters grew uneasy. Only a heavy sea on Friday prevented Jane's journeying to Leghorn to investigate. That day a letter arrived from Hunt to Shelley. Mary opened it, but was so agitated that it dropped from her hands. Jane picked it up and read: " Pray write to tell us how you got home, for they say that you had bad weather after you sailed on Monday, and we are anxious." [51]

" Then it is all over," exclaimed Jane. But Mary, who had been dreading some vague calamity since Shelley's departure, refused to accept its apparent confirmation as final. She was far from well enough to travel, yet she insisted that they start at once for Leghorn to investigate. Passing through Lerici they were somewhat encouraged to learn that no wreck had been reported. Pisa lay on the route, and Mary, supposing Byron to be still at Leghorn, determined to go by the Lanfranchi Palace to see if Hunt had any news. After four years of separation to greet an old friend with the desperate question: " Do you know anything of Shelley? " — the very thought almost sent her into convulsions.

Hunt had gone to bed, but Byron and La Guiccioli saw her. They had no fresh news. Mary and Jane had been travelling since early morning and it was now midnight, but they refused all rest and set out for Leghorn, where they arrived between two and three o'clock in the morning. At six o'clock they found Captain Roberts at his inn and learned all that he had to tell them. At nine o'clock they started back to San Terenzo, and at Viareggio they saw and recognized the same wreckage that Trelawny had seen earlier. Either here or at Leghorn Trelawny joined them and accompanied them back to San Terenzo. As they were rowed across the little bay separating Lerici from San Terenzo they noticed that the hamlet was illuminated for some local fiesta. Five days of agonizing suspense followed. There was no further news — only the whistle of the sirocco, the sound of waves beneath the terrace, and the maddening, half-savage jubilation of the villagers, making the most of their fiesta.

Trelawny returned to Leghorn on the 19th to see if anything more could be done. On the same day a letter arrived from Roberts which he had expected and had left permission to open. Claire opened it without telling the others — and learned that two bodies had been cast up on the shore. Since a later official letter from Viareggio had stated that nothing had been found, she resolved to cling to this slight hope and withhold the news from the others. Yet she knew in her heart that Shelley and Williams were dead, and she wrote to Leigh Hunt begging him to come and break the news. "I assure you I cannot break it to them, nor is my spirit, weakened as it is from constant suffering, capable of giving them consolation, or protecting them from the first burst of their despair. . . . I know not what further to add, except that their case is desperate in every respect, and death would be the greatest kindness to us all." [52]

Meanwhile Trelawny had heard that two bodies had been washed up, one near Viareggio, the other three miles down the shore near the Bocca Lericcio.[53] He hurried to the scene. The first body, though the exposed parts were fleshless, was undoubtedly Shelley's; the tall, slight figure, the jacket, the volume of Sophocles in one pocket and of Keats in the other, identified him. The second body was much more mutilated, lacking not only most of the flesh, but most of the clothes as well. But one of Williams's boots that Trelawny had brought with him from San Terenzo matched the one boot left on the body, and the black silk handkerchief around the neck was Williams's. His watch and pocket-money were missing.[54]

All doubt now at an end, Trelawny returned to Casa Magni,

only a few hours after Claire had dispatched her letter to Leigh
Hunt. He now had to put an end to the hopes he had previously
tried to keep alive. His face must have borne his news, for the
maid shrieked when he entered the ground floor. Climbing
the stairs, he entered unannounced the room where the ladies
were sitting. No one spoke. Then Mary, unwilling to accept the
full implications of his silence, exclaimed: " Is there no hope? "
Without answering, Trelawny left the room and sent in the
servant with the children. Later he returned and won Mary's
undying gratitude by attempting no useless consolation, but
launching instead upon an eloquent eulogy.[55]

There was no reason for remaining any longer in a place
Mary had hated even before it became a home of tragedy. On
the next day, July 20, Trelawny took the whole household back
to Pisa.

The rather difficult funeral arrangements were undertaken
by Trelawny. Under the strict Italian quarantine laws both
bodies had been buried on the shore, with quicklime. Moving
them was out of the question. They could be burned, but there
was still a question as to whether the ashes could be carried
across state boundaries. Several states were involved: Lucca,
where Shelley's body had been cast up, Tuscany, where Williams's had been found, and Rome, where Shelley was to be
buried by the side of William Shelley. Mr. W. Dawkins, the
English minister at Florence, was very helpful in solving official
difficulties. Permission was eventually obtained to burn the
bodies where they lay and to transport the ashes.

On August 13 Trelawny placed on the *Bolivar* a sheet-iron
furnace, fuel, and spices,[56] and proceeded to the spot where
Williams's body was buried. There he was met by a military
guard, to assist him and also to see that the cremation did not
violate the quarantine laws. Everything was made ready, and
Byron and Hunt were notified to be present next morning. They
drove out from Pisa and were joined by a Tuscan military guard.
Wood was collected and piled up, the body was exhumed and
placed in its iron box, the torch was applied, and for some time
the fire burned furiously. As soon as they could approach the
furnace, Williams's friends threw frankincense, salt, wine, and

oil upon the body. By four o'clock in the afternoon (Byron and Trelawny having meanwhile taken a swim) the body had been reduced to ashes. The furnace was cooled in the sea, and Williams's ashes were placed in an oak box and given to Byron, who was to take them to Pisa, whence they were to accompany Jane Williams to England.

Next day the same ceremony was repeated with Shelley's body. As the diggers sought for the body Trelawny stood aside and thought what a desecration he was committing by this last necessary act of service to his friend. Why not leave him here with the sea in front and the wooded mountains behind him, in the midst of the solitude and natural grandeur that had given him such pleasure? Byron stood silent and thoughtful; Leigh Hunt had remained in the carriage, alone with his reflections. Trelawny had already spoken of Shelley's death as the loss of " all which made existence to me endurable." Quite possibly Byron was thinking, as he had written to Moore six days before: " There is thus another man gone, about whom the world was ill-naturedly, and ignorantly, and brutally mistaken " — a man " without exception," as he had previously written to Murray, " the *best* and least selfish man I ever knew." Hunt surely felt, as he did later, that for him the " land of sunshine " was now " smitten with darkness." [57]

A dull thud announced the location of the body. The ceremony of the previous day was repeated. Heat-waves from the fire and the sun made the air visible and tremulous; the quick-lime, the oil, and the salt made vari-coloured flames above the corpse. The iron box was now white-hot and the contents were slowly turning to grey ashes. A few bits of bone remained unconsumed, and, strangely, the heart also. Of the English party only Trelawny had fortitude enough to face this final scene. It would appear that the military officer also turned away, for Trelawny found an opportunity to rescue Shelley's heart, unobserved, though he burned his hand in doing so. The ashes were placed in a box and carried on board the *Bolivar*, and the spectators and participants went their various ways.

Leigh Hunt begged Shelley's heart from Trelawny, and received it. In some unknown manner he also procured a small fragment of Shelley's jawbone.[58] The ashes were sent to Mr. Freeborn, the English consul at Rome, who was requested to hold them until Trelawny could arrive and make arrangements for their burial in the Protestant Cemetery. It was Mary's desire that Shelley should be buried by the side of William Shelley. Trelawny was unable to go to Rome until the following March, and meanwhile Mr. Freeborn grew uneasy over his custody of the ashes. Joseph Severn, who had remained in Rome after the death of Keats, did what he could to represent Mary Shelley's interests. The old Protestant Cemetery having been closed to further burials, it was resolved to bury Shelley in the new cemetery and to transfer the body of William to the same grave. But William's body could not be found; the stone supposed to cover it was found to cover that of an adult. So Shelley was buried alone on January 21, 1823. A kindly English priest, the Reverend Richard Burgess, D.D., defied criticism to read the burial service over an enemy of the church, miscalled an atheist. Eight people were present: General Sir George Cockburn, Sir Charles Sykes, and Messrs. Kirkup, Westmacott, Scoles, and Severn, besides the two priests, the Reverend W. Cook and the Reverend Richard Burgess.[59]

Trelawny reached Rome in March and was dissatisfied with the location of the grave. In the shadow of the pyramid of Caius Cestius, in a niche formed by two buttresses of the old Roman Wall, he purchased enough space for two tombs. He secured masons, built the tombs, removed Shelley's ashes, and planted a row of young poplars near the graves. The extra tomb, though Trelawny does not say so in his books, was intended for himself. His official permission to place a blank stone over it is dated March 26, 1823. The simple inscription on Shelley's grave was suggested by Leigh Hunt and augmented, with Mary Shelley's subsequent approval, by three lines from *The Tempest* that Shelley had once been pleased to hear Trelawny quote. For more than a century Shelley's grave has remained undisturbed, except for an altercation over the land-title in 1891 between Lady Shelley and Trelawny's daughter. This was occasioned by Lady Shelley's desire to substitute for Shelley's simple slab an ornate monument by Onslow

Ford. The difficulty was tactfully composed by Sir Rennell Rodd, of the English embassy at Rome, and the monument was conferred upon University College, Oxford, where it still bears its part in preserving the misconception of Shelley as a beautiful, ineffectual angel.[60]

WITHIN little more than a year after Shelley's death all those most closely connected with him had scattered to different countries. Jane Williams, with her children, left Italy for England on September 17, 1822. In London she became friendly with the Gisbornes, and through them with T. J. Hogg, with whose fate she united her own in 1827, after a courtship not devoid of humour to the onlookers. Since they were never legally married, one might infer that the legal husband she had abandoned for Williams was still alive. Hogg was a good, if rather strict, father for Ned Williams's children,[61] and had one child by Jane who was named after Hogg's sister, Prudentia. Jane's close friendship with Mary was ruptured in 1827 by remarks on Shelley and Mary which deeply wounded Mary; though the friendship was resumed, it was never the same afterwards. Jane survived Hogg by twenty-two years, and died in 1884, at the age of eighty-six.[62]

Claire Clairmont left Italy only three days after Jane Williams. On September 20, with a light purse and a heavy heart, she quitted Florence to join her brother Charles in Vienna. Her last thoughts in Florence were bitter ones: "How hopelessly I had lingered on Italian soil for five years, waiting ever for a favourable change, instead of which I am now leaving it, having buried there everything that I loved." [63] For many years of a long life in Austria, Germany, Russia, and Italy she worked hard tutoring children whom for the most part she disliked. Her circumstances were made somewhat easier by inheriting her legacy from Shelley when his will finally became operative in 1844 upon the death of Sir Timothy Shelley. She never lost her love for Shelley, her friendship for Trelawny, her hatred of Byron, or her connection — occasionally antagonistic, but predominantly affectionate — with Shelley's family. In her old

SHELLEY'S GRAVE

Etching by A. Evershed, 1876, from a drawing by W. B. Scott. Reprinted from H. B.
Forman's edition of Shelley's Works, by permission of Mr. M. B. Forman

age she retired to Florence and became a Catholic. She died in Florence in 1879 at the age of eighty-one.[64]

Mary Shelley remained in Italy until July 25, 1823, living with the Hunts, first in Pisa and then, for nearly a year, in Genoa. She was without hope, without money, and almost without friends. Byron placed his London attorney at her disposal in settling the difficult matter of her relations with the Shelley family and was at first friendly with advice and offers of financial assistance. But he did not get on too well with Hunt, through whom much of Mary's business with him was carried on, and both Mary and Hunt considered that his attitude became more and more niggardly and ungenerous. In Pisa in 1821 Byron had lost a bet of a thousand pounds to Shelley which he said nothing of paying and which Mary and Hunt considered a just debt, though Byron may never have taken it seriously, or may have considered it discharged by his renunciation of a larger sum left him in Shelley's will.[65]

Living with the Hunts in the crowded household in Genoa was at first quite unsatisfactory. Hunt did what little he could for Mary out of his great friendship for Shelley rather than on her own account. She felt that he did not like her, and that both she and he were to blame. Whatever he had heard about the intimate relations of the Shelley household, he now thought that Mary had been unworthy of her husband. He had the almost unpardonable arrogance, on this ground, to refuse at first to surrender Shelley's heart to her. Soon, however, on the intervention of Jane Williams, he gave it up, and Mary ever afterwards had it near her.[66] A better feeling then succeeded between them.

Sir Timothy Shelley received the news of his son's death with a Christian fortitude not too difficult to achieve. Except for necessary business relations his elder son had long since been dead to him. He would do nothing for the widow, whom he held partly responsible for his son's evil course, and he would do little for Percy Florence, whose older half-brother, Charles Shelley, stood between him and the inheritance of the baronetcy and estate. Peacock, who was Shelley's other executor with Byron, did all he could to secure from Sir Timothy favourable treatment for Mary and her child. Mary cared little what arrangements might be made affecting only herself, but she would consent to nothing that would in any degree sacrifice her child's interests or her interests in the child. Percy Florence became thenceforth her dominant interest in life.

Hating England and loving Italy, Mary returned to England in 1823 in order to look after her son's interest. Sir Timothy Shelley finally made her an allowance, on condition that she publish no life of Shelley. He almost revoked it when she published his *Posthumous Poems* in 1824. For years Mary's life was devoted to her son, and she subsisted partly on her annuity and partly on her writings. The measure of Shelley's influence on her mind may be guessed from the inferiority of these writings to those produced during his lifetime.

Long years of semi-poverty and financial dependence combined with a latent yearning for respectability to carry Mary in her later years far from the radicalism she had once held so enthusiastically in common with Shelley. She regarded with horror the French revolution of 1848 and was thoroughly out of sympathy with the Chartists — some of whose leaders were doing their best to propagate the sale of *Queen Mab*. In personal relations, however, she continued firmly loyal to past associations — to her father, to the Hunts, to the increasingly contemptuous Trelawny, and to Claire, even though she sometimes spoke of her with a tinge of bitterness. As soon as Percy Florence came into his inheritance she saw to it that Hunt received an annuity for the rest of his life.

Many years after Shelley's death the half-melancholy reunion of Rosalind and Helen was duplicated in the lives of Mary Shelley and Isabel Booth. Mr. Booth had died after suffering financial reverses and Mary was a widow who had gone through years of hardship to attain a sober, thoughtful security in the end. In 1851, during Mary's last illness, Mrs. Booth wished to come to her bedside, but was persuaded by Sir Percy to defer the long journey until Mary's expected recovery. Mary's last deed of which there is any record was to express a wish, subsequently executed by Sir Percy, that Mrs. Booth should receive fifty pounds a year and a suit of mourning.[67]

Percy Florence Shelley became the direct heir to the family title and estates upon the death of Charles Bysshe Shelley in 1826, and inherited them upon the death of Sir Timothy in 1844. Largely under his mother's manipulation he married Jane St.John, who was an enthusiastic admirer of both Shelley and Mary. He was a passionate lover of amateur theatricals and also of yachting, the only taste in which he conspicuously resembled his father. He stood for Parliament as a conservative, but he loyally aided Lady Shelley in her collection of the voluminous materials which have added so greatly to Shelleyan biography. He not only defended Shelley against Hogg's irreverent biography; he also protected William Godwin as much as he could against the contempt which Professor Dowden could not wholly suppress in his biography of Shelley. Sir Percy and Lady Shelley had no children of their own, but an adopted daughter married Lord Abinger. Sir Percy died on December 5, 1889. The Shelley title and estates passed to the descendants of Shelley's younger brother John, and are now held by Sir John C. E. Shelley-Rolls. The Shelley papers collected by Lady Shelley were divided. A part of them are now held by Lord Abinger, a second part by Sir John C. E. Shelley-Rolls, and a third part by the Bodleian Library at Oxford.

Byron and Trelawny left Italy to take part in the Greek war of independence on July 17, 1823, a week before Mary Shelley started back to England. One of Trelawney's last actions in Italy was to provide Mary Shelley with enough money for her return to England. The *Liberal*, after four excellent issues, was a confessed failure. Byron's indifference and the mighty artillery of concerted conservative criticism had been too much for it. Leigh Hunt remained in Italy two gloomy years and returned to England rather bitter against Byron's memory.

In less than a year after he landed in Greece, Byron lay dead at Missolonghi; but Trelawny remained, the hero of exploits both martial and marital that equalled those of his youth. He lived longer than any of Shelley's friends — long enough to propose marriage to Mary Shelley and to write bitter words about her after his rejection, and long enough for a new series of rather discreditable adventures with wives and mistresses.

Tough, positive, and vigorous, he continued to worship Shelley's memory and to scorn most of Shelley's friends except Hogg and Claire Clairmont. He talked with, and outlived, some of Shelley's Victorian admirers. As an old man in his eighties he never missed his daily sea-bath, summer or winter. But in December 1880 the director of the Protestant Burial Ground at Rome received a letter from him: Trelawny explained about the grave he had prepared nearly sixty years before, enclosed an inscription for the blank stone, and stated that his ashes would be delivered in the near future to occupy their appointed place.[68] He died the next year at the age of eighty-nine, and his ashes were duly delivered and interred.

The friendship between Hogg, Peacock, and Leigh Hunt, which Shelley had initiated, had flourished during Shelley's lifetime in frequent meetings and long walks, probably productive of the amusing article " Dinner by the Amateurs of Vegetable Diet," which appeared in the *London Magazine and Theatrical Inquisitor* for July 1821. After Shelley's death this friendship continued for years and in the case of Hogg and Peacock included most of the members of both families.

It was Shelley who disrupted the friendship he had formed. Hogg's publication of his life of Shelley in 1858 excited Hunt's anger and evoked several quiet corrections from Peacock in his *Memoir of Shelley,* the first part of which appeared in *Fraser's Magazine* in 1858. Leigh Hunt was so angry that he referred to Hogg privately as an imbecile pretender and hinted in a note published in the *Spectator* that Hogg might not be quite in his right mind. Publication of Hogg's biography was stopped by Sir Percy and Lady Shelley and the manuscripts they had furnished were withdrawn; but Hogg persisted and is known to have finished a third volume. It is conceivable that this volume may still be found, though every effort so far has been unavailing. Hogg resented Peacock's implied criticisms, but their friendship was not completely broken off. Hogg died in 1862, four years before Peacock's death and three years after the death of Leigh Hunt.

Chapter XXX

SHELLEY'S

POSTHUMOUS REPUTATION

COMMENTS ON HIS DEATH;
GROWTH OF HIS EARLY REPUTATION; SPECIAL
INFLUENCES; HIS LATER REPUTATION

SHELLEY valued life so lightly as mere physical activity and so highly as the expression of undying spiritual values that it would be false to end this biography with his physical extinction. To Shelley those "kings of thought" who "waged contention with their time's decay" were the only really durable legacies of the past to the future. He had claimed for Keats, as he would have liked to hope for himself, a vitality of spirit that would long survive him in the world to which he was physically dead. It was a tremulous hope at best, and its slow abolition under his conviction of martyrdom was probably the worst hell that life imposed upon him. Yet even then the world was listening more than he perceived, and it eventually came to listen as enthusiastically as he had listened to his skylark. How this came about is surely a part of his biography, deserving fuller treatment than a final chapter can afford.

There were few signs of future admiration in the tone with which the British press received the news of Shelley's death. The most generous notice was the first, which appeared in the *Examiner* for August 4, 1822:

Those who know a great mind when they meet with it, and who have been delighted with the noble things in the works of Mr. Shelley, will be shocked to hear that he has been cut off in the prime of his life and genius. He perished at sea, in a storm, with his friend Captain Williams, of the Fusileers, on the evening of the 8th ult., somewhere off Via Reggia, on the coast of Italy, between Leghorn and the Gulf of Spezia. He had been to Pisa, to do a kind action, and he was returning to his country abode at Lerici to do another. — Such was the whole course of his life. Let those who have known such hearts, and have lost them, judge of the grief of his friends. Both he and Capt. Williams have left wives and children. Capt. Williams was also in the prime of life, and a most amiable man, beloved like his friend. The greatest thing we can say in honour of his memory (and we are sure he would think so), is, that he was worthy to live with his friend, and to die with him. — Vale, dilectissime hominum! Vale, dilectissime; et nos ama, ut dixisti, in sepulchro.

This tribute was from the pen of Leigh Hunt. On July 25 Hunt had conveyed the sad news to Horace Smith in Paris, just as Smith or one of his friends was beginning a review of *Hellas* for the Paris *Monthly Review*. The review was immediately turned into a generous obituary notice, in which Shelley's genius and personal character were highly praised. Leigh Hunt's letter, with which this notice concluded, was first quoted (in part) in England in the *Morning Chronicle* of August 12, 1822, without comment. Leigh Hunt had written: " But Shelley, my divine-minded friend — your friend — the friend of the Universe — he has perished at sea! " and after a few particulars of the tragedy had added: " God bless him! I cannot help thinking of him as if he were alive as much as ever, so unearthly he always appeared to me, and so seraphical a King [thing?] of the elements." [1]

On the same day the savagely Tory *John Bull* published a short scornful paragraph on Shelley's death. This drew from the *British Luminary and Weekly Intelligence* (August 18) a well-merited accusation of cant which Richard Carlile's *The Republican* reprinted without comment five days later. But the *John Bull* had still more to say. On August 19 it reprinted the *Morning Chronicle's* quotation from Leigh Hunt's letter as an example of " the ridiculous . . . and infinitely more of the disgusting." Disavowing any desire to speak ill of the dead, the article condemned Hunt's eulogium as blasphemous and proceeded at length to convict Shelley of blasphemy and treason.

The *Courier*, a leading Tory newspaper, wrote: " Shelley, the writer of some infidel poetry, has been drowned, *now* he knows whether there is a God or no." In the same article the *Courier* excoriated the radicals for attacking the memory of Lord Castlereagh, who had committed suicide on August 12. Both the *Examiner* (November 3) and the *Liberal* (No. 1, Preface) denounced this article as a specimen of hypocritical cant.

Two liberal periodicals, the *New Monthly Magazine* (October 1, 1822) and the *Drama, or Theatrical Pocket Magazine* (December 1822) made Shelley's death the occasion for a sympathetic appraisal of his works and character and a rebuke to his detractors. Two other liberal journals, the *Monthly Magazine* and the *Monthly Repository of Theology and General Literature* (both for September) contained brief notices of Shelley's death with the statement that he was " a man of highly cultivated genius." The three sentences of comment with which Richard Carlile's radical *Republican* (August 16) accompanied its first notice of Shelley's death were even more appreciative. On the other hand, the *Country Literary Chronicle and Weekly Review* (August 10) and the *Gentleman's Magazine* (September) could not publish short notices of Shelley's death without a damning implication. To the former he was " a man of extraordinary but perverted talents, and the author of the Cenci, Queen Mab, and some less censurable productions "; to the latter he was " unfortunately too well known for his infamous novels and poems," and as a man who " openly professed himself an atheist."

SHELLEY's death had been greeted with the same factionalism — hatred from the Tories, championship from the radicals, and a fairly generous desire for fair play from the liberals — which had obscured his recognition during life. After the obituaries he might have dropped at once out of public notice but for the verse-writers and the *Liberal*.

The *Liberal*, with which Shelley's name was associated, was not yet dead, nor was the Tory determination to smother it in obloquy. During 1823 a considerable number of reviews of the *Liberal* appeared. An "Illiberal" was written, but apparently not published. The *London Liberal* appeared as an antidote to the Italian one, and received several reviews. These various notices were principally unfriendly to the *Liberal,* but friendly or unfriendly, they generally included an incidental remark or two about Shelley.

To poets and poetasters Shelley's death provided a subject which seemed irresistible. Seven poems occasioned by Shelley's death appeared in 1822, five of them in the public journals and two in separate volumes of their own. Three of the authors, J. W. Dalby, Arthur Brooke [John Chalk Claris], and Bernard Barton, had previously published poems to Shelley. Like most of their brother commentators in prose, the poets agreed only in the mediocrity of their effusions. Bernard Barton's *Verses on the Death of Percy Bysshe Shelley,* published as a separate volume, is written in a spirit of genuine Christian charity for Shelley's "Errors and faults, alike gone by." Somewhat smug, but not entirely unsympathetic, a poem signed J. N. in the *Hermes* for December 14 draws the conclusion that "loathsome vice" and "reckless guilt"

> To memory leave a name, unlov'd, forlorn,
> For some to pity, — others hold in scorn!

The "Elegy on the Death of Shelley," published by F. in the *Bard* (November 16) moralizes somewhat pityingly on Shelley's pride and impiety.

The other poets were all Shelley's partisans. In the *Examiner* for August 25 a blank-verse poem signed B. prophesied:

> — while Genius is admired
> And Feeling loved — while Freedom still retains
> Amid the waters of Corruption's flood,
> An Ararat whereon to rest her foot, —
> Thy spirit still will be revered on earth,
> And commune with the minds of unborn men.

A similar conviction of Shelley's greatness appears in Arthur Brooke's seventeen-stanza *Elegy on the Death of Percy Bysshe*

Shelley, dated August 10 in the Advertisement and published
as a separate book:

> Thou poet's poet! whose sublimer strain
> To the extremest verge of human thought
> Soared, and the vulgar ken was stretched in vain
> To follow, till with baffled powers o'erwrought
> They turned their hooded eyes to earth again,
> And slandered what themselves had vainly sought;
> Effulgent spirit! splendour without peer!
> Brief comet of our intellectual hemisphere!

John Watson Dalby, who was later to write other poetic tributes
to Shelley, published in the *Troubadour* two elegies, signed respectively P and xxD, in both of which it is asserted that Shelley's influence for good will extend to future times.[2]

The last contemporary poem on Shelley's death was one dated
August 4 of the next year (Shelley's birthday) and published
unsigned in the *Literary Examiner* for September 20, 1823:

SONNET TO PERCY SHELLEY

> Hast thou from earth, then, really passed away,
> And mingled with the shadowy mass of things
> Which were, but are not? Will thy harp's dear strings
> No more yield music to the rapid play
> Of thy swift thoughts, now thou art turned to clay?
> Hark! Is that rushing of thy spirit's wings,
> When (like the skylark, who in mounting sings)
> Soaring through high imagination's way,
> Thou poureds't thy melody upon the earth,
> Silent for ever? Yes, wild ocean's wave
> Hath o'er thee rolled. But whilst within the grave
> Thou sleeps't let me in the love of thy pure worth
> One thing foretell — that thy great fame shall be
> Progressive as Time's flood, eternal as the sea!

With this poem the immediate reaction to Shelley's death may
be said to have died away. Thenceforth his reputation becomes
a part of the ocean of human thought to which he contributed.
For a while, like the waters of a distinctive stream, its colour and

current may be distinguished, as it seeks to amalgamate with the tides of opinion and change that make up the complex character of what is called Victorian England. Eventually it is " borne darkly, fearfully afar " until it merges indistinguishably with the elements of which it is a part.

FOR half a generation after Shelley's death it is possible to trace the history of his impression upon public opinion until he was clearly recognized as one of England's half-dozen greatest poets. For certain limited elements in the British public this conviction seems to have been reached ten years after Shelley's death, but it can hardly be regarded as general or reasonably secure before 1839–40. At that time his works in prose and poetry were first published by his widow in six volumes which received widespread and practically unanimous recognition.

During the eighteen years in which Shelley's reputation was being established there were more than eight hundred periodicals in England and America which might have mentioned Shelley more or less casually. Of these, at least a hundred and seventy-five did so. Their notices, ranging from trivial to weighty, and representing widely various quality, motives, and viewpoints, reach a total of at least five hundred and forty-five items. In addition there were several classes of books in which Shelley was presented to the public in various ways. Several elements in this mass of materials require separate comment, but it is first necessary to obtain an impression of the bulk and incidence of its principal ingredients. This I have attempted to present in the following table: [3]

TABLE I

	1823	1824	1825	1826	1827	1828	1829	1830	1831	1832	1833	1834	1835	1836	1837	1838	1839	1840	Total
1	3	1	0	3	1	0	5	3	3	3	1	2	0	2	0	0	5	2	34
2	5	8	5	4	3	8	8	6	8	26	12	1	5	3	1	4	31	4	142
3a	0	9	3	8	1	5	3	3	7	14	5	2	3	4	1	4	28	9	109
3b	0	1	0	0	0	0	0	0	0	1	1	0	0	1	0	0	0	0	4
3c	0	0	0	4	6	0	0	0	0	1	1	1	0	0	0	0	4	1	18
4a	6	9	3	3	2	7	4	8	5	10	3	6	3	3	4	0	1	1	78
4b	6	7	2	2	0	2	2	1	0	0	2	4	0	0	0	0	2	2	32
4c	1	8	2	5	1	2	4	11	6	4	3	9	2	3	4	5	12	6	88
5a	1	1	1	0	0	1	3	0	3	3	8	2	0	0	1	3	3	1	31
5b	0	1	1	0	0	0	0	0	0	1	0	0	0	0	0	0	0	0	3
5c	0	0	0	0	0	0	1	3	1	0	1	0	0	0	0	0	0	0	6
Total	22	45	17	29	14	25	30	35	33	63	37	27	13	16	11	16	86	26	545

394

KEY TO TABLE I

1. Books, authorized and unauthorized, by or about Shelley. Each publication of each work is counted separately.
2. Quotations of individual poems or prose passages, in periodicals, annuals, or anthologies. The count is by the number of publications rather than the number of selections, and does not include poems quoted as a part of reviews or other articles about Shelley.
3, a,b,c. Periodical articles and book-reviews devoted to Shelley. Articles in series are listed once for each separate publication. Items predominantly favourable in tone are listed under (a), unfavourable under (b), and indeterminate or neutral under (c).
4, a,b,c. Brief, incidental comments in books or periodicals, grouped (a), (b), and (c) as above.
5, a,b,c. Poems to or about Shelley grouped (a), (b), and (c) as above. Each poem counted as many times as it is separately published.

This table shows Shelley's rising fame in perspective. For several years after Shelley's death he was but slightly noticed by most people who expressed themselves publicly on literary matters. The publication of *Posthumous Poems* in 1824 elicited ten reviews and some incidental comment and quotation, but the book was considered such a bad risk that it had to be guaranteed by B. W. Procter, T. F. Kelsall, and T. L. Beddoes, all ardent admirers of Shelley. But for this publication Shelley's name would have survived in the years 1823–30 chiefly because of his incidental connection with Byron and the *Liberal,* and because a small group of unliterary radical admirers considered him a prophet.

The year 1832 marks the crest of a much broader interest which had been gathering head for two years and which dwindled rather rapidly to the low figures shown for the years 1835–8. That this relapse creates an exaggerated impression, however, and that the comparative popularity of the early 1830's had not been barren of effect is shown by the fact that in 1834 two pirated editions of Shelley's "Works" appeared, and in 1836 still another appeared, and also the fourth edition of *The Beau-*

ties of Percy Bysshe Shelley. In 1834 or 1835 Mary Shelley was offered six hundred pounds for an annotated edition of her husband's works.[4] When this edition appeared in 1839, it received over twice the number of reviews that *Posthumous Poems* had received, and the volume and tone of other comment in that year made it practically impossible, for at least a generation, that Shelley's name would slip back into semi-obscurity.

One other fact seems very clearly established by this table. The predominantly favourable items under 3, 4, and 5 outnumber the predominantly unfavourable ones by more than five to one, and the unfavourable items are very largely limited to incidental comments. During the eighteen years covered by these figures only four articles and three poems of a definitely unfavourable cast appeared. Now that Shelley was dead and his works apparently not likely to become popular, the great majority of English readers probably still felt that his views were as repugnant as ever. Many sincere eulogists of his poetry were still at pains to exculpate themselves from any participation in his social, economic, and religious beliefs, particularly the last. But they were no longer of the opinion which had dominated reviewing in the first quarter of the century. Shelley's " errors " were still " errors," but were lightly or compassionately touched. Even Wordsworth was quoted in the *Somerset House Gazette and Literary Museum* for June 26, 1824 as asserting that Shelley was " by far the most promising young poet of the day." [5] The British sense of fair play came into prominent if belated action, and a large number of the reviewers insisted that Shelley had been cruelly and unjustly treated while he was alive. Periodicals which had assailed him most vigorously either fell silent or limited themselves to incidental remarks in which praise of Shelley's genius was mixed with a condemnation of his principles which apparently strove to be as charitable as possible.[6]

It may be noticed in Table I that the years in which the total number of items is most numerous are generally years in which the greatest number of Shelley's books were printed. The relative importance of books appears more significant when to the editions of Shelley's works are added the various other books, principally about Byron, in which he was given some attention.

Not only was Shelley often spoken of in reviews of these books, but extracts from them about Shelley were frequently reprinted as separate little articles. During the same period Shelley was quoted in nine annuals and eight anthologies, and was requoted from them in magazines and journals. The most important single book was *Queen Mab*, of which at least nine pirated editions appeared after 1822 and before 1841. Others were Mrs. Shelley's edition of *Posthumous Poems* (1824); Medwin's *Conversations with Lord Byron* (1824); William Benbow's pirated *Miscellaneous and Posthumous Poems* (1826), *Posthumous Poems* (1826), and *The Cenci* (1827); Leigh Hunt's *Lord Byron and Some of His Contemporaries* (1828); the Galignani edition of the *Poems of Shelley, Keats, and Coleridge* (Paris, 1829); the Cambridge Apostles' edition of *Epipsychidion* (1829); four pirated editions of *The Beauties of Percy Bysshe Shelley* (1830, with later editions in 1831, 1832, and 1836); Moore's *Byron* and Galt's *Byron* (both 1830); a Philadelphia pirated edition of Shelley's *Works* (1831); Leigh Hunt's edition of *The Mask of Anarchy*, containing a valuable biographical sketch (1832); Medwin's *The Shelley Papers* and *Memoir of Shelley* (both republished in 1833 from the *Athenæum*); Ascham's two pirated editions of Shelley's *Works* (both 1834); Daly's pirated edition of Shelley's *Works* (1835); and Mrs. Shelley's edition of the *Poetical Works* in four volumes and also in one volume (both 1839) with her two volumes of *Essays, Letters from Abroad* in 1839 or 1840.[7] In addition Shelley appeared as an important character in three novels: Mrs. Shelley's *The Last Man* (1826) and *Lodore* (1834), and Disraeli's *Venetia* (1837).

The importance of some of the non-Shelleyan books in stimulating comment about Shelley may be judged from the fact that in 1828 six out of the total number of twenty-five items of all descriptions are traceable to Hunt's *Lord Byron and his Contemporaries* and in 1830 eight out of a total of thirty-five are traceable to the two lives of Byron by Moore and Galt. Thirty-three such books containing more or less important incidental notice of Shelley appeared during the eighteen years following his death. During the same time the thirty-four editions noted in Table I were responsible for at least sixty-three reviews, about forty of which were occasioned by Mary Shelley's four editions in 1824 and 1839–40.

THE relative importance of books in comparison with articles is so normal that it can be passed without further comment. It does little to explain how Shelley's reputation sailed with or against certain currents of the age, or what were the forces which constituted its impetus. Some of these forces may be suggested by a second table:

TABLE II

	1823	1824	1825	1826	1827	1828	1829	1830	1831	1832	1833	1834	1835	1836	1837	1838	1839	1840	Total
1	8	12	4	1	0	10	0	8	5	1	0	0	0	0	0	0	0	0	49
2	2	7	1	0	0	1	0	0	7	3	3	0	2	0	0	0	5	1	32
3	3	0	8	12	1	1	4	6	1	4	6	0	1	6	0	5	27	1	86
4	0	0	1	1	0	0	0	3	2	7	2	1	0	0	0	1	1	1	20
5	2	0	0	0	1	1	1	1	1	18	4	0	0	2	0	0	3	0	34
6	2	0	0	0	0	1	0	1	0	0	0	0	1	0	4	0	4	0	13
7	1	2	0	0	0	10	9	1	1	2	8	10	2	2	0	1	10	8	67
8	1	0	2	0	0	2	2	0	3	0	0	0	2	0	1	3	0	0	16
9	1	0	0	3	1	0	4	3	4	2	1	2	0	2	0	0	2	1[?]	26
10	2	1	0	0	0	0	1	0	0	1	2	0	0	0	0	0	2	2	11
Total	22	22	16	17	3	26	21	23	24	38	26	13	8	12	5	10	54	14	354
Total from Table I	22	45	17	29	14	25	30	35	33	63	37	27	13	16	11	16	86	26	545

KEY TO TABLE II

1. Items of all descriptions incidental to the *Liberal* or to the interest in Byron.
2. Items of all descriptions which originated (or probably originated) with Shelley's surviving friends.
3. Items of all descriptions reflecting the working-class radical interest in Shelley.
4. Items of all descriptions in working-class non-radical periodicals.
5. Items of all descriptions reflecting upper- or middle-class intellectual radicalism or extreme liberalism.
6. Items in journals primarily religious.
7. Items of all descriptions published in English in America, India, and France.
8. Items, mainly quotations, in anthologies and annuals.
9. Pirated editions.
10. Authorized or semi-authorized editions.

Following the totals I have brought forward the annual totals from Table I, for comparison. Discrepancies in the two totals are accounted for by a slight overlapping of categories in Table II, resulting in the duplication of some fifteen or twenty items, and by the fact that over a hundred items included in Table I do not fall within the limits of Table II.

One fact immediately obvious is that the first growth of Shelley's fame owed a noticeable debt to the accidental factor of his connection with Byron. Nearly ten per cent of the total number of items were stimulated by an original interest in Byron and the *Liberal*. This factor had no significance after 1832, but in the critical years before that time it accounts for nearly one-sixth of the total, and in the two years following Shelley's death to nearly a third.

On the basis of numbers, this accidental aid to Shelley's reputation would seem to be about twice as important as the efforts of Shelley's friends to establish his reputation on a just basis. The reverse ratio, however, would probably be nearer the truth. With the exception of Medwin's *Conversations with Lord Byron* and Hunt's *Lord Byron and Some of his Contemporaries* (which belong also in the second category) most of the notice which Shelley attracted by way of Byron was neutral rather than propagandistic. It merely helped to keep his name alive and perhaps stimulate curiosity.

Shelley's friends, on the other hand, were warm propagandists. In some of them Shelley had inspired almost a religious veneration that made of him something more than a mortal man. Emilia Viviani had expressed this feeling during Shelley's life, and it was echoed later by Mary Shelley, Claire Clairmont, Leigh Hunt, and Marianne Hunt. "My divine friend" Hunt had called him shortly after his death, adding, as quoted above: "I cannot help thinking of him as if he were alive as much as ever, so unearthly he always appeared to me, and so seraphical a King of the elements." His wife, Marianne, believed that she received visits from Shelley in 1823.[8] A devoted tribute to Shelley among some notes written about 1825 by Claire Clairmont stresses angelic, superhuman elements in his character. In her early widowhood Mary Shelley more than once conversed with him in her journal as if he were a spiritual presence. In the preface to Hogg's biography of Shelley she is quoted as saying: " I was the chosen mate of a celestial spirit. . . . Methinks my calling is high; I am to justify his ways. . . . I am a priestess, dedicated to his glorification by my sufferings." As late as August 13, 1859, in an article in the *Spectator*, Leigh Hunt maintained that " Shelley was not a man to be judged by ordinary rules of any kind. . . . He was one of those great and rare spirits, who, by a combination of the extremes of intellectual perceptiveness and nervous sensibility may be said . . . to be the founders of new faiths or improvers of the old. Inasmuch as they are human in the ordinary sense they may err; but inasmuch as they carry humanity to its highest and widest extent they approach divinity." Though Thomas Medwin and Jefferson Hogg lacked the note of semi-religious apostleship, and though Mary Shelley accused Medwin of attempted blackmail, and Lady Shelley later accused Hogg of seeking to make Shelley ridiculous, Medwin's friendship and personal devotion to Shelley are obvious enough to any reader, and even Hogg's are obvious to me.

Much of the service done to Shelley's reputation by these friends and missionaries cannot be tabulated. Mary Shelley and Leigh Hunt both had extensive connections in literary and journalistic circles. Thornton Hunt continued this influence with a younger generation of journalists. Undoubtedly they were responsible for a personal influence far beyond the published record, and beyond the evidence of such influence that is afforded by their extant letters. Mary Shelley, for example, seems to have arranged for the publication of Hogg's valuable articles in the *New Monthly Magazine* that resulted later in the first — and ill-starred — biography of Shelley.

Nearly every item published by this small group between 1822 and 1841 was of unusual importance. Medwin's *Conver-. sations with Lord Byron* and *Memoir of Shelley* presented Shelley to a large audience as Byron's moral and mental equal or superior, instead of the mere hanger-on he had been supposed

REMINISCENT BUST OF SHELLEY BY MARIANNE HUNT

By permission of the owner, Dr. A. S. W. Rosenbach

by many to have been. His *Shelley Papers* furnished new materials to a public which as yet had access only to a part of Shelley's works. The importance of Mary Shelley's edition of the *Posthumous Poems* has been shown already. Even more important to a full and fair estimate of Shelley (though not to the development of his reputation) were her editions of 1839 and 1840, which for the first time provided a full and accurate text, in addition to full, semi-biographical notes that have ever since proved invaluable. Her thinly disguised use of Shelley in her novels doubtless stimulated further thirst for knowledge about him.

Mary's activity would probably have been more abundant had not Sir Timothy Shelley, on whom her income largely depended, set himself sternly against the preservation of his son's name. He compelled the suppression of *Posthumous Poems*, forbade publication of a biography, and grudgingly consented to the editions of 1839 and 1840 only on condition that no biographical memoir should accompany them. The notes which accompanied these editions were an effort to comply with the letter of Sir Timothy's prohibition while evading its spirit. Her novels have also been so regarded, perhaps erroneously. As a novelist, after *Frankenstein*, Mary Shelley lacked invention, and wrote out of her own experience largely because she had to. Byron, whom she came to dislike and can hardly be suspected of wishing to apotheosize, occupies perhaps a larger place than Shelley in her novels. Sir Timothy's attitude could not prevent her writing a biography of Shelley to be published after her death and his. Her resort to subterfuge in the case of her notes argues that she would not have considered this dishonourable. The idea must have occurred to her more than once. Her failure to do so can most reasonably be attributed to the same reasons Leigh Hunt assigned for declining the same task. If she made herself liable for a biography she could not conscientiously suppress certain facts which, on the other hand, she could not bear to publish.

Leigh Hunt's contribution was not so obvious as during Shelley's lifetime. During 1824 the *Examiner*, presumably under his influence, though John Hunt was editor, three times presented specimens of Shelley's poems, reprinted a favourable passage from Medwin, gave *Posthumous Poems* an appreciative review, published an original poem on Shelley and Byron, twice condemned the slanderous story about Shelley in the *Narrative of Lord Byron's Voyage to Sicily,* and defended him against a charge of falsehood contained in a letter published by Southey. That the *Examiner* was silent thereafter may be attributed to the fact that it soon fell away both from its association with Hunt and from its earlier interest in literature. But Leigh Hunt's *London Journal* (non-political) contained in January 1835 two short quotations from Shelley; and three brief items relating to Shelley in the *Monthly Repository* of 1833 may have owed something to his association with that periodical. The *Tatler,* which was edited and largely written by Leigh Hunt, contained two poems on Shelley in 1831 (April 8 and 14), and two incidental items and one quotation between January 12 and March 30, 1832. Leigh Hunt's principal published contribution, however, was the memoir which accompanied his publication of *The Mask of Anarchy* in 1832. In the year of its appearance this publication was responsible for seven other items. The *Spectator,* of which Thornton Hunt was a managing editor, contained one favourable review in 1832 and three in 1839.

During his life Shelley had come to despair of his ability to reach the popular mind directly. As in *Prometheus Unbound,* he had directed his "passion for reforming the world" more to "the highly refined imagination of the more select classes of poetical readers," hoping that it would eventually filter down to the popular mind through the minds of others. During the eighteen years following his death this hope was not entirely fruitless.

One fine mind which listened while most others remained heedless was that of George Henry Lewes, later founder and editor of the *Contemporary Review.* As a young student in Germany Lewes wrote to Leigh Hunt in 1838 expressing his deep interest in Shelley, asking questions about him, and stating that he was writing a biographical and critical study of Shelley. On December 21, 1839 he requested Mary Shelley to read his manuscript.[9] Nearly two years before this, however, in 1838, the *National Magazine and Monthly Critic* for four successive months (January, February, March, and April) had included in its list of works in the press " The Life of Percy Bysshe Shelley. By G. H. Lewes." The book never appeared, nor is there to this day any record or knowledge of it in the Lewes family. Some of its ideas and values may have gone into the later work of William Michael Rossetti, whom Lewes is known to have helped in the preparation of his valuable *Memoir of Shelley* in 1869. Some of it may also have been preserved in the forty-one-page, enthusiastic, and genuinely critical article which Lewes published in the *Westminster Review* for April 1841. This was one of the best of all the reviews of *The Poetical Works of Percy Bysshe Shelley*. Carlyle had lectured on Heroes and Hero-Worship less than a year before. Lewes roundly proclaimed that Shelley was one of the two great Englishmen of the nineteenth century. He characterized him as " the original man, the hero," a fit object for hero-worship.

Another mind such as Shelley had hoped to inspire was that of young Robert Browning. In the year 1826 Robert Browning, then a youth of fourteen, came across Benbow's pirated *Miscellaneous Poems* of Shelley (1826). He had never heard of the author before, but he so admired this volume that he immediately sought Shelley's other works. It is eloquent testimony to the early neglect of Shelley that in 1826, four years after Shelley's death, Ollier still had on hand remainders of the first printings of every volume of Shelley's poetry that he had printed except *The Cenci*. From that moment until his death in 1889 Browning was a great admirer of Shelley. Somewhere he obtained a copy of *Queen Mab;* for two years he became an atheist and a vegetarian. His first published volume, *Pauline* (1833), showed the influence of this admiration and contained a long, passionate apostrophe to Shelley as the great " Sun-treader," first scorned and later ignored, who was too great and pure a spirit ever to die.[10] Twenty years later Browning offered to Victorian England one of its most influential appreciative essays on Shelley.

Throughout his life Browning sought the acquaintance of those who had known Shelley or who were writing about him.

He was a member of the Shelley Society in the late 1880's. But Browning was a liberal rather than a radical. In his home environment and in his education he was a product of the new middle-class liberalism of which the Reform Bill of 1832 was a fairly typical product. After the first few years his appreciation of Shelley was primarily as a rare soul and a great voice of passion and human charity, but not as a radical prophet. Even this admiration was greatly lessened by a disapprobation of Shelley's character after he heard Harriet's story from Thomas Hookham.

At this point it may be seen that the liberal trend of the times was a distinct advantage to Shelley's reputation. It brought about a new toleration and a genuine, though somewhat limited, appreciation and even enthusiasm. Such new liberal or radical-liberal periodicals as the *Westminster Review,* the *Athenæum,* the shortlived *Edinburgh Literary Journal,* the *Atlas,* the *Spectator,* the *Tatler,* and *Tait's Edinburgh Magazine* gave a distinctly more liberal tone to literary criticism. Among the 175 periodicals which noticed Shelley during the period with which we are here concerned, only eighteen carried more than five items, and among this number are to be found all of the periodicals just mentioned except the *Tatler* and the *Spectator,* which contained five and four items respectively. Two of these journals, the *Westminster Review* (six items) and *Tait's Edinburgh Magazine* (nine items) were Benthamite organs and were considered somewhat radical. But the radicalism of the Benthamites was a utilitarian radicalism. There is a considerable difference between Shelley's condemnation of commerce, in *Queen Mab,* and the *Westminster Review's* ideal of solving social and economic difficulties by stimulating trade and sharing more fully with the working classes the profit that trade creates. Otherwise there should have been more articles about Shelley in the *Westminster Review,* whose coterie included several of Shelley's friends and admirers.

THE MOST surprising factor in the rise of Shelley's reputation was the attention he received from the working classes. The ruthless employment of the Newspaper Stamp Tax to discourage radical political and religious opinions in journals for the workingman had placed periodical literature practically out of the reach of the labouring classes. This tax could be avoided by eschewing opinions on church and state. As a result, a whole class of cheap journals of information for the workingman appeared, and the English labouring classes began to read more extensively than had ever been possible before. These journals, whose cardinal policy was to avoid religious and political topics, nevertheless evinced a peculiar interest in Shelley. Of his opinions they had little to say, except an occasional vague word of regret for his lack of Christianity. Their interest was largely in anecdotes, in Shelley's romantic life, and his connection with Byron. They quoted his poetry only occasionally, and never the more radical passages. Nevertheless this interest was considerable, especially in the early 1830's, and resulted in some twenty items, fifteen of them in the *Mirror*. Only one periodical, the *Athenæum*, contained a larger total number of Shelley items. This interest, and other similar ones, must have been responsible for the success of repeated editions of such popular-priced piracies as *The Beauties of Percy Bysshe Shelley*, with its " revised edition " of *Queen Mab* " free from objectionable matter."

Side by side with these conservative workingmen's periodicals existed a vigorously radical labour journalism. A leader among these writers during the latter years of Shelley's life and until some years after the passing of the Reform Bill was the much-prosecuted Richard Carlile, whose second prosecution had inspired one of Shelley's most earnest letters. Carlile had wished to be the first publisher of *Queen Mab*, but had deferred to Shelley's objections. That distinction fell a little later to William Clark, a clerk in Carlile's radical book-shop, whose abject conduct under the ensuing prosecution by the Society for the Prevention of Vice showed, in Carlile's opinion, that he had been unworthy of the honour. Carlile then published two editions of *Queen Mab* in 1822 and a third and fourth in 1823 and 1826, having meanwhile bought up and sold all that remained of Shelley's original edition. On December 15, 1826 he published in his *Republican* some laudatory " Remarks on

the Genius and Writings of the late Mr. Percy Bysshe Shelley."
His later periodical, the *Lion,* contained in 1829 (March 13 and
April 3 and 17) three poems on Shelley by different unidentified
authors, and an article by Carlile on the history of *The Revolt
of Islam.* In 1832, while Carlile was serving one of his prison
terms, Mrs. Carlile and Sons brought out still another edition
of *Queen Mab.*

In 1825 eight fellow radicals entered Carlile's Fleet Street
shop determined to carry on his activities while he was imprisoned. They were at once arrested and sent to Newgate
prison, whence during 1825 and 1826 they published the *Newgate Magazine.* During the brief period of its existence this
magazine contained thirteen Shelley items of all descriptions,
a number exceeded (over a longer space of time) only by the
Athenæum, the *Mirror,* and the *New Moral World.* These items
include a number of quotations, a contributed letter, a sonnet
praising Shelley, and a series of five articles signed C. [Carlile?]
" On the Character and Writings of Shelley," in which *The
Cenci, The Revolt of Islam,* and *Queen Mab* (all radical piracies) are analysed. The last of this series, which is also the
last article in the last number of the magazine (August 1826),
maintains that Shelley's present obscurity can be explained on
no other basis than frightened prejudice.

Robert Owen, whom it is just possible Shelley may have
known, was perhaps even more influential than Richard Carlile
in spreading the knowledge of Shelley among English working-
class radicals. The Owenites, as Medwin had noticed, regarded
Shelley's *Queen Mab* almost as a Bible. Shelley was indeed the
patron saint of their periodical literature. The *Quarterly Review* (March 1840) and the *General Baptist Repository,* etc.
(May 1839), charged that Owen derived much of his doctrine
from Shelley. If, as has been claimed, Robert Owen was the
founder of British socialism, it is possible for modern socialism
to claim Shelley as a sort of grandfather.

The principal Owenite periodicals flourished between 1826
and 1841 and consisted of the *Cooperative Magazine and
Monthly Herald* (1826–9), continued in 1830 as the *London
Cooperative Magazine;* the *Magazine of Useful Knowledge and*

Cooperative Miscellany (1830); the *Lancashire Cooperator* (Manchester, 1830); the *Crisis* (1832–4); and the *New Moral World* (1835–41). Of these, the *New Moral World* was edited by Robert Owen, and the *Crisis* was edited by Robert Owen and his son Robert Dale Owen, who was partly responsible for an American *Queen Mab* piracy. All contained Shelley items, totalling twenty-five, of which fifteen appeared in the *New Moral World*. In 1841, seven more items appeared in this journal. Most of these Owenite items were quotations, but one in the *New Moral World* (January 27, 1838) was Robert Buchanan's poem "On Shelley." The same journal began on December 1, 1838 an intermittent series of "Reviews of Modern Poets and Illustrations of the Philosophy of Modern Poetry," which devoted the first two numbers to Shelley in general and two numbers each to analyses of *Prometheus Unbound* and *The Revolt of Islam*.

Still another class of radicals who found strength in Shelley and helped to advance his fame were such men as Henry Hetherington, James Watson, W. J. Linton, and J. G. Holyoake. These men worked for the Chartist cause and fought for freedom of speech for the labouring man. Hetherington's *Poor Man's Guardian* (1831–5), "Published in Defiance of the Newspaper Stamp Tax," eventually compelled the government to cease prosecutions under that law. Though the *Poor Man's Guardian* contains no articles on Shelley, it carries more advertisements of *Queen Mab* than any other journal. The *Freethinkers' Information for the People*, edited by Hetherington and Watson apparently in 1836, contains several short quotations from Shelley and an account of a visit to his grave. Both Hetherington and his friend Watson brought out pirated editions of *Queen Mab*. For the first six months of 1839 W. J. Linton edited the *National, A Library for the People*. In February and March this periodical contained eleven Shelley items. Most of them are quotations, but one is a biographical sketch and another a laudatory sonnet.

In 1841 Hetherington, Watson, and their friends made a clever use of *Queen Mab* to force the government to abandon discriminatory proceedings against radicals under the law of

blasphemous libel. Edward Moxon, a gentleman and a respectable publisher whom it would embarrass the government
to prosecute, had deleted the objectionable passages of *Queen
Mab* in Mary Shelley's four-volume edition of 1839, but in the
one-volume edition of the same year he yielded to her desire
for their restoration. The radicals forced a trial under the same
law that had been used against themselves, and when they inevitably won a verdict calmly announced that they would not
pray judgment, and that their interest was confined to making
the law unpopular. That they succeeded in this purpose is clear
enough from a full history of the case and its results.[11]

Queen Mab was by long odds the most frequently printed,
the most extensively advertised, and the most eagerly read of
Shelley's works for at least twenty years after his death. Its
vitality during that period was the largest single factor in the
vitality of Shelley's reputation. In his 1834 " Course of Lectures on Ancient and Modern Literature, their Intimate Connection and Relative Value," George Burgess, M.A., seems to
have restricted his remarks on Shelley to *Queen Mab.* The more
general radical interest of which *Queen Mab* was the back-log
accounts for a total number of eighty-six items in Table II — far
more than any other single strain of interest.

The results which have already been indicated will be clari-
fied and supported by the following list of all periodicals containing more than five Shelleyan items.

The presence in this list of the two last-named periodicals, and
possibly of one or two others, is more accidental than significant. The *Quarterly Review* spanned the whole period from a
time before Shelley's death and yet reviewed only one Shelley
edition; its attention was confined almost entirely to brief incidental references which were perhaps inescapable over so long
a period. *Stockdale's Budget,* on the other hand, was a purely
personal journal. Its interest in Shelley depended on the accident of Stockdale's having been Shelley's first publisher and
having in his possession facts and documents of which he could
make journalistic capital.

TABLE III

	Life of Periodical	Dates of Shelley Items	Number of Shelley Items	Group Total
A. Liberal Periodicals				
Athenæum	1828–1921	1828–39	26	
Atlas	1826–69	1828–40	6	
Edinburgh Literary Journal	1829–31	1828–30	8	
Metropolitan Magazine	1831–50	1833–40	7	
Monthly Chronicle	1839–41	1839–40	6	
Monthly Magazine	1796–1843	1834–40	7	
New Monthly Magazine	1814–84	1830–3	11	71
B. Middle-Class Liberal-Radical Periodicals				
Examiner	1808–81	1824	9	
Tait's Edinburgh Magazine	1832–61	1832–40	9	
Westminster Review	1824–40	1825–36	6	24
C. Working-Class Radical Periodicals				
National, A Library for the People	1839	1839	11	
Newgate Monthly	1825–6	1825–6	13	
New Moral World	1835–41	1835–40	15	39
D. Conservative or Non-Political Periodicals				
Fraser's Magazine (independent Tory)	1830–82	1830–8	6	
Magazine of the Beau Monde (fashion and taste)	1831–42	1832–9	8	
Mirror (working-class non-political)	1823–41	1826–40	15	
Quarterly Review (regular Tory)	1809, current	1826–40	6	
Stockdale's Budget (personal, non-political)	1826–7	1826–7	9	44
			Total	178

How largely Shelley's journalistic reputation was a product of new journalism may be noticed from the fact that only three of the eighteen journals listed were in existence when he was alive. It is also evident at a glance that the periodicals of liberal principles were those which exerted the largest influence in bringing about a general appreciation of Shelley. Undoubtedly the working-class radical journalism had far less influence upon general opinion, yet it becomes clear, if one makes due allowance for the frequency of the items within the time-limits in which they appeared, that Shelley's most ardent and devoted admirers were to be found among the readers and editors of these journals. Omitting the fourth group, one notices that out of a total of 175 journals and some 470 journalistic items of all descriptions, thirteen liberal and radical journals provided 134 items, or between a fourth and a third of the total.[12]

IT SHOULD not be supposed that the early Victorians deserted the judgment of their fathers and elder brothers as smoothly and unhesitatingly as a tabular study of the phenomenon might indicate. Reputations do not arise so easily out of the confused sea of varying opinions which characterize every generation. Cross-currents deflect and undertows retard at the same time that other currents accelerate. Throughout the whole period the reticences of many conservative journals and the constant note of apology common to most friendly criticism except that of the radicals (which was rather outside regular literary channels) indicate that the age continued a bit uncertain about Shelley and that his reputation, though almost secure by 1832, was not yet sailing on an even keel. Outside of radical circles two of the passages most frequently quoted from Shelley were the totally unrepresentative description of a calm winter night, from *Queen Mab*, and the prose essay on Love, neither of which could offend any possible prejudice.

The Cambridge Apostles, who discovered Shelley in 1829, printed *Epipsychidion*, and debated the merits of Shelley versus Byron with Oxford undergraduates, were interested primarily in Shelley's " pure poetry " and were said to have become later rather ashamed of their enthusiasm. Some of their Oxford antagonists admitted afterwards that they hadn't understood who Shelley was, and really thought they had been arguing about Shenstone.[13] In 1834, at the same time that the *Calcutta Literary Gazette* was disclosing Shelley's literary merits to India, his fame was first publicly welcomed at Oxford in a somewhat cautious eulogy in the *Oxford University Magazine* for May — which the Calcutta journal hailed (July 5) as " a striking indication of the change that has come over the spirit of the age." Nor was Oxford slower than Eton. The *Eton Miscellany*, which ran for six months in 1827 under the editorship of the same William Ewart Gladstone who participated for Oxford in the 1829 debate, makes no mention of Shelley. As late as the 1870's Eton's headmaster, Dr. Hornby, declined to receive a bust of Shelley for the school.[14]

In more than one genuinely enthusiastic appreciation Shelley was placed — as a climax — alongside Mrs. Hemans. The *Edinburgh Literary Gazette* of January 2, 1829, after sincerely praising Shelley's great poetic merit, asserted that it was less than that of Professor John Wilson. In 1830 the *British Magazine* remarked that Shelley was "gifted with powers almost equal to any poet who ever existed" — but the remark is a brief digression in an appreciation of the Reverend Mr. George Croly, who is dignified with a full sketch in a series on Popular Authors of the Nineteenth Century, from which Shelley is omitted. In January 1836 the *Edinburgh Review* could casually deprecate "the schoolboy popularity of Shelley," and in 1840 Ebenezer Elliott, in a Defence of Modern Poetry written for the Sheffield Mechanics' Institution and published in *Tait's Edinburgh Magazine* for May, praised Keats and Byron while completely ignoring Shelley.

It seems unnecessary to remark that the rise of Shelley's fame and influence, aided as it was by some accidental circumstances and retarded by others, derived its principal motive power from an inner vitality rather than from sheer accident. What this vitality consisted in has been one of the subjects of this biography and need not here be repeated. There have been accidental reputations, and revived reputations, but they have been evanescent, and their characteristic motion *diminuendo* rather than *crescendo*. A reputation which is purely the creature of its time dies with the period that creates it; Shelley's has grown greater since the disappearance of all the early nineteenth-century influences which aided, but could not have created, its emergence as a literary and social force.

THE MIDDLE and later Victorian students of Shelley produced more than a dozen biographies, scores of editions, and hundreds of critical essays, many of them from the most distinguished critics of the age. Led at first by Lady Shelley, they collected and preserved priceless materials for later biography and criticism. Without discrimination between editors, biographers, and critics, one needs only to call a list of distinguished names: Mrs. Angeli, Arnold, Bagehot, Bradley, Brailsford, Brooke, Browning, Clutton-Brock, Dowden, Forman, Garnett, Gosse, Hutton, Ingpen, Locock, Masson, P. E. More, Quiller-Couch, W. M. Rossetti, Salt, Shairp, Swinburne, Symonds, Francis Thompson, James Thomson, Todhunter, Wise, Woodberry, and Yeats. J. P. Anderson's bibliography appended to William Sharp's *Life of Shelley* (1887) contains over a hundred and fifty book titles in biography and criticism alone.

In 1886 a Shelley Society was formed, consisting of about four hundred members, among them Robert Browning, George Bernard Shaw, W. M. Rossetti, H. B. Forman, F. J. Furnivall, and T. J. Wise. For two years this society flourished and published volumes by or about Shelley, besides managing public productions of both *Hellas* and *The Cenci*. A number of papers were read at its meetings, including several distinctly able critical discussions. By 1887 forty or fifty of Shelley's lyrics had been set to music, as well as all the choral parts of *Hellas*.[15] In 1892 the centenary of Shelley's birth was celebrated at Field Place and Oxford. Numerous books and articles were published, including George Edward Woodberry's scholarly edition of Shelley's poetical works. In 1894 Eton accepted a bust of Shelley — while Dr. Hornby still wished, *sotto voce*, that Shelley had gone to Harrow.[16] Oxford accepted Sir Onslow Ford's sculpture and a part of Lady Shelley's accumulation of Shelleyana. In 1922 the centenary of his death was even more extensively noticed, not only throughout the English-speaking world, but in most European countries.[17] Again numerous books and articles were published, and *The Cenci* was produced on the stage in both London and Prague. By this time it was a commonplace not to be questioned in either Europe or America that Shelley was one of the great English poets.

It is a curious fact, demanding some reflection, that many of the most important authors and critics of the period did not join whole-heartedly in this general acclaim. Wordsworth re-

peated his earlier praise of Shelley's art, the Shelleyan enthusiasm of Browning and George Henry Lewes continued, and
Swinburne was a strong admirer. But there was an interesting
cautiousness or vagueness about much of the appreciation of
Shelley by many of the Victorians. Some of them were definitely antagonistic, echoing Charles Lamb's earlier statement
that " no one was ever the wiser or better for reading Shelley." [18]
Charles Kingsley vigorously accused Shelley of preaching " the
worship of uncleanness as the last and highest ethical development of ' pure ' humanity." [19] " Yon man Shelley," said Thomas
Carlyle, rudely interrupting a rhapsody by William Bell Scott,
" was just a scoundrel, and ought to have been hangèd "; publicly he uttered: " Hear a Shelley filling the earth with inarticulate wail; like the infinite, inarticulate grief and weeping of
forsaken infants." [20] Tennyson, while granting Shelley's " splendid imagery and colour," found in his poetry " a sort of tenuity," [21] and William Morris, a radical himself, charged that Shelley " had no eyes," and always floundered in narration.[22]

One might discount most of these statements as random remarks if their counterparts did not present themselves so embarrassingly in some of the most important and fully considered
critical essays of the age. Matthew Arnold's " beautiful and ineffectual angel, beating in the void his luminous wings in
vain," was protested by Stopford Brooke in his Shelley Society
inaugural address, but it remains to this day one of the most
influential critical dicta on Shelley. Walter Bagehot's weighty
essay is based upon the assumption that Shelley's actions were
motivated by impulse rather than reason or principle, Browning
expresses the belief that Shelley would eventually have turned
to Christianity, and Francis Thompson makes of him an angelic
creature of purely naïve and instinctive wisdom. With Thompson many an admirer has been glad to " peep over the wild mass
of revolutionary metaphysics " and discover that Shelley was
" to the last " an " enchanted child." [23] To Leslie Stephen, who
thought " the crude incoherence of his whole system too obvious to require exposition," a beautiful, iridescent mist above a
muddy pool of Godwinism, Shelley's appeal to most readers

seemed sentimentally pathetic — the poet and his readers were really weeping together over the " obstinate insubstantiality " of Shelley's hopes.[24]

In America it was much the same. There was abundant appreciation of the Victorian type. The poetry of Edgar Allan Poe showed some Shelleyan influences; that of his somewhat obscure predecessor Thomas Holley Chivers showed more, including a poetic tribute to Shelley. But in 1873 Emerson had hardly read Shelley and had never cared for him,[25] and about 1882 the president of Harvard University hesitated to accept from Captain Silsbee the manuscript of Shelley's " The Cloud." [26] One of America's foremost critics, Paul Elmer More, expressed a fair counterpart of Leslie Stephen's view by speaking of *Prometheus Unbound* and *The Revolt of Islam* as a " kind of elusive, yet rapturous, emanation of hope, devoid of specific content." [27]

THESE strains of disapprobation and limited appreciation demand explanation. What is their source and meaning and to what extent may they be expected to influence Shelley's future position?

Let us recall the most obvious conclusion from the story of Shelley's early reputation — that it grew and spread mainly in liberal and radical circles, who appreciated Shelley for two very different reasons. To the radicals he was the prophet of a new order, and only incidentally a poet. For them his poetry added passion and persuasion to his prophecy, but they were not interested in poetry for mere æsthetic pleasure. Even if they had possessed the necessary cultural tastes and background (which most of them lacked), they would have seen little meaning in art that conveyed no stimulating social, political, or economic message. They honestly exaggerated Shelley's radicalism in their desire to use him as an instrument of immediate reform. The liberals, on the other hand, were interested in Shelley primarily as a rare soul and a poet of lyric emotion. It was *Epipsychidion* that the Cambridge Apostles revived; and the poems which the annuals and magazines most loved to quote were

"The Sensitive Plant," "To a Skylark," "With a Guitar: To Jane," and the pathetic self-portrait from *Adonais*. Journalists were no longer oppressed by the fears and dreads that had afflicted their fathers and brothers and caused some of them to persecute "poor Shelley" because they could not afford to tolerate him. Shelley's enthusiasm for political freedom was something they could share in principle, while still regarding the details as premature or impractical. They admired the nobility of Shelley's private character. They could not afford to endorse his religious and social views (the Cambridge debaters of 1829 had been suspected of atheism by some of the audience), but they could afford to apologize for them. The keynote of early Victorian liberal criticism of Shelley was apologetic appreciation.

Later Victorian criticism of Shelley was the child of early Victorian liberal appreciation. The radical note, which had swelled so loud during the Reform Bill and Chartist agitations, died gradually without important issue with the failure of the Chartist movement. Thereafter there was no important great popular agitation in England for more than fifty years. There were still radicals, of course, and radicals who continued the old radical feeling toward Shelley, but it was a comparatively minor note. As for Freedom, the facts seemed to support Tennyson's assurance that Freedom was slowly broadening down from precedent to precedent. Were not the nineteenth-century French Revolutionists (whom Mary Shelley even regarded with aversion) "the red fool-fury of the Seine"? It was better for the middle and upper classes to make the precedents. England was steadily becoming stronger and richer, the increased comforts of life were "broadening down" also, child labour was being restricted, and public education was being extended. England was taking up the white man's burden with profitable resignation. Younger sons and discontented labourers knew where they could go — or if they didn't they could learn from a hundred novels that emigration solved all difficulties. Almost forgotten, the fierce hopes and fears engendered by the French Revolution and its aftermath belonged to a closed chapter of human progress. In this atmosphere one could appreciate Shelley a little more generously than the earlier liberals, and apologize a little less conspicuously and uneasily. But the fundamental attitude was the same. Shelley was one of the great English poets; practically everyone thought so now. Yet in everything that really mattered to *him* except his purely personal emotions and his fine art, he was dead wrong.

All that was most serious to Shelley the later Victorians seldom took the trouble to study seriously. There seemed no particular reason for doing so, and it must also be said that some of the letters and the important *Philosophical View of Reform* were not available. Mary Shelley herself was willing to minimize Shelley the radical, though she was honest enough to restore the *Queen Mab* notes. Lady Shelley's influence, through her control of Shelley materials, was a sentimentalizing one. It was resentment of this influence as much as an honest disapproval of much of Shelley's character and philosophy that caused J. Cordy Jeaffreson to flutter the Shelley Society dovecote with his crudely reactionary *The Real Shelley* (1885). Something of the old radical flavour persisted in H. N. Brailsford (*Shelley, Godwin and Their Circle*, 1913) and more in H. S. Salt, whose *Percy Bysshe Shelley, Poet and Pioneer* (1896) was written in protest against what he considered a ridiculous contemporary blindness to Shelley's true significance. George Bernard Shaw, one of Shelley's more radical admirers, suggested that the Shelley chapel at University College, Oxford, be decorated " with a relief representing Shelley in a tall hat, bible in hand, leading his children on Sunday morning to the church of his native parish." [28] And the explorer Henry M. Stanley warned an officer of the Shelley Society: " You are a funny people, you Shelleyites. You are playing — at a safe distance yourself, maybe, with fire. In spreading Shelley you are indirectly helping to stir up the great socialist question, the great question of the needs and wants and wishes of unhappy men; the one question which bids fair to swamp you all for a bit." [29]

It is too early to say that the vital radical force of Shelley, from which the early nineteenth-century reformers drew such

PORTRAIT OF SHELLEY BY WYON, SHOWING INFLUENCE
OF BUST BY MARIANNE HUNT

By permission of the British Museum

inspiration, is yet dead. To an appreciable extent, it helped stimulate Young Germany in the abortive revolution of 1848, and the Italian patriots of the Risorgimento.[30] Only a few years ago a group of Communists in a Milwaukee jail were reported to have attempted to convert fellow prisoners by reading *Queen Mab* aloud. We learn from the autobiography of Upton Sinclair, certainly one of the great radical voices of the age, that Shelley was one of the enthusiasms of his youth. A typically Shelleyan radical idea has recently been proved by Mahatma Gandhi to have enormous practical force. That it was suggested not by Shelley, but by Thoreau (who may have had it from the New Testament), does not affect the validity of the idea. Shelley was no communist; he was in some respects considerably less radical than his radical admirers supposed; but he was perhaps the greatest radical voice in poetry since Lucretius.

Professor Dowden, Shelley's authorized biographer, successfully maintained his independence of Lady Shelley's control, but he could not be independent of the dominant tendency of the age. His treatment of Shelley is apologetically and sentimentally protective. To him Shelley was great and good not because of, but in spite of, his major beliefs. He did not sufficiently perceive either the guiding purpose of Shelley's life or the strength of that purpose. This may explain why one so admirable in the collection and presentation of factual detail could be at the same time so glossily mediocre in his critical treatment of Shelley's ideas. It may also explain some of the excessive disgust with which Mark Twain treated the book in his " Defense of Harriet Shelley." Perhaps it is the same latent incongruity that prompted the opening paragraphs of Paul Elmer More's essay on Shelley (1910), in which he seeks to show, by very apposite quotations, that most criticism of Shelley is mealymouthed and straddling.

Undoubtedly a large part of Shelley's popularity for a hundred years has been based upon an evasion of the real Shelley. His great lyrics were to him for the most part only tangential to the controlling purposes of his life, for which he reserved his greatest poetic energies. To most of his admirers these splendid lapses constitute his main glory, and his main purpose in writing constitutes an utter failure which they are not quite frank enough to face squarely.

CAN a man be wrong in most of his major principles, lead his life, so far as possible, in passionate accord with those principles, and still be generally acclaimed as one of the chief glories of his country and age? Can "a kind of elusive, yet rapturous, emanation of hope devoid of specific content," added to a few short lyrics of a very high order, be a sufficient foundation for such a reputation as Shelley achieved in the later nineteenth century? If true, it is pure magic — which is of course possible in poetry. If false, then Shelley was greatly overpraised by the Victorians, and his reputation should already be waning. Yet his reputation increases. The tendency of more recent scholarship has been to find in Shelley an intellectual penetration, knowledge, and wisdom which his Victorian admirers did not perceive.

Have we then, in Shelley's later reputation, a real paradox or only the illusion of one? Shelley himself would have called it one — but would he have been right in doing so? Few will deny the grandeur, in itself, of what the Victorians admired as great, even though the admiration was an evasive one. Is it possible that Shelley offers two adequate bases for abiding admiration — bases which for most generations are mutually exclusive? The answer must lie with critics and biographers yet unborn, who will have achieved a perspective of the times in which this book is written.

Chapter XXXI

REVIEW AND INTERPRETATION

CONTRADICTIONS OF CRITICISM; SHELLEY'S
DOMINANT SENSE OF MISSION; HIS OBJECTS
AND LEADING IDEAS; SOME PECULIARITIES
OF HIS NATURE; HIS POETRY

A DETAILED biography must record all the pertinent facts in their fullness and in the order of occurrence. Now that the primary undertaking of this biography has been concluded, I venture to reassemble and interpret the most important facts, not as accident and time carelessly distributed their original occurrence, but as they fit my personal view of their significance.

When any man is assessed and assigned his proper place in history, it is generally in answer to the following questions: What were the man's purposes and how did he go about fulfilling them? What was his accomplishment? How did he impress his generation? How did he impress succeeding generations, and what is his significance today? These questions can hardly be answered without answering at the same time one that is perhaps even more fundamental: namely, what sort of person *was* he?

At the outset one is impressed by the controversy which has so long enveloped Shelley's name. At least four people who knew Shelley well have said — two of them in print — that he was one of the best men who ever lived and was, in sober fact, something a little more than mortal. But his father and his father's lawyer, after personal experience, called him a lunatic. Southey, who had known and liked him, settled down to the opinion that he was a scoundrel, William Godwin, his father-in-law, believed that he had a complete genius for falsehood. Walter Savage Landor refused to meet him because he disapproved his conduct — and a few years after Shelley's death he had so completely changed his opinion that he expressed his regret to Shelley's widow, sought earnestly to obtain a portrait of the poet, and urged Edward Trelawny to write a biography.

Contemporary journalists who did not know Shelley illustrated the same violent differences. One of the magazines indexed a casual reference to him as " Shelley, Percy Bysshe — an unmentionable subject." No other English poet of any importance ever experienced the combined volume and intensity of denunciation which Shelley experienced from a number of the most influential journals of his day. At the same time other journalists were praising him for his genius and high ideals, and one — Leigh Hunt — was asserting that he was a man whose private life was an extraordinary mixture of gentleness, benevolence, and good deeds. When Shelley died, one journal gloated that " Shelley, the writer of some infidel poetry is dead — now he knows whether there is a God or no," while another praised him as a " divine-minded " friend, and " friend of the universe." At the time of his death, and even before, magazine poets were hailing him as one of the great liberating spirits of the age — and others were publishing verses deploring his wasted and perverted life.

For almost a hundred years this sharp clash of opinion may be heard. The followers of Robert Owen, leader of a sect which was later to evolve into modern Socialism, habitually quoted from his works as a sort of Bible. Robert Browning in his first published poem addressed Shelley in an enthusiastic apostrophe as the great " Sun-treader." Charles Kingsley, on the other hand, accused Shelley of preaching " the worship of uncleanness as the last and highest ethical development of a ' pure ' humanity." Thomas Carlyle once interrupted a friend's panegyric on Shelley with the vigorous assertion: " Yon man Shelley was nothing but a scoundrel and ought to have been hangèd." And yet, by the time this last remark was made, statements had been published by at least one or two responsible critics in four different

European countries — England, Germany, France, and Italy — that Shelley was one of the two or three really great and enduring spirits of the nineteenth century. A great Victorian editor commissioned an artist to retouch Leonardo da Vinci's conception of the young man Christ and offered it seriously in two books as a portrait of Shelley.

The questions I proposed to attempt answering must be answered clearly indeed if the answers are to harmonize or explain this dissonance of a hundred years. But one important point is demonstrated by the dissonance itself. Its vitality and heat prove that the essence of yon man Shelley — if I can only make it clear — was certainly nothing superficial. To a certain extent he was to a good many people either a kind of Christ or a kind of Antichrist.

OUR first question was: What was this man trying to do? To anyone closely acquainted with his letters, his life, and his published work, the answer is clear — even though two generations of Victorian admirers almost succeeded in evading it. Stated briefly, Shelley was out to reform the world. He frankly acknowledged, in the preface of his greatest poem, *Prometheus Unbound*, what he called " a passion for reforming the world." How this passion arose, how it developed and changed, and what it involved, are our first and most important topics.

The origin of Shelley's master passion carries us back to his boyhood and youth. In 1792, when Shelley was born, the French Revolution was blowing like an irresistible gale against the rotten political and social structure which the eighteenth century had considered stable and enduring. Refugees from France were landing on the Sussex coast from every sort of boat, many of them passing within a mile or two of the Shelley home on their way up to London. William Godwin, Shelley's future father-in-law, was just finishing his *Political Justice*, the strongest, most lucid, most logical, and most highly priced of all the books which sought to remodel the whole structure of society in the spirit of revolutionary Reason. Burke had turned his eloquence against the Revolution, and Tom Paine had published in its defence his *The Rights of Man*. Mary Wollstonecraft was just publishing another revolutionary book, *The Rights of Woman*. Even in Sussex, one of the quietest and most conservative of English counties, whose slow-moving countrymen had a favourite saying: "We won't be druv," the future poet could hardly escape breathing the atmosphere of excitement and change that enveloped all of western Europe. It showed no particular signs of its effect on him, however, until he was about nineteen, ready to enter college.

Meanwhile he had been growing up in a household surrounded by younger sisters to whom he was a leader. All the anecdotes of his early boyhood emphasize his imaginative and emotional sensitiveness and his precocity. A few hard-headed people who knew him casually in boyhood and youth thought him a little crazy. From early days he was an extensive reader. Then and later he was extremely susceptible to influences from books. He read rapidly, with a quick comprehension and a most tenacious memory.

Some of these influences from books were quite peculiar and persistent and of considerable importance in determining his conduct. Among the first books he read, one notices Robert Paltock's novel, *Peter Wilkins*. The hero of this novel was a kind of Promethean light-bringer to an island populated by a mysterious, semi-human folk. Two of his children were adopted by royalty. At once we hear of the boy Shelley, mounted on his pony, scouring the countryside for a little gypsy girl to adopt. Until four years before his death he never quite gave up the notion of adopting a little girl. Just before his own daughter Clara was born, he did adopt a little girl as far as it was possible to adopt a child whose parents were living. Immediately after the death of his small daughter he adopted another little girl at Naples under such strange circumstances that for about a hundred years scholars have been puzzled by what they called the "mystery at Naples." This proneness to suggestion, as we shall see later, seems in some cases to be connected with delusions and in others with fixed ideas.

Shelley's greatest youthful reading was in the Gothic novel, that extraordinary class of fiction which our forefathers for two

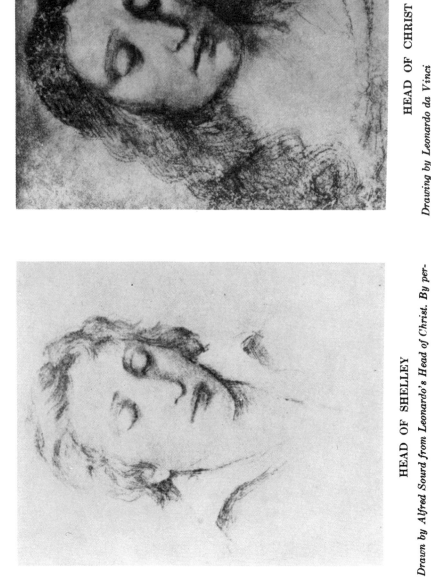

HEAD OF CHRIST

Drawing by Leonardo da Vinci

HEAD OF SHELLEY

Drawn by Alfred Sourd from Leonardo's Head of Christ. By per-

mission of Mr. M. B. Forman

generations read more avidly than we read its lineal descendant, the modern mystery story. In the Gothic novel all was
mystery, horror, violent action, and dull description. One notes
in the various anecdotes of Shelley's boyhood the prominence
of disguise, mystery, magic, and violent sensational ideas and
experiments. As late as 1815, when he was twenty-three years
old, Shelley was planning, in the manner of the sensational
novel, to abduct " two heiresses " from a boarding-school. In
these novels the tyrannical father, the maiden to be rescued,
the scheming, unscrupulous priest, were as common as black-
berries. Whether or not any causal relationship can be demonstrated, it is a fact that the tyrannous father, the maiden to be
rescued from oppression, and the conception of priests as evil,
self-seeking schemers soon became extremely prominent in Shelley's actual life.

Here was a youth who by reason of sensitiveness, intellectual
superiority, and physical unpreparedness was singularly unfitted for the brutalities of English public-school life. It was
to him

> a harsh and grating strife
> Of tyrants and of foes.

At some time before his nineteenth year he came to a remarkable
decision. He decided that he would devote his whole life to
a warfare against the oppressions which it seemed to him dominated all human society. A few years later, in two poems
("Hymn to Intellectual Beauty," 1816, and "Dedication" to
The Revolt of Islam, 1817), Shelley definitely described this
moment in his life:

> So, without shame I spake: — I will be wise
> And just, and free and mild, if in me lies
> Such power, for I grow weary to behold
> The selfish and the strong still tyrannize
> Without reproach or check.

This is from the Dedicatory poem to *The Revolt of Islam*; in
the parallel account of the same moment which is a part of the
"Hymn to Intellectual Beauty" he called upon "a thousand

hours of study" to bear witness to the zeal with which he had kept his vow and had sought to equip himself for its fulfilment.

How do we know that this autobiographical testimony is not mere rationalizing — that this young man, several years after embarking on a course, did not decide merely that it would be a good idea to provide that course with an earlier, more definite starting-point? The really important thing, the resolution itself, is abundantly evident in most of Shelley's later conduct and expressions. He referred to it later in both poems and letters. As a matter of fact, there are external indications that the story must be true in detail as Shelley told it. The time is not definitely fixed, but would appear to be either while Shelley was at Syon House Academy or a year or two before he left Eton College to enter Oxford. After the latter time it is easy enough to see in Shelley's conduct that the youth had a dominant purpose similar to the one he ascribed to himself.

At about the same time he happened to pick up in the streets a loose sheet from an old magazine, containing a translation of Schubart's German poem on the Wandering Jew, a character with whom Shelley had already formed a slight acquaintance in Lewis's *The Monk*. Here we have another instance of something like a fixed idea suggested by reading. Immediately this poem made a powerful impression on his mind. The Wandering Jew became almost at once for him the symbol of Heaven's eternal, unrelenting vengeance on one who was a rebel against its authority. That Shelley later thought this a false authority is a commonplace, but it is significant that he must have thought so *at this time* to be so tremendously impressed by the symbol. His first inquiry at the Bodleian Library was an effort to get more information about this poem. At different times during the next few years he made copies of it. He immediately wrote a poem of his own on the subject; he quoted a part of the translation in the notes to his *Queen Mab;* throughout his poems for the rest of his whole life one finds occasional allusions to the Wandering Jew; several of his best-known shorter poems slightly echo the language of the original translation. The Wandering Jew appears as a character in his first long poem, *Queen Mab*, and in the last poem he published, *Hellas*.

At the very time that Shelley discovered the Wandering Jew, his first love-affair was beginning to drift into disaster, obviously because of his unorthodox opinions. Harriet Grove was fond of her cousin, but she was certainly no young revolutionary. The informal engagement was definitely broken off during the Christmas vacation, shortly after Shelley had entered Oxford. Shelley was wild with disappointment; his letters on the subject to his new-found bosom friend, Thomas Jefferson Hogg, are almost incoherent with his sense of oppression. In the midst of one of the wildest of these outbursts Shelley adopted as his own, obviously without realizing it, a whole sentence from Schubart's " The Wandering Jew." In his view he was the victim of two oppressions, one parental, the other religious. His earlier acquaintance with parental tyranny in the Gothic novel was now reinforced by the authority of William Godwin, one of whose tenets was that parental authority is often unjustified and tyrannous. The works of his future father-in-law had only a few months earlier stimulated Shelley to an admiration destined to become far more disastrous than his broken engagement. But it was Religion that Shelley held to be his principal enemy. Here, within a year or so of his original self-dedication, we get another one fully as impassioned, in a letter to Hogg. This time there can be no question at all of reality:

O! I burn with impatience for the moment of Christianity's dissolution; it has injured me. I swear on the altar of perjured Love to revenge myself on the hated cause of the effect. . . . Indeed I think it is to the benefit of society to destroy the opinion which can annihilate the dearest of its ties.

The idea that parental and religious tyranny are naturally and viciously allied forms the basis of Shelley's powerful *The Cenci*, written nine years after he first felt himself their victim.

The inextricably complicated interactions of many diverse and apparently unrelated circumstances which flow together to make the motives for an individual life are not to be diagrammed too dogmatically. No one could possibly possess all the evidence for doing so. But with due allowance for probable incompleteness and exaggeration, I submit that the transition in Shelley from an affectionate, extraordinarily bright and sensitive small boy to a youth with a conviction of oppression and a feverishly intense mission for quelling tyrannies and establishing freedom is accounted for by the circumstances I have mentioned. A highly suggestive mind had merged with the theoretical world of French revolutionary literature and the sensational world of Gothic romance; and the colouring it had thus acquired was intensified and made fast by unfortunate personal experience.

IT is just possible the youth might in time have forgotten his self-dedication if it had not been followed so soon by his expulsion from Oxford and the hopeless estrangement from his father. After this there was no change; his life was almost completely dominated by his purpose. Soon after his expulsion he eloped with Harriet Westbrook, a young schoolgirl whom he did not love until later, because it was the only way to rescue her from parental and pedagogic tyranny. He brought into his household Elizabeth Hitchener, a Sussex school-teacher with emancipated views, whom he expected to become a fellow emancipator with himself and Harriet. When he became disillusioned he got rid of her, but his numerous and zealous letters to her testify to the strength of his enthusiasm for their common purposes. His young wife shared his views at first and studied hard to fit herself for her rôle. Eventually, however, it became evident to both that she could not keep the pace. Her first child was born, and her views (probably much influenced by her dominating older sister) changed radically. Shelley experienced a brief period of miserable struggle between natural affection and duty on one side (for love was probably dying) and all that he hoped to accomplish in life — and for a moment duty and affection seemed victorious.

Then Shelley met Mary Godwin, the daughter of William Godwin and Mary Wollstonecraft, in his opinion the two most godlike people of the age. She seemed the ideal partner for his life's purpose, and she was also the victim of the second Mrs. Godwin's parental tyranny. She encouraged his love, and then, frightened, sought vainly and against her own will to discourage it. The elopement that followed was the result of a domination too strong for either to resist. I would not say that the sole reason for deserting Harriet and eloping with Mary was the unfitness of the one and the fitness of the other for Shelley's ruling purpose in life, but it is assuredly one very important reason. The journals kept from this time until after Shelley's death by both Mary and Claire Clairmont (who came into the family with Mary) are devoted largely to their reading and study, which was conducted mainly under Shelley's direction and was designed to fit them for their rôles as emancipators. Shelley was doing the same thing for himself throughout his whole life. He read and studied assiduously, with extraordinary penetration and memory, and his range included seven languages — English, French, German, Italian, Spanish, Latin, and Greek.

Previous to his elopement with Mary Godwin, Shelley had lost no opportunity of advancing his declared purpose. He had tried to aid Peter Finnerty, an oppressed Irish journalist; he had printed an eloquent letter to Lord Ellenborough protesting against the unjust sentence of Daniel Isaac Eaton for radical publications; he had tried to start a public subscription for Leigh Hunt and his brother when they were imprisoned for telling the truth about the Prince Regent; he had sought to raise money for the families of Yorkshire workmen who had been executed for frame-breaking; he had given time and money to building the Tremadoc Embankment, which was to reclaim thousands of acres from the sea and put them (as Shelley first thought) to philanthropic use; and he had spent some months in Ireland seeking to ameliorate the condition of an oppressed people. He had printed copies of a Declaration of Rights, and a servant of his had been imprisoned for posting them on walls; he had addressed a great public meeting in Ireland, published two addresses to the Irish People, and printed (but *not* published) a long revolutionary poem, *Queen Mab* — all between the ages of nineteen and twenty-two.

Critics who have treated some of this activity as irresponsible

and ridiculous have missed the most important fact in emphasizing a minor and even doubtful one. The important fact is
the guiding purpose, amounting almost to an obsession. Certainly some of the attendant circumstances are ridiculous —
such as dropping leaflets from a balcony in Dublin and setting
documents afloat in bottles. Certainly the financial aspects of
most of these adventures were reckless and irresponsible, nor
did Shelley ever achieve any reasonably consistent financial
prudence before his twenty-eighth year, in Pisa. But not even
the Irish episode was as quixotic as it has been commonly pictured. In the two addresses to the Irish people you will find no
violent and reckless suggestions, no demands that have not long
since been granted and that would not be regarded today as
moderate, no expectation of quick political miracles, no hope
of progress that is not based upon an improvement in the education, temperance, and tolerance to be achieved by the Irish
themselves.

After his elopement with Mary Godwin there were times
when the all-consuming purpose had to be laid aside temporarily for reasons of health, money, or personal and family
difficulties. The whole social, political, and economic pattern
which Shelley believed in so many respects to be wrong, but
which nevertheless was the framework within which he must
live, was far from sympathetic with his activities. The resentment of William Godwin (oddly combined with his demands
for money); the estrangement from his father's family; the mis-
management of his finances; the suicides of his dear friend
Fanny Imlay and his legal wife, Harriet; the Chancery suit
which deprived him of his children by his first wife and made
him fear a criminal prosecution; the deadly venom with which
the conservative reviewers convinced a majority of their readers
that he was a moral monster; the death of two children in Italy;
a secret rift in his happiness with his second wife that drove
him for a short time almost insane — these and other circumstances limited and at times intermitted the prosecution of his
self-imposed mission. Though he may be justly accused of something like a persecution complex, there was considerable real
basis for the feeling. In *Adonais* he described himself as

> a herd-abandoned deer, struck by the hunter's dart,

and

> A Love in desolation masked; a Power
> Girt round with weakness. . . .

Yet even in his deepest personal despair, which is represented by his poem " Julian and Maddalo," Shelley refers in one place to the moment of self-dedication he had already described in two poems, and in another he says that personal misfortune will never stop his opposition to tyranny and oppression.

Since the spring of 1818 Shelley had been living in Italy, but his interest in English affairs continued. Just before leaving England he had written two pamphlets advocating reform. In Italy he wrote his " Mask of Anarchy " to denounce the Manchester Massacre; he wrote (as he had written before) to reprove Wordsworth's desertion of the liberal cause; and he sent back from Italy a long letter which he asked Leigh Hunt to print in the *Examiner* condemning the sentence of Richard Carlile for publishing radical literature. Every abortive Italian and Spanish revolt against oppression that took place during his life was hailed in his poetry as a sign of better times. The Greek War of Independence caused him to write *Hellas,* the last poem that he published.

It may be truly said that Shelley's whole life was astonishingly — even terribly — consistent with his youthful self-dedication. " I always go on until I am stopped," he once remarked quite simply, "and I never am stopped." It has been said of him that his principal difference from other people was that he *practised* his professed beliefs. How far he dared go may be seen from his willingness to share both Harriet and Mary with Hogg, a willingness defeated only by Harriet's scruples and (in Mary's case, one believes) by circumstances. It is still true, however, as he protested to Byron, that he regarded some of his beliefs as valid ideals, but as impracticable in the society in which he lived.

BUT while Shelley was invariably true to his sense of mission, a significant change is to be observed in his own view of the mission. Prior to 1815 he was impetuous and headlong. It still seemed possible that direct, personal action could accomplish some immediate, significant change. Even then he realized *with his mind* that the process of human betterment was a long, slow process, as his Irish pamphlets show. His impetuous character, however, often decided his conduct rather than his more sober reason. But in August 1815 he wrote to his friend Hogg that he was trying to become more dispassionate and more historical-minded in his judgment of the political events of the day. Something over a year later he wrote to Leigh Hunt: " I am undeceived in the belief that I have powers deeply to interest, or substantially to improve mankind. . . . Perhaps I should have shrunk from persisting in the task which I had undertaken in early life, of opposing myself in these evil times and among these evil tongues, to what I esteem misery and vice."

This tempering of Shelley's earlier impetuosity appears to have begun in Ireland. His expulsion from Oxford and his estrangement from his father had scarcely affected it, because they had really interfered very little with his chosen way of living. In Ireland he obtained at first hand a perfectly appalling view of the evils he had set out to correct. By his own testimony, he was sobered and dejected, but he was not stopped. A much greater sobering factor, because it altered his personal life and seriously interfered for a time with his mission, was the immediate result of his elopement with Mary. Bailiffs harried him, old friends silently fell away or sneered at him. Harriet behaved with a strange antagonistic stubbornness which he could not reconcile with principles he could not doubt, and Godwin, his spiritual godfather, spurned him with a loathing and disgust that seemed a betrayal of principles they had held in common. Had this situation not been lightened by the opportune death of his grandfather, Shelley's elopement with Mary must in the end have proved as disastrous to his hopes as life with Harriet had become.

But the greatest shock came some months after the letter quoted above, with the deaths of Harriet and of Fanny Imlay. One was certainly and the other probably an indirect result of Shelley's second elopement. He was fond of Fanny Imlay and

had loved Harriet. He could see nothing wrong in his impetuous elopement, and yet it had led to Harriet's death and possibly
Fanny's. Shelley was deeply shaken. He had only Mary and
his own invincible sense of rectitude to sustain him. If he permitted the latter to falter he was ruined. I believe this is a partial explanation of the unadmirable account of Harriet's death
which he sent to Mary from London. Yet even to Shelley it was
clear that a headlong action he still regarded as right and necessary had resulted fatally. He regarded himself as the victim of
circumstances and of malicious misinterpretation, but thereafter
he was no longer unrestrained, even in prosecuting his mission.

About a year later he published his longest poem, *The Revolt of Islam,* designed to present a picture of a true revolution
in human society that would avoid the errors which had made
the French Revolution a partial failure. The revolution he described was in fact stamped out in the end by the forces of reaction, after a brief period of success. This fact is explained by
the fable with which Shelley introduced the poem — a fable
describing the never ending conflict between a serpent, representing good, and an eagle, representing evil. In the particular
phase of this eternal conflict described in the fable, evil is triumphant, but the poet is assured by a prophetess that the defeat
is only temporary — the serpent perpetually recruits its strength
and perpetually returns to the conflict. A similar view is stated
in Shelley's preface, where he proclaims his confidence, not in
a rapid, miraculous improvement of society, but in what he calls
" a slow, gradual, silent change."

We follow this moderated view still further, to *Prometheus
Unbound,* commonly regarded as Shelley's greatest poem, written two years afterwards, in 1818–19. It was in the preface to
this poem that he confessed to the desire to reform the world,
which I quoted earlier. " But it is a mistake," he continued,
" to suppose that I dedicate my poetical compositions solely to
the direct enforcement of reform, or that I consider them in any
degree as containing a reasoned system on the theory of human
life. Didactic poetry is my abhorrence. . . . My purpose has
hitherto been simply to familiarize the highly refined imagination of the more select classes of poetical readers with beautiful

431

idealisms of moral excellence, aware that until the mind can love and admire and trust and hope and endure, reasoned principles of moral conduct are seeds cast upon the highway of life which the unconscious passenger tramples into the dust."

The meaning of this explanation becomes clearer when we examine the grounds on which Shelley based his belief, stated in his " Defence of Poetry " (1821), that poetry is the great enlightener of the human spirit, a force which " lifts the veil from the hidden beauty of the world," and makes of poets the " unacknowledged legislators of mankind." This was so, he believed, because poetry was the most authentic voice of the imagination — and the imagination, with Shelley as with Wordsworth and Coleridge, was an almost divine quality of the human mind. It could at times perceive almost by intuition truths not perceptible to the ordinary reason operating within long-familiar boundaries. Only as the imagination enlarged mental boundaries and refined human sympathies and perceptions could ordinary reason develop new territory. Only by imagination could we use wisely the immense store of technical knowledge whose tendency otherwise was merely to exaggerate social and economic inequalities.

In pursuing this point Shelley furnishes incidentally the reason for his repeated statements that he abhorred what he called " didactic " poetry. For as an ordinary man the poet was bound to be influenced by his human environment of time, place, and class; but as a mouthpiece of the imagination he was above his environment. Consequently, if he attempted to prescribe too specifically for his generation — that is, to be didactic — he was liable to error. The imagination, on the other hand, taught men *how* to think and feel justly, not specifically *what* to think and feel.

It is a far cry from this mature point of view to his early rather quixotic forays into direct action and the vigorous didacticism of his first long poem, *Queen Mab.* In *Queen Mab* it seemed a relatively simply matter to free the human spirit by destroying certain institutions. In *Prometheus Unbound* Shelley realizes that the evil is in the very mind of man. The worst torture that Prometheus has to endure is the sight of Christ on the cross and the perception that Christ's agony proceeds from the knowledge that his good principles will be turned to evil purposes. The final victory of Prometheus is not possible until he has recalled his curse upon Jupiter and abjured revenge. As in *The Revolt of Islam*, Shelley is able no longer to regard any victory over evil as final except within time limitations. The last speech in the poem points out that in time the forces of evil may again control the world, but they can always be reconquered by repeating the experience of Prometheus. This is no easy formula, but an agonizing ordeal:

> To suffer woes which Hope thinks infinite;
> To forgive wrongs darker than death or night;
>   To defy Power, which seems omnipotent;
> To love and bear; to hope till Hope creates
> From its own wreck the thing it contemplates;
>   Neither to change, nor falter, nor repent;
> This, like thy glory, Titan, is to be
> Good, great and joyous, beautiful and free;
> This is alone Life, Joy, Empire, and Victory.

The numerous frustrating forces of life which Shelley had to stop and deal with, when viewed in connection with this vastly increased respect for the difficulties of his mission, and his growing feeling of personal inadequacy to it, might easily lead to the conclusion that after about 1815 his sense of mission was no longer the controlling motive of his life. In fact he had made no real change in purpose or direction; the changes were only in emphasis, speed, and method of procedure. The evils which he condemned in *Queen Mab*, with one or two trifling exceptions such as the evil of eating flesh, were the same evils that he condemned to the end of his life. The remedies for these evils were in general the same, and the virtues he sought to cultivate were the same. Hope, which Wordsworth had called " the paramount duty," was always so for Shelley, though an enlarged experience and knowledge of human depravity and fallibility made it no longer the easy duty it had once been. In Italy, at a time of personal depression, he began wearing a ring with the inscription: " *Il buon tempo verrà* " — the good time will come. In *Hellas*, the last long poem that he published, he declares:

433

> Life may change, but it may fly not;
> Hope may vanish, but can die not;
> Truth be veiled, but still it burneth;
> Love repulsed — but it returneth —

and adds in the next two stanzas that the soul of all these forces is liberty, without which they are powerless and dead.

FROM what has been said already about Shelley's distrust of didactic poetry and the moderation which he learned to apply to his expectations of life, one would look for his more specific notions of reform in his prose and in his earlier poems. This is in fact where we find them. Let us now see what they are.

Christianity was for Shelley probably the greatest single despoiler of the human spirit. *Queen Mab* began with a motto that had been Voltaire's battle-cry against Catholicism: "*Écrasez l'infâme*" — crush the scoundrel. Long after Shelley could properly be described as an atheist — if the term was ever quite applicable to him — he wrote *atheos* after his name in more than one hotel album, mainly to signify his opposition to Christianity. As he later told Edward Trelawny, he accepted the appellation of atheist as a gage of battle. This error in tactics cost him dearly, for the *atheos* inscription was copied by Robert Southey and repeated in the public journals.

At first Shelley's opposition to Christianity included Christ himself, all the supernatural part of fundamental Christian doctrine, and the Christian Church as an institution. Soon, however, he developed a veneration for Christ as one of the greatest human spirits. Two of Shelley's own most emphatic principles — namely, forgiveness of injuries, and the necessity of opposing brute force by spiritual resistance only — have always been too intensely Christian even for most professing Christians to achieve. In his mature poems when Shelley attacks Christianity he means only the human institution which has grown up around Christianity, and the actual practices in the name of Christianity which went on around him. The institution was in his eyes a vested interest, a collection of robber-priests who exploited a vicious fable for their own selfish interests and mercilessly exterminated all enlightening dissent. Their Old Testament God seemed to him, as to Tom Paine and other revolutionists, an imaginary bloody tyrant whom they had set up to debase men's minds to their own selfish ends.

To an equal or almost equal extent Shelley hated political tyranny, or kingship, as he called it. Kings were drones and wastrels who supported luxurious establishments, corrupted morals, maintained favourites, built useless, extravagant monuments, constricted the lives and liberties of millions of people, and led them into murderous wars — merely to feed their own luxury or vanity. Kings and priests were almost invariably in alliance against true freedom. About them clustered a privileged class of money-lenders, traders, and military officers whose interests were practically identical with theirs. A whole system of corrupt customs had been built up by successive generations of these tyrannies; Custom itself, as an abstraction, was their ally.

Various individual customs were tremendous shackles upon the natural rights of humanity. One of the most vicious of these was the system of finance and commerce, which promoted the taste for luxury, with ensuing depravities, and also caused unnecessary want and misery. Another was the institution of marriage. " A system could not well have been devised more hostile to human happiness than marriage," he declared. Yet he himself married twice, contrary to his own creed, because he did not wish his principles to be the instrument of suffering to others. Marriage could have no binding moral force, he maintained, any longer than both parties were happy within its bonds. Beyond that point it became an intolerable tyranny. It was the principal reason for the degradations of prostitution and the generally enslaved state of women.

All these views appear most fully and vigorously in *Queen Mab* and its notes, but with less emphasis they are to be found again and again in Shelley's more mature poems, until his death. Obviously they are not at all unique; they are a quintessence of all the radicalisms of the later eighteenth century. Undoubtedly in its earliest expressions Shelley's radicalism laid far too much stress on the evils inherent in institutions and too little on that inherent in the human nature which created the institutions. His more mature poems corrected this error — but found the same institutions still evil. Even in the early poems he emphasized the value of the positive virtues of frugality, benevolence, knowledge, courage, and endurance. A considerable mass of testimony shows that he sought personally to exercise them himself and encourage them in others. As his knowledge and experience developed he tended more and more to perceive that the important thing was to stimulate the imagination to perceive beauty and freedom for what it was, and to encourage the will-power to attain them through knowledge, hope, and endurance. He no longer believed, like the psalmist, that the ungodly are not so. He now perceived that the final citadel of evil was in the human mind itself and could be vanquished only by the enlightened will. " It is our will," he says several times in different phrasings:

It is our will
That thus enchains us to permitted ill.

Shelley's steady opposition to violence in revolutionary changes was based probably upon his conviction that violence perpetuated the very vices upon which all injustice was founded. Like Wordsworth and Coleridge, he believed that the partial disintegration of the French Revolution was due to the spirit of violence with which it was prosecuted. He also believed, long before Gandhi, that non-violence was good revolutionary tactics. Soldiers were hirelings, he maintained, but they were also men, who could not submerge altogether their fellow-feeling with other men. By training they would shoot and stab whoever opposed or fled from them; but if faced by an unyielding, but non-violent opposition, they would pause and think, and eventually come over to the people.

Shelley's poetry represented an ideal, which he hoped might be at least partly achieved, but only when and if men's minds were ready for it. In some of his prose one may see that his view of what was immediately to be recommended was quite different. He believed the suffrage laws should be liberalized, but not yet to the point of including women, or even all men. Civil disabilities for religious reasons should be abolished at once. Tithes should also be abolished. Like Cobbett, he believed that the national debt had become an intolerable burden upon the people of England; it should be liquidated by an assessment on all the physical property in the island. The Union with Ireland should be repealed. Kingship should be retained until it was possible to end it without civil warfare. On almost any of the moderate reforms that he thought immediately needed he professed himself ready to compromise, provided only enough reform were accomplished to keep alive the determination to achieve the others in time, without the bloodshed that might nullify their value.

Shelley practised one form of radicalism which he did not particularly seek to propagate. He believed that Custom always degraded language and modes of expression just as it debased institutions and conduct. Words, like creeds, naturally wore smooth and meaningless and lost their original brightness. It was the function of poets to revitalize language as well as thoughts. With Shelley this was a common practice rather than a mission. It took the form of unusual figures of speech, and the use of symbols for suggesting a meaning beyond the worn literal meaning of words alone. Caves, veils, clouds, streams, and boats have generally a symbolic meaning in Shelley. The frequent charges of obscurity brought against such poems as *Prometheus Unbound* and *Epipsychidion* are partly due to this practice, the purpose of which Shelley never made quite clear. For the modern reader, who is much less inclined than Shelley's contemporaries to use Pope as a poetic yardstick, the so-called obscurities of Shelley offer only incidental difficulties; but even the modern reader does not fully recognize that they are a logical extension of Shelley's general philosophy and are an expression of a curious, consistent mental subtlety rather than of careless or cloudy thinking.

It should now be quite clear why Shelley was, of all the major English poets, the one most hated and feared by conservative contemporary reviewers. These reviewers were no more stupid than most people are in a period of crisis and transition. During

the decade 1812–22, in which most of Shelley's publishing occurred, English public journals were oppressed with an extreme and justifiable fear, either of foreign invasion or of domestic revolution. Any attack upon settled institutions seemed
to increase the danger. There was more radicalism among
gifted writers than ever before — the Poet Laureate sounded
a public warning against them as the Satanic School. Most of
these writers, however, as usual, were radical only in certain
respects and conservative in others. Shelley alone was radical
in his religious, social, economic, and political beliefs and also
in his poetic technique. The remarkable thing is that under
these circumstances Shelley was appreciated by practically as
many journals as attacked him.

I HAVE not yet discussed two of the most peculiar aspects of
Shelley's beliefs, which are under the surface pretty much the
same — his worship of Intellectual Beauty and his philosophy
of Love. Under the dominance of eighteenth-century materialistic philosophy Shelley's god at the time he wrote *Queen Mab*
was Necessity. This was simply the belief that an impersonal
force called Necessity ruled all thought and action through a
chain of consequences which led back to the first moment of
time and prescribed everything irrevocably. Such a force left
little scope for freedom of the will, which Shelley wished to
assert at the same time; and it was too negative and impersonal
for Shelley's impulsive, sympathetic nature. By the time he
wrote *Alastor* (1815) he was already searching for a more satisfactory deity. When he wrote his "Hymn to Intellectual
Beauty" (June 30, 1816) he had found his goddess and had
named her Intellectual Beauty, which is about the same thing
as the Platonic ideal Beauty. Later Shelley often called her
Love, but the difference is more in name than in nature.

Intellectual Beauty was to Shelley an ideal of beauty and
sympathy capable of being dimly recognized by the mind, but
far too intensely bright ever to be seen except through various
veils of human thought. In his "Hymn to Intellectual Beauty"
Shelley emphasizes both its practical remoteness and its power:

> The awful *shadow* of some *unseen* Power
> Floats though *unseen* amongst us, — visiting
> This various world with an *inconstant* wing
> As summer winds that creep from flower to flower.

This inconstant shadow of an unseen loveliness, he goes on to say, touches every human heart; but it also vanishes, and its absence causes human misery. If it could only be established firmly in the human heart, misery could be abolished, for even its fitful and veiled appearance is what " Gives grace and truth to life's unquiet dream." All the efforts of sages and prophets have been vain attempts to understand why this spirit is so imperfectly in contact with the human spirit, which it could immortalize. The poem closes with a personal testimony of Shelley's own blind groping for this spirit in boyhood and his passionate dedication in early youth to its service — one of the self-dedication passages to which I referred earlier.

From this time on, Intellectual Beauty, or Love, is the goddess whom Shelley's poetry serves with a truly religious devotion. " The Sensitive Plant," one of his best-known shorter poems, would undoubtedly seem to the casual reader to be only a beautiful picture of a garden which is radiant while the Lady who attends it is present, but loathsome with decay in her absence. Possibly the picture is a little sentimental; it is certainly so if taken merely at face value. But the garden is really a little world, and its beautiful lady is really Intellectual Beauty. And within this little world is also the little personal world of the Sensitive Plant — the poet, including the poet Shelley, whose personal world had experienced both happiness and blight as he felt the spiritual companionship or the spiritual alienation — recently experienced — of Mary Shelley.

Prometheus Unbound shows how the human mind, having achieved a victory over evil by " Gentleness, virtue, wisdom and endurance " while keeping alive the love of Intellectual Beauty through almost intolerable sufferings, crowns the victory by a union with this long-separated spirit. It might almost be regarded as a vast dramatic fulfilment of the faith expressed in the " Hymn to Intellectual Beauty." As Asia journeys to join Prometheus she is addressed by a Voice from the air in one of

Shelley's most intense lyrics, in which she is hailed successively as the Life of Life, Child of Light, and Lamp of Earth, whose beauty makes the cold earth fire and is insupportable to human gaze unless veiled.

> Lamp of Earth! where'er thou movest
>   Its dim shapes are clad with brightness,
> And the souls of whom thou lovest
>   Walk upon the winds with lightness,
> Till they fail, as I am failing,
> Dizzy, lost, yet unbewailing!

And when Prometheus greets her she is called:

> Asia, thou light of life,
> Shadow of beauty unbeheld

— that is to say, Intellectual Beauty.

About a year later Shelley could not resist a playful impulse to furnish Intellectual Beauty with a genealogy, a slight sense of mischief, and complete apparatus for taking her station as a new young goddess in the Græco-Roman pantheon. The result was his delicately beautiful poem "The Witch of Atlas." We cannot pause now to wander through its leisurely mazes; one stanza of description must suffice:

> For she was beautiful; her beauty made
>   The bright world dim, and everything beside
> Seemed like the fleeting image of a shade;
>   No thought of living spirit could abide,
> Which to her looks had ever been betrayed,
>   On any object in the world so wide,
> On any hope within the circling skies
> But on her form, and in her inmost eyes.

Seeing which, the Lady wove for herself a magic veil, to shield men from the too great splendour of her beauty.

In *Adonais,* which many critics agree with Shelley in regarding as his "least imperfect poem," Intellectual Beauty is the radiant force which alone remains unchanged in a world that Shelley had come to regard as not really very substantial or significant in the eye of Eternity:

> The One remains, the many change and pass;
>   Heaven's light forever shines, Earth's shadows fly;
> Life, like a dome of many-coloured glass,
>   Stains the white radiance of Eternity,

and, two stanzas later, he returns to the characterization:

> That Light whose smile kindles the Universe,
> That Beauty in which all things work and move,
> That Benediction which the eclipsing Curse
> Of birth can quench not, that sustaining Love
> Which, through the web of being blindly wove
> By man and beast and earth and air and sea,
> Burns bright or dim, as each are mirrors of
> The fire for which all thirst, now beams on me
> Consuming the last clouds of cold mortality.

A still more fervid description of Intellectual Beauty may be found in *Epipsychidion*.

Two poems, *Alastor* (written near the beginning of his career) and *Epipsychidion* (written near its close), present Shelley as actually seeing this goddess in a vision. In the first the young poet who represents Shelley pursued the vision to the exclusion of all human love, and even to his death, without ever being able to clasp in actual life what was physically unattainable. In *Epipsychidion* the same pursuit begins, but turns into a search for a human partner who should be the nearest approximation to his conception of Intellectual Beauty. In veiled language the poem refers to several such episodes in Shelley's life in which he had been invariably disappointed or disillusioned. Then, for one brief, almost insupportable moment, Shelley realizes the fulfilment of his vision in the beautiful Emilia Viviani. Never in all his poetry, and seldom in the whole range of English poetry, occur such impassioned declarations of love as abound in this poem.

It might be interesting to pause here for a brief backward glance at the various women in whom Shelley thought at different times be recognized the shadow of Intellectual Beauty. Harriet Grove, the beautiful, normal-minded cousin whom he loved in youth and never quite ceased idealizing; Elizabeth Hitchener, the Sussex country school-teacher of libertarian views who became in Shelley's words to her "the sister of my soul" and later, in his words about her, "the Brown Demon," and "an ugly, hermaphroditical beast of a woman"; Mary Godwin, the only instance, after the somewhat shadowy episode of Harriet Grove, where intellectual love and physical love coincided for a while; Emilia Viviani, who he soon after confessed had turned out to be a cloud rather than a Juno — their stories comprise no small portion of Shelley's biography. There are two more whose idealizations were probably never quite complete in Shelley's mind: Claire Clairmont, who deserted the possibility of becoming Shelley's spiritual mistress in order to become Byron's physical one, and Jane Williams, to whom some of the most beautiful shorter lyrics of Shelley's last months were written. A few months before the end of his life, in confessing his disillusion in Emilia Viviani, Shelley delivered his own mournful conclusion on such episodes: "I think one is always in love with something or other; the error, and I confess it not easy for spirits cased in flesh and blood to avoid it, consists in seeking in a mortal image the likeness of what is perhaps eternal."

Many readers, critics, and biographers have misunderstood Shelley through putting a false construction upon these idealizations. It is indeed hard to read some of the most intense love-poetry ever written, as in *Epipsychidion,* and not construe it as one normally construes similar poetry that is far less impassioned. But in this poem Shelley himself warns Emilia:

> To whatsoe'er of dull mortality
> Is mine, remain a vestal sister still.

The point was already understood between them, for as Shelley wrote the poem he had before him an essay by Emilia in which she expressed the same idea of love. It was an idea quite similar to that expressed by Plato, Dante, and Petrarch, all of whom Shelley greatly admired. In his much earlier correspondence with Elizabeth Hitchener, Shelley had made the same reservation. In a well-known lyric, addressed either to Emilia Viviani or Jane Williams, he had said plainly:

> One word is too often profaned
> For me to profane it,
> One feeling too falsely disdained
> For thee to disdain it,

concluding:

> I can give not what men call love,
> But wilt thou accept not
> The worship the heart lifts above
> And the Heavens reject not:
> The desire of the moth for the star,
> Of the night for the morrow,
> The devotion to something afar
> From the sphere of our sorrow?

This is for most mortals — even for a Shelley — a dangerous distinction in love, but for Shelley it was a real one, as his words and conduct clearly testify. Harriet Shelley (when he idealized Elizabeth Hitchener) and Mary Shelley (when he idealized Emilia Viviani) both seem to have taken Shelley's words at face value.

If we now turn briefly to Shelley's prose we may see more clearly what he meant by a word which he used almost seven hundred times in his poems. In his fragmentary essay " On Love " he defines it as " that powerful attraction toward all that we conceive, or feel, or hope, beyond ourselves . . . the bond and sanction which connects not only man with man, but with everything that exists." In his " Discourse on the Manners of the Ancients Relative to the Subject of Love " he calls it " a universal thirst for a communion, not only of the senses, but of our whole nature, intellectual, imaginative, and sensitive "; and in his " Defence of Poetry " as " a going out of our own nature, and an identification of ourselves with the beautiful which exists in thought, action, or person not our own."

The biological and sensational function of love was for Shelley " what men call love," and is nowhere rejected by him; it was merely a different thing from spiritual love, on a far different, and inferior, plane of living. As may be seen from his definitions, Shelleyan love was simply an intense longing for

complete sympathy. The highest love between two human beings was their common perception, in each other, of the shadow
of Intellectual Beauty and their common aspiration toward a
more complete unity with Intellectual Beauty. The thirst for
Intellectual Beauty and the desire to free oneself, and the world,
from evil and ignorance were really one and the same thing.
That is why, in the "Hymn to Intellectual Beauty," Shelley
describes his youthful awakening to a sense of mission as a devotion to Intellectual Beauty, and in the prefatory poem to *The
Revolt of Islam* describes it as the beginning of a crusade against
tyranny. And that is why, in summarizing my impression of this
unique personality, I have concentrated so largely on emphasizing its truly amazing unity and consistency.

How could this emphasis be true of a man whose biography
furnishes so many anecdotes of eccentric behaviour, a man who
seemed to his intimates the victim of so many illusions, a man
who was regarded by so many people in his youth as slightly
crazy, who believed that his father wished to place him in an
insane asylum, and who represented three of his palpably autobiographical characters as passing through periods of madness?

It is a commonplace which every layman will accept that
madness, after all, is but an extreme variation from normal men-
tality, and may be caused, among other things, by a subnormal
or a supernormal capacity for emotional, sensational, and intellectual excitement. No one supposes that Shelley was subnormal in these respects; but it can easily be shown that in all
of them he was highly supernormal. It would be hard to find
anywhere any more intense emotional sensitivity than one finds
in *Epipsychidion* or "Julian and Maddalo," or some of Shelley's
early letters to Hogg or Elizabeth Hitchener. In "Julian and
Maddalo" he speaks of himself as

> a nerve o'er which do creep
> The else unfelt oppressions of this earth.

From a letter to William Godwin one glimpses the pathological
extremes of physical sensation of which Shelley was capable,
especially in ill health:

" My feelings at intervals are of a deadly and torpid kind, or awakened to a state of such unnatural and keen excitement, that, only to instance the organ of sight, I find the very blades of grass and the boughs of distant trees present themselves to me with microscopical distinctness."

But it is the intensity of his mental reactions that is most remarkable. As a small boy he could read a poem once, and then repeat it. During the last year of his life his friend Trelawny once saw him standing in front of a mantelpiece reading a book, with his untasted breakfast or lunch on a plate beside the book. Returning hours later to dinner, Trelawny noticed that his friend's position was exactly the same as before; and when he urged Shelley to come in to dinner, Shelley remarked absently that he had just finished his dinner, and pointed to the still untasted meal that Trelawny had observed earlier.

This quality of utter absorption in what was going on in his mind was undoubtedly the cause of many of the odd incidents which Shelley's friend Hogg told later simply as amusing anecdotes. It is also very closely connected with the unusual suggestibility mentioned earlier. As a child he was constantly trying to re-create in his physical world the experiences he had encountered only in his world of reading or imagination. This is not unusual with highly imaginative children, but with Shelley it lasted throughout life. Those critics, like Francis Thompson, who have regarded Shelley as the Eternal Child were partly right. His direct manner of discussing, as remembered by young Thornton Hunt, his confraternity with the Newton and Hunt children, his frequent disregard of conventional considerations, and the significant connections to be observed between his boyhood ideas and conduct and those of his later life, all argue that in his maturity Shelley retained far more of his childhood than is usual. Much of what is commonly called abnormal in Shelley is probably explicable on this basis. The only error in this point of view is the rather serious one that the " child " was at the same time an adult with an extremely subtle and comprehending mind.

Children are far more likely than adults to abolish convention and confound the actual world with a world of their own imagining. If a child could read extensively and still "imagine things," he would draw many of his confusions of fact and reality from books, as Shelley did. Shelley's elopement with Harriet Westbrook rather closely resembles the conduct of the hero and heroine of a novel that Harriet had persuaded him to read only a week or two earlier; at three separate times thereafter he seemed to be trying to walk in the very footsteps of Fleetwood, the hero of one of Godwin's novels which he especially admired; at another time he seemed to have identified himself with Godwin's Caleb Williams to the extent of believing himself in danger of assassination from a wholly imaginary pursuer. Fanny Imlay even accused him of acting or thinking from novels, and Alfred Boinville expressed a similar suggestion about Shelley's elopement with Mary. His feeling of martyrdom was at times so strong that he told of three separate personal assaults that he had sustained in Keswick, at Tremadoc, and in Pisa. Of these assaults the first may possibly have occurred, though the neighbours doubted it; but the second and third were quite imaginary. Yet Shelley believed for several years that he still suffered from an injury sustained in one of these imaginary assaults, which were for him more real than physical facts. "No man," Mary Shelley once remarked with great insight, "had such keen sensations as Shelley. His nervous temperament was wound up by the delicacy of his health to an intense degree of sensibility, and while his active mind pondered for ever upon, and drew conclusions from his sensations, his reveries increased their vivacity till they mingled with, and made one with thought, and both became absorbing and tumultuous, even to physical pain."

One of Shelley's autobiographical characters, the Madman in "Julian and Maddalo," speaks of his acknowledged ability to see the absent as though present. In actual life Shelley thought he saw Claire Clairmont's dead daughter alive again, and he thought he encountered himself, or, as we should say today, his own astral body. He must have talked of these delusions more often and convincingly than the records show, for his friend Jane Williams was sure that she too had seen Shelley's astral body when his physical body was elsewhere; and after his death Mrs. Leigh Hunt was sure that she received visits from him.

All these projections of purely mental phenomena into the world of physical reality show that Shelley's mental world was from the first so intense that it sometimes abolished his physical world. It is the proper background for a view of his conscious philosophy of reality and unreality. In his youth and early manhood, dominated as his philosophy then was by eighteenth-century rationalism, he not only accepted physical reality for what it seemed to be, but made the physical senses the test of truth, as in his pamphlet misnamed *The Necessity of Atheism.* When, at the age of twenty, he first became acquainted with Berkeley's philosophy of immaterialism, he definitely rejected it. But by his twenty-fifth year he was a convert to Berkeley, a change doubtless made easier by his recent admiration for Plato. This change practically coincided with the first appearance of his idea of Intellectual Beauty, which might otherwise have been difficult. Thereafter the world of so-called physical realities became less and less real for Shelley. In " The Sensitive Plant " he concluded that all the phenomena of the garden might well be only false creations of the mind. Life itself, he suggested in *Adonais,* was a distortion of reality; only the dead are alive, and the alive are really dead:

> 'Tis we, who, lost in stormy vision keep
> With phantoms an unprofitable strife
> And in mad trance, strike with our spirit's knife
> Invulnerable nothings.

Even time, in the human sense of past, present, and future, he suggests in *Hellas,* is a false notion. The only true Greece is not the Greece struggling at the moment for independence, but the Greece that exists in men's minds as an idea, of which the past and the future are as much a part as the present.

At every stage of such explanations as these we must remind ourselves that life is infinitely more complicated than the rationalizer ever supposes. Every act and utterance of Shelley's mature life which may be significantly connected with his boyhood ran, between its two termini, a gauntlet of influences set

447

up by external events and by an extremely large acquaintance with books that were read with unusual intelligence, imagination, and memory. Thus the passage I have just quoted from *Adonais* may in one sense be regarded as made up entirely of three literary influences — Petrarch's assertion, in his *Triumphs,* that the dead are alive and the living are dead, Socrates's identical assertion in Plato's *Gorgias,* and the air-drawn dagger scene in *Macbeth.* The passage in *Hellas* next mentioned might be regarded as a combination of Prospero's finest speech in *The Tempest* and Calderón's *Life Is a Dream.* The hands of Spenser, Milton, Keats, and Forteguerri may all be seen in " The Witch of Atlas," which was written almost impromptu and is a thoroughly Shelleyan poem. But in most such cases the established bent is more important than the literary " influence " and generally even dictates its choice. After his direction was determined Shelley was as unlikely to be deflected by literary influences as he was to be deeply influenced by any of his friends. And it is a fact that none of the several people who were influenced by Shelley ever really influenced him counter to his established course.

The preceding comments on Shelley's philosophy and peculiar mental qualities have led us some distance from the point at which they started: namely, the relation of Shelley's extraordinary sensational, emotional, and intellectual sensitivity to the question of insanity. It was Shelley's consciousness of this intensity that made him speak of himself as having already lived a hundred years; it is the reader's consciousness of it that makes it so hard for him to realize as he reads that this extraordinary young man was not quite thirty when he died. Returning now to the point of departure, one can readily perceive that without being insane Shelley might easily enough have caused various casual, unimaginative observers of his youth to believe him so. One might go to the other extreme and suggest the paradox that such a highly penetrating and sympathetic intelligence, when functioning in balance, might well make the so-called normal mind appear insane by comparison. Such a mind, however, would obviously have greater trouble than the normal mind in preserving its sanity. Tom Medwin, the only writer about Shelley who was with him both in his boyhood and in his last years, said that throughout his whole life Shelley was on the brink of insanity. Such a person might easily be pushed over the brink by an attack of ill health or by a great emotional shock. I am inclined to think that this may actually have happened to Shelley for very brief periods at two or three times in his life — that Shelley may have been in the very shadow of such a period when he wrote " Julian and Maddalo " and possibly just before he eloped with Mary Godwin. Beyond this, however, the testimony of his acquaintances and the evidence of his works is overwhelming. They show that he possessed one of the most subtly penetrating minds of his age, and that it was usually very justly balanced.

The same considerations that illuminate Shelley's supposed occasional insanity may be brought to bear upon the question of his truthfulness. Godwin asserted bitterly that Shelley had a peculiar genius for falsehood, while Leigh Hunt thought him extraordinarily, almost uniquely truthful. The antagonistic J. Cordy Jeaffreson devoted a chapter of his biography to a rather indiscriminate presentation of Shelley's " lies." That Shelley falsely accused Harriet in order to ensure Mary's elopement seems incontrovertible, and it is also clear that he made in at least three legal documents statements that no normal-minded person could make without knowing them to be false. But how certain can one be that they seemed lies to Shelley at the time? Before his elopement with Mary he was, according to two witnesses, so distraught that he can hardly be held accountable for knowing what he said. His various " delusions " cannot have been both lies and delusions. It is quite possible that Shelley regarded his legal lies as not culpable, since they injured no one and were necessary to purposes that were in themselves laudable. And it is also clearly evident that such a mind as Shelley's was capable of seeing some lies as the truth, merely because in his own view they *had* to be true. If so, he may have been Jesuitical or casuistic, but not necessarily insincere. Beatrice's false denial of her guilt in *The Cenci,* apparently with Shelley's approval, and for no dramatic purpose, is significant. She might almost be thought to believe her own denial, because (as Leigh Hunt suggested) to admit the parricide, in the construction that society put upon it, was to her the only real lie.

DIFFICULT as it is to reach satisfying conclusions about so complicated a personality as Shelley's, it is even more difficult to explain the miracle of Shelley's greatness as a poet. We can perceive that he studied diligently to be a poet and applied constantly to that purpose a fine mind and memory, and extremely subtle and intense emotional and physical sensibilities — but others have done the same without becoming great poets. If we have discerned a poet's purpose, leading ideas, and dominant emotions, we may still be far short of perceiving what gives them compelling power in his poems. Even the maddest prophet could not have foretold that *Poetry by Victor and Cazire,* one of the poorest volumes of juvenilia ever published by a great poet, would lead in nine years to *Prometheus Unbound.* Nor could even a Coleridge tell *how* it led there. Even if he knew, the same inadequacy of words which so many poets have sought to circumvent would come between him and his object. Probably that is why the greatest poetry, simply *as* poetry, is generally degraded by prose exposition, and will speak only directly to the reader. And that must be my excuse for having said little either in this biography or in this concluding chapter about Shelley's greatness as a poetic artist, though I have purposely quoted many passages which assert this fact more convincingly than any attempted exposition could do.

A few generalizations may be hazarded, however, as an indication of the range and effectiveness of Shelley's poetic powers. Though he furnishes numerous colourful and picturesque descriptions, he offers few if any natural scenes in which the reader can feel as much at home as in many that are to be found in the poems of Wordsworth or Keats. And yet his unpretentious, unfinished " Evening: Ponte al Mare, Pisa," instantly springs to mind as an exception. His poems contain many isolated fine and just perceptions of natural beauty — which may be matched easily enough, however, among the other great English poets. Alone among his compeers he emphasizes beauty of seasonal order and change as a symbol of the naturalness and inevitability of revolution in men's minds and in the social order. Sometimes, as in " To a Skylark," " The Cloud," and the address to spring in *Prometheus Unbound,* it is the beauty or fitness of the rhythm, as much as the words themselves, that accomplishes the desired effect.

Shelley's range of effective rhythms, even in *Prometheus Unbound* alone, is greater than that of most English poets. The fitness of these rhythms to the suggestion they are meant to convey is often extraordinary. Since the days of Dryden, for example, the five-stress couplet had been primarily a medium for intellectual verse. Leigh Hunt and Keats had recently loosened its structure and made it a vehicle of sensuous description and familiar poetry. In his " Letter to Maria Gisborne " Shelley used it for familiar purposes better than Hunt or Keats, principally by improving the dignity of its diction. Some of the rejected passages for *Epipsychidion* show that this later poem was probably begun in a similar tone. But before it was finished Shelley had converted to a new use what was formerly one of the coldest and most controlled, and latterly one of the loosest, least dignified forms of English verse by making it a perfectly fit vehicle of intense personal emotion. In " With a Guitar: To Jane," which is based upon a whimsical parallelism with *The Tempest,* he took the verse-form of Shakespeare's Epilogue and modified its tone to suit the graceful tenderness of his conceit. So firmly fixed a verse-form as *terza rima* had been skilfully used by Shelley in his unfinished " Prince Athanase," but when he came to write his " Ode to the West Wind " he modified it boldly into a stanza form in which concluding couplets, conventionally used to establish a full stop, became a device for increasing suspense and cumulative force. Since Spenser's day many English poets had put his famous stanza to a variety of uses. In *Laon and Cythna* Shelley had used it with success, but without particular originality. In " The Witch of Atlas," however, he captures the deliberate pace and rich music and colour of Spenser's stanza and mixes it with other ingredients, but in *ottava rima* — and within less than a year he was writing Spenser's stanza in *Adonais* with a flavour far more Miltonic than Spenserian, but

451

predominantly his own. His blank verse alone ranges from the vigorous, somewhat plain directness of *Queen Mab*, through the flexible, quasi-Miltonic harmonies of *Alastor* and the Miltonic grandeur and power of *Prometheus Unbound*, to the purely objective Shakespearian-Websterian quality of *The Cenci*.

Shelley's notebooks, with their many fragments of unfinished verse, offer me no significant light as to the origin and development of his wonderful metrical power. Any reader can feel qualities in Shelley's rhythms which he is at a loss to duplicate in earlier English poetry. I can only suggest, as a weak guess, that some of it comes direct from music. Among the pleasures which he keenly enjoyed were opera and the singing of Claire Clairmont, Sophia Stacey, and Jane Williams. In every case this singing stimulated him to poetry, so that it might be reasonable to suppose that the poems retained some of the quality of their stimulus. The music of *Prometheus Unbound*, considered as a whole, has always seemed to me more like that of an opera than a long poem. The "Ode to the West Wind" has a sustained harmony that seems to me primarily more orchestral than poetic. I can never read "To Jane: 'The keen stars are twinkling'" without hearing the notes of Jane's guitar in the delicate, unusual music of the stanzas. Similarly there is a quality — perhaps the sure sense of knowing when and how to break the regular rhythm of set verse-forms — that reminds me of music in such short poems as the "Indian Serenade," "Hymn of Pan," "To Night," "A Lament," and others. If it is but a wild suggestion that music was a part of the origin of many of Shelley's most admired shorter lyrics, there is at least no guess-work as to how such poems have affected musicians. Between forty and fifty of Shelley's poems were set to music by Victorian composers.

Shelley's sense of structure was often notably inferior to his genius for verse-harmony. *Laon and Cythna* is certainly indifferently planned and proportioned. It might even be questioned whether the fourth act of *Prometheus Unbound* — save for the final speech and the lines leading up to it — was altogether well advised. A severe critic might find slight flaws of proportion and emphasis in *Adonais*, regarded by Shelley as his "least imperfect" poem. *Epipsychidion* is thrown out of perfect balance and proportion by the account of an imaginary elopement which contains signs of having been attached to a poem already finished. The charge of disproportion against "Julian and Maddalo," however, is principally the result of failure to understand its real meaning. And few poems, if any, have ever been written with a finer sense of structure than the "Ode to the West Wind."

The most characteristic and at the same time the most appealing qualities of Shelley's poetry seem to me to be its peculiar intensity, its unique sense of loneliness, and its superb faith in human destiny. The intensity is a large element in its persuasive power; combined with Shelley's music, it makes him one of the most hypnotic of English poets. The sense of loneliness voices the feeling which no sensitive person can always entirely escape, of the utter isolation of his own personality. These two traits, mainly, were sufficient to make him a great poet in the eyes of generations that could ignore or belittle his faith in human destiny and his courageous self-dedication to the advancement of human freedom. It was well for him that he could be exalted on these traits alone. But the last quality is his greatest glory. For if the future which we now face has in store a period of repressive reaction, Shelley's will be one of the voices to inspire the inevitable rebels. If we are, on the other hand, to improve upon the present state of freedom and justice, some of our reformers will turn to Shelley, not for a specific program, but for inspiration. More persuasively than any other English poet, Shelley voices that desire for social justice which will perhaps never be fully satisfied and which it is hard to think can ever be extinguished.

APPENDIX I

UNPUBLISHED OR UNCOLLECTED LETTERS BY
SHELLEY, WITH ONE BY HARRIET SHELLEY

Some twenty or thirty letters by Shelley listed in sales records and catalogues have never been published. Of these I have been able to locate only those here printed, with the following exceptions:

1. Shelley to William Godwin, postmarked November 13, 1816. The text is to be found in Mr. Seymour de Ricci's *Bibliography of Shelley's Letters* (Paris, 1927), 85. It evidently seemed doubtful to the editors of the Julian edition, who omitted it. It was once offered for sale (Anderson Art Galleries, December 9, 1909) as "possibly a forgery." Without having seen the MS., I feel certain on internal evidence that the letter is not Shelley's.

2. Shelley to T. J. Hogg, October 22, 1821. Bodleian Library, MS. Shelley Adds d. 4. This letter was to have been published here but was omitted when I found that it had been previously published in R. Brimley-Johnson: *Shelley–Leigh Hunt* (London, 1928) 333–5. I understand that it is also to be included in Professor George Stuart Gordon's forthcoming *Shelley Letters*.

1

TO EDWARD FERGUS GRAHAM

LONDON

Field Place, near
Horsham, Sussex

My dear Graham
    My father arrived to day, I have as yet had no opportunity of conversing on money matters but when I do you may depend

on the 5£. I enclose you 3£ more, but that is to do a commission for me. — It is to get the octavo edition of the Lady of the Lake — the cheapest edition of Locke on the Human Understanding, of a Leonora such as Elisabeth has — then [these?] I wish you to send to

> Miss Harriet Grove
> Fern
> Salisbury
> Wiltshire —.

Now, you know, dear Graham, that as this is to Harriet the sooner you send it the better. In a day or two I shall have the pleasure of sending [?] 5£. Philipps the Horsham printer has undertaken our poetry, — 1500 copies are to be taken off but I shall have to write to you again on that subject

Meanwhile I remain

> Your most affectionate
> friend
> PERCY B. SHELLEY

Saturday Night
[?] Pray write when you have performed my commission — I dont tell my mother or they would quiz me —.

[ADDRESSED:]   [POSTMARKED:]
Edward Fergus Graham, Esq.   *Aug. 13, 1810*
29 Vine Street   [*Shelley seal*
*   Piccadilly, London*   *almost intact*]
    [On the reverse:]
After John's [we . . . ?] I
            [medicine?]
    [and below]
I hope you will be [better?]

Owned in September 1935 by Arthur Pforzheimer, 26 East Fifty-sixth Street, New York City, and printed here with his permission.

Listed in De Ricci: Bibliography of Shelley's Letters, *90: " John Davies' sale (9 September 1851, p. 20, n. 235) 11 sh. to Lidstone."*

2

TO JOHN WILLIAMS

YNYS TOWN

Dear Sir

I had understood until this moment that I was your creditor for the Coals you were so good as to procure for me. I am just undeceived and not having a sixpence of ready money am placed in a most awkward situation by the mistake.

I write, earnestly to request that you would satisfy the man for the present. I think you ought to have made me acquainted with the real state of the business at first, knowing the economy of my affairs.

Yours [servant?]

P. B. SHELLEY

[UNDATED AND WITHOUT
POSTMARK; ADDRESSED TO:]   [ENDORSED ON BACK:]
Mr. John Williams   *Mr. Shelley, Decr*
  Ynys Town   *4th 1812*

Owned in September 1935 by Gabriel Wells, 145 West Fifty-seventh Street, New York City, and printed here with his permission.
   Listed in De Ricci: Bibliography of Shelley's Letters, 281: *" Charles W. Frederickson's sale (New York, 24 May 1897, p. 218, n. 2310) $21 to Haines." It had been previously sold at Sotheby's, July 16, 1894, and was last sold at the Miller sale, American Art Association, December 5, 1934. Julian* Works, IX, 26, *note, quotes a sentence from the Frederickson Catalogue, and states that the letter is dated Dec. 4, 1812, and is addressed to Ynys Towyn.*

3

SIX LINES OF AN UNDATED LETTER

Mr. Shelley would [3 or 4 words cut off at top] favour if, particularly during his stay in town, the printer could be urged to expedition. The printing is remarkably accurate, and a revise will only be required when there shall happen to be made any considerable corrections of language.

Fragment owned in September 1935 by Gabriel Wells, 145 West Fifty-seventh Street, New York City, and printed here with his permission. Last sold at the Conway sale, American Art Association, December 16, 17, 1929.

4

TO THOMAS LOVE PEACOCK

Geneva
May 15, 1816

My dear Peacock

After a journey of ten days, we arrived at Geneva. The journey like that of life was variegated with intermingled rain and sunshine, though these many showers were to me as you well know, April showers, quickly passing away, and foretelling the calm brightness of summer —

The journey was in some respects exceedingly delightful but the prudential considerations arising out of the necessity of preventing delay the continual attention to pecuniary disbursements, detract terribly from the pleasure of all travelling schemes.

The manners of the French are interesting, although less attractive, at least to an Englishman than before. The discontent and sullenness of their minds perpetually betrays itself. I despise this nation so much the less [MS. illegible] and well fit for slavery as it is because it has learned to wear its chains with smiles of sycophantic gratitude. The best thing would be that they should love and practice true liberty, — but it is well that the vilest servitude can extract one murmur.

You live by the shore of a tranquil stream among low and woody hills. You live in a free country, where you may act without restraint, and possess that which you possess in security; and so long as the name of country and the selfish conceptions which it includes shall subsist, England, I am persuaded, is the most free and the most refined.

Perhaps you have chosen wisely. But if I return and follow your example, it will be no subject of regret to me that I have seen other things. Surely there is much of bad and much of good, there is much to disgust, and much to elevate, which he will never feel or know who has never passed the limits of his native land.

So long as man is such as he now is, the experience of which I speak will never teach him to despise the country of his birth — far otherwise, like Wordsworth, he will never know what love subsist[s] between himself and it until absence shall have made its beauty heartfelt; our poets and our philosophers, our mountains and our lakes, the rural lanes and fields which are ours so especially are ties which, until I become utterly senseless, can never be broken asunder.

These, and the memory of them, if I never should return, these and the affections of the mind, with which, having once been united, they are inseparably united, will make the name of England, my country, dear to me for ever, even if I should permanently return to it no more. Yes, they constitute my country, and are the general coin [?] under which all that is so dear to me in that thought must be vitally comprehended.

But I suppose you did not pay the postage of this letter in the imagination that you would hear nothing but sentimental gossip. But I fear it will be long before I shall play the tourist deftly I will, however, tell you that to come to Geneva we have crossed the Jura branch of the Alps.

The mere difficulties of horses and high bills and postillions and cheating, lying aubergistes, you can easily conceive. Fill up this part of the picture according to your own experience, and it cannot fail to resemble.

The mountains of Jura are a very high ridge of Alps. They exhibit scenery of wonderful sublimity. Pine forests of impenetrable thickness, and untrodden, nay, inaccessible expanse, spread on every side. Sometimes descending, they follow the route into the valleys, clothing the precipitous rocks, and struggling with knotted roots between the most barren clefts. Sometimes the route winds on high into the regions of frost, and there these forests become scantier and are loaded with the snow.

The trees in these regions are incredibly large, but stand in scattered clumps in the white wilderness. Never was scene more awfully desolate than that which we passed on the evening of our last day's journey.

The natural silence of that uninhabited desert contrasted strangely with the voices of the people who conducted us. For it was necessary in this part of the mountain to take a number of persons, who should assist the horses to force the chaise through the snow, and prevent it from falling down the precipice.

We are now at Geneva, where, or in the neighbourhood, we shall remain probably until the autumn. I shall return almost immediately, within a fortnight or three weeks, to attend to the last exertions which L[ongdill] is to make for the settlement of my affairs; of course I shall then see you; in the meantime it will interest me to hear all that you have to tell of yourself.

Mary is engaged in writing or she would have written in Latin a language that will not express my thoughts. I do not require you to imitate what doubtless you will consider an inexcusable piece of barbarism in me.

Very truly your friend
P. B. SHELLEY

Original in the Harvard Library Poetry Room. Published by permission. This letter was first published by Peacock in his Memoirs, *and all subsequent publications have used Peacock's text. This text is so seriously erratic and incomplete that the letter is here accurately printed for the first time.*

5

TO BROOKES, ESQ., BANKER

CHANCERY LANE, LONDON.

Bath, December 4, 18[16].

Sir

I have taken the liberty of referring a person, to whom it is essential to me that I should afford evidence of my respectability and identity to you, for that information.

It is only necessary to state, that you know me, as the eldest son of Sir Timothy Shelley, and as keeping such and such pecuniary accounts at your house.

In complying with this request, you would exceedingly oblige, Sir, Your very obedient and humble Servt,

PERCY BYSSHE SHELLEY.

[POSTMARKED:]
Bath, Dec. 4
[*and*] *E, Dec.* 5, 1816
[ADDRESSED:]   [ENDORSED:]
*Brookes, Esq*ʳ, *Banker*   *P. B. Shelley*
Chancery Lane   4 *Decbr* 1816.
       London.

Original in the Bodleian Library, MS. Shelley Adds. d. 4. *Published by permission. Not listed by De Ricci.*

6

TO LORD BYRON

My dear Lord B.

I am so dreadfully sleepy that I cannot come tonight. Will you have the goodness to send us — the " Fudge Family " the " Quarterly " and my Plato . . .

Truthfully [Gratefully?] Yours

P. B. SHELLEY.

Between sleep and awake
Oct. 17. 1818.

[NO POSTMARK.]
[ADDRESSED:]
Right Hon-Lord Byron
Casa Nova Mocenigo.

From a photograph of the original MS. published in the catalogue
of Roderick Terry sale (American Art Association and Anderson
Galleries) New York, May 2–3, 1934. Since that date the MS. has
been owned by Mr. W. T. H. Howe. Not listed by De Ricci.

7

TO CANE & SHERBORNE

LONDON

Marlow,
Feb. 28, 1817.

Gentlemen

On my arrival at Marlow, I have received your letter dated
Jany. 31 — and beg to inform you that when I come to London
(certainly within a fortnight) I will call on you on the subject —

Your obed. Servant

PERCY B SHELLEY

[ADDRESSED:]   [POSTMARKED:]

Messrs. Cane & Sherborne   *MARLOW*
185 *Strand*   [*and*]
    London   *C*
                                         1 MR 1
                                         1817

Owned by the Hispanic Society of America, 156th Street, New
York City, and printed with its permission.

Listed in De Ricci: Bibliography of Shelley's Letters, 289. *The*
two entries of letters dated Feb. 28, 1817 probably refer to this let-
ter, as De Ricci suggests. De Ricci's sales record: "Robert Cole's
sale (29 July 1861, I, p. 144, n. 1132) 11 sh. to Stamp." "Offered for
£ 125 *(with the other autograph below) by Pearson,* Catalogue of
a superb collection of holograph manuscripts . . . [*about* 1918],
p. 135, n. 193 and sold to the Library of the Hispanic Society, New
York."

8

TO C. AND J. OLLIER

Marlow, July 24, 1817.

Dear Sir

Be so good as to send me " Tasso's Lament " a poem just published; and Taylors Translation of Pausanias. You will oblige
me by sending them without delay, as I have immediate need
for them. —

Your obliged and faithful Svt

P. B. SHELLEY.

P.S. I have desired a parcel for me to be sent to your House;
which you will have the goodness to enclose with the books.

[ADDRESSED:]   [POSTMARKED:]
Mess. Ollier — Booksellers   MARLOW
31 *Welbeck St.*   [*and*]
   London   C

25 JY 25

1817

*Owned by the Maine Historical Society, Portland, Maine, and
printed with its permission.*

Listed in De Ricci: Bibliography of Shelley's Letters, 289: " *Lewis
J. Cist's sale* (*New York,* 5 *October* 1886, *I, pp.* 262–263, *n.* 2869)."
The addressee is not identified in De Ricci.

9

TO HAYWARD

LONDON

Pisa, Aug. 27, 1820.

Dear Sir

I should be exceedingly obliged to you, for an exact account
of the state of my debt, upon the annuity granted by me to your

client Mr. ———. the interest of which is now due for more than two years; that is the exact amount of the entire sum, principal and interest, now due. —

I am, sir,
Your obliged Servant
PERCY B. SHELLEY

[ADDRESSED:]   [POSTMARKED:]
— *Hayward, Esq.*   *FPO — Se — 1820*
  Solicitor   *Pisa* [*stamped or*
  Tooke's Court   *engrossed in upper*
  Chancery Lane   *right-hand corner*]
  London
Angleterre.   [ENDORSED ON BACK:]
                                " *August 17, 1820,*
                                from Mr. Shelley."

Owned by the Massachusetts Historical Society, 1154 Boylston Street, Boston, Mass., and printed with its permission.

Not listed in De Ricci: Bibliography of Shelley's Letters. *One of a number of autograph letters collected by the Reverend Robert Cassie Waterston and bequeathed to the Massachusetts Historical Society. Received by the society in November 1899.*

10

TO C. OLLIER

LONDON

Pisa, Oc. 11, 1821.

Dear Sir

I forgot the other day to inclose the corrections of Adonais.

My dramatic poem called " Hellas " will soon be ready — you may advertise it, and as the subject is in a certain degree of a transitory nature, I send it you, instead of printing it here, in the full confidence that you will at my request not delay to send it to the press. It is short and Aeschylean.

How is Adonais liked? I should be glad to see what the reviews may say — having attacked them.

463

Expect Charles the 1st or Troilus and Cressida in the spring — If I had had notice of Hunt's coming I should have wished you to have given him several books for me to bring out — Should this letter be yet in time send me by him if they are not included in the box any of my list that I should like to receive before the others. Exercise your own discretion in sending me a few books (not like the poetical decameron) — and include Mill's India.

Dear Sir — Your most obliged Svt.

PERCY B. SHELLEY

[ADDRESSED]   [POSTMARKED:]
Messrs Ollier, Booksellers   *Pisa*
Vere Street   [and]
Bond Street   *F. P. O. Oct. 27, 1821.*
London
Angleterre.

Owned by the Henry E. Huntington Library and Art Gallery, San Marino, California, and printed here with its permission.

Listed in De Ricci: Bibliography of Shelley's Letters, 202, *with the query: " Is this letter of unquestionable authenticity? " De Ricci gives no sale record.*

The letter bears a seal and the paper is watermarked with a flowering plant in a pot. The only reason I can see for Mr. De Ricci's query is the absence of a history. The Huntington Library possesses no history for the letter beyond the fact that it was in the library before 1925. All the other evidence seems to me to furnish adequate authentication. The request for Mill's India *comes at a time when Shelley was hoping Peacock might secure him an appointment there.*

11

HARRIET SHELLEY TO JOHN WILLIAMS

My dear Sir

I have received the Boxes safe and am much indebted to you for them — How is poor dear Mr. Nanney is he at Gwynfryn tell him if there I will come and see him. This is the least I

464

can do for his kindness to us and help to cheer his spirits in hopes of hearing from you soon I remain

Yours truly
H SHELLEY

April 14th
  23 Chapel St.

[POSTMARKED:]
BAP 14

[ADDRESSED:]   [ENDORSED:]
Mr. John Williams   *Mrs. Shelley*
Innys Towynn   *14th April, 1815.*
Tremadoc
Carnarvonshire, North Wales.

From MS. Shelley Adds d. 4, in the Bodleian Library, by permission.

APPENDIX II

There are in *Shelley and Mary* a number of letters to the Shelleys still unpublished, principally letters from Horace Smith, William Godwin, Charles Clairmont, and Mr. and Mrs. Gisborne. There is scarcely space to include these letters in an appendix to this volume; moreover *Shelley and Mary* itself is now accessible in five public or semi-public libraries in England and America, counting a photostatic copy in the Library of Congress. It is to be hoped that some day its journal and unpublished letters will be published. I have made an exception in publishing the letters of Emilia Viviani because it was in some cases possible to correct and augment the incomplete versions given in *Shelley and Mary* and because they have hitherto been translated only in part.

The Marchesa Enrica Viviani Della Robbia, a descendant of a collateral branch of Emilia Viviani's family, who has written a life of Shelley's Emilia entitled *Vita di una Donna* (Florence, 1936), has very graciously translated for me all letters and portions of letters not translated in Professor Dowden's biography of Shelley. The present translations, therefore, are composite translations by Professor Dowden and the Marchesa Enrica Viviani Della Robbia, except in those letters ignored completely by Professor Dowden and except in two cases where an oversight has resulted in my own responsibility for the translation of the last two paragraphs of letter 12 (with the very useful assistance of Mr. Creighton Gilbert) and the whole of letter 16.

The present collection of Emilia's letters is still doubtless incomplete, as are also some of the individual letters. But it is more complete than any other, on account of the fact that the letters furnished to the Marchesa Enrica Viviani Della Robbia

for her *Vita di una Donna* by Sir John C. E. Shelley-Rolls are
not identical with those printed in *Shelley and Mary,* but in
some cases supplement and in some cases are supplemented by
the *Shelley and Mary* texts. One letter in *Shelley and Mary*
does not occur in *Vita di una Donna* and two letters in the latter
do not occur in the former.

1

EMILIA VIVIANI TO SHELLEY

To my good Friend Percy.
                                        December 10, 1820.
My Dear Brother,
    Your courteous attentions overwhelm me, for I know that in
no wise do I deserve them. Beside the trouble Claire takes to
teach me your native tongue, you give me books! O my good,
my dear friend! How can I prove to you my gratitude and make
a return for your favours? My situation prevents me from doing
this, notwithstanding my will, my duty, and the affection which
I bear you. Pity me, therefore, and be assured of my eternal
gratitude. Call me always, if you like, your sister, for so sweet
a name is very dear to me; and I too will always call you my
dear brother, and will consider you as though you were such
indeed. You have already seen that I had anticipated you in
this, which means that our hearts understand each other, that
they have the same sentiments, and were created to be bound
by a strong and constant friendship. I embrace my very dear
and beautiful sister Mary, whose company is so agreeable to me.
Adieu, *sensibile* Percy, take every care of your health, and do
not forget you most affectionate sister and friend
                                        TERESA EMILIA.

    Shelley and Mary, *III*, 554; Vita di una Donna, 71; *as translated
entire by Dowden: Life, II, 373.*

2

EMILIA VIVIANI TO MARY SHELLEY

To my beautiful Mary.   *Tuesday*
   My dearest Sister,
   I send you back " Corinne " with my liveliest thanks. It is a beautiful story, though sad and such as to make a soul sensitive and "*passionée*" like mine shed tears. Unhappy Corinne! But how many unhappy ones there are whose lot is the same as thine? . . .
   This weather is really against me, as it obliges me to give up the company of my most beloved friends, or rather of the *only ones* that I love. How profoundly I feel my sorrows! And those of my Friends! No, it will never be possible that I accustom myself to them. Although they are afflicting me since so long, yet I always feel them as if it was for the first time. I am obliged to live always in tumult. And never a moment of peace!
   I thank you for your blotting-paper that I will use with great pleasure. Farewell, dear; sympathize with my deep sadness, which in spite of me will show itself every moment. Pray with my brother to the supreme being for me. You both whose divine souls are so like Him, who created them, beg him to change my destiny or to take from me this very heavy life. Hide this sad letter from my friend. But salute him tenderly for me.
   Good-bye, dearest Mary, I embrace you with all my heart.
             Your sister and friend
                        TERESA EMILIA

Shelley and Mary, *III*, 571; Vita di una Donna, 72, 73; *translated in part by Dowden:* Life, *II*, 376–7.

3

EMILIA VIVIANI TO MARY SHELLEY

Tuesday

My beloved Mary,

Although I recognize myself unworthy of your love, be sure that it is not lost, for I am returning it with my greatest tenderness and gratitude. Continue, then, to like me, my dearest, otherwise, I should feel even unhappier than before. Since Heaven, moved with pity of my sorrows, sent his *three* angels to comfort me, I have never felt unhappy. From this lucky moment consolation entered into my heart, which had been for so long empty, and I felt as if a sweet hand were healing the wounds of my soul. The sky that I always saw so cloudy over me, suddenly cleared up, and I became able to perceive the way of the future more smiling than it has ever been, when the thorns and the bushes which overcrowded it, made my heart so often bleed, and my eyes weep. My poor life had become as confused as a labyrinth, making me despair to be ever able to get through it. But I do not distinguish these dreadful things any more and the same way appears to me strewn all with flowers.

I don't flatter myself that I shall see you today, because the weather is too bad, and you already know that your health is a thousand times dearer to me than my *pleasure*. It is infinitely more valuable than my own, for you are all my life, and if I know you are ill or suffering, I can't be myself otherwise. I beg you to take great care of your health.

Your troubles are more mine than my own; they are greater even than my pain in living always in this prison. But what do these words mean? Nothing compared to the feelings of my heart. I should grow angry with myself for not being able to tell you better my love, which is as *great* as my talent is small, which makes me unable to give it vigorous expression.

In case I may not have the joy of seeing you, please send me news of your health. I should grow very uneasy if I remained a day alone without it. Mine is rather good except my inability to sleep at night, a most troublesome thing indeed. However true it is that this is time *gained* for life, yet the *gain* is neither agreeable nor useful!

Good-bye, my beloved Friend. Give many kisses to my Claire and many tender salutations to my generous-spirited Brother. I trust to your care the recovery from your cold, I beg you to remain my faithful friend and to accept all my love. I embrace you heartily

Your invariable Friend
TERESA E.

P.S. How is your Cousin? I am sorry that he is not well.

Shelley and Mary, *III*, 557; Vita di una Donna, 73–5; *not in Dowden.*

4

EMILIA VIVIANI TO MARY SHELLEY

Friday.

To my dear Mary.
My dear Sister and Friend,

It is very long since I saw you last, and I am, for this reason, very anxious. The prospect which Destiny holds before my eyes is indeed terrible. Oh! How many things make me anxious! I am unhappy, and I shall always be so; I see that it is inevitable.

But your friendship for me will always endure, I hope, and that Shelley and Claire will like me too, and that none of you, the only ones who are dear to me, will leave me. In the same way that your affection has sweetened my present lot, it will diminish the grief of my future. I hope it will be so; if not my despair would indeed be limitless. Heaven! What will become of me! Yes, it is true, " there are people in this world, who seem to be only born to be unhappy." I am myself an incontestable proof of it.

Farewell, Mary, give me your affection. Maybe you will do it for a short time, for I feel that my pains will overwhelm me in

such manner that they will soon cause me to die. I embrace
you, dear Mary

Your constant Friend

T. Emilia

Shelley and Mary, *III*, 571; Vita di una Donna, 75; *not in Dowden*.

5

EMILIA VIVIANI TO SHELLEY

To my dear Brother.

Monday

Dear Brother,

How are you? You must have suffered horribly from those
spasms. May heaven grant that they have now ceased! Dear
friend, you cannot think how much your lot interests me, and
how sensible I am to all that befalls you! I know that you are
very unhappy, and to see myself incapable of alleviating or
healing your unmerited ills is for me the greatest of all pains.
There are no sacrifices I wouldn't make with joy if I could help
you, my dear Friend! Alas! Afflicted as you are by past sorrows,
and misfortunes, and by your health too . . . everything per-
secutes you and makes a veritable martyr of you. You! whose
virtue deserves the reward of every happiness, and whose generous feelings ought to attract the regard and the love of everyone! What a cruel injustice! But God is good and omnipotent.
If He has delayed the justice and recompense which are your
due, it is not, I hope, that He has forgotten it. And the day
will come, if He is just, which will compensate you for the horrible pains which torture you so undeservedly. Farewell, my
good and innocent friend. Please take care of your health,
which concerns me more than any other thing in this world!
Take heart! Take some food, in order to prevent getting weak.
Good-bye. Be assured that you have in me a tender Sister and
Friend, and that I will cherish you always, whatever fate the
future is preparing for me.

Your E.

Shelley and Mary, *III*, 569; Vita di una Donna, 76–7; *translated
in part by Dowden: Life, II, 375–6.*

6

EMILIA VIVIANI TO SHELLEY

December 12th, 1820, 10 *o'clock in the afternoon.*
My dear Brother,

To show you that your familiarity does not displease, but, on the contrary, gratifies me, and in order that you should not take as a rebuke my treating you in any other way, I write to you in your own tone of confidence and sweet friendship. My Claire, if she reads this, will say that she is *jealous:* but let her reflect that I do not write thus save to her good brother and to mine.

This evening I wished to tell you many things, but my vigilant argus has hindered me from so doing. I will now tell you a part of them. You console me by engaging yourself to effect my liberation. Here I fare ill in both spirits and health, and suffer very much in every way, so that by taking me from here you would give me a new existence. I leave the *how* to you, who have that wisdom and experience in which I am wanting. But I dread that the plan of the Archduchess will not turn out well, for my parents never will consent to it, and it is not sure that Her Royal Highness will deign to interest herself for my sake. Ah, God pardon my mother! She could make me contented if not happy, and on the contrary it is she who is the chief cause of my misfortunes. I love her still, and wish her every good. I feel that nature speaks and lives in my heart. Although she forgets that she is my mother, I remember that I am her daughter; but if she were to have pleasures as many as are and have been the sorrows which she has brought upon me, no woman would be more fortunate than she. I ought to pass over this in silence, and to hide it in my heart, but this poor heart is so affected by its cruel wounds that I cannot prevent its giving vent to its grievance with you, my Percy, and to shed upon this paper a drop of the sadness that fills my soul; I beg you to pity me, and to believe me no worse than I am, in speaking so frankly.

You say that my liberation will perhaps *divide* us. O my

friend! My soul, my heart, can never be parted from my brother and from my dear sisters. My person, once delivered from this prison, will attempt all things in order to follow my heart, and Emilia will seek you everywhere, even were you at the utmost boundaries of the world. I do not love, nor shall I ever be able to love anything or person so much as your family; for it I would abandon everything, and should lose nothing, since in it are included all that can exist of beautiful, virtuous, amiable, *sensible*, and learned in the world. What will be my lot? I pray always to God to grant that I may live with you always.

Yes, my soul is simple and sincere like the blue of the sky on a fine day of spring. I am happy that you know it, and I know that since you do, you will do me justice. I always was candid, and although this quality sometimes has done me wrong with those people who were not like me, I cannot lay it aside, nor would I do it for all the gold in this world. I hate deception so much that if I were able to deceive once only, I would never respect myself; and self-esteem is one of the chief goods of this earth. If the others do not esteem me, if they blacken my name, it may make me sorry, but I can console myself for their malice with the sense of my innocence. But if I behave so as to merit my blame too, this pain would be far greater than the first one. What should then repay me for the loss of my self-esteem? Therefore I will always be sincere, and my face, like my mouth and my pen, will always express the motions of my heart. People fixing their eyes on my face will be able to read my feelings and my defects, and all that is within me. Turning over my letters they will get the same impression, and listening to my words it will be still the same.

You say well; in *friendship* everything must be in common; few, indeed, very few, are the persons who know this sublime and sweet divinity; but we know it, and that is enough.

I thank you very much for your kind offer. You do too much for me, and I don't deserve it, but be assured that in need, I should apply to you alone.

According to your wishes, I take no more opium, but the want of sleep is a very troublesome thing.

My Claire's departure afflicts me, excessively, as the mere thought afflicts me. I love her so much. I hope for the rest that you both will not abandon me, and that the beautiful Mary, so dear to me, and you, will come to see me, and bring me letters from my dear friend Claire. Mary does not write to me. It is possible that she loves me less than the others do? I should be very much pained by that. I wish to flatter myself that it is only her son and her occupations that cause this. Is not this the case?

What a long letter have I written, without being aware of it! Excuse me if I forgot to be brief.

Pray tell Mary the same things I have just written to you. Remember that your company is a great pleasure to me, always be fond of me, and rest yourself from this long reading!

Your Sister and affectionate Friend
T. Emilia.

Shelley and Mary, III: 555–6; Vita di una Donna, 80–3, with a photograph of page 1 of the original MS. on p. 76. Translated in part by Dowden: Life, II, 374, 377. From "I hate deception . . ." the remainder of the letter is given in Shelley and Mary, III, 575–6, as if it were another letter. The time should have been translated 10 p.m.

7

EMILIA VIVIANI TO MARY SHELLEY

December 14th, 1820

I am very sorry, my dear [Mary], that you are not as well as I wish; take every care of your health, for the sake of your beautiful son, and for your friends who love you dearly. I have been so glad to receive your letter. I covered it with my kisses and pressed it several times to my heart. Its strong palpitations will tell you how dear you are to me. A visit of yours when you will be able to come will give me a great pleasure, the more so as I shall be more sad and melancholy than I am, on account of my little Claire's absence! But now take my advice and don't go out till you are perfectly recovered from your cold, because these colds are generally turning bad this year, if neglected. How sweet the thought of your friendship is for my heart! You angelic creatures! How shall I be able to tell you my feelings? I like you, I adore you even, I consider and admire you like three Divinities. I would do everything to give you a proof of my sincere affection. But I know that I don't tell you anything with these words! I am not able to find any more efficacious ones, because my love is so great, so intense, that it can't be expressed through words. How glad I was to get your affectionate letter! How much your good thoughts pleased me, adorned by your poetical ideas! You have much talent, my Mary, which, together with your virtue and your excellent heart, makes you one of the loveliest of God's or Nature's creatures.

I will study your beautiful and useful language, but I am afraid that my little talent will prevent my learning it thoroughly. However, being aware of this, I shall be satisfied with my mediocrity and you will be my guide.

Please give many kisses to my dearest Friend and tell her she must not go out during this ugly weather, for I think more about her health than about my own pleasure, and I wish her to take great care of it. I passed a bad night, dreading that the rain had done some ill to her and to Percy last evening. I wish eagerly to receive good news from them, and from you also. I fear that it hurt them indeed. Your health is such an important thing that I am never so much in pain as when I know you are not well.

Give my tenderest salutations to your dear husband and my good brother. Last night Claire narrated to me part of his history. His many misfortunes, his unjust persecutions, and his firm and innate virtue in the midst of these terrible and unmerited sorrows, filled my heart with admiration and affection, and made me think, and perhaps not untruly, that he is not a human creature; he has only a human exterior; but the interior is all divine. The being of all beings has doubtless sent him to earth to accredit virtue and to give an exact image of himself. I can scarcely believe that he has enemies and that his virtue is not known by everyone. Take care, however, to

475

tell your affairs to a few people only; I gave the same advice to Clara already. Good-bye, my dearest Mary, I am very proud to be your

Friend and affectionate Sister
TERESA EMILIA

Shelley and Mary, *III*, 573; Vita di una Donna, 77–8; *translated in part by Dowden:* Life, *II*, 376.

8

EMILIA VIVIANI TO MARY SHELLEY

December 24th, 1820, in the evening.

My adored Friend,

Although after the gift of your friendship you can offer me no other gift so precious, or more dear to me, yet I have been exceedingly pleased by the slender *chain*, which must be the symbol of that which binds and will eternally bind our hearts. Your generous ways, besides, overwhelm me, and I am much mortified not to be able to do as much towards you, that I might show you a part of the immense gratitude which lives in my heart, and tell you how much I love you. But in the same way that I don't know how to thank you for your affection, I never shall be able to thank you for your other gift. Excuse my insufficiency, and be assured that I know the full worth of Mary.

So you are not well. How sorry I am! You did right not to go out in this bad weather. I say this out of regard for your health, for to see you is a great pleasure to me. You seem to me a little cold sometimes, and that causes me an uncomfortable feeling; but I know that your husband said well when he said that your apparent coldness is only *the ash which covers an affectionate heart.*

It is unnecessary, unless you so desire, for one of you to go to see the Signora Taddeoli, to make up for the impossibility of Claire's going. Tomorrow Mrs. Barsanti is going to the same house, and I will write and send her a note in Claire's name, making her excuses. Thus you will be spared too great an intimacy with a person, good and fine, no doubt, but who, I think, would not be very congenial to you either in *feeling* or thought. I have known her a long time, but I have never felt like becoming her *Friend*. Excuse my frank language, but I am speaking with my sweet Sister.

Also I shall be going home tomorrow and, according to the ill humour, or good humour, of my Parents, will see what I can say on the matter which is so very important to me. But whatever it may be, I hope that Eusta will succeed in attaining it, for she is rather beloved by my family. And in a few days I will then have the pleasure of embracing you in your own home.

Thank you for the good wishes you sent me for the Christmas holidays; I send them back to you a hundredfold both for you and for all your family and friends; and I pray that God will grant completely all that you desire, with good health and many long years — of which I pray Him to permit me to pass many in your incomparable company.

Shelley and Mary, III, 558; Vita di una Donna, 83–4; translated in part by Dowden: Life, II, 375.

9

EMILIA VIVIANI TO SHELLEY

Mr. Shelley

Saturday morning.

Dear Brother,

I don't send my Cousin to you, because I must give the matter better consideration, in order that my business may not grow more confused than it already is. We can do it in good time a little later. I am obliged to go home tomorrow, although I do not like it at all, for several good reasons, but I can't decline it. Therefore, I am prevented the sweet pleasure of seeing Mary. But if she could come a moment today, immediately after dinner, or after her walk, before they shut the Convent, I should be very happy indeed, provided it won't trouble her.

My spirits are in the same condition as ever, my health is getting better. Don't afflict yourself on my behalf, my dear Friend, and don't be uneasy on my account. I am not at all miserable, if I can keep such sympathetic Friends who are taking such an interest in me. Moreover, God will help me, I hope. He sees the injustice and the cruelty with which they use me, and He will make them cease, at length. Meanwhile continue, my dear Brother, to give me your affection, which softens every pain, and adds to every pleasure. I entreat you to take care of your precious health. My sorrows are great enough without being increased by the thought of your grief.

Remember me tenderly to my dear good Sister. I thank you and Mary very much for the two nice little birds, which have given me the greatest pleasure. They shall never be separated, and I will always like them. Many thanks for everything. Don't be afflicted on my account; I am better! Good-bye!

Your faithful Friend and Sister E.

Shelley and Mary, *III*, 570; Vita di una Donna, 85; *not in Dowden*.

10

EMILIA VIVIANI TO MARY SHELLEY

Mrs. Mary Shelley
December 28th, 1820.

My dearest Friend,

I am sorry that the weather is so bad, as it will hinder us from seeing each other today. Alas! Everything is against me! But if my dear Friends will be faithful to me, I shall laugh at everything, and I won't feel my sorrows so much. How are you and how is my dear only Brother? This is always my thought during the Night and my first one in the morning.

I flatter myself that you will write to me, but as I have no servants of mine here, so the one I am sending to you can't wait for your answer. Please forgive my cruel situation, and send me your letter through one of your maids, when it ceases raining.

Farewell, my adorable Mary. I send you many kisses. Re-

member me tenderly to your husband, and preserve me your
affection.

Your constant Friend and Sister
Theresa Emily

Vita di una Donna, 86. *Not in* Shelley and Mary *or Dowden. Unlike the others, this note is in French.*

11

EMILIA VIVIANI TO SHELLEY

Friday evening, 1821.

My dear Friend and Brother,

I write to you by moonlight. I can't resolve to take another
light than this. It would be like doing an injury to this clear and
splendid Daughter of Heaven. What sweetness is mine, looking at it! What an inexpressible enchantment! But you know it
too, and you understand it as well as I, because you are like me.

Did you observe the sunset this evening? If you were free
at that moment, it is impossible you didn't admire the sight of
the Clouds, here and there gathered into groups, or becoming
scattered again, and their colour gold and blue.

I stood at a window, thinking of my misfortunes, and thinking
of those people who are so dear to me. I listened in silence
with all my soul to the never silent language of Nature. A
thousand thoughts, some sweet, tender, or even melancholy,
overcame me. I felt surprised finding myself so absorbed in
reverie that I did not know any more where I was, shuddering
and frightened before the gloomy walls of my prison and the
malefic ghosts which surrounded me everywhere. From that
place I could gaze upon the Mountains, partly painted in purple
by the rays of " the first Planet," and partly quite blue. Oh,
what a feeling! How I should like to abolish those rustic houses
which are spoiling the line of those beautiful mountains!

Nature, divine Nature! I lose myself in your sublime immensity, while an invincible sense of veneration urges me to
prostrate myself before your majesty. I said my evening prayer

by the window, upon my knees, and I said it more devoutly than ever. Stupid persons might think that I adore the Moon; No, it isn't so; but I adore in the Moon and in the sight of Heaven the two finest works of our Supreme Being. My fervour grows exceedingly before them, and they remind me of the almighty power of a Christ hanging lacerated upon a cross, whose figure wrings my heart and shows the cruelty and perfidy of men. But enough. How are you? Farewell! This letter in not at all tender, but I will end it by telling you (hoping that Mary won't be *jealous*): " I love you with all my heart, dear Brother! "

I am tenderly your Sister and Friend

EMILY

Vita di una Donna, 87–8. *Not in* Shelley and Mary *or Dowden.*

12

EMILIA VIVIANI TO MARY SHELLEY

January 14th, 1821.

My dear Sister,

Few, very few things happen according to our wishes! If man does not have what he desires, he is restless, and even after the fulfilment of some of his wishes he does not achieve peace, for his ebullient temper imagines and invents new needs and new plans. But alas! How often they are delusions! And our souls become empty and very bitter.

I wished to see you today, and to learn many things in your amiable company, but the rain is playing a trick on me and depriving me of this pleasure. Heaven has grown very sad for its being separated from the Earth, its beloved one, and is shedding its tears over her fruitful bosom and over her changing face. This Lover receives its weeping like a sweet nectar, and joins, perhaps, her own to it. I also am sighing for being separated from my dear Friends, and some tears rise from my heart to my eyes.

This morning I saw Miss Moray in spite of her promise to come at ten o'clock. You can believe that *this* did not bother

me at all, but *they* maddened me all morning, and I passed it
laughing, and, at the same time, becoming more and more
anxious. Now I will tell you briefly why. About half past eight
Pacchiani came with Esopo and the other little boy whom he
has undertaken to teach. He came expressly to tell me to do my
best with Miss M. to get her to advise some friend or relative
of hers (what it concerns he himself is unaware) to take Esopo
as Italian master. He does not speak of it to her himself, because he does not wish to appear to have anything to do with
it. Then he talked a little about you, and told me that you were
extremely charmed by Signora Bernardini, the *prima donna* of
Italy. Afterwards he left with all his train, and at ten Esopo
returned to wait for Miss M., to whom he was to present her,
and with whom he had orders to speak English. But this lady
was not to be seen; Esopo waited; at eleven Pacchiani returned. . . .

My dear sister . . . Do you not know where they found the
notorious rascal [Pacchiani]? After much searching at Pisa, and
at Florence, the police found him at Leghorn, living in a tiny,
dark hovel, lower than he was, in which he stayed hidden the
whole day, and from which he went out only when " The day
departed." . . . They made the search because, occupying the
post of Professor in the University, and receiving a salary for
it, he should in consequence give the due lessons, which he has
not given and now they have arranged about his pay. . . .

Shelley and Mary, *III*, 637–8; Vita di una Donna, 89; *not in*
Dowden. *Only the first two paragraphs of this translation are to be
found in the Italian in* Vita di una Donna. *The rest is in* Shelley and
Mary, *but a paragraph in* Vita di una Donna *describing the rest of
the letter contains quoted phrases which show that a part of the
letter has been omitted in* Shelley and Mary *also.*

*The Italian from which the last two paragraphs are translated
seems to have become garbled either in transcribing or in printing.
In the first sentence the sense requires " I did not see Miss Moray."
At the end of the first paragraph " present her " is nonsense; ap-
parently Esopo was to introduce himself, a translation which the
Italian text will not admit.*

481

13

EMILIA VIVIANI, APPARENTLY TO SHELLEY

My dear Friend,

I am indeed unhappy! What a fate! I suffer heavily, and am the cause of a thousand griefs to others. Oh God! Were it not better that I should die? Then I should cease to suffer, or at least to make others suffer. Now I am the object of hatred to others and to myself. I afflict the most courteous and beloved persons. O my incomparable Friend, Angelic Creature, did you ever suppose that I should be the cause of so much anguish to you? You see what a person you have come to know. Pardon me, my friend, pardon me! You are obliged to bear so many pains and anxieties on my account that your health even suffers through them. How remorse is torturing me! How many misfortunes have I caused! It would be better if you had never known me!

Shelley and Mary, *III*, 554; Vita di una Donna, 93; *translated in part by Dowden:* Life, *II*, 374.

14

EMILIA VIVIANI TO SHELLEY

Saturday morning

My dear Shelley,

I beg you to come no more to St. Anna, yourself or any of your family. My parents desire that I should henceforth see no one. Every attempt would be in vain; we should be humiliated without obtaining anything. The Signora Eusta acts in concert with them. She treated me yesterday in a most insolent manner, and uttered an impertinence to me which not even a servant-maid would have endured. They are all my enemies. I am really sensible of this blow, because I love you all with my sincerest friendship, but what shall I do? Ah! You know that

" right can do nothing against power." Everything in the world
is tyranny, everything! Console yourself meanwhile, and do not
afflict yourself on account of such proceedings. Consider that
in a few days I shall be delivered from this odious prison, and
then I shall be permitted to enjoy your amiable and virtuous
society. This hope sweetens my misfortunes. Please, write to
my Claire and tell her what happened, so that she won't grow
angry with me, hearing no more from me. I am watched very severely. I beg Mary and Claire to maintain their faithful friendship to me, and I beg you also to do it. And the favour which
I now ask of you is that you do not come any more to Saint Anna
either now or ever. You must have not the least relationship
with my enemies, who have always persecuted me, trying by
all means to send me to the grave. I require this favour from
you; otherwise I should no more be able to consider you a
Friend.

Lastly, don't take any steps, for it would be quite useless.
Send your servant to me Monday morning; I will return you
some books. Let me know if you wish also your little writing-
desk and the " Nouvelle Héloïse." If you will write, tell her to
deliver your letter into my own hands only. Good-bye, dear
Friend, good-bye until happier days. Oh! They will arrive, yes!
they will arrive! My heart, which is seldom mistaken, tells me
to be sure of it.

Remember me tenderly to Mary. Many thanks to you all for
the continued kindness you have shown me hitherto. Be assured that I will be always grateful to you, and that I will love
you till death. Courage! I must drink to the last drop the bitter
cup of sorrows.

Take care of your precious health, be quiet, and don't get
angry. Let nobody come into your house who is related to me,
because they are all rascals.

Farewell again. I am and will be for ever

Your affectionate Friend

T. Emily

Shelley and Mary, III, 576; Vita di una Donna, 115–16; *translated in part by Dowden*: Life, II, 377.

15

EMILIA VIVIANI TO MARY SHELLEY

Tuesday

My always dear Mary,

I hope you will forgive me for my delay in answering your two dear letters and for not having yet given you some news of my health. But during these days something has happened which has made me very angry, although it didn't concern me directly. Now this matter is nearly well over.

I am very happy that my Friend Claire is well. Please, when you write, remember me heartily to her, and let her know that I cannot write on account of the " retreat," and this is the reason of my silence. I hope you all continue well too. Tell Shelley that I think this weather is too bad for going to Leghorn and it could do him some harm. It would be better if he didn't go there. Please remember me to him.

Good-bye, beautiful and good Mary! Don't write tomorrow, for these annoying and very stupid people will grumble if we write to each other in these days during our " retreat." Never mind if they read this letter; I only spoke the truth. I hope you will write to me next Friday; you may behave yourself as usual. In so far I send you many kisses with all my heart.

Your faithful Friend

T. EMILY

P.S. My health is good enough.

Shelley and Mary, *III*, 572–3; *not in* Vita di una Donna *or Dowden*.

16

EMILIA VIVIANI TO SHELLEY

3 September.

Mr. Shelley
His Own Hands
In Haste.
My dear Friend,

I have received your much cherished letter. But I am greatly disappointed that your health is not good. Oh God! how very unfortunate we are in this world! You will have received my other letter in which I asked a favour for my Friend [feminine]. Indeed I know I have presumed, but I hope, my dear, that you will feel as I do and will not give me the great unhappiness of not granting my request and of having to see a virtuous, sensitive Friend, who deserves much, suffer and be destroyed by sorrow. If Lord Byron comes to Pisa, as you tell me, you could ask him to join you to make up the amount indicated; but if this seems too risky, I would then be content with less. In case you wish to do me this favour, which for me would be a very great one, then do it at your convenience. And then handle the matter so that you (if you wish) will not appear in it and I will tell you to whom to give the money so that no one could form unworthy suspicions of me. It would be enough for me now to have a promise which would make certain the redemption of my pledged word to my Friend. Reply immediately, for in a few days now I shall not be in Pisa, and this matter is of extreme concern to me. I will think to send to get your letter tomorrow morning; that is, Friday.

When I am married, if you wish to write to me, I should be pleased, but please be very prudent in all your expressions, and use the formal pronoun.

My dear friend, farewell. Salute all your family for me, a thousand times, see that you re-establish your health and tranquillity of spirit, and believe in the unchanging affection

Of your sincere Friend,

E.

Shelley and Mary, *III*, 691; Vita di una Donna, 131–2; *not in Dowden.*

17

THOMAS JEFFERSON HOGG TO SHELLEY

London Christmas day
1820

My Dear Shelley,

Last Friday our friend Hunt received in my presence a long letter in the Etruscan idiom, wch we read together, he being seated at the pianoforte, whilst I stood behind him, & we found two locks of hair & much entertainment, in addition to the welcome intelligence, that you were all well.

Hunt has been very somewhat indisposed, but he is now much recovered, & in better spirits; he begins to discern certain *indications* of prosperity, & seems to have great pleasure in following his Cuculus Indicator to the hives, where he is well rewarded with honey. This kind of publication exactly suits him; & is a more nutritious pap for babes in knowledge, than the generality of dry nurses afford to the toothless little mouths of ordinary little readers. I see Hunt as often as his unfortunate attachment to a nest amidst the brick-fields of some remote suburb will permit, & I always find him as agreeable & friendly, as I left him. When I returned from the north in November, I found a letter from you, dated, I think, in July, treating at length about a certain upholsterer; as it was so long since you had written the letter, I presumed that the matter was settled, & did not interfere indeed if I had known that it were, I sh^d have had my doubts as to adopting the course you desired. I have no doubts that the man will come to reasonable terms, &, if he will not, I cannot understand why you sh^d make yourself uneasy, so long as you intend to remain in Italy, about the notions of a Cabinet-maker at Bath respecting Post-obit bonds, however erroneous they may be, whilst I am in a state of tranquil indifference as to the opinions of Mrs. Mason's Milliner at Pisa concerning the intercourse of the sexes, & the obligation of the nuptial vow; why you sh^d hire an attorney at a great price to regulate the former, while I permit the latter, without even an expostulation, to fulfil her destinies in her own way. You surely must have discovered by this time that Creditors, who are the most oppressed class in the community, especially if they have been so unfortunate as to trust conscientious & enlightened men, will do almost any thing for kind treatment, to wch they are so little accustomed.

Many persons are afraid of being out-lawed; they seem to have some strange mysterious notion of this process wch is nothing but a matter of form at worst: if we are to take our information from German Romances, & not from real life, we shall cer-

tainly have reason to dread this ceremony, for we find there, that
an Outlaw, or a person under the ban of the Empire, stands
trembling all day & all night in a dark cave in a vast forest, up
to his chin in blood, or, in his happiest moments, squats in the
long grass, like a hare, but with a far greater length of hair, of
whiskers, & of ears, ready to start from his form at the least
squeak of the least puppy of the hounds of Justice, " deep,
dreadful, dark, daemoniac ministers." I will frankly own, without pretending to more courage, than my neighbours, that, if
I were told that certain judicial rites had been duly performed,
or rather that a narrative had been written upon parchment in
a hand, that I co^d with difficulty read, in some Court at Naples
of such rites having been performed, I sh^d not feel my self
bound on the sudden to renounce for ever my comb & razor
to dwell unhoused in Bisham wood in a state of praeternatural
hairiness. I received from Ollier a copy of Prometheus Unbound. I am at present occupied with the Greek orators &
with their prince Demosthenes; orations are at best tiresome
things, but the best orations are those of the Greeks, & the best
of the Greek orations are those of Demosthenes, & even Demosthenes some times fatigues me: he is often sublime, his language
always perfect, & his love of liberty & Athenian democracy
singularly interesting. In reading or hearing a speech we often
suffer this

> viz. we are either persuaded at the beginning of the speech to
> agree with the speaker, or we feel that no arguments can ever
> persuade us; & whatever arguments are offered after we are
> persuaded, or

when we know that we have formed an opposite opinion, that
cannot be shaken, are useless, & consequently irksome. Thus
an oration proving that the religion of Mahomet is false, wo^d
fatigue us, because we are already convinced, so, if it attempted
to shew that it is true, because we can never be persuaded that
it is true. I have nearly finished the public orations & I expect
more pleasure from those of a private nature, for private life
is more entertaining than politics, & I hope for curious information touching society & manners in Athens. I strictly observe

the Sabbath by a long walk & by a dinner at some snug little Inn in the country; Peacock is generally one of our party. I wish you co⁽ᵈ⁾ come every Saturday in a balloon to join us, as I used to go to Bishopsgate by Sadlers coach. Peacock deprecates the wrath of winter by the sacrifice of a Turkey, by libations & other solemnities, at wch I am to assist today at 4 o'clock precisely. I was sorry to find that the Gisbornes were gone, when I returned to Town; pray remember me kindly to them & to Mary; write to me soon; excuse my long silence & believe [me] ever, my Dear Friend, most truly & affectionately yours

T. J. Hogg.

[ADDRESSED:]
al signor P. B. Shelley
  Pisa
     Italia   C
ferma in posta

[POSTMARKED:]
Chambery
F 1820

[OTHER POSTMARKS ILLEGIBLE]

From the original in the Ashley Library, with the permission of Mr. T. J. Wise.

APPENDIX III

LETTERS ABOUT SHELLEY

The following letters on Shelley at Eton have not been quoted fully in any biography of the poet, though they were used by Professor Dowden, and were later quoted by Mr. Edmund Blunden in his *Shelley and Keats as They Struck Their Contemporaries* (London, 1925), 1–9.

The " A. A. " of the second letter is of course the Andrew Amos referred to in the first letter. By consulting the editorial file of the *Athenæum* Mr. Blunden ascertained that the first letter was contributed by Merle. This was the W. H. Merle erroneously supposed by Dowden to be the author of " A Newspaper Editor's Reminiscences."

The two letters first appeared in the *Athenæum*, March 4 and April 15, 1848, under the titles: " Shelley at Eton," and " Shelley and His Contemporaries at Eton."

For copies of the letters regarding Shelley in Wales I am indebted to Mr. W. M. Richards, of Portmadoc, North Wales, and for permission to use them to Mr. Adrian Stokes, of the firm of Breese, Jones, Casson, and Stokes in Portmadoc. Following my own examination of a collection of old papers of the Madocks Estate (which is still handled by the firm of Breese, Jones, and Casson), the National University of Wales sent an investigator to search more extensively. Among the rafters above one of the rooms these letters were found. They are now in the National Library of Wales at Aberystwyth.

1

W. H. MERLE TO THE *ATHENÆUM*

After an absence of some months I have been reading up my *Athenæums:* — and came upon the review of " The Life of P. B. Shelley, by Capt. Medwin." (See *Athenæum*, Nos. 1038–1039.)

489

As an old Etonian, allow me to express my surprise that in all the Memoirs of Shelley so little has been collected in illustration of his days at Eton. Shelley as a boy was a being never to be forgotten. He stood apart from the whole school. I have the list before me now for the year 1807 — amounting to 440 boys; and I will venture to say there is not a man of them living who does not remember Shelley for his wild and marked peculiarity. For years and years, and long before I knew that Shelley the boy was Shelley the poet and friend of Byron, he dwelt in my memory as one of those strange and unearthly compounds which sometimes, though rarely, appear in " the human form divine." Though death has thinned our ranks, I am convinced that any biographer of Shelley might have collected many and many an anecdote highly interesting as showing the man in boyhood, — with much that stamped its force on the original bent of his sensitive and poetical mind. Either from natural delicacy of frame or from possessing a mind which in boyhood busied itself in grasping at thoughts beyond his age — probably from something of both — he shunned or despised the usual games and exercises of youth. This made him with other boys a byword and a jest. He was known as " Mad Shelley "; — and many a cruel torture was practised upon him for his moody and singular exclusiveness.

Shelley was my senior; and I, in common with others, deemed him as one ranging between madness and folly, until one who then lived in the same house with Shelley — a boy his senior and well able to appreciate in others that talent which he largely possessed within himself — told me that in " Mad Shelley " there were seeds to overflowing of meditation deep and of that wild originality which is the attribute of genius. The boy, my informant, was the present barrister, Mr. Amos. For some reason or other Amos subsequently came to my tutor, the Rev. T. Carter; and it was while living under the same roof that I gathered his opinion of the " Mad Shelley." I cannot but think that if time and inclination served, this gentleman could furnish more than any other interesting details of the poet in embryo. In those days, as doubtless in these, there were a certain number of " extra masters," — some of whom resided at the college, took boarders, and held an amphibious rank between "the tutor" and "the dame." Among these was one "Mr. Hexter"; who professed to be a teacher of writing, — though it must be confessed that the boys under his roof made a much greater proficiency with their knives and forks than they did with their pens in the writing school. It was with this professor of pot-hooks and hangers that Percy Bysshe Shelley was placed. The house was small, the number of boarders few; and I doubt much if within those walls any intimacy was formed that grew with its growth and ripened in after life. There was, as already shown, a friendly and right understanding between Amos and himself, — but nothing more. Indeed, if I remember rightly, Shelley made no friends at Eton. He probably sought, but in vain, for a spirit congenial to his own. With the mass he had nothing in common. They could not enter into his spirit, nor he into theirs. They deemed him mad, and he despised them as fools. Singly they dared not insult him, — for " there was a method in his madness " which taught repentance: but the herd unite against the stricken, — and boys, like men, envy the strongest and trample on the weak.

These thoughts remind me of those occasions when poor Shelley's anguish and excitement bordered on the sublime. Conscious of his own superiority — of being the reverse of what the many deemed him — stung by the injustice of imputed madness, by the cruelty, if he were mad, of taunting the afflicted, his rage became boundless. Like Tasso's jailer, his heartless tyrants all but raised up the demon which they said was in him. I have seen him surrounded, hooted, baited like a maddened bull, — and at this distance of time I seem to hear ringing in my ears the cry which Shelley was wont to utter in his paroxysm of revengeful anger.

It may not be uninteresting to tell when and where these things occurred. At the same time it is but justice to state that the bigger boys frequently interfered to prevent acts of tyranny towards the smaller. But Shelley in his days of trial was not " a little boy "; and it often happened that one amongst the biggest of the big was singled out as the victim. In the dark winter evenings it was the practice to assemble under the cloisters previous to mounting to the "upper school." Sometimes some wicked wag would introduce a foot-ball into the forbidden ground; and the cloistered square would echo with shouts and laughter as some hapless "dandy" of the day was "nailed," — or in other words, received a blow from the muddy, bounding ball. Poor Shelley, though anything but a fop, was often marked out for this trial of temper. But there was another practice infinitely more galling. The particular name of some particular boy would be sounded by one, taken up by another and another, until hundreds echoed and echoed the name. At the same time, especially if the selected were a "big fellow," a path was usually made and a space opened for the one on whom a hundred tongues were calling. Such, I well remember, was the joke which was practised on one who certainly did not *rejoice* in the name of "Hornby," — one who dwells in my early memory as a square-built, big boy, looking very like a staid and rather elderly gentleman, harmless and kind, and having no offence beyond the carrying a gold quizzing-glass and white cambric pocket-handkerchief and eschewing all manly sports. In his case it was "*vox et præterea nihil*" : — but with poor Shelley it was different. The Shelley! Shelley! Shelley! which was thundered in the cloisters was but too often accompanied by practical jokes, — such as knocking his books from under his arm, seizing them as he stooped to recover them, pulling and tearing his clothes, or pointing with the finger, as one Neapolitan maddens another. The result was, as stated, a paroxysm of anger which made his eyes flash like a tiger's, his cheeks grow pale as death, his limbs quiver, and his hair stand on end.

Another circumstance I perfectly remember; — and name it because I feel certain that it called into active play a host of thought and feeling. In Shelley's days there used to be one "Walker" who lectured on astronomy, chemistry, mechanics, &c. I allude to the "Old Walker" as he was called; a man self-taught for the most part, but possessing much of talent, and being in his nature a thousand times more clever than much learning could ever make his son. Shelley and myself and many others attended "Old Walker's" lectures; and it may easily be imagined how the wonders of heaven, earth and electricity

would seize on a mind like Shelley's. Boys have fashions in their
playthings — and experimental electricity became the rage.
" Like master like man," says the adage — and " Old Walker's "
servant and assistant had picked up a smattering of his master's
knowledge sufficient to enable him to make small electrical
machines. These found a ready sale amongst the boys; much
to the encouragement of infant science — and proving that the
philosopher's man had found out the philosopher's stone. He
made a small fortune for the time. Shelley was amongst the
purchasers, — and, so daring and bold in his experiments, that
he nearly blew up himself and Mr. Hexter's house into the
bargain. Astronomy, like electricity, seized upon his imagination. His jubilee was night. His spirit bounded on the shadow
of darkness, and flew to the countless worlds beyond it.

It was doubtless in moments like these that he conceived the
rich fountains of poetry which subsequently burst forth from
his heart, — that he pictured —

> Heaven's ebon vault
> Studded with stars unutterably bright,
> Through which the moon's unclouded grandeur rolls
> To curtain her sleeping world. Yon gentle hills,
> Robed in a garment of untrodden snow; —
> Yon darksome rocks, whence icicles depend
> So stainless that their white and glittering spires
> Tinge not the moon's pure beam.

I have only to add, that about this time Shelley would often pass
the hour of dinner in pursuing the unearthly wanderings of
his muse. He delighted in invoking the subtleties of theory and
vision, and clothing them in imagery too daring for the utterance of his pen. He saw much, but dimly — yet was too proud
to lean upon a guide. He felt that knowledge is power — but
paused not to reflect that both are dangerous when applied in
ignorance. No wonder that he all but blew up his tutor's house
in boyhood, — and his own fortunes when a man.

2

ANDREW AMOS TO THE *ATHENÆUM*

My attention having been recently drawn to your number of the 4th of March last, in which my early intimacy with the poet Shelley is mentioned, I write a few lines concerning Eton College as it was in the first decade of the present century; in hope that your readers — or, at all events, your correspondent on this subject — may feel an interest in such reminiscences.

At Mr. Hexter's, mentioned by your correspondent, there were only three lower boys (or fags) — Shelley, another boy since deceased, and myself. We consequently messed together, and saw a great deal of each other. Shelley and I used to amuse ourselves in composing plays, and acting them before the other lower boy, — who constituted our sole audience. Shelley entered with great vivacity into this amusement; and from the circumstances attending the theatre of our triumvirate, and other facts connected with the developement of Shelley's early genius, I incline to think that if the slightest encouragement had been given at Eton to merit in English composition, verse or prose, it is highly probable that Shelley would have devoted himself with ardour to the studies of the place, and the irregularities of his mind would have been chastised by habits of patient study. Walker's lectures, mentioned by your correspondent, were perhaps an unfortunate occurrence for Shelley; as they supplied him with the means of producing interesting and dazzling results requiring very little application of mind, and as they increased his aversion to the studies of the school. By the way, your correspondent will perhaps recollect that " Old Walker " on the occasion of one of his lectures, at which both Shelley and myself were present, said, " Perhaps in the time of my son, if not in my own, it may come to pass that he or I shall get down from London to lecture here without being drawn by horses, but impelled by steam," — and that thereupon there was a deafening shout of derision from nearly three hundred boys at this Warner and his Eureka.

After attending Walker's lectures, Shelley became transported with a love of chemical experiments. He did not, however, I believe, study any scientific works upon the subject: — and I think it would have been happy for him if the multitude of boys at a public school had not rendered it almost impracticable for the tutors to watch, and endeavour at least to exercise some control in directing, the pursuits and dispositions of their pupils. Whilst the characteristic of nine-tenths of Shelley's contemporaries while at school was that of listlessness to excitements derived from intellectual sources, here was a youth carried away by an impetuous enthusiasm for producing and witnessing the phenomena of nature. But no Mentor was near him, — who, not discouraging his mental activity, might at the same time have governed and directed it at a period of life when judgment is rarely dominant, and less so perhaps in proportion to the early vigour of the mind.

I think I hear, as if it were yesterday, Shelley singing, with the buoyant cheerfulness in which he often indulged, as he might be running nimbly up and down stairs, the Witches' songs in " Macbeth." I fancy I still hearken to his

> Double, double, toil and trouble,
> Fire burn, and cauldron bubble.

From this period my intimacy with him slackened. Not following his new passion with the same zeal as himself, we now seldom walked or boated together in the hours between school-times. He used to call me — in a tone not altogether unfriendly, but still evincing displeasure approaching to bitterness — by the appellation of *Apurist;* indicating classically thereby one who did not appreciate properly the element of *fire.* I, on the other hand, just at this period, had begun to devote nearly all my play-hours to Latin composition, — being induced thereto by the master who presided over my *form,* and who is now Archbishop of Canterbury. [Remainder of paragraph describing the author's relations with the Archbishop when he was an Eton master omitted.]

[Non-Shelleyan paragraph relating a schoolboy prank omitted.]

495

I have already exceeded the limits I proposed to myself in this letter. Perhaps, if any interest shall attach to what I have written, I may indite more reminiscences concerning Shelley and his contemporaries; and among them, Matthews, the deceased author of "The Diary of an Invalid," — who was master, or *fagger*, to Shelley and his *co-faggee*, myself. But, in conclusion, I may inform my correspondent that I have an excellent neighbour who was at Eton in the time of Shelley, and who repeats an "Eton alphabet" precisely in the time and manner of the head master reading over an exercise "for good." Each letter of the alphabet introduces a well-known character of the Eton world at the beginning of this century, and each line recounts his peculiarities. *H* stands for *Hexter*. This writing-master was also a major in the volunteers, — whence he was often called *Hector;* and his writing pupils were in the habit of saying to him, "Major, will you mend my pen?" *Apropos* of the conventional tone of reading over an exercise "for good," your correspondent will perhaps recollect the circumstance of a boy at Carter's who was overheard by his companions, whilst he was sitting solitarily in his own room, reading over a copy of verses of his own making in the conventional tones of Dr. Goodall, the head master, and then concluding with — "A very good exercise, a very excellent composition; it does you very great credit indeed; you are a very clever boy."

I am, &c.

A. A.

3

S. GIRDLESTONE TO JOHN WILLIAMS, YNYS TOWYN, CARNARVON, NORTH WALES

London,

Sept: 17th 1812.

For W. A. Madocks.

My dear Sir,

However desirable it may be to let Tanyrallt, I am afraid we can make nothing of the present offer.

I should certainly refuse to let the house furnished for a single year to any one; indeed it is my wish to sell the furniture, tho' were an unexceptionable tenant to offer, I think an arrangement might be made as to the furniture — in respect to Mr. Shelley however good his connexions may be, they do not seem at present much avail to him. He being himself under age, no security he can give will be at all binding, consequently if any treaty were to go on between us I should expect it to be carried on with some one whose covenants would be available. I have this day applied to Mr Westbrooke pursuant to your direction, and he informs me that Mr Shelley is the person he represents himself to be, and that he has married his daughter, but he declines giving any guarantee for rent or anything and even declines saying which plan for taking Tanyrallt is or is not proper for the young couple, and says that any application on those subjects or on any means of his future subsistence must be made to Mr Shelley's own relations — in short his answers are in no respect satisfactory — under these circumstances I must explicitly declare the only terms on which I can treat with Mr Shelley — namely that he takes the furniture at a valuation and pays for it, I engaging to retake the same at a valuation at the end of a year if he then wishes to quit the place. I will then let him the house grounds etc at a rent to be agreed upon for one year, he however giving such collateral security as I shall approve of for the payment of the rent and performance of the covenant to keep up the place in a proper state of repair and under the circumstances I have this day learnt from Mr. Westbrooke I should not wish this or any arrangement to take place without the consent of his own family and friends. The circumstances of his being under age, and of his being at variance with his own family must make it very cautious how I deal with him, especially as I understand he has only a present allowance from his Father which may at any moment be withdrawn. In order that there may be no misunderstanding with Mr S. you had better to read to him my letter to this point.

Indeed my dear Sir, I am afraid that Mr S. would by no means prove a sort of tenant that would be useful to us, a young man who has I suspect married much beneath him, and thereby offended his family, with a confined and dependant income, would most probably be ill able to pay his rent, and would besides incur debts with the tradesmen in the town which he would be unable to pay — if indeed his residence was to be sanctioned by his friends, he might prove a valuable tenant, they being highly respectable and opulent, but without their consent I am afraid he would only prove a burden — you must take especial care to not let Mr Shelley into possession of the house or premises for if he gets in we may have great difficulty in getting him out again.

You will hear from me again in a day or two and I hope see me by the middle of next week.

I remain,

Yours &c

S. Girdlestone

Lincolns Inn,
17th Sept 1812.

4

ELIZA WESTBROOK TO JOHN WILLIAMS,
YNYSTOWYN, TREMADOC

My dear Mr Williams,

As Mr Shelley and myself have determined against our residing again at Tanyrallt we shall be obliged if you will send the boxes remaining there to my Father's with proper directions 23 Chapel Street, Grovenor Sqr.

My good friend though disappointed you cannot be surprised at our not returning, the unpleasant scenes which occurred there would ever make that situation disagreeable, lovely as is the spot by nature, the neighbourhood is too corrupt for us ever to take delight in Tanyrallt again, particularly as a fixed residence. We are going to tour through the South of Ireland, and the Carriage is now at the door waiting, all are engaged writing necessary letters. Mr Shelley will write himself soon. They unite in kindest remembrances with

Yours very truly,

E. W. [Eliza Westbrook]

498

I forgot to mention the boxes must be forwarded to London immediately as there are Library Books in them which is of consequence to have returned as soon as possible. Direct your letters as usual 35 Great Cuffe Street.

The Shelleys left Dublin for the Lakes of Killarney about March 21 or 22 and were back in Dublin on March 31. Hence this letter should be dated about March 21, 1813. The figure 13 is decipherable in the frank mark.

5

S. GIRDLESTONE TO JOHN WILLIAMS, CONDUIT STREET, BOND STREET, LONDON

My dear Sir,

Mr Madocks was unfortunately detained out of town the whole of last week by the illness of his Brother, and consequently I could not see the contents of your letter to him, nor judge of Mr Shelley's offers, and now upon receiving it, your letter does not go so far as to enable [me] to form any decisive opinion, because tho you say there is a copy of a deed in Doctors' Commons which will prove that Mr Shelley will when he comes of age come into the possession of a large property, yet you do not tell me how I am to get a sight of that Deed, nor in whose hands it is, from your mentioning Doctors' Commons, I think it must be Will and not a deed which he alludes to, if so, let him send me the name of the Testator and when and where he died, and I shall then be able to make the search and get at the copy. If however he is entitled under any deed, he must inform me in whose hands a copy of it is and how I can get a sight of it. And to show how desirous I am to accommodate Mr S. I will add that if upon search I find that Mr Shelley on coming of age will be in the possession of a considerable fortune, I will notwithstanding his present lack of means, let him Tanyrallt.

His views and proposals certainly seem not honourable [dishonourable?] but however much in earnest he may be, I must see that he does not deceive himself. If he will really have the command of property to the amount he specifies I might be able to chalk out something which might be as beneficial to himself as it would be to Mr M, but I must previously know his means. The intended dissolution of Parliament which will probably take place in a day or two has very much disconcerted all my plans. Mr M. must I believe go off for Boston tomorrow. I hope there will not be any opposition there. I shall, however, think you will see me by the end of this week, so dont you or Mr Shelley come posting off to London in the expectation of seeing me or Mr M. as the motions of both are at present wholly uncertain. You will hear from me again in a day or two.

I remain, Dear Sir,
Yours,
S. GIRDLESTONE.

Lincolns Inn,
28th September 1813.

Misdated or miscopied for 1812? Shelley was already of age on September 28, 1813.

6

D. E. VARNEY TO JOHN WILLIAMS, YNYSTOWYN, TREMADOC

24 *New Ormond Street,*
20th May [1815]

My dear Sir,

Upon application to Mr Shelley's Solicitors I have been informed that my name does not appear in the list of Creditors, but your name is set down as a creditor to the amount of 350 £ under a Bond with a penalty for 700 from whence I am led to conclude that the bond includes my debt as well as your own, the Solicitor further said that the arrangement for payment is as follows: — that those debts for the payment of which no security has been given are to be discharged very speedily — the cash being ready, but those creditors who have procured securities for their money, of which number you unfortunately are, must wait a year longer for payment; tell me therefore in which class of creditors am I to be numbered. Mr. Madocks dined here yesterday and seemed much oppressed with the

hopeless state of the concerns, as mentioned to you in my letters
of yesterday, and Girdlestone as well as I fear his health may
be again thereby affected. I shall call on him the instant I have
closed my letters.

A consultation with Mr Murray is to be fixed some early day
next week.

I am, Dear Sir,
Sincerely Yours,
D. E. VARNEY.

7

D. E. VARNEY TO JOHN WILLIAMS,
YNYSTOWYN, TREMADOC

Knowle,
20th June 1815.

Dear Sir,

I received your last letter two days since, and am much obliged to you for the account you give upon the proceedings on
the Embankment. I calculate your present expenses at about
£136 per month, and if we employ the same force, the £700
will last till about the 18th October, which seems to me to be
a good time to give over working, provided the Bank can then
be pronounced in a good state of security: — that is to say,
provided it should then be completed in every part, equal to
the work commenced and finished last winter on the Merionth-
shire side, if that were done and any money remained in hand,
I should still be of opinion that the work ought to be suspended
that the money might be reserved to meet some future storm
possibly threatening a breach; such is my opinion, and it is a
pleasure to me to observe that you very generally concur in
my opinions upon this subject.

I have been informed that you have received £150 of the
debt due from Shelley, all the money provided for the payment
of Shelley's debts is now exhausted and that act of justice must
be suspended till more money comes in which will be in November next, the money has failed in consequence of Shelley

stating his debts less than they are, and in order to justify this statement he is actually guilty of abundant falsities, in order to get rid of the £100 due to me for hire of furniture, he said, that he had resided at Tanyrallt only two months, and that the instant he had quitted it, I sold the furniture; Did you ever hear of a more ungrateful fellow? His Attorney however promises that all his debts will be paid by the Father —‚ in November next.

I have written to inform him that he cannot have either the carpet or linen upon the terms of hiring them. I must make myself up to this disappointment and search for some other fund to pay the workmen.

You will be glad to hear that Mr Girdlestone is recovering very nearly as much himself as ever, and that I hope he will suffer little further interruption from Mr Madock's creditors; he had indeed suffered very much from them, nor has he ever received the least aid from Mr M's friends; Not one of Mr M's friends would sign the Bond which procured for him the liberty of the Fleet and thereby enabled him to feed his miserable wife and children during his confinement, whence he was discharged by the Insolvent Act.

I began this letter at Uffington, but am finishing it at a small public house half way between Warwick and Birmingham.

I travel very slowly with the view of sparing a very young horse, and do not expect to reach Tremadoc till Sunday afternoon, if you can give me a well aired bed on Sunday night I shall be obliged, for I shall thereby not only save my horse, which will have travelled from Bettws on that day, but I shall be at hand to inspect the Bank on Monday morning, as the money now laying out is evidently brought forth at my strong instance and advice, I feel bound in duty to give the application as much personal attention as possible; this I have promised to do and I think I could not feel a stronger and more anxious interest in the success of it, if the whole were my own.

I remain Dear Sir,

Yours sincerely,

D. E. VARNEY.

Do not let it be generally known that I intend being with you on Sunday.

8

CHARLES CLAIRMONT TO FRANCIS PLACE

12 January, 1815 [for 1816]

My Dear Sir,

You were kind enough, when I applied to you some months ago, to say you would have no objection to render me any little assistance in your power to enable me to cast about and undertake some employment for my own subsistence. I was at that time engaged in a negotiation concerning a business in Ireland, the basis of which was founded on Shelley's assistance. I refrained from mentioning this to you at the time, because I was very well aware of your sentiments toward Shelley and was afraid they were even so inimical that you would perhaps have instantly renounced all advice or assistance on the ground of rejecting anything in which he was connected. After a more mature consideration on that point, however, I feel convinced this fear was needless. You have expressed in very strong terms your dislike of Shelley; but you have been prejudiced against him. I think Godwin's treatment of Shelley unjust; yet he is most peculiarly circumstanced with regard to him; and it is I believe from Godwin alone that you have received your accounts. I do not know exactly how the case has been stated to you, but I judge in the most unfavourable light. I trust that you will not for a moment infer that I think Godwin capable of having asserted untruths in the matter; yet you must be aware that it is possible so to state mere facts, that without deviating from the truth, one may make an argument appear on which side of a question one pleases, while the fairest deduction, perhaps, lies in the middle. — As the good respect I should be glad to obtain in your eyes may hang upon your forming a just decision on this subject, I wish, whatever are your opinions, to give you mine, in order that you may be convinced of my integrity with regard to Shelley and my sisters and that you may understand my sentiments to be general principles, and not merely the adoption of interested motives. You are acquainted with the facts; I will not therefore enter into them, however unfavourably they may have been stated to you; but simply give you my reasons why I think Shelley unjustly treated and why I am his friend.

Here is a young man of the greatest refinement and learning, and the most uncommon talent, by a puerile, inexperienced thoughtlessness married to a pretty trifling girl, of the most slender capacity, whose only pleasures and occupations are balls and theatres and such frivolous amusements. The particulars of the original connection between them are of a very remarkable nature, yet they are too long for insertion here. Suffice it at present to assure you he never had for her any strong attachment; he thought her certainly a pretty woman, and was married to her *when quite a boy,* under circumstances so very peculiar as could never have happened to any but one of so very strange a turn of mind as himself. Her love toward him was precisely of the same cold nature; this she most fully proved at the time of their separation. Her love for Shelley was absolutely none! So long as he was the minister of her pleasures and her respectability, she pretended a sympathy with his principles and an admiration of his character; but so soon as her interest became unconnected with his, she became his secret enemy and the enemy of his friends. Godwin, especially, though she knew his sentiments were inimical to Shelley's conduct, for he both wrote to her and called on her, was instantly the object of her blackest calumny and invective. I know of facts concerning her misrepresentations of Godwin, which place the weakness and treachery of her nature in a conspicuous light. She associated (I do not at all mean what the world calls criminally) with an Irish adventurer whom she commissioned to take all possible legal advantage of Shelley. She knew his embarrassed circumstances at the time, and yet glutted her revenge by running up the most extravagant and needless bills against him, among tradesmen where she knew she could obtain credit. In short, it was only her impotence to injure that rendered her innocent of the most wide spreading blasting mischief. My Dear Sir, I am susceptible of the most compassionate feeling for a woman placed in such a situation; and I would not require of her a compromise of that dignity and self-respect which is the property of every female who thoroughly feels the extent of her claims as a woman and a wife; I would not require of her that she become a crouching, puling, begging suppliant; she has certainly every right to feel her pride injured; yet still I cannot think that a woman who sincerely loved, could descend to the low revenge of abuse and scurrility — Such conduct is neither affection, or virtue, or dignity, or even reconcilable with these properties.

But now even suppose Mrs. Shelley's passion for her husband had been as intense as that which Shelley felt for my sister; still I cannot see that this would have been sufficient to entitle her to the preference when it was a question with whom Shelley should associate and domesticate for life. A certain portion of unhappiness necessarily falls to her whose love is unreturned: would cohabitation have remedied this evil? Shelley felt he could not esteem her; would a generous hypocrisy have procured the effects of passion? and if it could, how would the wretched victim of such a melancholy farce, a man of sensibility and virtue, have deserved this hopeless solitude of the heart? Because he is exquisitely framed to perceive and adore true excellence, must he be everlastingly chained to dullness and sickening folly? And who is she for whom this mighty sacrifice is prepared, for whom his happiness (and so far as depends on his life and reason) his usefulness is bartered? — She is totally unlike her companion. She delights in frivolous amusements, and despises from her heart all literature or learned accomplishments. Her fondness for her husband induces her to adopt principles, which she has neither the understanding or the courage to prefer for their intrinsic worthiness. Their intercourse must be full of irritating discomfitures. Their natures are distinguished by antipathies which no despotism but that of marriage could ever attempt to coalesce. I am persuaded that he who leaves such a woman for another in every respect more suited to his intellectual nature, acts neither selfishly or sensually. If it be true that a person is justified in terminating a connection thus unsatisfactory, when the other party has feelings in some degree inimical to the proceeding, surely the

505

justice is much more evident when the reluctance to the separation clearly arises out of the most vicious and ignoble motives that can disgrace the human heart.

What love can the person who enjoys frivolity and parade bear to the solitary student? Love is produced by a real or supposed sympathy of tastes and dispositions; subtract these causes; what remains but avarice or sensuality? — Perhaps you may think my sentiments too wild and undigested for a maturer age; yet if so I still hope you will agree with me in their bulk and main tenor. I believe you to be a thoroughly unprejudiced man, and I think I must have been wrong in supposing you would allow your judgement to be shackled on this subject. This long account is no doubt troublesome and tedious to you; yet I am afraid it was necessary; I want you not to withdraw from me your assistance; and as the arrangements I am desirous of making render me closely connected with Shelley, I judged it proper to convince you of the purity of my feeling in being so.

[*Charles goes on to explain that he has left Godwin's house with the latter's consent, because he is of no use there, and that about two months ago he went over to Ireland to investigate a distillery business which he felt was an excellent investment, promising 20 or 25 per cent return, and gives further account of its advantages. Then:*]

I am only prevented from an immediate accession to this very advantageous prospect by the abominable and unavoidable delays which have occurred in Shelley's now pending arrangements with his father. Shelley wishes to provide me with the necessary capital and on which I am to pay him the same interest he would acquire on it in the funds. He is willing even to make a present sacrifice, in order to procure a speedy arrangement, and to obtain for me the money on the same terms as he is now settling with his father, which is about £100 for £65. If I allow this sacrifice of course it would be my duty to see it afterwards made up to him; but I think this way of managing the thing out of the question, as the largest profits of the most prosperous business on earth could scarcely make it worth while to incur so heavy a loss. It is on this affair that I come to demand your consideration; some method may strike your

experienced and active mind of accomplishing my object; but
if this is impossible you will still be able to give me very valuable
advice concerning some occupation for a present immediate
subsistence. . . .

*The letter ends by offering to show estimates, letters, and documents
on the distillery project.*

*Original in British Museum, Add. MSS 35,152, folios 191–4. Sum-
marized in part in Helen Rossetti Angeli:* Shelley and His Friends
in Italy *(London, 1911), 76.*

*The same manuscript volume contains Place's reply, dated Jan. 14,
1816, showing that Clairmont's date of 1815 should be 1816.*

*Place briefly replied that if the project looked as promising to him
as to Clairmont he would not invest his own money in it on his own
account, and " of course I cannot agree to withdraw it [i.e., his money
from present investments] to lend it to another, neither can I consent
to take the chance of being involved in any transaction between you
and Shelley." He promised to continue to help Charles find employment.*

APPENDIX IV

BRIEF FOR SHELLEY'S DEFENCE IN THE CHANCERY
SUIT OVER HARRIET'S CHILDREN

In the late 1870's or early 1880's Mr. Harry Buxton Forman had copies made of the documents in the Chancery suit which was instituted to deprive Shelley of the custody of his two children by Harriet. These papers were used by Professor Dowden in his life of Shelley. All but one of them, apparently, were later published by Mr. Forman in Appendix III of his edition of Medwin's *Revised Life of Shelley*, pages 463–86. The present brief was in Mr. Forman's possession at that time and earlier; it is mentioned in a footnote on page 466 as " the brief prepared by Shelley's Solicitor, Longdill, for the use of his chief Counsel, Mr. Wetherell, a paper in my possession, from which Professor Dowden drew some interesting particulars." Why it was not published with the others I do not know. At some time after Mr. Forman's death it became a part of the Luther A. Brewer collection, now in the library of the University of Iowa. It is here published by the kind permission of the librarian.

Numerous notes appear on the backs of the pages of the original manuscript, evidently written down hastily as memoranda or points to be used in rebuttal. They are all difficult to decipher, and except for one note on the back of page one, which is here appended, they seem too fragmentary or insignificant to include with the original document.

IN CHANCERY

Eliza Ianthe Shelley and Charles Bysshe Shelley infants by John Westbrooke their maternal Grandfather and next Friend . . . Plaintiffs . . .

BETWEEN   and

Elizabeth Westbrooke spinster John Hig-

Brief for Defend-   ham Esq. Percy Bysshe Shelley Esq. Sir
ant P. B. Shelley   Timothy Shelley Baronet and John West-
                      brook Esq. . . . Defendants . . .

To the right Honorable the Lord High Chancellor of Great Britian.

The humble Petition of the said Plaintiffs — SHEWETH/

That in the month of August in the Year 1811 the s⁴ Percy Bysshe Shelley married Harriet Westbrook who was the daughter of the s⁴ John Westbrooke and that your Petitioners are the only issue of the s⁴ marriage and that after the birth of your Petitioner Eliza Ianthe Shelley and while the said Harriet Shelley was pregnant with your Petitioner Charles Bysshe Shelley the said Percy Bysshe Shelley became acquainted with a Wm. Godwin the Author of a Work called Political Justice and other Works and with a Mary Godwin his Daughter and that the s⁴ Percy Bysshe Shelley about 3 years ago deserted his s⁴ wife and unlawfully cohabited with the s⁴ Mary Godwin And that thereupon the said Harriet Shelley returned to the House of her father the s⁴ John Westbrooke and brought your Petitioner Eliza Ianthe Shelley with her and soon afterwards your Petitioner Charles Bysshe Shelley was born in the House of the s⁴ John Westbrooke And your Petitioners have ever since continued and are now in the Custody and under the care and protection of the said John Westbrooke and of his Daughter the s⁴ Eliza^b Westbrooke the Sister of the said Harriet Shelley.

That from the time the s⁴ Harriet Shelley was deserted by her said Husband until a short time previously to the time of her Death she lived with the s⁴ John Westbrooke her father And that in the Month of December last she died and that the s⁴ Percy Bysshe Shelley ever since he so deserted his said Wife has unlawfully cohabited with the s⁴ Mary Godwin and is now unlawfully cohabiting with her and has several illigitimate Children by her.[1]

---

[1] Here the following marginal note appears: "Cohabiting with Mary Godwin." The writing appears to have been done by the same hand making the notes on the backs of the sheets of the document.

That the s⁴ Sir Timothy Shelley the Father of the s⁴ Percy Bysshe Shelley did in the Year 1815 concur with the s⁴ Percy Bysshe Shelley in making a Settlement of certain Estates belonging to the s⁴ Sir Timothy Shelley and Percy Bysshe Shelley whereby the s⁴ Percy Bysshe Shelley became and is now indebted to a Yearly rent Charge or Annuity of £1000 subject to the payment there out of the Yearly Sum of £200 to the s⁴ Harriet Shelley during her life.

That while your Petitioners lived with the said John Westbrooke they were supported partly by their Mother and partly by the said Jn. Westbrooke and the s⁴ Percy Bysshe Shelley did not contribute to their support.

That the s⁴ Defendant Percy Bysshe Shelley vows himself to be an Atheist and that he hath since his s⁴ Marriage written, published a certain Work called "Queen Mab" with notes and other Works that he hath therein blasphemously derided the Truth of the Christian revelation and denied the existence of a God as the Creator of the Universe.

That since the Death of the s⁴ Harriet Shelley the s⁴ Deft. Percy Bysshe Shelley has demanded that your Petitioners should be delivered up to him and that he intends if he can to get possession of their Persons and Educate them as he thinks proper.

That in order to make some Provision for your Petitioners the s⁴ John Westbrooke hath transferred the sum of £2000 4 Cent. Bank Annuities into the names of the s⁴ Defts. Elizb. Westbrooke and John Higham And that the same is now standing in their names.

That an Indenture bearing date the 2ⁿᵈ day of Janry 1817 has been duly made between the s⁴ Jn. Westbrooke of the 1ˢᵗ Part your Petitioners Elizᵇ Ianthe Shelley and Charles Bysshe Shelley of the 2ⁿᵈ part and the s⁴ Defts Elizᵇ Westbrook and John Higham of the 3ʳᵈ Part And that the same has been executed by your Petitioner John Westbrooke and the said Defendants Elizabeth Westbrooke and John Higham And that by the s⁴ Inre After reciting the s⁴ transfer it was agreed that they the s⁴ Defts. Elizᵇ Westbrooke and John Higham and the Survivor of them and the Executors and Admors of such

Survivor should stand possessed of and interested in the said
Sum of £2000 4 Cent consol^d Bank Annuities. Upon trust
for your Petitioners equally to be divided between them
share and share alike and to be paid assigned or transferred
to them respectively in manner following that is to say One
Moiety or half part thereof to be paid assigned or transferred
to your Petitioner Eliza Ianthe Shelley when she shall attain
the Age of 21 Years or be married (with the consent in writing of your Petitioner John Westbrooke or of such Person as
he shall by Deed or Will appoint) which shall first happen
And the other Moiety or half part thereof to be assigned or
transferred to your Petitioner Charles Bysshe Shelley when
he shall attain the Age of 21 Years But in case your s^d Petitioner Eliza Ianthe Shelley shall happen to depart this Life
under the Age of 21 Years and without having married with
such consent as afores^d or your Petitioner Chars. Bysshe Shelley shall depart this Life under the Age of 21 Years Then in
that Case the whole of the s^d sum of £2000 4 Cent consol^d
Bank Annuities shall go and be paid to the Survivor of your
Petitioners Eliza Ianthe Shelley and Chas. Bysshe Shelley
at such time as is mentioned with respect to her or his original
Moiety of the s^d Trust Moneys and upon Trust in the meantime and until your Petitioners or the survivor of them shall
become intitled to an absolute vested Interest in the s^d trust
monies to pay and apply all or a sufficient part of the divi-
dends and annual Produce of the s^d trust fund for and
towards the maintenance and education as afores^d Upon
trust to accumulate the same upon the same Trusts as are
declared concerning the said Sum of £2000 4 Cent Consol^d
Bank Annuities and without making any distinct^n in the
shares from which such accumulations shall arise And, upon
further Trust that in case your Petitioners should depart this
Life before the Interest of either of them in the s^d Trust
Monies sho^d become payable and transferable under the
Trusts before set forth then that the s^d Trustees or Trustee
for the time being shall stand possessed of and interested
in the s^d Trust fund in trust for the s^d Defendant Jn. Westbrooke his Exors Admors and Assigns to and for his and

their own use and benefit absolutely Provided always and it is thereby declared and agreed that it shall and may be lawful to and for the s^d Trustees and the Survivor of them or other the trustees or Trustee for the time being of the s^d Bank Annuities by and with the consent in Writing of the s^d Jn. Westbrooke if living but if dead then by and of the proper Authy. of the same Trustees respectively to raise any sum of Money by and out of the s^d trust fund not exceeding in the whole £300 and to apply the same for the preferment and advancement in the world or other benefits and advantage of your Petitioner Charles Bysshe Shelley as they the s^d Trustees or other the trustees or trustee for the time being thereof shall in their his or her discretion think fit notwithstanding your Petitioner Chas Bysshe Shelley shall not then have attained his Age of 21 Years.

That your Petitioner Eliza Ianthe Shelley is now of the Age of 3 Years and a half or thereabouts and your Petitioner Chas. Bysshe Shelley is of the Age of 2 Years or thereabouts.[1]

That your Petitioners have lately filed their Bill in this Honorable Court setting forth the matters afores^d and praying amongst other Things that the Fortunes of your Petitioners and their Persons may be placed under the protection of this Honorable Court and that a proper Person or proper Persons may be appointed to act as their Guardian or Guardians and that all proper directions may be given for their maintenance and education and that the Trusts of the s^d Indenture may be performed and that if necessary the said sum of £2000 4 Cent Bank Annuities may be transferred into the name of the Accountant General of this Honorable Court upon the Trust of that Indenture and that in the mean time the s^d Percy Bysshe Shelley may be restrained by the Injunction of this Honorable Court from taking Possession of the Persons of your Petitioners Eliza Ianthe Shelley and Chas. Bysshe Shelley and for general relief.

[1] The age of Eliza Ianthe Shelley is blurred, but in the margin is written " 3½ " and " 2," the last number evidently referring to the age of Charles Bysshe Shelley.

PRAYER

That it may be referred to one of the Masters of this Honorable Court to appoint the s^d Jn. Westbrooke and the s^d Eliz^b Westbrooke or some other proper Person or Persons to act as the Guardian or Guardians of your Petitioners and to approve of a proper Plan for their maintenance and education and that the s^d Percy Bysshe Shelley may be restrained by the Injunction of this Honorable Court from taking Possession of the Persons of your Petitioners or either of them or that your Lordship will make such other order therein as shall be just.

AND your Petitioners shall ever Pray thee.

AFFIDAVIT of Elizabeth Westbrooke
one of the above named Defts.
sworn 10th Janry. 1817.

STATES

That she knows and is well acquainted with the Handwriting of Percy Bysshe Shelley Esq. one of the above named Defts. in this cause having frequently seen him write. That she hath looked upon certain paper Writings now produced and shewn to her at the time of swearing this her Affidavit and marked respectively 1. 2. 3. 4. 5. 6. 7. 8. 9. That the s^d Paper Writings are all of the Hand writing of the s^d Deft Percy Bysshe Shelley and were resptively addressed by him to Harriet his late Wife deced the sister of this Defent. That the female ment^d or referred to in the s^d Letters marked respectively 2. 4. 6. 9. under the name or designation of "Mary" and in the s^d other Letters by the Character or description of the Person with whom the s^d Deft. had connected or associated himself is Mary Godwin in the Headings of this Cause named whom the s^d Deft Percy Bysshe Shelley in the Life time of his s^d Wife and in or about the middle of the Year 1814 took to cohabit with him and hath ever since continued to cohabit and still doth cohabit with That she hath looked upon a certain other paper Writing produced and shewn to this Depont. now at the time of swear-

ing this her Affidavit and marked 10 That the same Paper
Writing is of the Hand Writing of the s^d Deft. Percy Bysshe
Shelley and was addressed by him to this Depont. since
the dece. of her s^d Sister the late wife of the s^d Percy
Bysshe Shelley That the Person referred to in the last men^d
Letter " As the Lady whose Union with the s^d Deft. this Deft.
might excusably regard as the Cause of her Sisters ruin " is
also the s^d Mary Godwin That she hath looked upon a certain
printed Book produced and shewn to this Depont. now at
the time of swearing this her Affidavit and marked with the
Letter A and entitled " Queen Mab " with notes subjoined
thereto and a certain printed Book a Pamphlett marked with
the Letter B entitled a Letter to Lord Ellenborough occasioned by the sentence which he passed on Mr. D. I. Eaton
as publisher of the 3rd part 'of Paines Age of Reason That
the s^d Books marked resptively. A B were resptively. written
and published by the s^d Deft. Percy Bysshe Shelley as she
this Dept. knows she having frequently seen the manuscript
of such respective Books in the Handwriting of the s^d Deft.
and having repeatedly seen him engaged in writing the same
That the s^d Printed Books now produced were presented by
the s^d Deft to his s^d late Wife the Sister of this Depont. That
she hath since the death of her s^d Sister received several applications from the s^d Deft Percy Bysshe Shelley and from
Mr. Leigh Hunt on his behalf demanding the s^d Pts. to be delivered up to the s^d Deft Percy Bysshe Shelley.

FURTHER AFFIDAVIT of the said
Elizabeth Westbrooke sworn
13th Jan. 1817
STATES

That in the Month of Aug. in the Year 1811 the above
named Deft Percy Bysshe Shelley married Harriet Westbrooke a Daughter of the above named Deft. John Westbrooke and Sister of this Depont. and the s^d Pts. are the only
Issue of the s^d Marriage That after the birth of the s^d Pt. Eliza
Ianthe Shelley and while the s^d Harriet Shelley was pregnant
with the s^d Chas. Bysshe Shelley he the s^d Percy Bysshe Shel-

ley deserted his Wife and as this depont. hath been informed
and verily believes unlawfully cohabited with Mary Godwin
in the Pleadings in this cause named And thereupon the s⁴
Harriet Shelley returned to the House of her s⁴ Father and
took the pt. Eliza Ianthe Shelley with her and soon afterwards the Pt. Chas. Bysshe Shelley was born in the House
of the s⁴ Jn. Westbrook and the s⁴ Pts. have since continued
and are now in the Custody or under the care and protection of the s⁴ Jn. Westbrooke and of this Depont. and from
the time the s⁴ Harriet Shelley was deserted by her s⁴ Husband until a short time previously to her Death she lived with
or under the protection of the s⁴ John Westbrook her Father
And that in the Month of Dec. last she died That while the
s⁴ Ptt. lived with or under the Care of the s⁴ Jn. Westbrooke
they were supported partly by their Mother and partly by
the s⁴ Jn. Westbrooke and in order to make some Provision
for the s⁴ ptts. the s⁴ Jn. Westbrooke hath transferred the Sum
of £ 2000   Cent Bk. Annus. into the names of this Depont.
and the above named Deft. Jn. Higham upon certain Trusts
declared thereof in and by the Indre. dated the 2nd Day
of Janry Inst. in the Pleads. of this cause men⁴ and the same
is now standing in their Names.

OBSERVATIONS

Mr. Shelley being extremely anxious to have the care of his
Children, hopes that such a Case is not made out by Mr. and
Miss Westbrooke, as will induce the Lord Chancellor to de-
prive him of the natural rights of a Father.

Little can be said in defence of " Queen Mab." It was however written and printed by Mr. Shelley when he was only 19
and as to the Publication of it, it was merely distributed to
some few of his personal Friends; not 20 ever got abroad. The
Copy which is referred to by Miss Westbrooke appears to be
one which Mr. Shelley confidentially gave to his late Wife. Mr.
Shelley has not been able to get a Copy of his Letter to Lord
Ellenborough. A very few Copies of that were printed and
none ever publickly circulated.

Notwithstanding Mr. Shelley's violent Phillippics against the "Despotism of Marriage," as a Contract "against delicacy and reason" and as a system hostile to human happiness and notwithstanding his anticipated delights of the free enjoyment of "choice and change" which would result from the "abolition of Marriage" (see page 147 et seq of Queen Mab) Mr. Shelley married twice before he is 25! — he is no sooner liberated from the despotick chains which he speaks of with so much horrour and contempt, than he voluntarily forges a new set, and becomes again a willing victim of this horrid despotism! It is hoped that a consideration of this marked difference between his speculative opinions and his actions, will induce the Lord Chancellor not to think very seriously of this boyish and silly, but certainly unjustifiable Publication of Queen Mab.

There appears to be no case in print in which the Chancellor has exercised his right of taking Children from the care of their Father on account of his religious or irreligious opinions *alone*. The objection as to the adulterous connexion with Miss Godwin is at an end, and certainly no danger is *at present* to be apprehended as to effect which the religious principles of the Father may have on the minds of the Children.

As a Question involving the worldly Interest of the Children, it is conceived that the Lord Chancellor should, in this case, be very cautious how he exerts the Power which he is now called upon to exercise. Mr. Shelley is, under the Family Settlements, Tenant in Tail of the Shelley Estates in Sussex, which are probably of the value of £60000. In these Estates he has, by suffering a Recovery, acquired a base fee, and he has besides not very remote prospects of a still larger Inheritance. If the Effect of taking these Children (one of whom he has never seen) from his care should be an estrangement of all feelings of parental affection on one hand and of filial piety on the other, it is much to be feared that he may be led to look on the Children which he may have by his present Wife (by whom he has one born during the late Mrs. Shelley's life) as the sole objects of his affection, as well as of his pecuniary consideration.

Part of the Prayer of the Petition is that Mr. and Miss Westbrooke should be appointed Guardians. That part of the

Prayer it is presumed can not in the present state of the Affair
be granted, but it is thought right to say that Mr. Westbrook
formerly kept a Coffee House, and is certainly in no respect
qualified to be the Guardian of Mr. Shelley's Children. To Miss
Westbrooke there are more decided objections — she is illiter-
ate and vulgar, and what is perhaps a still greater objection, it
was by her advice and with her active concurrence, and it may
be said by her *management* that Mr. Shelley when of the Age
of 19 ran away with Miss Harriet Westbrooke, then of the age
of 17, and married her in Scotland. Miss Westbrooke the proposed Guardian was then nearly 30, and if she had acted as
she ought to have done as the Guardian and Friend of her
Younger Sister, all this misery and disgrace to both Families
would have been avoided.

Note on Reverse of Page 1
Objective — The Plaintiff's father is alive, and therefore nobody can have the Guardianship of him, by reason of the
patriae populia; consequently this Court has not, and if so the
Court cannot interfere. But this Court does not act on the *foot
of Guardianship* or Wardship: the latter is totally taken away
by the *Stat. Car:* 2, and without claiming the *former,* and dis-
claiming the latter, has a general right delegated by the Crown
as *pater patria,* to interfere in particular cases, for the benefit
of such who are incapable to protect themselves. *And it is no
objection that the father* of such *persons* is living; for infants
in the life of the father, are in this Court by *prochim amy* and
defend by Guardian. This Court will protect the Estate of the
Infant against the father, and prevent its coming into the
father's hands.

APPENDIX V

THE PORTRAITS AND BUSTS OF SHELLEY

There are no portraits or sketches of Shelley that may be fully relied upon as true likenesses. The portrait which most nearly corresponds to verbal descriptions has hitherto never been published; and the portrait most beloved by twentieth-century Shelleyans will be shown in this discussion to be not Shelley at all, but Leigh Hunt. Thornton Hunt believed that imperfect portraiture was responsible for many misconceptions of Shelley's character and described the accepted portraits as resembling Shelley "about as much as a lady in a book of fashions resembles real women" (*Atlantic Monthly*, XI, 184 and 202). Peacock, Medwin and Trelawny were of similar opinion, and the former even considered that the best representation of Shelley's appearance was to be found in the portrait of another man, Antonio Leisman, in the Florentine Gallery.

The difficulty of securing a reliable likeness of Shelley was fully realized by Mary Shelley, who on August 28, 1819 answered the Hunts' request for a portrait: "The Italian painters are very bad; they might make a nose like Shelley's, and perhaps a mouth, but I doubt it; but there would be no expression about it." In her next letter, September 24, she added: "Italian artists cannot make portraits. We may chance to find an English or German at Florence, and if so I will persuade Shelley to sit."

Two paintings of Shelley are known to have been made during the last years of his life, both by amateurs. Miss Amelia Curran did an oil painting of him in Rome in 1819, but was soon dissatisfied with it and threw it aside. It was a mere accident that she did not burn it and was able later to reclaim and finish it to satisfy Mary Shelley's intense longing for a portrait of her dead husband. Edward Williams did a small water-

colour shortly before the poet's death. De Quincey saw a pen
and ink sketch of the poet said to have been done while Shelley was at Oxford. Claire Clairmont's journal for January 7
and 9, 1820, mentions that a Mr. Tomkins, then associating
with the Shelleys in Florence, "takes Shelley's likeness." This
was probably in fulfilment of Mary Shelley's promise to Marianne Hunt, quoted above. From another source of information Lady Shelley knew of this likeness in July 1883 and
spoke of it as having been done "in black chalk" (*Letters
about Shelley*, 80). It seems rather probable that Lady Shelley spoke of it as a sketch still extant, for her knowledge of it
would not have come from the only written source, since Claire
Clairmont's journal makes no mention of the black chalk. She
could have learned of it, however, from Mary Shelley's conversation. Nothing has been heard of it since. Like all the others
except the Curran painting, it seems now to have been lost.

The portrait made by Clint after the poet's death was "composed" from the amateur efforts of Miss Curran and Edward
Williams, plus the oral suggestions and descriptions of Jane
Williams and the poet's widow. This seems to have satisfied
Trelawny as a fair likeness. From this portrait and from the
original by Miss Curran descend most of the portraits now current, except those of Shelley as a boy. There are extant three
other alleged portraits of Shelley supposedly done from life,
but the questions to which they give rise are so extensive that
I reserve them for special treatment at the end of this note.

Two portraits of Shelley as a boy are still extant, one of them
completely authenticated, the other dubious. In the Pierpoint
Morgan Library in New York is an unsigned miniature oil painting of a brown-haired, fair-skinned boy of seven or eight labelled on the frame "P. B. Shelley" and endorsed on the back
of the frame: "This miniature was given to me by my poor
dear friend Shelley in the presence of Lord Byron. Leigh Hunt."
The handwriting is undoubtedly Hunt's, and the portrait has
an unbroken history as a Hunt family heirloom until about 1909,
when it was purchased by Mr. Morgan from Mrs. Cheltman
(née Jacintha Shelley Leigh Hunt) the youngest daughter of
Leigh Hunt. From the fact that it could have been given to

Hunt only during the first week in July 1822 one may even reconstruct with fair certainty the circumstances of the gift. Nearly three years earlier the Shelleys had received a portrait of Hunt with a request for their own portraits in return. Mary had promised a portrait of Shelley if a satisfactory English or German artist could be found when they got to Florence. For some reason or other the promise was not fulfilled, though a Mr. Tomkins did make a sketch of Shelley in Florence early in January 1820. On the first day of July 1822, when Shelley set out in the *Don Juan* to meet Hunt in Leghorn, he must have been disturbed by Mary's almost hysterical reluctance to see him leave. Yet he remembered the boyhood portrait that must have been moved from Pisa with his other furniture and resolved to greet his friend with the fulfilment of an old promise that under the circumstances might easily have been forgotten.

A supposed portrait of Shelley as a boy, said to have been painted by the Duc de Montpensier, is owned by Sir John C. E. Shelley-Rolls. There is no authentication beyond traditional belief, and it does not fully agree with Shelley's features, as later described. From the portrait, this boy is several years older than he could have been if the portrait was painted before the time that the Duc de Montpensier is known to have ceased painting. Thus Richard Garnett was quite correct in asserting that either the portrait is not Shelley or the artist is not the Duc de Montpensier.

Next comes a group of reminiscent or imaginary portraits, interesting for their history and their effect on the popular notion of Shelley's appearance rather than for their somewhat slight contribution toward real truth or understanding.

Either in July 1822, a few days before Shelley's death, or else within a year afterwards, Mrs. Leigh Hunt made a cut-paper silhouette of Shelley which apparently has been lost. An engraving from it by S. Freeman was published by R. Ackerman on October 6, 1826. It is not now to be found in the British Museum, however. Mrs. Hunt's better-known silhouette of Byron is proof of her amateur skill in this early nineteenth-century art. Mary

PERCY BYSSHE SHELLEY

Painting by George Clint after the Curran portrait and the Williams
miniature

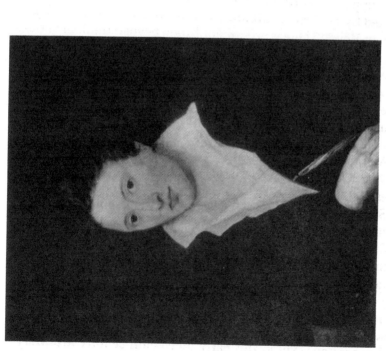

PERCY BYSSHE SHELLEY IN 1819

Painting by Amelia Curran. By permission of the National
Portrait Gallery

Shelley, who had seen the silhouette of Shelley before her departure from Italy in 1823, thought highly enough of it to seek to borrow it for use as a help to Miss Curran in improving the somewhat unsatisfactory oil portrait which Miss Curran was then (1823–4) completing for her. On the end fly-leaf of Leigh Hunt's copy of *Letters of Mr. Pope and Several Eminent Persons* is a pencil profile, resembling the Curran portrait, which the London *Times* (September 9, 1930) suggested is a sketch of Shelley done by Thornton Hunt as a boy. Its resemblance, its genuineness, and its present whereabouts are equally unknown.

Afterwards, in 1829, Mary Shelley herself did a pencil sketch of Shelley based partly on memory and partly on the Curran portrait. This sketch was the basis of an unsatisfactory engraving that was published in Galignani's Paris edition of Shelley, Coleridge, and Keats in 1829. Mary had received drawing-lessons in both England and Italy, but her sketch is rather wooden and conventional and suggests her own stricture on Italian portrait-painters — that they conventionalize their subjects to types seen only in the tradition of their art. It is now in the library of the University of Texas, and has been published in Professor W. E. Peck's *Shelley: His Life and Works*, II, 441.

A reminiscent sculptured bust of Shelley was done after Shelley's death by Mrs. Leigh Hunt, who was an amateur sculptress as well as a maker of silhouettes. It was owned at one time by Browning and is now in the possession of Dr. A. S. W. Rosenbach, of New York and Philadelphia. An etching from this bust was done by William Bell Scott, somewhat "improving" the features, and was published by H. B. Forman in his edition of Trelawny's letters (London, 1910, p. 270). A photograph of the bust appears as the frontispiece of my *The Unextinguished Hearth*. The bust is at least consistent with verbal descriptions in its representation of nose, chin, eyes, and cheeks. In these respects it is probably truer than the Curran and Clint portraits. But it emphasizes these particulars considerably more than the verbal descriptions warrant. On seeing it Thomas Carlyle coarsely remarked that Shelley seemed to have swallowed his chin, and to have disliked it. Yet it differs so greatly from the Curran and Clint portraits, which must certainly possess some validity of another sort, that it is probably a bad general likeness, as Trelawny pronounced it. Why, then, should Leigh Hunt have pronounced the likeness — "at times" — to be "startling"? I suspect that "at times" refers to those times when both Hunt and his wife had seen Shelley in moods of melancholy or deep abstraction. "I should conceive no one so difficult to pourtray," Medwin remarked, apropos of the Williams portrait (*Revised Life,* 313), "the expression of his countenance being ever flitting and varied, — now depressed and melancholy, now lit up like that of a spirit, — making him look one moment forty and the next eighteen."

In 1845 Joseph Severn produced his full-length oil painting of Shelley writing *Prometheus Unbound* among the ruins of the Baths of Caracalla. This painting now hangs in the Keats-Shelley Memorial at Rome. It is in the "one frail form" vein and as genuine portraiture has only such value as may inhere in an indifferent copy of a poor model, embellished in a misleading tradition. Mary Shelley considered it distinctly bad, and in a note to Marianne Hunt (*Bodleian Quarterly Record,* autumn, 1937, VIII, 419) pronounced the nose wrong and the mouth and facial contour defective.

Several palpably fraudulent portraits and one false bust have turned up from time to time. The recumbent full-length figure of Shelley in white marble at University College, Oxford, is obviously the record of a sentimentally false idea and was never intended as a faithful representation of the poet's appearance. The bust of Shelley which appears on the monument at Viareggio represents a more manly conception, but is still the portrait of a sculptor's idea rather than of Shelley himself.

Not only are the authenticated and partly authenticated portraits and bust confusing in their differences, but the Curran-Clint tradition — the dominant one — is plainly idealized and conventionalized beyond any close resemblance to truth. It was somewhat so in the beginning, and the tendency has been greatly extended by various Victorian engravings which sought to conform Shelley still more to the Victorian ideal.

This Victorian idealization reached its climax in a truly remarkable portrait twice printed by Mr. H. B. Forman — once in his edition of *The Shelley Note Books* (Boston, 1911) without legend, and again in his edition of Medwin's *Revised Life of Shelley* (London, 1913) over two lines from Shelley's poems, described in the List of Illustrations as "Portrait of Shelley: Photogravure by Henry Dixon and Son, from a drawing by Alfred Soord." Alfred Soord was a Victorian artist who could not possibly have drawn Shelley from the life; otherwise the portrait might well have been taken as a genuine one, as it doubtless has been by members of a later generation to whom the artist is unknown. Miss Keith Glenn, of Cambridge, Massachusetts, first called my attention to the fact that it is an entirely faithful copy of Leonardo da Vinci's Head of Christ, with only the necessary changes in hair and dress to fit it to Shelley's historical period. In a letter to Miss Glenn, dated August 12, 1935, Mr. Maurice Buxton Forman has explained the matter thus:

My father and my uncle (Alfred Forman, the translator of Wagner, etc.) coming upon the Leonardo "Head of Christ" one day were struck by the likeness to Shelley and it occurred to them that Shelley's head posed at the same angle as the Leonardo, would make a wonderful representation of the lines facsimiled below the print in the Medwin Life of Shelley (Oxford University Press, 1913) I fancy they brooded over this for some time and then one day my father came upon some work of Mr. Soord's and he decided that he was the man to carry out the idea. Soord was living in Hampstead at the time, liked the idea, and carried it out. I have the original here, and a very beautiful piece of work it is.

In a later letter (October 24, 1935) Mr. Forman permitted my use of this information, adding: "but please make it clear that it comes from me and not from my father, because, as I was abroad at the time, I may be quite wrong about the intention."

We now come to the three alleged contemporary portraits mentioned earlier and reserved for later discussion. Two of these, which have hitherto been almost entirely neglected, are probably genuine contemporary portraits. The third, which since 1905 has been almost universally accepted as one of the two undoubtedly genuine portraits of Shelley in his maturity, I will show is certainly not a portrait of Shelley.

Some years ago Mr. Gabriel Wells sold to Mr. George A. Plimpton for his portrait collection what he considered to be the Williams portrait of Shelley. This portrait is a thin, somewhat expressionless pencil sketch, previously published only in a newspaper. In a letter of August 21, 1939 Mrs. Plimpton tells me that when it was recently taken out of its frame the discovery was made that there was another sketch of the same subject on the reverse side. It was sold without any authenticating documents. Both sides bear inscriptions stating that the sketches are of Shelley, done by E. E. Williams on November 27, 1821, at Pisa — a date on which Shelley and Williams were together at Pisa. On one side is a pasted-on paper bearing Mary Shelley's name and address in an unidentified hand. The latter could have no value as evidence, but if the handwriting of the other two inscriptions could be verified as that of either Mary Shelley or Jane Williams the authentication would be absolute, since these two women alone were in a position to make such a statement from first-hand knowledge. But Jane Williams wrote an utterly different hand from the one here shown. Mary Shelley's hand is in general similar to the one here shown and shares one or two peculiarities with it. However, Professor Frederick L. Jones, who is better acquainted with her handwriting than I am, assures me after careful comparison with a number of specimens that in his opinion the handwriting is not hers. The sketches are themselves so thin and apparently extempore that I cannot believe either of them to have been the portrait by Williams which is known to have been used by Clint. The only acquaintance of Shelley who knew and described the Williams portrait was Medwin (*Revised Life*, 313). Medwin speaks of Williams as highly talented in producing " sketches " that were " spirited and masterly " and refers to his portrait of Shelley as a " sketch " and " not a very happy miniature." The term " sketch " (and also " drawing ") might in English usage apply to one of the pencil sketches under discussion, but it could also apply to a water-colour. Tradition refers to Medwin's portrait as a sketch,

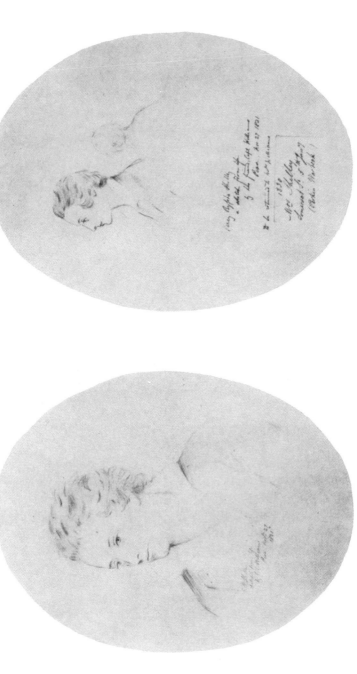

PENCIL SKETCH, SUPPOSEDLY OF SHELLEY,
BY EDWARD ELLERKER WILLIAMS

Here first published by permission of the owner,

Mrs. George A. Plimpton

PENCIL SKETCHES, SUPPOSEDLY OF SHELLEY,
BY EDWARD ELLERKER WILLIAMS

Here first published by permission of the owner,

Mrs. George A. Plimpton

a drawing, and a water-colour sketch, but prefers the last. Medwin's "miniature," however, could refer only to a portrait in colour, and could hardly apply to a portrait so large as the pencil sketch, which is $12\frac{3}{4}$ by $10\frac{1}{4}$ inches.

Nevertheless, though Medwin's reference does not apply, and though the documentation seems inconclusive, I believe these sketches actually to be sketches of Shelley by Edward E. Williams. They violate no known detail of Shelley's appearance, and they could easily be regarded as sketches by the same man, and of the same subject, as the small water-colour portrait which I shall next attribute to Williams. The similarities of dress, eyes, eyebrows, ears, and shoulder seem to me to be more reasonably attributable to the fact that subject and artist are the same than to a coincidence which also coincides with verbal descriptions.

The phrases of Medwin's reference to the Williams portrait apply readily enough to a small water-colour, $6\frac{1}{16}$ by $4\frac{7}{16}$ inches, hitherto unpublished, which came into the possession of Mr. H. B. Forman in 1912. This portrait was purchased of James Gunn, a respectable dealer in Bedford Street, Strand, and bears the following inscriptions:

Directly under the portrait:

Percy Bysshe Shelley

Lower right-hand corner of mounting paper:

R. Hancock, fec. Clifton.

On back of portrait:

Drawn by R. Hancock Clifton.

On back of portrait, faintly pencilled:

Mr. P. B. Shelley the Poet.

Robert Hancock was a fairly well-known painter of porcelain in Clifton, near Bristol, who died in 1817 at the age of eighty-seven. His porcelain work was sometimes signed " R. Hancock, fec.," and he is known to have done in 1796 the crayon portraits of Lamb, Wordsworth, Southey, and Coleridge that were purchased for the National Portrait Gallery in 1877, but I can find no evidence that he painted portraits in oil or water-colour.

The dealer who sold this portrait to Mr. Forman specified in his bill of sale (still owned by Mr. M. B. Forman) that he would not guarantee the signature. Mr. Forman himself came to believe that it was the lost Williams water-colour and began writing a paper expressing this belief. This paper was left unfinished at his death, and at the sale of his library the portrait was bought for Mrs. R. Murray Crane, as the Williams portrait. Recent examination of a photograph of this portrait has elicited from the National Portrait Gallery (through the kind offices of Mr. M. B. Forman) the emphatic opinion that it is in every detail plainly the work of an amateur, and could not possibly have been painted by R. Hancock, a professional.

This judgment seems final. Unfortunately no signature of Hancock could be found for comparison with the signature on the Shelley portrait. However, if the portrait were a genuine portrait of Shelley painted in 1815 one would expect that Shelley's name written under it would be Shelley's signature or else Shelley's name written honestly in an entirely different hand. I reproduce this ascription below, with Shelley's genuine signature and Mary Shelley's signature of a letter copied for Shelley. These signatures show that the first could not have been written by either Shelley or Mary, but is probably intended as an imitation of Shelley's signature.

From the water-colour:

Percy Bysshe Shelley

Shelley, August 27, 1820:

Percy. B. Shelley

Mary Shelley, October 22, 1821:

P. B. Shelley

Since this portrait cannot be what it pretends to be, how did the pretence arise? One thinks at once of the water-colour portrait of Shelley by Edward Williams. This portrait was lost or stolen at some time prior to 1869. The probable imitation of Shelley's signature under the picture strongly suggests that it was stolen. A stolen portrait whose authentication depends upon the testimony of witnesses who cannot be invoked by the thief must be supplied with another authentication and another artist if it is to be sold. The same reasoning would apply if the portrait was lost and later believed to be Shelley's. The impostor needed only to find an artist who could have been in the same place with Shelley at the same time, and who was no longer alive. R. Hancock, of Clifton, painted small portraits, and was not too well known to suit the impostor's purpose. From *Shelley Memorials,* published in 1859, anyone could have learned that Shelley had been in Clifton in 1815. If Hancock's signature was available it was probably imitated as Shelley's was.

Let us now examine more closely the possibility that the portrait falsely attributed to R. Hancock — a portrait without authentication — may be the lost portrait of Shelley by Edward Williams — an authentication, so to speak, without a portrait.

Medwin's rather vague but undoubtedly authentic account of the Williams portrait fits it exactly. W. M. Rossetti's mention of it (*Letters About Shelley,* 29) as a small water-colour portrait also fits, as far as it goes, and probably has behind it the authority of Rossetti's conversations with Trelawny. The water-colour has some points of resemblance to the pencil-sketches supposed to be by Williams and is in no way really inconsistent with them.

This is rather vague and negative evidence, but it does establish the necessary point that the alleged Hancock portrait *could* be the Williams portrait of Shelley. We can now go a step further and show that *if* it is a portrait of Shelley it *must* be the Williams portrait. This follows from the known fact that the only painted portraits of Shelley after he left England were those by Williams and Miss Amelia Curran.

It may be significant that the portrait is labelled Shelley in two different hands; even though the other labels are false, there must have been some genuine reason for calling it Shelley rather than someone else. Miss Curran's portrait is of little direct use in identifying this one, because it is known to have been different, and also unsatisfactory. One has to fall back upon Marianne Hunt's reminiscent bust (also unsatisfactory) and upon the verbal descriptions of the poet. It would be too cumbrous to compare the portrait with all the verbal descriptions; one can only say that they furnish no details which could throw suspicion on the painting as a portrait of Shelley. But since Williams's portrait must have been painted between January, 1821 and July, 1822, and was probably painted in 1822, let us quote the most detailed description of Shelley at that time. Its probable author was Leigh Hunt, and it was first published in 1838 in the *Literary and Pictorial Repository:*

This great poet . . . was about five feet ten or eleven in height, and peculiarly slim, so as to give him an aspect even of fragility. His hair and complexion were light, the face finer than the handsomest could possibly be. The eyes were produced, watchful, and full of the most impassioned feeling; brilliant, yet of a mild thoughtfulness which softened what would otherwise have been their wild expression. The nose was straight and small, and finely carved; the mouth narrow, the lip protruding, the upper one being, a sculptor might think, too long; but it was at all events not sufficiently so to mar the sensitiveness and tremulous firmness (if I may be allowed the expression) which characterized it. The chin receded, and was small and pointed. The cheeks were slightly sunken; the forehead was broad, but not intellectual in the phrenological sense of the word. . . . His dress, when I saw him in Italy, a short time previous to his death . . . consisted of a large-brimmed leghorn hat, such as are worn by planters; a jane jacket and waistcoat, and nankeen trousers, all fitting loosely to the body. His collar he wore up; but because it was supported by no neckcloth it seldom long retained its erect position, or if one side of it did, the other did not, having upon the whole the appearance not decidedly the reverse of negligé.

This is by far the fullest, most detailed, objective, and unromanticized description of Shelley, and it has the advantage of being Shelley within a few months of the time the Williams portrait was painted. Practically every detail in it receives some confirmation from other sources. It explains more fully Shelley's own reference to his nose, and Mary Shelley's mention of the difficulty of painting his lips and eyes and mouth. Trelawny constantly mentions the jacket Shelley wore at this time, and it is mentioned in the official Italian report of the discovery of his body.

This description is strikingly in accord with Marianne Hunt's bust, which reproduces — and amateurishly exaggerates — nearly all of the peculiarities mentioned in it. It is not in accord with the Curran portrait principally in those irregularities which were in Mary Shelley's opinion hard to paint and which may be presumed to form the basis of her objection to that portrait, as they did to the Severn portrait which was based on it. But when this description is compared with the falsely labelled " Hancock " portrait, it is immediately obvious that the portrait is in no respect inconsistent with the description, and that several details are surprisingly corroborated. The jacket, the careless collar without neckcloth, the " produced," slightly wild-looking eyes, the small, pointed, receding chin, extraordinary upper lip, slightly sunken cheeks, and broad forehead — all are in such evident correspondence that the portrait could only have been painted from the written description or from life.

It is true that the figure in the portrait can scarcely be called " peculiarly slim," but in this detail the writer must have been thinking of Shelley as he had appeared in England, for Thornton Hunt, describing Shelley as in July 1822, makes particular mention of the greater fullness of his figure and says that Shelley's chest appeared to have developed to the extent of about four inches. There is another detail of possible significance, not mentioned in the description. According to Medwin and Trelawny, Shelley's hair was beginning in 1822 to show a slight touch of gray. This fact is definitely suggested by this portrait, and by no other. In short, the water-colour resembles both the descriptions of Shelley and Marianne Hunt's bust of Shelley too closely to be a portrait of anyone but Shelley. It seems fantastic to suppose that such a portrait could have been painted from oral descriptions only. Therefore it must be a portrait of Shelley from life, and, if so, it can be no other than the lost water-colour "miniature" painted by Edward Williams.

This conclusion is supported by an examination of the Clint portrait and the self-portrait of Antonio Leisman. The Clint portrait is known to have been an effort to correct the errors of the Curran portrait by combining it with the Williams portrait. When the Clint and Curran portraits are compared, it will be found that Clint did little more than copy Miss Curran. In the Clint portrait the forehead is perhaps slightly higher and broader, the chin slightly more receding. These differences — if they are clearly perceptible — are in the direction both of the verbal description and of the portrait which I now venture to call the Williams portrait. A more perceptible variation is in the upper lip, which in the Clint portrait appears to be a true compromise between the Curran and the Williams portraits. Though the eyes are darker in the Clint and Curran portraits, all three could be easily taken for portraits of the same man. If we now turn to the self-portrait of Antonio Leisman which Peacock said resembled Shelley more than any of the published portraits, we can easily see why. The nose, the upper lip, and the chin correspond almost exactly with the description I have quoted and with the Williams portrait — more so than either the Clint or the Williams portrait. Also, like the Williams portrait, it is more masculine and vital.

The conclusion that the portrait I have used as my frontispiece to Volume I must be the lost portrait of Shelley by Williams can be incorrect only if the resemblances I have traced are all meaningless coincidence. But since these resemblances are matters of individual opinion I can hardly claim to have *proved* my conclusion. More objective proof might have been forthcoming through an expert comparison of the water-colour with Williams's authenticated self-portrait in the British Museum. This examination had already been arranged when the outbreak of the present war forced its indefinite postponement.

If I have so far failed to mention the oil painting by William E. West which has become almost the darling of Twentieth-Cen-

SELF-PORTRAIT OF ANTONIO LEISMAN

Zinco-line facsimile of Lasinio's engraving, called by Peacock

the best likeness of Shelley's features

PENCIL SKETCH BY WILLIAM E. WEST

Commonly supposed to be of Shelley in 1821. Reprinted

from the Century Magazine, October 1905

tury Shelleyans it is because I have strong grounds for a conviction that it is not a portrait of Shelley at all. These grounds are sufficiently lengthy and detailed to demand a separate and rather extended treatment.

The genuineness of West's portrait has hitherto never been publicly questioned. This painting, formerly owned by Mrs. N. P. Dunn, of Richmond, Virginia, and now by the University of Virginia, was first publicly produced as a portrait of Shelley in October 1905, in an illustrated article in the *Century Magazine* by Mrs. N. P. Dunn. From that time it has been fully accepted, its genuineness apparently established by the following undated statement attributed to West by his niece, Mrs. A. P. Bryant, and published in Mrs. Dunn's article:

> While painting the portrait of Lord Byron at Monte Nero, a summer resort on the hills near Leghorn, where Byron had come to spend the warm months at Villa Rossa, the home of Guiccioli and the Gamba family, during one of the sittings, which Byron gave me from three to four o'clock, Shelley, who lived up on the coast not far from Leghorn, called at the villa, and was at once ushered into the room where I was at work. Byron sprang up with delight, and after a warm greeting, seated him facing my easel, which gave me the opportunity to study his face and listen to his interesting conversation for more than an hour. I was so impressed by the man's charming individuality I picked up my pencil and slyly made a sketch of him. Byron thought this sketch an excellent likeness, and after seeing Shelley again in Leghorn, I determined to paint a picture of him while his image was fresh in my memory.

Two earlier statements by West, giving fuller details of the time he spent with Byron, seemed to add verification to West's story. Both are mentioned in the *Century Magazine* article, and the second, in most that concerns Shelley, is quoted. Yet it is these same early accounts which should have first raised a serious doubt about West's veracity.

The first of these appeared in the *New Monthly Magazine* in 1826 (XVI, 243–8, Part I, Original Papers); the second in Henry T. Tuckerman's *Artist-Life, or Sketches of American Painters* (1847), from " a late conversation with Mr. West."

Both accounts contain inaccuracies about Byron and some about Shelley that need not detain us here, since their significance may be extraneous. The first account, though unsigned, was presumably written by West himself, since in March 1897 his niece sent Mrs. Dunn a copy of it in his handwriting. It is by far the more detailed relation, yet it does not mention either Shelley or Leigh Hunt. Even in 1825 or 1826, when Shelley's name appeared insignificant, it seems odd that so great an admirer as West had already become (according to his second and third versions) would fail to mention a sketch and a portrait of him. It will be seen later that both sketch and portrait must have been in his rooms as he was writing. West's failure to mention his portrait of Shelley was repeated in 1828, when an article in the Portland (Maine) *Yankee* for March 19 gives West as the source of a rather vague personal description of Shelley and yet ignores his supposed portrait.

The second version (1847) tells the same story as the first one, except that it brings in both Shelley and Leigh Hunt and gives a warm and detailed account of the former. It does not, however, make the slightest mention of the sketch and the portrait which (according to the third story) had been in his possession since 1822. West was talking with an author whom he knew to be writing a sketch of him as an artist. In 1847 a new portrait of Shelley would have been of sensational importance. If under these circumstances West failed to mention his sketch and portrait, can it be explained on any other ground than that West did not then have, and had never had, a sketch or portrait which he knew to be of Shelley? Any other conclusion seems psychologically impossible. As the story unfolds, it will be seen that there were three other very similar psychological impossibilities.

Perhaps it is worth while under these circumstances to glance a little more closely at West's account of meeting Shelley. He speaks of Shelley as wearing " a loose dress of gingham " because of the sultriness of the day, and as describing, " in the most vivid and glowing terms, a cave that he had discovered while coasting along the Mediterranean the day previous," and had entered in his boat and explored. If we now pause to fix the precise time of this alleged interview the results will show that these two details must be absurdly false.

Byron's residence at Montenero, where his portrait and La Guiccioli's were painted by West, began between May 20 and 26 (according to his letters) and ended on July 2 (according to Edward Williams's diary and a letter written by Byron next day, which is headed Pisa, July 3). The letter suggesting that West should paint Byron's portrait has been printed (Byron's *Letters and Journals*, VI, 73, note) and shows that West could not have begun work before May 25, 1822, the date of the letter. Thus the time in which West could have made his alleged sketch of Shelley at Montenero is definitely fixed as not earlier than May 25 and not later than July 2, 1822. This period is covered by the diaries of Edward Williams and Mary Shelley, who were Shelley's daily companions. It is touched upon at different times by the recollections of Edward Trelawny and the letters of the Shelley-Byron group. From the evidence of all four sources it is abundantly clear that during this period, until July 1, Shelley never came nearer to Montenero than San Terenzo, Viareggio, or Lerici, some forty or fifty miles distant. Shelley and Williams landed in Leghorn on the morning of July 2, and on July 3 Byron and Shelley were in Pisa.

Thus West's alleged sketch could only have been made on July 2. On the morning of that day Byron and the Gambas were in Leghorn, four miles from Montenero. Williams met the Gambas as they were leaving the police station where they had just received notice to quit Tuscany within a few days. He also met and said good-bye to Byron, who was returning at once to Pisa to install the Leigh Hunts and pack his own belongings. Considering that Byron generally slept late in the mornings and was nevertheless in Pisa next day — three or four hours' journey — it would appear that Byron left that afternoon rather than in the evening or early next morning. Nevertheless it is possible that he returned to Montenero in the afternoon and found West waiting there for his usual afternoon sitting. Byron may have been accompanied by Shelley, or Shelley may have dropped in later. West claimed only that he saw Shelley *once* at Montenero, and this is the one and only possibility.

It seems incredible, however, that Byron should have given West his usual sitting on that afternoon — his last afternoon at Montenero, on the most crowded, exciting, and irritating day of his sojourn there. On that day, the only possible one, West could hardly have had the opportunity of making his alleged sketch. Moreover, though he may possibly have seen Shelley then, his account of Shelley's dress and conversation is so incredible as to throw doubt on even this possibility. There is no other record that Shelley ever wore a " loose dress of gingham " or even a dressing-gown. Leigh Hunt often wore the latter, but not Shelley. During the months in question Shelley constantly wore a jacket, which Mary wished him to discard because she thought it peculiar, and which he was wearing when he began the fatal return journey to San Terenzo on the afternoon of July 8. It is mentioned both in Trelawny's account of finding the body and in the Italian official report. Shelley had just left his boat when West saw him — *if* he saw him — and it is absurd to suppose that he had dressed himself for landing in any such garment as West describes. Incidentally, West's sketch does not show any such garment. The person sketched wears what appears to be a dressing-gown of medium weight, with either a rolled collar or a scarf around the neck, a garment rather similar to that worn by Leigh Hunt in the sketch of him by J. Hayter. The oil painting allegedly made from the sketch shortly afterwards again changes the dress to a long, rather formal dark coat.

Similarly Shelley could never have told the colourful, detailed story of exploring a sea-cave in his small boat on the previous day (July 1). For Byron (as well as Edward Williams, who set it down in his diary) knew that on July 1 Shelley, Williams, and Captain Roberts were sailing toward Leghorn in a boat far too large for any such exploits.

West's claim that he saw Shelley later in Pisa, after which he decided to make a painting from his sketch, is possible. It can be neither proved nor disproved. Shelley was in Pisa with Byron and the Hunts between July 3 and 8; and if West followed Byron to Pisa immediately, as he says, he would very possibly have seen Shelley during these days. It was only in his last account, however, that West made this claim.

One other detail in this last account seems almost impossible. How could Byron, who is alleged to have seen and approved the sketch, have kept silent on the subject to Mary Shelley, when he was in contact with her for a year afterwards and knew how anxious she was to secure a portrait of Shelley?

From the chronology, from the absurdities of West's story, and particularly from Byron's silence on the subject to Mary Shelley and West's silence to Tuckerman in 1846 or 1847, it is a fairly certain conclusion that West never made a sketch, and later an oil portrait, of Shelley. Who, then, was the subject of the portrait that West later presented as Shelley? The answer to this question adds incidentally some very strong confirmation of the conclusion already reached.

I have mentioned that in his first account of meeting Shelley, and before he claimed to have sketched him, West spoke of Leigh Hunt's presence on the same afternoon. I have also shown that the clothing attributed to Shelley and the clothing that appears in the sketch violate our knowledge of Shelley's clothing and accord neatly with Leigh Hunt's well-known habit of moving among his informal guests in a dressing-gown, and also with the Hayter portrait of Hunt. Everyone who has compared West's portrait with the demonstrably genuine Curran portrait of Shelley has been surprised at the difference. On the other hand, a comparison of West's portrait with Samuel Lawrence's portrait of Leigh Hunt surprises by an unusual similarity. Lawrence's portrait is somewhat unlike all the others, but Thornton Hunt regarded it as by far the best likeness and used it as the frontispiece of his *Correspondence of Leigh Hunt*. The late Mr. Walter Leigh Hunt, who owned the portrait, is quoted by Roger Ingpen in his edition of Hunt's *Autobiography* as continuing the family tradition of considering it far above the others as a likeness.

The similarity of West's painting to the portrait of Leigh Hunt has been noted before, but it has never been pointed out publicly, since after all it might be mere coincidence, as long as it could not be shown from other evidence that West actually painted Leigh Hunt's portrait. This hitherto unknown fact is proved by the following extract from Hunt's letter of November 6, 1824, published in Luther A. Brewer's *My Leigh Hunt Library: The Holograph Letters* (Iowa City, 1939, p. 137). Hunt is writing from Florence to his sister-in-law, Elizabeth Kent:

Mr. West, another American artist of that name, has gone from here to England, taking with him a portrait which he has done of me, as well as one of Lord Byron and [one of] his lady. I have given him a letter to Novello and should have added one to yourself or Mr. Hunter. . . . I tell you of him, however, thinking it might be a satisfaction to you to see a likeness so lately done of your dear friend. Would to Heaven I could have bought it for you, but that was impossible.

From this letter it is evident not only that West made a portrait of Hunt in Florence in 1824, but that the portrait remained in West's possession and accompanied him to England. That it was seen there by Mary Shelley is established by her letter of August 12, 1826 to Leigh Hunt, not very long after Hunt's return to England:

I trust that we shall find you on our next walk up the Hill as well as England has made you ever since your return — looking how unlike West's Florentine picture, how unlike when I first saw you in the Vale of Health, better and younger than either.

Since West retained the portrait, Mary Shelley must have talked with him when she saw it. They had too many friends in common — Hunt, Byron, and La Guiccioli — not to have talked about them. Mary would have been obliged to see and talk about the portraits of Byron and La Guiccioli that West had in his rooms. She was then living in Kentish Town, a London suburb, and could easily have seen West a number of times.

The facts brought out by these two letters establish two amazing phenomena which simply cannot be true if West's story of his Shelley portrait is true. West's later "authenticating" story states that Hunt was present on the afternoon in 1822

PAINTING BY WILLIAM E. WEST

Commonly supposed to be of Shelley in 1821. By permission of the owners, the Alderman Library of the University of Virginia

LEIGH HUNT

Painting by Samuel Lawrence. By permission of the National Portrait Gallery

when he sketched Shelley. How could West, knowing Hunt's devotion to Shelley, have failed to mention, while sketching or painting Hunt, his previous sketch of Shelley; and how could Hunt have failed to inform Mary Shelley, who was eagerly seeking a portrait of Shelley, that one was soon coming to England? For Hunt knew that West was leaving Florence for good and taking everything with him. Again, how could West have talked to Mary Shelley about his portraits of Byron and Hunt without mentioning one of Shelley that was in the same room with the others? If West had told either Hunt or Mary, the fact would now be known. He did not, and the only explanation is that he possessed no sketch or painting of Shelley to tell about.

If at any time later during the lives of Mary Shelley or Leigh Hunt, West had produced a portrait of Shelley, both Mary Shelley and Leigh Hunt would have wondered why it had been concealed from them. If the portrait of Hunt should be produced and called a portrait of Shelley, they were both in a position to denounce it. Mary Shelley died in 1851, West in 1857, and Hunt in 1859. At some time between 1847 and 1857 West is said to have told his " authenticating " story in his family, but he never made it public, nor was it ever made public until 1905.

If West's " authenticating " story was true, there was no reason for withholding it until Mary Shelley and Hunt were dead; if it was false, it could not have been published while they lived. We have seen that his own account is false in several details and doubtful in all. We have also seen that even had the story attributed to West been plausible, it would still have been refuted by the total irreconcilability of his subsequent conduct with the story. The same conduct, however, reconciles itself perfectly with the assumption that the sketch and painting produced in 1905 as portraits of Shelley were in 1824, 1828, and 1847 a sketch and a portrait of Leigh Hunt. At no time in West's life did he claim publicly to have made a portrait of either Shelley or Hunt. At no time did he claim privately to have painted both. When he admitted privately to have painted Hunt he said nothing of Shelley; when he later claimed privately to have painted Shelley, he said nothing of Hunt. The two paintings never had simultaneous existence. It seems impossible, therefore, to reach any conclusion except that the real painting of Hunt became the alleged painting of Shelley. The same conclusion may be reached, on purely visual evidence, by comparing West's portrait with the Lawrence portrait of Hunt.

After this investigation had been concluded I learned that Mrs. N. P. Dunn, owner of the West portrait, had presented it to the Alderman Library of the University of Virginia, together with a voluminous correspondence concerning it. From my examination of this correspondence a number of minor details might be added to the foregoing discussion. But since they do not impair, but support, a conclusion which seems evident already, they may be summarily abridged. They show that both Richard Watson Gilder, editor of the *Century Magazine*, and Robert Underwood Johnson, assistant-editor, had uneasy fears — the former that the pencil sketch was really of Leigh Hunt, and the latter that the painting was of Leigh Hunt. Mr. Gilder was reassured by Richard Garnett's confidence that both painting and sketch were genuine — an opinion, incidentally, in which Professor Dowden later concurred and from which H. B. Forman dissented. Mr. Johnson's suggestion that the sketch might be of Shelley and the painting of Hunt seems barely possible from a comparison of both sketch and portrait with portraits of Hunt and Shelley. From the other evidence, however, it seems unlikely. Mrs. Bryant, the real authority for West's claims, vigorously denied the possibility of such an error.

The correspondence makes it abundantly clear that Mrs. Dunn was an innocent victim either of an honest error or a fraud. Whether any fraud was intended, either by West or Mrs. Bryant, is in my opinion left unproved. Since it is no part of my purpose to saddle any individual with a possibly false imputation of dishonesty, I must add my personal conclusion that Mrs. Bryant's letters are not inconsistent with an assumption that she was honestly mistaken, and that West's substitution of Shelley for Hunt might have been the honest mistake of a memory which his own stories prove to be remarkably inaccurate.

APPENDIX VI

When Mary and Shelley began a joint journal immediately after their elopement, the one detail to which they at first gave most careful attention was their daily reading. When, very soon, the journal fell almost entirely into Mary's keeping, the close attention to reading was continued. At the end of each year Mary drew up a list of books read by each during the year. For constant readers such a list is never complete, even when it is a summary of daily entries; and Mary's lists omit a few titles which the daily entries show were read at least in part. Moreover, after the first year in Italy Mary's daily reading entries, particularly for Shelley, became more and more desultory, and she failed to make her yearly summary for the years 1819, 1821, and 1822. Incomplete as they are, Mary Shelley's lists are a valuable aid to the understanding of Shelley's interests; and as they have never been previously published complete, it seems well to make them all available in one place. Except for words and phrases in brackets, the lists are given *literatim* from *Shelley and Mary*.

LIST OF BOOKS READ IN 1814

Mary

*(Those marked * Shelley has read also.)*

*Letters from Norway [by Mary Wollstonecraft]. *Mary. A Fiction [by Mary Wollstonecraft]. *Wordsworth's Excursion. *Madoc, by Southey. 2 vols. *Curse of Kehama. *Sorcerer. A Novel. *Political Justice. 2 vols. *The Monk. By Lewis. 4 vols. *Thalaba. 2 vols. *The Empire of the Nairs [by Sir

James Lawrence]. *St. Godwin [a parody on Godwin's St. Leon]. *Wrongs of Woman. 2 vols. [by Mary Wollstonecraft]. Caleb Williams. 3 vols. *Zadig. *Life of Alfieri. By himself. 2 vols. *Essay on Sepulchres [by Godwin]. *Louvet's Memoirs. Carnot's Memorial. *Lives of the Revolutionists By Adolphus. 2 vols. *Edgar Huntley. 3 vols. *Peregrine Proteus. 2 vols. *The Italian. 3 vols. *Prince Alexy Haimatoff [by Hogg]. Philip Stanley, By Brown. Miss Baillie's Plays. *Moore's Journal [Dr. John Moore]. *Agathon. *Mungo Park's Travels in Africa. 1st Part. *Barrow's Embassy to China. Milton's Letter to Mr. Hartlib. Emilia Galotti [Lessing]. *Bryan Edwards's History of the West Indies. *View of the French Revolution. By M. W. G. [Mary Wollstonecraft Godwin]. *Candide. *Kirke White. 62 *Volumes.*

Shelley

Diogenes Laertius. Cicero Collectanea. Petronius. Suetonius. Barrow's Embassy to China. Mungo Park's Travels. 60 *Volumes.*

LIST OF BOOKS READ IN 1815

Mary

*(Those marked * Shelley has read also.)*

Posthumous Works [of Mary Wollstonecraft Godwin]. 3 vols. Sorrows of Werter. Don Roderick. By Southey. *Gibbon's Decline and Fall. 12 vols. Paradise Regained. *Gibbon's Life and Letters. 1st Edition. 2 vols. *Lara. New Arabian Nights. 3 vols. Corinne. Fall of the Jesuits. Rinaldo Rinaldini. Fontenelle's Plurality of Worlds. Hermsprong. Le Diable Boiteux. Man as he is. Rokeby. Ovid's Metamorphoses in Latin. *Wordsworth's Poems. *Spenser's Fairy Queen. *Life of the Phillips. — 2. *Fox's History of James II. The Reflector. Fleetwood. Wieland. Don Carlos. *Peter Wilkins. Rousseau's Confessions. Leonora: a Poem. Emile. *Milton's Paradise

Lost. *Life of Lady Hamilton. De l'Allemagne. By Madame de Staël. Three vols. of Barruel. *Caliph Vathek. Nouvelle Héloïse. *Kotzebue's Account of his Banishment to Siberia. Waverly. Clarissa Harlowe. Robertson's History of America. *Virgil. *Tale of a Tub. *Milton's Speech on Unlicensed Printing. *Curse of Kehama. *Madoc. La Bible Expliquée. Lives of Abélard and Héloïse. *The New Testament. *Coleridge s Poems. First vol. of Système de la Nature. *Castle of Indolence. Chatterton's Poems. *Paradise Regained. Don Carlos. *Lycidas. *St. Leon. Shakespeare's Plays (part of which Shelley read aloud). *Burke's Account of Civil Society. *Excursion. Pope's Homer's Iliad. *Sallust. Micromejas. *Life of Chaucer. Canterbury Tales. Peruvian Letters. Voyages round the World. Plutarch's Lives. *2 vols. of Gibbon. Ormond. Hugh Trevor. Labaume's History of the Russian War. Lewis's Tales. Castle of Udolpho. Guy Mannering. *Charles XII. By Voltaire. Tales of the East.

Shelley

Pastor Fido. Orlando Furioso. Livy's History. Seneca's Works. Tasso's Gerusalemme Liberata. Tasso's Aminta. Two vols. of Plutarch in Italian. Some of the Plays of Euripides. Seneca's Tragedies. Reveries of Rousseau. Hesiod. Novum Organum. Alfieri's Tragedies. Theocritus. Ossian. Herodotus. Thucydides. Homer. Locke on the Human Understanding. Conspiration de Rienzi. History of Arianism. Ockley's History of the Saracens. Madame de Staël sur la Littérature.

LIST OF BOOKS READ IN 1816

Mary

*(Those marked * Shelley has read also.)*

*Moritz, Tour in England. Tales of the Minstrels. *Park's Journal of a Journey in Africa. Peregrine Proteus. *Siege of

Corinth, Byron's Parisina. 4 vols. of Clarendon's History.
*Modern Philosophers. Opinion of various Writers on the Punishment of Death. By B. Montagu. Erskine's Speeches. *Caleb
Williams. *3rd Canto of Childe Harold. Schiller's Armenian.
Lady Craven's Letters. Caliste. Nouvelles Nouvelles. Romans
de Voltaire. Reveries d'un Solitaire, de Rousseau. Adèle et
Théodore. *Lettres Persanes de Montesquieu. Tableau de
Famille. Le Vieux de la Montagne. *Conspiration de Rienzi.
Walther, par la Fontaine. Le Vœux Téméraires. Herman
d'Una. Nouveaux Nouvelles de Mad. de Genlis. Contes Moraux de Marmontel. *Christabel. Caroline de Lichtenfeld.
*Bertram: *Le Criminel Secret. Vancenza. By Mrs. Robinson.
Antiquary. *Edinburgh Review. No. LII. Chrononhotonthologus. *Fazio. Love and Madness. Memoirs of Princess of
Bareith. *Letters of Emile. The latter part of Clarissa Harlowe.
Clarendon's History of the Civil War. *Life of Holcroft.
*Glenarvon. Patronage. The Milesian Chief. O'Donnel.
*Don Quixote. *Vita Alexandri Quintii Curtii. Conspiration
de Rienzi. Introduction to Davy's Chemistry. Les Incas de
Marmontel. Bryan Perdue. Sir C. Grandison. *Castle Rackrent. *Gulliver's Travels. *Paradise Lost. *Pamela. *3 vols. of
Gibbon. 1 book of Locke's Essay. Some of Horace's Odes.
*Edinburgh Review No. LIII. Rights of Women. De Senectute.
By Cicero. 2 vols. of Lord Chesterfield's Letters to his Son.
*Story of Rimini.

Shelley

Works of Theocritus, Moschus, &c. Prometheus of Aeschylus
(Greek). Works of Lucian (Greek). *Telemacho. La Nouvelle Héloïse. *Blackwell's History of the Court of Augustus.
Lucretius de Rerum Natura. Epistolae Plinii. Annals. By Tacitus. Several of Plutarch's Lives (Greek). Germania of Tacitus.
Mémoires d'un Détenu. Histoire de la Révolution. Par Rabault et Lacretelle. Montaigne's Essays. Tasso. Life of Cromwell. Locke's Essay. Political Justice. Lorenzo de Médicis.
Coleridge's Lay Sermon.

LIST OF BOOKS READ IN 1817

Mary

(*Those marked* * *Shelley has read also.*)

2 vols. of Lord Chesterfield's Letters. *Coleridge's Lay Sermon. Memoirs of Count Grammont. Somnium Scipionis. Roderick Random. Comus. Knights of the Swan. Cumberland's Memoirs. Junius's Letters. Journey to the World Underground. Duke of Buckingham's Rehearsal, and the Restoration. Countess of Pembroke's Arcadia. By Sir P. Sidney. Round Table. By W. Hazlitt. Cupid's Revenge. Beaumont and Fletcher. Martial Maid. Wild Goose Chase. *Tales of my Landlord. Rambler. *Waverly. Amadis de Gaul. Epistolae Plinii Secundi. *Story of Psyche in Apuleius. Anna St. Ives. Vita Julii Caesaris. Suetonius. *Defoe on the Plague. *Wilson's City of the Plague. Miss Edgeworth's Comic Dramas. Fortitude and Frailty. By Holcroft. 3rd canto of Childe Harold. Quarterly Review. *Lalla Rookh. By T. Moore. *Davis's Travels in America. *Godwin's Miscellanies. *Spenser's Fairy Queen. *Manuscript venu de St. Hélène. Buffon's Théorie de la Terre. Beaumont and Fletcher's Plays. *Volpone, Cynthia's Revels, The Alchemist, Fall of Sejanus, Catiline's Conspiracy. La Nouvelle Héloïse. Lettres Persiennes. Miss Edgeworth's Harrington and Ormond. Arthur Mervyn. *Antony and Cleopatra. Othello. Missionary. Rhoda. Wild Irish Girl. Glenarvon. The Anaconda. Pastor's Fireside. Amelia. Sir Launcelot Greave. Strathallan. Two penny Postbag. Anti-Jacobin Poetry. Miseries of Human Life. *Moore's Odes and Epistles. Les Lettres d'une Péruvienne. Confessions et Lettres de Rousseau. *Lamb's Specimens. Molière's George Dandin. Le Testament. Family of Montorio. Querelles de Famille. German Theatre. Eugenie and Mathilde. *Mandeville. *Laon and Cythna. *Lady Morgan's France. The Three Brothers. 1st vol. of Hume's Essays. Annalium C. Cornelii Taciti.

Shelley

Symposium of Plato. Plays of Aeschylus. Plays of Sophocles (Greek). Iliad of Homer. Arrian's Historia Indica. Homer's Hymn. Histoire de la Révolution Française. Apuleius. Meta-- morphoses (Latin). Coleridge's Biographia Literaria. Political Justice. Rights of Man. Elphinstone's Embassy to Caubwl. Several vols. of Gibbon.

LIST OF BOOKS READ IN 1818

Mary

Clarke's Travels. Aeneid. Terence. Hume's Dissertation on the Passions. Sterne's Tristram Shandy. Sentimental Journey and Letters. 2 vols. of Montaigne. Schlegel on the Drama. Rhododaphne. Aminta of Tasso. Oeuvres de Molière. 2 books of the Odes of Horace. Aristippe, and Les Abderites de Wie- land. French Translation of Lucian. Monti's Tragedies. Or- lando Furioso.

1819 – [NO LIST]

LIST OF BOOKS READ IN 1820

Mary

*(Those marked * Shelley has read also.)*

The remainder of Livy. *The Bible until the end of Ezekiel. *Don Juan. *Travels before the Flood. La Nouvelle Héloïse. The Fable of the Bees. Paine's Works. Utopia. *Voltaire's Memoirs. *The Aeneid and Georgics. Brydone's Travels. Rob- inson Crusoe. Sandford and Merton. *Astronomy in the En- cyclopedia. Vindication of the Rights of Woman. *Boswell's

Life of Johnson. Paradise Regained and Lost. Letters from
Norway and Posthumous Works. Ivanhoe, Tales of my
Landlord. Fleetwood, Caleb Williams. *Ricciardetto. *Mrs.
Macaulay's History of England. *Lucretius. The first 3 Ora-
tions of Cicero. Muratori Antichita d'Italia. Travels and Re-
bellion in Ireland. Segreno's Life of Castruccio. *Boccaccio
Decamerone. *Keats's Poems. *Armata. Corinne. The First
Book of Homer, Oedipus Tyrannus, a little Spanish, and much
Italian.

Shelley

The New Testament. Muller's Universal History. Hobbes.
Political Justice. Locke. Robertson's America and History of
Charles V. Ancient Metaphysics. Gillies's Greece. Solis's His-
tory of Mexico. Several of the Plays of Calderon. Sophocles.
Plato's Republic, Phaedon, Phaedrus. Euripides. Greek Ro-
mances. Apollonius Rhodius.

1821 AND 1822 – [NO LISTS]

APPENDIX VII

DOCUMENTS CONCERNING ELENA ADELAIDE SHELLEY

In October 1936, through the courtesy of Mr. Coert Du Bois, American Consul-General at Naples, I engaged Professor Alberto Tortaglione to search the birth-records and death-records of Naples for the mysterious " Neapolitan ward " mentioned in Shelley's letters of June 1820 to Mr. and Mrs. Gisborne. The following documents were found, for which Professor Tortaglione supplied the English translation:

Birth Registry

[Estratto dai Registri delle Nascite della Sezione Chiaia — Città e Provincia di Napoli — Italia — conservati presso il Regio Archivio di Stato.]

Numero d'Ordine centosessantaquattro. —
L'anno milleottocentodieciannove a ventisette del mese di Febbraio ad ore dicinove Avanti di Noi — Marchese di Civita — Eletto ed Ufficiali dello Stato Civile del Comune di Chiaia — Provincia di Napoli — è comparso PERCY SHELLEY d'Inghilterra — di anni ventisei — di professione Proprietario — domiciliato Riviera di Chiaja — Numero duecentocinquante — ed ha dichiarato che ai ventisette del mese di Dicembre passato anno milleottocentodieciotto, nacque nella sua propria casa da lui dichiarante e da Maria Padurin sua moglie legittima — d'Inghilterra — di anni ventisette — una femina che ci ha presentato, a cui si è dato il nome di Elena Adelaide.
La presentazione e dichiarazione si è fatta alla presenza di Francesco Florimonte di anni cinquantasette — di professione casolio — domiciliato Fondo Pennino — Numero centoven-

OFFICIAL BIRTH REGISTRATION OF ELENA ADELAIDE SHELLEY

From the State Archives of Naples, by permission

totto, e di Antonio Di Lorenzo — di anni ventitre — de professione Parrucchiere — domiciliato alla Riviera di Chiaia — Numero duecentoventitre.

Il presente Atto è stato letto tanto al dichiarante che ai Testimoni ed indi firmato da Noi.

[Fto]: PERCY SHELLEY
[Fto]: FRANC° FLORIMONTE
[Fto]: ANTONIO DI LORENZO

Battezzata nella Parrocchia di San Giuseppe a Chiaia

[Fto]: CIVITA — Eletto
[Fto]: N. PENNASILICO — Canc.

Ventisette Febbraio 18dieccinove

[Fto]: CIVITA — Eletto —

Translation:

[Extract from the Birth Records 1819 of the District of Chiaia — City and Province of Naples — Italy — kept at the Regio Archivio di Stato.]

No. of Certificate, 164.

On the twenty-seventh day of the month of February One Thousand Eight Hundred and Nineteen at 7 p.m. Before Me — Marchese di Civita — Elect and Registrar of Vital Statistics for the District of Chiaia — Province of Naples — has appeared PERCY SHELLEY of England — aged twenty-six — Proprietor — domiciled at Riviera di Chiaia — Number 250 — who has declared that on the twenty-seventh day of the month of December One Thousand Eight Hundred and Eighteen, was born to him and to Mary Padurin, his legitimate wife — of England — aged twenty-seven — a girl whom he has presented us and to whom the name of Elena Adelaide was given.

The presentation and declaration were made in the presence of Francesco Florimonte — aged fifty-seven — occupation cheesemonger — domiciled at Fondo Pennino — Number one hundred and twenty-eight — and of Antonio Di Lorenzo — aged twenty-three — occupation Hairdresser — domiciled at Riviera di Chiaia — Number two hundred and twenty-three.

This present Act has been read both to the declarer and to the Witnesses, after which duly signed by Us.

[Sgd]: PERCY SHELLEY
[Sgd]: FRANCESCO FLORIMONTE
[Sgd]: ANTONIO DI LORENZO   Baptized at the Parish of
St. Joseph, Chiaia, the
[Sgd]: CIVITA — Elect   Twenty-seventh of February
[Sgd]: N. PENNASILICO — Canc.   eighteen-nineteen
[Sgd]: CIVITA — Elect.

From a photograph and a manuscript copy of this document officially attested and stamped by the Superintendent and the Secretary of the State Archives of Naples, in my possession.

Certificate of Baptism

Parrocchia di S. Giuseppe a Chiaia
Certifico che dal Reg: déi nati libro XXIV — pag: 276 risulta che: Elena Adelaide figlia di Percy Shelley e di Maria Godwin leg: nata dom. Riviera di Chiaia 250 Battezzate il 27–2–1819 dal Rev: D. Francesco Boccaccio Lev: Gaetana Musto.
Napoli, 8 Marzo 1937

Il Parroco
Lac. M. Gilberti

Translation:

Parish of St. Joseph
     Chiaia
     I hereby Certify that from the Records of the births — Book XXIV° — at page 276 — appears that Elena Adelaide daughter of Percy Shelley and of Mary Godwin lawfully begotten — domiciled at Riviera di Chiaia No. 250 was baptized in this Parish Church on the 27–2–1819 — by the Rev'd Francesco Boccaccio. Midwife: Gaetana Musto.
     Naples, 8 March 1937

The Parish Priest
Sgd: Rev. M. Gilberti

The original of this document is an official form signed by the parish priest and stamped with the seal of the parish, in my possession.

Certificate of Death

[Estratto dai Registri dei morti della Sezione di Montecalvario — Città e Provincia di Napoli — Italia — conservati presso il Regio Archivio di Stato.]

Numero d'Ordine 513 —

L'anno milleottocentoventi, il dì dieci del mese di Giugno alle ore quindici Avanti di Noi, Marchese di Casalnuovo Pignatelli — Eletto ed Uffiziale dello Stato Civile del circondario di Montecalvario — Comune di Napoli — Provincia di Napoli, sono comparsi Antonio Liguori di Napoli di anni venticinque, di professione caciolio, domiciliato Vico Canale No 48 e Pasquale Fiorenzano di Napoli, di anni ventidue di professione cajonzaro, domiciliato Vico Lungo Trinità dei Spagnuoli No 59. I quali hanno dichiarato che nel giorno nove del mese di Giugno anno corrente alle ore tre di notte è morta nella propria casa *ELENA SCHELLY* di Napoli di mesi quindici e giorni dodici, di professione —— domiciliata Vico Canale No 45, figlia di Bercy Schelly — Possidente — e di Maria Gebuin — domiciliati in Livorno.

Per esecuzione della Legge, ci siamo trasferiti insieme coi detti Testimoni presso la persona defunta e ne abbiamo riconosciuta la sua effettiva morte. Abbiamo indi formato il presente Atto che abbiamo iscritto sopra i due registri, e datane lettura à dichiaranti, si è nel giorno, mese ed anno come sopra segnato da Noi e da essi.

[Fto]: Antonio Liguori
[Fto]: Pasquale Fiorenzano
[Fto]: Pignatelli — Eletto —

Translation:

[Extract from the death Records 1820 of the District of Montecalvario — City and Province of Naples — Italy — kept at the Regio Archivio di Stato.]

No. of Certificate, 513 —

On the tenth day of the month of June One Thousand Eight Hundred and twenty, at three p.m. — Before me, Marchese di Casalnuovo Pignatelli — Elect and Registrar of Vital Statistics — for the District of Montecalvario — City of Naples — Province of Naples — have appeared Antonio Liguori of Naples, aged twenty-five, occupation cheesemonger, domiciled at Vico Canale No 48 — and Pasquale Fiorenzano of Naples, aged twenty-two, occupation potteryman, domiciled at Vico Lungo Trinità dei Spagnuoli No 59.

They have declared that on the ninth day of June, current year, at three a.m. has died at her home *ELENA SCHELLY* of Naples, aged fifteen months and twelve days, occupation ——————————— domiciled at Vico Canale No 45, daughter of Bercy Schelly — Proprietor — and of Maria Gebuin — domiciled at Leghorn.

In conformity with the law we have visited, together with the aforesaid Witnesses, the deceased person whose actual death is herein recognized and have therefore drawn up this present Act and written it on two registries. After reading same to the witnesses, we have on the day, month and year as above annexed our respective signatures.

[Sgd]: Antonio Liguori
[Sgd]: Pasquale Fiorenzano
[Sgd]: Pignatelli — Elect —

From Professor Tortaglione's manuscript copy of the original record.

SOURCES AND NOTES
Chapter XIX

GENERAL SOURCES

The journal of Claire Clairmont (MS.), *Shelley and Mary*, Shelley's *Works*, *Lord Byron's Correspondence* (ed. Murray, London, 1922), Medwin's *Revised Life*, Harper's *Letters of Mary Shelley*, *Correspondence of Leigh Hunt* — all as previously cited.

NOTES AND REFERENCES

[1] Shelley to Leigh Hunt, March 22, 1818, Julian *Works*, IX, 291. Shelley had written briefly to Hunt from Calais.

[2] Journal for March 26, *Shelley and Mary*, II, 264, quoted in Julian *Works*, IX, 292.

[3] Ibid., 292–3, and 293, note; Claire's journal, April 8, 1818, p. 21.

[4] Shelley to Maria Gisborne, July 16, 1818, Julian *Works*, IX, 311–12.

[5] Journal for March 26, as cited above.

[6] Mary Shelley to Leigh Hunt, July 30, [1823], Bodleian MSS Adds d. 5, folios 71–73. This letter is printed in Mrs. Marshall's *Life and Letters of Mary Wollstonecraft Shelley*, II, 85–6, as if entire, but the continuation, dated Pont Bon Voisin, August 1, is omitted.

[7] Claire's journal, April 8, 1818, p. 22.

[8] Ibid., 23.

[9] Ibid., 24.

[10] Shelley to Peacock, April 1818 [postmarked F. P. O., Ap. 23, 1818], Julian *Works*, IX, 293–4.

[11] Mary Shelley to the Hunts, April 1818, Harper: *Letters of Mary Shelley*, 44–5.

[12] Claire's journal, April 9, 1818.

[13] Shelley to Peacock, April 1818, Julian *Works*, IX, 294; and Mary to the Hunts, April 1818, in Harper, op. cit., 46.

[14] Shelley to Peacock, April 20, 1818, Julian *Works*, IX, 297.

[15] Ibid., 297–8.

[16] Claire's journal, April 12, 1818.

[17] Shelley to Byron, April 13, 1818, Julian *Works*, IX, 295–6.

[18] Byron to J. C. Hobhouse, April 24, 1818, in Murray's *Lord Byron's Correspondence*, II, 79.

[19] Julian *Works*, IX, 301–2. The latter third of the letter repeats his invitation to Byron to join the Shelleys at Como, saying that Claire was willing to absent herself and that there could be no gossip. Shelley tells Byron about Allegra's nurse, and gracefully waves aside Byron's willingness to pay the expenses of Allegra up to this time.

[20] Shelley to Byron, April 30, 1818, Julian *Works*, IX, 304.

[21] Shelley to Claire Clairmont ["Postmark? March 26, 1822"], Julian *Works*, X, 366.

[22] This inn Professor Dowden (*Life*, II, 203) conjectures to be that of Pietra Mala, described by Lady Morgan (who stopped there during Shelley's stay in Italy) as a rude dark hostelry, the only visible habitation in a wild landscape.

[23] Claire's journal, May 25, 1818.

[24] Shelley to Peacock, April 20, 1818, Julian *Works*, IX, 299–300. There is a somewhat similar passage in Shelley's letter of April 30 to Hogg, ibid., 306.

[25] Claire's journal, May 25, 1818. Mary's journal has a briefer, similar entry for May 7, 1818.

[26] Medwin: *Revised Life*, 268, describes Shelley's later reaction to the sight of chained and guarded convicts.

[27] Shelley to Peacock, June 5, 1818, Julian *Works*, IX, 309. Cf. Claire's journal for May 25. At the time of their departure from Leghorn the Shelleys seem to have been living at the Croce di Malta (Mrs. Gisborne to Shelley, June 21, 1818, in *Shelley and Mary*, II, 288).

[28] Shelley to Peacock, June 5, 1818, Julian *Works*, IX, 309.

[29] Godwin to Mary, June 1, 1818, in *Shelley and Mary*, II, 279–80.

[30] Hunt to Shelley, August 23, 1820, *Correspondence of Leigh Hunt*, I, 157.

[31] Shelley to Peacock, August ("probably 22"), 1819, Julian *Works*, X, 72.

[32] Shelley to Hogg, July 25, 1819, ibid., X, 65.

[33] Peacock: *Memoirs*, II, 452. The tone of Shelley's last letters to John Gisborne suggests that by 1822 Shelley agreed with Peacock's opinion.

[34] Shelley to Peacock, May 16, 1820, Julian *Works*, X, 169.

[35] Shelley's rhymed "Letter to Maria Gisborne," which was written in Henry Reveley's room, probably July 1, 1820.

[36] Mary Shelley to the Hunts, May 13, 1818, Harper, op. cit., 50, 51.

[37] Shelley to Peacock, April 20, 1818, Julian *Works*, IX, 298. Shelley's letter of April 30 to Hogg, ibid., 307, contains a similar statement.

[38] Mary Shelley to Maria Gisborne, June 15, 1818, in *Shelley and Mary*, II, 283–5. Professor Dowden (*Life*, II, 211, note) discovered that in 1817 Signor Chiappa's first floor rented for twenty-eight sequins monthly.

[39] Mary Shelley to Maria Gisborne, June 15, 1818, and Maria Gisborne to Mary Shelley, June 21, 1818, in *Shelley and Mary*, II, 283–5 and 288–90. Mary's letter appears in *Shelley Memorials*, 98–100. See also Julian *Works*, X, 7, *re* kaleidoscope.

[40] Little is known of Anacharsis the Scythian except indirectly through other classical writers. Shelley's knowledge was based upon the work of the Abbé J. J. Barthélemy (whom he mentions in his "Discourse on the Manners of the Ancients," etc.), *Voyage du jeune Anacharsis en Grèce vers le milieu du quatrième siècle avant l'ère vulgaire* (5th ed., Paris, 1817, 7 vols). This lengthy and learned work uses the travels of the vaguely known Anacharsis merely as a framework for presenting as thorough a picture of Greek history and society as the author could bring together from his extensive reading in Greek literature.

[41] Mary Shelley to Maria Gisborne, July 2, 1818, in *Shelley and Mary*, II, 291–2 (published in *Shelley Memorials*, 100–1). In August 1820 Shelley climbed alone to the shrine on Monte Pellagrino.

[42] Shelley to the Gisbornes, July 16, 1818, Julian *Works*, IX, 311–12. This letter is probably misdated for July 11. See note, ibid.

Il Prato Fiorito made a considerable impression on Shelley's memory. Two or three years later he described to Thomas Medwin the overpowering sweetness of the jonquils there, which almost caused him to faint (*Revised Life*, 198). Professor Dowden (*Life*, II, 215) has suggested that this experience is the source of lines 450–3 of *Epipsychidion*, where such an effect of jonquils is described. See also "Ode to the West Wind," iii, 35–6.

[43] So called in Mary's journal. The correct title was *Classical Tour through Italy*. Both Shelley and Mary ridiculed his account of contemporary Italians as absurdly favourable.

[44] Shelley to Peacock, July 25, 1818, Julian *Works*, IX, 314.

⁴⁵ Mrs. Shelley in her Note on *Prometheus Unbound* speaks of that poem and the projected dramas on Tasso and Job as belonging to the first year in Italy.

⁴⁶ *Adonais*, stanza 54.

⁴⁷ Julian *Works*, VII, 206–7. The two preceding paragraphs of Diotima's discourse, too long to be quoted in the text, are of great importance to the understanding of Shelley's ideas.

⁴⁸ Julian *Works*, VII, 228–9.

⁴⁹ Shelley to Peacock, August 16, 1818, Julian *Works*, IX, 320.

⁵⁰ It had been sent by July 5. The Shelleys do not mention its receipt, but two months after leaving Bagni di Lucca Shelley loaned Byron a book that was among the contents of the box. The box may have reached Bagni di Lucca during these two months and have been forwarded.

⁵¹ Godwin to Mary Shelley, June 20 and July 7; Peacock to Shelley, May 30, July 5, 1818; all in *Shelley and Mary*, II, 290A–B, 296–7, 277–9, 293–5. Godwin's second letter has been published in *Shelley Memorials*, 101–2; and Peacock's letters appear in Peacock's *Works* (London and New York, 1934), VIII, 192–9.

⁵² Shelley to Godwin, July 25, 1818, Julian *Works*, IX, 317.

⁵³ Shelley to Peacock, July 25, 1818, Julian *Works*, IX, 315. Professor Dowden has suggested (*Life*, II, 218, note) that the following fragment of verse, written in 1818, is another record of Shelley's disappointment in Wordsworth:

> My head is wild with weeping for a grief
>   Which is the shadow of a gentle mind,
> I walk into the air (but no relief
>   To seek, — or haply, if I sought, to find;
> It came unsought); for to wonder that a chief
>   Like the wild spirits, should be cold and blind.

But it is quite possible that this refers to Shelley's own mysterious grief of 1818, as discussed fully in Chapter xx.

⁵⁴ Julian *Works*, loc. cit.

⁵⁵ Godwin to Shelley, June 8, 1818, in *Shelley and Mary*, II, 281, published in *Shelley Memorials*, 96–8.

⁵⁶ The *Quarterly Review*, XVIII, 324 (May 1818), quoted in my *The Unextinguished Hearth*, 124. Peacock quoted most of this passage to Shelley in his letter of June 14 and Hunt refers to it in his letter of August 4, noting that the *Quarterly* quoted *atheos* but not *philanthropos*. It also ignored Shelley's *demokratos*.

[57] The *British Critic*, X, 94 (July 1818).

[58] Shelley to Peacock, July 25, 1818, Julian *Works*, IX, 315. Cf. Shelley to Hunt, December 22, 1818, ibid., X, 9–10.

[59] Ibid., IX, 311.

[60] Ibid., IX, 330.

[61] Mr. Peck's suggestion (*Life*, II, 72) that A. B. was one of Godwin's aliases is unconvincing. "A. B." was the writer of the note, not necessarily the beneficiary. Shelley's payments to Godwin after Shelley's marriage to Mary were made without employing aliases; moreover, Ollier knew Godwin, a fact which would have made the alias useless. Nor would there have been in 1818 any reason why Ollier should not mention Shelley's name to Godwin. If this letter does not relate to something quite beyond our present knowledge of Shelley it is possibly connected with some quixotic charity or some petty money-lender with whom he did not wish to be connected by name, or more probably with Shelley's recent instructions to his bankers not to pay certain claims (Julian *Works*, IX, 319).

[62] Shelley to Peacock, July 25, 1818, in Julian *Works*, IX, 314. I can find no basis in Mary's journal for Professor Dowden's statement (*Life*, II, 217) that Shelley still suffered frequently and acutely from the old pain in his side, though his letter of August 20, 1818 (Julian *Works*, IX, 322) shows that he had suffered with his side shortly before that date.

[63] Shelley wrote Peacock on October 8: "We left . . . on a visit to Venice partly for the sake of seeing the city and partly that little Alba might spend a month or two with Clare . . ." (Julian *Works*, IX, 334).

[64] Shelley to Mary [August 20, 1818], ibid., IX, 322.

[65] Shelley to Mary [August 20, 1818], ibid., IX, 323–4. The reference in the last line is to Mary's work on *Frankenstein* while Shelley was absent on his boat-trip with Byron on the Lake of Geneva. The work Shelley wished her to undertake was a tragedy on Charles I. He thought Godwin's recent suggestion of a book on the Commonwealth men excellent, and "precisely the subject for Mary," but supposed she would not be able to begin it without access to more books than were available at Bagni di Lucca. The drama on Charles I seems to have been settled on as a substitute requiring fewer books.

Chapter XX

GENERAL SOURCES

Shelley's letters (Julian *Works*, IX, X); "Julian and Maddalo"; Shelley's Poems of 1818 with Mrs. Shelley's Notes; *Shelley and Mary*, Vol. II; *Correspondence of Leigh Hunt; Lord Byron's Correspondence; Life and Letters of Mary Wollstonecraft Shelley* (Mrs. Marshall); Harper's *Letters of Mary Shelley;* Peacock's *Works*, Vol. VII — all as previously cited.

NOTES AND REFERENCES

[1] Shelley to Mary, [August 20, 1818], Julian *Works*, IX, 322.

[2] Ibid., 323.

[3] Ibid., 323–4.

[4] Shelley to Mary, [August 23, 1818], ibid., 325–6.

[5] Ibid., 325.

[6] Shelley to Mary, "5 o'clock in the morning" [August 24, 1818], ibid., 327.

[7] Shelley to Peacock, October 8, 1818, ibid., 334–5; also "Julian and Maddalo," 89–92. Cf. the more extended picture of Venice in "Lines Written among the Euganean Hills."

[8] "Julian and Maddalo" (1818), 43–8. The details of the meeting are drawn from this poem and from Shelley's letter to Mary describing the same meeting (August 24, 1818, Julian *Works*, IX, 327–8).

[9] Shelley to Peacock, October 8, 1818, Julian *Works*, IX, 334.

[10] Shelley to Mary [August 24, 1818], ibid., 329–30.

[11] Such a journey is to be inferred from Mary's letter of August 17, 1818, to Maria Gisborne (Mrs. Marshall, op. cit., I, 219) as planned to take place shortly after the equinox.

[12] Mary's journal, August 28–September 5, 1818. On September 13, a Monday, Shelley informed Byron of their arrival "last Sun-

day," by which he probably meant "yesterday a week ago." This would indicate that he had meanwhile informed Byron that Mary had not accompanied him to Padua, as Byron had been allowed to suppose at first.

[13] Mrs. Shelley's Note on the Poems of 1818 and her letter to Maria Gisborne, "September, 1818" (Mrs. Marshall, op. cit., I, 225).

[14] Mary's journal, September 5, 1818, *Shelley and Mary*, II, 328.

[15] Mary Shelley's Note on the Poems of 1818.

[16] Shelley to Byron, September 13, 1818, Julian *Works*, IX, 331.

[17] Mary's journal, September 5–24, is very brief and omits September 6–15 inclusive. It mentions the beginning of *Prometheus Unbound* on September 5 and thereafter makes no further mention of Shelley's writing until long after they had left Este. Her notes on Shelley's poems, written twenty years later, show that "Julian and Maddalo" and Act I of *Prometheus Unbound* were written at Este; and Shelley dated "Lines Written among the Euganean Hills" "October, 1818." Shelley's letter of September 22 to Mary shows that twenty-six sheets of *Prometheus Unbound* were then written, and his letter of October 8 to Peacock speaks of the first act as "just finished."

[18] Shelley to Mary [? September 22, 1818], Julian *Works*, IX, 332. The conjectured date of the letter is validated by Mary's journal for September 24.

[19] *Correspondence of Leigh Hunt*, I, 119–24; Peacock's *Works* (ed. H. F. B. Brett-Smith), VIII, 200–4. All three are in *Shelley and Mary*.

[20] Shelley to Mary [? September 22, 1818], Julian *Works*, IX, 332.

[21] Mary Shelley's Note on the Poems of 1818.

[22] Shelley to Claire Clairmont [September 25, 1818], Julian *Works*, IX, 333.

[23] Since the Shelleys later sustained a great injury at the hands of the Hoppners, it is only fair to pause and consider their early behaviour and the impression it left. When Shelley first met them he thought them the "most amiable people I ever knew." Mr. Hoppner, like his father, was a painter, and was on the eve of departing for the Julian Alps on a sketching excursion. Both had become so interested in helping Shelley and Claire that they had postponed their excursion to do so. Mrs. Hoppner, a native of Switzerland, seemed to Shelley kind, beautiful, not wise or philosophic, but unprejudiced in the best meaning of the word. From

the start he was attracted by her hazel eyes and sweet looks, which he found "rather Maryish" (Shelley to Mary, August 24, 1818, and to Peacock, October 8, 1818, Julian *Works,* IX, 328, 334).

24 Godwin to Mary, October 27, 1818, in *Shelley and Mary,* II, 338A. Unsigned and apparently incomplete. Godwin's letter to Shelley (November 13, 1818, *Shelley Memorials,* 107) speaks of the "great depression of spirits" revealed in Mary's letters.

25 Mary's journal dated "October" (between September 30 and October 5) reads: "Transcribe 'Mazeppa,' copy the Ode." Byron's "Ode to Venice," written in July 1818, seems to be the only poem to which "Ode" could refer. Incidentally it has some general points of resemblance to part of Shelley's "Lines Written among the Euganean Hills," which appears to have been composed while the "Ode" was in Mary's possession.

26 Shelley to Peacock, October 8, 1818, Julian *Works,* IX, 336.

27 "Julian and Maddalo" (1818), 144–53.

28 "Lines Written among the Euganean Hills," 335–6. Certain phrases about Venice and the plains of Lombardy in Shelley's letter of October 8 to Peacock suggest that the letter and the poem may have been written at about the same date. The same letter is full of Shelley's indignation at the tyranny and decadence that was impressed upon him by his visit to the dungeons of the Venetian state.

29 Professor Raymond D. Havens, in his article "Julian and Maddalo" (*Studies in Philology,* XXVII, 648–53, October 1930), calls attention to the disproportion and offers the ingenious suggestion that it is due to Shelley's interest in Tasso. The name Maddalo was used by Shelley in one of his Tasso fragments written shortly before "Julian and Maddalo," and Tasso's madness, Professor Havens thinks, is also the madness of Shelley's Madman. Tasso's life, like the Madman's, he argues, must have been developed by Shelley around the central fact of a guilty and secret love. The presence of another woman, however (with whom Shelley's Madman appears to be more deeply in love), Professor Havens himself points out as irreconcilable with the Tasso theory. Tasso, moreover, was regarded by Shelley as a flatterer of tyranny, whereas the Madman is the reverse.

It seems to me possible that Tasso was in Shelley's mind as he wrote, but in the background rather than in the foreground. Shelley was interested in madness, with reference to *himself,* long before he was interested in Tasso's madness. It was possibly an important cause of his original interest in Tasso. Shelley's two previous autobiographical characters, Lionel and Laon, each passed through a period of madness, and Shelley was convinced that his father once wished to confine him as a madman.

I agree with Professor Havens in dismissing completely the argument by Miss Arabella Shore (*Gentleman's Magazine,* October 1887, 329–42) and Mr. H. S. Salt (*Shelley Society Papers,* Series I, No. 1, Part II, 1891, 325–42) that the Madman represents Shelley in relation to his first wife — a theory modified and developed by Professor Peck (*Life,* II, 103–6). The woman who deserted the Madman is still living and is still loved by him; in the end she rejoins him. Nor is there any reason to suppose that Shelley, whose happiness with Mary had long since obscured the memory of Harriet, should revert to that memory with such intense passion at a time when he had far different reasons for deep sorrow. Needless to say, I agree with the theory of Professor Carl Grabo (*The Magic Plant,* 1936, pp. 267–71), which in part anticipates my own.

My disagreement with the interpretation of Professor John Harrington Smith ("Shelley and Claire Clairmont," *P.M.L.A.,* LIV, 785–815, September 1939) will appear in other notes in this chapter.

[30] Shelley to the Olliers, November 10, 1820, Julian *Works,* X, 220.

[31] Shelley to Charles Ollier, December 15 [or 25], 1819: "Have you seen my poem 'Julian and Maddalo' . . . for I mean to write three other poems, the scenes of which will be laid at Rome, Florence, and Naples, but the subjects of which will be drawn from dreadful or beautiful realities, as that of this was" (Julian *Works,* X, 135). Also Shelley to Leigh Hunt, August 15, 1819: "I send you a little Poem to give to Ollier for publication but *without my Name* [*sic*]. . . . It was composed last year at Este; two of the characters you will recognize; the third is also in some degree a painting from nature, but, with respect to time and place, ideal" (ibid., 68). By "the third" Shelley must have meant the Madman, for Allegra's position is quite subordinate, and Shelley knew perfectly well that Hunt would recognize her as well as Byron and Shelley.

[32] Line 195.

[33] Lines 380–3. Cf. "Hymn to Intellectual Beauty," stanzas 5 and 6; and "Dedication" to *The Revolt of Islam,* stanzas 3, 4, 5.

[34] Lines 442–6 and 449–50.

[35] See note 31, above.

[36] Lines 415–19.

[37] Lines 357–68.

[38] Lines 494–9.

[39] Lines 328–9. These lines rather militate against Professor Smith's theory, discussed elsewhere, that the Lady was Claire.

The remainder of this paragraph is quoted from or based on lines 529, 347–8, and 383–4 respectively.

[40] Lines 304–15.

[41] Lines 337–43.

[42] Mary Shelley's Note on the Poems of 1818, first published in 1839.

[43] But Shelley's advertisement to *Rosalind and Helen*, dated Naples, December 20, 1818, shows that Mary had read " Lines Written among the Euganean Hills " some time before that date.

[44] Professor John Harrington Smith, in his article " Shelley and Claire Clairmont " (*P.M.L.A.*, LIV, 785–814, September 1939), rejects the possibility that the defaulting lady may be Mary Shelley, on the grounds that Mary is more clearly to be identified as the Madman's " spirit's mate " addressed in lines 337–43. This is to judge abnormal utterances by normal standards, which calls for caution. Every completed poem Shelley is known to have written between the death of Clara and his departure from Naples indicates that during that period he considered that he had no " spirit's mate." Mary was only a former " spirit's mate " whom he hoped would be so again, and it is the Mary-who-was that is addressed. With any ordinary writer, even, this would not rule out the alien Mary-who-is, and even less so with Shelley.

Professor Smith ignores Shelley's very pronounced idea of double personality. This idea was a constant one with him. To Claire in 1816 he had analysed her character as that of " two Claires "; in 1822 he spoke of more than one occasion on which he had met (as he thought) his own ghost. He had evidently spoken of it often enough to make Jane Williams think she saw the same thing. In Act I of *Prometheus Unbound*, which Shelley was writing at the same time as " Julian and Maddalo," he uses the phantasm of Jupiter as a coexistent personality of Jupiter himself and pauses in the poem (lines 191 ff.) to suggest a basis for the idea. In " Lines Written among the Euganean Hills " he seems to have thought of himself as buried with Clara and as also writing the poem. In one of his letters from Naples he spoke of " two Italys " radically different yet coexistent in his mind, and the same distinction about Greece is clearly implied in his *Hellas*. He spoke of hypnotism as a possible proof that the mind could separate itself from the body. The long persistence of this idea, and its immediacy at the time "Julian and Maddalo" was written, indicate that a double identity for Mary, under the circumstances, is not to be dismissed as impossible or fantastic, but on the contrary is natural and almost to be expected.

There is indeed one passage in the poem which, as Professor Smith reads it, seems irreconcilable with the identification of the Madman's defaulting lady with Mary Shelley. In lines 420–38 the Madman says that in her revulsion his Lady has given emphatic utterance to the wish that she had never seen or heard him, or endured his embrace. She even wished that he had emasculated himself —

> so that ne'er
> Our hearts had for a moment mingled there
> To disunite in horror.

If one reads the quoted lines as stating that there was only one moment of sexual union between the two, then the passage cannot refer to Mary. The passage would then mean that his love for his Lady, as the Madman describes it, turns on one climactic moment — which is rather absurd. But the phrase "ne'er for a moment" is plainly intensive only (never *even* for one moment), just as the word "never" or "ne'er" is used for "never even" four times previously in the same sentence. In this sense it fits perfectly with the state of mind I have imputed to Mary following Clara's death — or rather with Shelley's possibly exaggerated view of it.

[45] An existing love for Claire will not fulfil the circumstances of the poem. If Claire is thought of as the Lady, the love would have been one of long duration during which, as the Madman says, there was no infidelity — and Shelley's love for Mary during much of this period would have been infidelity to Claire. If Mary is thought of as the Lady and a secret love for Claire as the "falsehood," the situation is even more evidently inconsistent with the Madman's assertion of fidelity to the Lady.

Anyone who believed in the "Hoppner scandal" (to be discussed later in this chapter) might suppose that the Lady is indeed Mary and the secret falsehood the fact that a child was to be born to Shelley and Claire soon afterwards in Naples. This would still violate the Madman's assertion of fidelity to the Lady — and even more his clear belief that his secret was within his own keeping. If one thinks of Claire as the Lady, then the child to be born was certainly not a secret the Madman could speak of (as he does) as one he concealed from *her*. Moreover, the Lady under such circumstances would surely not have abandoned her lover with scorn and contempt at the very time he was most needed.

In his recent article (cited in the previous note) Professor John Harrington Smith argues for a long, intermittent love-affair between Shelley and Claire and asserts that Claire is the Madman's Lady in "Julian and Maddalo," though he considers Shelley's love at that time to be more reminiscent (or temporarily recrudescent) than active and enduring. I have already commented sufficiently on Claire's asserted identity with the Lady; but I must add my conviction that Professor Smith has misunderstood most of the evidence by which he has sought to build up his general situation between the two. I can find no passage cited in support of his view which necessarily runs counter to the view expressed in this book, nor do I find any such passage in my own reading of all the letters, journals, and poems of the parties involved. He has too often failed to discriminate between passages that can support a view already chosen but are also capable of different interpretation, and passages that *inevitably* support that view *alone*. I can find none of the latter, which are absolutely necessary to sound conclusions. Professor Smith's passages seem to me to have been chosen (and often interpreted) arbitrarily, without due regard to the mass of other materials from which one would presume a more regular relationship.

⁴⁶ Lines 383–4.

⁴⁷ Shelley sent the poem to Hunt on August 15, 1819, for publication by Ollier, "*without my name*." Shelley's letter of January 2, 1821 shows that Claire objected to the publication and assures her (contrary to his apparent intention at the time) that it would not be published. But the most obvious basis for Claire's objection is not the Madman's story, which she may not have understood, but the account of Allegra, which would be immediately clear if the poem were published with Shelley's name.

⁴⁸ Lines 359–60.

⁴⁹ Shelley to Peacock, November 9, 1818, Julian *Works*, IX, 347.

⁵⁰ See note 30, above.

⁵¹ See Chapter xiv, conclusion, and note 80 to that chapter.

⁵² In 1818 the fragment "To Mary," written at Este, expressed despondency at Mary's absence. Though it may have been written before Mary's arrival there and refer only to a physical absence, if it was written after Clara's death it certainly refers to her spiritual

absence. It is quite similar to two fragments of the same title written in 1819, evidently inspired by the effect upon Mary of the death of William Shelley. The poem "Love's Philosophy," with the fragment usually printed as "Follow," which is evidently a part of it (both written before December 28, 1819 though dated 1820 by Mary Shelley and subsequent editors), may represent, after the situation had changed, a more hopeful wooing of Mary than the despondent wooing of "Invocation to Misery." If so, it would be still easier to understand why Shelley in presenting the poem to Sophia Stacey and also in giving it to Leigh Hunt for publication left off the stanza that is so evidently a part of it and that troubled Mr. H. B. Forman (*The Shelley Notebooks*, II, 11) as Shelley's "only licentious stanza" — because with the stanza added it is definitely a personal rather than a generally philosophic poem. Cf. Chapter xxiii, notes 51 and 52.

"Is Not To-day Enough?" (1819) is an eight-line fragment in which the deeply despondent speaker who has fled from a "cheerless home" tells himself he must return "charged with the load that makes thee faint and mourn." The plant in "The Sensitive Plant" (1820) has long been identified with Shelley, and the Lady of the garden in that poem with Love, or Intellectual Beauty. This remains quite true, but it may now be seen also that the deserted plant and garden of that poem correspond exactly, though in a far mellower and more impersonal mood, with the deserted Madman of "Julian and Maddalo" and the deserted Shelley of 1818. Shelley said that the Lady of the garden was an "anticipated cognition" of Jane Williams, but she corresponds to the two Mary Shelleys of "Julian and Maddalo" and to Shelley's Mary before and after the alienation following Clara's death. "The Question" (1820) represents a poet gathering beautiful flowers but in despair of finding a recipient for them. "The Two Spirits — An Allegory" (1820) is a short debate between a spirit who discourages aspiration and a spirit determined to aspire because "within my heart is the lamp of love"; it closes with mention of a traveller who dreams of "the silver shape like his early love" and awakes to find night turned to day. Hitherto there has been no allegory apparent in this poem in spite of the title; there is at least a possible one now, however, in the restored love of Shelley and Mary. "Time Long Past" (1819) and "Death" (1820) contain only vague, possible connections in mood with the other poems under consideration. However, the seven-line fragment "To thirst and have no fill," which Mary Shelley dated 1817 and connected with the mood of "Prince Athanase," may well be, as Forman conjectured, a cancelled passage of "Julian and Maddalo." In it the despondent speaker feels condemned

> To nurse the image of unfelt caresses
> Till [dizzy] imagination just possesses
> The half-created shadow.

Also another short lyric entitled "Death," published by Mary Shelley as written in 1817, fits so well into the group of the sad poems accompanying "Julian and Maddalo" (and especially the "Invocation to Misery") that one suspects it may belong there, instead of to Shelley's grief over the deaths of Harriet and Fanny Imlay.

[53] "The Choice," lines 23–36, Shelley's *Works* (ed. Forman, 1876), I, 4.

Mary's remorse in this poem has hitherto been understood to apply to her conduct in the months immediately preceding Shelley's death. No doubt these months are included in her apology, but these lines cannot be taken to apply solely to that time, for they say that Shelley had *often* written of his dejection and imply that it was caused by "unrequited love." Moreover, Mary's conduct in 1822 was not a matter of "cold neglect, averted eyes"; it was a simple case of unreasoning, hysterical fear directly traceable to her pregnancy at the time. The lines apply fully, however, to the situation in the autumn of 1818, which was probably repeated in milder form after the death of William Shelley in 1819.

In this connection one wonders that the usually sympathetic and charitable Leigh Hunt could have judged Mary so severely simply on the basis of her obviously hysterical conduct at San Terenzo in 1822, of which Shelley is known to have told him. Obviously the Williamses, who were witnesses, did not judge so harshly. Only by supposing that Shelley also told Hunt of the events of 1818 does Hunt's behaviour seem in character. Many years later Hunt explained to a correspondent that he would not review Middleton's life of Shelley or write a life himself because there were truths he could not suppress without falsifying the biography, nor utter without deeply injuring the living. (Leigh Hunt to Edmund Ollier, February 2, 1858, in Luther A. Brewer: *My Leigh Hunt Library — The Holograph Letters*, Iowa City, 1938, p. 114.)

[54] Shelley to Peacock, December [22], 1818, Julian *Works*, X, 12, 13.

[55] Mary Shelley to Mrs. Gisborne, December (no day) 1818, in *Shelley Memorials*, 107.

[56] Julian *Works*, IX, 337–42. Mary's journal for the same days runs as follows:

Thursday, Nov. 5. — Go as far as Rovigo. Bad roads and cloudy weather.

Friday, No. 6. — Very bad roads; our horses could hardly draw the carriage; we get oxen where we can. Pass by farm-house filled with the finest oxen in the world. Sleep at Ferrara.

Saturday, Nov. 7. — Remain all day at Ferrara. Visit the Public Library, where we see the armchair and inkstand of Ariosto, his handwriting, also that of Tasso. Visit the carcere of Tasso. Read Montaigne. Shelley reads Plato's "Republic."

[57] Toward the end of the letter, as Shelley philosophizes about painting in relation to the other arts in a passage that definitely foreshadows a part of his "Defence of Poetry," one wonders if Guido's painting may not be the starting-point of his "Song of Proserpine," written in 1820, in the same way that he imagined the lost paintings of antiquity may have stimulated Homer and Æschylus.

[58] Shelley to Peacock, Monday [November 9, 1818], Julian *Works*, IX, 346. Dated November 9 by Mary Shelley in Shelley's *Essays, Letters from Abroad* (1840), II, 153. But it is mentioned in *Shelley and Mary* as written Tuesday, November 10.

[59] Mary's journal, *Shelley and Mary*, II, 339–40, November 14–20.

[60] Shelley to Peacock, November [20], 1818, Julian *Works*, X, 4. This letter should probably be dated November 21, since Shelley says in the opening sentence that he has yet seen nothing in Rome except St. Peter's and the Vatican. Mary's journal shows that the Vatican was visited on November 21 and that on the 22nd a number of historic places were visited. Thus the letter was probably written after a visit on the 21st and before those of the 22nd.

[61] Ibid., 4–5.

[62] Shelley to Peacock, December [22], 1818, ibid., X, 13.

[63] Mary Shelley to Mrs. Gisborne, December [no day], 1818, in *Shelley Memorials*, 108.

[64] "The Coliseum: A Fragment" fills nearly eight pages in the Julian *Works* (VI, 299–306). It consists of a conversation between an old man and his daughter and a youthful stranger, in the Colosseum, which is excellently described. The young stranger's physical appearance is much like Shelley's in his various self-descriptions; the old man, however, is Shelley's mouthpiece. His prayer to Love may be connected with the situation existing between Mary and

Shelley: "O Power . . . Thou which interpenetratest all things, and without which this glorious world were a blind and formless chaos . . . Two solitary hearts invoke thee, may they be divided never!" etc.

⁶⁵ Shelley to Peacock, December [22], 1818, Julian *Works,* X, 13–14.

⁶⁶ Mary Shelley to Mrs. Gisborne, December (no day), 1818, in *Shelley Memorials,* 108.

⁶⁷ Shelley to Peacock, December [22], 1818. Julian *Works,* X, 15.

⁶⁸ So stated by Shelley in an official document quoted in Appendix VI.

⁶⁹ Shelley to Peacock, December [22], 1818, Julian *Works,* X, 15.

⁷⁰ Shelley to Peacock, February 25 [1819], ibid., 28.

⁷¹ Shelley to Leigh Hunt, December 22, 1818, ibid., 10.

⁷² Shelley to Peacock, January 24 and February 25, 1819, Julian *Works,* X, 27 and 34. Charles MacFarlane, in his *Reminiscences of a Literary Life* (London, 1917) , 6, gives the surgeon's name as "Mr. Roskilly" and quotes him (p. 9) as saying that Shelley's health was "in a very poor way" when he left Naples.

⁷³ Mary Shelley to Mrs. Gisborne, February 19, 1819, in *Shelley and Mary,* II, 362.

⁷⁴ "Ode to the West Wind," iii, 32–6. The moss and seaweed as well as the sunken ruins are described in Shelley's letter to Peacock that constitutes the only account of this excursion (December [22?], 1818; Julian *Works,* X, 12–19). The last line of the quotation is possibly a reminiscence of Shelley's earlier visit to the Prato Fiorito, from Bagni di Lucca.

⁷⁵ Shelley to Peacock, ibid., 17.

⁷⁶ Shelley to Peacock, ibid., 17–19.

⁷⁷ Shelley to Peacock, January 24, 1819, ibid., 25, 26. Two years later, in his "Ode to Naples," Shelley describes his feelings at Pompeii in lines 1–11.

⁷⁸ Charles MacFarlane, op. cit., 1–12. Professor Peck (*Life,* II, 113), the only biographer who has mentioned Shelley's acquaintance with MacFarlane, supposes the visit of Shelley and MacFarlane to Pompeii to be the one described in Shelley's letter. But MacFarlane speaks of meeting Mary after the return from Pompeii and makes it quite clear that he made the visit with Shelley alone, whereas Mary's journal for December 22 makes it clear that she was present with Shelley in Pompeii and does not mention MacFarlane. This was two months before the Shelleys left Naples; MacFarlane's visit was

only a few days before their departure. MacFarlane's account was written thirty-seven years later and may be both padded and inaccurate, but we must either suppose two separate visits or else suppose MacFarlane's account entirely fictitious. If he had based a fictitious account on Shelley's letters from Italy published by Mary Shelley in 1840 he would have made it conform to Shelley's account instead of clashing with it. Hence his account should be accepted as genuine, and hence Shelley made two visits to Pompeii. Mary's journal for February 25 mentions also a visit to Pompeii on the return journey from Pæstum, but does not mention MacFarlane.

[79] Shelley to Peacock, February 25, 1819, Julian *Works*, X, 30–2.

[80] Mary's journal under the dates given, and Shelley's letters to Peacock, December [22], 1818 and February 25, [1819], ibid., 19, 28, 29, and 32–4. For Rossetti, see MacFarlane's *Reminiscences*, 3–5.

[81] See Mary Shelley's letter of August 11, 1821 to Madame Hoppner, quoted in Chapter xxvii. It is unfortunate that Mary's letter does not fix the date of Paolo's discharge. Shelley's letter of December [22?] to Peacock shows that Paolo was present on the expedition to Vesuvius (December 16) and presumably was in his employ when the letter was written. The next letter to Peacock (January 24, 1819) states that "Elise has just married our Italian Servant and has quitted us; the man was a great rascal, and cheated enormously: this event was very much against our advice" (Julian *Works*, X, 27).

[82] Madame Hoppner to Mary Shelley, January 6, 1819, in *Shelley and Mary*, II, 357–8.

[83] Leigh Hunt to the Shelleys, November 12, 1818, in *Correspondence of Leigh Hunt*, I, 125; and Shelley to Leigh Hunt, December 22, 1818, in Julian *Works*, X, 9–11.

[84] Peacock to Shelley, November 29 and December 15, 1818, and January 13, 1819; in Peacock's *Works*, ed. Brett-Smith, VIII, 207, 211, 214; also in *Shelley and Mary*.

[85] Shelley to Peacock [January 24, 1819], Julian *Works*, X, 21.

[86] Mary Shelley's Note on the Poems of 1818.

[87] Shelley to Leigh Hunt, December 22, 1818, Julian *Works*, X, 10.

[88] In the Preface to *Essays, Letters from Abroad*, etc. (1840) Mary Shelley quotes a maxim of Shelley's: "'When we take people merely as they are, we make them worse; when we treat them as if they were what they should be, we improve them as far as they can be improved.'"

[89] For examples, Dowden (*Life*, II, 252–3), W. M. Rossetti (*Memoir of Shelley*, section xx), Helen Rossetti Angeli (*Shelley and His*

Friends in Italy, 54–5). Mrs. Marshall and Professor Peck mention the Hoppner scandal, but discuss no mystery.

90 See conclusion of Chapter xiv, and note 80 to that chapter.

91 See note 31, above.

92 The three official documents establishing the birth, baptism, and death of Elena Adelaide Shelley are given in Appendix vii.

93 Shelley to the Gisbornes, June 30, July 2, 1820, and an undated letter to the Gisbornes, probably written in July 1820 (Julian *Works*, X, 180, 182, 184).

94 Mary Shelley to Marianne Hunt, June 29 and November 24, 1819; Harper: *Letters of Mary W. Shelley*, 66, 80.

95 The silence of Mary's journal might mean little on this point, since at Marlow Mary's journal ignored the constant presence in the house of the semi-adopted Polly Rose. But the later evidence of Elise Foggi is here almost conclusive. Elise said the child was spirited out of the house immediately after its birth and that Mary never knew of it. Elise and Paolo were discharged between December 22 and January 24. To have known of the child at all, which they certainly did, they must have been with the Shelleys at the time of its " birth." Its presence or absence in the house for any length of time after its birth is a point in which Elise could not possibly have been mistaken. Though I believe Elise misunderstood what she saw and heard, she would hardly have made a wilful misstatement about the child's absence knowing that probably half a dozen witnesses could prove it false. If the child had remained in the house Elise would have welcomed the fact as a demonstrable confirmation of her story, instead of asserting the contrary.

96 See conclusion of Chapter xiv and note 80 on that chapter.

97 To the extent that circumstantial evidence can be deduced from the known facts between the time the Shelleys left England and the time of their Neapolitan residence, every consideration weighs against both hypotheses:

1. It is rather hard to suppose Shelley capable of a purely sordid or even a purely impulsive casual liaison, especially at a time when he was continually on the move. His letters of 1818 speak more than once of a mental and physical disgust for Italian women. It is difficult to suspect him of a sneaking liaison with either of the two maidservants. If, nevertheless, Elena was the child of Shelley and Milly Shields, assuredly her fellow-servant Elise Foggi would have been aware of the facts and would not have substituted an apparently improbable story for the true one. And if Elise herself was

the mother of Shelley's child she would have told no story at all. Medwin's mysterious " lady " might be a possible mother if her very existence were not so doubtful, but even then (when the time-elements are closely examined) there would be difficulties of circumstance and opportunity that would render such a hypothesis rather ridiculous. To the extent that circumstantial evidence permits conclusions, we may safely conclude that Elena Adelaide Shelley was not the daughter of Shelley and an unknown mother.

2. If Elena was the daughter of Claire and an unknown father, the Shelleys would certainly have kept her existence a secret (which they did) on account of the Byron-Allegra complication. But in that event Mary would have known in advance. Shelley might even have been willing to conceal the facts from Mary, for Claire's sake, but Claire, in the peculiar relations existing among the three, would never have dared allow Mary to suspect that the child was hers and Shelley's. It is unthinkable that she would not have abolished this possibility in advance. However unwillingly, Mary would then have assisted Claire. She had done so under exactly similar circumstances when Allegra was born.

Claire's journal is missing for nearly six months before and more than two months after Elena's birth, and the silence of Mary's journal about Elena is no certain proof that she either knew or did not know that Claire was to have a child. She had been equally silent when Allegra was born. The testimony of Elise Foggi, however (as given in full in Chapter xxvii), is clear on this point. Mary did *not* know of any birth at the time. If Elise's story was a malicious fabrication, a hundred inventions would have occurred to her as more credible than the assertion that the child was born and the mother restored to strength under Mary's eyes without her knowledge. Experienced doctors disagree on the mere possibility. Certainly there could have been no doubt in Elise's mind that such details were both unnecessary and dangerous – unless she really believed them herself. Evidently Elise believed that Mary knew nothing of this mysterious birth, and Elise was in a position to know. Moreover, Claire Clairmont, though she had been Byron's mistress, was a fastidious person hardly to be suspected, unless there were definite evidence, of a sordid, overnight hotel immorality with a stranger – an affair, moreover, for which her opportunities during the journey from Calais to Pisa were extraordinarily limited.

⁹⁸ The text of Elise's story as repeated in a letter from R. B. Hoppner to Byron is quoted in Chapter xxvii, with the comments

of both Shelley and Mary at the time. For Elise's unconvincing repudiation of her story, see Chapter xxviii, text and note 51.

[99] William Graham: *Last Links with Byron, Shelley, and Keats* (London, 1898). The book has been regarded by most Shelleyans as untrustworthy, or worse.

[100] Julian *Works*, X, 150, 152, and 367.

[101] Shelley to Byron, May 26, 1820, ibid., 194.

[102] In order to consider every possible circumstance that might support Elise's story, two other particulars should be mentioned. In 1822 when Claire was in frequent consultation with Elise and Elise was repudiating her former story, Claire's journal contains several passages that have been carefully crossed out. It might be presumed that this was to destroy references to Elena. But these passages are all short, and by infra-red photography I have deciphered some of them completely and all of them partly, without encountering a single word that could refer to the Naples affair, or to any other matter that might seem to require deletion.

The other circumstance is Shelley's mysterious letters of June 28 and August (no day) 1818 to Ollier, discussed in Chapter xix. One might suppose the sums there mentioned to be payments for medicines sent to Shelley to procure an abortion. The real purpose of these letters is unknown, and the truth of Elise's charges would have to be demonstrated first to establish such a meaning for these letters. Meanwhile they are more credible as financial transactions which for unknown reasons had to be kept secret. See Chapter xix, note 61.

[103] Shelley to the Gisbornes, dated by the editors "June or July, 1820," Julian *Works*, X, 184; and Mary to Shelley, undated [August 10, 1821?], Dowden: *Life*, II, 426.

[104] See note 93, above. Shelley's use of *my* instead of *our* is significant in connection with the name Elena. The name, Elena, complimenting Mary, was evidently given in anticipation of Mary's approval; the *my* suggests the failure of this hope.

[105] I can find no person in Shelley's acquaintance or family who bore Elena's second name, Adelaide. A possible but rather far-fetched source for the name would be Mrs. Opie's *Adelina Mowbray, or Mother and Daughter,* which impressed Shelley considerably just before his elopement with Harriet. A poet's ear would hardly approve Elena Adelina, and Adelaide may have resulted from a combination of Adelina and Mowbray. And Shelley had previously conferred the name Constantia on Claire from a novel.

[106] " Shelley, he says, attempted suicide in Naples "; W. M. Ros-

setti's reports of conversations with Trelawny, in the *Athenæum* for July 15, 1882 (No. 2855, p. 79). Cf. "Julian and Maddalo," 494–9, where the Madman rejects the constant temptation to suicide and lives only because the Lady's lot is rendered less defenceless by his doing so.

[107] An annotation to this act in Halsbury's Statutes of England (London, 1929), IX, 827, states: "Before the passing of this act adoption had never been recognized by the law, though agreements may have been made which for many purposes place a stranger *in loco parentis.*" Complete legal status, with a definite system of legal adoption, was not available in England until the British Adoption of Children Act, in 1926 (*Encyclopædia Britannica,* 14th ed., art. "Adoption"). For this information I am indebted to Professors J. S. Bradway and Douglas Maggs of Duke University Law School.)

[108] For a similar case, involving a well-known Canadian author, see *Time,* XXXII, 52 (December 5, 1938).

[109] A further suggestion that Mary knew occurs in Shelley's letter of April 6, 1819 to Mrs. Gisborne (Julian *Works,* X, 50): "A combination of circumstances which Mary will explain to you, leads us back to Naples in June, or rather at the end of May, where we shall remain until the ensuing winter." Also Mary's letter of August 17, 1820 to Amelia Curran, quoted in Chapter xxv (II, 215).

[110] See note 109 above.

[111] Mary Shelley to Maria Gisborne, February 19, 1819, *Shelley and Mary,* II, 362–3.

[112] Medwin: *Revised Life,* 116.

Chapter XXI

GENERAL SOURCES

Shelley's letters (Julian *Works,* IX, X); Shelley's poems, with Mrs. Shelley's Notes and her Preface to *Essays, Letters from Abroad,* etc.; *Shelley and Mary,* Vol. II; journal of Claire Clairmont; *Correspondence of Leigh Hunt; Life and Letters of Mary Wollstonecraft Shelley* (Mrs. Marshall); *Letters of Mary Shelley* (Harper); *Shelley Memorials* — all as previously cited — and Mrs. Helen Rossetti Angeli: *Shelley and His Friends in Italy* (London, 1911).

NOTES AND REFERENCES

¹ Mary's journal, March 5, 1819. Claire's journal becomes again available beginning March 7, and is the basis for the statement about their places of residence. Shelley's letter to Peacock, March 23, 1819, gives an excellent account of the journey to Rome.

² Shelley to Peacock, March 23, 1819, Julian *Works*, X, 38–9.

³ Ibid., 40–1.

⁴ Claire's journal for March 9, 1819; also Shelley to Peacock as cited in note 2 above.

⁵ The Shelleys were using at the time J. C. Hobhouse's notes on Canto iv of *Childe Harold's Pilgrimage*, J. C. Eustace's *Classical Tour through Italy* (1813), and Joseph Forsyth's *Remarks on Antiquities, Arts and Letters during an Excursion in Italy in the Years 1802 and 1803*.

⁶ Shelley to Peacock, Julian *Works*, X, 42, 43.

⁷ Ibid., 41.

⁸ Mary Shelley to Marianne Hunt, March 12, 1819, Harper, op. cit., 55.

⁹ Shelley to Leigh Hunt, September 3, 1819, Julian *Works*, X, 76, 77.

¹⁰ *Shelley Memorials*, 113.

¹¹ Shelley to Peacock, April 6, 1819, Julian *Works*, X, 46–7.

¹² Mary Shelley to Mrs. Gisborne, April 26, 1819, *Shelley Memorials*, 113. Signora Dionigi is not mentioned by name, but the characterization seems intended for her and is so taken by Mrs. Marshall in her life of Mary Shelley and by Mrs. Helen Rossetti Angeli in *Shelley and His Friends in Italy*, 65.

¹³ Godwin to Mary Shelley, March 5, 1819, in *Shelley and Mary*, II, 364 A.

¹⁴ Mary Shelley to Leigh Hunt, April 6, 1819, Harper, op. cit., 64.

¹⁵ Mary Shelley to Marianne Hunt, March 12, 1819, ibid., 55, 56.

¹⁶ Shelley to Peacock, April 6, 1819, Julian *Works*, X, 48.

¹⁷ The portrait of William Shelley was a great comfort to Shelley and Mary after William's death. Presumably it descended to Sir Percy Florence Shelley, but, like Mary's portrait, secured and kept by Trelawny in 1923, it appears never to have been printed. The portrait of Claire was owned by Edward Trelawny in 1882 (W. M. Rossetti: "Talks With Trelawny," in the *Athenæum*, July 15, 1882, p. 79).

[18] See Appendix V.

[19] Mrs. Shelley's Note to *The Cenci,* and Shelley's Preface.

[20] Shelley to the Gisbornes, April 6, 1819, Julian *Works,* X, 50.

[21] Mary Shelley to Mrs. Gisborne, April 26, 1819, *Shelley Memorials,* 112. Mary's invitation is in a postscript omitted in *Shelley Memorials,* but included in *Shelley and Mary,* II, 376.

[22] Shelley to Hogg, July 25, 1819, Julian *Works,* X, 64.

[23] Mary Shelley to Mrs. Gisborne, May 30, 1819, in *Shelley and Mary,* II, 379.

[24] Julian *Works,* X, 52. The letter was first ascribed to Miss Curran by Lady Shelley, in *Shelley and Mary,* and her ascription has been accepted by Professor Dowden and Mr. Ingpen. A recent study of the MS. by Professor Frederick L. Jones (*Times Literary Supplement,* July 10, 1937) shows that it is endorsed by Mrs. Gisborne: " C. C. and M. W. S."

[25] Mary Shelley to Marianne Hunt, August 28, 1819, in Marshall, op. cit., I, 252.

[26] Shelley to Hogg, July 25, 1819, Julian *Works,* X, 64.

[27] Hogg to Shelley, July 2, 1819, in *Shelley and Mary,* II, 385.

[28] Leigh Hunt to Mary Shelley, July (no day) 1819, *Correspondence of Leigh Hunt,* I, 132–3.

[29] Mary Shelley to Amelia Curran, Marshall, op. cit., I, 249–50.

[30] Mary Shelley to Marianne Hunt, June 29, 1819, Harper, op. cit., 66–7, 68.

[31] Mary Shelley to Marianne Hunt, August 28, 1819, Marshall, op. cit., I, 252.

[32] William Godwin to Mary Shelley, September 9, 1819, Marshall, op. cit., I, 254–6.

[33] Mary Shelley's Note on *The Cenci;* also Mary Shelley to Marianne Hunt, August 28, 1819, Harper, op. cit., 69, 70.

[34] Shelley to Peacock, August ("Probably 22") 1819, Julian *Works,* X, 72.

[35] Mary Shelley to Marianne Hunt, August 28, 1819, Harper, op. cit., 73.

[36] Shelley to Peacock, June [20 or 21?] 1819, Julian *Works,* X, 57.

[37] Shelley to Peacock, April 6, 1819, Julian *Works,* X, 49. Mary Shelley to Marianne Hunt, November 24, 1819, Harper, op. cit., 81.

[38] Shelley to Peacock, July 6, 1819, Julian *Works,* X, 59.

[39] The location of William Shelley's grave is unknown. The white marble pyramid supposed to have been placed over it was placed by mistake over the body of an adult, and the error was not dis-

covered until after Shelley's death, when it was desired to place the
child's body by the father's ashes. See Chapter xix; also Helen Rossetti Angeli's *Shelley and His Friends in Italy*, 318–19.

⁴⁰ " It is not to be supposed that a mind so full of vast ideas concerning the universe . . . should be content with a mere logical
view [i.e., Shelley's " Essay on a Future State "] of that which even
in religion is a mystery and a wonder. I cannot pretend to supply
the deficiency, nor say what Shelley's views were — they were vague,
certainly; yet as certainly regarded the country beyond the grave as
by no means foreign to our interests and hopes — " Mary Shelley's
Preface to *Essays, Letters from Abroad*, etc. (1840). Byron asserted
Shelley's belief in immortality, and Trelawny quoted Shelley as denying any such belief (Byron to Moore, March 6, 1822, Prothero:
Letters and Journals, VI, 35; and Trelawny's *Recollections*, II, 190).
Cf. Chapter xxv, note 62.

⁴¹ Shelley to Leigh Hunt, August 15, 1819, Julian *Works*, X, 69–70.

⁴² Mary's journal states that it was finished August 8. But in a
letter to Hunt dated August 15, Shelley refers to the poem as on the
eve of completion. Shelley's dedicatory letter to Leigh Hunt is
dated Rome, May 29, 1819.

⁴³ Louise du Plantis. An unpublished letter of Charles Clairmont's
to Mary and Claire (Vienna, February 26, 1820, in the Bodleian
Library, MSS Shelley Adds. d. 5, folios 6–8) shows that Madame du
Plantis, whom he despises, has written to prefer vague charges
against him and Claire and to break off all relations. Charles seems
both angry and amused at this, and states that he answered temperately. Madame du Plantis seems to have been an acquaintance
of Mrs. Clairmont's. Her charges may have concerned either Allegra
or Elena Adelaide, of both of whom Charles was probably still
ignorant. He believes them to have been trumped up and asks for
further information. For Shelley's comment on Charles and Louise,
see Julian *Works*, X, 93.

⁴⁴ Shelley to Peacock, September 21, 1819, Julian *Works*, X, 83.

⁴⁵ In late December " Julian and Maddalo " was still unpublished,
and as late as May 14, 1820 Shelley still wished it published anonymously, if at all. The delay was probably due to Claire Clairmont's
objections, which Shelley pacified by assuring her that the poem was
never intended for publication. Nevertheless, early in 1821 Shelley
supposed that it had been published according to his directions,
though as a matter of fact it was first published by Mrs. Shelley in
1824. Claire's objections may have been based on the presence of

Allegra in a poem where Byron, at least, was sure to be recognized. (Shelley to Hunt, August 15, 1819; to Ollier, December 15 [or 25], 1819; May 14, 1820; and February 22, 1821; to Claire Clairmont, January 2, 1821; in Julian *Works*, X, 68, 135, 168, 243, 228.)

[46] Nevertheless, *The Cenci* has had a rather interesting stage history. Before 1886 it was several times considered by managers, only to be rejected as unsuitable. Miss Genevieve Ward even attempted to organize a private production. On March 10, 1886 the Shelley Society, having been refused a licence for a public performance, gave a "private" production at the Grand Theatre, Islington, witnessed by an audience variously estimated at the time as from 2,300 to 3,000 people, including such notables as Robert Browning, James Russell Lowell, George Meredith, and Bernard Shaw. Despite brilliant acting of the principal rôles by Alma Murray (Mrs. Alfred Forman) and Herman Vezin, the verdict was almost unanimous that the play was unsuited to the modern stage. The Shelley Society never carried out its intention of repeating the performance.

In 1922 a translation by Dr. Otakar Fisher was produced at Prague by Dr. Karel Čapek, author of *R. U. R.*, with Madame Dostalåva as Beatrice and with strikingly unusual cubist stage-settings, mostly by Joseph Čapek. In the same year, for four successive Mondays beginning November 13, public matinées were given at the New Theatre, St. Martin's Lane, London, with Miss Sybil Thorndike as Beatrice.

For the earlier history see Shelley Society *Notebook* and *Papers;* E. S. Bates: *A Study of Shelley's Drama, "The Cenci"* (New York, 1908); the Alma Murray pamphlets, and my article: "Shelley's Debt to Alma Murray," in *Modern Language Notes*, XXXVII, 411–15 (November 1922). For the 1922 performance see the *Observer* (London), October 8, 1922 and numerous press clippings in Vol. IX of *Shelley after 100 Years*, Bodleian Library, 2796.c.2.

[47] Julian *Works*, X, 79, 83, 134–5, 81.

[48] Leigh Hunt to Mary Shelley, July (no day) 1819, *Correspondence of Leigh Hunt*, I, 133.

[49] Leigh Hunt to Shelley, July (no day) 1819, *Correspondence of Leigh Hunt*, I, 132.

[50] Shelley to Peacock, August 15, 1819, Julian *Works*, X, 69.

[51] Shelley to Peacock, August (probably 22) 1819, Julian *Works*, X, 73. The last sentence restates Shelley's poem, "The Past."

[52] Shelley to Mr. Dorville, October 18, 1819 (Julian *Works*, X, 97), and Mary Shelley to Miss Curran, September 18, 1819, quoted

(in part) from *Shelley and Mary* without date by Mrs. Marshall, op. cit., I, 256. It was during this period of six months that the Hoppners heard and believed Elise's scandalous story about the birth of Elena Shelley. They communicated the story to Byron on September 16. This probably accounts for part of the silence from Venice. The Shelleys were unaware as yet of Elise's story.

⁵³ The quotations and some other details in this paragraph are drawn from Professor A. Stanley Walker's " Peterloo, Shelley and Reform," *P.M.L.A.*, XL, 128–64 (March 1925).

⁵⁴ Shelley to Ollier, September 6, 1819, Julian *Works*, X, 80.

⁵⁵ Shelley to Peacock, September 9, 1819, ibid., 82.

⁵⁶ " He reads the ' Trionfe della Morte ' aloud in the evening . . ." (Mary Shelley's journal for September 17, 1819).

⁵⁷ Shelley to Leigh Hunt [November 1819] Julian *Works*, X, 129.

⁵⁸ " Lines Written during the Castlereagh Administration"; " Song: To the Men of England "; " To Sidmouth and Castlereagh "; " Fragment: To the People of England"; " A New National Anthem "; " Sonnet: England in 1819."

⁵⁹ Mrs. Shelley's Note on the Poems of 1819.

⁶⁰ Mary Shelley to Leigh Hunt, September 24, 1819, Harper, op. cit., 77.

⁶¹ Ibid., 75.

⁶² William Godwin to J. Marshall, August 2, 1800, in C. K. Paul's *William Godwin*, I, 369–70.

⁶³ Claire Clairmont is so quoted by Dowden (*Life*, II, 317) and Mrs. Angeli (*Shelley and His Friends in Italy*, 89), from an unspecified source of which I am ignorant.

⁶⁴ Mrs. Mason to Shelley and Mary, November 14, 1819; also two undated letters ("November or December"), and " Friday — 14," 1819, in *Shelley and Mary*, II, 444–51.

Chapter XXII

GENERAL SOURCES

Shelley's works and letters in the Julian edition, as previously cited.

Contemporary reviews of Shelley as reprinted in my *The Un-*

extinguished Hearth (Durham, N. C.: Duke University Press; 1938).

My own unpublished doctoral dissertation: *Shelley's Dramatic Poems,* Harvard, 1918, MS. in Widener Library.

Carl Grabo: *A Newton Among Poets* (Chapel Hill: University of North Carolina Press; 1930).

Carl Grabo: *"Prometheus Unbound"* — *An Interpretation* (Chapel Hill: University of North Carolina Press; 1935).

NOTES AND REFERENCES

[1] "Julian and Maddalo," 170–1.

[2] Julian *Works,* X, 40, 47.

[3] Claire Clairmont's journal, March 12, 1819.

[4] *Prometheus Unbound,* Act II, Scene i, lines 1–12.

[5] Ibid., Act II, Scene iii, lines 54–62.

[6] Ibid., Act II, Scene v, lines 60–71.

[7] Ibid., Act III, Scene i, lines 71–4. I do not intend by this paragraph to endorse the many attempts, which I consider absurd, to find a regular allegorical machinery in the poem. On this point I have expressed myself more fully in an article entitled "*Prometheus Unbound,* or Every Man His Own Allegorist," in *Publications of the Modern Language Association of America,* XL, 172–84 (March 1925).

[8] *Prometheus Unbound,* Act III, Scene iii, lines 6–7.

[9] Ibid., lines 55–6.

[10] Many readers of the poem have been misled by the rapidity of the changes noted by the Spirit of the Earth into concluding that Shelley expected an immediate change. If we could think of the human mind as changed to the extent Shelley presupposes, even an immediate change in dependent matters would not be unreasonable. But the changes here described are probably viewed by Shelley from the almost timeless point of view of his characters, for other passages in the poem and in his other works show that his conception of change in the actual world was gradual. This is especially emphasized when he deals specifically with the actual world in *A Philosophical View of Reform* and in his letters.

[11] *Prometheus Unbound,* Act III, Scene iv, lines 126–204.

[12] Ibid., Act IV, lines 562–78.

[13] It may be that in one or two details the optimism breaks through

its intellectual restraint. When the Spirit of the Earth (III, iv, 80–3) describes birds that after Jupiter's overthrow eat deadly nightshade berries unharmed, the reader may see no connection with the human will or human vices and virtues. When Asia and Prometheus propose to spend their freedom in a lonely cave, it may seem a poor and dangerously passive way of enjoying, or at least of preserving, freedom. These discrepancies may be partly explained as symbols. The cave, at least, is almost certainly not merely a literal cave. Perhaps it is also a remnant of Shelley's early desire to retire to Wales with Harriet and later with Mary, which he repeated two years after *Prometheus Unbound* in a letter to Mary and in the idealized solitude he imagined for himself and Emilia Viviani. In any case it would have been almost as difficult to imagine a plausible future for Prometheus and Asia as to solve in human language the riddle of good and evil. But to explain is not necessarily to justify. Both instances seem to me to be flaws of taste and temperament, but minor flaws only, since the main structure stands easily without them.

14 See Dowden: *Life*, II, 263–4.

15 Shelley to Charles Ollier, June 8, 1821, Julian *Works*, X, 273.

16 Shelley to Charles Ollier, December 15 [or 25], 1819, ibid., 135; cf. ibid., 95. Nearly forty references to the poem in Shelley's letters from 1818 to 1822 show the extent of his interest in it.

17 Chapter xiv of this work.

18 Professor Carl Grabo has made a study of the science of Shelley's day and of Shelley's scientific reading and interests, the results of which are to be found in his *A Newton among Poets* (1930) and *Prometheus Unbound* (1935). In these works he demonstrates beyond question the extent and accuracy of Shelley's scientific knowledge and links a number of passages in Shelley's writings with passages in scientific works that Shelley is known to have read. Other passages in Shelley are shown to have a similar resemblance to scientific passages which Shelley may have read. The evidence is sufficient to show an undeniable connection in general, though not in every particular case. This influence, I am convinced, is limited to the imagery and does not extend to the general philosophy of the poem. Also it is largely the result of remembered, rather than current, reading. *Shelley and Mary* provides a detailed account of Shelley's daily reading after his elopement with Mary. This record, which was available to Professor Grabo only in the scanty printed excerpts, shows that Shelley did very little scientific reading after 1815. Most of the parallels cited by Professor Grabo from *Prome-*

theus Unbound occur in the fourth act, which was written some months after Shelley considered the poem finished. The fact that Shelley's Spirit of the Earth is described in terms corresponding rather closely with current scientific knowledge of electricity does not necessarily indicate that Shelley was adapting electricity to his fable of human regeneration, though it does show that he was neglecting no means, through his imagery, of stimulating the imagination. The same seems true also of Shelley's indebtedness to Newton, Erasmus Darwin, and Herschel, and his possible debt to Father Beccaria and others.

[19] This parallel is fully developed by Grabo (*A Newton among Poets*, 140–2), who fully explains both descriptions in terms of nineteenth-century scientific knowledge and speculation.

[20] Professor Grabo thinks (ibid., 132–3) that Shelley found in electricity the physical counterpart of Love; that as Love was to Shelley the unifying principle spiritually, so electricity, or fire, was the unifying principle of the physical universe. Elsewhere in the volume (p. 141) he shows how Shelley's scientific reading may have made him regard electricity as the unifying principle of matter. Thus he regards Shelley as producing a mystical synthesis of two ideas of unity derived from his metaphysical and his scientific interests. The idea seems to me quite plausible. Shelley was obviously deeply interested in both electricity and Love and in arriving at an idea of unity beyond the specious and jarring diversity of appearances. But I would insist, far more than Mr. Grabo seems to think necessary, that the use of electricity in this concept of unity is symbolic rather than literal. It furnished, at least to Shelley's mind, a powerful suggestion of the possibility of a unifying principle in the midst of apparent diversity. It may even have been a part of his general theory of ultimate reality. Shelley could never have expected electricity to bear a significant part in the moral regeneration which is the centre of the poem.

[21] In the *Examiner* for June 23, 1822 Leigh Hunt, in attacking the *Quarterly's* method of demonstrating that *Prometheus Unbound* was obscure, quoted as a parallel the following from Cary's translation of Dante's *Paradiso*, turning the blank verse into prose:

Every orb, corporeal, doth proportion its extent unto the virtue through its parts diffused. . . . Therefore the circle, whose swift course enwheels the universal frame, answers to that which is supreme in knowledge and in love. . . .

Shelley was familiar with the *Paradiso* before writing *Prometheus Unbound* and Mrs. Shelley was reading it at the time. Also both Shelley and Mary were reading frequently in the Old and New Testaments and may well have been impressed anew with the wheel in Ezekiel.

22 The word "phantasm," with a suggestion of the meaning Shelley gives it, may have come into his mind from the *Confessions* of Saint Augustine, which he quoted from in his motto to *Alastor,* as early as 1815. But there are doubtless other possible sources in Shelley's philosophic reading from which he could have derived his phantasms. Professor Grabo has shown that Shelley's imagery was often coloured by his reading in Neo-Platonic philosophy.

23 See *Power and Elusiveness in Shelley,* by the late Oscar W. Firkins (Minneapolis, 1937). Professor Firkins devoted short chapters to each of the three categories I have mentioned.

24 Ibid., 58. I am indebted to this volume for a part of my discussion of the imagery of *Prometheus Unbound.* The same imagery becomes much more impressively characteristic when traced through the whole body of Shelley's poetry, as in Professor Firkins's study.

25 The *Literary Gazette,* September 9, 1820; and the *Quarterly Review,* October 1821. The texts of these and all other contemporary reviews of *Prometheus Unbound* may be seen in my *The Unextinguished Hearth,* 217–50.

26 Shelley to C. and J. Ollier, March 6, 1820; to Hunt, May 26, 1820; to Charles Ollier, February 16, 1821; and to John Gisborne, January 26, 1822; Julian *Works,* X, 148, 171, 237, 354.

27 Shelley to Peacock, November 7, 1818, ibid., IX, 340.

28 *Prometheus Unbound,* Act III, Scene iii, lines 113–14.

29 Mary Shelley's Note on *The Cenci.*

30 The production was reviewed by at least eighty-one periodicals in 1888. See the list, with copious extracts, in *The Shelley Society Notebook.*

31 Cf. Wilhelm Wagner: *Shelleys " The Cenci," Analyse, Quellen und innerer Zusammenhang mit des Dichters Ideen* (Rostock, 1903), 90, 93.

32 Samuel Phelps, who had wished to stage the play at Sadler's Wells, gave it up on the opinion of Jonas Levy and R. H. Horne that the dramatic interest ended with Cenci's death (*Notebook of the Shelley Society,* I, i, 187). Kean and Macready both considered producing the play, but their motives for not doing so are unknown.

33 *The Cenci* has been called " the greatest tragedy of modern

times" by R. W. Griswold (1875), W. M. Rossetti (1878), R. P. Scott (1878), H. S. Salt (1887), and William Sharp (1887); "the greatest English tragedy since Shakespeare" by George Griffin (1845), Lady Shelley (1858), and John Addington Symonds (1879) — all as quoted by E. S. Bates, in *A Study of Shelley's Drama, "The Cenci"* (New York, 1908), 20. Professor S. C. Chew, in his *The Dramas of Lord Byron* (Baltimore, 1915), 14, and Algernon Charles Swinburne in his Preface to *Les Cenci* (Paris, 1883) both call it the greatest English drama of the nineteenth century. Perhaps the limit of admiration is reached by Alfred and H. B. Forman in the introduction to the Shelley Society's reprint of the play in 1886: "Companionship for The Cenci must be sought in the *Œdipus Tyrannus* of Sophocles, in the *Medea* of Euripides, in Shakespeare's *King Lear*, and in the masterpiece of French classic drama, *Phèdre*."

[34] It had been the "life-long ambition" of both Alma Murray (Mrs. Alfred Forman) and Miss Glyn to act the part of Beatrice, and Miss Genevieve Ward had almost succeeded in organizing a private performance several years before the Shelley Society, with the material assistance of Alma Murray, staged the "private" performance of 1886 (*Daily Telegraph* for May 8, 1886, as quoted in *Shelley Society Notebook*, 55–6. See also my "Shelley's Debt to Alma Murray," in *Modern Language Notes*, November 1922, XXXVII, 411–15).

[35] Mary Shelley's Note on *The Cenci*, 1839.

[36] From the original draft of Shelley's Preface, as printed by H. B. Forman in *Notebooks of Shelley* (1911), II, 97. Erroneously quoted in *Shelley Memorials*, 117, as from "another letter." Other references to *The Cenci* in Shelley's letters may be found in Julian *Works*, X, 61, 79, 134, 148, 151, 159, 166, 172, 192, 194, 232, 235, 237.

[37] Shelley to Thomas Medwin, July 20, 1820, Julian *Works*, X, 192.

[38] See the chapter entitled "Prometheus Bound" in Mr. Ellsworth Barnard's *Shelley's Religion* (Minneapolis, 1937).

[39] There is no reference to *A Philosophical View of Reform* in Mary's journal, but on December 23, 1819, while Mary was transcribing the last act of *Prometheus Unbound*, Shelley wrote John and Maria Gisborne: "I am engaged in a political work," and on May 26, 1820 he asked Leigh Hunt's help in finding a publisher for *A Philosophical View of Reform*, as if it were practically complete (Julian *Works*, X, 136, 172). The discussion of Spanish affairs in the work itself would indicate that at least part of it was written at about the same time as "An Ode, Written October, 1819, before

the Spaniards had Recovered Their Liberty." Mary Shelley's letter of March 26, 1820 to Maria Gisborne (*Shelley and Mary,* III, 484) conveys the recent news of Spanish freedom.

⁴⁰ Professor Dowden described the work in his *Transcripts and Studies* (London, 1888); it was first published in 1920 by T. W. Rolleston. The passages quoted in this chapter are from the later text of the Julian edition, VII, 333 ff.

Chapter XXIII

GENERAL SOURCES

Shelley's letters (Julian *Works,* X), Shelley's *Works,* Mrs. Shelley's Notes, Medwin's *Life,* Leigh Hunt's *Correspondence, Shelley and Mary,* Mrs. Marshall, Harper, and Mrs. Angeli — all as previously cited. The *Quarterly Review,* the *Examiner,* the *Monthly Magazine,* and *Blackwood's Edinburgh Magazine.*

NOTES AND REFERENCES

¹ Mrs. Angeli, op. cit., 90. I doubt if the house number was so high.

² From an undated letter of Mrs. Gisborne's to the Shelleys, written apparently in December 1819, it would appear that Madame du Plantis or her daughter had formerly been a tutor or governess in the family of Mr. Webb, an English merchant at Leghorn with whom the Shelleys were acquainted (*Shelley and Mary,* II, 443).

³ Mary Shelley to Maria Gisborne, December 28, 1819, ibid., II, 460. Parts of this letter only are printed in *Shelley Memorials,* 129. Professor Dowden (*Life,* II, 318, note) misreads this passage as referring either to Mrs. Mason or to Mrs. Meadows. The context shows that " Madame M." refers to Madame Merveilleux du Plantis.

⁴ Shelley to Maria Gisborne, October 13 or 14, 1819, Julian *Works,* X, 93.

⁵ Shelley to Maria Gisborne, October 13 or 14, 1819, ibid., 94. To Hogg, on April 20, 1820, Shelley wrote that he had dedicated

every sunny day in Florence to study at the art galleries. He praised especially the statue of Niobe and her children. "No production of sculpture, not even the Apollo, ever produced on me so strong an effect as this Niobe" (ibid., 159).

6 Mary Shelley's Note on the Poems of 1820.

7 Shelley's "Notes on Sculptures in Rome and Florence," sixty in number, ranging in length from a mere phrase to two or three pages. Medwin first printed eight of them in 1832 and three more in 1847; the rest were first printed by H. B. Forman in 1879. Most of them are brief descriptions; some, like "The Arch of Titus," "The Laocoon," "Bacchus and Ampelus," "Venus Anodyomene," "Minerva," "Marsyas," "A Bacchus by Michaelangelo," and "Niobe," contain excellent touches of delicate, typically Shelleyan observation.

8 *The Man of Kent or Canterbury Political and Literary Weekly Messenger*, Saturday, November 21, 1818, pp. 157–60. The general tone and two or three phrases in this review suggest Hunt's previous review in the *Examiner*. It is also signed with the figure of a hand, a common signature with Hunt.

This review, which I overlooked in my *The Unextinguished Hearth*, was called to my attention by Mr. W. S. Ward.

9 Medwin: *Revised Life*, 225. This story may still be true, but it should be noted that on October 15 Shelley acknowledged receipt of both the *Quarterly* article and Hunt's reply to it, sent by Ollier (Julian *Works*, X, 95). Medwin's later version of the same story (*The Angler in Wales*, London, 1834, II, 190) is, as Forman remarks, "instructively different."

10 Shelley at first supposed it to have been written by Southey, and later by Milman (Julian *Works*, X, 95, 103, 275).

11 Shelley to Ollier, October 15 and December 15 [or 25], 1819, ibid., 96, 134. (Mr. Charters, who never received full payment for the coach he sold Shelley, would probably not have regarded Shelley's jest as very humorous.)

12 Ibid., 97. The fragment is dated only 1819, and presumably was not completed or sent. Shelley's quotation from the review shows that he meant the April number when he wrote "Sept. no."

13 The *Quarterly Review*, XXI, 460–71 (April 1819).

14 The *Monthly Review*, LXXXVIII, 323 (March 1819). A part of this article, including the sentences I have quoted, was copied in the *Fireside Magazine or Monthly Entertainer*, of Stamford, I, 187 (May 1, 1819).

[15] " The Quarterly Review, and Revolt of Islam," in the *Examiner* for September 26 and October 3 and 10, 1819, pp. 620–1, 635–6, 652–3. The last instalment could not have been included in the packet sent by Ollier and acknowledged on October 15, but in November Shelley thanked Hunt for the friendly sentiments he had expressed in it.

[16] See my note on this review in *The Unextinguished Hearth*, 125.

[17] *Blackwood's Edinburgh Magazine*, IV, 475–82 (January 1819).

[18] Ibid., V, 268–274 (June 1819).

[19] Ibid., VI, 148–54 (November 1819).

[20] Shelley to Ollier, December 15 [or 25], 1819, Julian *Works*, X, 134.

[21] Mary Shelley to Maria Gisborne [December 15], 1819, *Shelley and Mary*, II, 463, quoted inaccurately and in part in *Shelley Memorials*, 129.

[22] Shelley to Leigh Hunt [November 13], and to Amelia Curran, November 18, 1819, Julian *Works*, X, 122, 127.

[23] Mary Shelley to Marianne Hunt, November 24, 1819 (Harper, op. cit., 80), and Mrs. Mason to Mary Shelley, " Friday — 14, 1819," in *Shelley and Mary*, II, 451. Also *Shelley Memorials*, 128.

[24] Godwin's letter is not extant, but it is partly described in Shelley's letter of August 7, 1820 to Godwin, Julian *Works*, X, 198.

[25] Shelley to Amelia Curran, November 18, 1819, ibid., 128.

[26] Mrs. Mason to Shelley, " November or December, 1819," *Shelley and Mary*, II, 447–8.

[27] Shelley to the Gisbornes, November 6, and to John Gisborne, November 16, 1819, Julian *Works*, X, 120, 123.

[28] Mrs. Gisborne to Mary Shelley, undated, in *Shelley and Mary*, II, 419, quoted in Julian *Works*, X, 92.

[29] Shelley to Henry Reveley, December 7, and to John and Maria Gisborne, December 23, 1819, Julian *Works*, X, 132, 136.

[30] Shelley had drawn a bill of £175 and possibly another of £50 on Brookes & Co. instead of Messrs. Coutts, and they had protested the first bill. Through Mr. Webb, of Leghorn, Shelley had drawn in early October a bill of £200 with which to aid Henry Reveley. This bill was also protested. (Shelley to John and Maria Gisborne, October 28, and to Brookes & Co., October 30 and December 7, 1819; Julian *Works*, X, 100, 101, 131.)

[31] Henry Reveley to Shelley, November 10 and 12, 1819, in *Shelley and Mary*, II, 436–7, and Julian *Works*, X, 126; and Shelley to Henry Reveley, November 17, 1819, in Julian *Works*, X, 126–7.

[32] Shelley to Hunt [November (no day) 1819], and November 3, 1819, Julian *Works*, X, 130–1, 119.

[33] For a brief eyewitness account of Carlile's trial, see Henry Crabb Robinson's journal for October 12, 13, 14, 1819. Carlile was sentenced to three years in prison, was fined £5,500, and was required to give security of £1,200 for good behaviour during life. He had previously (in 1817) served four months for publishing parodies on the Book of Common Prayer. In 1831 and 1834 he was imprisoned for three years and for four months respectively. All together he spent nine years, seven months, and one week in prison. After serving his three-year sentence beginning in 1819 he was compelled to serve an additional three years for non-payment of fines. His publishing business, which went on during his imprisonments, was several times ruined by the government. So sober a person as Francis Place cautioned him against being poisoned in prison; another friend reported to him in 1830 that the government was secretly discussing the revival of flogging for his special benefit.

Like Leigh Hunt, Carlile was permitted to write while in prison. During five of his six years in Dorchester Gaol Carlile wrote almost single-handed his thirty-two-page weekly *Republican* and a life of Tom Paine. Other radical periodicals published and largely written by him were the *Deist*, the *Moralist*, the *Lion*, the *Prompter*, the *Gauntlet*, the *Christian Warrior*, the *Phœnix*, the *Scourge*, and the *Church*.

It was one of Carlile's shopmen, William Clark, who published in 1821 the first pirated edition of Shelley's *Queen Mab*, after Carlile had vainly sought Shelley's permission to publish it in 1819. In 1822, while still in jail, Carlile purchased and offered for sale the remaining copies of Shelley's original edition, and printed articles about Shelley in the *Republican*.

In later years, as the result of difficulties with the wife who had ruined herself for his sake, he maintained a common-law wife. His disposition seemed not to have been always the most amiable — Crabb Robinson (a barrister) was offended by his pertness in court in 1819. But he was shrewd, courageous, and energetic, and though his portrait now hangs in the National Portrait Gallery, England has never yet sufficiently acknowledged his services and sufferings in the cause of free speech. (See mainly his *Republican* and *The Battle of the Press, as Told in the Story of the Life of Richard Carlile. By his Daughter*, Theophila Carlile Campbell, London, 1899.)

[34] For further details of this episode in the relation of radicals to

law enforcement see my article "Literature and the Law of Libel: Shelley and the Radicals of 1840–42," in *Studies in Philology*, XXII, 34–47 (January 1925).

[35] Shelley to Leigh Hunt, November 3, 1819, Julian *Works*, X, 118. Mary Shelley's journal records this letter as written November 5.

[36] According to Mary's journal, "Shelley reads Peter Bell," October 24, and she copied it October 28 and finished copying it November 2, 1819.

[37] See the introductory poem to "The Witch of Atlas," and Medwin: *Revised Life*, 250.

[38] Mrs. Mason to Mary Shelley (no month) —— 14, 1819, *Shelley and Mary*, II, 449.

[39] Maria Gisborne to the Shelleys, undated (December, 1819?), ibid., 440.

[40] Shelley to Hunt [November 13, 1819], Julian *Works*, X, 122.

[41] Shelley to Medwin, January 17, 1820, ibid., 140.

[42] Mary Shelley to Maria Gisborne, January 18, 1820, in *Shelley and Mary*, II, 469.

[43] Mary Shelley to Maria Gisborne, undated, ibid., 465.

[44] In one of Shelley's notebooks occurs a stanza beginning "'Twas the twentieth of October" and containing the comparison of dead leaves to ghosts that occurs in the "Ode to the West Wind." From this Mr. H. B. Forman (*Shelley Notebooks*, I, 165) deduces that the "Ode to the West Wind" was written at about this date, October 20, 1819.

[45] Shelley to Maria Gisborne, November 16, 1819, Julian *Works*, X, 124.

[46] Claire Clairmont's journal, January 7 and 9, 1820. See Appendix V.

[47] In Mrs. Helen Rossetti Angeli's *Shelley and His Friends in Italy*. Mrs. Angeli informs me that she had the journal from Mr. C. S. Catty, the son of Sophia Stacey, and that she extracted and printed practically all the Shelley material. Mr. Catty himself describes the journal in a letter to the *Athenæum*, April 18, 1908. The journal seems meanwhile to have disappeared. On May 13, 1936 Mr. Charles S. Catty, the grandson of Sophia Stacey, who inherited her Shelley relics, wrote to me: "I have not the faintest idea what has become of my grandmother's journal. . . ."

[48] Helen Rossetti Angeli, op. cit., 97. Mrs. Angeli adds: "The Italian is very incorrect, but should apparently translate as follows:

'I saw the signal: the light of the lamp. He spoke of his sisters. I am to give his regards to Mr. Parker. His adventures in youth — Authors — Ink — We talked about music — He listened to the songs (or possibly 'I listened to his verses') — A very interesting man.'"

⁴⁹ Mary Shelley to Maria Gisborne, December 1, 1819, in *Shelley and Mary*, II, 453, also *Shelley Memorials*, 128. Mrs. Angeli (op. cit., 96) says that Mary's description of Miss Jones is "prejudiced and unfair," that she was "a very cultivated woman."

⁵⁰ Helen Rossetti Angeli, op. cit., 104.

⁵¹ Sophia Stacey's journal for December 28, 1819, as cited by Mrs. Helen Rossetti Angeli, op. cit., 99. Mary Shelley and subsequent editors have misdated all three poems 1820. Cf. Chapter xx, note 52.

⁵² First printed by H. B. Forman in *The Shelley Notebooks* (II, 11). Professor Peck (*Life*, II, 161) reprints this stanza as the second stanza of "To Sophia," which it does not fit either in form or in thought. "Love's Philosophy" was written presumably while Sophia Stacey was in Florence and was published in the *Indicator* a week before her departure, but has no demonstrable connection with her. Cf. Chapter xx, note 52.

The mistaken attribution of a stanza which Mr. Forman called Shelley's only licentious one to a poem addressed to Miss Stacey, together with her own statement that she watched Shelley's window for a signal, apparently suggested to Professor Peck a guilty quality in the relations of Shelley and Miss Stacey. (It also suggests that Miss Stacey was quite a fool to make such an entry in her journal if anything but an innocent interpretation had occurred to her as possible.) I have been unable to locate the original journal either to prove or to disprove this possibility, which on other grounds I see no reason for taking seriously. Mrs. Helen Rossetti Angeli assures me that Sophia Stacey's journal contained nothing of Shelleyan significance which she did not quote in *Shelley and His Friends in Italy* and nothing whatever to suggest that the friendship was more than a mildly sentimental one.

⁵³ Shelley to John Gisborne, January 25, 1820, Julian *Works*, X, 142; also Claire Clairmont's journal for January 26, 1820.

Chapter XXIV

GENERAL SOURCES

Shelley's letters (Julian *Works*, X), Shelley's *Works* with Mrs. Shelley's Notes, *Shelley and Mary*, Claire Clairmont's journal — all as previously cited; contemporary reviews (as reprinted in *The Unextinguished Hearth*), and the manuscript journals of Maria and John Gisborne.

NOTES AND REFERENCES

[1] Mary Shelley, Note on the Poems of 1820.
[2] Shelley to Hunt, April 5, 1820, Julian *Works*, X, 153–4.
[3] "Poor Shelley got into a scrape about me with Byron," Landor wrote to his biographer, John Forster, on April 26, 1858, "yet, ardent as he was in my favour, I refused his proffered visit. His conduct towards his first wife had made me distrustful of him." After Shelley's death Mary Shelley wrote to Landor to tell him that Shelley's enthusiasm for his poetry lasted through life. Landor also heard of Shelley's admiration from Hogg. In 1826, according to an unpublished letter of Charles Brown to Leigh Hunt (Brit. Mus. Add. MSS 38,109, folio 30), Landor was seeking a portrait of Shelley; and in 1829 he was urging Trelawny to write Shelley's biography (Mrs. Julian Marshall: *Life and Letters of Mary Shelley*, II, 192). His disapproval of Shelley's early life seems largely based on his correspondence with Southey. "It was my intention," wrote Forster, ". . . to have made allusion to the effect produced on Landor by a detailed narrative (I found it among his papers) of all the circumstances of Shelley's first marriage, and its disastrous issue, communicated from a source unhappily only too authentic. Later reflection has however convinced me that no good can now be done by reviving a subject so inexpressibly painful." See *The Life of Walter*

Savage Landor by John Forster (London, 1869), I, 95, 114; and II, 167, 176, 375, 453, 537, note.

[4] Claire's journal, January 30, 1820.

[5] Mary Shelley to Maria Gisborne, undated, but between March 9 or 10 and 15, in *Shelley and Mary*, III, 480. Claire's journal fixes the date of the encounter as March 8. This is the same Colonel Finch whose letter to Mr. Gisborne furnished Shelley with particulars of Keats's death. He is mentioned briefly in Byron's letters and Polidori's *Diary*.

[6] Medwin: *Revised Life*, 239–41. The identification of the assailant as an officer in the Portuguese service would seem to be Medwin's rather than Shelley's. The details of this story seem to fix it absolutely at Pisa and in the first half of 1820, if the reference to the *Quarterly Review* article (which appeared in April 1819) has any significance. Though the story is impossible as it has been told, Shelley did have some sort of "adventure at the Post Office" in Rome on May 6, 1819, according to both journals. This would have been too early to have been stimulated by the *Quarterly* article, but it may have furnished the suggestion for the later story. Peacock (*Memoirs*, II, 354) tells the same story only to label it pure imagination, but places the scene at Florence. The journey from Florence to Genoa and back, however, is also impossible if the daily details of Mary's journal at that time are to be believed.

[7] Shelley to Medwin, April 16, 1820, Julian *Works*, X, 158.

[8] These details of Mrs. Mason are derived respectively from Claire's journal for February 13, February 27, April 21, Shelley's letter of April 20 to Hogg (Julian *Works*, X, 159), and Medwin's *Revised Life*, 265.

[9] Comparing the anticipated visit from the Gisbornes mentioned in this letter with the journal accounts of their visits, one suspects that this letter should have been dated by the Julian editors (X, 161) April 18 rather than April 23, 1820.

[10] Mary Shelley to Mrs. Gisborne, undated [between March 6 and 15], another on March 15; Shelley to Mr. Gisborne, March 19; Mary to Mrs. Gisborne, March 24, and also between March 26 and Good Friday, 1820 — all in *Shelley and Mary*, III, 478–87.

[11] Federico del Rosso was born October 29, 1780 and died November 19, 1858. When Shelley met him he had been a practising advocate in Leghorn for nearly eighteen years, and for two years had been conducting a novel school in which parents collaborated in educating one another's children. He was also a contributor of

papers to the Livornese Academy. He was a very religious man and was probably also conservative politically, as he certainly was later.

In 1824 the Grand Duke of Tuscany appointed him a lecturer on law at the University of Pisa, where he served with distinction until in 1850 he was made tutor in Philosophy and Law to the son of the Grand Duke, who rewarded him in 1856 with his most valuable decoration, Al Merito. In the 1830's and 1840's he was the author of some half-dozen legal treatises, all anonymous. In 1842 he was assaulted by students who resented his conservative loyalty to the Grand Duke.

Two of his living descendants have answered inquiries in a way that makes it seem extremely doubtful if any papers of his exist that could relate to his early connection with Shelley. A search of the legal archives at Leghorn reveals no sign that the dealings with Paolo Foggi ever reached a trial.

(This information is all based upon researches conducted for me in Pisa and Leghorn by Professor Giovanni Maresca, of Leghorn.)

[12] Mary Shelley's Note on the Poems of 1820. Cf. also Shelley to Hogg, April 5, 1820, and to Peacock, May 16, 1820, Julian *Works*, X, 154, 170.

[13] Shelley to Peacock, May 16, 1820, Julian *Works*, X, 170.

[14] Mrs. Shelley's Note on the Poems of 1820, and Shelley to Hunt, April 5, 1820, Julian *Works*, X, 154.

[15] Shelley to Ollier, postmarked May 30, 1820, Julian *Works*, X, 177.

[16] Details of this and the preceding paragraph are based on Shelley's letters of April 5 to Hunt (Julian *Works*, X, 153); to Ollier, April 30 and May 14 and 30 (ibid., 162, 167, 177); to Peacock, "early in March" (ibid., 147); to Samuel Hamilton and to Baldwin & Co., July 1 (ibid., 184, 185); and Sir Timothy Shelley to William Whitton, January 18, 1820 (Ingpen: *Shelley in England*, II, 539).

[17] Byron to Hoppner, April 22, 1820 and Claire Clairmont to Byron, undated, in *Letters and Journals of Lord Byron* (ed. Prothero), V, 14, 15.

[18] Shelley to the Gisbornes, May 26, 1820, Julian *Works*, X, 176.

[19] Shelley to Leigh Hunt, April 5, 1820, ibid., 154.

[20] "Orpheus," lines 50–3. The preceding lines present Shelley's familiar figure of the poet as a stag chased by hounds and wounded by arrows. And the lines immediately following (54–8) continue the appositeness of the passage to the situation between Shelley and Mary:

And then he struck from forth the strings a sound
Of deep and fearful melody. Alas!
In times long past, when fair Eurydice
With her bright eyes sat listening by his side,
He gently sang of high and heavenly themes.

[21] Shelley to Peacock, "early in March, 1820," Julian *Works*, X, 147.

[22] Shelley to Hunt, May 1, 1820, ibid., 164.

[23] *Shelley and Mary*, III, 484.

[24] Shelley to Hunt, April 15, 1820, Julian *Works*, X, 154.

[25] In sending the poem to Peacock on July 12 to be included in the *Prometheus Unbound* volume Shelley empowered him to insert an asterisk or asterisks for "some expressions" in these two stanzas (Julian *Works*, X, 187). The word *King* was therefore printed with four stars. The *Quarterly* reviewer (October 1821 — quoted in my *The Unextinguished Hearth*, 249) quotes Shelley's reference to the "Galilean serpent," line 119, and then skips nearly a hundred lines to condemn this passage, printing the four stars as six, to suggest Christ. Leigh Hunt indignantly exposed this piece of dishonesty in the *Examiner* for June 16, 1822 (quoted in *The Unextinguished Hearth*, 310). In quoting the same stanza the *London Magazine and Theatrical Inquisitor* (*The Unextinguished Hearth*, 260) correctly printed *King* instead of the four stars.

[26] Shelley to Leigh Hunt, May 26 and May 1, 1820, Julian *Works*, X, 172, 164.

[27] Shelley to Leigh Hunt, April 5, 1820, ibid., 155.

[28] The proof was actually read by Peacock, however.

[29] Details about publication in this and the preceding paragraph are drawn from Shelley's letters to Ollier, the Gisbornes, Medwin, Hunt, and Peacock, between March 6 and May 26, 1820, Julian *Works*, X, 168, 177, 167, 175, 155, 148, 170, 163, 168, 166, 162, 167, 151, 171, 163, and 171, in order.

[30] The *Examiner*, March 19; the *Monthly Magazine*, April; the *Literary Gazette*, April 1; the *London Magazine and Monthly Critical and Dramatic Review*, April; the *Theatrical Inquisitor*, April; the *New Monthly Magazine*, May; the *Edinburgh Monthly Review*, May; the *London Magazine*, May; and the *Indicator*, July 19 and 26. For the texts of these reviews see my *The Unextinguished Hearth*, 1938.

[31] Shelley to Ollier, January 20, 1820 [misdated for 1821], Julian

Works, X, 232. Shelley's brief "Lines to a Reviewer," written in the latter half of 1820, suggests that it must be poor sport to hate when the hatred is not returned.

[32] Southey's letters to Shelley may be found in Edward Dowden's edition of *The Correspondence of Robert Southey with Caroline Bowles* (London, 1881), 357–66, along with Shelley's replies.

[33] Letters and Letter Books of Sir Henry Taylor, Bodleian MS. Eng. Letters d. 6, folios 381, 383.

[34] Details for this and the preceding paragraph are from the unpublished journal of Maria Gisborne, in the Ashley Library, British Museum, 41, 56, 64, 68, 73, 58, 54, 62.

[35] Unpublished journal of Maria Gisborne, August 24, 1820, 71 and 70.

[36] Mary Shelley to Maria Gisborne, June 18, 1820, *Shelley and Mary,* III, 504–5.

[37] Shelley to the Gisbornes, June 30, 1820, Julian *Works,* X, 180.

[38] The official records are printed in Appendix VI.

Shelley's phrase "to us" in his letter of July 2 is here printed as it is given in the Julian edition. In the text of the letter in *Shelley and Mary* it is: "She is to come as soon as she recovers." I have been unable to locate the original MS., and am inclined to accept the Julian edition text as the more reliable. The difference seems insignificant.

[39] Shelley to the Gisbornes, Julian *Works,* X, 184. Dated "June or July, 1820" by the editors, but obviously written shortly after July 2.

[40] Unpublished journal of Maria Gisborne, entry for August 28, 1820, which includes Mrs. Gisborne's conversation with Godwin on August 24. In telling Godwin that Claire's liaison with Byron was little known, Mrs. Gisborne added that it "might be rendered more public through the villainy of P. . . ."

Of course any widespread scandal about Shelley alone might possibly give added currency to an old scandal about Claire, but Mrs. Gisborne (who had only recently enlightened Godwin himself on the subject) knew that outside of Shelley's household probably the only people in Italy who knew of Claire's liaison with Byron were the Masons, the Hoppners, and Byron himself. To regard the present danger to Claire as worth any alarm she would have had to know that Paolo's story involved Claire.

[41] Godwin to Shelley, undated. Dowden (*Life,* II, 322) quotes three sentences from this letter, which he must have read in MS., as

I am unable to find it in *Shelley and Mary* or elsewhere in print. Possibly it is the letter referred to in Mary's letter of March 15, 1820 to Mrs. Gisborne as having caused "great evil" by being delayed more than a month in being forwarded from Leghorn to Pisa.

42 Shelley to the Gisbornes, May 26, 1820, Julian *Works*, X, 176.

43 *Shelley and Mary*, III, 505.

44 Shelley to the Gisbornes, June 30, 1820, Julian *Works*, X, 179.

45 Ibid., 181.

46 The following extracts from Godwin's chapter on Promises in *Political Justice* may illuminate a dispute on the subject between two eminent admirers of the book. They may also suggest that Shelley had scriptural authority in *Political Justice* for his dilatory treatment of ordinary debtors:

. . . promises and compacts are in no sense the foundation of morality. The foundation of morality is justice.

Upon this ground it may be my duty to relieve upon some occasions the wretchedness of my neighbour, without having first balanced the debtor and creditor side of my accounts. . . . Upon this ground every promise is considered as given under a reserve for unforeseen and imperious circumstances, whether that reserve be specifically stated or no. (*Political Justice*, Philadelphia, 1796, I, 162, 172–3.)

47 Shelley to Godwin, August 7, 1820, Julian *Works*, X, 200–1.

48 Shelley to the Gisbornes, June or July 1820, ibid., 182–3.

49 Mary Shelley's journal for June 25, 1820.

50 Shelley to Peacock, July 12, 1820, Julian *Works*, X, 187.

51 Shelley to Godwin, August 7, 1820, ibid., 202.

52 Dowden (*Life*, II, 333) prints the story of the quarrel, for the details of which textual authority is lacking, with the following note: "Miss Mathilde Blind recovered this story, and Mr. Rossetti printed it. The quarrel is referred to in an unpublished letter of Mrs. Shelley to Mrs. Gisborne."

53 Maria Gisborne's journal and her letters to Mary Shelley show how each of these friends impressed her. Coleridge still had one of the finest minds she had ever known. Godwin she spoke of with respect but hardly admiration. She liked Hunt, was inclined to dislike Peacock (who failed to call), liked Horace Smith mildly, but was painfully impressed by his formal dinner; and was quite favourably impressed by Hogg.

⁵⁴ Mary Shelley's Note on the Poems of 1820. In her journal for June 22 Mary mentions a " Walk to the sea," presumably with Shelley. The only other walk mentioned on which Shelley could have accompanied her was on July 14, after which Shelley wrote his translation of the Homeric " Hymn to Mercury." In an article entitled " Probable Dates of Composition of Shelley's ' Letter to Maria Gisborne ' and ' To a Skylark,' " in *Studies in Philology* (XXXVI, 524–8, July 1939), I have shown from the chronology of letters, journals, and the *Prometheus Unbound* volume that the " Letter " was in all probability written June 15 and the " To a Skylark " June 22 or soon afterwards.

Mr. Gisborne thus described the spot which he associated with Shelley and skylarks:

> We passed by the side of the brook, over those breezy and luxuriant meadows of which one in particular was most dear to our remembrance. It is the favourite resort of innumerable larks, and other sweet-voiced birds! How often, pursuing our early morning walks over this lovely expanse, we have beheld the speckled songsters, burst forth from their bed of rich herbage and soar fluttering — gladdening the very air with their incessant and thrilling notes — to a height at which the straining eye could scarcely ken the stationary and diminutive specks into which their soft and still receding forms had at length vanished. The steep banks of the brook were overgrown with myrtles and other sweet shrubs and embellished with an infinite variety of gaudy, delicate and odorous flowers. . . . We returned home . . . by the Conduits, which recalled mournfully to our remembrance a delightful walk we had once taken in that direction with a dear friend who no longer lives but in the indelible sympathies of his surviving and enthusiastic admirers. (Unpublished journal of John Gisborne, formerly in the Ashley Library, now in the British Museum, entry for October 20, 1827.)

⁵⁵ Shelley to Mary, July 30, 1820, Julian *Works*, X, 196; and Mary's journal, August 5, 1820; and Claire Clairmont's journal, August 5, 1820.

⁵⁶ Mr. Gisborne's letter has been lost. But Mrs. Gisborne's unpublished journal contains four interesting glimpses of Keats (June 23, 28, July 12, and August 20), all of which Miss Amy Lowell made use of in her biography of Keats.

⁵⁷ Shelley to Keats, July 27, 1820, Julian *Works*, X, 194. This letter, and Keats's reply (with a photograph of the latter), are re-

printed in *Mary Shelley, A Biography* (London, 1938), by R. Glynn Grylls, 125–7. Shelley's tactful warning against " mannerism " seems to be a hint to avoid the influence of Leigh Hunt's poetic style, which Shelley thought false. But this was a discovery Keats had already made for himself.

[58] Charles and Mary Cowden Clarke: *Recollections of Writers* (London, 1878), 151.

Chapter XXV

GENERAL SOURCES

Shelley's *Works* (Julian edition) and Mrs. Shelley's Notes, Shelley's letters (Julian edition, X), the journals of Mary Shelley and Claire Clairmont, *Shelley and Mary* (Vol. III) — all as previously cited. Also Thomas Medwin: *Revised Life of Shelley*, ed. H. B. Forman, London, 1913; and Enrica Viviani Della Robbia: *Vita di una Donna*, Firenze, 1936.

NOTES AND REFERENCES

[1] Claire Clairmont's journal, August 5, 1820; and note 55, p. 594.

[2] Mary Shelley to Maria Gisborne, September 25, 1820, *Shelley and Mary*, III, 539.

[3] Mary Shelley to Amelia Curran, August 17, 1820, *Shelley Memorials*, 145. In a letter to Miss Curran dated January 2, 1825 (*Shelley and Mary*, IV, 1054–6, quoted by Mrs. Marshall, op. cit., II, 130–2) Mary spoke of the Baths of Pisa as the scene of " the happiest years of my life."

[4] Mrs. Shelley's Note on the Poems of 1820, and also her journal for August 14, 15, 16, 1820.

[5] Mary Shelley's Note on the Poems of 1820.

[6] Shelley to the Olliers, " January 20, 1820 [misdated for 1821]," Julian *Works*, X, 232.

7 Professor Carl Grabo: *The Meaning of " The Witch of Atlas "* (Chapel Hill, N.C., 1935), 3, 25.

8 Dowden (*Life*, II, 334), suggested that "the playful form of speech common to the 'Hymn to Mercury' and 'The Witch of Atlas'" and "not found elsewhere in Shelley's poetry" might be due to *Ricciardetto*.

9 Here I am obliged to give reasons for not accepting most of the results of Professor Carl Grabo's learned study: *The Meaning of " The Witch of Atlas "* (as cited above).

Ranging widely through the scientific writings of Shelley's age, and also through the writings of the ancients, especially the neo-Platonists, on myths and symbols, Professor Grabo finds scientific ideas to which Shelley's fancies in the poem seem to correspond, ancient parallels from which he interprets Shelley's supposedly symbolic words, a genealogy for Shelley's Witch in ancient writings on mythology, and neo-Platonic ideas on the rationalizing of myth, all of which seem to him to give new significance to the Witch. He concludes that the Witch is in various aspects Minerva, the earthly Venus, Isis, the moon-goddess, and Intellectual Beauty; that her special realm is the air, that her power is that of electricity, which Shelley also thought of as magnetism (as hypnotism was then called) making of it both a spiritual and a physical force. Thus Shelley is supposed to have fused ancient myth, contemporary science, ancient metaphysical speculation, and his own concept of Intellectual Beauty into a new and subtly complicated mythological figure.

I agree with Professor Grabo that such a complex creation, and such a purpose, would not be unnatural in Shelley. It is hardly to be doubted that in much of his later poetry Shelley sought to reinvigorate and in some cases reinterpret ancient myth. He was probably familiar with the ancient rationalizing of myth, and he had read Wordsworth's *Excursion*, in which the essential validity of ancient myth is so powerfully argued (iv, 630–762). He had read Keats's reinterpretation of ancient myths in *Endymion*. *Prometheus Unbound* shows him professedly remaking ancient myth; " Arethusa " (1820), "The Hymn of Apollo " (1820), and the " Hymn of Pan " (1820) show him revitalizing it. In remaking or revitalizing any myth for his own age, Shelley might well have made use of modern science, and indeed appears to some extent to have done so in *Prometheus Unbound*. He might seek to imply metaphysical suggestions, in accord with his own belief in the illusory nature of reality, and he might also make use of the symbols that had occurred frequently in his poetry before. Actually he does show his usual fondness for water, boats, winds, caves, but whether symbolically or not cannot be proved, since they make perfectly good sense literally, and no poet has ever limited himself to a purely symbolic use of such common properties. They are all used unsymbolically in *Ricciardetto.*

Shelley was a highly intellectual poet, quite capable of combining all these elements in a subtle interpretation of the new deity he was delineating with evident care and tenderness. A somewhat analogous process is demonstrable in his " The Cloud " (1820), where the cloud clearly symbolizes the natural cycle of growth and destruction and is described symbolically, naturally, and scientifically all at once. In the " Ode to the West Wind," the wind, symbolizing both destruction and regeneration, is at the same time a personal, a natural, and a social force. If he did something similar in "The Witch of Atlas," it was for himself alone, and he refrained from furnishing anyone else with the key. It may easily be regarded as complete without such a meaning, whether or not the added meaning exists.

But actual intent and deed do not follow automatically from possible intent and deed. Professor Grabo supposes his case established by the similarities between ideas which he finds in the scientific and neo-Platonic writers and ideas which he finds in the poem. Even if the " similarities " were always conclusive (which is doubtful), still it must be remarked that parallels mean nothing unless a bridge can be made to connect them, either by strong verbal links or by definite proof of a connection between the author and his putative source. Otherwise we must assume, for example, that most vegetarians derive their ideas direct from Pythagoras.

" He [Shelley] must," says Professor Grabo, " for years, have read the neo-Platonists and the scientific philosophers of his own day " (p. 111). He must indeed, to have produced the results ascribed to him. But that is precisely what Shelley did *not* do. Of about thirty scientific and metaphysical writers mentioned in Professor Grabo's index who might have been read by Shelley, only about a third can be shown to have been actually read in any of their works. Of the larger number of specific books by these authors, the books from which Professor Grabo's parallels are drawn, only five were certainly read by Shelley, and two of these were encyclopædias. Thus it can be shown that Shelley read Plutarch, but not his *Morals;* Thomas Taylor, but not his neo-Platonic writings.

Moreover, of the five books which Shelley can definitely be shown to have read, there is no evidence that he read more than two (one of the encyclopædias, possibly, and the works of Diodorus Siculus) within six years of writing "The Witch of Atlas." These figures would be significant in any case, considering the necessity of actually connecting Shelley with the books from which he is supposed to have drawn ideas. They are particularly so in Shelley's case, however, for from July 1814 Shelley and Mary kept obviously careful daily records of the books they read. In scientific and metaphysical matters these records show no special interest whatever — only the occasional interests of an omnivorous reader who has not suffered two of his earlier interests to die out completely. Shelley's memory was tenacious. We have seen in an earlier chapter that his meteorological science, which Professor Grabo attributes to Father Beccaria, may have come from the Syon House and Eton College lectures of Adam Walker. But no one would claim that after more than six years of only casual interest his memory alone would furnish the fullness of knowledge which Professor Grabo himself recognized must have come from full and constant reading.

This tremendous gap between Shelley's supposed reading and his demonstrable reading is a weighty objection when we consider that the Shelleys kept careful reading records. Far less important is such a trivial slip as attributing to Plutarch on page 15 an anticipation of neo-Platonic doctrines by which on page 17 he is said to have been influenced.

But another chronological confusion turns out to be very destructive indeed. Professor Grabo lays considerable emphasis upon magnetism as the moral counterpart of electricity. It is in his interpretation the source of the Witch's power over men's minds. His sole basis for Shelley's knowledge of hypnotism is Medwin's account, which makes it quite clear that Shelley knew nothing of hypnotism before Medwin's arrival. Yet Medwin arrived on October 22 and "The Witch of Atlas" was finished nearly two months before, on August 16. Thus the whole element of electrical magnetism in Professor Grabo's interpretation can have no bearing upon the actual meaning of the poem.

Professor Grabo's study completely ignores Forteguerri's *Ricciardetto*, which Shelley had only finished reading. This poem certainly furnished Shelley the stanza, the magic, and something of the tone of "The Witch of Atlas." It contains some of the details (whether borrowed therefrom by Shelley or not) for which in Shelley's poem Professor Grabo finds other provenience in books Shelley cannot be shown to have read.

The identification of the Witch with Minerva seems indicated to Professor Grabo (p. 24) by her dwelling upon Mount Atlas, for, according to Thomas Taylor's translation of Proclus (which Shelley may never have read), Minerva, goddess of the intelligible, dwelt on Atlas as the highest point of earth. But there is a simpler explanation, involving neither Minerva nor Proclus, depending upon data that are fully demonstrable. Shelley composed the poem while climbing Mount Pellegrino and wrote it down immediately after his return. There was a shrine on the mountain. Why not a mountain-shrine for his Witch? And since it had to be named, and Atlas was a high mountain, and his Witch (as daughter of one of the Atlantides) a granddaughter of Atlas, why not Mount Atlas? Shelley's last preceding poem had been his translation of the Homeric " Hymn to Mercury," in which Mercury's birth in a mountain cavern is described.

Since Professor Grabo's book appeared, two studies have demonstrated other influences on the poem which he has overlooked: namely, a number of verbal reminiscences from Keats, and influences from both Milton and Spenser on both style and idea. (" The Witch of Atlas and Endymion," by John Livingston Lowes, in *P.M.L.A.*, LV: 203–7 [March, 1940]; and " Spenser and Shelley's Witch of Atlas," by C. H. Baker, to appear in *P.M.L.A.* probably in September, 1941).

Finally (pp. 3, 25) Professor Grabo mistakenly assumes that the last stanza of Shelley's introductory poem announces that " The Witch of Atlas " contains a mystery and offers a challenge for its solution. As I have pointed out in this chapter, what Shelley is actually saying is that to attempt to unveil Intellectual Beauty (the Witch, not the poem) is deadly. Rightly interpreted, the introductory poem does not establish a presupposition of hidden philosophical meanings, but by its lightness, borne out by the poem itself, it suggests the contrary.

[10] Professor Grabo thinks the poem combines a scientific and mythological interest in the moon and its goddesses Isis and Diana. I can perceive no evidence of this in the poem itself, but it would have been possible to derive even a slight moon-interest from *Ricciardetto*. The *maga* Lirina on one occasion descends to meet Ricciardetto " from the mountains of the moon," and some of the action takes place on an Island of the Moon, really Madagascar.

[11] The only mention of the poem in either journal is Mary's entry for August 25: " On the 24th . . . Shelley writes an Ode to Naples . . . begins Swellfoot the Tyrant."

[12] " Ode to Naples," lines 51–5 and 62–5.

[13] Mary Shelley's Note on *Œdipus Tyrannus,* and her journal for August 25, 1820.

[14] Except for Mary Shelley's statement in her note that the book was suppressed, all knowledge of its publication depends upon a manuscript note in the copy of the book formerly owned by Mr. H. B. Forman. This copy, one of the four extant, sold in 1920 for $6,100. See H. B. Forman: *The Shelley Library,* etc. (London, 1886), 97–100, and T. J. Wise: *A Shelley Library,* privately printed (London, 1924), 56–7.

[15] See my article " Shelley's Swellfoot the Tyrant in Relation to Contemporary Political Satires," *P.M.L.A.,* XXXVI, 332–46 (September 1921). The article by Professor Porson was first cited by Peck: *Life,* II, 174–5, 394.

[16] Byron to Shelley, August 25, 1820, in *Shelley and Mary,* III, 532A. Not in Byron's collected letters.

[17] Shelley to Byron, September 17, 1820, Julian *Works,* X, 207–8.

[18] Mary Shelley's Note on the Poems of 1820.

[19] Medwin: *Revised Life,* 234.

[20] Shelley to Claire Clairmont, October 29, 1820, Julian *Works,* X, 214.

[21] Trelawny: *Recollections of the Last Days of Shelley and Byron,* II, 167.

[22] Medwin, op. cit., 233–4.

[23] Shelley to Claire Clairmont, October 29, 1820, and to John Gisborne, same date, Julian *Works,* X, 216.

[24] Shelley to Peacock, November [probably 15], 1820, ibid., 223.

[25] Mary Shelley to Mrs. Gisborne, September 25, 1820, and Mr. Gisborne to Mary Shelley, October 3, 1820, *Shelley and Mary,* III, 539, 540; and Shelley to the Gisbornes, October 11, 1820, Julian *Works,* X, 210.

[26] William Godwin to Mrs. Gisborne, September 15, 1820, *Shelley and Mary,* III, 536–7.

[27] Shelley to Claire Clairmont, October 29, 1820, Julian *Works,* X, 215–16.

[28] Shelley to Jane Clairmont, November (probably 18), [1820], ibid., 226.

[29] Mary Shelley to Marianne Hunt, December 2, 1820, Brit. Mus.

MSS 38,523, folio 56; quoted by R. Glynn Grylls: *Mary Shelley, A Biography,* 115, note.

[30] Medwin, op. cit., 259.

[31] *Shelley and Mary,* III, 534–5.

[32] See II, 212, and note.

[33] Medwin, op. cit., 259–60.

[34] Medwin, op. cit., 261, and Shelley to Peacock, February 15, 1821, Julian *Works,* X, 235.

[35] Shelley to Marianne Hunt [?October 27, 1820], ibid., 212.

[36] Medwin, op. cit., 235. Mrs. Shelley's journal mentions Medwin's illness first on November 5: " Mr. Medwin ill."

[37] Medwin, op. cit., 236.

[38] Shelley to Byron, September 17, 1820, Julian *Works,* X, 209.

[39] Shelley to Claire Clairmont, October 29, 1820, ibid., 215.

[40] Mary Shelley to Marianne Hunt, undated (spring of 1820), H. H. Harper: *Letters of Mary Shelley* (Boston, 1918), 86–7.

[41] Mary Shelley's journal, November 12, 1820.

[42] Medwin, op. cit., 268.

[43] Ibid., 238.

[44] Ibid., 250.

[45] Ibid., 242–3. Medwin professed that his own later translation of the *Prometheus* owed much to these readings.

[46] Ibid., 243–4. Medwin mentions that Shelley was particularly impressed with the Fool in the play. Cf. Shelley's Fool in the fragment of " Charles I." Shelley's letter of November 1820 to John Gisborne (Julian *Works,* X, 221) speaks with enthusiasm of " bathing myself in the light and odour of the starry autos."

[47] Medwin, op. cit., 244–5. This translation, with Guido's *Rape of Proserpine* (see Chapter xx, note 57), was probably the basis for Shelley's exquisite " Song of Proserpine," written during the next winter.

[48] Medwin, op. cit., 256.

[49] Ibid., 262–3. The opinions quoted previously in this paragraph are from Medwin, op. cit., 255, 256, 263–4, 262. Not all of the opinions quoted by Medwin could have been expressed by Shelley in the winter of 1820–1. Shelley read *Anastasius* and possibly one or two of the other works later. But all of the opinions could have been expressed to Medwin while the latter was at Pisa.

[50] Medwin, op. cit., 251, 257–8, 259, 260–1, and Shelley to Marianne Hunt [?October 27, 1820], and to Peacock, February 15 and March 21, 1821, Julian *Works,* X, 211, 234, 248.

⁵¹ Medwin, op. cit., 255.

⁵² Ibid., 268–9.

⁵³ Ibid., 237–8.

⁵⁴ Shelley to Peacock, April 6, 1819, Julian *Works*, X, 48. This passage is quoted by Medwin (op. cit., 239) as describing Shelley's dejection.

⁵⁵ Medwin, op. cit., 237.

⁵⁶ Ibid., 267.

⁵⁷ Ibid., 269.

⁵⁸ Ibid.

⁵⁹ Ibid., 269. Cf. Thornton Hunt's earlier account of one of Shelley's spasms, p. 500.

⁶⁰ Medwin, op. cit., 269–70.

⁶¹ Claire Clairmont's journal, December 15, 1820.

⁶² Medwin, op. cit., 270. There is no passage in Shelley's poems, letters, or prose fragments that clearly shows a belief in or a denial of immortality in the sense of a survival of mundane personality. *Adonais*, his nearest approach, seems to fall far short of the ordinary belief in immortality. Cf. Chapter xxi, note 40, and Ellsworth Barnard, *Shelley's Religion* (Minneapolis, 1937), index, under "Immortality."

⁶³ Those on Byron are sharp and amusing and show some insight. The two on Shelley are perhaps worth quoting: "Caricature for poor [*Shelley* crossed out] S. He looking very sweet and smiling. A little [*child playing* crossed out] Jesus Christ playing about the room. He says. Then grasping a small knife and looking mild [*I'll quietly hide that little child,* crossed out] I will quietly murder that little child. Another. Himself and God Almighty. He says If you please, God Almighty, I had rather be damned with Plato and Lord Bacon than go to Heaven with Paley and Malthus. God Almighty, It shall be quite as you please, pray don't stand upon ceremony. Shelley's three aversions, God Almighty, Lord Chancellor and didactic Poetry" (Claire Clairmont's journal, November 8, 1820).

⁶⁴ Shelley to Claire Clairmont, October, 29, November [18?], 1820, and [January 2 and 16], 1821, Julian *Works*, X, 213, 216, 225, 229.

⁶⁵ Details on Pacchiani drawn partly from Medwin and partly from Enrica Viviani Della Robbia: *Vita di una Donna* (Firenze, 1936), chapter on Pacchiani.

⁶⁶ Mary Shelley to Marianne Hunt, December 3, 1820, Harper, op. cit., 95.

⁶⁷ Claire Clairmont's journal, December 11, 1820.

[68] Claire Clairmont's journal, December 9, 1820.

[69] Mary Shelley to Maria Gisborne, January 1821, *Shelley and Mary*, III, 568.

[70] Claire's journal for December 23, 1820, and Mary's for February 22, 1821. Mary's journal for December 23 mentions Pacchiani's departure, but ignores Claire's.

[71] *Encyclopedia Italiana*, " Tommaso Sgricci." Several years after Shelley's death Sgricci performed in London. He died in 1836. The *Encyclopedia Italiana* cites W. Viviani: *Un genio aretino, Tommaso Sgricci, poeta tragico improvvisatore*, Arezzo, 1928.

[72] Mary Shelley to Marianne Hunt, December 3, 1820, Harper, op. cit., 96.

[73] Mary Shelley to Marianne Hunt, December 29, 1820, Harper, op. cit., 101–3. In an article, " The English in Italy," in the *Westminster Review*, VI, 325–41 (October 1826). Mary Shelley gives an account of three performances of Sgricci witnessed by her in Italy.

[74] According to a description of Mavrocordato in 1823, in Julius Millingen's *Memoirs of the Affairs of Greece*, 65, 66, as quoted by Dowden: *Life*, II, 362.

[75] See note 74; also Mary to Marianne Hunt, January 1, 1821, Harper, op. cit., 107.

[76] Shelley to Peacock, March 21, 1821, Julian *Works*, X, 249.

[77] Medwin, op. cit., 263–4.

[78] Shelley to Peacock, as cited in note 76, above.

[79] Shelley to Claire Clairmont, undated (spring of 1821), and June 8, 1821, Julian *Works*, X, 264, 273. In 1824 Trelawny characterized Mavrocordato to Mary as " your wooden god, Mavrocordato . . . I hope, ere long, to see his head removed from his worthless and heartless body. He is a mere shuffling soldier, an aristocratic brute " (*Letters of E. J. Trelawny*, London, 1910, p. 82).

[80] Journal of John Gisborne (MS.), October 9, 1827 — " Foggi also called, in consequence of my letter to him which I had sent to Pisa. He had in a most liberal and handsome manner paid up the full arrears of our rent. . . . I consider this a rather remarkable instance of faith in absent friends."

On April 27, 1821, while the Gisbornes were making the Shelleys a short visit, Mary's journal records: " The Williams and Foggi in the evening."

[81] Shelley to Claire Clairmont [April 29, 1821], Julian *Works*, X, 260, quotes a specimen line from the translation: " I Mantuan, capering, squalid, squalling." It is uncertain whether or not Count

Taafe really possessed the title claimed; he is usually referred to as "Mr." by the Shelleys.

⁸² Dowden: *Life*, II, 364–5. The original MSS. of Shelley's letter proposing the book to Ollier, and of a letter of Taafe's to Murray inquiring about delay in publication, are to be found in a grangerized edition of Moore's Byron in the British Museum.

⁸³ On January 2 Shelley wrote Claire Clairmont: "I have not been able to see until the last day or two," and on January 20 he wrote to Vincent Novello that he had recovered, though "My eyes even yet are very inadequate to the fatigue of writing" (Julian *Works*, X, 228, 231).

Chapter XXVI

GENERAL SOURCES

Shelley's letters (Julian *Works*, X), Shelley's *Works*, Mrs. Shelley's Notes, *Shelley and Mary*, the journals of Mary Shelley and Claire Clairmont, Medwin's *Revised Life of Shelley*, and Enrica Viviani Della Robbia: *Vita di una Donna* — all as previously cited.

NOTES AND REFERENCES

¹ Claire Clairmont's journal, November 29, 1820. The school was also called the Conservatory of St. Anna. Though the Shelleys regularly referred to it as a convent, the account of it given in *Vita di una Donna* shows that after the Napoleonic Wars it could hardly have been a typical convent school. It was controlled more by the Grand Duke of Tuscany than by the church, and a man, Professor Pacchiani, had been one of the faculty.

² Mary Shelley to Marianne Hunt, December 3, 1820, Harper, *Letters of Mary W. Shelley*, 98–9. At this time Emilia expected to be married to a young attorney named Biondi. Medwin's account (*Revised Life*, 277) of a jealous stepmother who was responsible

for Emilia's confinement is evidently without basis. According to *Vita di una Donna* (p. 170), Emilia's mother died in 1826.

³ Enrica Viviani Della Robbia, op. cit., 27. This volume is also the source of my impression of Emilia's father.

⁴ Medwin, op. cit., 281–4, quotes and translates the document entire, under the title " Il Vero Amore." Two sonnets are quoted in *Vita di una Donna*, 94–5.

⁵ Medwin, op. cit., 277. This seems unjust to Niccoló Viviani, in that Emilia eventually married Biondi, to whom she was affianced at the time, and presumably received a *dot* of 7,500 scudi, as specified in the marriage contract. The contract is printed in *Vita di una Donna*, 135–41.

⁶ Medwin, op. cit., 279. Mary Shelley's description of Clementina in *Lodore* (1835, II, 185), obviously intended as a portrait of Emilia, conforms almost exactly to Medwin's description, but adds a few imperfections. " Her smile was deficient in sweetness, her voice wanted melody . . . she gesticulated too much," etc.

⁷ Medwin, op. cit., 279. One of Mary Shelley's gifts to Emilia had been " *uccelli* " (birds).

⁸ All the extracts from Emilia Viviani's letters here quoted are taken from the text as translated in Appendix II.

⁹ Shelley to Claire Clairmont [February 18], 1821, Julian *Works*, X, 241.

¹⁰ Shelley to Claire Clairmont [January 2] and [16], 1821, ibid., 228, 230.

¹¹ Mary Shelley to Hunt, December 29, 1820, Harper, op. cit., 105. Many years later, in *Lodore,* Mary Shelley still gave Emilia (Clorinda) many attractive qualities, though she also gave her an ungovernable temper. In this novel Mary represents Savile's (Shelley's) interest in Clorinda previous to their marriage as purely Platonic.

¹² Emilia Viviani to Mary Shelley, January 14, 1821. The preceding quotation is from the same letter. In *Shelley and Mary* (III, 637) parts of this letter are omitted, including both these expressions. In *Vita di una Donna* (89), where the letters appear to have been printed from photographs of the manuscript, these passages are included, but the Marchesa Della Robbia omitted them from the translations in Appendix II of the present work, possibly because they appear in *Vita di una Donna* as isolated passages only, for which the basic complete photographs may have been lost.

¹³ The poem is printed as a fragment of fourteen lines and dated

March 1821. Probably the flowers were not sent to Shelley individually, but to " tua famiglia." The only gift of flowers mentioned in
either journal is in Claire's for December 8, 1820: " In the evening
a letter and flowers from Emilia." This suggests that the poem may
have been written in the second week of December 1820.

¹⁴ The date of this essay is uncertain. Both Rossetti and Forman
date it 1815, but Mrs. Shelley seems to have supposed it to have been
written about 1820 or 1821. Mrs. Shelley makes the significant comment that it " reveals the secrets of the most impassioned, and yet the
purest and softest heart that ever yearned for sympathy."

¹⁵ The approximate date is determined by three other dates —
February 16, when Shelley sent the finished poem to Ollier; January 19, when the Williamses arrived at Pisa; and January 31, when
Shelley read Dante's *Vita Nuova* aloud to Mary. The poem quotes
the *Vita Nuova* in the Advertisement and echoes it in several places
in the text. This may have happened *before* almost as easily as *after*
Shelley read the *Vita Nuova* to Mary; but Shelley would hardly have
been addressing Jane and Edward Williams by familiar nicknames
in the poem within less than two weeks after their arrival. Hence
the poem was probably written in the first two weeks of February.

Here I must correct an error in the Julian *Works*, X, 236, where
Mary Shelley's letter of December 29, 1820 is quoted to show that
the poem had been completed by that date. This letter was first
printed in part in *The Correspondence of Leigh Hunt,* with an
editorial insertion of the word *Epipsychidion* into the text. The complete text in Harper's *Letters of Mary Shelley* shows clearly that
Mary's reference was to a poem by the Pisan professor, Rosini.

¹⁶ Shelley to Charles Ollier, February 16, 1821, Julian *Works*, X,
236. Since Mary Shelley's journal for this day records that Shelley
spent the whole evening at the Masons', leaving her at home alone,
one suspects that he may have gone there purposely to write this
letter and to make his fair copy of *Epipsychidion.*

¹⁷ Shelley to Claire Clairmont [April 29 and 2, 1821], Julian
Works, X, 259, 251. Psychologists might find in this passage and
in " Julian and Maddalo" and *Epipsychidion* clear examples of
manic-depressive phenomena, but I cannot see that the phenomena
are made clearer by classifying them — on the contrary, there seems
some danger of warping the individual phenomenon by assigning it
a type-name.

¹⁸ Professor Peck (*Life*, II, 207) considers that Shelley desired

an actual elopement. The poem itself, with its inclusion of Mary and its reassurance that Emily is to " remain a vestal sister still," renders this impossible — not to mention the absurdity of writing a long poem in advance to advertise a secret and dangerous elopement.

[19] The italics are mine, to mark the passage used by Shelley (in Italian) as a motto. The translation is Medwin's, who quotes the entire essay in both Italian and English, *Revised Life*, 281–4.

[20] Mary Shelley to Maria Gisborne, March 7, 1822, Mrs. Marshall, op. cit., I, 331.

[21] " To —— (One word is too often profaned)," 1821. This poem is usually supposed to have been addressed to Jane Williams, but unless it was written very late in 1821 it may very well have been addressed to Emilia Viviani.

[22] Shelley to Charles Ollier, February 16, 1821, Julian *Works*, X, 236.

[23] Shelley to John Gisborne, June 18, 1822, ibid., 401.

[24] Professor Peck (*Life*, II, 191) has suggested that this passage refers to an unknown affair at Oxford and that " electric poison " may be a venereal disease. Elsewhere (see Chapter v and notes) I have shown that he is mistaken in his supposed factual bases for an Oxford entanglement. But even if such an episode existed, how could it possibly have been considered by Shelley as an idealization? *Epipsychidion* is a professed record of idealizations.

[25] Cancelled lines of the dedication to Mary, as follows:

> Nor ever found I one not false to me:
> Hard hearts and cold, like weights of icy stone,
> That crushed and withered mine.
> She whom I found was dear but false to me,
> The other's heart was like a heart of stone
> Which crushed and withered mine.

[26] As early as 1817, in his unfinished poem " To Constantia," Shelley employed the same symbolism of the moon to express a feeling of the incompleteness of Mary's love:

> The rose that drinks the fountain dew
>   In the pleasant air of noon
> Grows pale with blue and altered hue —
>   In the gaze of the nightly moon;

For the planet of frost, so cold and bright,
Makes it wan with her borrowed light:
Such is my heart — . . .

[27] See Chapter xx.

[28] Shelley to John and Maria Gisborne [June or July 1820], Julian
Works, X, 184.

[29] It has been suggested (F. G. Fleay: "The Story of Shelley's
Life in His Epipsychidion," in *Poet Lore,* 1890) that Claire may have
been intended by the Planet (line 309). The same article anticipates
my identification of Claire as the Comet. But Shelley is plainly following a chronological sequence of events, in which the episode of
the Planet is the last Incarnate Sympathy before Emilia. This could
only place the Planet in 1819 or 1820, a time when it is perfectly
certain Claire could not have been intended. Moreover, Shelley's
astronomical imagery throughout the poem is scientifically correct.
He could hardly have made the ignorant blunder of calling Claire
both a Planet and a Comet.

[30] Medwin, op. cit., 281.

[31] See the note on *Epipsychidion* in Julian *Works,* II, 428.

[32] The approximate date of publication is fixed by an incidental
comment in the *Gossip* (Brighton) for May 19, 1821, in which it
is attributed to "that frantic fellow S-ll-y" (No. 12, p. 91). The
same magazine printed two reviews in different styles, June 23 and
July 14, 1821, pp. 129–35 and 153–9. *Blackwood's Edinburgh Magazine,* February 1822 (XI, 237–8), remarks upon the poem in "A
Letter from London."

[33] Mary Shelley to Claire Clairmont, undated, but shortly after
May 8, 1821, Julian *Works,* X, 262. Since Shelley wrote the latter
part of this letter, he probably read the first part, and hence knew
and perhaps concurred in Mary's view that the friendship with
Emilia was a misfortune. The reference may be to nothing more
than its obviously bad effect on Shelley's health.

[34] Shelley to Peacock, February 15, 1821, ibid., 234.

[35] Shelley to Charles Ollier, February 22, 1821, ibid., 242–3.

[36] Shelley to Peacock, March 21, 1821, Julian *Works,* X, 248.

[37] The "Defence of Poetry" was later edited by John Hunt for
the *Liberal,* omitting some passages referring directly to Peacock's
views. But the *Liberal* did not live long enough to publish it and
it was first published, as edited by John Hunt, by Mary Shelley in
1840 in *Essays, Letters from Abroad,* etc.

[38] Shelley's reading of the *Apologie* at this time is not directly demonstrable, but Mary's journal shows that she was reading it (alone or with Shelley) and the general similarity of the two essays on many points argues that Shelley was reading it also.

[39] Shelley to John and Maria Gisborne [July 13, 1821], Julian *Works*, X, 283: "Poets, the best of them, are a very camœleonic race; they take the colour not only of what they feed on, but of the very leaves under which they pass."

[40] Claire Clairmont's journal, November 8, 1820: "Shelley's three aversions, God Almighty, Lord Chancellor, and didactic poetry."

[41] *Hellas*, lines 38–45.

[42] The same paragraph in Shelley's "Defence of Poetry" offers in its succession of metaphors a parallel to Shelley's poetic method in "To a Skylark."

[43] Wordsworth: *The Prelude*, XIV, 190–2.

[44] Shelley to John and Maria Gisborne, July 19, [1821], Julian *Works*, X, 287: "The poet and the man are two different natures; though they exist together they may be unconscious of each other and incapable of deciding upon each other's powers and efforts by any reflex act."

[45] Professor Dowden (*Life*, II, 413, note) supposed that Shelley was engaged at this time on an ambitious work called "The Creator." In his letter of June 5, 1821 to the Gisbornes Shelley referred to the probable loss of a box containing materials for his "Charles I," and added: "If the idea of the *Creator* had been packed up with them, it would have shared the same fate; and that, I am afraid, has undergone another sort of shipwreck" (Julian *Works*, X, 270). In writing to Mrs. Gisborne on June 30, 1821, Mary Shelley said: "The 'Creator' has not yet made himself heard" (Mrs. Julian Marshall, op. cit., I, 291). Without the second statement, the first would seem clearly to refer to the creator of "Charles I." An examination of the original manuscript of Mary's letter destroys the second statement — Mary did not write "Creator," but "cicala." Thus the whole supposition falls down. See Elizabeth Nitchie in *Times Literary Supplement*, April 30, 1938.

[46] Shelley to Peacock, February 15, 1821, and to Claire Clairmont [February 18, 1821], Julian *Works*, X, 234–5 and 240–1.

[47] Mary Shelley's journal, April 1, 1821.

[48] Mary Shelley to Claire Clairmont [April 2, 1821], Julian *Works*, X, 250–1. On April 5 Mary wrote to Mrs. Gisborne in the same strain (*Shelley and Mary*, IV, 602–3).

⁴⁹ Prince Alexandro Mavrocordato to Mary Shelley, April 3, 1821, *Shelley and Mary*, IV, 600–1.

⁵⁰ Shelley to Claire Clairmont, undated, Julian *Works*, X, 264. The letter was written a few days after the Shelleys returned to the Baths of Pisa, which was on May 8, 1821.

⁵¹ Trelawny's *Recollections*, II, 168, and *Journal of Edward Ellerker Williams*, ed. Richard Garnett, London, 1902, p. 21 (October 26, 1821).

⁵² Leigh Hunt to Shelley, March 1, 1821, *Correspondence of Leigh Hunt*, I, 161–3.

⁵³ Marianne Hunt to Mary Shelley, January 24, 1821, *Shelley and Mary*, III, 578–9.

⁵⁴ Early in May Mary wrote to Claire Clairmont (Julian *Works*, X, 262): "Then we are drearily behindhand with money at present — Hunt and our furniture has swallowed up more than our savings."

⁵⁵ Horace Smith to Shelley, April 3, 1821, *Shelley and Mary*, III, 598–600.

⁵⁶ Shelley to Dr. Hume, February 17, 1820 (supposed by the Julian editors, X, 238, to have been misdated for 1821).

⁵⁷ Horace Smith to Shelley, April 17 and 19, 1821, *Shelley and Mary*, III, 610–12A and 616. The first encloses a fine, dignified protest from Smith to Sir Timothy Shelley, and the second encloses Sir Timothy's brief reply, denying all knowledge of the affair. On June 15 Horace Smith wrote Shelley that the Chancellor had settled the matter by decreeing that Dr. Hume's £30 be regularly reserved from Shelley's income, leaving Shelley £220 quarterly (ibid., III, 639).

⁵⁸ Shelley to Claire Clairmont [April 2, 1821], Julian *Works*, X, 252. If Shelley did not write the letters in question one would suspect Henry Reveley, the only other intimate of Claire's who would have been likely to know Shelley's habit of drawing trees in his margins. But it is a little difficult to imagine such letters from an actual lover, and Claire wrote much later in one of her journals that she declined an offer of marriage from Henry in 1820.

⁵⁹ Mary Shelley to Claire Clairmont, spring, 1821 (a few days after May 8), ibid., 260–2.

⁶⁰ Evidently referring to the distance between Pisa and the Baths of Pisa, which were four miles away. Allowing for some walking within the city, the distance appears exaggerated either by Shelley or Henry Reveley. *Shelley and Mary*, III, 605.

⁶¹ Shelley to Henry Reveley, April 17 and 19, 1821, Julian *Works*, X, 256–7.

⁶² Shelley to Henry Reveley, April 17, 1821, ibid., 256. See Henry Reveley's Notes, in *Shelley and Mary*, III, 605–6, and Mrs. Shelley's Note on the Poems of 1821. Both voyages are briefly chronicled in Mary's journal for April 16 and May 2 respectively. The misadventure of April 16 is casually mentioned in Shelley's letter of April 29 to Claire Clairmont, Julian *Works*, X, 259. Mrs. Shelley's Note mistakenly reverses the order of the two voyages.

⁶³ Shelley to Claire Clairmont, undated [April 29, 1821], Julian *Works*, X, 259. The steamboat was broken up and sold.

⁶⁴ Mary Shelley's Note on the Poems of 1821.

Chapter XXVII

GENERAL SOURCES

Shelley's letters (Julian *Works*, X), Shelley's poems, Mrs. Shelley's Notes, *Shelley and Mary*, the journals of Mary Shelley and Claire Clairmont, and Enrica Viviani Della Robbia: *Vita di una Donna* — all as previously cited.

NOTES AND REFERENCES

¹ Shelley to Byron, July 16, 1821, Julian *Works*, X, 285.

² Mary Shelley's journal for May 8 and November 1 and Claire Clairmont's journal for the last days of October. No specific date is given for the return to Pisa, but Williams's journal states Oct. 25.

³ Mary Shelley's Note on the Poems of 1821.

⁴ "Evening: Ponte Al Mare, Pisa," stanzas 1–3. The third stanza is incomplete, and the fourth and final stanza describes the western sky.

⁵ Williams wrote his play during the first three months of his residence at Pisa. It was never produced or published. Shelley praised it in his letter of August 22, 1821 to Medwin (Julian *Works*,

X, 317). The manuscript of Acts II, IV, and V is in the Bodleian
Library and contains many corrections in Shelley's hand, all of
which have been noted by Professor Peck in his *Life* (II, 365–80).

6 Mary Shelley's Note on the Poems of 1821.

7 "The Aziola" (1821), lines 10–20.

8 About May 8 (cf. Chapter xxvi) Shelley wrote to Claire: "W[il-
liams] I like, and I have got reconciled to Jane." On June 8 he wrote
to Claire that he liked Jane "much better than I did," and on August 22 he wrote to Medwin: "my regard for them is every day
increased; I hardly know which I like best, but I know that Jane is
your favourite" (Julian *Works*, X, 264, 272, 317).

9 "The Boat on the Serchio," 1821. Mary's journal for May 25
records: "Shelley and Williams go down the Serchio to the sea."

10 Keats died on February 23, 1821. Leigh Hunt's letter of March 1
(received April 4) stated that Keats was "dying" at Rome. When
and how the Shelleys received definite information is uncertain, but
on April 19 Mary Shelley wrote to Mrs. Gisborne (*Shelley and Mary*,
III, 617): "Henry will have told you perhaps that poor Keats is
dead at Rome." Claire Clairmont received the news on April 21,
in a letter from Shelley and Mary.

11 For a collection of Byron's opinions on Keats see T. J. Wise: *A
Bibliography of Byron* (privately printed, London, 1933), II, 15–23.

12 Shelley to Byron, July 16, 1821, Julian *Works*, X, 284.

13 Shelley to John and Maria Gisborne, postmarked June 6, 1821,
ibid., 270. There is no mention of *Adonais* in Mary's journal.

14 Shelley to Charles Ollier, June 8, 1821, Julian *Works*, X, 273.
See also Shelley to Ollier, June 11, 16, and undated, ibid., 275, 276,
286; and Shelley to Claire Clairmont, postmarked June 22, 1821,
ibid., 279.

15 See Shelley's letters of July 16, 1818 and September 27, 1819,
ibid., IX, 312 and X, 86; also Medwin: *Revised Life*, 262.
The idea that death may be life and life death had possibly been
encountered by Shelley in his reading of Plato's *Gorgias:*
Soc. Well, well, as you say, life is strange. For I tell you I should
not wonder if Euripides' words were true, when he says:

> Who knoweth if to live is to be dead,
> And to be dead, to live?

and we really, it may be, are dead, etc. (W. M. R. Lamb., trans. Loeb
Classics *Gorgias*, 415. I am indebted to Miss Ellen Frey for the passage.) Shelley read *Gorgias* October 22, 1821, and perhaps earlier.

[16] Stanza xxvii.

[17] See the rejected passages for *Adonais* recently recovered from the notebooks and printed by Sir John C. E. Shelley-Rolls and Roger Ingpen in *Verse and Prose from the Manuscripts of Percy Bysshe Shelley* (London, 1934), 43.

[18] Shelley to Claire Clairmont, undated, but written from Bagni di Pisa, i.e., shortly after May 8, 1822. Julian *Works*, X, 263–4.

[19] Shelley to Claire Clairmont [April 29, 1821], ibid., 259–60.

[20] Shelley to Mary, August 7, 1821, ibid., 297.

[21] On July 23 Claire wrote in her journal: " Emilia says that she prays always to a Saint, and every time she changes her lover, she changes her Saint, adopting the one of her lover." Professor Dowden (*Life*, II, 372) has taken this remark as significant of Emilia's light character. This seems to me an injustice, in that it contradicts the tone of all of Emilia's extant letters. She had only two suitors and no other known lovers. Possibly the remark was made flippantly and was set down by Claire because it amused her; but more likely it is a perfectly serious example of naïve piety, and amused Claire on that account. In neither case does it support Professor Dowden's insinuation.

[22] Shelley to Claire Clairmont, postmarked June 22, 1821, Julian *Works*, X, 278, 279.

[23] Shelley to Claire Clairmont, undated (shortly after May 8, 1821), ibid., 264.

[24] Shelley to John Taafe, July 4, 1821, ibid., 281–2.

[25] Mary Shelley to Amelia Curran, May 14, 1821, *Shelley and Mary*, III, 624. The friend here mentioned in connection with Lake Como is identified as Count Taafe by Shelley's letters to him dated July 4, 1821, Julian *Works*, X, 282.

[26] Shelley to Claire Clairmont, June 8, 1821, Julian *Works*, X, 272. What Shelley received, if anything, for the wreckage of the steamboat is unknown. In later years Henry Reveley's wife asserted that Shelley owed him £1,000 (*Letters about Shelley*, 29).

[27] Shelley to Claire Clairmont, June 8, 1821, Julian *Works*, X, 272.

[28] Shelley to John Gisborne, October 22, 1821, and to Claire Clairmont, postmarked June 22, 1821, ibid., 333 and 280.

[29] Hogg to Shelley, June 15, 1821 (*Shelley and Mary*, III, 640–3); Leigh Hunt to the Shelleys, July 10, and to Shelley, August 28, 1821 (*Correspondence of Leigh Hunt*, I, 163–9); and Peacock to Shelley, June 3, 1821 (*Shelley and Mary*, III, 634–5, and Peacock's *Works*, Halliford ed., VIII, 220).

³⁰ Shelley to Peacock, "August [probably 10], 1821," Julian *Works*, X, 306.

³¹ Memorandum of conversations with T. Hookham by J. Mitford, quoted by Peck (*Life*, II, 410).

³² Leigh Hunt to Shelley, July 11, 1821, *Correspondence of Leigh Hunt*, I, 166.

³³ In *The Spirit of the Age*, 1821. Two or three slurring incidental references to Shelley in the *London Magazine* in 1820 and 1821 may also have been by Hazlitt.

³⁴ See my *The Unextinguished Hearth*, 24–8, for a more extended comment on Shelley's attitude toward the reviewers.

³⁵ These reviews are quoted in my *The Unextinguished Hearth*.

³⁶ These and all other reviews of Shelley from which I quote are reprinted in my *The Unextinguished Hearth*.

³⁷ Thomas Noon Talfourd to James Ollier, September 9, 1820, printed in T. J. Wise: *A Shelley Library*, 101–2.

³⁸ For fuller details see my *The Unextinguished Hearth*, 365–8.

³⁹ Shelley to Charles and James Ollier, January 20, 1821 [misdated 1820], Julian *Works*, X, 233.

⁴⁰ A fourth review of *Adonais* appeared in the *Examiner* for July 7, 1822.

⁴¹ Shelley to Leigh Hunt, January 25, 1822, Julian *Works*, X, 351.

⁴² See H. B. Forman: *The Shelley Library;* T. J. Wise: *A Shelley Library;* and my *The Unextinguished Hearth*, 95–8, 368.

⁴³ See George T. Goodspeed: "The 'First American' Queen Mab" in the *Colophon*, New Graphic Series No. 1, 25–33 (spring, 1939). And cf. Chapter xiii, note 137.

⁴⁴ Shelley to John Gisborne [June 16, 1821], Julian *Works*, X, 278.

⁴⁵ Shelley to the Editor of the *Examiner*, June 22, 1821, ibid., 280–1. Published in the *Examiner* and reprinted in *St. Tammany's Magazine*, New York, November 9, 1821. A similar estimate of *Queen Mab* is to be found in Shelley's letter of November 22, 1817, to Mr. [or Mrs.?] Waller (*Verse and Prose from the Manuscripts of Percy Bysshe Shelley*, 1934, p. 129).

⁴⁶ These two reviews are reprinted in my *The Unextinguished Hearth*.

⁴⁷ See Richard Carlile's *Republican* for February 1, 1822, quoted in my *The Unextinguished Hearth*, 95.

⁴⁸ *The Monthly Repository of Theology and General Literature*, XVII, 717–18 (November 1822).

⁴⁹ "The Atheist," in the *Literary Gazette* for June 2, 1821, signed

C., is reprinted in my *The Unextinguished Hearth*, 344–5. Dalby's poem, without title, occurs in a letter in the *Literary Chronicle* for June 9, 1821, p. 362, signed J.W.D * * *. I am indebted to Professor George L. Marsh for my knowledge of it, which came too late for inclusion in *The Unextinguished Hearth*. Its text follows:

> Percy Bysshe Shelley! the unearthly brightness
>> And wild expression of thy fearful eye
> Prove thou hast forfeited thy bosom's whiteness,
>> And leagued thy soul to shame and perfidy.
> And then thy " gait perturbed," — its wondrous lightness, —
> Thy long unequal strides — all these supply
> The clearest proofs, that if thou'rt not the devil,
> Thou art his equal in all kinds of evil.
>
> Percy Bysshe Shelley! while almost a child,
>> You wrote a profligate and wicked book,
> At which it seems you ne'er were weak and wild
>> Enough to let the public have a look;
> But one it seems has printed it, beguiled
>> By hope of gain, — and so, by hook or crook,
> We'll heap on you slander, reproach, and shame,
> And play the very devil with your name.

⁵⁰ Shelley to Mary [August 1, 1821], Julian *Works*, X, 293.

⁵¹ Mary Shelley's journal, August 2 and 3, 1821, and Claire Clairmont's journal, August 3 and 4, 1821.

⁵² Shelley to Mary, August 6, [1821], Julian *Works*, X, 295–6.

⁵³ John Murray: *Lord Byron's Correspondence*, II, 180–2.

⁵⁴ Byron to R. B. Hoppner, October 1, 1820, Murray, op. cit., II, 183.

⁵⁵ Shelley to Mary, August 7, 1821, Julian *Works*, X, 298–9. In *Shelley and Mary* this letter omits some of the details of the charges against Shelley. Dowden, however (*Life*, II, 423), prints the text without these omissions.

⁵⁶ Shelley to Mary [August 9, 1821], Julian *Works*, X, 300.

⁵⁷ Mary Shelley to Shelley, undated, enclosing a letter to Mrs. Hoppner dated August 10, 1821, in Dowden: *Life*, II, 424–5.

⁵⁸ Murray, op. cit., II, 185–8. This letter has been printed by both Mrs. Marshall in her *Life and Letters of Mary Shelley* (I, 298–300) and Dowden (*Life*, II, 425–7) with important omissions: viz., all of paragraphs 5, and part of 6, 7, and 11, which are included

only in the text as printed in John Murray as cited above. Lady Shelley, who copied the letter in *Shelley and Mary* from the papers of Lady Dorchester, is responsible for the omissions. The MS. of her copy in the Bodleian Library mentions that she suffered from a headache while making the copy. It is a rather curious coincidence that Mrs. Marshall in dealing with Mary Shelley's letter to Mrs. Hoppner (op. cit., 298) conceals Mary's frank admission of Claire's illness by saying falsely that the manuscript reads E. (for Elise) instead of C. (for Claire).

[59] Shelley to Mary [August 16, 1821], Julian *Works*, X, 313–14. Shelley's reference to the *Literary Gazette* in this and the former letter is doubtless to the following footnote in the *Literary Gazette's* review of *Queen Mab*, May 19, 1821, apropos of condemning Shelley's behaviour to Harriet:

> We are aware that ordinary criticism has little or nothing to do with the personal conduct of authors, but when the most horrible doctrines are promulgated with appalling force, it is the duty of every man to expose, in every way, the abominations to which they irresistibly drive their odious professors. We declare against receiving our social impulses from a destroyer of every social virtue; our moral creed, from an incestuous wretch; or our religion from an atheist, who denied God, and reviled the purest institutes of human philosophy and divine ordination, did such a demon exist.

It is possible that the charge of incest refers to Elise's story, but it seems easier to suppose that it is an echo of current gossip about the relations of Byron, Shelley, Mary, and Claire at Geneva in 1816.

[60] Shelley to Mary, August 7, 1821, and Shelley to Medwin, August 22, 1821, Julian *Works*, X, 296, 316.

[61] Shelley to Mary, August 7, and to Medwin, August 22, 1821, ibid., 296, 317. The servant who waited on Shelley during this visit was Battista Falcieri, Byron's gondolier at Venice, and the "Tita" of *Don Juan*, ii, 56. In 1820 he became the servant of Disraeli and was one of the sources of Disraeli's knowledge of Byron and Shelley in his *Venetia*. See William Flavelle Moneypenny: *The Life of Benjamin Disraeli* (New York, 1916), 383–5.

[62] Shelley to Peacock, August [probably 10], 1821, Julian *Works*, X, 306–7.

[63] Shelley to Mary [August 10, 1821], ibid., 303.

[64] Shelley to Byron, September 14, 1821, ibid., 322.

[65] Shelley to Mary [August 16, 1821], ibid., 315.

[66] Shelley to Mary [August 15, 1821], ibid., 310–11.

[67] Ibid., 312.

[68] Shelley to Medwin, ibid., 316.

[69] Mary's last recorded visit to Emilia is on June 22, Claire's on June 23, and Shelley's on June 22 (but not with Mary apparently). Shelley's letter of August 22 (see note 68, above) indicates that Emilia's letter breaking off communications had been received by that time.

[70] *Shelley and Mary*, III, 576, published in *Vita di una Donna*, 115. A possible echo of this prohibition is to be found in Shelley's letter of August 15 to Mary (Julian *Works*, X, 311), in which he thinks Emilia might recommend a tutor for Allegra " if you can see or write to Emilia." The text of Emilia's letters, as given in Appendix II, indicates that the prohibition was probably a temporary one, during the period of " retreat."

[71] Enrica Viviani Della Robbia, op. cit., 143. Biondi was the son of Francesco Biondi, President of Good Government and Councillor of State, of Pomerance.

[72] Shelley to Byron, September 14, 1821, Julian *Works*, X, 322.

[73] Shelley to John Gisborne, January 26, 1822, ibid., 255.

[74] " Ginevra " (1821), lines 58–69. For the Italian story, see H. B. Forman, Shelley's *Works*, IV, 545–8.

[75] Shelley later sent this poem to Jane Williams with a note very suggestive of the one that had accompanied his present of " On a Faded Violet " to Sophia Stacey:

> Dear Jane, — If this melancholy old song suits any of your tunes, or any that humour of the moment may dictate, you are welcome to it. Do not say it is mine to any one, even if you think so; indeed it is from the torn leaf of a book out of date. . . .

[76] Professor Peck (*Life*, II, 207) has preceded me in suggesting the connection of these poems with Emilia Viviani, and also the similar connection of " The Fugitives " and " Ginevra."

[77] Shelley to Hogg, October 22, 1821, in George Stuart Gordon: *Shelley Letters*, galley proofs.

[78] Mary Shelley to Maria Gisborne, March 7, 1822, Mrs. Marshall, op. cit., I, 331.

[79] Shelley to John Gisborne, June 18, 1822, Julian *Works*, X, 401.

[80] Charles Ollier to Mary Shelley, November 17, 1823, in *Shelley and Mary*, IV, 990–1. Ollier says he is delivering 160 unsold copies

to Leigh Hunt. This would indicate that he printed probably 200 copies instead of the 100 Shelley first suggested, and that not more than forty were disposed of.

[81] The story of Emilia's later life is to be found in Enrica Viviani Della Robbia's *Vita di una Donna* (Firenze, 1936).

Chapter XXVIII

GENERAL SOURCES

The letters and works of Shelley; letters of Mary Shelley; of William Godwin; of Leigh Hunt; contemporary reviews; the journals of Mary Shelley and of Claire Clairmont; Trelawny's *Recollections;* Medwin's *Revised Life; Journal of Edward Ellerker Williams* — all as previously cited.

NOTES AND REFERENCES

[1] Peacock to Shelley, October (no day) 1821, *Works of Thomas Love Peacock,* ed. H. F. B. Brett-Smith and C. E. Jones, London, 1934, VIII, 225–6.

[2] Mary Shelley to Maria Gisborne, November 30, 1821, Mrs. Marshall, op. cit., I, 317.

[3] Godwin to Mary, June 29, October 10, October 30, 1821, in *Shelley and Mary,* III, 698A, 698C, and 704A. In 1819, when the case involving the rent of Godwin's house had first come before the courts, judgment had been reserved on the question of whether or not Godwin was entitled to a notice to vacate, despite the fact that he paid no rent. The case came up again on October 26, 1821. Opinion was practically unanimous that Godwin would be thrown out of his house and his property sold for debt. Godwin's sole reliance was a promise of £400 from Horace Smith, which Smith had withdrawn on the 25th. The next day, contrary to all opinion and to the judge's charge, the jury granted Godwin another extension.

[4] Shelley to Horace Smith, May (no day) 1822, Julian *Works*, X, 392.

[5] Shelley to John Gisborne, October 22, 1821; Shelley's Preface; Shelley to Horace Smith, April 11, 1822; Shelley to John Gisborne, April 10, 1822, Julian *Works*, X, 333, 377, 370.

[6] *Journal of Edward Ellerker Williams*, entries for October 26 and November 6–10.

[7] " A Discourse on the Manners of the Ancients Relative to the Subject of Love," Julian *Works*, VII, 223.

[8] Trelawny, op. cit., II, 200–1.

[9] Shelley to John Gisborne, April 10, 1822, Julian *Works*, X, 370. Mr. Gisborne was acting as Shelley's agent in London and probably saw *Hellas* through the press.

[10] Reprinted in my *The Unextinguished Hearth*, 303–8. The Paris *Monthly Review* for August 1822 contained a favourable obituary notice of Shelley entitled " Hellas, A Poem." See *The Unextinguished Hearth*, 326–9.

[11] Shelley to Byron, October 21, 1821, Julian *Works*, X, 330–1. The similarity of the last chorus to Byron's " Isles of Greece " is noticed by Medwin, op. cit., 354.

[12] *Hellas*, lines 776–85 and 792–802.

[13] W. M. Rossetti supposed it to have been written about 1815; A. H. Koszul has shown that the notebook in which it was written was used in 1817 and later. See Chapter xiv, note 32, and the editorial note on the essay, Julian *Works*, VI, 364.

[14] Mary Shelley to Maria Gisborne, November 30, 1821, Mrs. Marshall, op. cit., I, 317–18. The two desks were recovered soon after Shelley's death. Mary's had been broken open and some of Shelley's letters taken. These letters are supposed to have been the basis for the forged Shelley letters of 1852, which deceived Robert Browning.

[15] Mary's journal for November 1, and Shelley to Byron, September 14, 1821, Julian *Works*, X, 321.

[16] Claire's journal, November 1, 1821. Other details in this paragraph are from Mary Shelley to Maria Gisborne, November 30, 1821, Mrs. Marshall, op. cit., I, 317, and Shelley to John Gisborne, October 22, 1821, Julian *Works*, X, 332.

[17] Shelley to Peacock, dated " probably January 11 " by the Julian editors, Julian *Works*, X, 341–3.

[18] Shelley to John Gisborne, October 22, 1821, ibid., 332–3.

[19] Shelley to John Gisborne, January 12, 1822, ibid., 346.

²⁰ Shelley to Claire Clairmont, December 31, 1821, ibid., 341. For further details of Mrs. Beauclerc, see Medwin, op. cit., 362, 367–9.

²¹ Leigh Hunt to Shelley, September 21, 1821, *Correspondence of Leigh Hunt,* I, 172–3. The plan for the *Liberal* had been formulated by Byron and Shelley at Ravenna. Julian *Works,* X, 318.

²² Mary to Maria Gisborne, December 21, 1821, in *Shelley and Mary,* III, 719.

²³ Mary Shelley to Maria Gisborne, December 20 and 21, 1821, *Shelley and Mary,* III, 719; also Medwin, op. cit., 327. In a later letter to Mrs. Gisborne, on April 10 (Mrs. Marshall, op. cit., I, 340), Mary says: " Shelley has been much better in health this winter than any other since I have known him. . . ." Trelawny's account also shows Shelley's health unusually good, and Thornton Hunt drew similar conclusions from Shelley's appearance in July 1822.

²⁴ Mary Shelley's journal does not mention Rogers's presence, but see Williams's journal for April 20, 1822 and the *Reminiscences and Table Talk of Samuel Rogers,* ed. G. H. Powell, London, 1903, pp. 183–4. Rogers mentions an argument at dinner between Byron and Shelley, on Shakespeare.

²⁵ Medwin, op. cit., 331.

²⁶ Ibid., 334–5, 356–7, 377; and Samuel Rogers, as cited in note 24.

²⁷ Medwin, op. cit., 378. Trelawny's and Williams's comments on the relations of Byron and Shelley support Medwin's account.

²⁸ Shelley to Claire Clairmont, December 31, 1821, Julian *Works,* X, 340.

²⁹ Shelley to Peacock, dated by the Julian editors " probably January 11," 1822, ibid., 342.

³⁰ Shelley to John Gisborne, October 22, 1821, ibid., 334.

³¹ Shelley to John Gisborne, January 12, and to Horace Smith, January 25, 1822, both ibid., 346.

³² Mary Shelley's journal for December 12 and 13, 1821, and Medwin, op. cit., 364–7. There is a slight disagreement in the two accounts, which I have attempted to reconcile.

³³ Mary's journal mentions " church at Dr. Nott's " on December 9 and reads " Go to church " December 16, February 24, March 3.

³⁴ Medwin, op. cit., 360–4, and Mary Shelley to Maria Gisborne, March 7, 1822, quoted by Mrs. Marshall, op. cit., I, 329–31, from *Shelley and Mary,* III, 761–4.

³⁵ Trelawny, op. cit., II, 172.

³⁶ Mary Shelley to Maria Gisborne, February 9, 1822, as quoted from *Shelley and Mary* in Mrs. Marshall, op. cit., I, 324–5.

[37] Williams's journal for April 10, 1822. The description of the Pirate is from Mary Shelley's Note on "An Unfinished Drama." It has been suggested with some plausibility (Sylva Norman: *After Shelley*, London, 1934, p. xvi) that the lady who converses with the Indian youth in this fragment is Jane Williams.

[38] E. E. Williams to E. J. Trelawny, December (no day) 1821, in Trelawny's *Recollections*, II, 170; also ibid., 207, 206, and Williams's journal for January 15, 1822. The direct conversation is part of a note appended by Mary Shelley to her transcript of Williams's journal opposite the entry cited above, as quoted by Dowden: *Life*, II, 465.

[39] Trelawny, op. cit., II, 189–90.

[40] Ibid., II, 197 and 194–6.

[41] Shelley to Horace Smith, January 25, 1822, and to Claire Clairmont, postmarked March 26, 1822, Julian *Works*, X, 346, 365. It will be noted incidentally that Shelley asked for the advance of seventy or eighty guineas and referred to it later as six or seven napoleons, the cost of the sheet music only.

[42] Jane Williams to Leigh Hunt, April 28, [1824], Brit. Mus. Add. MSS 38,523, folio 85. Published in part in Edmund Blunden: *Shelley and Keats as They Struck Their Contemporaries* (London, 1925), 55–7. For a full copy of this letter I am indebted to Professor Frederick L. Jones. The same letter shows that Shelley had mentioned this state of affairs to Hunt in July 1822.

[43] Shelley to Edward Williams, dated by the Julian editors January 26, 1822, Julian *Works*, X, 353. Mrs. Shelley printed this poem as written in 1821, which, if true, supports the statement in Shelley's letter that he found it in " the portfolio in which my friend used to keep his verses." But if it was actually written in 1821, which is doubtful, Shelley thought it apposite in January 1822, for Williams's journal shows that he first saw it on that day. The same journal shows that there was not at this time the slightest interruption of Shelley's daily intimacy with the Williamses.

If the poem was written in 1822 with the Williamses in mind, one might suspect that Mary's objection was not so much to his association with them as to his discussing his spiritual loneliness with them. What Edward Williams thought of the situation in Shelley's home in January and February of 1822 may be partly inferred from two separate, cautious remarks in his journal. On January 8, apropos of Shelley's resumption of " Charles the First," he remarked upon Shelley's need of encouragement: " a mind such as his, powerful as it is, requires *gentle leading.*" And when he received Shelley's sad poem on January 26 he characterized it as " beautiful but too melancholy."

44 Maria Gisborne to Mary Shelley, February 9, 1822, in *Shelley and Mary,* III, 743.

45 John Gisborne to Shelley, February 19, 1822, ibid., III, 751; and Shelley to Gisborne, dated by the Julian editors March 7, 1822, and to Ollier and Co., April 11, 1822, Julian *Works,* 363, 376.

46 Shelley to John Gisborne, April 10, 1822, Julian *Works,* X, 373–4.

47 Shelley to Leigh Hunt, January 25, 1822; to Byron, February 15, 1822; to Hunt, February 17, and March 2, 1822; ibid., 349, 356, 357, 361.

48 T. J. Hogg to Shelley, January 28, 1822, in *Shelley and Mary,* III, 735.

49 Dowden: *Life,* II, 486–7, from Claire Clairmont papers that I have been unable to locate. According to Claire's statement, the Shelleys were kept ignorant of Mr. Mason's journey, lest they unwittingly betray it to Byron.

50 Shelley to Claire Clairmont, undated, apparently in early February 1822, Julian *Works,* X, 356. Mary's letter referred to is printed in Dowden: *Life,* II, 488–90.

51 Claire's journal for February 7 mentions meeting Elise. On March 18 she mentions that Elise " writes to Mad. Hoppner," and on April 12: " Call upon Elise — to write the letter to Madame H." Elise's two notes of denial (printed in John Murray's *Lord Byron's Correspondence,* II, 190, 191) are dated April 12. Three days before this a letter from Claire to Mary (*Shelley and Mary,* III, 778) concludes: " I wish you would write me back what you wish Elise to say to you, and what she is to say to Madame H. I have tried in vain to compose it." On April 11 Claire received " a letter from M. and S." It would thus appear that Elise failed to execute a promise to write to Madame Hoppner on March 18 and that her two letters of April 12 may have been dictated by Mary or Claire. Since Elise's two notes constitute a sweeping denial of what she had certainly told Mrs. Hoppner, they must have been written primarily to prevent Mrs. Hoppner from repeating the story.

52 Claire's pathetic and dignified letter is quoted entire in Dowden: *Life,* II, 484–6. Byron had ignored two previous letters.

53 Shelley to Claire Clairmont, postmarked March 26, 1822, Julian *Works,* X, 365.

⁵⁴ Shelley to Claire Clairmont, postmarked April 11, 1822, ibid., 375.

⁵⁵ Shelley to Claire Clairmont, undated (probably late in March 1822) and also May 31, 1822, ibid., 367, 396.

⁵⁶ *Journal of Edward Ellerker Williams*, February 7–11, and April 26–30, 1822.

⁵⁷ Details of the Masi affray are drawn from Edward Williams's journal, March 24–30, 1822; Trelawny's *Recollections*, II, 213–15; and the letters of Byron, Shelley, and Mary Shelley, particularly Mary's letters of April 6 and June 2, to Maria Gisborne, in Mrs. Marshall, op. cit., I, 337, 356. In 1936 I examined cursorily a collection of letters, depositions, and other documents bearing upon the affray, which was at that time in the possession of Mr. Gabriel Wells.

Byron's servant, when released, fled to the Shelleys, who had meanwhile moved to San Terenzo. He was later returned to Byron. A prosecution was begun against Serjeant-Major Masi for his assault on Shelley. After Masi's recovery Shelley wished to drop the legal proceedings, but deferred to Byron's opinion that they should be prosecuted. Shelley died before Masi could be brought to trial.

⁵⁸ Mary Shelley to Maria Gisborne, June 2, 1822, Mrs. Marshall, op. cit., I, 358, reprinted from *Shelley and Mary*.

⁵⁹ This extract from some later memoranda of Claire Clairmont kept with her journals is printed in full, with Claire's characterization of Mary, in R. Glynn Grylls: *Claire Clairmont*, 255.

⁶⁰ The *Examiner*, January 20, June 9, 16, 23, pp. 35, 355–7, 370–1, 389–90; and July 7, pp. 419–21 (reprinted in my *The Unextinguished Hearth*).

⁶¹ See *The Unextinguished Hearth*, 375.

Chapter XXIX

GENERAL SOURCES

Trelawny's *Recollections;* Mary Shelley's letters, journal, and Notes on the Poems of 1822; Shelley's letters and poems; and the journal of Edward Williams — all as previously cited.

NOTES AND REFERENCES

[1] Here, as elsewhere, I have based my account on Trelawny's earlier *Recollections* (1858) rather than his later *Records* (1878), because his earlier memories seemed likely to be more reliable and also because in the interval Trelawny's attitude toward Mary Shelley had become less friendly and at times even contemptuous. With a person of such violent prejudices as Trelawny this circumstance might easily affect his later account in other details than his obviously altered treatment of Mary.

Trelawny's memory and understanding were excellent, but his habits of expression were those of the raconteur rather than the accurate scholar. His reputation for truthfulness was not impeccable. In Greece Byron remarked more than once to George Finlay, the historian: " If we could but make Trelawny wash his hands and speak the truth, we might make a gentleman of him " (as quoted in *The Life of Frances Power Cobbe,* by Herself, Boston and New York, 1894, I, 236). But it has been often observed that he is at his best in writing of Shelley. His remarks on Shelley have in general the indefinable ring of truth; they are well supported by Medwin's earlier account (of which he certainly availed himself), and by other incidental records. They can safely be taken as true in general, though liable to occasional exaggeration and inaccuracy. Thus in his several accounts of the cremation of Shelley's body he varies the circumstances of the preservation of Shelley's heart and mentions a bird hovering over the scene, which is called a different kind of bird in each of the three accounts. But the variation of detail scarcely affects the essential general truth of his narrative.

The *Records* contain documents, conversations, and several anecdotes not present in the earlier book. Most of the added documents are available elsewhere. The conversation sounds less genuine than that of twenty years earlier and is surely none the more accurate and reliable for not having been included in the first volume. Of the anecdotes, two are among his best-known. These, the only new ones of possible importance, are the stories of Shelley's appearing naked before dinner guests as he returned to his room at Casa Magni after losing his clothes on the beach, and his proposal to Jane Williams at about the same time to " solve the great riddle " by allowing Williams's little coracle to sink beneath them, as they were drifting around in the bay. The latter story has been told to me by Jane's grandson, Mr. R. Wheeler Williams, as a family tradition heard from his father. Yet I cannot help wondering why such capi‑ tal stories were not printed until Mary Shelley and Jane Williams were no longer alive to contradict them. The former story is not sup‑ ported by any mention in Williams's or Mary's journal of a visitor from Genoa, and Mary was in such poor health at the times of both Trelawny's visits to Casa Magni that the dinner party itself sounds somewhat doubtful.

A brief but excellent general description of Shelley at this time, possibly by Leigh Hunt, appeared in the *Literary and Pictorial Repository*, London, 1838, and is quoted in Appendix V.

[2] Details in this paragraph are based on Trelawny's *Recollections*, II, 227, 188–9, 202, 186, 194, 202, 203.

[3] This paragraph and the next are based on ibid., II, 194, 206, 190, 191, 203.

[4] Paragraph based on ibid., II, 189, 187, 175, 179, 203, 202.

[5] Paragraph based on ibid., II, 189, 175, 227, 194, 189, 190.

[6] Mary Shelley's Note on the Poems of 1822, and Trelawny's *Recollections*, II, 205, 240, and Mary to Maria Gisborne, August 15, 1822, Mrs. Marshall, op. cit., II, 12–13.

Descriptions of the house as it appeared in the early 1900's may be found in the *West Sussex Gazette* for July 6, 1922 and in the London *Daily Mail*, August 20, 1925.

[7] Mary Shelley, Note on the Poems of 1822.

[8] Mary Shelley to Maria Gisborne, August 15 and June 2, 1822, Mrs. Marshall, op. cit., II, 11, and I, 359; Shelley to Claire Clairmont, May 29, 1822, Julian *Works*, X, 396; Mrs. Mason to Shelley, May [no day] 1822, Mrs. Marshall, op. cit., I, 353; Jane Williams to Leigh Hunt, April 28, [1823], and Leigh Hunt to Elizabeth Kent, undated [before April 28, 1823], both published in part in Edmund Blunden: *Shelley and Keats as They Struck Their Contemporaries*, 55–7.

In his *Recollections* Trelawny gives no hint of any discord between Shelley and Mary, but he mentions in his later *Records* that he had since learned that Shelley suffered from Mary's jealousy. In his later letters he sometimes spoke disparagingly of Mary, but not very definitely of her attitude toward Shelley. In 1870 (*Letters about Shelley*, 36–7) Lady Shelley bought and destroyed some Shelley materials. The late Mr. T. J. Wise assured me these were some Trelawny letters, and that they were destroyed because they spoke of Mary as a whining, nagging wife.

⁹ Shelley to Mrs. Godwin, May 29, 1822, and to Claire Clairmont, May 29, 1822, Julian *Works*, X, 393, 395.

¹⁰ Shelley to John Gisborne, June 18, 1822, ibid., 402. See also note 8, above, and 41, below.

¹¹ Mrs. Mason to Shelley, May [no day] 1822, Mrs. Marshall, op. cit., I, 352; Shelley to Mrs. Godwin, May 29, 1822, Julian *Works*, X, 393.

¹² Shelley to Horace Smith, May [no day] 1822, Julian *Works*, X, 392; and Horace Smith to Shelley, June 5, 1822, *Shelley and Mary*, III, 812–15.

¹³ William Godwin, Jr., to Mary Shelley, June 24, 1822, in *Shelley and Mary*, III, 824A.

¹⁴ Trelawny felt that there was nothing seriously wrong with Shelley's health at this time, and Thornton Hunt commented on how much stronger and healthier Shelley looked than in England. For Mary's similar testimony see Mrs. Marshall, op. cit., II, 11, 12–13, 20; and for Shelley's see Julian *Works*, X, 396, 402.

¹⁵ Mary Shelley wrote of her to Mrs. Gisborne as lacking imagination, and Trelawny wrote of her to Mary as somewhat commonplace. Shelley admitted to John Gisborne her lack of literary refinement, and Leigh Hunt wrote of her to Elizabeth Kent as having " not quite intellect enough " to understand truly the situation between Shelley and Mary (Mrs. Marshall, op. cit., II, 14, 48, Julian *Works*, X, 403, and Edmund Blunden, op. cit., 57).

¹⁶ That this poem was intended as a sequel to " Lines Written in the Bay of Lerici " seems indicated by the first poem's description of a parting to which the second poem seems to refer, and the parallel between the concluding lines of each poem.

How much of these poems may belong to Shelley's ideal plane of living and how much to the plane of actual life is uncertain, but obviously they belong at least partly in the actual plane. It is quite possible (and in my opinion probable) that the incident was a relatively trivial one, heightened and magnified by an idealizing mood. Mr. Peck (*Life*, II, 199) states: " His affection, indeed, for Jane . . . if we are to trust an unpublished letter written by Shelley to Byron . . . led to the actual fulfillment of passion, one evening, after an Italian *fiesta* which they together had attended." I am convinced that Mr. Peck is here citing either an imaginary or a forged letter which he takes to be genuine. Diligent inquiry of various Shelley scholars and collectors has failed to reveal to me a single person other than Mr. Peck who had ever heard of the letter in question. Mr. Peck does not state the ownership, location, or date of this letter, so that the basis of his statement cannot be tested. There are so many extant Shelley and Byron forgeries (and Mr. Peck himself edited a group of the latter without recognizing them as forgeries) that no letter of Shelley's or Byron's that is protected from scrutiny should be given final authority. In 1928 I wrote to Mr. Peck in care of his publishers requesting more information about this letter, but received no reply — very possibly he never received my letter. But in December 1938, when I repeated this question to Mr. Peck orally, he replied that the letter was " in the Shelley family papers."

The lapse of time between this statement and the publication of Mr. Peck's biography, and also the somewhat hurried circumstances of my talk with Mr. Peck, may account for the unsatisfactory nature of this statement. Had any such letter ever been a part of the Shelley family papers (instead of in the Lady Dorchester papers, where they belonged, with all Shelley's other letters of this period to Byron), Lady Shelley would inevitably have destroyed it, long before Mr. Peck could have seen it. Moreover, Mr. Peck's book gives no evidence of access to any Shelley family papers not commonly accessible to others at the time and since. Further, there is no evidence in the journals of E. E. Williams and Mary Shelley, or elsewhere in published letters, that Jane and Shelley ever attended a fiesta together. Nor, if the story itself were true, would Shelley ever have confided it to Byron, in whom he had come to have no real confidence and to whom such a letter would have seemed to confirm the old scandal about Shelley and Claire in Naples.

No one could well assert the impossibility that there was an " actual fulfillment of passion "; but if there was, Professor Peck's letter probably has nothing to do with it. The only authentic record of the high-water mark of Shelley's attraction to Jane Williams is Shelley's own poems. From these the only tenable conclusion to be reached is that in May, probably, at San Terenzo, Shelley committed some indiscretion which would seem trivial in the plane of ordinary living but which to an idealist could form the basis for the poem " We Meet Not as We Parted." What happened can never be known, but a kiss or a passionate declaration, followed by a rebuke, could have produced the known results.

In 1828 Jane Williams "talked." Specifically what she said has never been stated, but the effect on Mary was to make her consider that her dearest friend had turned malicious. It is known that the talk concerned Shelley's attitude toward Jane, and Mary's treatment of Shelley, and it is felt by Mary's biographers (I believe truly) that the talk was exaggerated and irresponsible. It would appear that Jane asserted that Shelley was actually in love with her at San Terenzo.

If Jane's talk was exaggerated by the retrospective vanity with which she has been charged, then its actual basis may well have been the circumstance vaguely in the background of "We Meet Not as We Parted." If so, and if she was not exaggerating, then the basis of the poem was less trivial than I suppose, even though the exact extent of Jane's claim is unknown. In such circumstances it seems to me that a better indication of the situation in May 1822 is to be had from the contemporary documents and circumstances, which to me suggest that there was either no particular incident or a relatively trivial one.

[17] Shelley to Claire Clairmont, May 29, 1822, Julian *Works*, X, 396.

[18] Edward Williams's journal; Mary Shelley to Mrs. Gisborne, June 2, 1822, Marshall, op. cit., I, 359; Trelawny: *Recollections*, II, 207; Medwin: *Revised Life*, 378.

[19] Shelley to Trelawny, May 16, 1822, Julian *Works*, X, 390. On June 18 Shelley made through Trelawny a final payment of 154 Tuscan crowns, which, with 60 crowns previously paid, made the cost of the boat 214 crowns, or £80.

[20] Edward Williams's journal for May 17, 1822; Mary Shelley to Maria Gisborne, June 2, 1822 in Mrs. Marshall, op. cit., I, 359; and Shelley to Claire Clairmont, May 29 and May 31, 1822, Julian *Works*, X, 395, 397. See two letters on the subject by Professor Frederick L. Jones in *Times Literary Supplement*, January 18, 1936 and April 22, 1939.

[21] Williams's journal for June 12, 13, 1822.

[22] The chronology of Trelawny's visit is somewhat confusing. In his *Recollections* (II, 209) he speaks of only one visit, "not long after" receiving a letter from Shelley dated June 18. But Shelley, in that letter, refers to a conversation with Trelawny "the other night." Mary Shelley's journal does not mention Trelawny's arrival, but does mention his departure on June 16. Williams's journal does not mention either his arrival or departure, but contains (in the printed version) no entries between June 13 and 19, and on the

13th describes encountering the *Bolivar* with Byron and Roberts on board. From this I suppose that Trelawny made a first visit from June 13 to June 16. In her letter of August 15, 1822 to Maria Gisborne, Mary speaks of Trelawny's presence at Casa Magni " the day before I was taken ill." By this she must have meant the day before her miscarriage, which she dates as June 16, rather than the day before her threatened miscarriage, which in the same letter she dates June 8 (" I think "). Williams's journal gives June 9 as the date of Mary's illness, with the word " miscarried " inserted in editorial brackets, from which I conclude that Williams was referring only to Mary's first seizure. In any event, Trelawny can hardly have been present before June 13.

In his *Records* Trelawny does not distinguish between his two visits, but relates several events as if they occurred during his presence at Casa Magni, or, more probably, Lerici, where Roberts was staying. One of these was Shelley's sleep-walking scene, which is dated by Williams's journal Sunday, June 23, and which Mary Shelley's letter dates "I think . . . the Saturday after my illness " — which would have been June 22. Trelawny's second visit, therefore, would appear to have begun between June 18 and 22, and to have lasted only a few days. Trelawny's silence about Mary's serious illness may be explained by supposing that on his first visit he sailed from Lerici before eight in the morning of the 16th and hence did not know until later of her seizure at that hour. On his return Mary was better, though she was thrown into a relapse by Shelley's sleep-walking of June 23. At neither time does Mary's known state of health accord very satisfactorily with Trelawny's references to her behaviour, but they suit the second period, up to June 23, as well as the first; and Trelawny's account of Shelley's sleep-walking could only belong to a second visit. See note 28, below.

[23] Trelawny: *Recollections*, II, 209–11.

[24] The date of Claire's arrival is not mentioned in Mary's journal, and Claire's journal contains no entries for over four months after Allegra's death. In a letter postmarked May 31 Shelley urged Claire to visit them. In a letter to Mrs. Gisborne dated June 2 Mary said that she did not know if Claire would visit them again. Mrs. Marshall (op. cit., I, 360) dates Claire's return on July 6; Miss Grylls (*Claire Clairmont*, 151) June 7. Mary's journal for June 6 says: " Shelley and Clare go to Via Reggio," which I take to be a slip for " Shelley and Williams go to Via Reggio for Clare." Williams's journal for that date describes an attempt to reach Viareggio in the

boat. Being becalmed, they rowed to shore at Massa, where they had to produce pistols before the lone guard would permit their landing. They returned to Casa Magni next day without having reached Viareggio, and Claire must have arrived from Viareggio by herself on either June 6 or June 7.

25 Shelley to John Gisborne, June 18, 1822, Julian *Works*, X, 403. Both Mrs. Mason and Mary Shelley also noted the change in Claire.

26 Mary Shelley to Maria Gisborne, August 15, 1822, Mrs. Marshall, op. cit., II, 12.

27 Journal of Edward Williams, May 6, 1822.

28 Mary Shelley to Maria Gisborne, August 15, 1822, Mrs. Marshall, op. cit., II, 13–14. From Mary's letter it is to be inferred that Jane's and Shelley's visions of Shelley's phantasm preceded the sleep-walking scene. According to Mary's letter of August 15, Trelawny was with Jane at the time of her illusion. See notes 22 and 27, above.

Thomas Moore, in *Letters and Journals of Lord Byron: With Notices of His Life* (London, 1830, II, 617), states that friends once saw Shelley walking in a wood near Lerici when he was really far away in another direction.

29 Shelley to John Gisborne, June 18, and to Horace Smith, June 29, 1822, Julian *Works*, X, 403, 411.

30 Journal of Edward Williams, 31, under December 30, 1821; Trelawny: *Recollections*, II, 199.

31 Shelley to Leigh Hunt, January 25, 1822, Julian *Works*, X, 351.

32 E. J. Trelawny: *Records of Shelley, Byron and the Author* (New York, 1887), 70. This statement does not occur twenty years earlier in his *Recollections*.

33 Shelley to Trelawny, June 18, 1822, Julian *Works*, X, 405.

34 Shelley to Claire Clairmont, dated by the Julian editors April 29, 1821, ibid., 259.

35 Professor Dowden (*Life*, II, 506) noted that Shelley's model was Petrarch's "Triumph of Love," but the suggestion has been ignored by most or all commentators on the poem, who have supposed the *terza rima* to be Dante's rather than Petrarch's. It is true that the poem more closely resembles the first of Petrarch's triumphs than any other, but several circumstances suggest that Shelley's model was the *Triumphs* as a whole, rather than merely the first one. Petrarch's six triumphs are different phases of the same vision, culminating in the "Triumph of Eternity." They are obviously highly integrated parts of one unified conception. Shelley was an enthu-

siastic admirer of Petrarch by July 1818; on September 7, 1819 he had read the "Triumph of Death" aloud to Mary. He had shown in *Adonais* the influence of Petrarch's conclusion. No better statement of the essence of Petrarch's *Triumphs* could be imagined than Shelley's

> Life, like a dome of many-coloured glass,
> Stains the white radiance of Eternity.

Petrarch's first four triumphs — "Love," "Chastity," "Death," and "Fame" — include a fairly complete poetic view of life. Shelley condenses a similar view under one name — with considerable difference, however, because of the more generalized approach. To Petrarch, as to Shelley, life in its most intense reality was the life of a "god-like" spirit in the "white radiance of Eternity." Had Petrarch made his general title a specific rather than a generic one he could hardly have found one more descriptive than the Triumphs of False and True Life.

Supposing that Shelley's model was only the first triumph, Professor Dowden concluded that Shelley's poem would not have been a long one. But this supposition is untenable when Shelley is seen to be including the whole group in his range of ideas, even though probably intending to write only one triumph. This did not compel Shelley to write one poem as long as Petrarch's six, but it does imply a poem probably two or three times the length of the fragment. Such a view is supported by Shelley's treatment of Rousseau, which occupies about half the fragment and is longer than any of Petrarch's comparable episodes. Rousseau was for Shelley always a splendid spiritual failure, never one of the few supremely great spirits. His treatment in the fragment appears grotesquely disproportionate unless we assume that additional episodes of similar length, and more congenial to Shelley's notion of spiritual grandeur, were intended. Such a person as Rousseau would hardly have been chosen by Shelley as his only or most important mouthpiece.

Shelley's Italian prose parable "Una Favola" (1820) has obvious similarities both to Petrarch's idea of life and to the idea of "The Triumph of Life." In this fable the poet is in love with two mistresses at different times, Life and Death, but the true lover is Death. If Death is considered only as the necessary gateway to Eternity — as Shelley did consider it at times — the fable is both Petrarchan and Shelleyan.

³⁶ Shelley to Horace Smith, June 29, 1822, Julian *Works*, X, 410.

³⁷ Mary Shelley to Leigh Hunt, first published (misdated) by Lucy Madox Rossetti in *Mrs. Shelley* (1890), p. 157.

³⁸ Journal of E. E. Williams for June 20, 1822; Shelley to Hunt, June 24, and to Horace Smith, June 29, 1822, Julian *Works*, X, 408, 410; and Mary Shelley to Maria Gisborne, August 15, 1822, Mrs. Marshall, op. cit., II, 14.

³⁹ Edward Williams to Jane Williams, July 6, 1822, in Trelawny: *Recollections*, II, 212–13.

⁴⁰ Thornton Hunt: " Shelley, by One Who Knew Him," in *Atlantic Monthly*, XI, 191 (February 1863).

⁴¹ Mary's letter has been lost, but Shelley spoke of it to both Hunt and Williams, and Mary referred to it in her letter of August 15 to Maria Gisborne. In her letter of April 22, 1824 to Leigh Hunt (Brit. Mus. Add. MSS, 38,523, folios 85–6), Jane Williams reminds Hunt of the pain he saw Shelley suffer on reading it. In his letter of July 6 to Jane, Edward Williams describes it as " of the most gloomy kind "; and this fits Mary's own mention of it to Mrs. Gisborne. Mary explained to Mrs. Gisborne that her apprehensions were for young Percy rather than Shelley.

The precise time when the Hunts and Shelley went to Pisa is fixed by Marianne Hunt's journal, as published in the *Bulletin and Review of the Keats-Shelley Memorial*, No. 2 (Rome, 1913), 71.

⁴² Edward Williams to Jane Williams, July 6, 1822, in Trelawny's *Recollections*, II, 212–13; Shelley to Mary, July 4, 1822, Julian *Works*, X, 412; and Mary Shelley to Maria Gisborne, August 15, 1822, Mrs. Marshall, op. cit., II, 17.

⁴³ Byron had just loaned Shelley £50, and either Shelley or Williams had other cash sums, as Captain Roberts later recovered $400 from the wreck (Byron to W. Webb, September 2, 1822, *Lord Byron's Correspondence*, II, 229; Captain Roberts to Byron, July 16, 1822, in Bodleian MSS Shelley Adds. d. 4, folio 13, and to Trelawny, September [no day] and September 18, 1822, in Trelawny: *Recollections*, II, 229).

Shelley's bankers were Guebhard & Co. Another banker, Mr. De Young, of the house of Bell, De Young & Co., claimed to have accompanied Shelley to the pier and to have argued vainly against his departure, according to the MS. diary of Captain Gorham P. Low in the Library of Congress, as quoted by Richard Rice in the *Spectator*, CXXIX, 873 (December 9, 1922).

⁴⁴ I follow Trelawny's *Recollections*. But Trelawny wrote four

other accounts of Shelley's last voyage, in which the time and some other minor circumstances vary. See *Times Literary Supplement,* London, December 9, 1920, pp. 838–9.

⁴⁵ From the conversation of Mr. Taafe in 1826, as reported in the *Journal of Clarissa Trant* (London, 1925), 198–9. The passage is quoted in Peck: *Life,* II, 287.

In 1875 Trelawny's daughter, while travelling in Italy, heard and repeated to Trelawny a story that an old sailor had confessed to a priest that he was one of a crew which had run down the *Don Juan,* supposing Byron to be on board with much money. Trelawny believed that this story was true and adopted it in his *Records.* Undoubtedly the confession was made, but no writer on Shelley except Trelawny has regarded it with anything except scepticism. The money was not stolen, and it is hard to see how such a robbery could have been planned with any prospect of success. The " confession " hardly accords with the stories of other Livornese sailors who claimed to have hailed the boat. No one in San Terenzo believed the confession. See the *Athenæum,* December 25, 1875, for documents throwing doubt on the confession.

⁴⁶ Captain Dan Roberts to Trelawny, September 18, 1822, Trelawny: *Recollections,* II, 229–30.

The *Don Juan* was raised by Captain Roberts and sold at auction. In 1827 she was bought by a group of military officers at Zante, where she was often used for short cruises. Finally she broke her moorings in a gale and was smashed to pieces. See letter of Ernest Law in *The Times,* London, July 10, 1922.

⁴⁷ Trelawny: *Recollections,* II, 190, 211, and *Records,* Chapters x and xiii, pp. 91 and 137 in the New Universal Library edition, London and New York, n. d.

⁴⁸ Mary Shelley to Maria Gisborne, September 10, 1822, Mrs. Marshall, op. cit., II, 27.

⁴⁹ Mary Shelley to Maria Gisborne, August 15, 1822, Mrs. Marshall, op. cit., II, 20.

⁵⁰ In 1926 Elinor Wylie published a novel, *The Orphan Angel,* founded upon this supposition.

⁵¹ This paragraph and the two following are based on Mary Shelley's long letter of August 15, 1822 to Maria Gisborne, as given in Mrs. Marshall, op. cit., II, 11–21.

⁵² Claire Clairmont to Leigh Hunt, July 18, 1822, MS. in the Ashley Library, British Museum, quoted in part in R. Glynn Grylls: *Claire Clairmont,* 155–6.

[53] Except where otherwise specified the details of the remainder of this and the next eight paragraphs are drawn from Trelawny's *Recollections*, II, 216–27.

[54] Trelawny supposed that the watch and money had either been stolen from the body or lost in the water. But the watch had been given to Jane Williams before the journey and is now in the Bodleian Library at Oxford, and the money was found in Williams's trunk in the *Don Juan*. It was not until ten or eleven days later that Charles Vivian's body was found two miles from the others, reduced to a skeleton.

[55] Mary Shelley to Maria Gisborne, September 10, 1822, Mrs. Marshall, op. cit., II, 26.

[56] The bill for these items, totalling £413, has been printed by Mr. Peck (*Life*, II, 405–6) from the MS. in the British Museum.

[57] Trelawny to Hunt, July 11, 1822, in Bodleian MSS Shelley Adds. d. 4, folio 20; Byron to Murray and to Moore, August 3 and 8, 1822, R. E. Prothero: Byron's *Letters and Journals*, VI, 99; and Hunt to Arthur Brooke, undated but probably early in 1823, printed in part in the catalogue of the Harry B. Smith sale, New York, April 8 and 9, 1936.

[58] Later deposited by Walter Leigh Hunt in the Keats-Shelley Memorial at Rome, where it is preserved in a marble urn. It is alluded to in Marianne Hunt's journal for September 19, 1822, published in the *Bulletin and Review of the Keats-Shelley Memorial*, No. 2 (Rome, 1913), 72.

[59] William Severn to C. A. Brown, January 21, 1823, as published in the *Bulletin and Review of the Keats-Shelley Memorial*, No. 2 (Rome, 1913), 54; also the recollections of Dr. Richard Burgess, as published (in part) in Mrs. Angeli's *Shelley and His Friends in Italy*, Appendix. Burgess's recollections were written down over fifty years after the event and have misled previous biographers into supposing that only two laymen attended the burial. Neither Burgess nor Severn mentions the criticism Burgess received for giving Christian burial to an atheist, but it is a tradition in his family.

The exact date of Shelley's burial is fixed by the register of burials, as quoted by H. Nelson Gay on p. 52 of the same article, cited above, in which Severn's letter is quoted.

[60] Mary Shelley to Trelawny, May 10, 1823, as quoted in Mrs. Marshall, op. cit., II, 75–7; Trelawny: *Recollections*, II, 225–6; and Sir Rennell Rodd: "The Protestant Burial Ground in Rome (A Personal Reminiscence)" in the *Bulletin and Review of the Keats-*

Shelley Memorial, No. 2 (Rome, 1913), 66; also H. Nelson Gay, as cited in note 59.

[61] Mr. J. Wheeler Williams, Jane's grandson, told me in 1936 that this was the impression he had received from his father, Edward Medwin Williams.

[62] For further information on Hogg and Jane Williams see Sylva Norman: *After Shelley: The Letters of Thomas Jefferson Hogg to Jane Williams* (London, 1934).

[63] Claire Clairmont's journal for September 20, 1822.

[64] A somewhat unreliable picture of Claire in her last years is to be found in William Graham: *Last Links with Byron, Shelley and Keats* (London, 1898). The only biography is *Claire Clairmont,* by R. Glynn Grylls (London, 1939).

[65] A dinner-table bet that Lady Noel would die before Sir Timothy Shelley, won for Shelley soon afterwards by Lady Noel's death. Williams was quite indignant when Byron made no move to pay. See Medwin: *Revised Life,* 375.

[66] On the death of Mary Shelley it was found in her desk, dried to dust, and wrapped in a copy of *Adonais.* It was buried in 1889 with the body of Sir Percy Florence Shelley, in the vault he had built in St. Peter's Churchyard, Bournemouth, which also contains the bodies of Mary Shelley, William Godwin, and Mary Wollstonecraft Godwin — the last two having been removed from St. Pancras Churchyard. See Maud Rolleston: *Talks with Lady Shelley* (London, 1925), 30–2; and an anonymous article entitled " The Real Truth about Shelley's Heart," in *My Magazine,* London, November 1933, pp. 939–43.

[67] Sir Percy Florence Shelley to Mrs. Booth, three MS. letters, two undated, one dated January 3, 1851, Bodleian MSS Shelley Add. d. 5, folios 105–11.

[68] Written statement by A. John Trucchi, Director of the Protestant Burial Ground in Rome, quoted in *Bulletin and Review of the Keats-Shelley Memorial,* No. 2 (Rome, 1913), 57–8.

Chapter XXX

GENERAL SOURCES

Principally the files of English and American periodicals, 1822–40.

NOTES AND REFERENCES

[1] Printed " thing " in the *Morning Chronicle.* But Mr. T. J. Wise, owner of the MS., printed " King " in *A Shelley Library* (1924), 107.

[2] For copies of Dalby's two poems I am indebted to Professor Louise S. Boas, of Wheaton College. The other poems of 1822 are reprinted in my *The Unextinguished Hearth.*

[3] In collecting the materials summarized in this and the following tables I am indebted to my wife for extensive and valuable assistance. A dozen or more American items were contributed by the late Professor Lewis Chase, and several others by my colleague Professor Jay B. Hubbell.

For the years 1823–40 inclusive, every available periodical in the Harvard Library and the British Museum was searched by title and index, and many by a rapid page-by-page inspection. Other libraries were used less systematically. Possibly some files or separate volumes were overlooked and some articles thereby missed. Certainly a number of incidental references were missed. But I regard the results as so nearly complete that further additions could not significantly vary my conclusions.

For none of these tables may be claimed the finality and accuracy of detail which the form of presentation suggests. Not only are the data incomplete, but the distinctions between favourable, unfavourable, and neutral items are necessarily based upon individual judgment which would certainly in some cases vary according to the judge. Nor are the classifications always quite free from overlapping. But while these considerations forbid regarding any figure in these tables as more than approximately accurate, their significance is too slight to affect relative values. And it is relative and not absolute values that I seek to indicate.

⁴ Mary Shelley to Mrs. Gisborne, February [no day] 1835, Mrs. Julian Marshall, *Life and Letters of Mary Wollstonecraft Shelley*, II, 263.

⁵ In 1827 Wordsworth said: "Shelley is one of the best *artists* of us all: I mean in workmanship of style" — Norwell E. Smith: *Wordsworth's Literary Criticism* (London, 1905), 259. Quoted also in Christopher Wordsworth's *Memoirs of William Wordsworth* (London, 1851), II, 474. Cf. John Morley's *Life of Gladstone* (London, 1903), I, 136, where Wordsworth is quoted in 1836 as seeing in Shelley "the lowest form of irreligion, but a later progress toward better things."

⁶ Between 1822 and 1841 *Blackwood's Edinburgh Magazine* made incidental reference to Shelley in January 1823, April 1830, and August 1834. Of these the first was unfavourable, the second colourless, and the last favourable. In December 1830 it printed a poem to Shelley by T. L. Beddoes.

The *Quarterly* in the same years contains six items, all but the first incidental. The first was a mildly unfavourable review of *Posthumous Poems*, June 1826. The incidental notices were slightly unfavourable.

The *Literary Gazette* reviewed *Posthumous Poems* (July 17, 1824), *The Beauties of Percy Bysshe Shelley* (November 3, 1832), and *The Mask of Anarchy* (November 10, 1832); and made incidental reference to Shelley on June 16, 1830 and March 2, 1839. The first review was kindly in tone, but somewhat unfavourable; the two following were moderately favourable, as was the last of the two incidental references.

In 1824 both the *New Times* and the *John Bull* continued the old unscrupulous attitude and were denounced by the *Examiner* of November 7, 1824.

⁷ Though the one-volume *Poetical Works* and the *Letters, Essays from Abroad*, etc., are both dated 1840 on their title pages, both were reviewed in 1839 — the former on November 23 in the *Atlas* and the *Spectator* and on November 27 in the *London Weekly Review;* and the latter on December 14 and 28 in the *Athenæum.* Two other reviews of the latter are mentioned by Mary Shelley in a letter of December 19 to Moxon.

⁸ Marianne Hunt to Mary Shelley, October 4–November 7, 1823, Bodleian MSS Shelley Adds. d 5., folios 42–44.

⁹ George Henry Lewes to Leigh Hunt, November 15, 1838 and December 21, 1839, Brit. Mus. Add. MSS 38,523, folios 182 and 200. Very possibly Mary Shelley requested Lewes not to publish.

¹⁰ For detailed information about Browning's first acquaintance with Shelley see Frederick A. Pottle: *Shelley and Browning — A Myth and Some Facts* (Chicago, 1931).

¹¹ For fuller discussions of the growth of Shelley's reputation among the labouring classes see my two articles " Literature and the Law of Libel: Shelley and the Radicals of 1840–1842," in *Studies in Philology,* XXII, 34–47 (January 1925); and "Shelley and the Active Radicals of the Early Nineteenth Century," in the *South Atlantic Quarterly,* XXIX, 248–61 (July 1930).

¹² In the large mass of materials under analysis there are several noteworthy reviews and discussions that do not fall readily into place under the classifications adopted. Chief among these are an able review, followed by a discussion in the *Noctes Ambrosianæ* manner, in *Knight's Quarterly Magazine* for August 1824; Hazlitt's somewhat grudging review in the *Edinburgh Review* for July 1824 (for which he was rebuked in *McPhun's Glasgow Magazine* for November 1824, possibly by Leigh Hunt); an essay, signed D. C. [Derwent Coleridge?], in the *Metropolitan Quarterly Magazine* (1826, pp. 191–202) "On the Poetic Character of Percy Bysshe Shelley, and on the Probable Tendency of His Works," which seeks to soften the " horror " with which " the majority " regard Shelley's works; and two able Irish appreciations, " The Works of Percy Bysshe Shelley," and " Modern Poetry," in the *Dublin Literary Gazette and National Magazine* (August 1830 and No. 3, no date, 1831). Both Irish articles, with the usual apologies for Shelley's views, ranked him at the top of nineteenth-century poetry, but the first of them drew a spirited rebuke from the *Christian Examiner and Church of Ireland Magazine* (November 1830).

¹³ T. Wemys Reed: *Life, Letters, and Friendships of Richard Monckton Milnes* (London, 1890), II, 162. For other recollections of the event see Sir F. H. Doyle: *Reminiscences and Opinions* (London, 1886), 108–13; and G. B. Smith: *Life of Gladstone* (New York, 1880), 27. Perhaps the Bodleian Library was to blame for some of the Oxford ignorance. Five years earlier the Bodleian Library had listed *Alastor* as one of the books which it declined to accept under the Copyright Act. Commenting upon the whole list, the *Man of Letters* (April 21, 1824) remarked that probably no one but Cockneys would criticize this exclusion, but wondered

how the rejection of Hannah More's *Sacred Dramas* and Mrs. Opie's *Simple Tales* was to be explained.

[14] H. S. Salt: *Percy Bysshe Shelley, Poet and Pioneer* (London, 1896), 16.

[15] As listed in J. P. Anderson's bibliography, cited in the text. A later list may be found in the *Musical News* for December 16, 1922, which states truly that " Midvictorian composers tumbled over one another to set Shelley to music." Between 1837 and 1880, fourteen different musical settings for the " Indian Serenade " were published.

[16] H. S. Salt, op. cit., 17. See also note 19, Chapter iii.

[17] Previous to this point I have not considered Shelley's American reputation separately, because its phenomena are in general the same as the British. I have seen (too late to use it) Miss Julia Powers's *Shelley in America in the Nineteenth Century: His Relation to American Critical Thought and His Influence* (University of Nebraska Studies, 1940).

Shelley's reputation in Germany, France, and Italy has been treated respectively in the three following books: *Shelley in Germany,* by Solomon Liptzin (New York, 1924); *Shelley et la France,* by Henri Peyre (Paris, n.d., 1935?); and *Shelley e l'Italia,* by Maria Louisa G. de Courten (Milan, 1923).

In all three countries the first interest in Shelley seems to have been awakened and sustained by the greater interest in Byron; and later interest seems in the main to have paralleled contemporary English interest. In all three countries it has also been handicapped by the difficulty of adequately translating Shelley's most characteristic poems. Perhaps this partly explains why *The Cenci* was one of the first works to attract attention.

Until the middle 1830's Shelley's reputation in Germany was relatively insignificant. Goethe became acquainted with *Posthumous Poems* in 1824 and found no special merit in them. By 1835 Gustav Kühne's novel, *Quarantäne im Irrenhaus,* could treat Shelley (with Hegel and Goethe) as one of the three great spirits of the age; and an article in the *Telegraph für Deutschland* in 1837 could rank him among the three writers to be called " gods." By 1839 Alfred Meissner was translating and imitating Shelley's poems, and Julius Seybt was beginning his five years' labour of translating Shelley's complete poetical works.

Shelley's influence in Germany reached its height in the decade before the revolution of 1848. " Young Germany " regarded him as a brother in arms, and emphasized the radical import of his life and works. After the failure of the revolution Shelley became a romantic character in several German novels and plays, among which the most noteworthy were Wilhelm Hamm's *Shelley, eine biographische Novelle* (Leipzig, 1858) and Emil Claar's *Shelley, Trauerspiel in fünf Aufzügen* (Vienna, 1876) — the latter intended for stage presentation, but vetoed by the censor until 1918. During the 1850's two of Germany's most influential critics, Hebbel and Julian Schmidt, led a reaction against Shelley. Since the reaction to the revolution of 1848 Shelley cannot be said to have exercised any important influence in Germany except in scholarly circles. But in scholarly circles since 1880 he has been the subject of almost innumerable theses. The scholarship of Richard Ackerman, Helene Druskovitz, Helene Richter, and others has contributed considerably to the knowledge of Shelley, not only in Germany, but elsewhere.

Shelley's reputation in France seems to have been based almost entirely on æsthetic and romantic grounds. Not until the 1840's was he seriously noticed, although a few of his poems were translated in the 1830's. Balzac, de Musset, de Vigny, and Sainte-Beuve either esteemed him but lightly, or apparently did not know him. But between 1843 and 1858 it became fairly commonplace for French writers on English literature to rank Shelley above Byron and his other contemporaries. The poetry of the French symbolists was in several respects akin to Shelley's, but evidence of Shelley's influence is very slight. He may have influenced to a slight degree Baudelaire and Victor Hugo. Paul Bourget was an admirer of Shelley. Shelley occupies a restricted but distinguished place in Taine's *History of English Literature* (1864). In 1833 and 1884 Madame Tola Dorian published her translations of *The Cenci* and *Hellas*, the former with an introduction in French by Swinburne. During the 1880's distinguished works on Shelley were produced by Gabriel Sarrazin and Félix Rabbe, most of which were translated into English and helped influence Shelley's later Victorian reputation. Félix Rabbe published in 1886 the first French translation of Shelley's complete works, and in 1887 the first French biography. In 1895 appeared A. Beljame's translation of *Alastor* and in 1906 M. Catelaine's translation of *Hellas*. One of the most penetrating biographical studies of Shelley in any language is A. Koszul's *La Jeunesse de Shelley* (1910), which with his other contributions ranks this author among the foremost Shelleyans of the century. André Maurois's *Ariel* (1923), though in some ways superficial, is the most popular biography of Shelley ever written. The centenary of Shelley's death attracted more attention in French journals than that of any other foreign poet except Goethe.

The first published translation of Shelley into any foreign language was Damas Parato's Italian translation of *Adonais* in 1830. But it was not much noticed, for Italians at this time were much more interested in Byron. Shelley seemed too metaphysical, and in addition he offended the religious orthodoxy of Catholics and the æsthetic orthodoxy of classicists. During the 1830's and 1840's a sort of critical feud existed (as to a less extent in other countries) between Shelleyans and Byronians, with the Shelleyans eventually gaining the upper hand. But Shelley's reputation in Italy grew very slowly until after 1844. In that year G. B. Niccolini published his *Beatrice Cenci,* which he called an imitation of Shelley's *The Cenci,* but which was in reality a translation. In the same year a part of G. Blenio's translation of *Alastor* appeared in Mazzoni's *Fiori e gloria della letteratura inglese.* G. Aglio's translation, *Opere poetiche scelte di P. B. Shelley,* was published in 1858.

The flowering of Shelley's Italian reputation in the late 1840's and the 1850's corresponded with Italy's first unsuccessful effort to unite, the following years of oppression, and the achievement of independence. This may explain why Shelley's reputation in Italy, much more than elsewhere, was for many years based mainly on his championship of freedom. Afterwards the appreciative writings of E. Nencioni and G. Chiarini made him appreciated as " the greatest modern lyrist." Leopardi has been said to have been influenced by him, and Carducci was an admirer, calling him in " Presso l'urna di P. B. Shelley " the " soul of a titan in the body of a virgin." In 1892 Gabriele d'Annunzio celebrated Shelley's centennial by elaborating upon one of Sarrazin's essays. Perhaps the greatest single service to Shelley's Italian reputation has been the translations of A. de Bosis — *The Cenci* (1898), *Prometheus Unbound* (1922), and *Lyrics* (1928). Other recent Italian Shelleyans whose works have had weight beyond Italy are G. Biagi, M. Renzuli, and Mario Praz.

[18] Charles Lamb to Bernard Barton, August 17, 1824, in E. V. Lucas: *The Letters of Charles and Mary Lamb* (London, 1912), VI, 698. Lamb is quoting Hazlitt's opinion and making it his own.

[19] *Fraser's Magazine,* XLVIII, 570–1 (November 1853).

[20] Hall Caine: *Recollections of Rossetti* (London, 1928), 169; and Thomas Carlyle: " Characteristics," in *Critical and Miscel-*

laneous Essays of Thomas Carlyle (London, 1899), III, 31. But
Carlyle was not without some appreciation of Shelley's lyric qualities, and a letter from Robert Browning to Carlyle in October 1851
implies Carlyle's approval of Browning's essay on Shelley (*Letters of
Robert Browning,* ed. Thurman L. Hood, New Haven, 1933, p. 36).
See also W. Minto, ed.: *Autobiographical Notes of the Life of William Bell Scott* (London, 1892), I, 88, 89, 91, 128. In the last passage
Scott, an ardent admirer of Shelley, speaks of him as "that great
poet, though only half-matured intellect."

[21] *Tennyson and His Friends,* ed. Hallam, Lord Tennyson (London, 1911), p. 269.

[22] J. W. Mackail: *The Life of William Morris* (London, 1901),
I, 178.

[23] *Shelley,* by Francis Thompson (London, 1909), 30, 45.

[24] Leslie Stephen: "Godwin and Shelley," in *Hours in a Library*
(London, 1894), III, 64–101.

[25] *Letters of Charles Eliot Norton,* ed. Sara Norton and M. A. De
Wolfe Howe (Boston and New York, 1913), I, 508.

[26] The episode is related in a manuscript by Eliot Norton, in the
Harvard Library. Eliot Norton, a son of Charles Eliot Norton, witnessed the interview between Captain Silsbee and Dr. Charles Eliot.

[27] "Shelley," by Paul Elmer More, in *Shelburne Essays,* Seventh
Series (Boston and New York, 1910), 18.

[28] *Albemarle Magazine,* September 1892, as quoted by H. S. Salt,
op. cit., 19.

[29] For this quotation I am also indebted to Mr. Salt, op. cit., 13.

[30] See note 17.

INDEX

EXPLANATION

This index covers the text, notes, and appendices of the two volumes. A small number of names of persons and places which occur only once or twice and are otherwise insignificant have been omitted. I have also made no effort to list the numerous individual citations of some half-dozen books which are cited so often in the notes that a list of citations would bewilder the reader with scores and hundreds of unimportant and confusing page-references. These books are specified in the index itself. Except for special reasons, quotations of less than three lines have not been indexed.

The number of references for the most important subjects is so large that an effort has been made to simplify their presentation by the use of several sub-topics. This has been done in the hope of making the index more easily usable, and not with the idea of providing complete separate indices for the subjects thus isolated. References already at hand were put into these categories, but no full re-indexing of the two volumes was undertaken to make the categories complete. Consequently any interested reader may expand these categories for himself, both from the volumes and from cross-reference within the index.

Because of its importance to the further study of Shelley, however, I have given rather special attention to bibliographical matters, and have sought to include in the index all of Shelley's reading mentioned in the two volumes, and short titles of all the works which I have cited.

Where no volume number is given before the first page-reference after a topic or sub-topic, Volume I is intended.

i

and Claire Clairmont's situation with the Bojtis, II, 227, 238; Mary and Claire Clairmont's visits to, II, 240, 241; Claire Clairmont corresponds with, II, 285; and Allegra Clairmont, II, 317; on living conditions at Casa Magni, II, 361; Mrs. Godwin writes to, on Godwin's distress, II, 362; her last view of Shelley, II, 376; dreams of disaster to Shelley, II, 378; letter of, quoted, II, 162, 170; *passim*, II, 246, 281, 297, 335, 353, 486, 582, 592, 606; *and see* Mountcashell, Lady

Massa, II, 630

Massachusetts Historical Society, Shelley letter owned by, II, 463

Massinger, Philip: Shelley reads, II, 171; Shelley claims *The Cenci* no more indelicate than, II, 194

Masson, David, II, 412

Masten, C. H. K., Vice-Provost of Eton in 1938, 568, 569, 570, 571

Matthews, Henry, Shelley's fagmaster at Eton, 570, II, 496; *Diary of an Invalid*, 570

Maurois, André: *Ariel* (1923), II, 640

Mavrocordato, Prince: calls on Shelleys, II, 240, 241, 281; account of, II, 245; Shelleys on, II, 245; *Hellas* dedicated to, II, 245, 329; Shelley argues with, on Greek revolution, II, 246; prepares to take part in Greek Revolution, II, 282; departure for Greek Revolution, II, 298–9; in Greece, II, 328; Trelawny's scorn of, II, 603;

Lady Morgan's acquaintance with, 651

Maxse, James, student at University College with Shelley, 587

Mayence, 358

Mayne, Ethel C.: *Byron* (2nd ed., Boston, 1924), 716

Mazzoni, Guido: *Fiori e gloria della letteratura inglese*, translation from *Alastor* in, II, 641

Meadows, Mr. and Mrs., acquaintances of Shelleys in Florence, II, 171

Medwin, Thomas Charles: lends Shelley money, 153; advises Shelley on his marriage to Harriet, 167; Shelley exonerates of aid in elopement, 168; Shelley writes to, on his finances, 177, 222–3, 231; Shelley seeks aid of, 296–7; warns Shelley against post-obits, 297

Medwin, Thomas, Jr.:

as an associate of Shelley: student at Syon House, 19; with Shelley at Field Place, 54; collaborates with Shelley on "The Nightmare" (lost), 55; interests Shelley in Felicia Browne, later Hemans, 61; receives *Necessity of Atheism*, 112; sees Shelley after expulsion from Oxford, 119; with Shelley in London, 132–3; receives copy of *Queen Mab*, 653; Shelley writes to, on his health, II, 170; invited to visit Shelleys, II, 212; and "The Witch of Atlas," II, 219; joins Shelleys at Baths of Pisa, II, 227; reminded of Shelley in India, II, 228; talks of Shelley in Geneva,

Q

Shelley, Percy Bysshe (continued)

8; reading in 1812, books ordered, 648; books ordered in 1812, list quoted, 638; reading in 1813, 309–10; reading in 1815, 406, 407–8, 695; reading at Marlow (1817), 506; reading in Naples, II, 66; reading in Florence (1819), II, 171; reading in early 1820, II, 188; reading at Baths of Pisa, II, 215; idea of a good library, II, 234

SHELLEY'S READING ALPHABETICALLY ARRANGED

(*including, with a very few apparently safe exceptions, only items definitely stated by some contemporary authority to have been read; for other items and more accurate phrasing of some titles, see under separate authors and titles in general index*):

Adolphus: *Lives of the Revolutionists*, II, 540; Æschylus, II, 188, 245, 524; Æschylus: *Agamemnon*, 524, II, 179–80 (with Mrs. Mason), II, 245 (with Mavrocordato); Æschylus: *The Persians*, II, 21; Æschylus: *Prometheus Bound*, II, 542; Albertus Magnus, 41, 52; Alfieri: *Life of*, II, 540, and Tragedies, II, 541; "Ancient Metaphysics," II, 215, 545; Apollonius Rhodius, II, 215, 245; Apuleius, II, 544: *Golden Ass*, story of Psyche in, II, 543; Ariosto, II, 17, 19, 20 (criticized); Ariosto: *Orlando Furioso*, 310 (with Hogg), II, 541; Aristophanes, II, 21: *Clouds*, II, 19, *Lysistra-*

Shelley, Percy Bysshe (continued)

ta, II, 19, *Plutus*, II, 19; Arrian: *Historia Indica*, II, 544; *Armata*, II, 545; "Astronomy" in [Nicholson's?] *Encyclopedia*, II, 544; "Athenaius," II, 188; Bacon: *Novum Organum*, II, 541; Barrow: *Embassy to China*, II, 540; Barthélemy: *Anacharsis*, II, 19, 21; Beaumont and Fletcher, II, 171: *Bonduca*, II, 188, *The Gentle Shepherdess*, 523, *The Maid's Tragedy*, II, 21, *Philaster*, II, 21, *Rule a Wife and Have a Wife*, 522, *Thierry and Theodoret*, II, 188; William Beckford: *Caliph Vathek*, II, 541; Berkeley, 277, 552; Bertram: *Le Criminel Secret*, II, 542; Bible, 124, II, 171, 541, 544, 580; Blackwell: *History of the Court of Augustus*, II, 542; Boccaccio (aloud), II, 215; Boccaccio: *Decameron*, II, 545; Boswell: *Life of Johnson*, II, 544–5; Charles Brockden Brown: *Edgar Huntly*, II, 540, *Wieland*, 721; Buffon, 158; Burke: *Account of Civil Society*, II, 541; Byron: *Childe Harold's Pilgrimage*, II, 39 (aloud), II, 329, 542, *Don Juan*, II, 544, *English Bards and Scotch Reviewers*, 120, *Lara*, II, 540, *Siege of Corinth*, II, 541–2; plays of Calderón, II, 100 (with Maria Gisborne), II, 233 (with Medwin), 341, 545; Cervantes: *Don Quixote*, 469, II, 542, "Little Novels" (with Medwin), II, 233; Cicero: *Collectanea*, II, 540,

W

II, 335; Shelley's intended gift to, II, 338–9; and Shelley, II, 343–7; hypnotizes Shelley, II, 345–6; Shelley's poems to, II, 345–6, 452, 607, 617; on the domestic frictions of Shelley and Mary, II, 346, 621; her dissatisfaction at Casa Magni, II, 361; Shelley's probable impropriety with, II, 364; sees vision at Casa Magni, II, 368–9; alarm and distress over disappearance of the *Don Juan*, II, 379; seeks news of the *Don Juan*, II, 379–80; estrangement from Mary Shelley, II, 384, 628; later life of, II, 384; and "The Sensitive Plant," II, 563; in Shelley's "An Unfinished Drama," II, 621; Shelley proposes solving "the great riddle" with, II, 624; intellectual limitations of, II, 626; and Edward Williams's watch, II, 634; and T. J. Hogg, II, 635

Williams, John: Shelley meets, 255; and Shelley's arrest at Carnarvon, 256; his tribute to Shelley, 257; Madocks's letter to, on Shelley (quoted), 258; Elizabeth Hitchener's letters to, 264, 265; Shelley works with, for Tremadoc Embankment, 267; Shelley's friendship for, 269; alleged source of Leeson story of Shelley's radical activities, 269, 646; on alleged Tanyrallt assault, 281, 285; Shelley's debts to, 325, 643; Shelley's possible delusion about, 433; Madocks's letters to, unpublished, 642; unpublished letter of Shelley to (quoted), II, 456; unpub-

lished letter of Harriet Shelley to (quoted), II, 464–5; letter of S. Girdlestone to (quoted), II, 496–8, 499–500; Eliza Westbrook's letter to (quoted), II, 498; D. E. Varney's letter to, about Shelley (quoted), II, 500–1, 501–2; *passim,* 266, 300, 408, II, 236

Williams, Mrs. John: on Robert Leeson, 258; on Shelley's aid to the Tremadoc Embankment, 267; her tribute to Shelley's benevolence, 268; *passim,* 646, 649

Williams, Orlo: *Lamb's Friend, the Census Taker: Life and Letters of John Rickman* (Boston, New York, London, 1912), 620

Williams, Owen, brother of John Williams, Shelley borrows from, 275, 647

Williams, Robert, "Robin Pant Ifan," q. v.

Williams, Sir Robert, on Shelley's aid to the Tremadoc Embankment, 257

Williams, Rosalind, daughter of Edward Ellerker and Jane Williams, II, 283

Williams, Rumsey, solicitor in Carnarvon, and Shelley's arrest, 643

Williams, William, brother of John Williams, 398, 650

Williams-Ellis, Mrs.: and Shelley's sketch of his Tanyrallt assailant, 649; on "Robin Pant Ifan," 650

Wilson, Eunomus, on *Queen Mab,* in the *Theological Inquirer* (May 1815), 410

Wilson, John: review of *Laon and Cythna* in *Blackwood's*